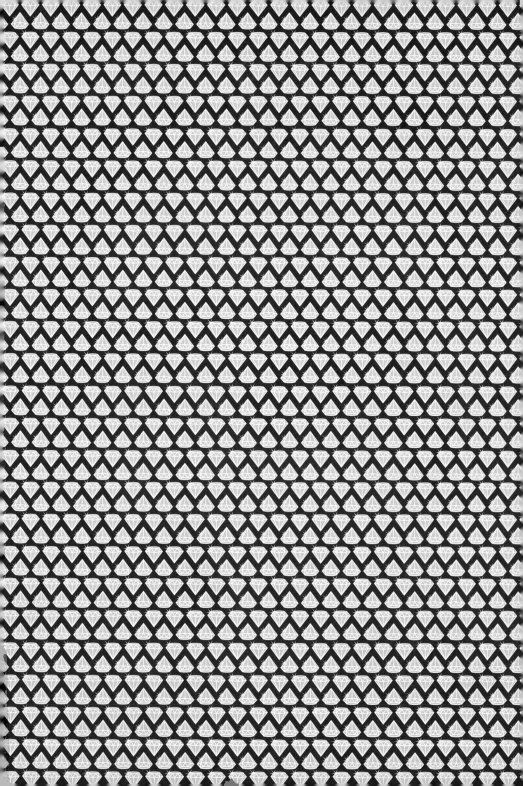

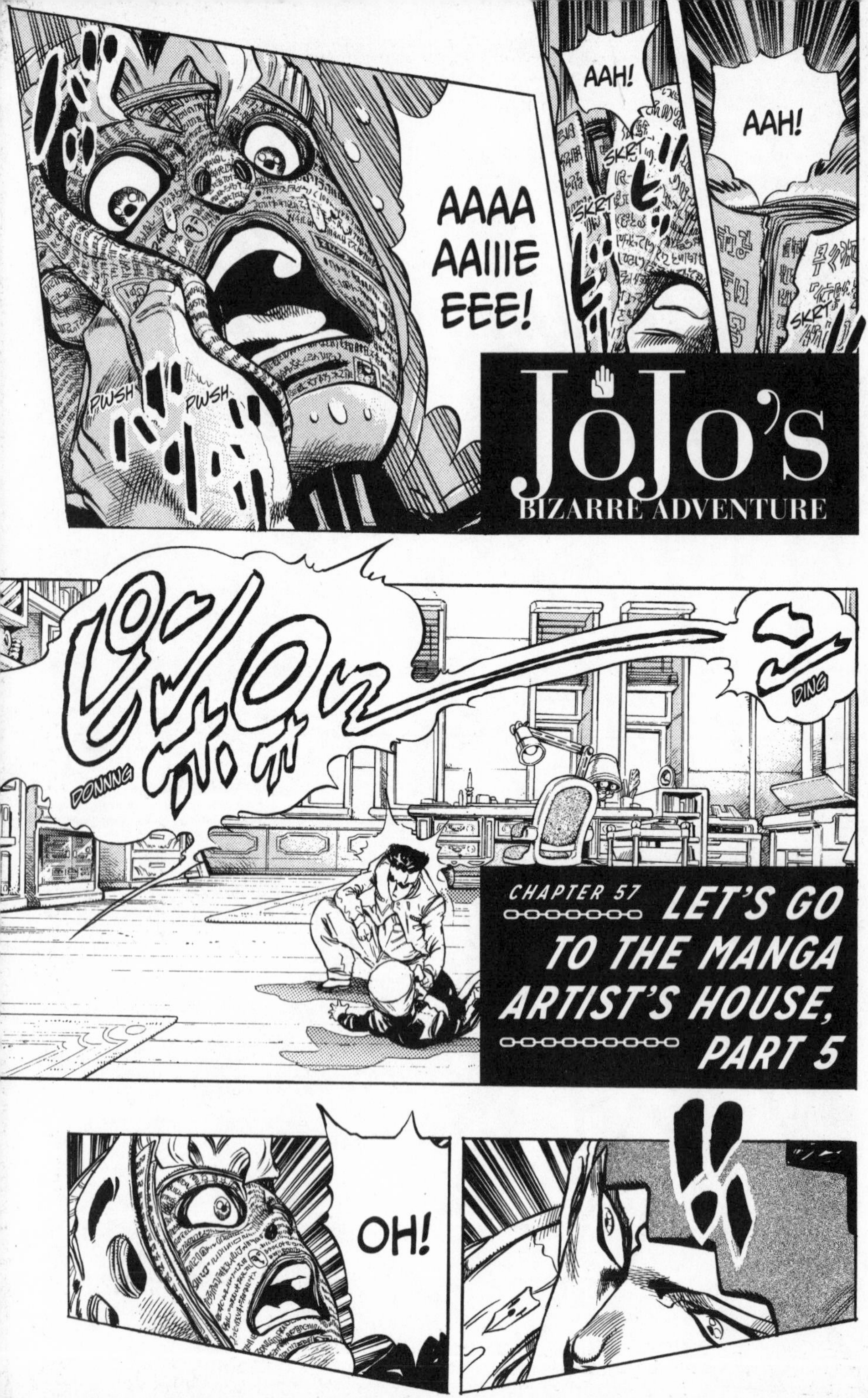

AAH!
AAH!
SKRT
SKRT
SKRT
AAAA AAIIIE EEE!
PWSH
PWSH
JoJo's
BIZARRE ADVENTURE
DING
DONNNG
CHAPTER 57
LET'S GO TO THE MANGA ARTIST'S HOUSE, PART 5
OH!

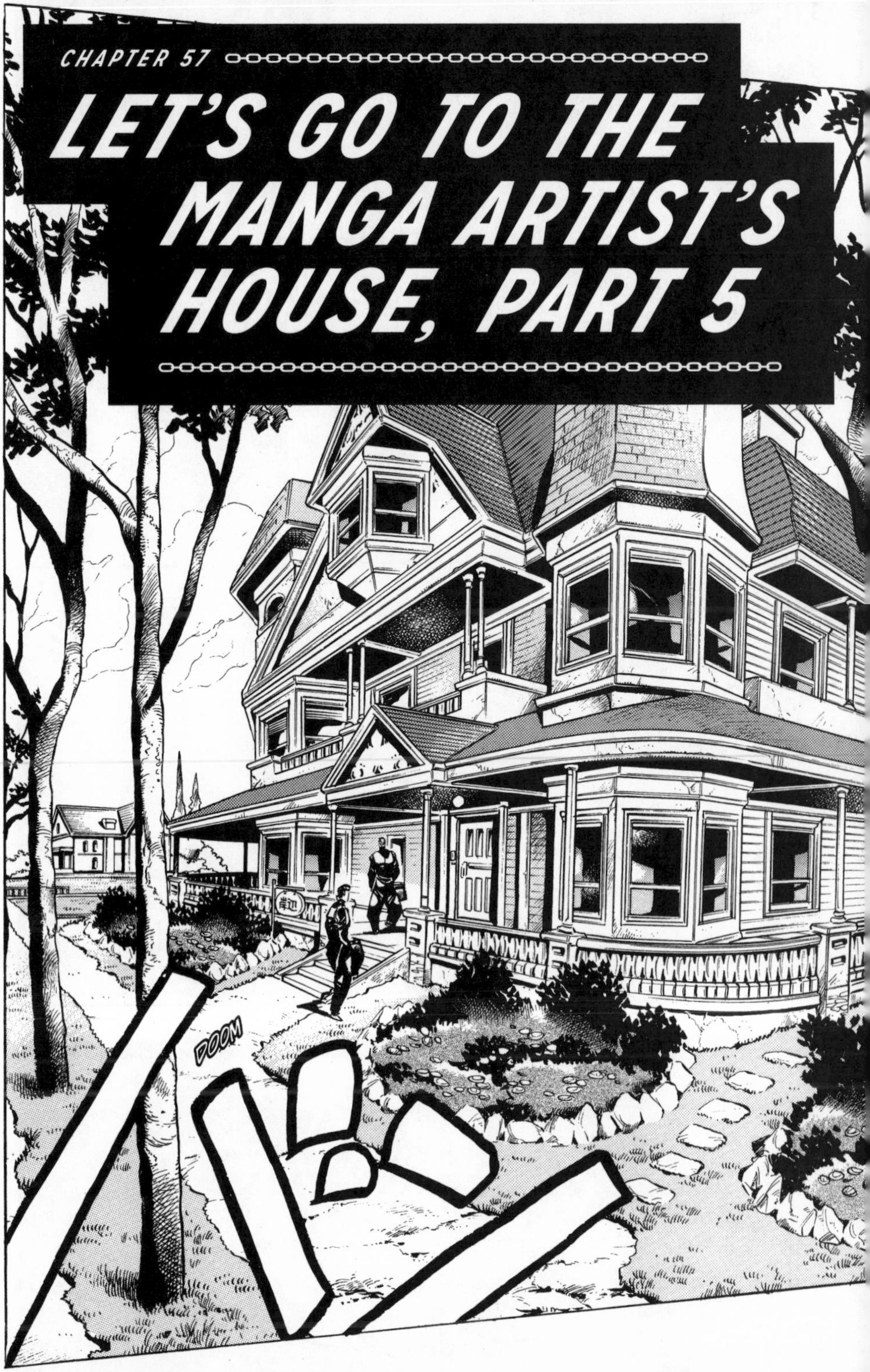
CHAPTER 57
LET'S GO TO THE MANGA ARTIST'S HOUSE, PART 5
DOOM

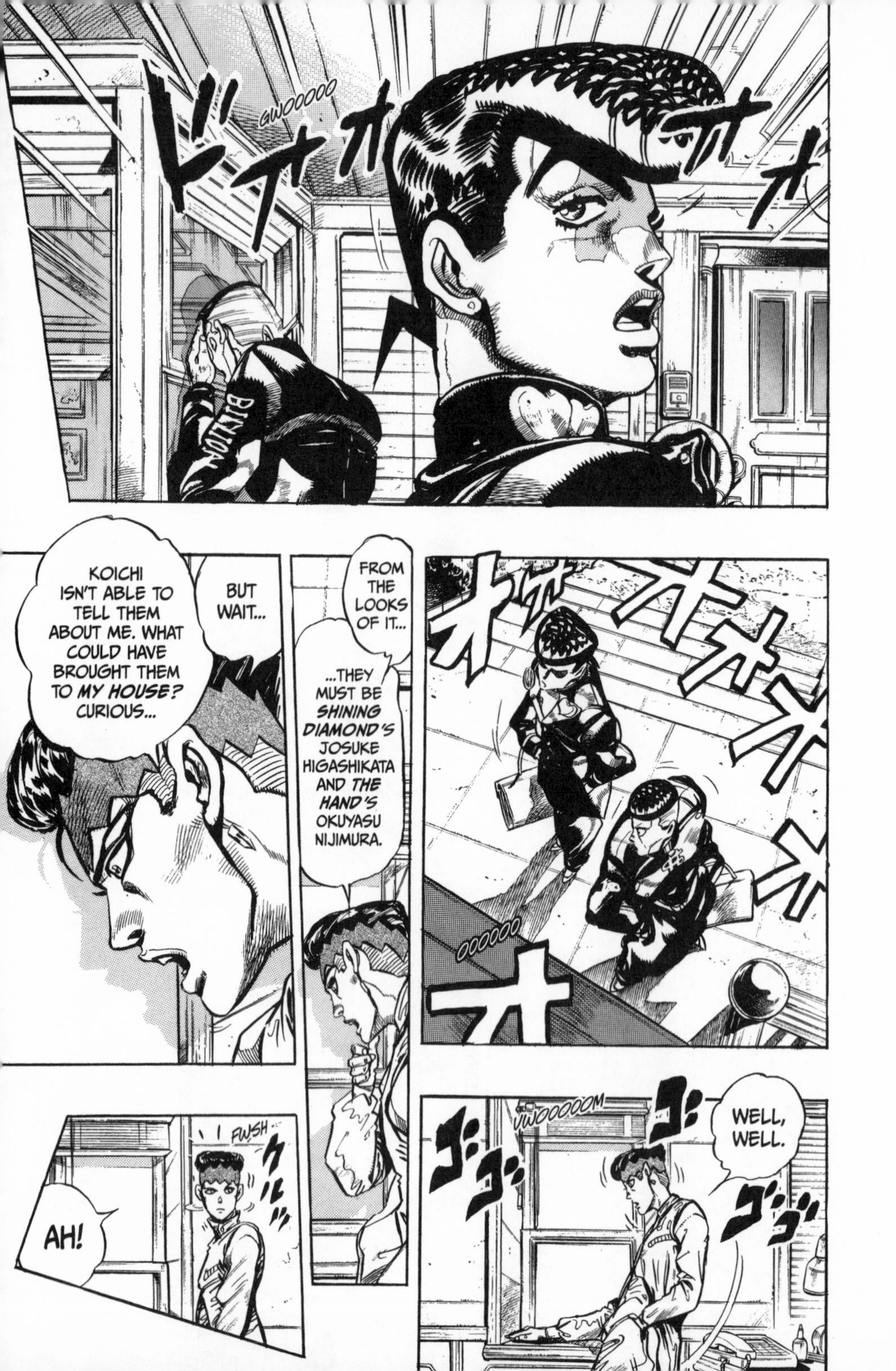
GWOOOOO
OOOOOO
FROM THE LOOKS OF IT...
...THEY MUST BE *SHINING DIAMOND'S* JOSUKE HIGASHIKATA AND *THE HAND'S* OKUYASU NIJIMURA.
BUT WAIT...
KOICHI ISN'T ABLE TO TELL THEM ABOUT ME. WHAT COULD HAVE BROUGHT THEM TO *MY HOUSE?* CURIOUS...
VWOOOOOM
WELL, WELL.
FWSH
AH!

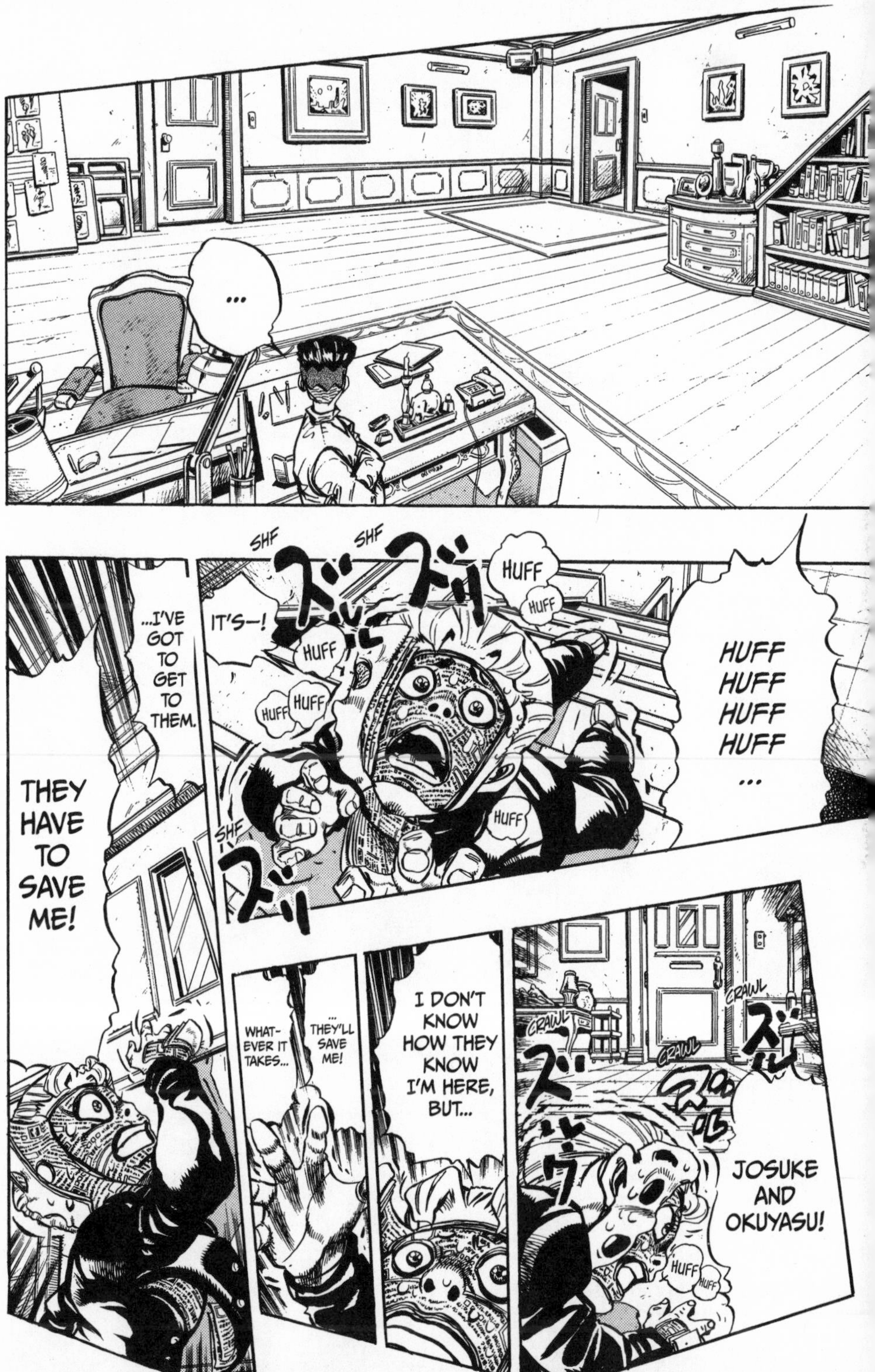

...
HUFF HUFF HUFF HUFF ...
SHF
SHF
HUFF
HUFF
IT'S—!
HUFF
HUFF
HUFF
HUFF
SHF
...I'VE GOT TO GET TO THEM.
CRAWL
CRAWL
CRAWL
JOSUKE AND OKUYASU!
HUFF
HUFF
I DON'T KNOW HOW THEY KNOW I'M HERE, BUT...
...THEY'LL SAVE ME!
WHAT-EVER IT TAKES...
THEY HAVE TO SAVE ME!

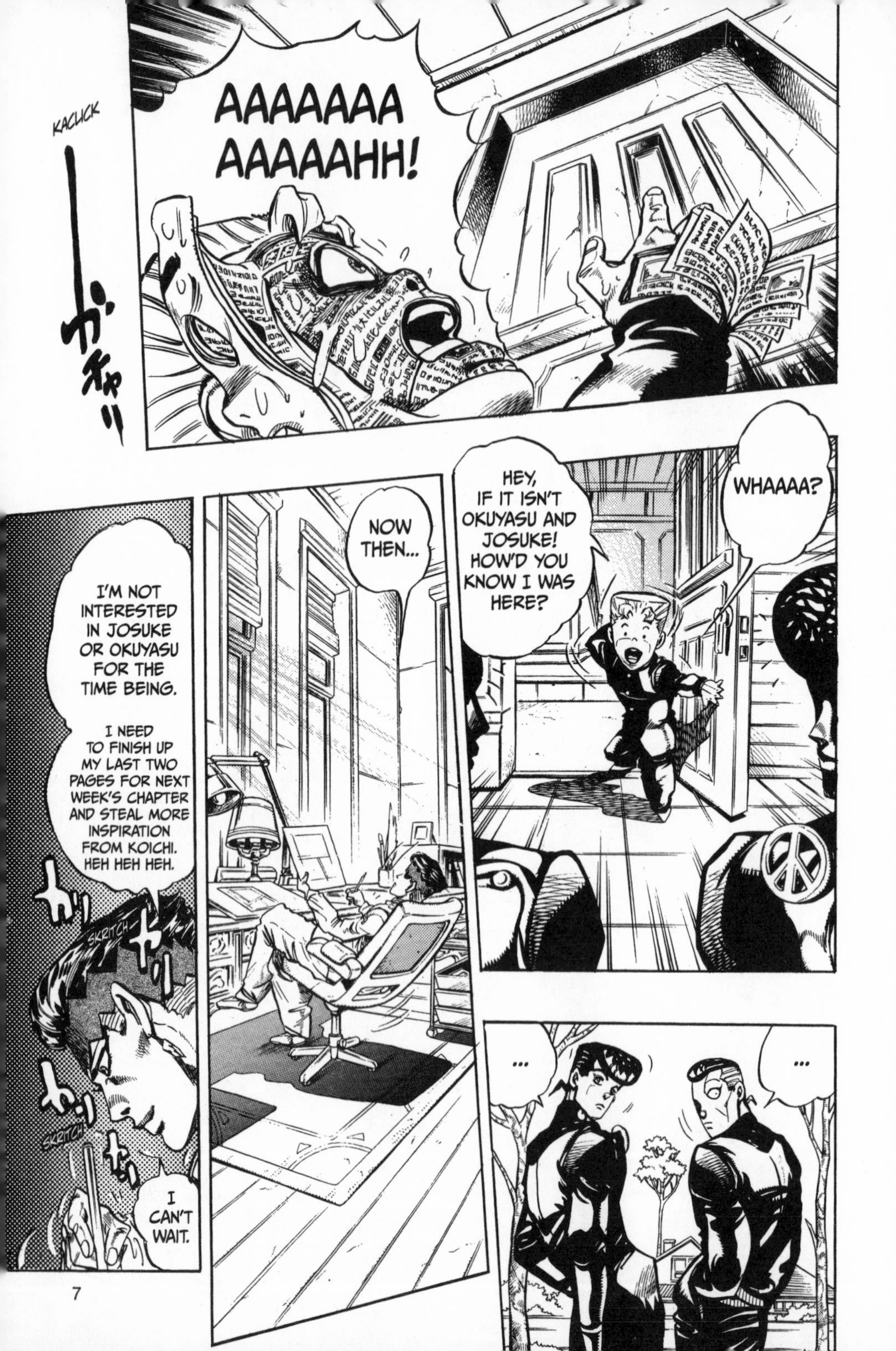
KACLICK
AAAAAAA AAAAAHH!
ガチャリ
WHAAAA?
HEY, IF IT ISN'T OKUYASU AND JOSUKE! HOW'D YOU KNOW I WAS HERE?
...
...
NOW THEN...
I'M NOT INTERESTED IN JOSUKE OR OKUYASU FOR THE TIME BEING.
I NEED TO FINISH UP MY LAST TWO PAGES FOR NEXT WEEK'S CHAPTER AND STEAL MORE INSPIRATION FROM KOICHI. HEH HEH HEH.
SKRITCH
SKRITCH
I CAN'T WAIT.

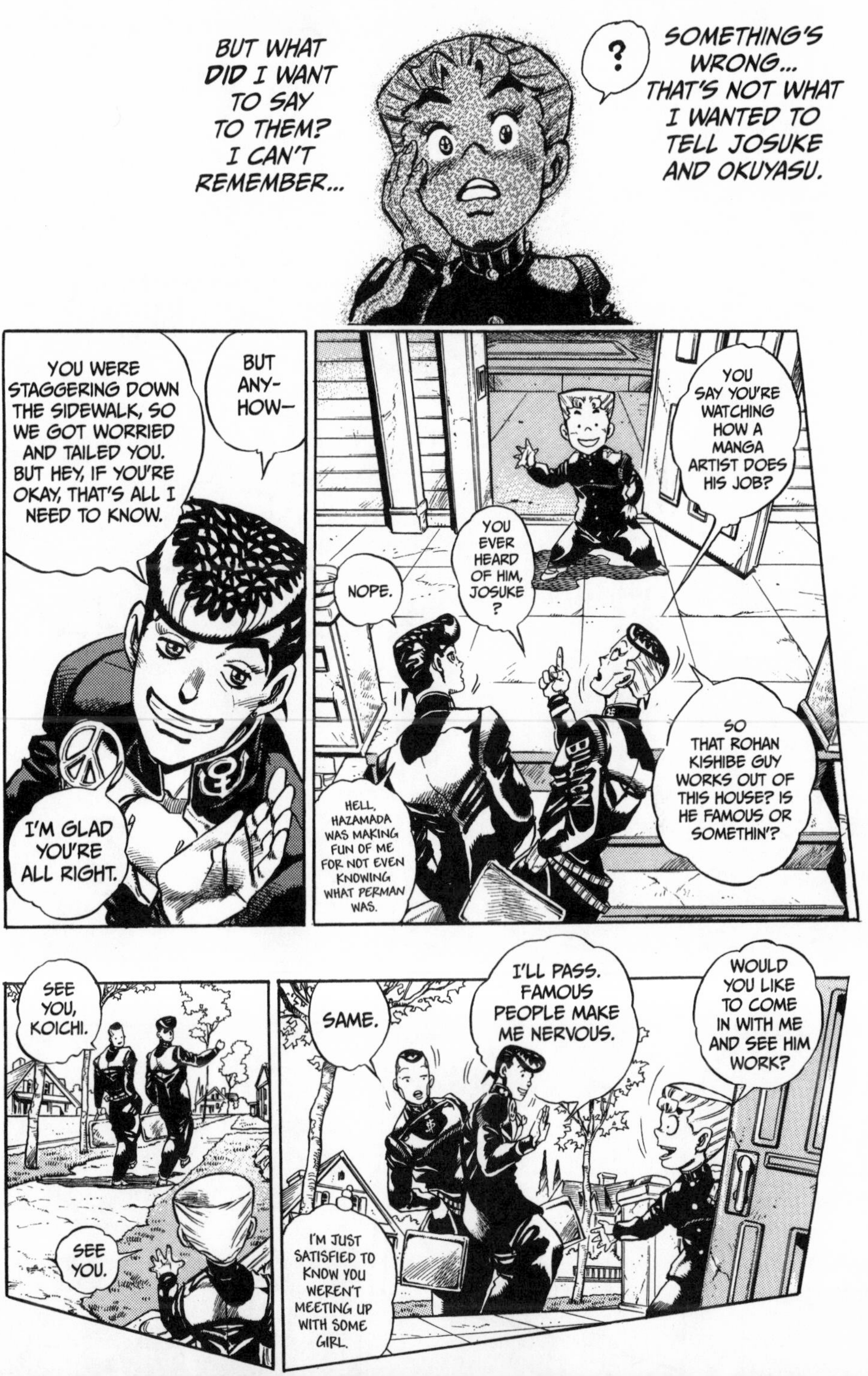
SOMETHING'S WRONG... THAT'S NOT WHAT I WANTED TO TELL JOSUKE AND OKUYASU.
?
BUT WHAT DID I WANT TO SAY TO THEM? I CAN'T REMEMBER...
YOU SAY YOU'RE WATCHING HOW A MANGA ARTIST DOES HIS JOB?
SO THAT ROHAN KISHIBE GUY WORKS OUT OF THIS HOUSE? IS HE FAMOUS OR SOMETHIN'?
YOU EVER HEARD OF HIM, JOSUKE?
NOPE.
HELL, HAZAMADA WAS MAKING FUN OF ME FOR NOT EVEN KNOWING WHAT PERMAN WAS.
BUT ANY-HOW—
YOU WERE STAGGERING DOWN THE SIDEWALK, SO WE GOT WORRIED AND TAILED YOU. BUT HEY, IF YOU'RE OKAY, THAT'S ALL I NEED TO KNOW.
I'M GLAD YOU'RE ALL RIGHT.
WOULD YOU LIKE TO COME IN WITH ME AND SEE HIM WORK?
I'LL PASS. FAMOUS PEOPLE MAKE ME NERVOUS.
SAME.
I'M JUST SATISFIED TO KNOW YOU WEREN'T MEETING UP WITH SOME GIRL.
SEE YOU, KOICHI.
SEE YOU.

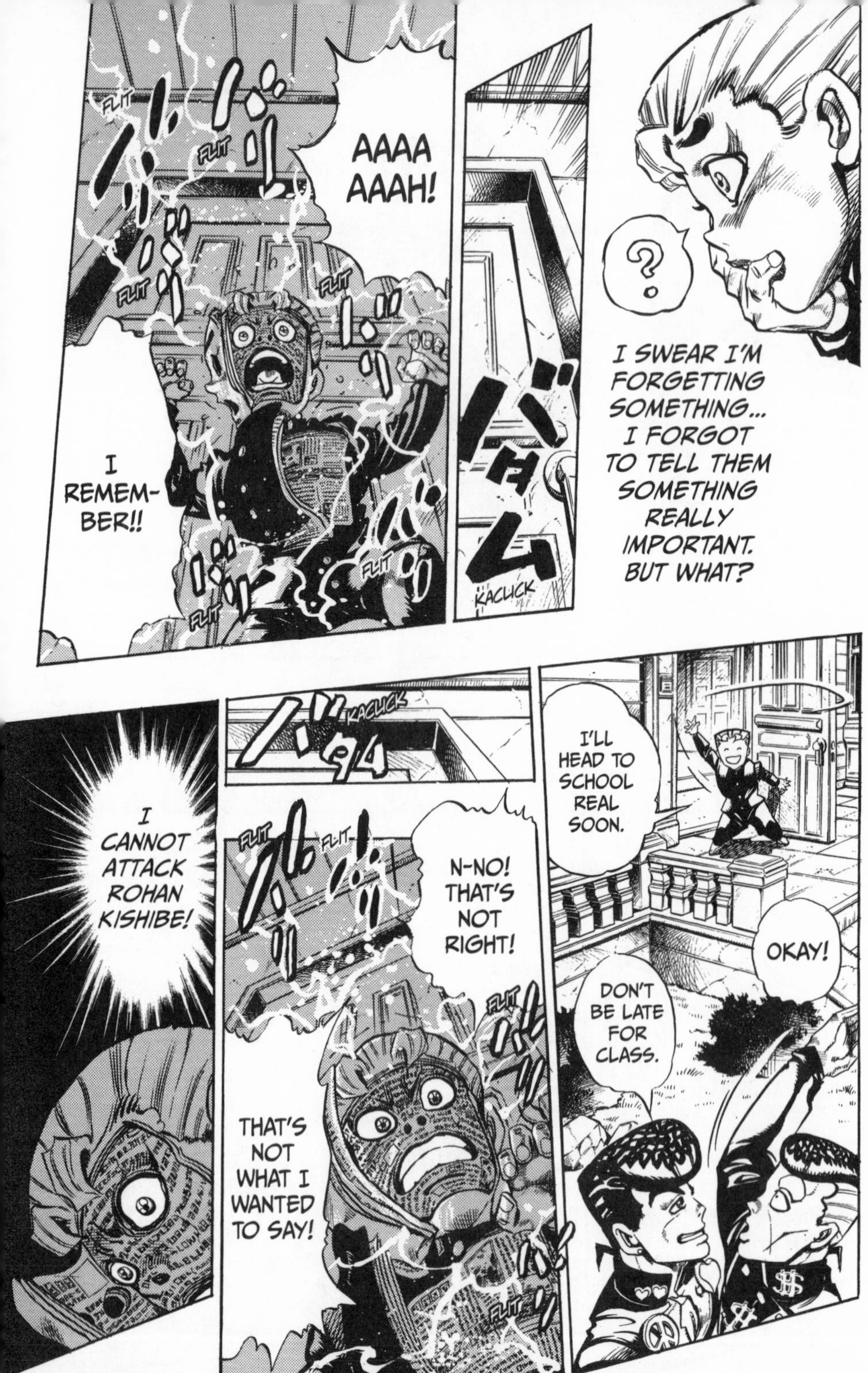
?
I SWEAR I'M FORGETTING SOMETHING... I FORGOT TO TELL THEM SOMETHING REALLY IMPORTANT. BUT WHAT?
KACLICK
AAAA AAAH!
FLIT
FLIT
FLIT
FLIT
FLIT
FLIT
I REMEMBER!!
I'LL HEAD TO SCHOOL REAL SOON.
OKAY!
DON'T BE LATE FOR CLASS.
KACLICK
FLIT
FLIT
N-NO! THAT'S NOT RIGHT!
FLIT
THAT'S NOT WHAT I WANTED TO SAY!
FLIT
I CANNOT ATTACK ROHAN KISHIBE!

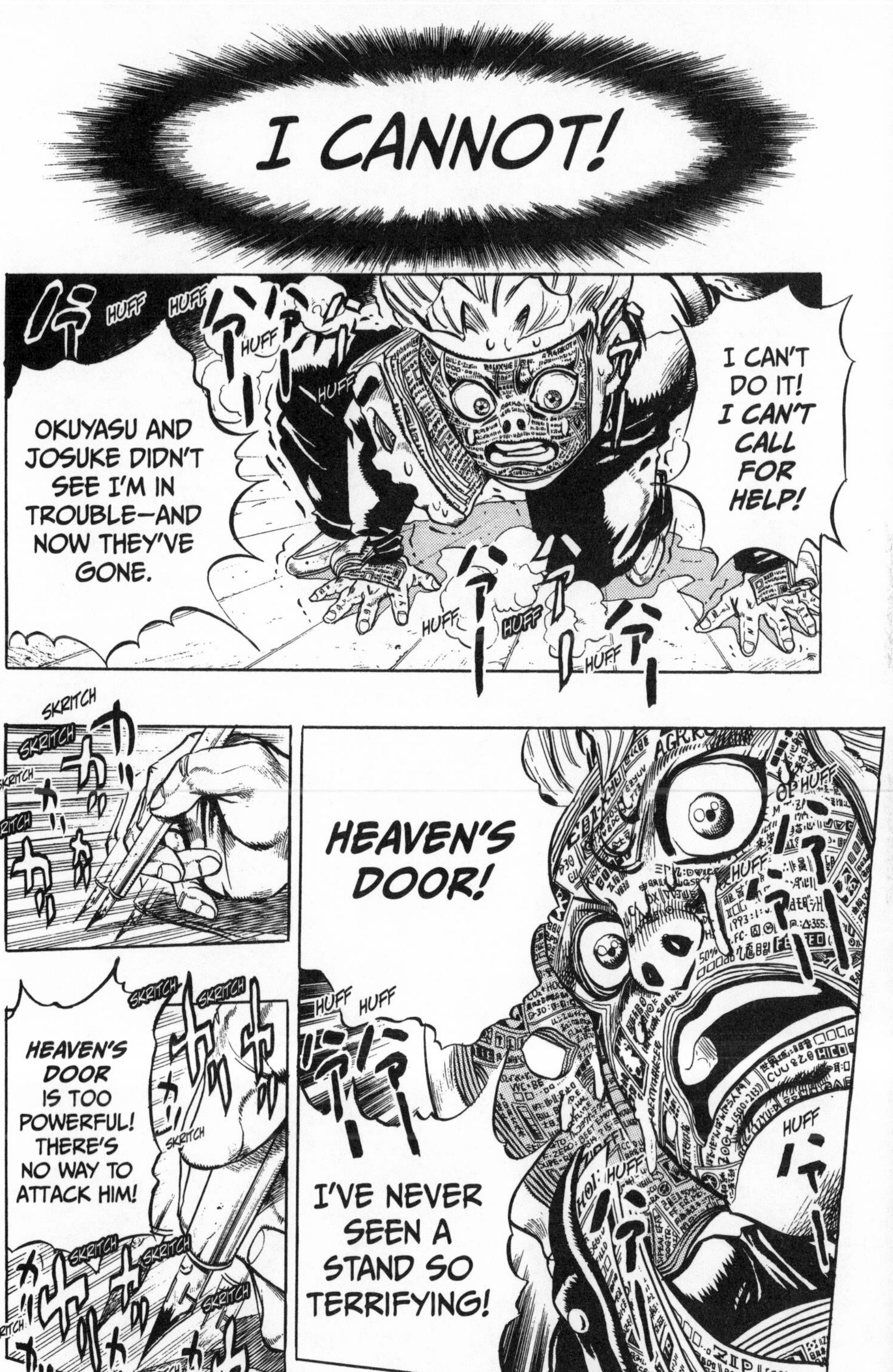
I CANNOT!
I CAN'T DO IT! I CAN'T CALL FOR HELP!
HUFF HUFF HUFF HUFF
OKUYASU AND JOSUKE DIDN'T SEE I'M IN TROUBLE—AND NOW THEY'VE GONE.
HUFF HUFF HUFF
HUFF
HEAVEN'S DOOR!
HUFF HUFF
I'VE NEVER SEEN A STAND SO TERRIFYING!
SKRITCH SKRITCH SKRITCH SKRITCH
SKRITCH SKRITCH
HEAVEN'S DOOR IS TOO POWERFUL! THERE'S NO WAY TO ATTACK HIM!
SKRITCH SKRITCH SKRITCH SKRITCH SKRITCH SKRITCH

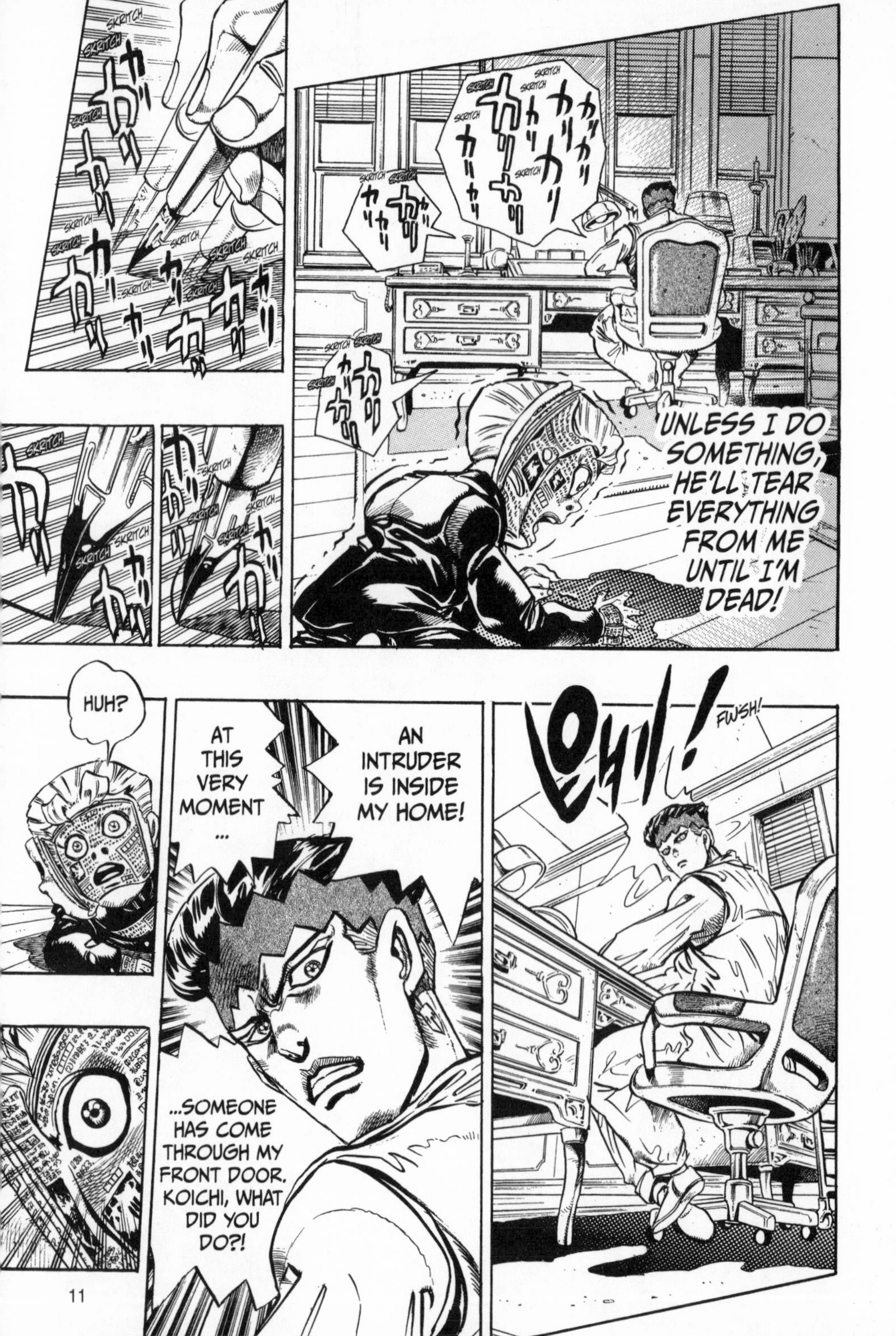
SKRITCH
SKRITCH
SKRITCH
SKRITCH
SKRITCH
SKRITCH
SKRITCH
SKRITCH
UNLESS I DO SOMETHING, HE'LL TEAR EVERYTHING FROM ME UNTIL I'M DEAD!
SKRITCH
SKRITCH
SKRITCH
SKRITCH
SKRITCH
SKRITCH
SKRITCH
SKRITCH
SKRITCH
SKRITCH
SKRITCH
SKRITCH
SKRITCH
FWSH!
AN INTRUDER IS INSIDE MY HOME!
AT THIS VERY MOMENT ...
...SOMEONE HAS COME THROUGH MY FRONT DOOR. KOICHI, WHAT DID YOU DO?!
HUH?

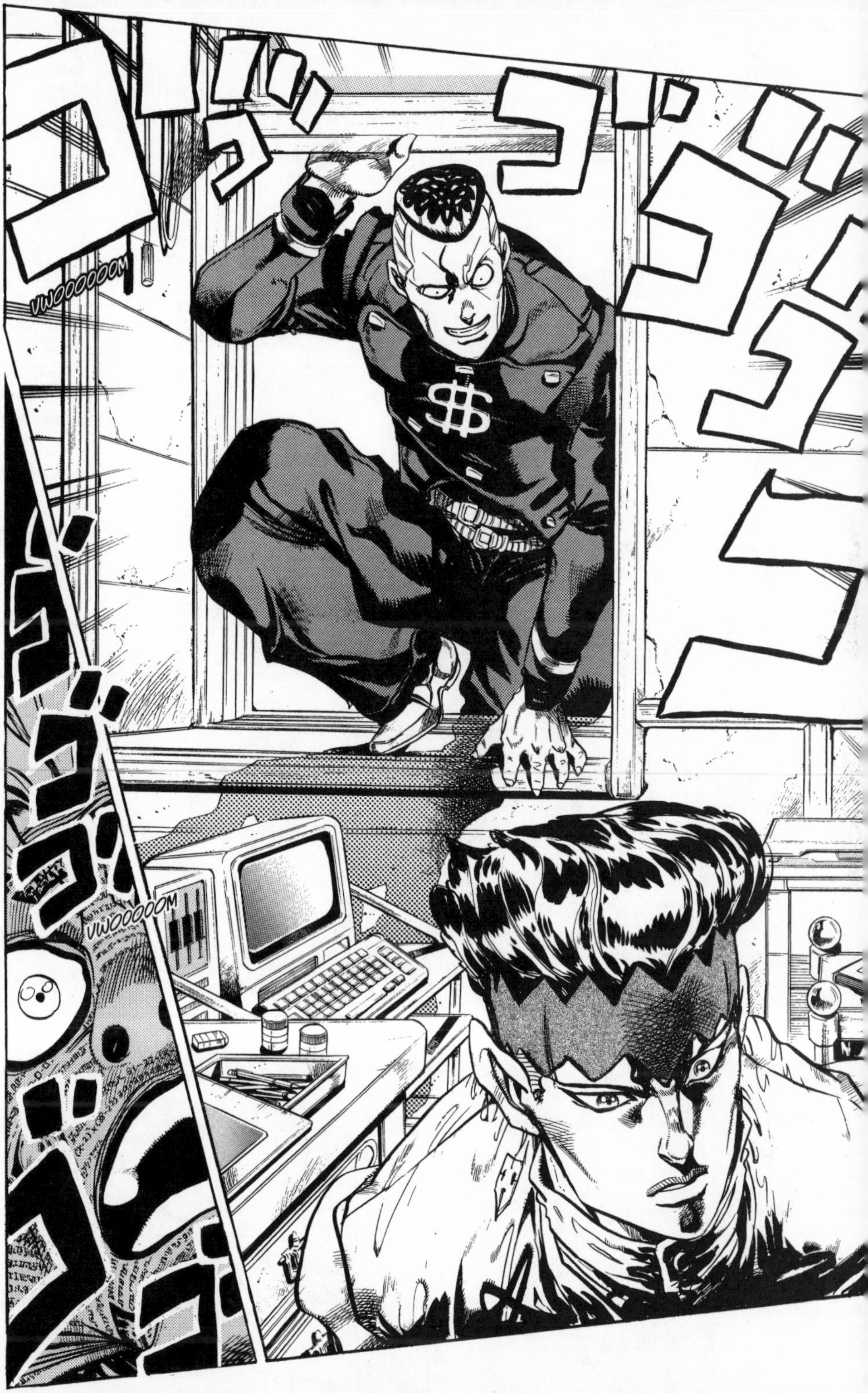
VWOOOOOOOM
VWOOOOOM

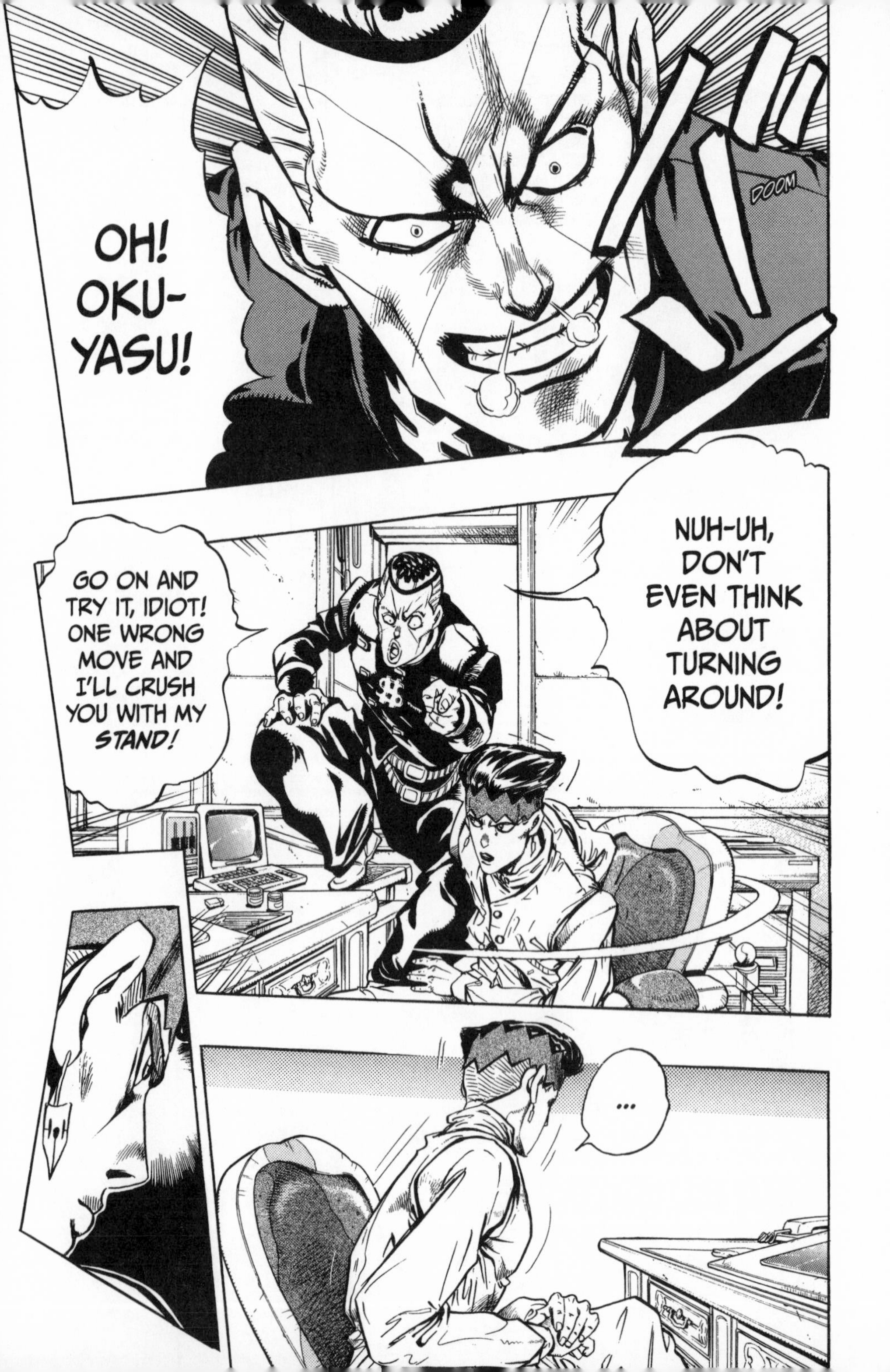
OH! OKU-YASU!
DOOM
NUH-UH, DON'T EVEN THINK ABOUT TURNING AROUND!
GO ON AND TRY IT, IDIOT! ONE WRONG MOVE AND I'LL CRUSH YOU WITH MY *STAND*!
...

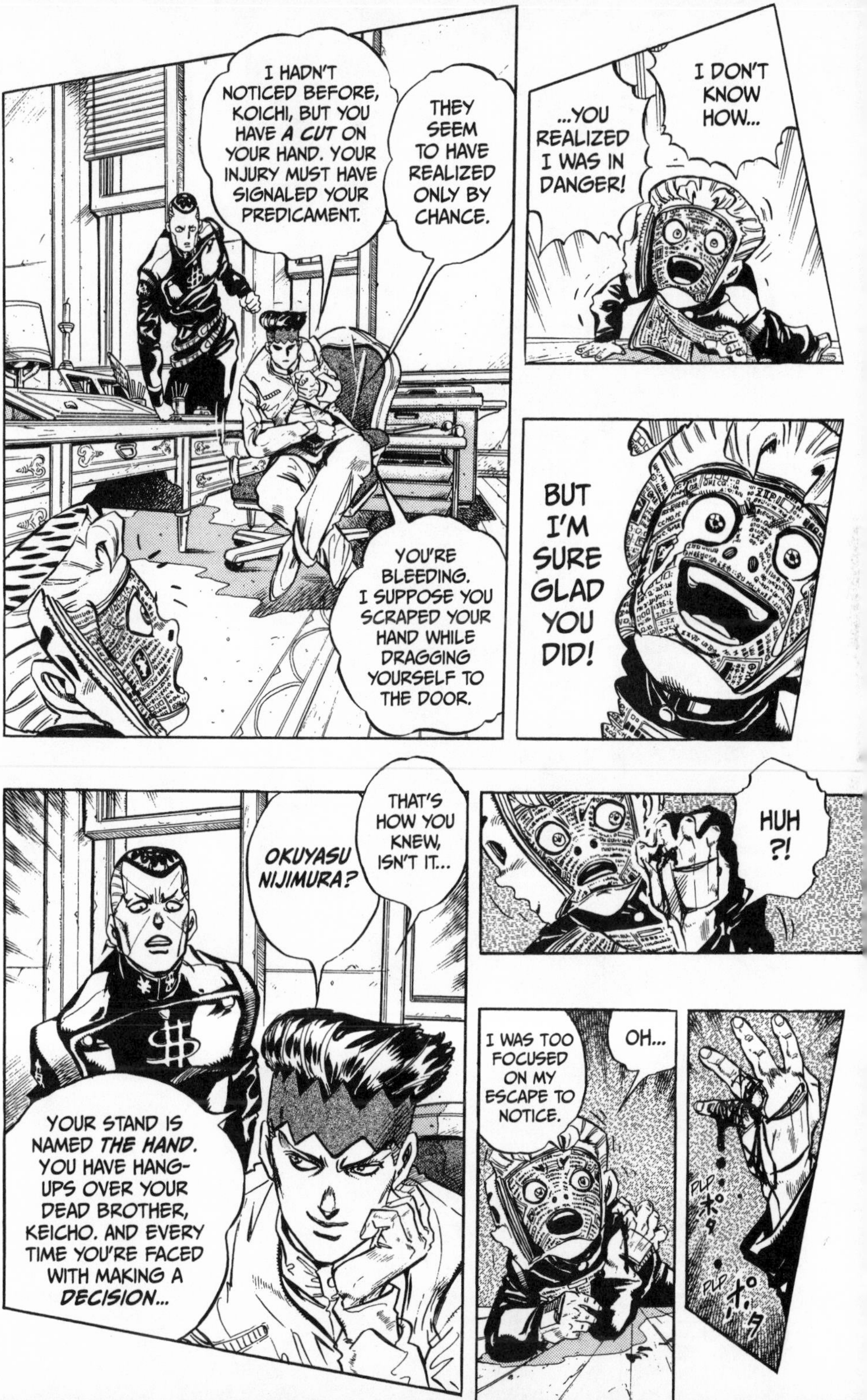
I DON'T KNOW HOW...
...YOU REALIZED I WAS IN DANGER!
BUT I'M SURE GLAD YOU DID!
THEY SEEM TO HAVE REALIZED ONLY BY CHANCE.
I HADN'T NOTICED BEFORE, KOICHI, BUT YOU HAVE *A CUT* ON YOUR HAND. YOUR INJURY MUST HAVE SIGNALED YOUR PREDICAMENT.
YOU'RE BLEEDING. I SUPPOSE YOU SCRAPED YOUR HAND WHILE DRAGGING YOURSELF TO THE DOOR.
HUH?!
PLP ポタ
PLP ポタ
OH...
I WAS TOO FOCUSED ON MY ESCAPE TO NOTICE.
THAT'S HOW YOU KNEW, ISN'T IT...
OKUYASU NIJIMURA?
YOUR STAND IS NAMED ***THE HAND***. YOU HAVE HANG-UPS OVER YOUR DEAD BROTHER, KEICHO. AND EVERY TIME YOU'RE FACED WITH MAKING A ***DECISION***...

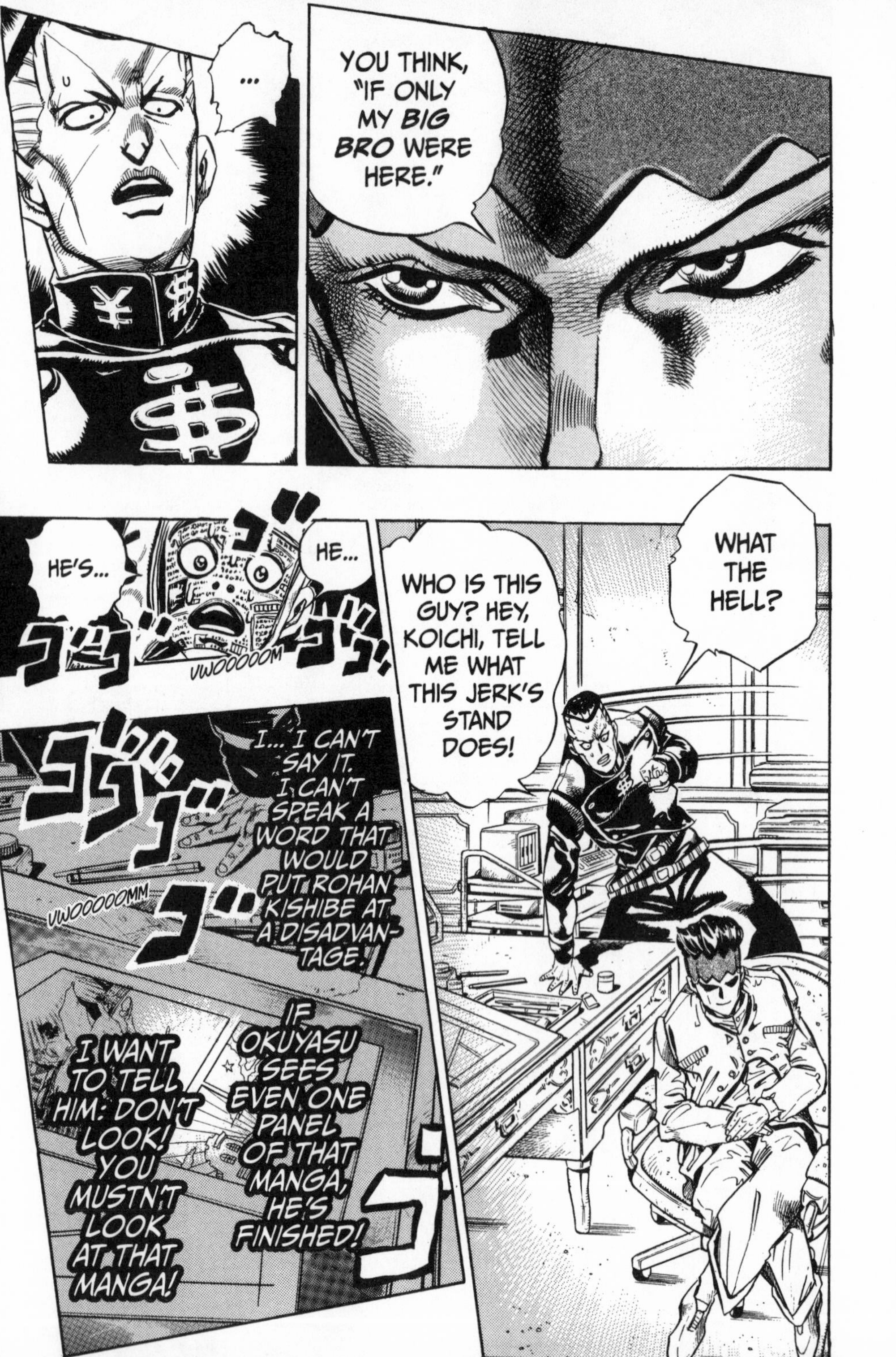
YOU THINK, "IF ONLY MY BIG BRO WERE HERE."
...
WHAT THE HELL?
WHO IS THIS GUY? HEY, KOICHI, TELL ME WHAT THIS JERK'S STAND DOES!
HE...
HE'S...
VWOOOOOM
I... I CAN'T SAY IT. I CAN'T SPEAK A WORD THAT WOULD PUT ROHAN KISHIBE AT A DISADVANTAGE!
VWOOOOOMM
IF OKUYASU SEES EVEN ONE PANEL OF THAT MANGA, HE'S FINISHED!
I WANT TO TELL HIM: DON'T LOOK! YOU MUSTN'T LOOK AT THAT MANGA!

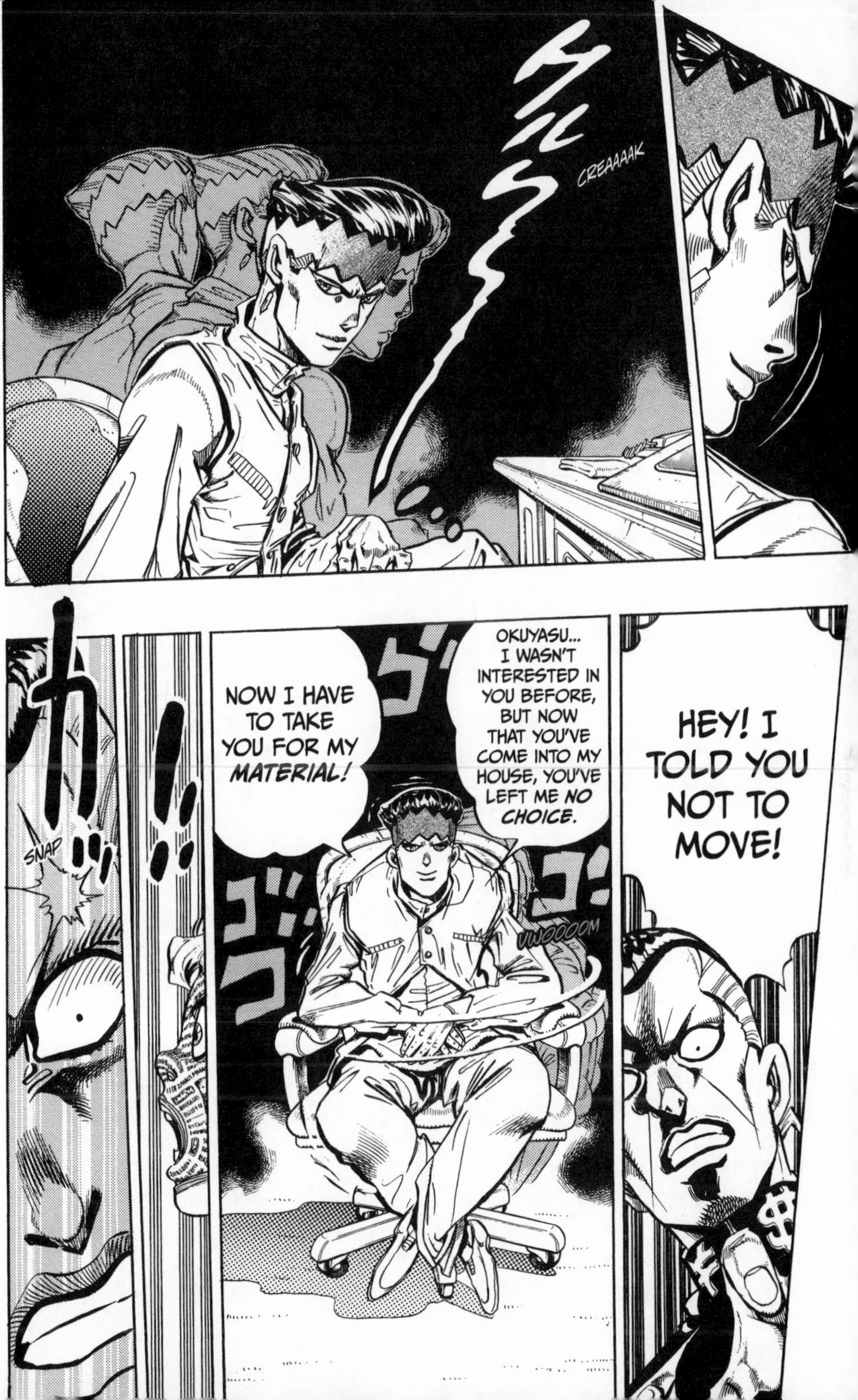
CREAAAAK
HEY! I TOLD YOU NOT TO MOVE!
OKUYASU... I WASN'T INTERESTED IN YOU BEFORE, BUT NOW THAT YOU'VE COME INTO MY HOUSE, YOU'VE LEFT ME *NO CHOICE*.
NOW I HAVE TO TAKE YOU FOR MY *MATERIAL*!
UWOOOOM
SNAP

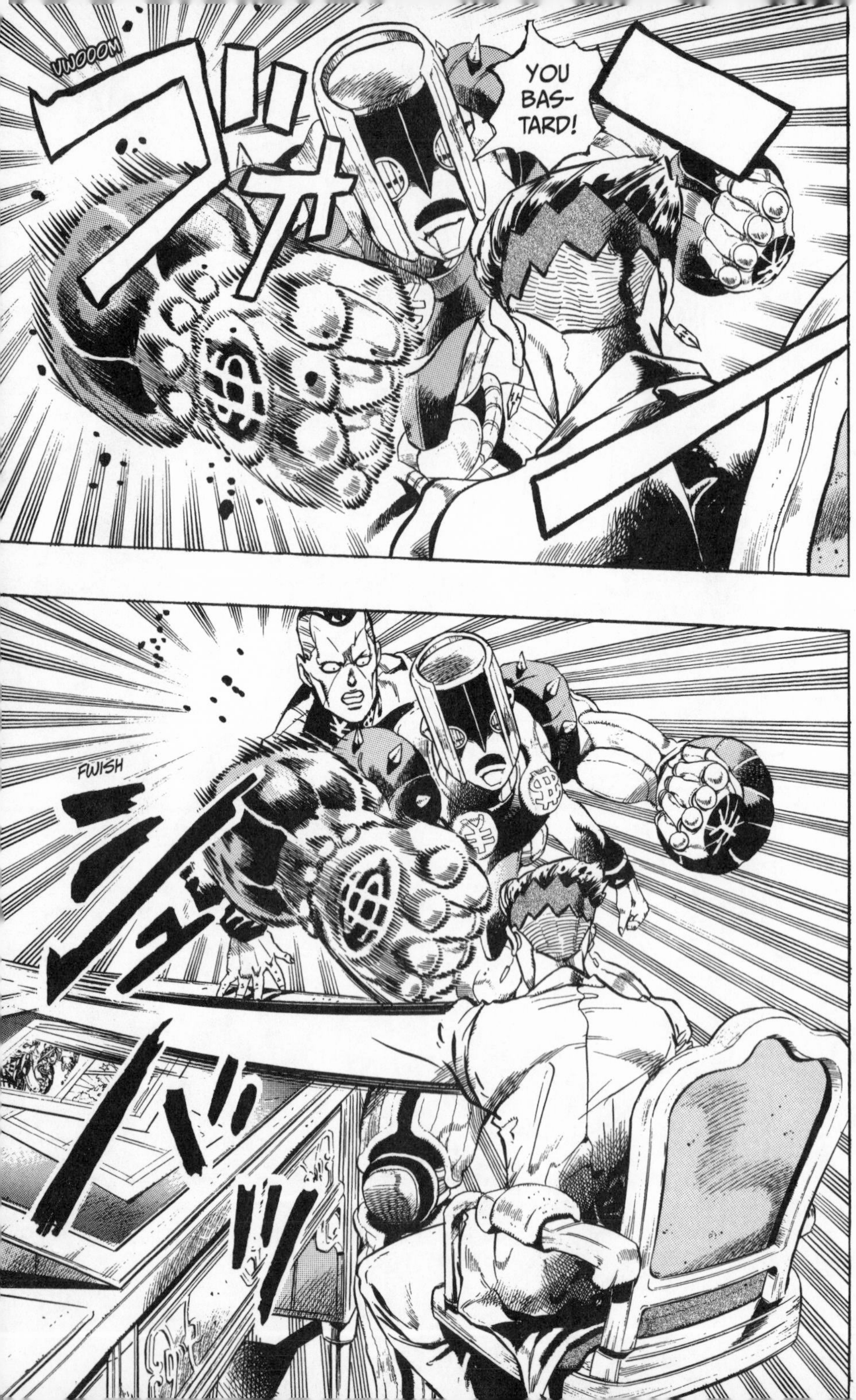
YOU BAS-TARD!
UWOOOM
FWISH

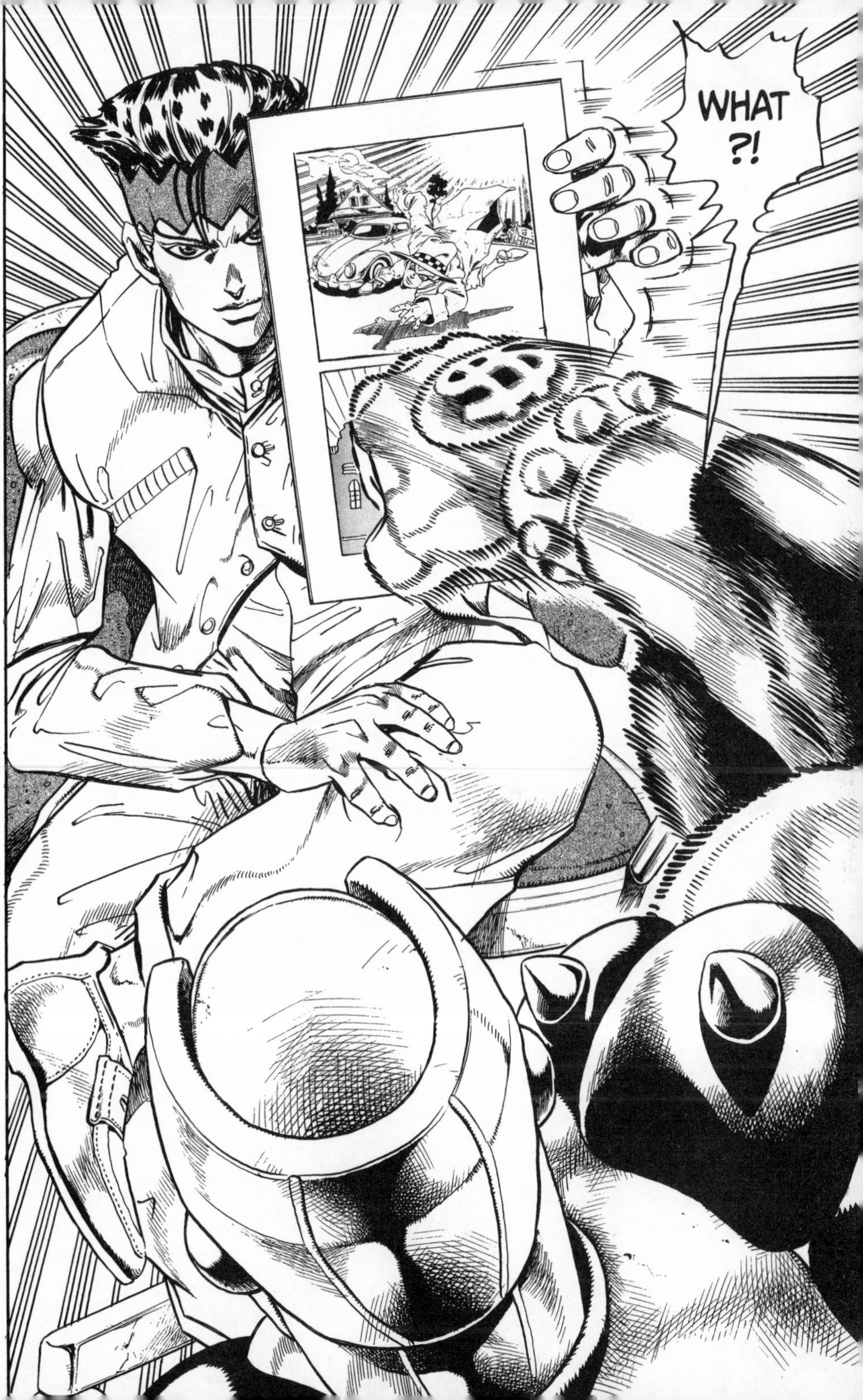
WHAT ?!

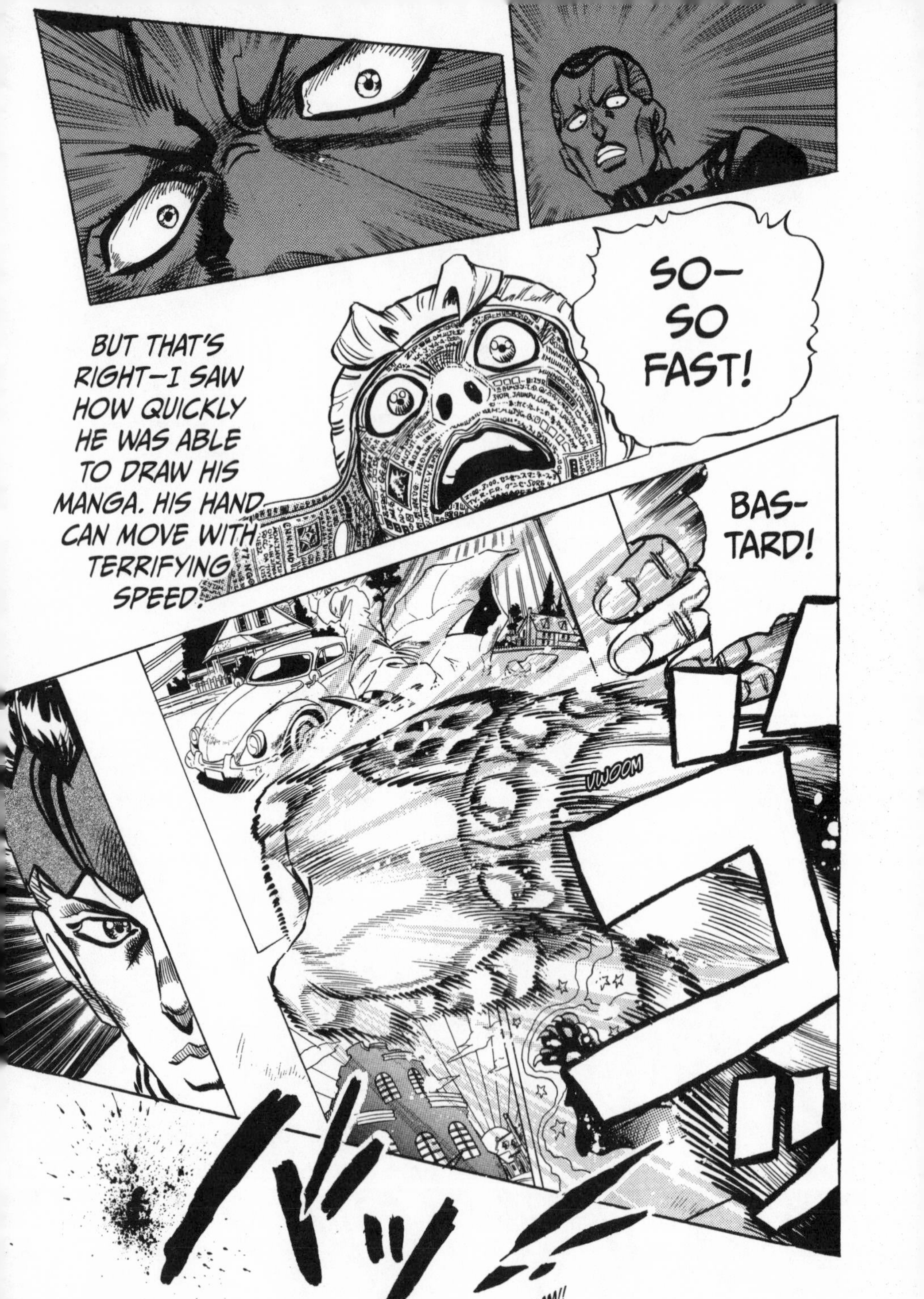
SO-SO FAST!
BUT THAT'S RIGHT—I SAW HOW QUICKLY HE WAS ABLE TO DRAW HIS MANGA. HIS HAND CAN MOVE WITH TERRIFYING SPEED!
BAS-TARD!
UWOOM
BAM!!

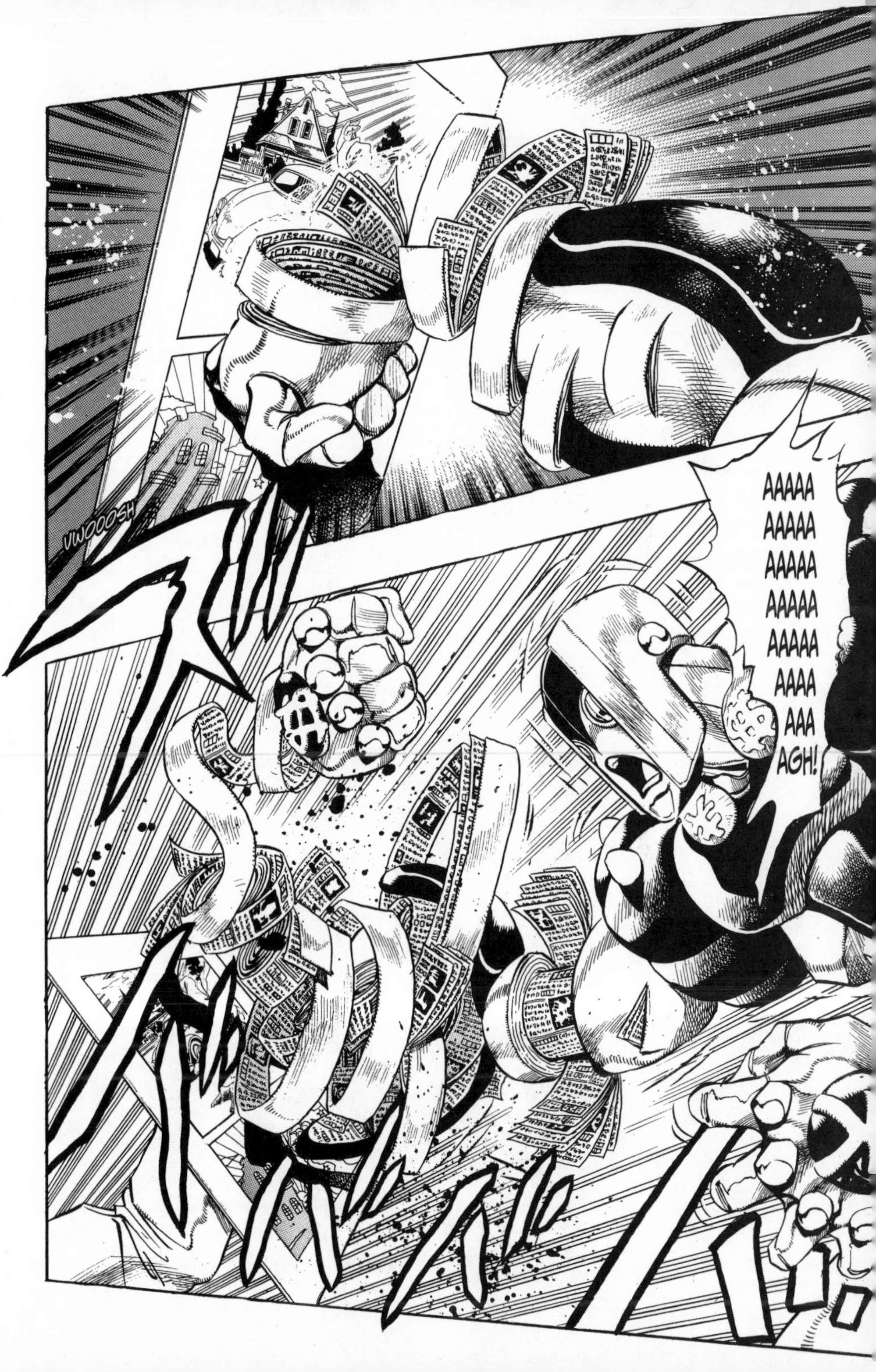
AAAAAAAAAAAAAAAAAAAAAAAAAAAAAAAAAAAAAAAGH!
VWOOOSH

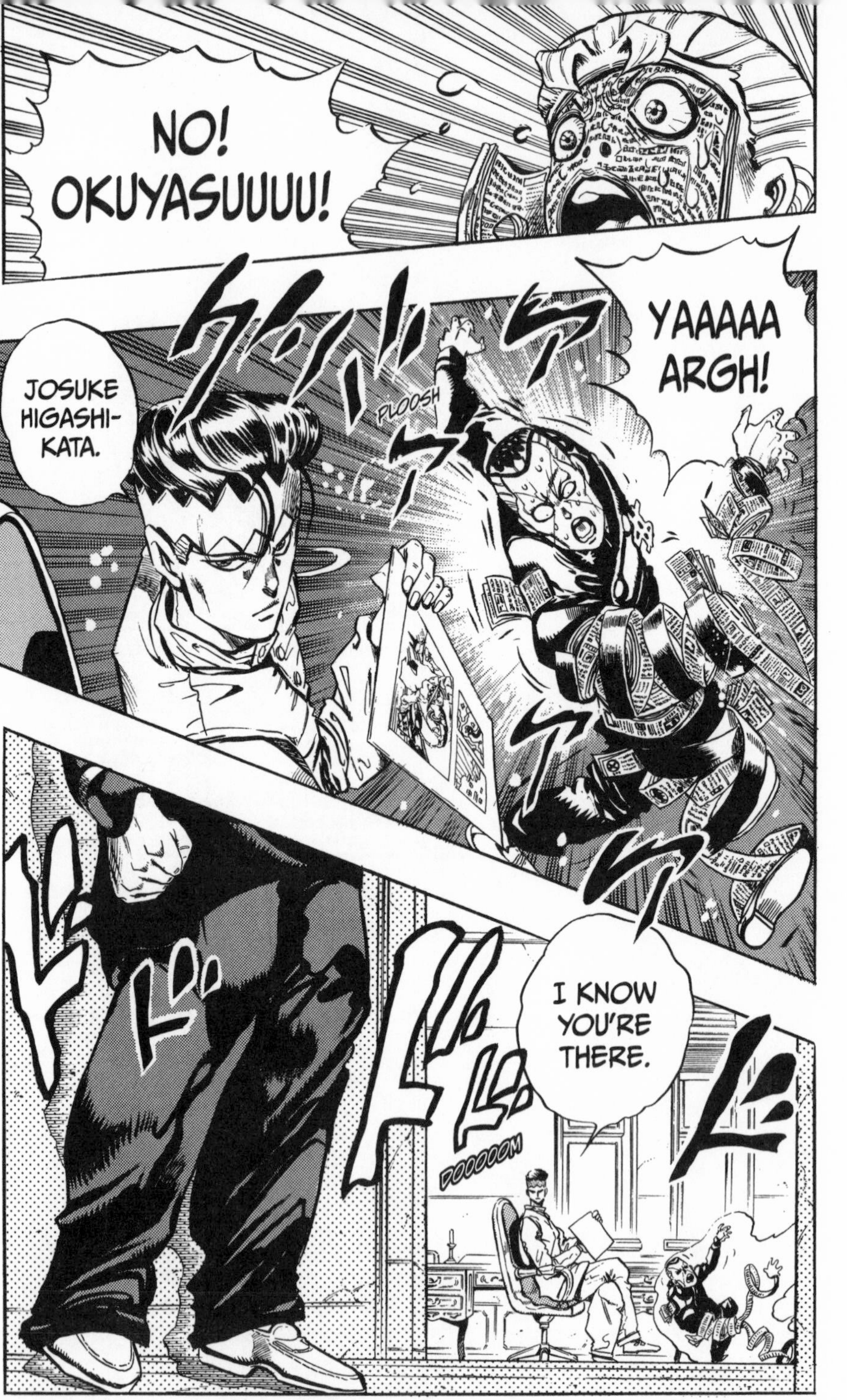
NO! OKUYASUUUU!
YAAAAA ARGH!
PLOOSH
JOSUKE HIGASHI-KATA.
I KNOW YOU'RE THERE.
DOOOOOM

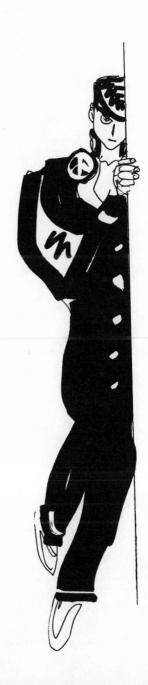

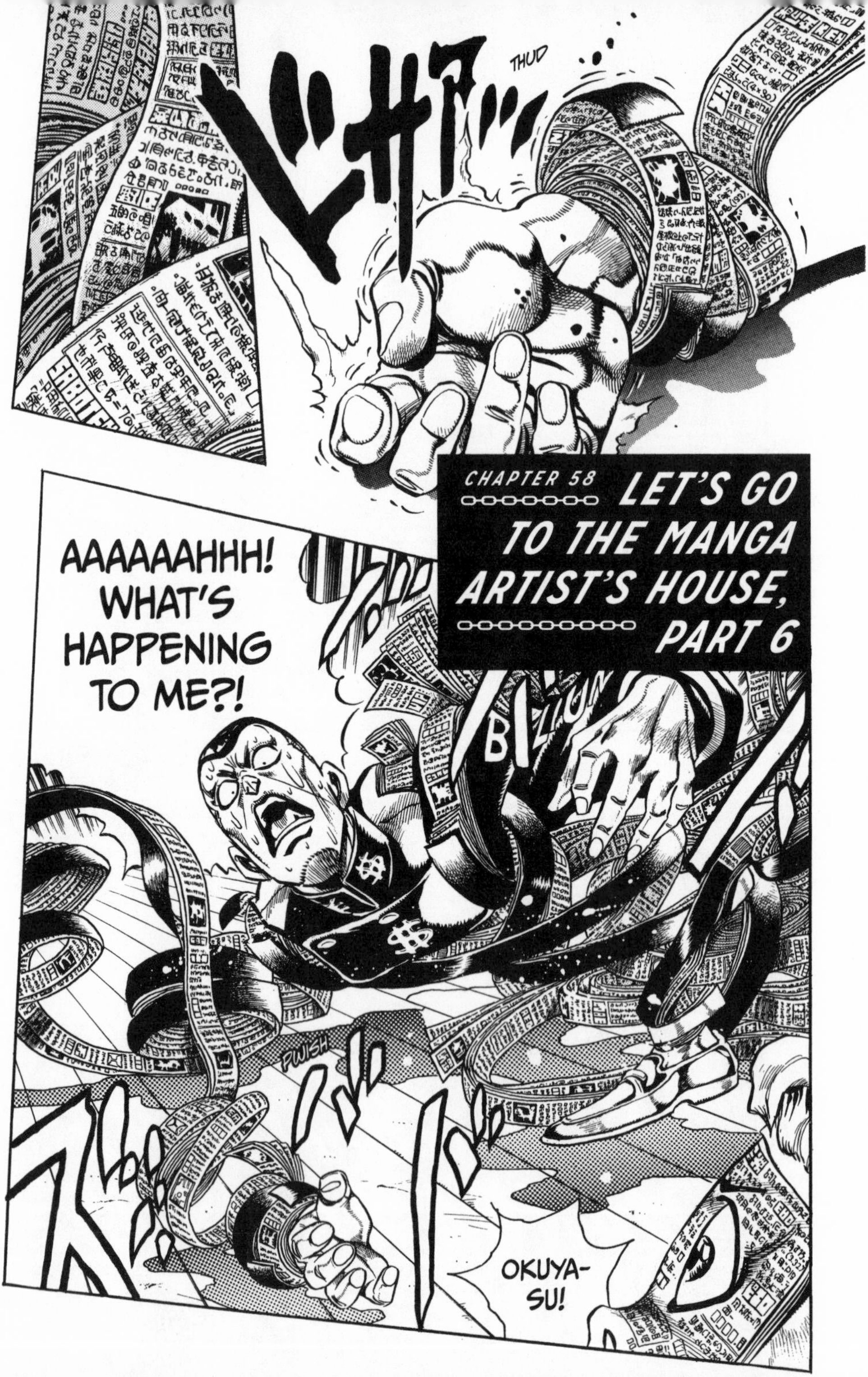
THUD
CHAPTER 58
LET'S GO TO THE MANGA ARTIST'S HOUSE, PART 6
AAAAAAHHH! WHAT'S HAPPENING TO ME?!
PWISH
OKUYA-SU!

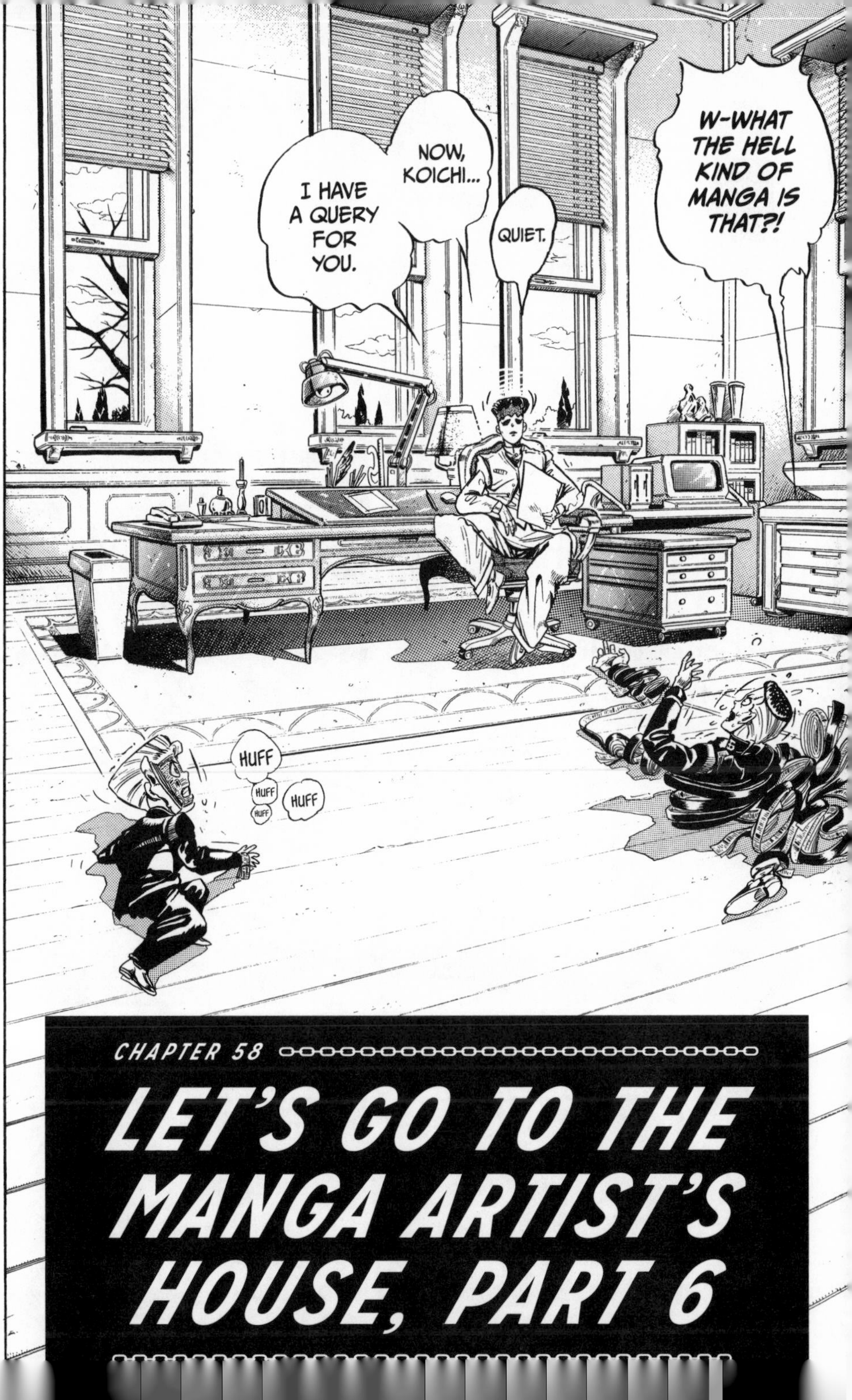
W-WHAT THE HELL KIND OF MANGA IS THAT?!
QUIET.
NOW, KOICHI...
I HAVE A QUERY FOR YOU.
HUFF
HUFF
HUFF
HUFF

CHAPTER 58

LET'S GO TO THE MANGA ARTIST'S HOUSE, PART 6

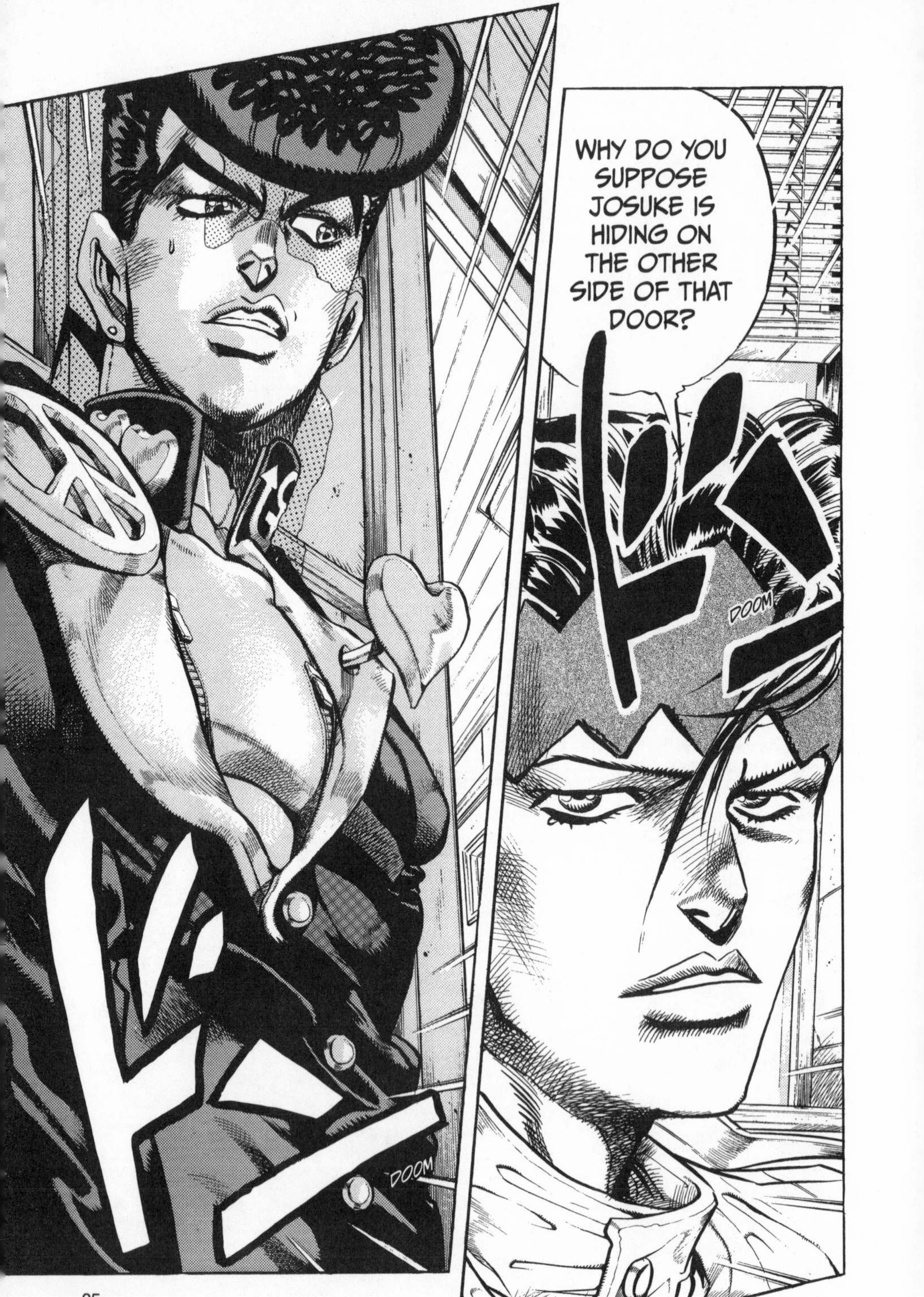
WHY DO YOU SUPPOSE JOSUKE IS HIDING ON THE OTHER SIDE OF THAT DOOR?
DOOM
DOOM

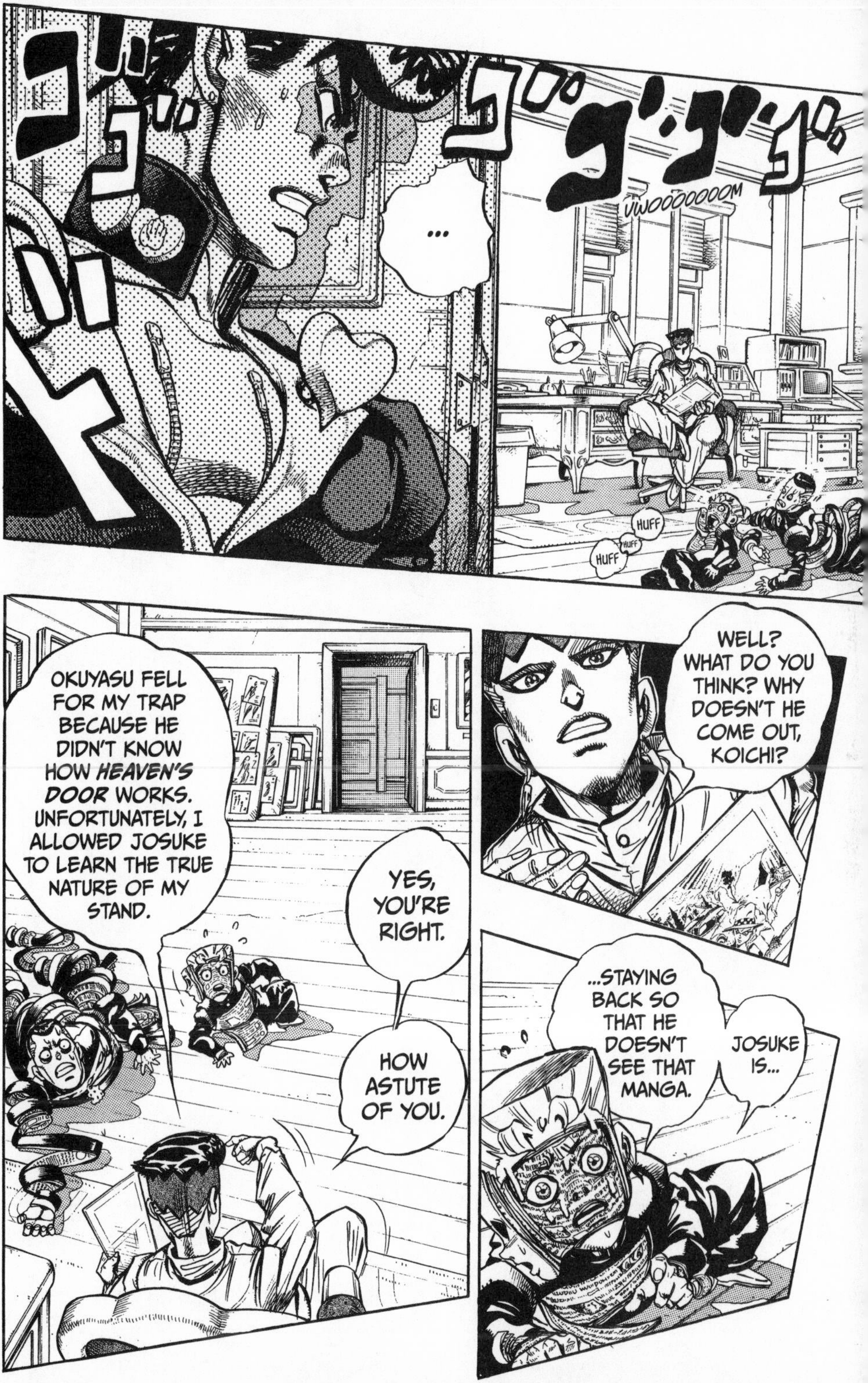
UWOOOOOOOM
HUFF
HUFF
HUFF
...
WELL? WHAT DO YOU THINK? WHY DOESN'T HE COME OUT, KOICHI?
JOSUKE IS...
...STAYING BACK SO THAT HE DOESN'T SEE THAT MANGA.
OKUYASU FELL FOR MY TRAP BECAUSE HE DIDN'T KNOW HOW *HEAVEN'S DOOR* WORKS. UNFORTUNATELY, I ALLOWED JOSUKE TO LEARN THE TRUE NATURE OF MY STAND.
YES, YOU'RE RIGHT.
HOW ASTUTE OF YOU.

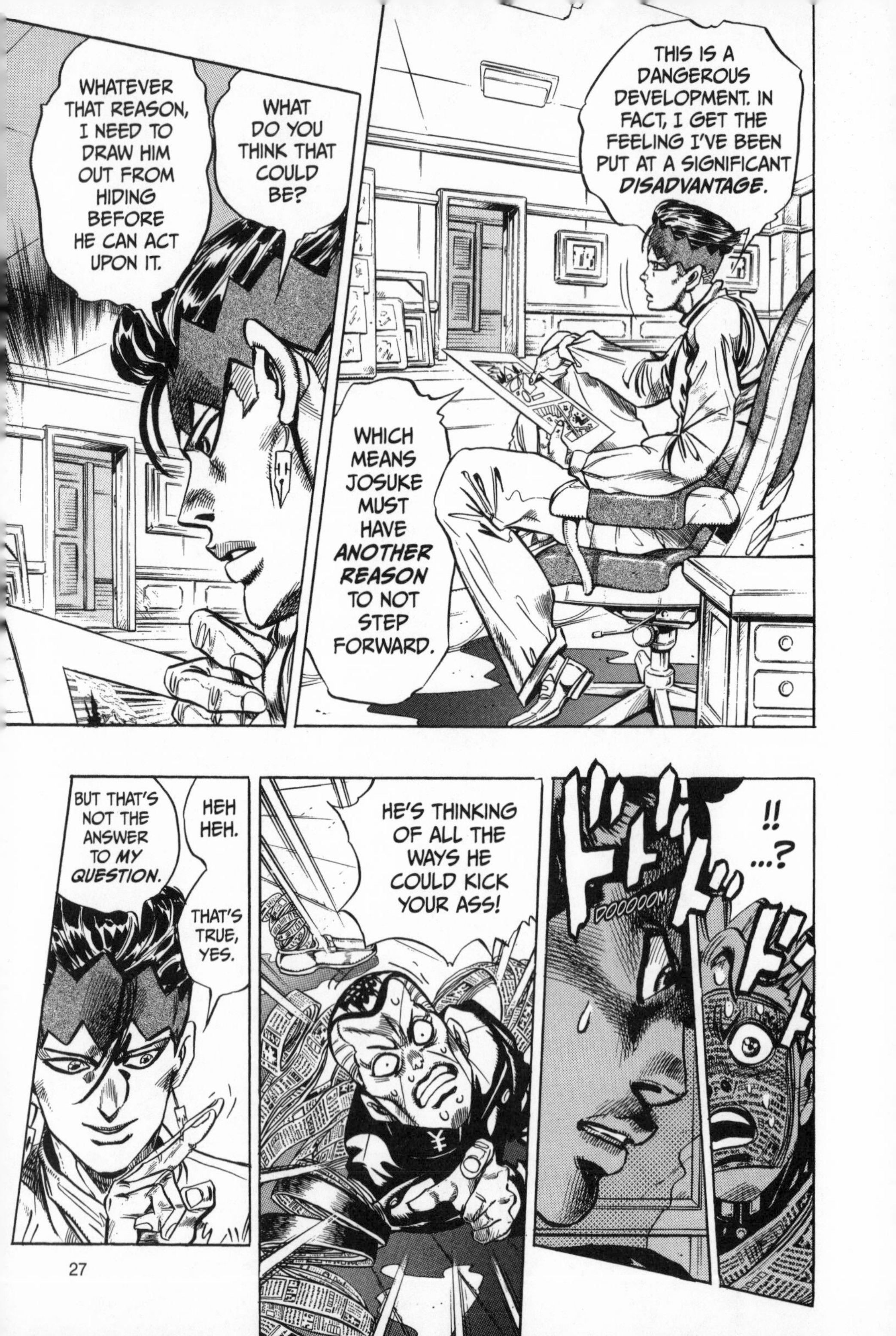
THIS IS A DANGEROUS DEVELOPMENT. IN FACT, I GET THE FEELING I'VE BEEN PUT AT A SIGNIFICANT *DISADVANTAGE*.
WHICH MEANS JOSUKE MUST HAVE *ANOTHER REASON* TO NOT STEP FORWARD.
WHAT DO YOU THINK THAT COULD BE?
WHATEVER THAT REASON, I NEED TO DRAW HIM OUT FROM HIDING BEFORE HE CAN ACT UPON IT.
DOOOOOM
!! ...?
HE'S THINKING OF ALL THE WAYS HE COULD KICK YOUR ASS!
HEH HEH.
BUT THAT'S NOT THE ANSWER TO *MY QUESTION*.
THAT'S TRUE, YES.

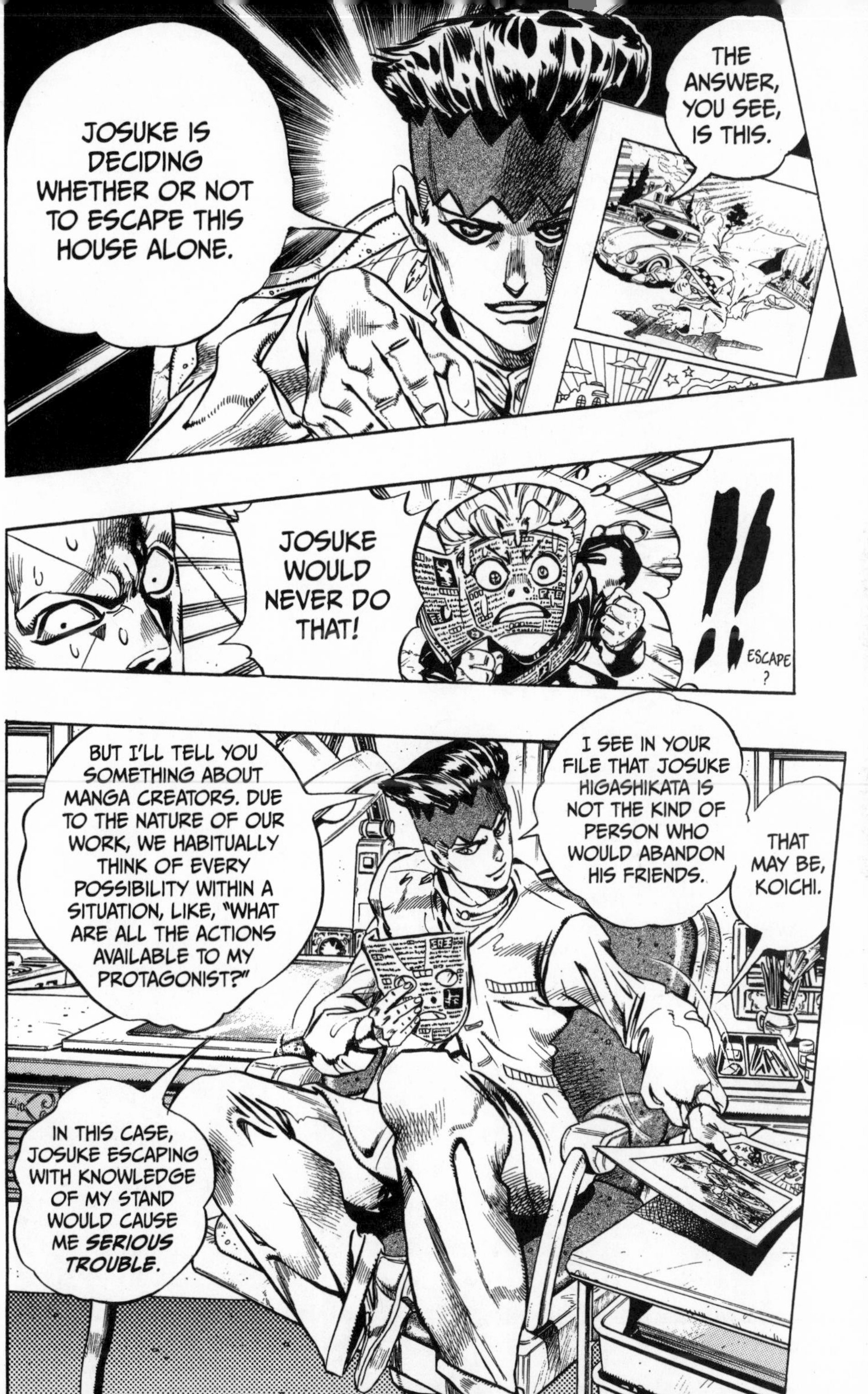
THE ANSWER, YOU SEE, IS THIS.
JOSUKE IS DECIDING WHETHER OR NOT TO ESCAPE THIS HOUSE ALONE.
!!
ESCAPE ?
JOSUKE WOULD NEVER DO THAT!
I SEE IN YOUR FILE THAT JOSUKE HIGASHIKATA IS NOT THE KIND OF PERSON WHO WOULD ABANDON HIS FRIENDS.
THAT MAY BE, KOICHI.
BUT I'LL TELL YOU SOMETHING ABOUT MANGA CREATORS. DUE TO THE NATURE OF OUR WORK, WE HABITUALLY THINK OF EVERY POSSIBILITY WITHIN A SITUATION, LIKE, "WHAT ARE ALL THE ACTIONS AVAILABLE TO MY PROTAGONIST?"
IN THIS CASE, JOSUKE ESCAPING WITH KNOWLEDGE OF MY STAND WOULD CAUSE ME *SERIOUS TROUBLE*.

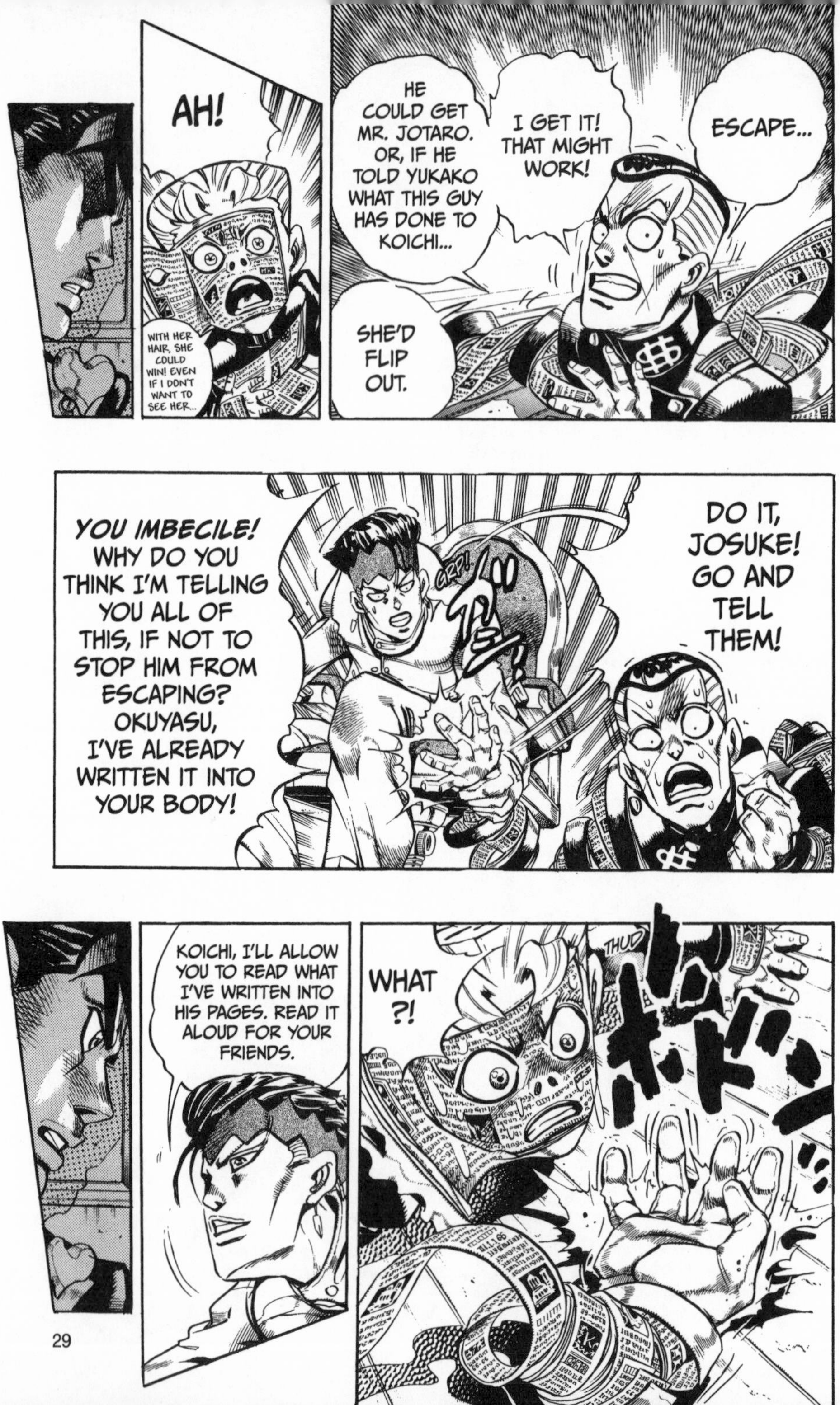
ESCAPE...
I GET IT! THAT MIGHT WORK!
HE COULD GET MR. JOTARO. OR, IF HE TOLD YUKAKO WHAT THIS GUY HAS DONE TO KOICHI...
SHE'D FLIP OUT.
AH!
WITH HER HAIR, SHE COULD WIN! EVEN IF I DON'T WANT TO SEE HER...
DO IT, JOSUKE! GO AND TELL THEM!
CRP!
YOU IMBECILE! WHY DO YOU THINK I'M TELLING YOU ALL OF THIS, IF NOT TO STOP HIM FROM ESCAPING? OKUYASU, I'VE ALREADY WRITTEN IT INTO YOUR BODY!
THUD
WHAT ?!
KOICHI, I'LL ALLOW YOU TO READ WHAT I'VE WRITTEN INTO HIS PAGES. READ IT ALOUD FOR YOUR FRIENDS.

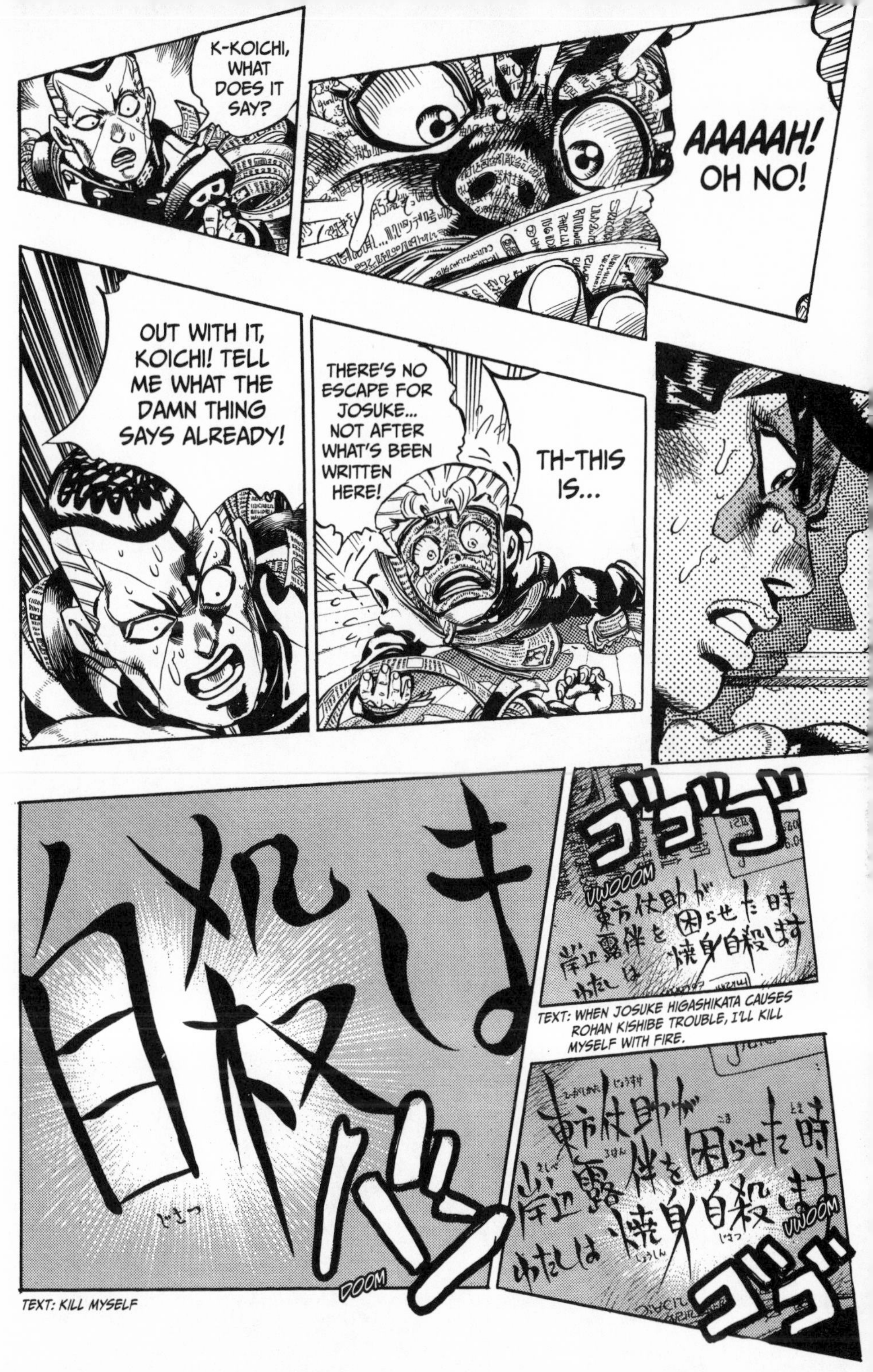
AAAAAH! OH NO!
K-KOICHI, WHAT DOES IT SAY?
TH-THIS IS...
THERE'S NO ESCAPE FOR JOSUKE... NOT AFTER WHAT'S BEEN WRITTEN HERE!
OUT WITH IT, KOICHI! TELL ME WHAT THE DAMN THING SAYS ALREADY!
ゴゴゴ
UWOOOM
東方仗助が岸辺露伴を困らせた時
わたしは焼身自殺します
TEXT: WHEN JOSUKE HIGASHIKATA CAUSES ROHAN KISHIBE TROUBLE, I'LL KILL MYSELF WITH FIRE.
東方仗助が岸辺露伴を困らせた時
わたしは焼身自殺します
UWOOOM
ゴゴ
自殺します
DOOM
TEXT: KILL MYSELF

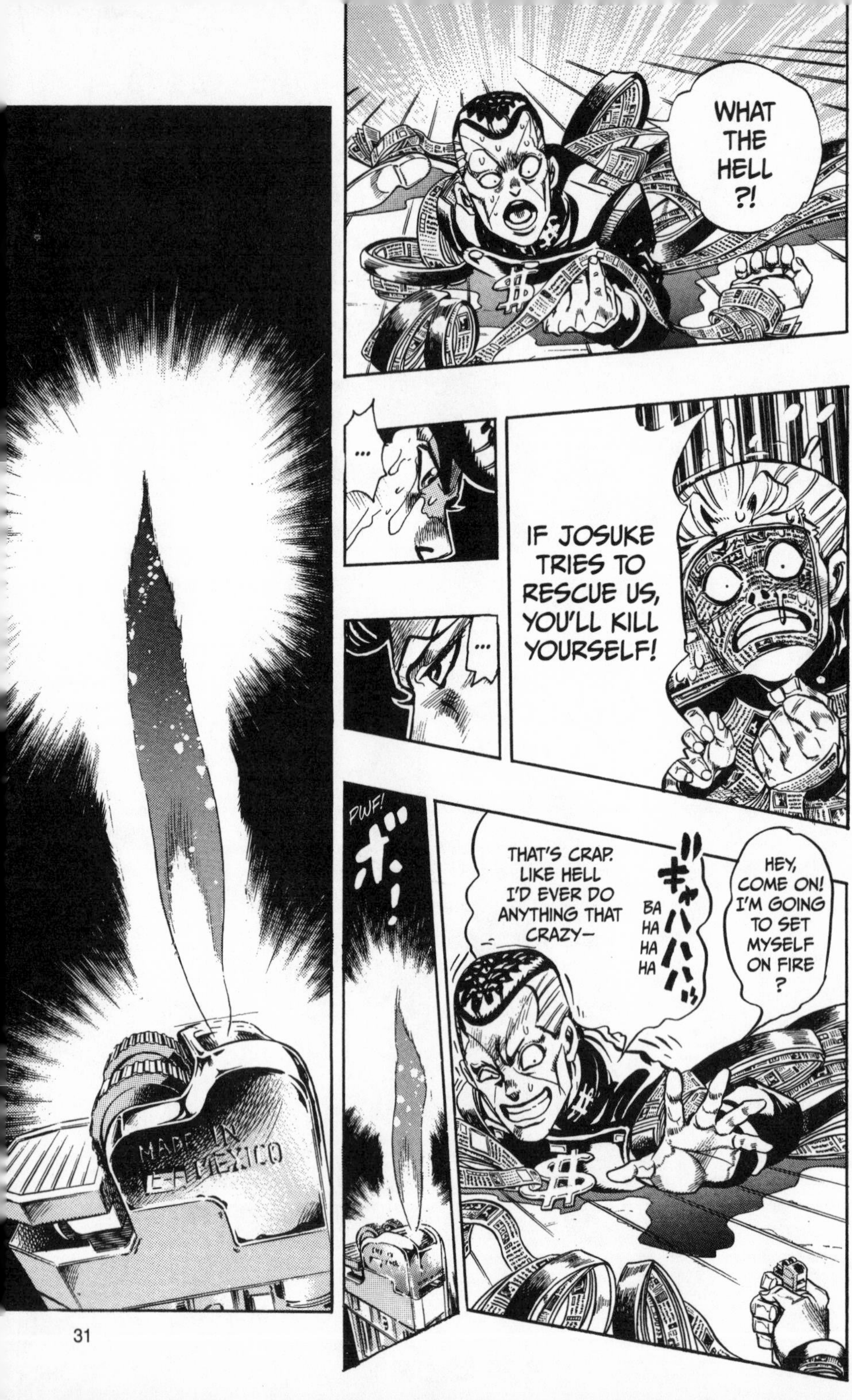
WHAT THE HELL ?!
IF JOSUKE TRIES TO RESCUE US, YOU'LL KILL YOURSELF!
...
...
HEY, COME ON! I'M GOING TO SET MYSELF ON FIRE ?
BA HA HA HA
THAT'S CRAP. LIKE HELL I'D EVER DO ANYTHING THAT CRAZY—
PWF!
MADE IN MEXICO

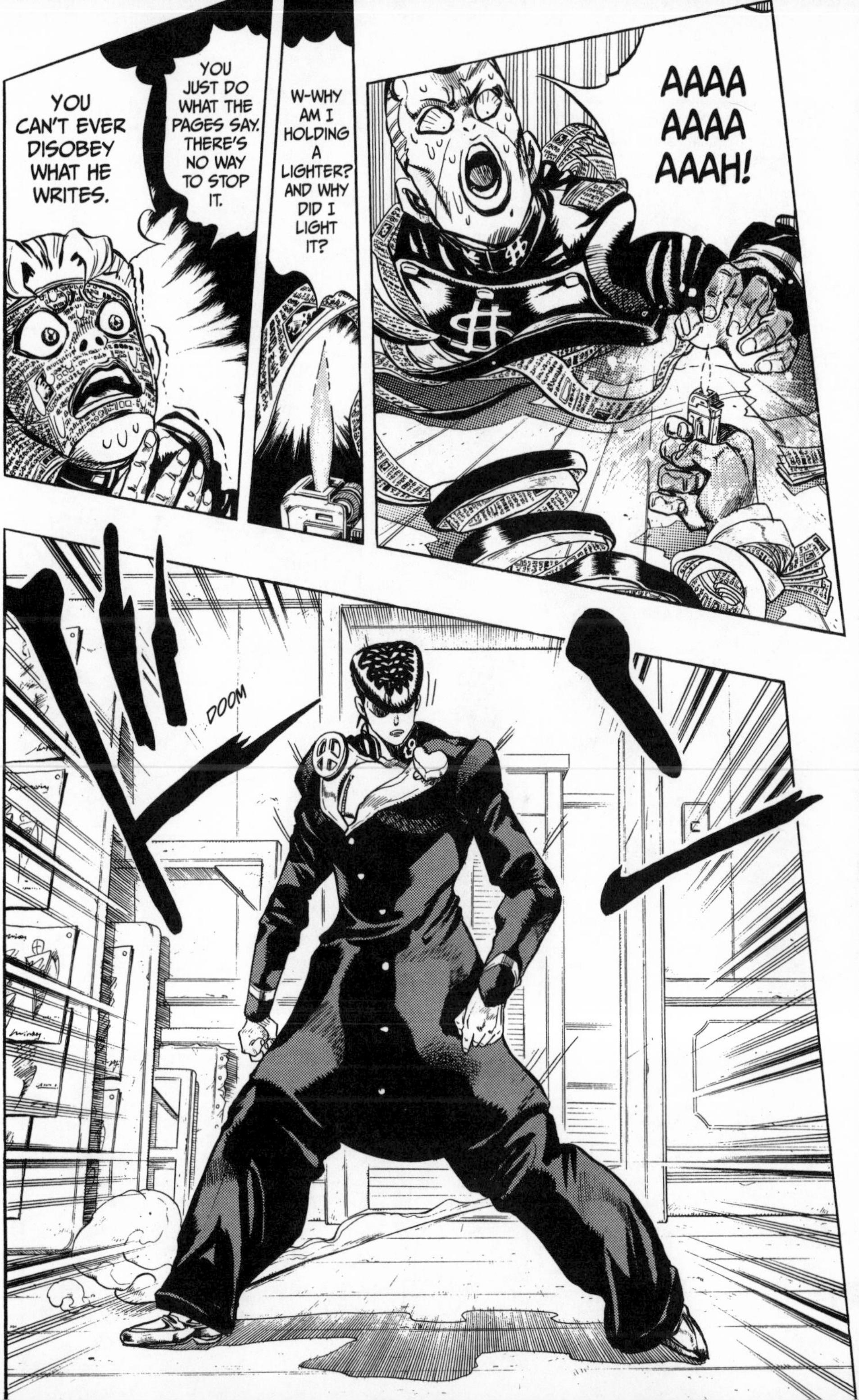
AAAA AAAA AAAH!
W-WHY AM I HOLDING A LIGHTER? AND WHY DID I LIGHT IT?
YOU JUST DO WHAT THE PAGES SAY. THERE'S NO WAY TO STOP IT.
YOU CAN'T EVER DISOBEY WHAT HE WRITES.
DOOM

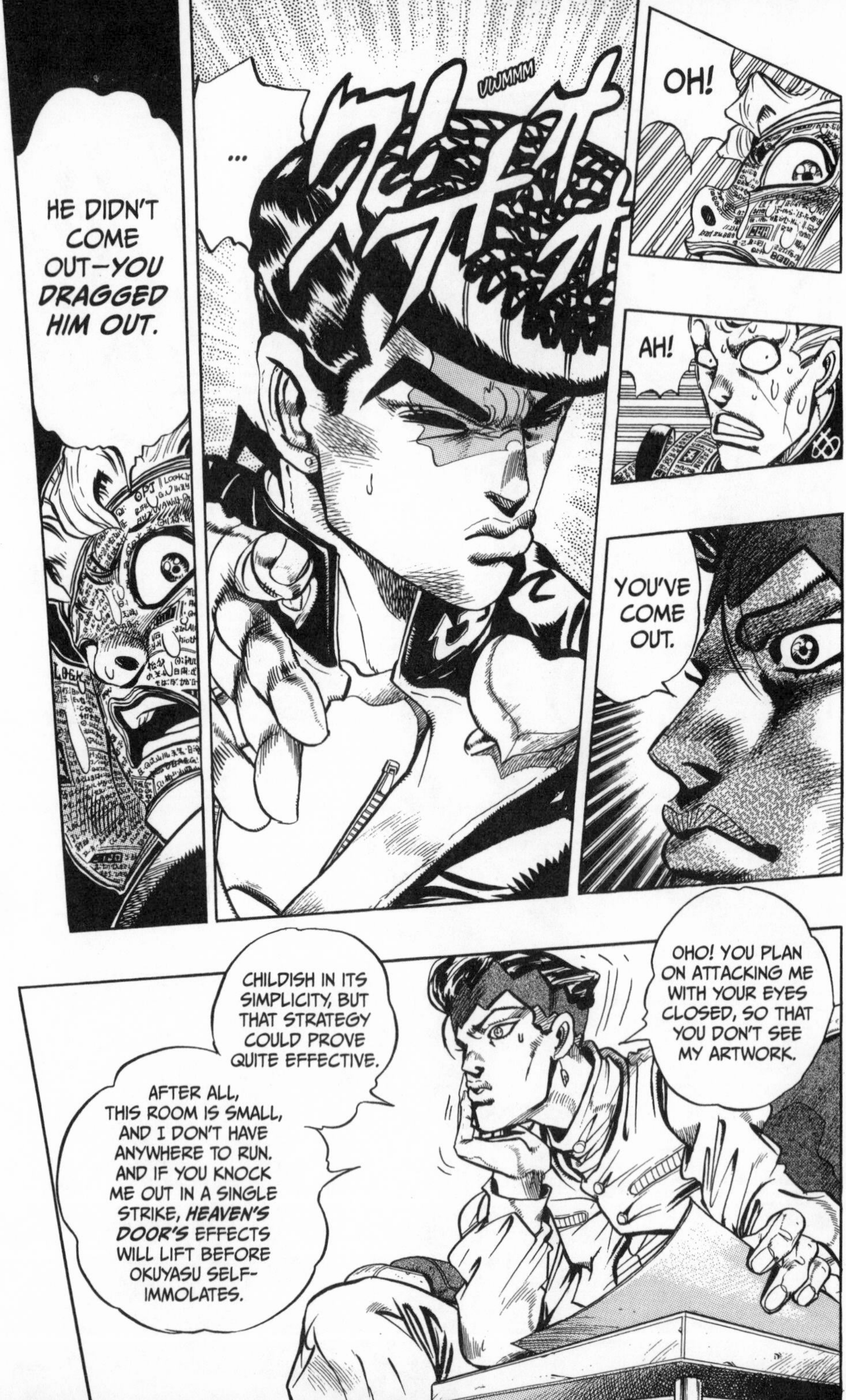
OH!
AH!
YOU'VE COME OUT.
VWMMM
...
HE DIDN'T COME OUT—*YOU* DRAGGED HIM OUT.
OHO! YOU PLAN ON ATTACKING ME WITH YOUR EYES CLOSED, SO THAT YOU DON'T SEE MY ARTWORK.
CHILDISH IN ITS SIMPLICITY, BUT THAT STRATEGY COULD PROVE QUITE EFFECTIVE.
AFTER ALL, THIS ROOM IS SMALL, AND I DON'T HAVE ANYWHERE TO RUN. AND IF YOU KNOCK ME OUT IN A SINGLE STRIKE, ***HEAVEN'S DOOR'S*** EFFECTS WILL LIFT BEFORE OKUYASU SELF-IMMOLATES.

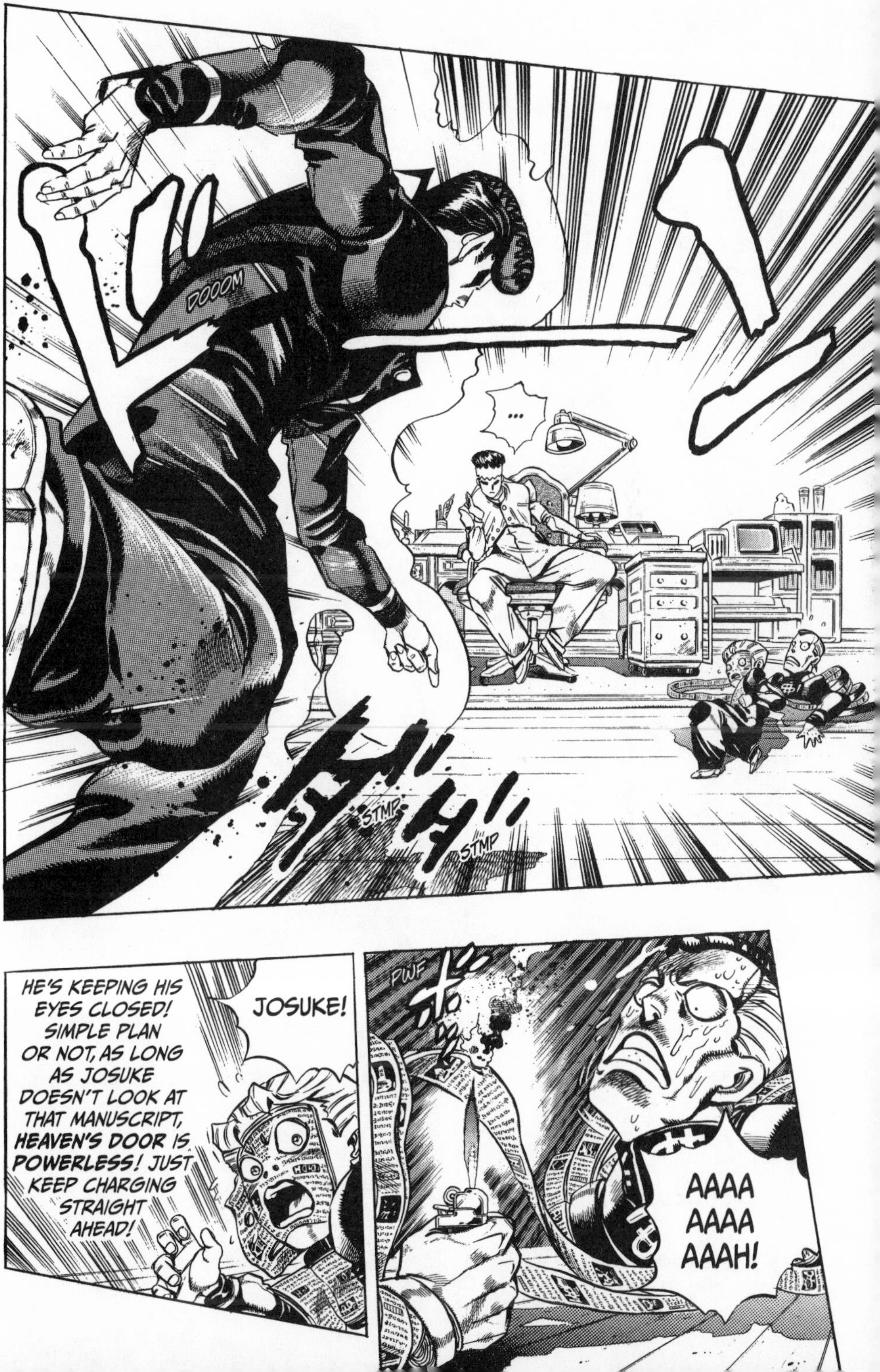
DOOOM
...
STMP
STMP
PWF
AAAA AAAA AAAH!
JOSUKE!
HE'S KEEPING HIS EYES CLOSED! SIMPLE PLAN OR NOT, AS LONG AS JOSUKE DOESN'T LOOK AT THAT MANUSCRIPT, **HEAVEN'S DOOR** IS **POWERLESS!** JUST KEEP CHARGING STRAIGHT AHEAD!

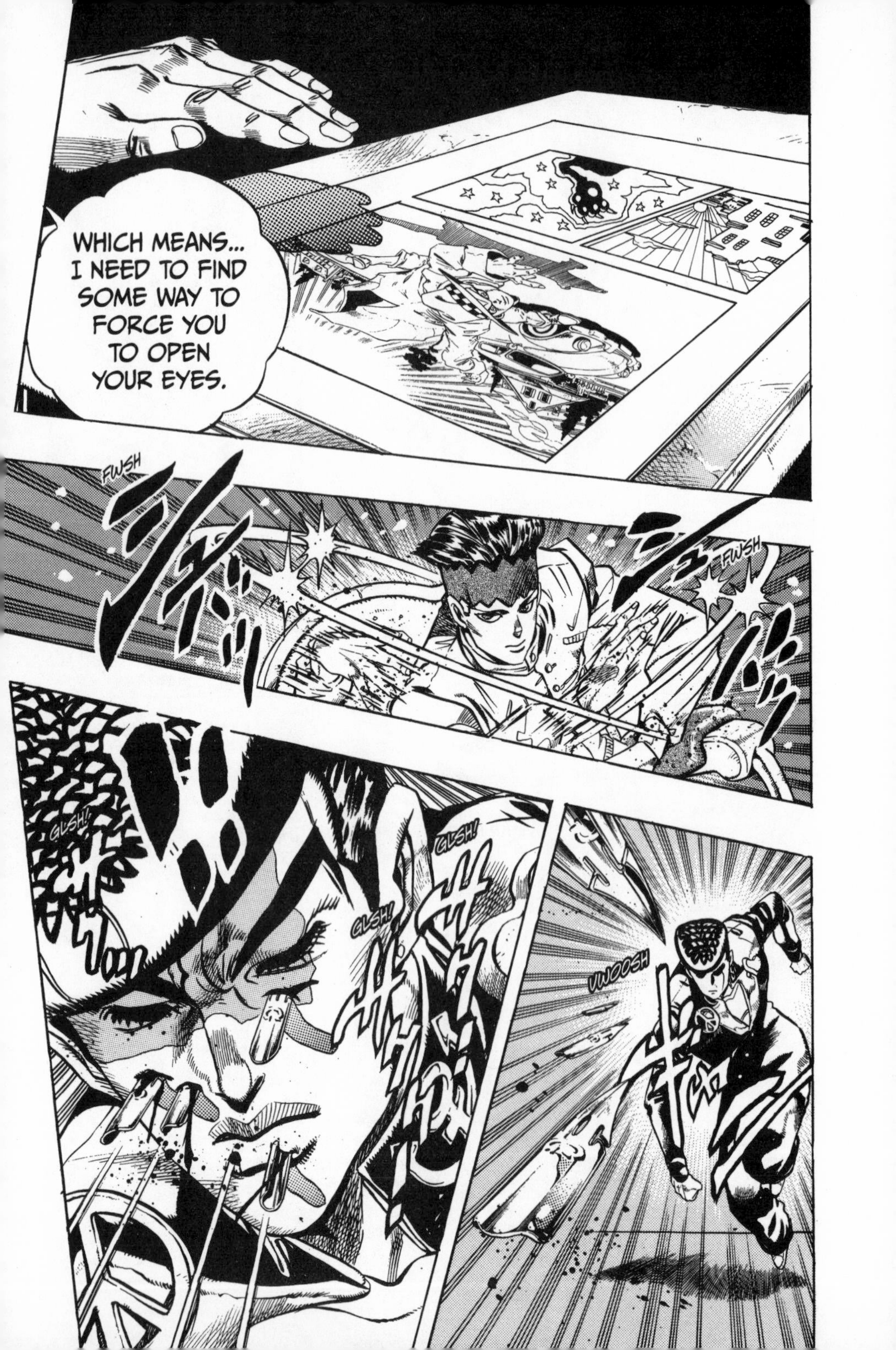
WHICH MEANS... I NEED TO FIND SOME WAY TO FORCE YOU TO OPEN YOUR EYES.
FWSH
FWSH
VWOOSH
GUSH!
GUSH!
GUSH!

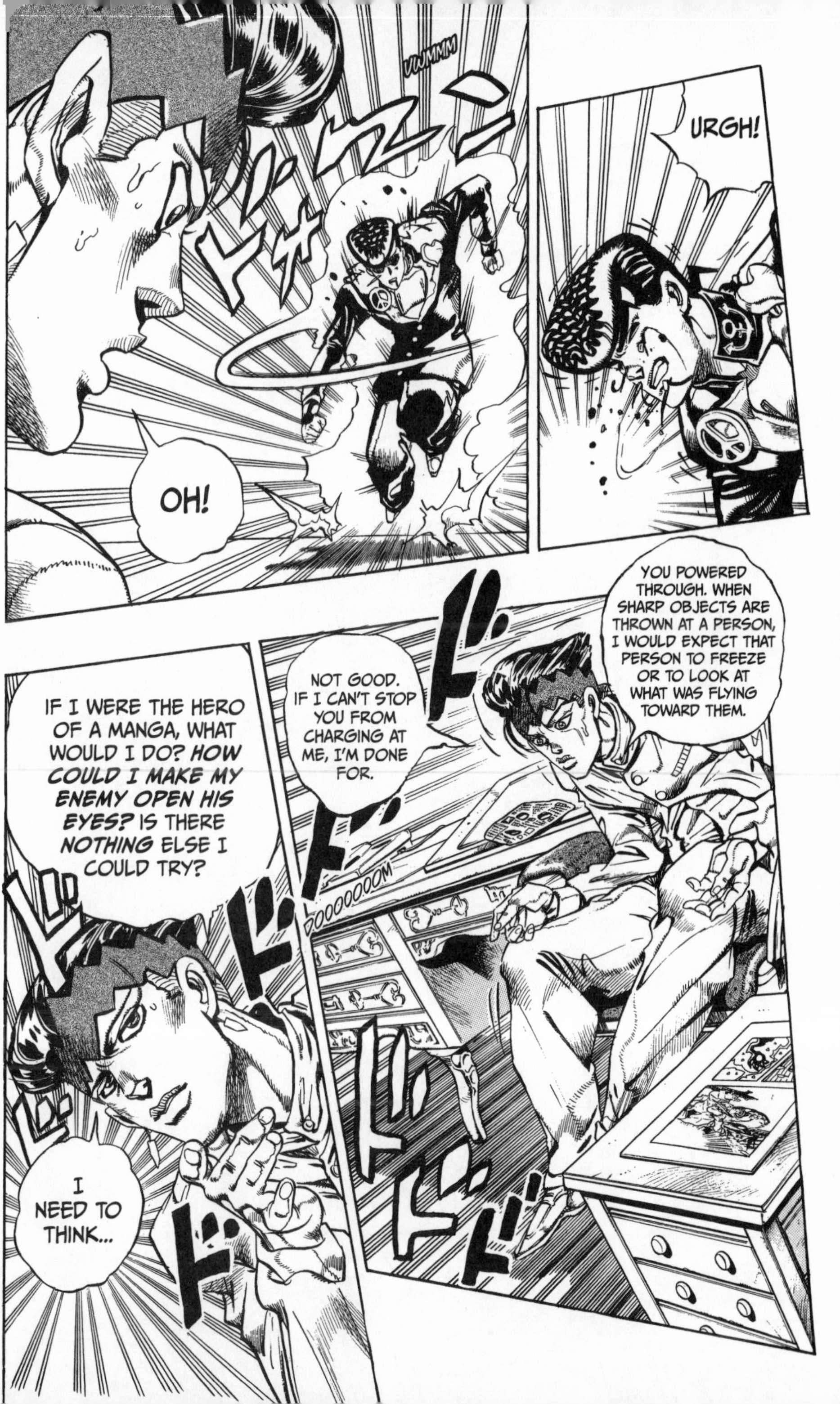
URGH!
VWMMM
OH!
YOU POWERED THROUGH. WHEN SHARP OBJECTS ARE THROWN AT A PERSON, I WOULD EXPECT THAT PERSON TO FREEZE OR TO LOOK AT WHAT WAS FLYING TOWARD THEM.
NOT GOOD. IF I CAN'T STOP YOU FROM CHARGING AT ME, I'M DONE FOR.
DOOOOOOOOM
IF I WERE THE HERO OF A MANGA, WHAT WOULD I DO? *HOW COULD I MAKE MY ENEMY OPEN HIS EYES?* IS THERE *NOTHING* ELSE I COULD TRY?
I NEED TO THINK...

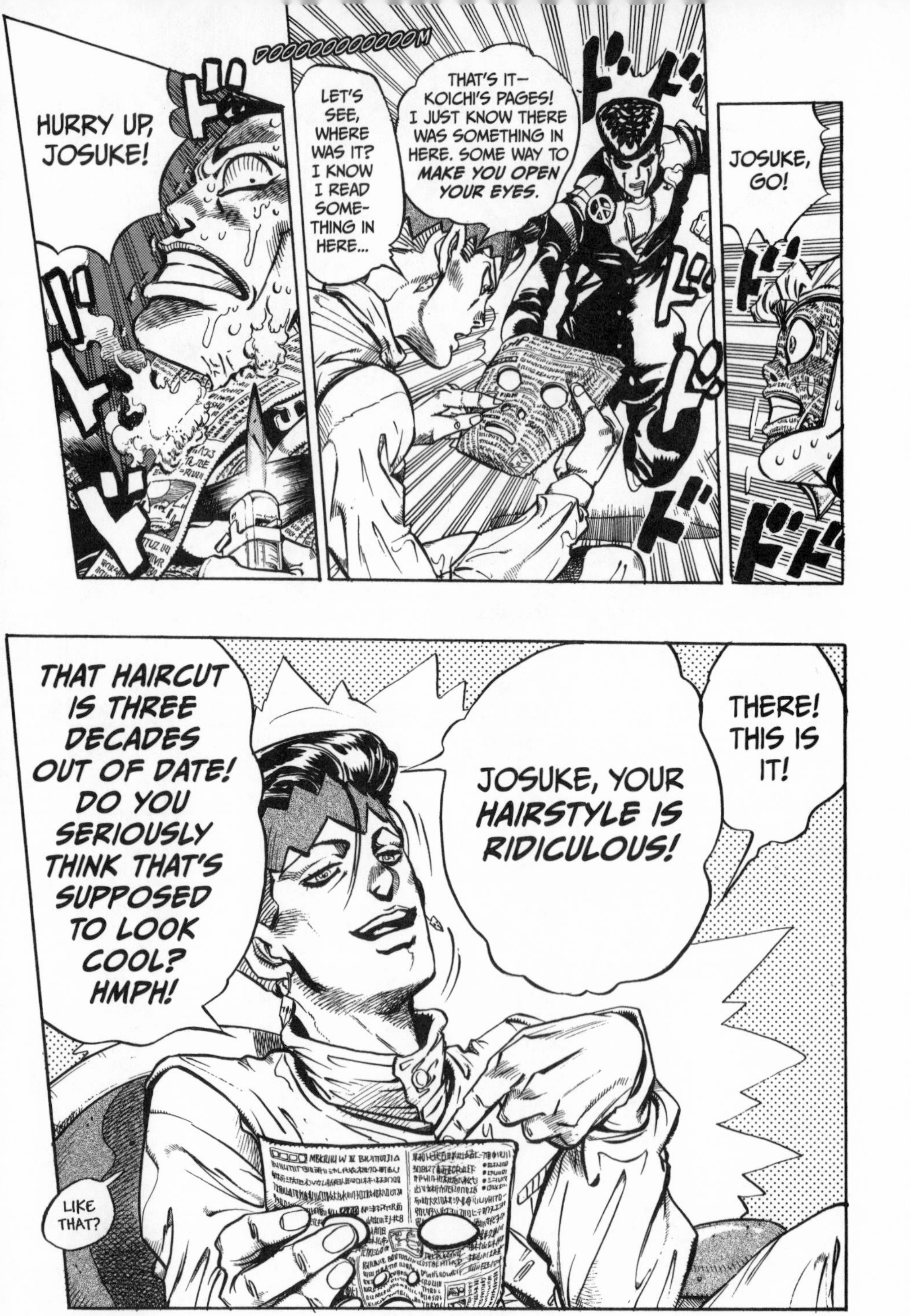
JOSUKE, GO!
DOOOOOOOOOOOM
LET'S SEE, WHERE WAS IT? I KNOW I READ SOME-THING IN HERE...
THAT'S IT—KOICHI'S PAGES! I JUST KNOW THERE WAS SOMETHING IN HERE. SOME WAY TO *MAKE YOU OPEN YOUR EYES.*
HURRY UP, JOSUKE!
THERE! THIS IS IT!
JOSUKE, YOUR HAIRSTYLE IS RIDICULOUS!
THAT HAIRCUT IS THREE DECADES OUT OF DATE! DO YOU SERIOUSLY THINK THAT'S SUPPOSED TO LOOK COOL? HMPH!
LIKE THAT?

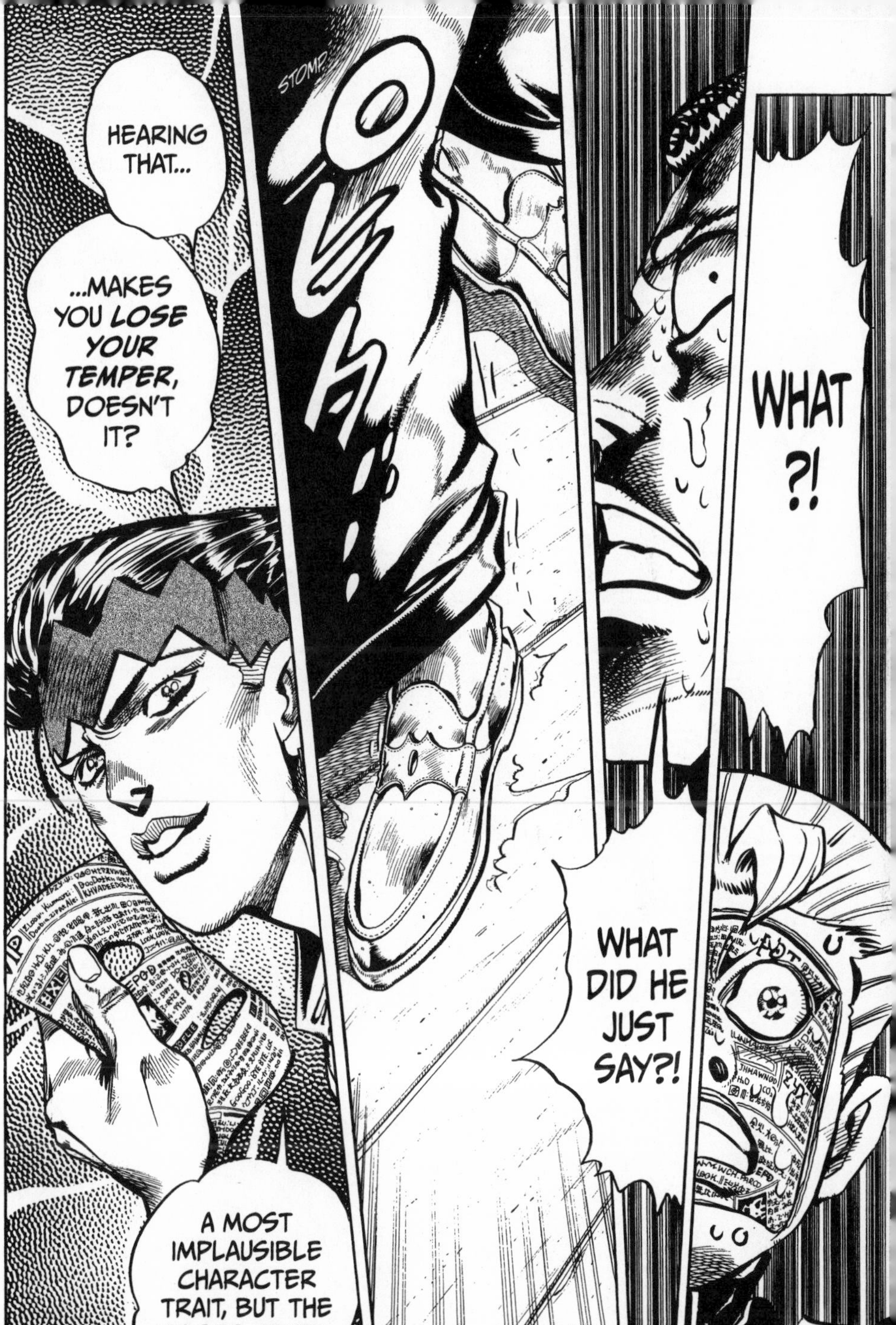
WHAT ?!
WHAT DID HE JUST SAY?!
STOMP
HEARING THAT...
...MAKES YOU *LOSE* YOUR *TEMPER*, DOESN'T IT?
A MOST IMPLAUSIBLE CHARACTER TRAIT, BUT THE PAGES NEVER LIE.

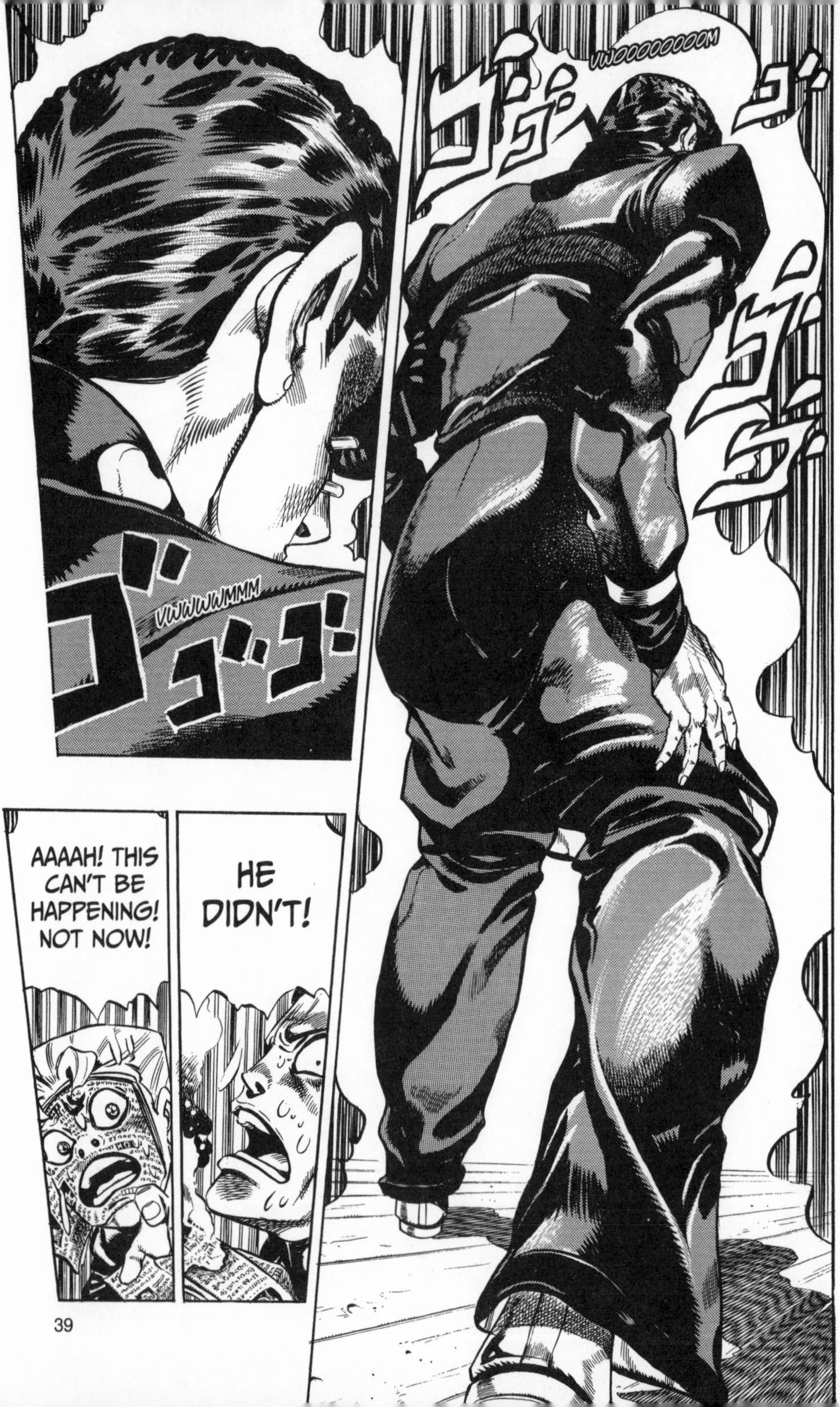
VWOOOOOOOOM
VWWWWMMM
HE DIDN'T!
AAAAH! THIS CAN'T BE HAPPENING! NOT NOW!

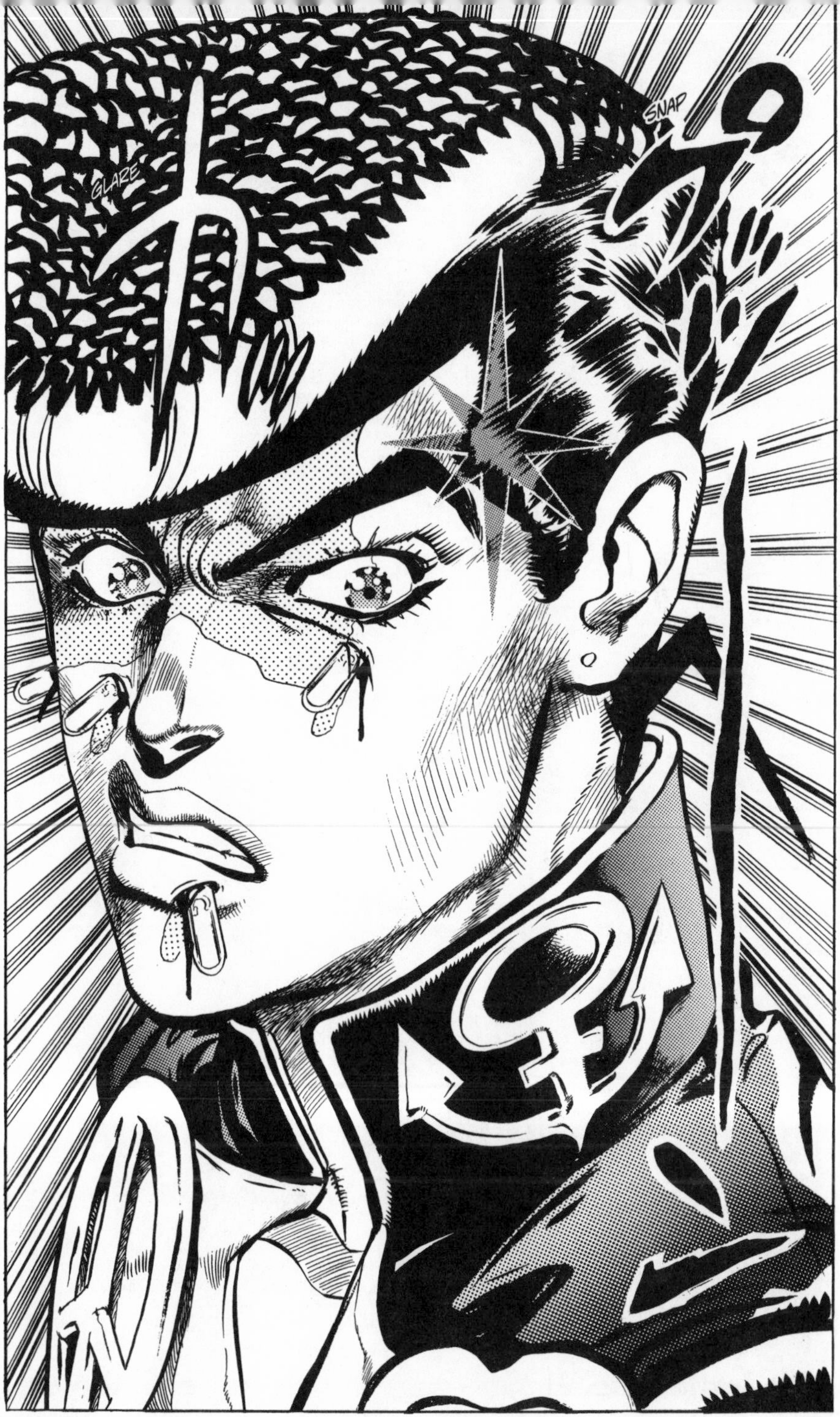
SNAP
GLARE

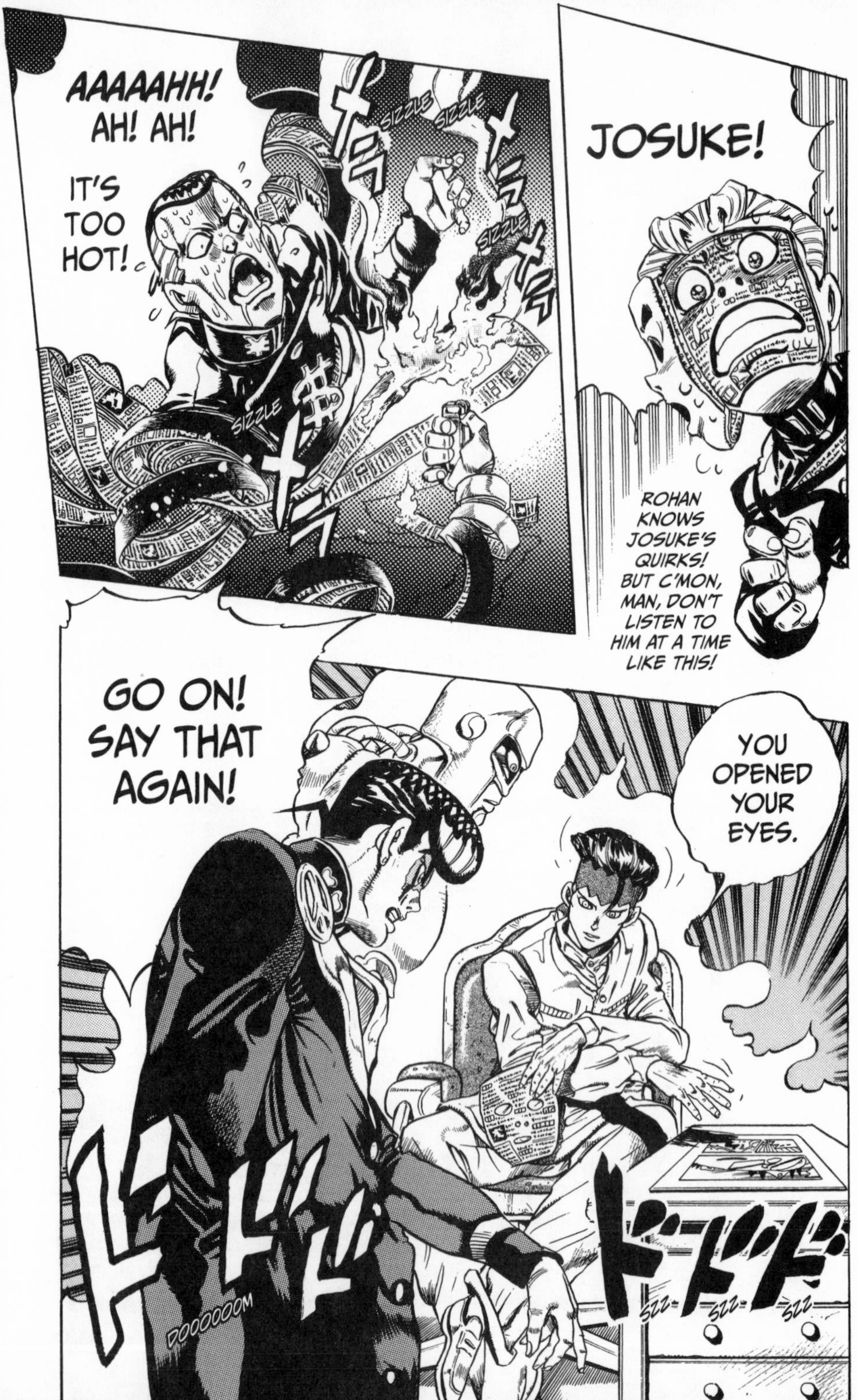
JOSUKE!
ROHAN KNOWS JOSUKE'S QUIRKS! BUT C'MON, MAN, DON'T LISTEN TO HIM AT A TIME LIKE THIS!
AAAAAHH! AH! AH!
IT'S TOO HOT!
SIZZLE SIZZLE
SIZZLE
SIZZLE
YOU OPENED YOUR EYES.
GO ON! SAY THAT AGAIN!
DOOOOOOM
SZZ SZZ SZZ

Morioh Places of Interest #3:
"Rohan Kishibe's House"

Lot: 3,665 square feet
7 bedrooms plus an attic

Directions: If you visit, he'll pretend to not be home.

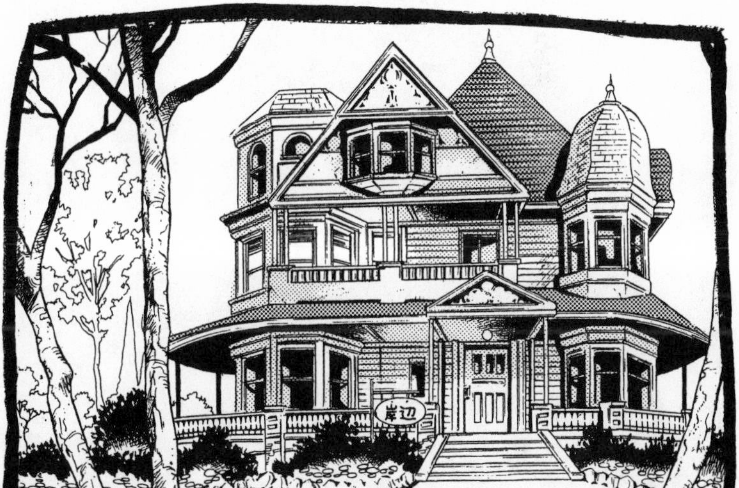
岸辺

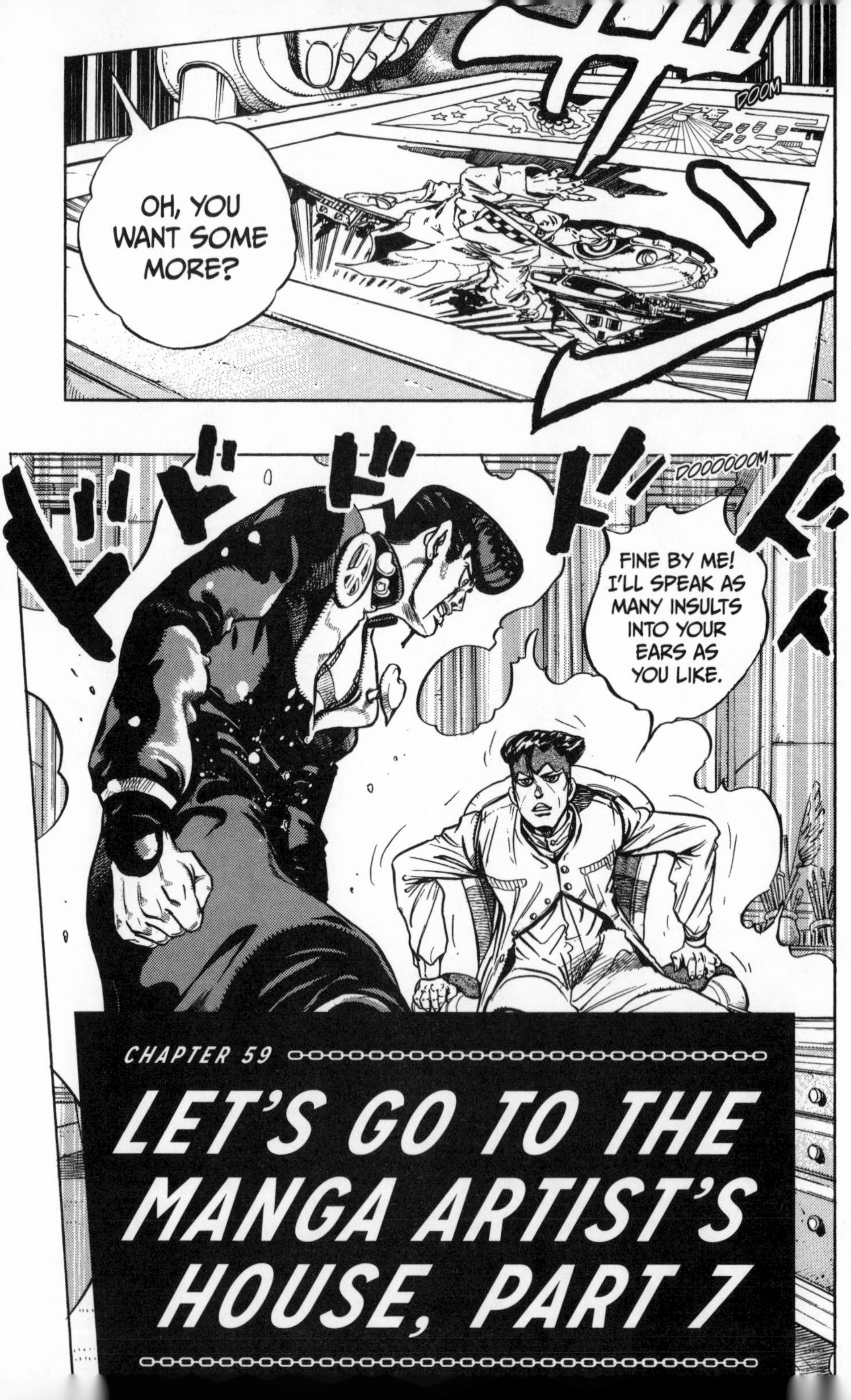
DOOM
OH, YOU WANT SOME MORE?
DOOOOOOM
FINE BY ME! I'LL SPEAK AS MANY INSULTS INTO YOUR EARS AS YOU LIKE.
CHAPTER 59
LET'S GO TO THE MANGA ARTIST'S HOUSE, PART 7

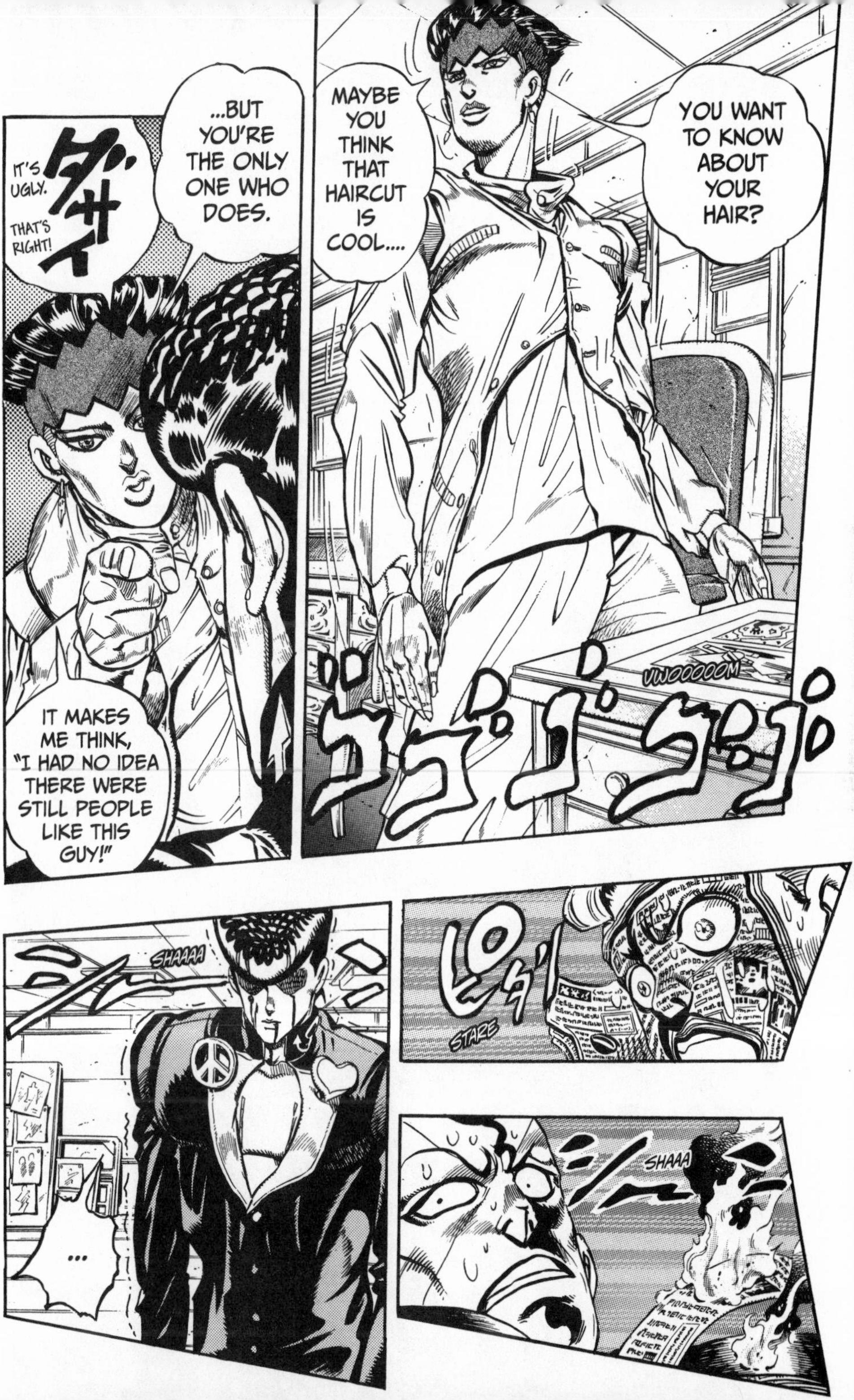
YOU WANT TO KNOW ABOUT YOUR HAIR?
MAYBE YOU THINK THAT HAIRCUT IS COOL....
VWOOOOOM
...BUT YOU'RE THE ONLY ONE WHO DOES.
IT'S UGLY.
THAT'S RIGHT!
IT MAKES ME THINK, "I HAD NO IDEA THERE WERE STILL PEOPLE LIKE THIS GUY!"
STARE
SHAAA
SHAAAA
...

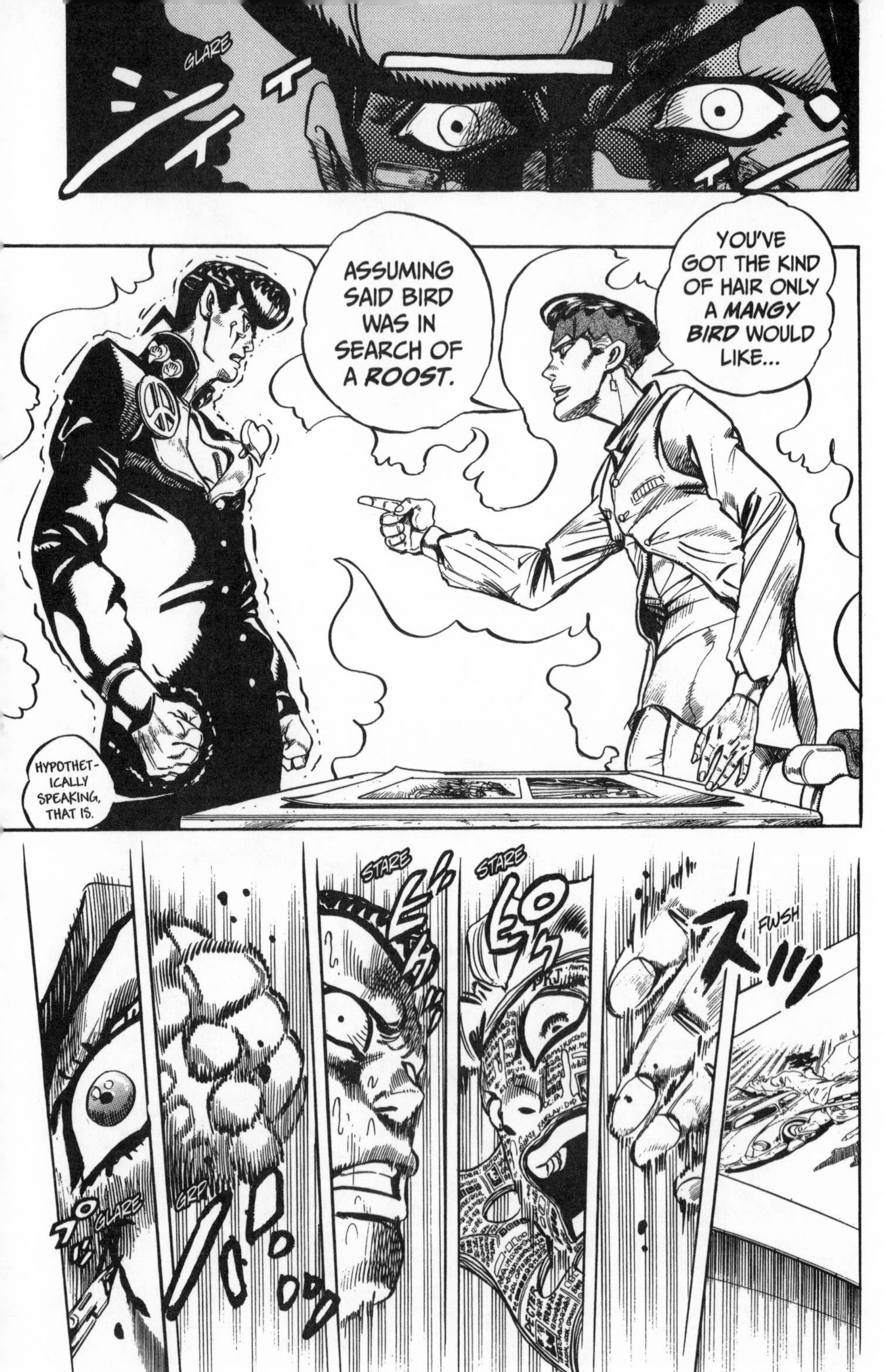
GLARE
YOU'VE GOT THE KIND OF HAIR ONLY A *MANGY BIRD* WOULD LIKE...
ASSUMING SAID BIRD WAS IN SEARCH OF A *ROOST*.
HYPOTHET-ICALLY SPEAKING, THAT IS.
FWSH
STARE
STARE
GRP
GLARE

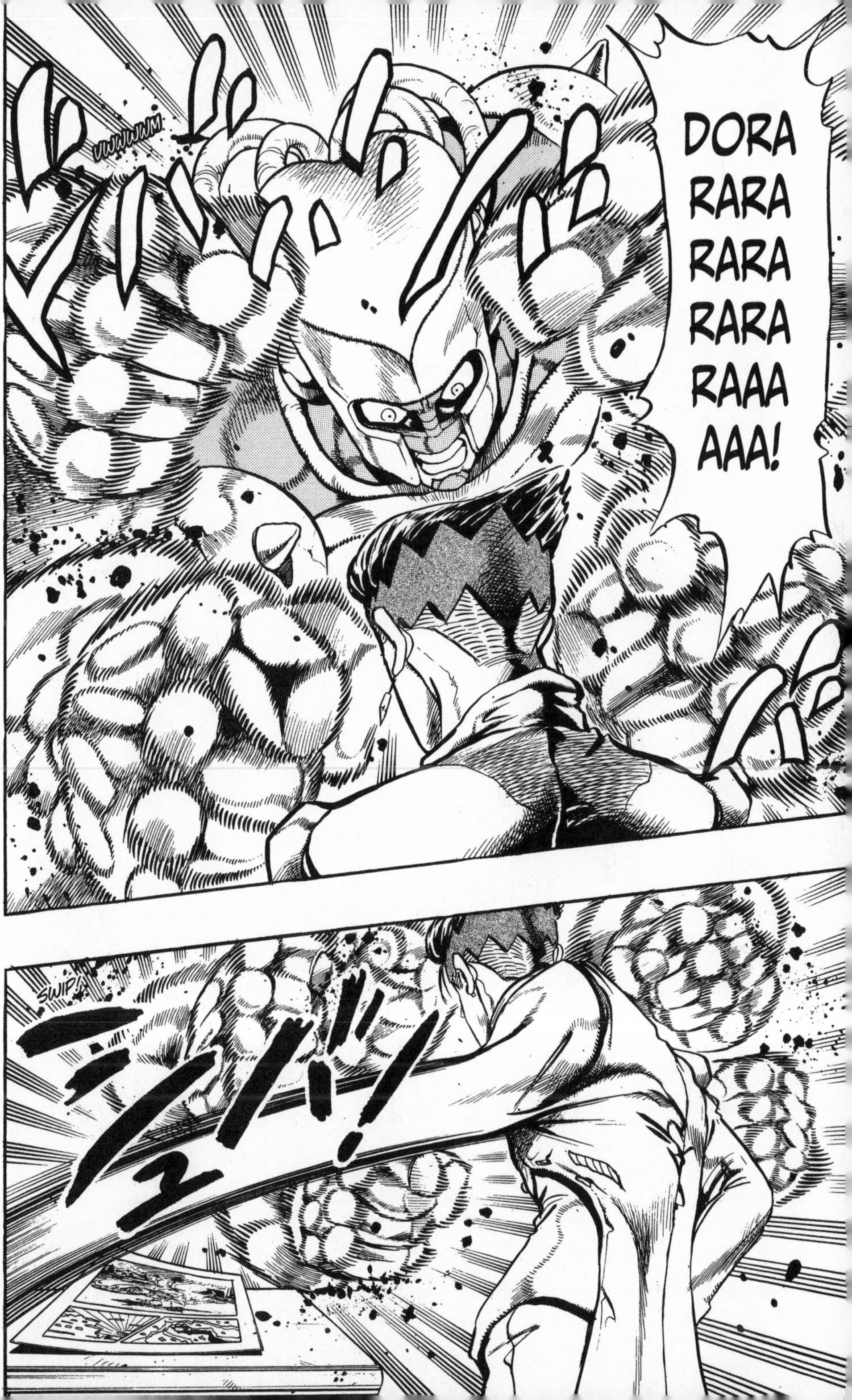
DORA RARA RARA RARA RAAA AAA!
VWWWWM
SWIP!

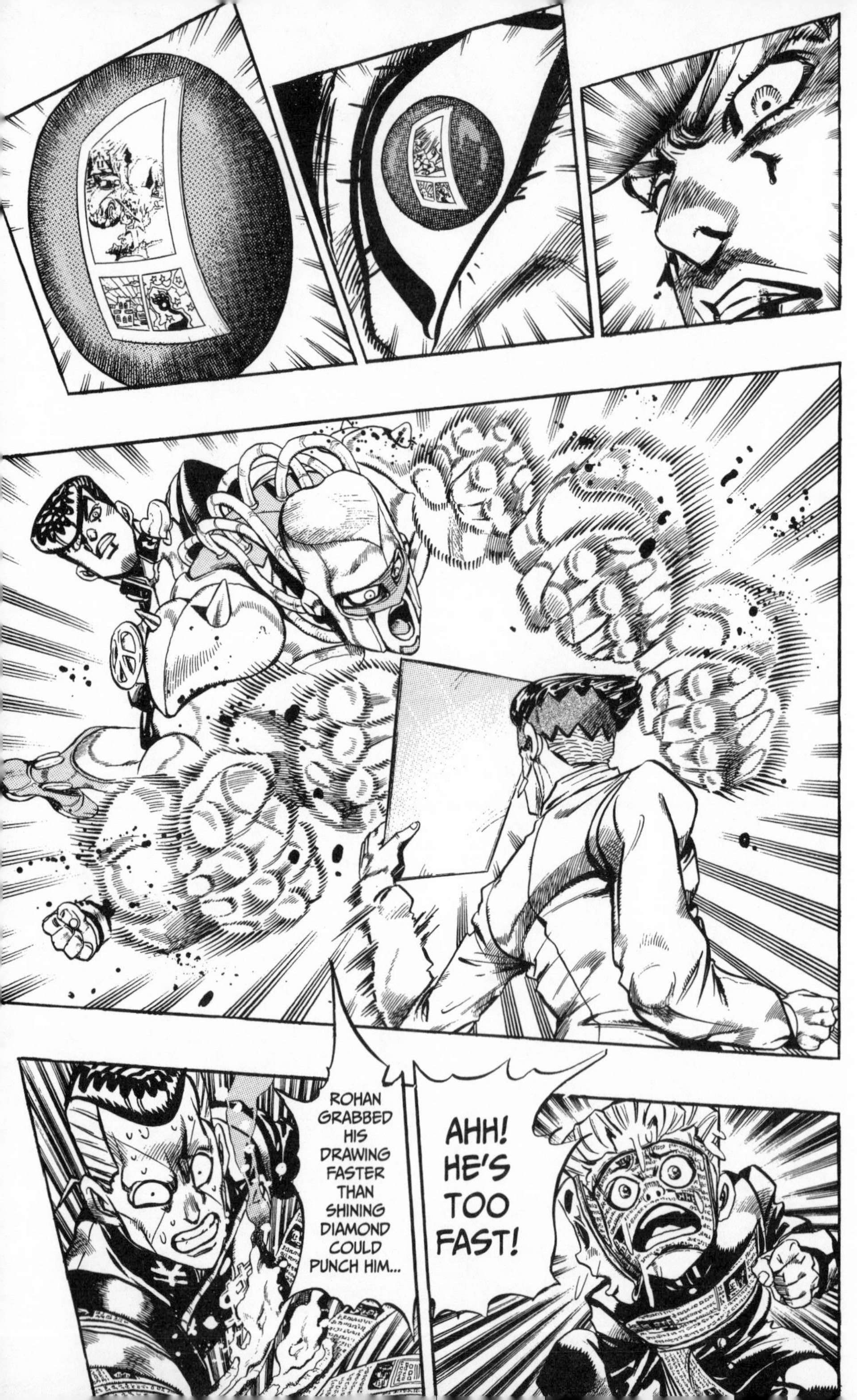
AHH! HE'S TOO FAST!
ROHAN GRABBED HIS DRAWING FASTER THAN SHINING DIAMOND COULD PUNCH HIM...

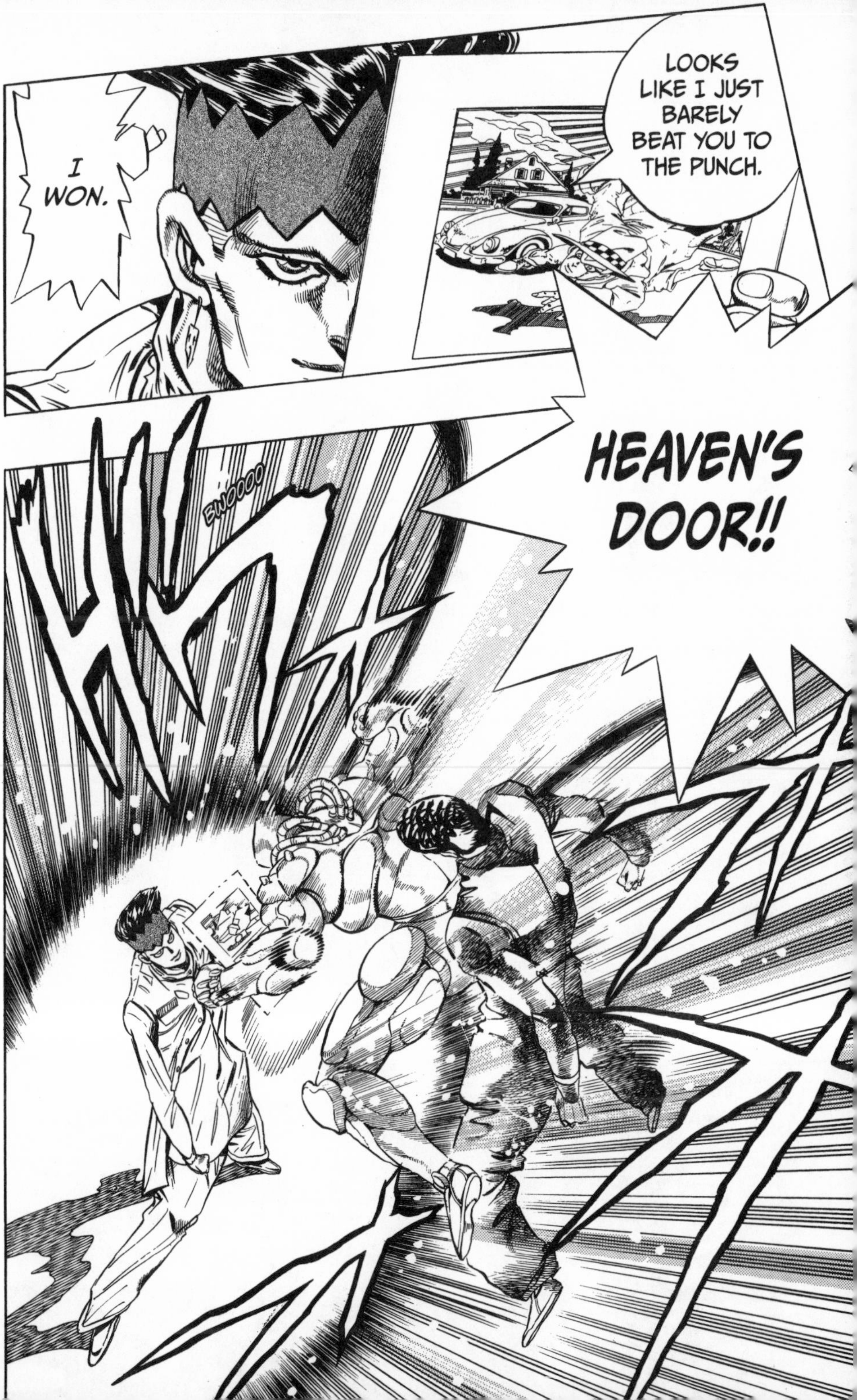
LOOKS LIKE I JUST BARELY BEAT YOU TO THE PUNCH.
I WON.
HEAVEN'S DOOR!!
BWOOOO

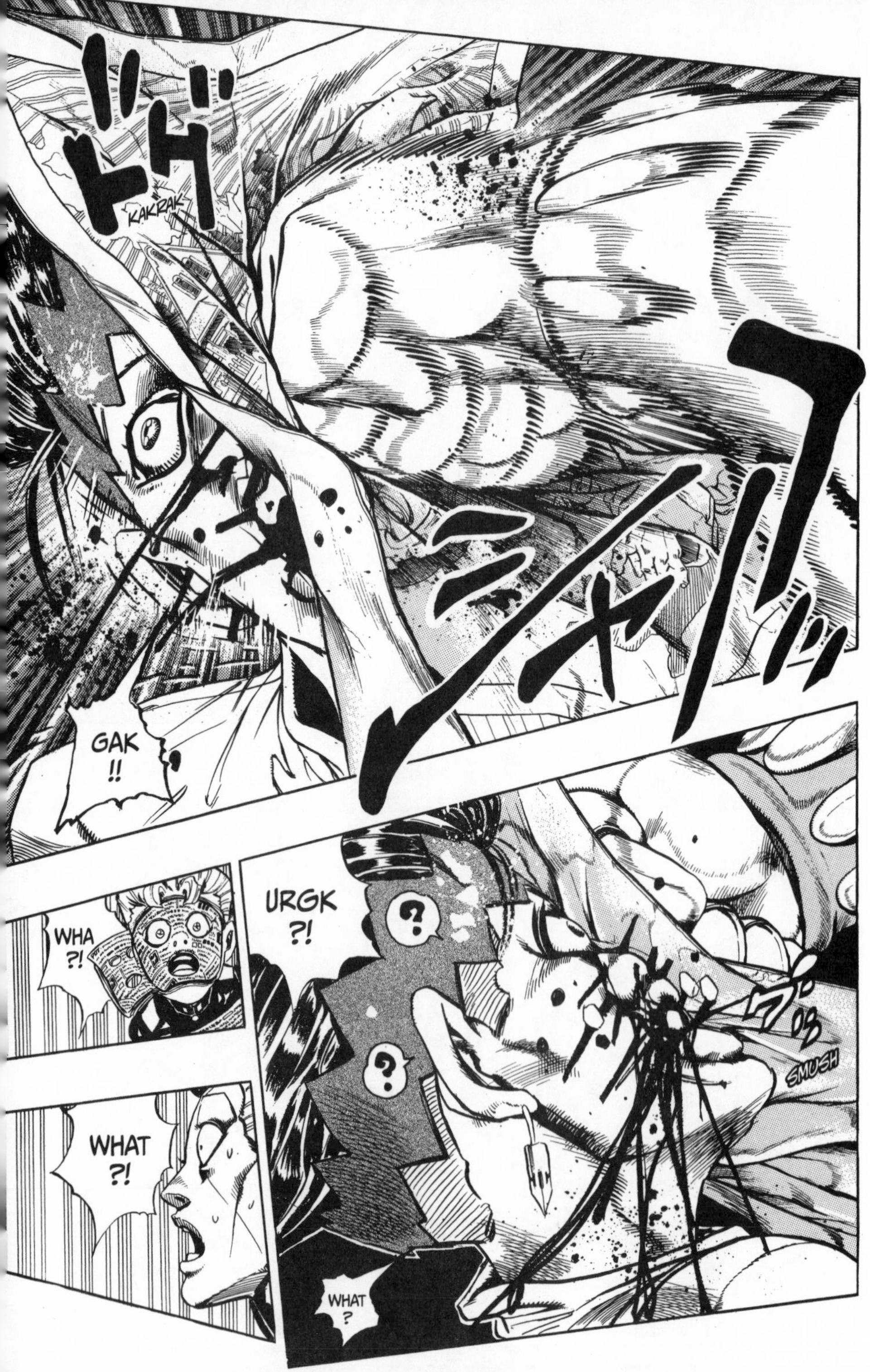
KAKRAK
GAK !!
URGK ?!
?
?
SMUSH
WHAT ?
WHA ?!
WHAT ?!

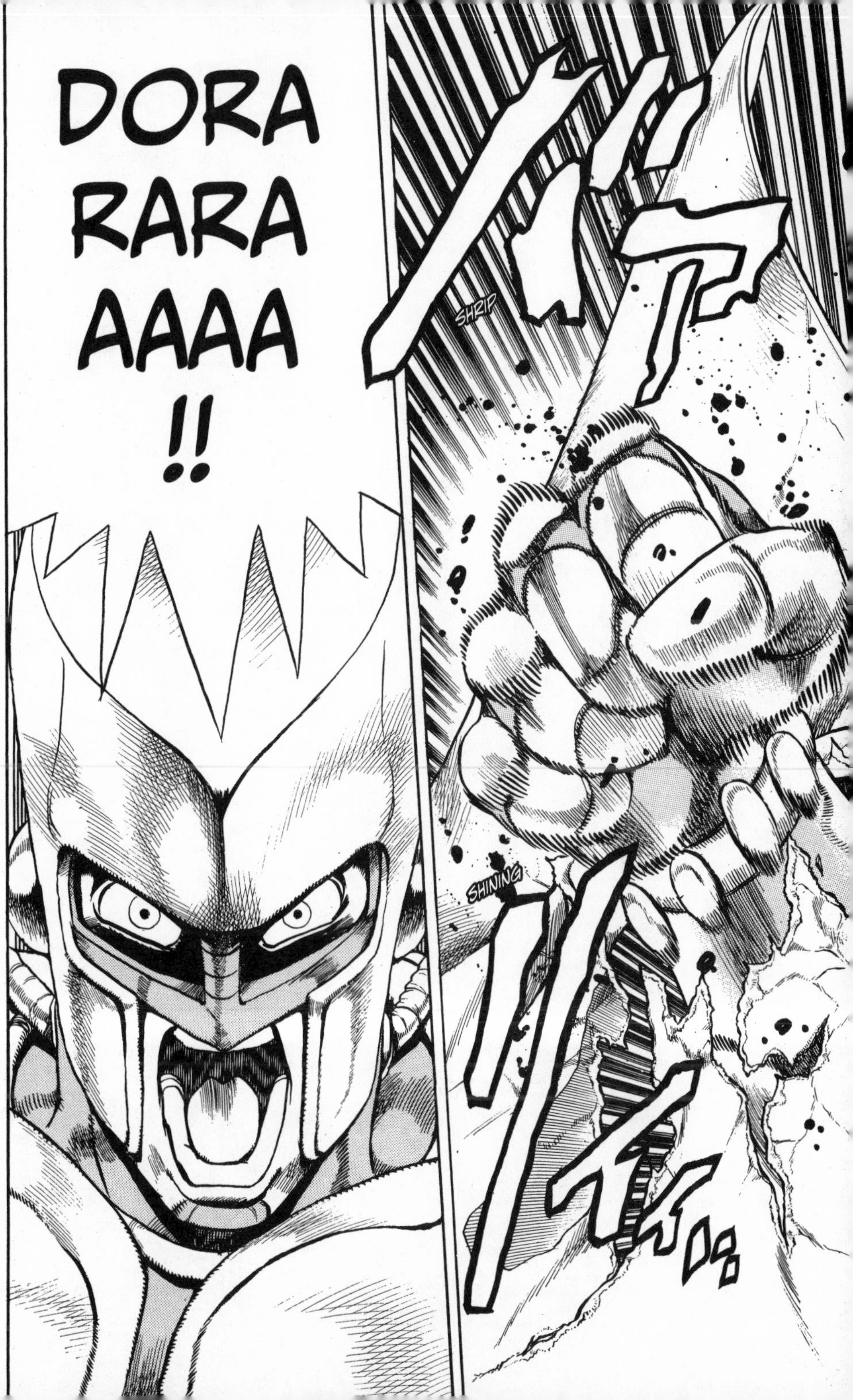
SHRIP
SHINING
DORA RARA AAAA !!

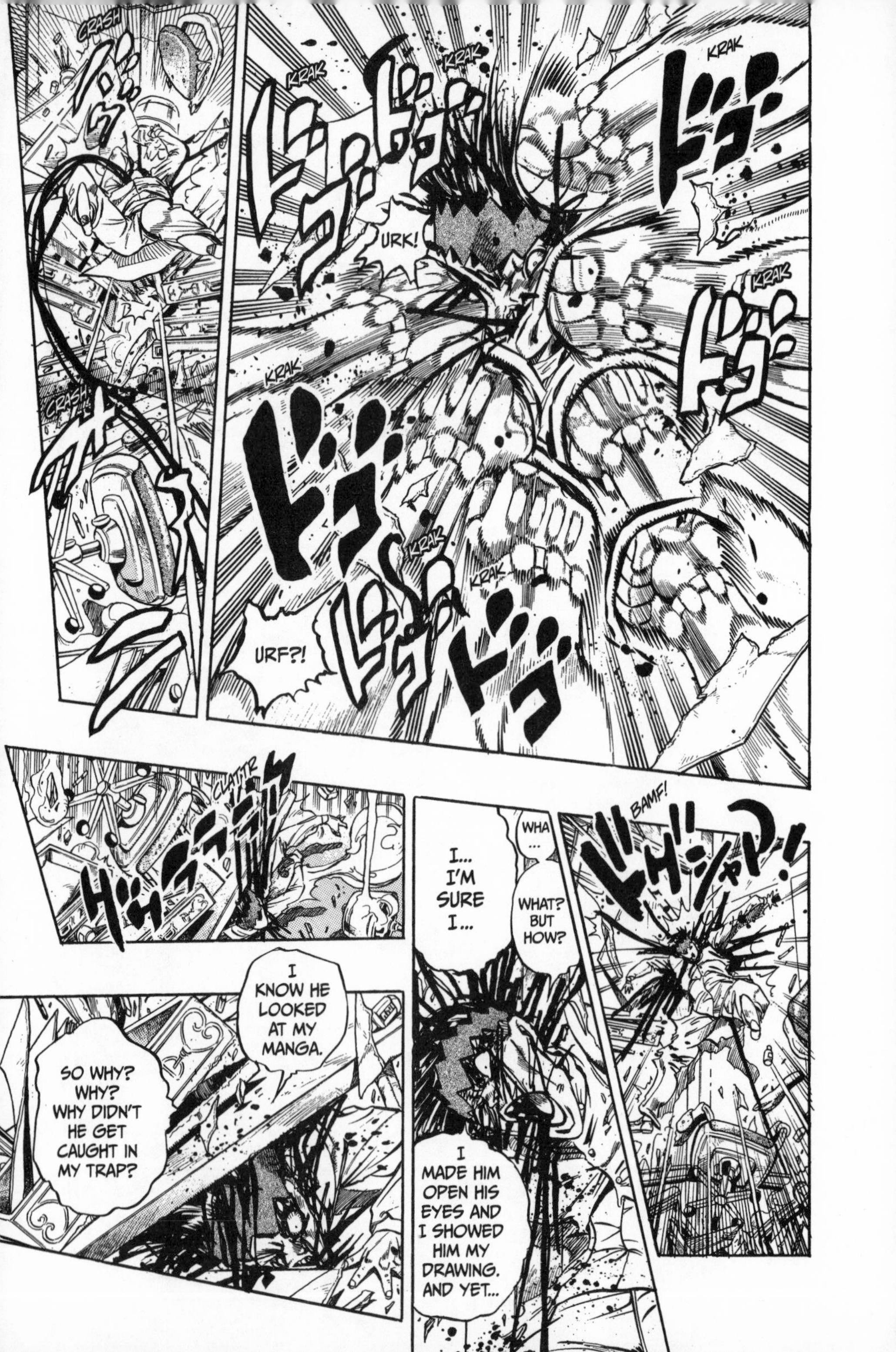
KRAK
KRAK
KRAK
URK!
KRAK
KRAK
KRAK
KRAK
URF?!
CRASH
CRASH
BAMF!
WHA...
WHAT? BUT HOW?
I... I'M SURE I...
I MADE HIM OPEN HIS EYES AND I SHOWED HIM MY DRAWING. AND YET...
CLATTR
I KNOW HE LOOKED AT MY MANGA.
SO WHY? WHY? WHY DIDN'T HE GET CAUGHT IN MY TRAP?

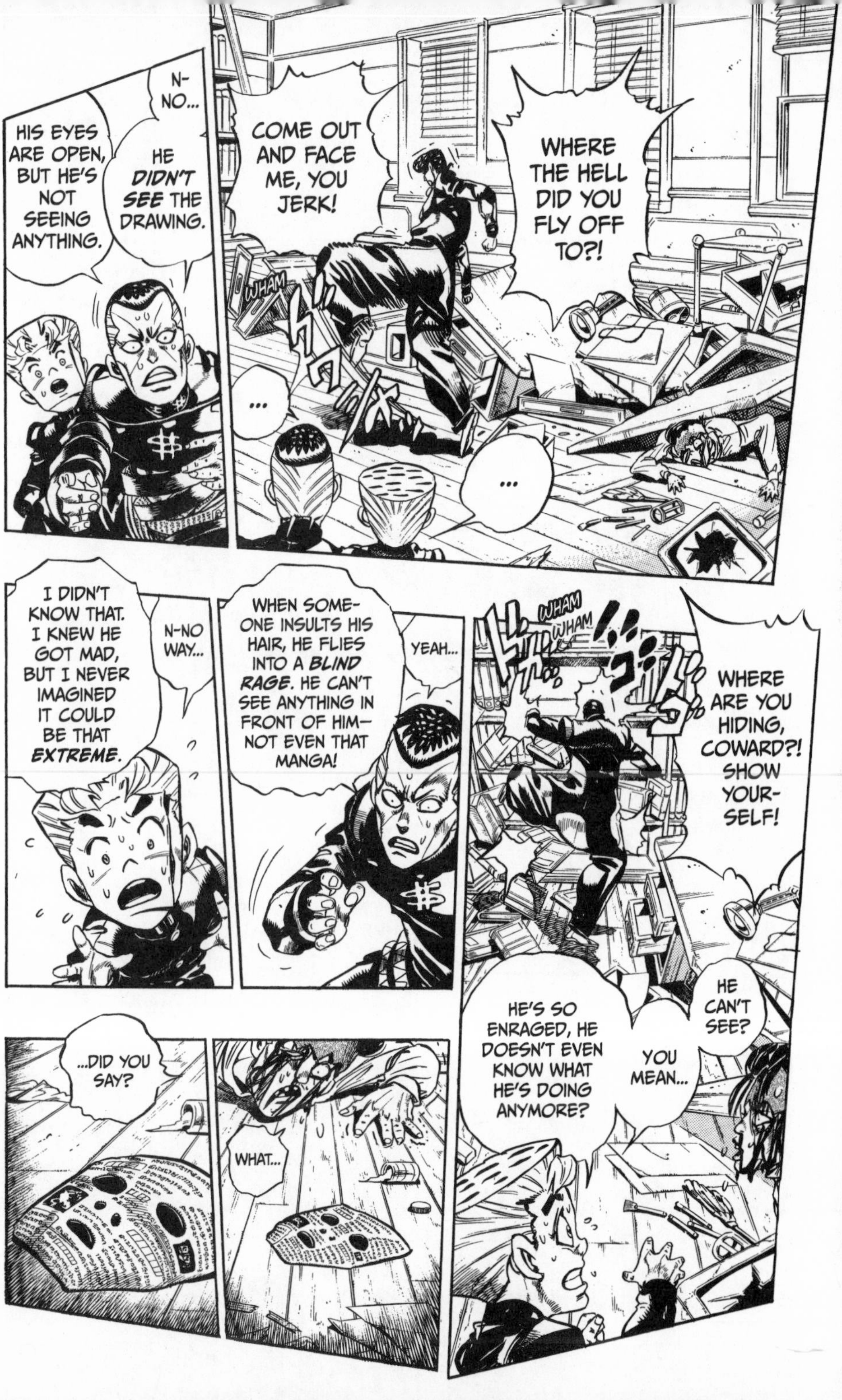
WHERE THE HELL DID YOU FLY OFF TO?!
COME OUT AND FACE ME, YOU JERK!
WHAM
...
...
N-NO...
HE *DIDN'T SEE* THE DRAWING.
HIS EYES ARE OPEN, BUT HE'S NOT SEEING ANYTHING.
WHAM
WHAM
WHERE ARE YOU HIDING, COWARD?! SHOW YOURSELF!
YEAH...
WHEN SOMEONE INSULTS HIS HAIR, HE FLIES INTO A *BLIND RAGE*. HE CAN'T SEE ANYTHING IN FRONT OF HIM—NOT EVEN THAT MANGA!
N-NO WAY...
I DIDN'T KNOW THAT. I KNEW HE GOT MAD, BUT I NEVER IMAGINED IT COULD BE THAT *EXTREME*.
HE CAN'T SEE?
YOU MEAN...
HE'S SO ENRAGED, HE DOESN'T EVEN KNOW WHAT HE'S DOING ANYMORE?
WHAT...
...DID YOU SAY?

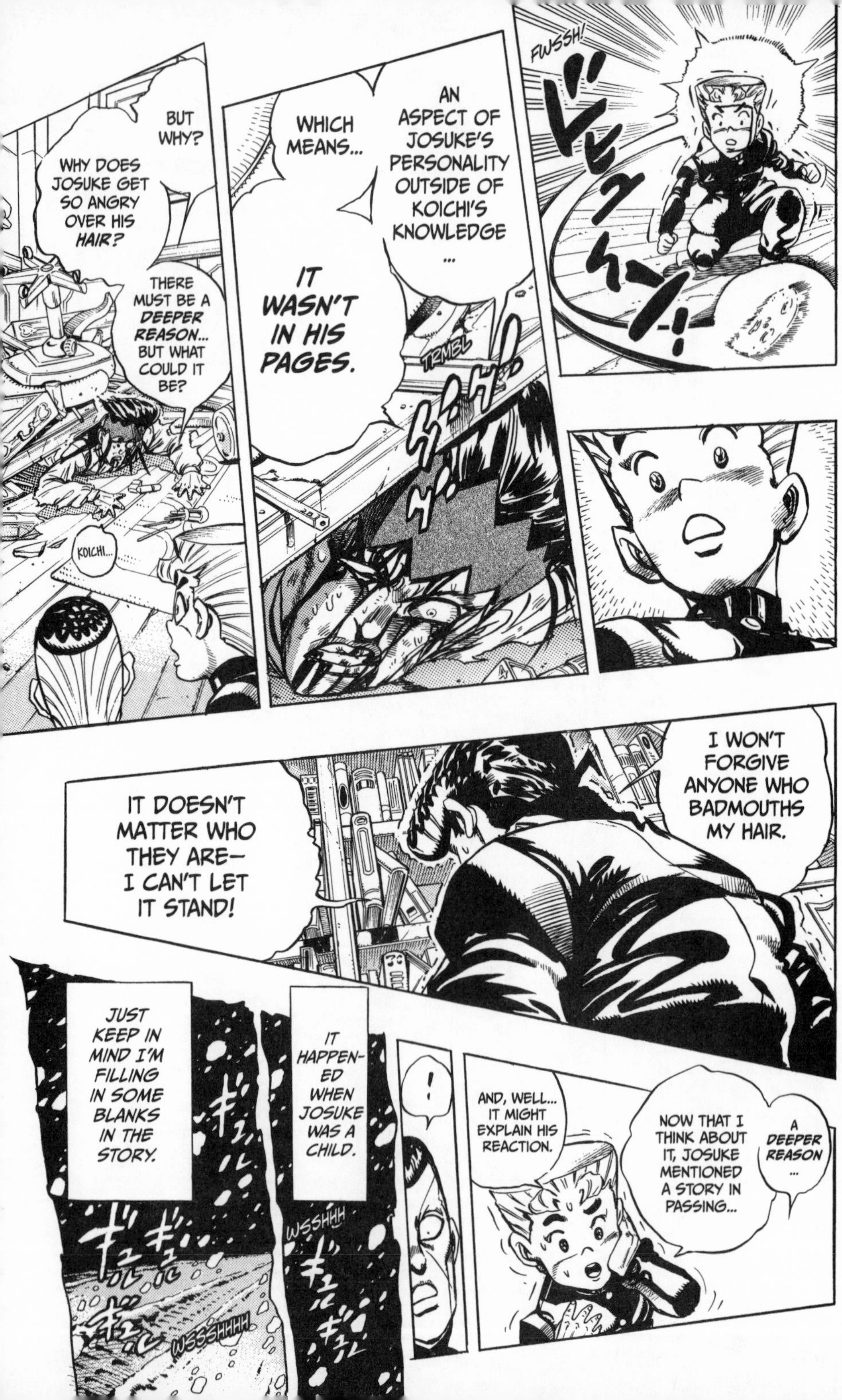
FWSSH!
WHICH MEANS...
AN ASPECT OF JOSUKE'S PERSONALITY OUTSIDE OF KOICHI'S KNOWLEDGE...
IT WASN'T IN HIS PAGES.
TRMBL
BUT WHY?
WHY DOES JOSUKE GET SO ANGRY OVER HIS HAIR?
THERE MUST BE A DEEPER REASON... BUT WHAT COULD IT BE?
KOICHI...
I WON'T FORGIVE ANYONE WHO BADMOUTHS MY HAIR.
IT DOESN'T MATTER WHO THEY ARE— I CAN'T LET IT STAND!
A DEEPER REASON...
NOW THAT I THINK ABOUT IT, JOSUKE MENTIONED A STORY IN PASSING...
AND, WELL... IT MIGHT EXPLAIN HIS REACTION.
!
IT HAPPENED WHEN JOSUKE WAS A CHILD.
WSSHHH
JUST KEEP IN MIND I'M FILLING IN SOME BLANKS IN THE STORY.
WSSSHHHH

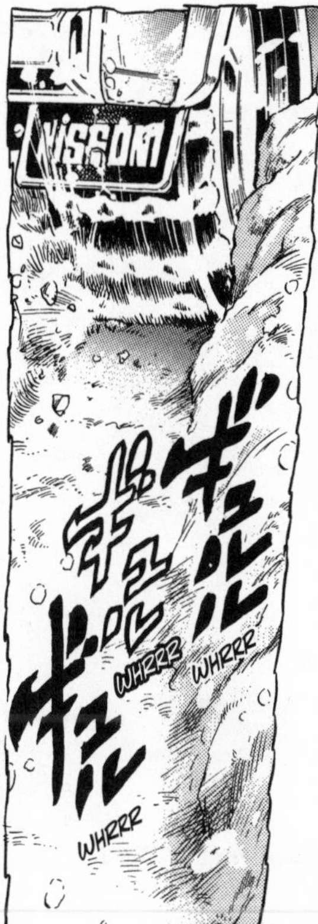
WHRRR
WHRRR
WHRRR
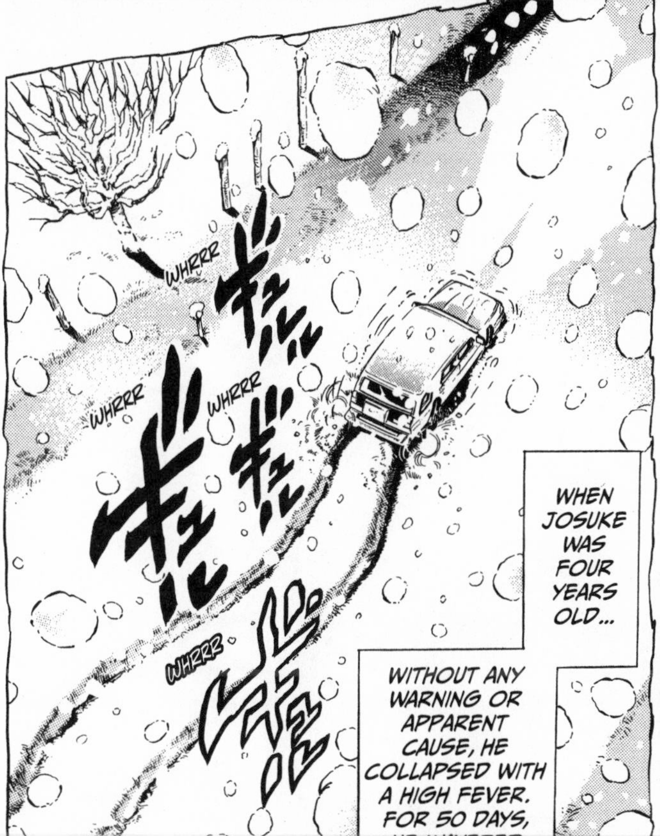
WHRRR
WHRRR
WHRRR
WHRRR
WHEN JOSUKE WAS FOUR YEARS OLD...
WITHOUT ANY WARNING OR APPARENT CAUSE, HE COLLAPSED WITH A HIGH FEVER. FOR 50 DAYS, HE WAVERED ON THE BRINK OF DEATH.
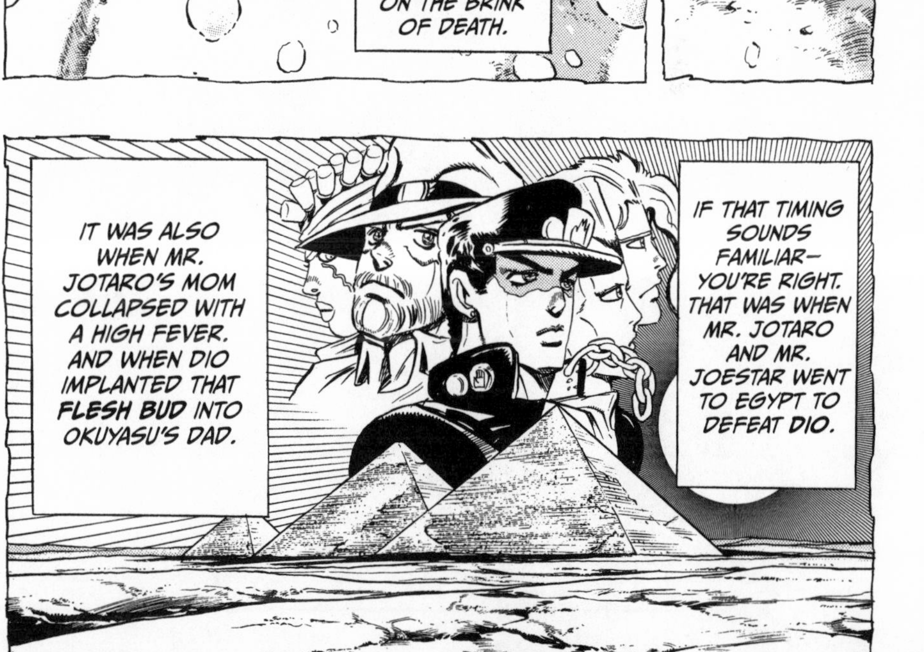
IF THAT TIMING SOUNDS FAMILIAR— YOU'RE RIGHT. THAT WAS WHEN MR. JOTARO AND MR. JOESTAR WENT TO EGYPT TO DEFEAT **DIO**.
IT WAS ALSO WHEN MR. JOTARO'S MOM COLLAPSED WITH A HIGH FEVER. AND WHEN DIO IMPLANTED THAT **FLESH BUD** INTO OKUYASU'S DAD.

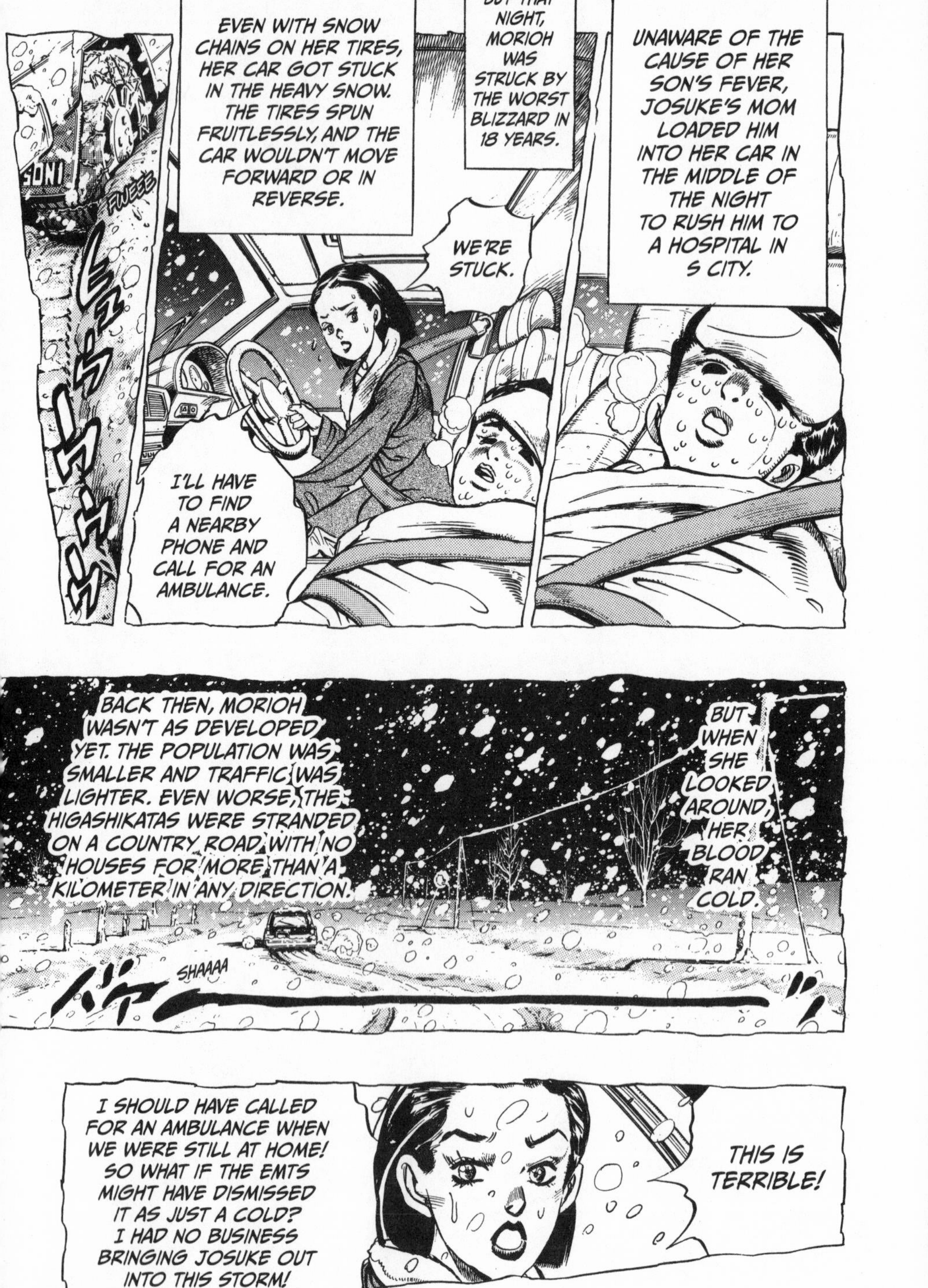
UNAWARE OF THE CAUSE OF HER SON'S FEVER, JOSUKE'S MOM LOADED HIM INTO HER CAR IN THE MIDDLE OF THE NIGHT TO RUSH HIM TO A HOSPITAL IN S CITY.
BUT THAT NIGHT, MORIOH WAS STRUCK BY THE WORST BLIZZARD IN 18 YEARS.
EVEN WITH SNOW CHAINS ON HER TIRES, HER CAR GOT STUCK IN THE HEAVY SNOW. THE TIRES SPUN FRUITLESSLY, AND THE CAR WOULDN'T MOVE FORWARD OR IN REVERSE.
WE'RE STUCK.
I'LL HAVE TO FIND A NEARBY PHONE AND CALL FOR AN AMBULANCE.
FWEEB
BUT WHEN SHE LOOKED AROUND, HER BLOOD RAN COLD.
BACK THEN, MORIOH WASN'T AS DEVELOPED YET. THE POPULATION WAS SMALLER AND TRAFFIC WAS LIGHTER. EVEN WORSE, THE HIGASHIKATAS WERE STRANDED ON A COUNTRY ROAD WITH NO HOUSES FOR MORE THAN A KILOMETER IN ANY DIRECTION.
SHAAAA
THIS IS TERRIBLE!
I SHOULD HAVE CALLED FOR AN AMBULANCE WHEN WE WERE STILL AT HOME! SO WHAT IF THE EMTS MIGHT HAVE DISMISSED IT AS JUST A COLD? I HAD NO BUSINESS BRINGING JOSUKE OUT INTO THIS STORM!

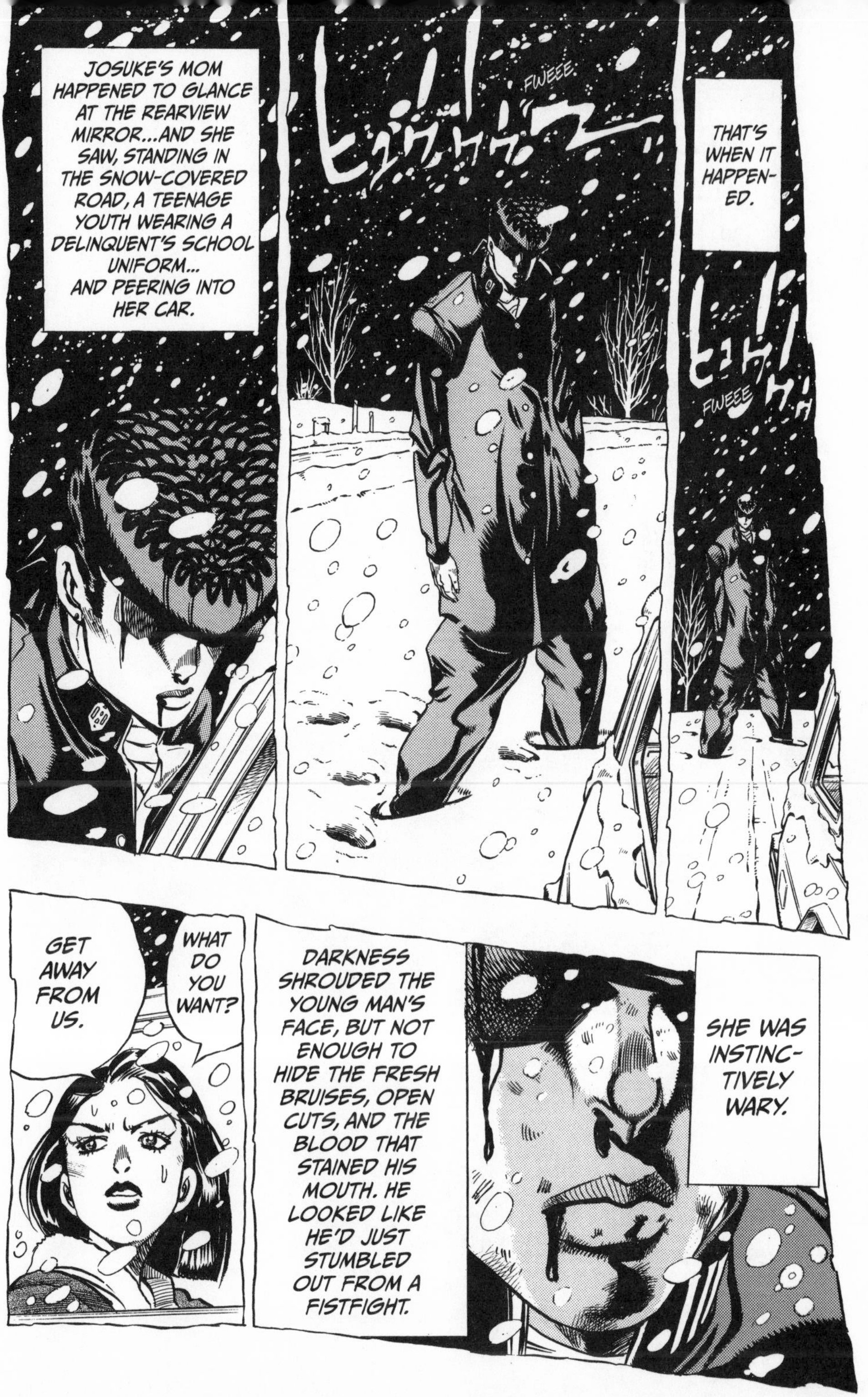
THAT'S WHEN IT HAPPEN-ED.
FWEEE
FWEEE
JOSUKE'S MOM HAPPENED TO GLANCE AT THE REARVIEW MIRROR...AND SHE SAW, STANDING IN THE SNOW-COVERED ROAD, A TEENAGE YOUTH WEARING A DELINQUENT'S SCHOOL UNIFORM... AND PEERING INTO HER CAR.
SHE WAS INSTINC-TIVELY WARY.
DARKNESS SHROUDED THE YOUNG MAN'S FACE, BUT NOT ENOUGH TO HIDE THE FRESH BRUISES, OPEN CUTS, AND THE BLOOD THAT STAINED HIS MOUTH. HE LOOKED LIKE HE'D JUST STUMBLED OUT FROM A FISTFIGHT.
WHAT DO YOU WANT?
GET AWAY FROM US.

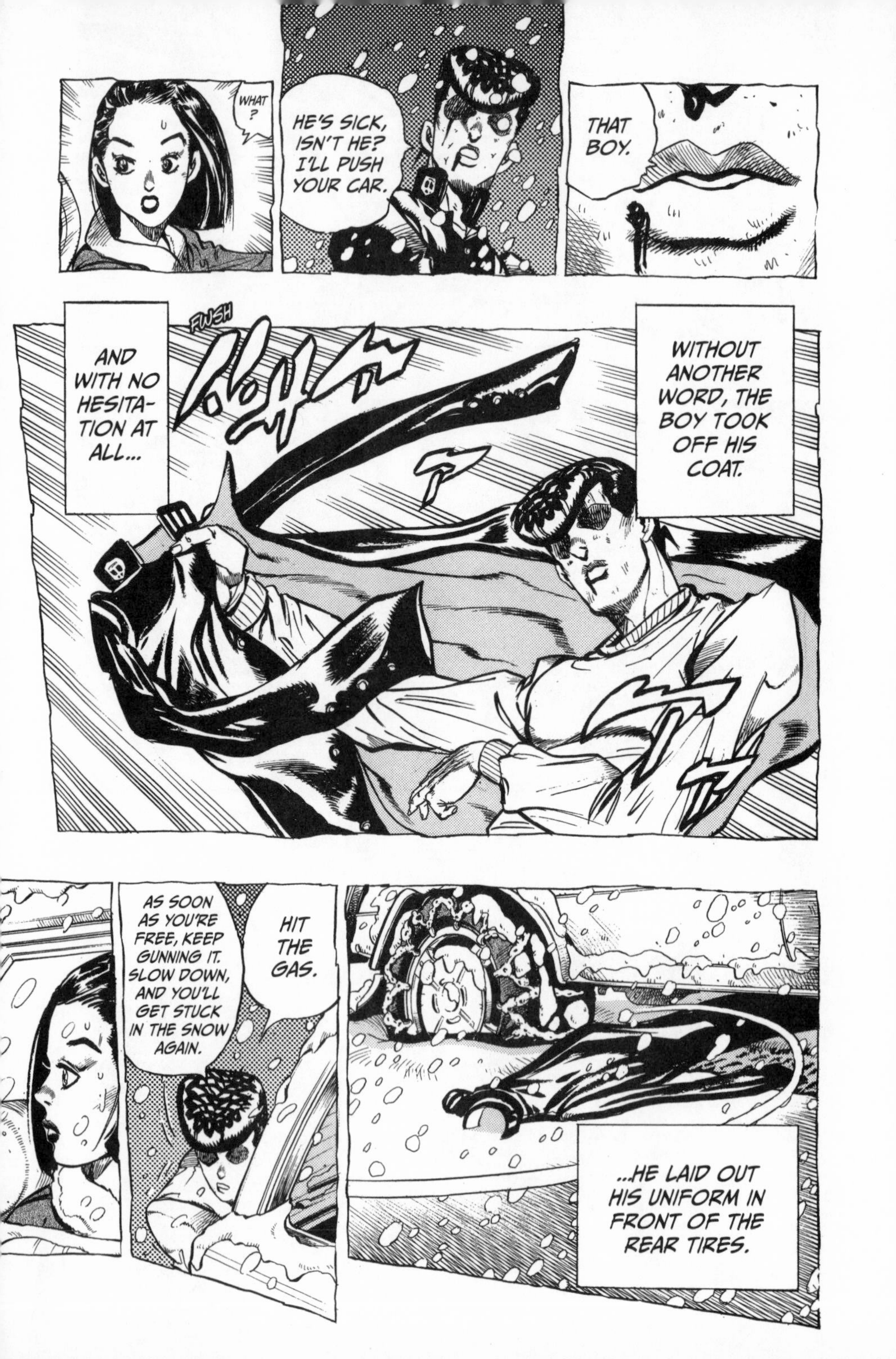
THAT BOY.
HE'S SICK, ISN'T HE? I'LL PUSH YOUR CAR.
WHAT?
WITHOUT ANOTHER WORD, THE BOY TOOK OFF HIS COAT.
FWSH
AND WITH NO HESITATION AT ALL...
...HE LAID OUT HIS UNIFORM IN FRONT OF THE REAR TIRES.
HIT THE GAS.
AS SOON AS YOU'RE FREE, KEEP GUNNING IT. SLOW DOWN, AND YOU'LL GET STUCK IN THE SNOW AGAIN.

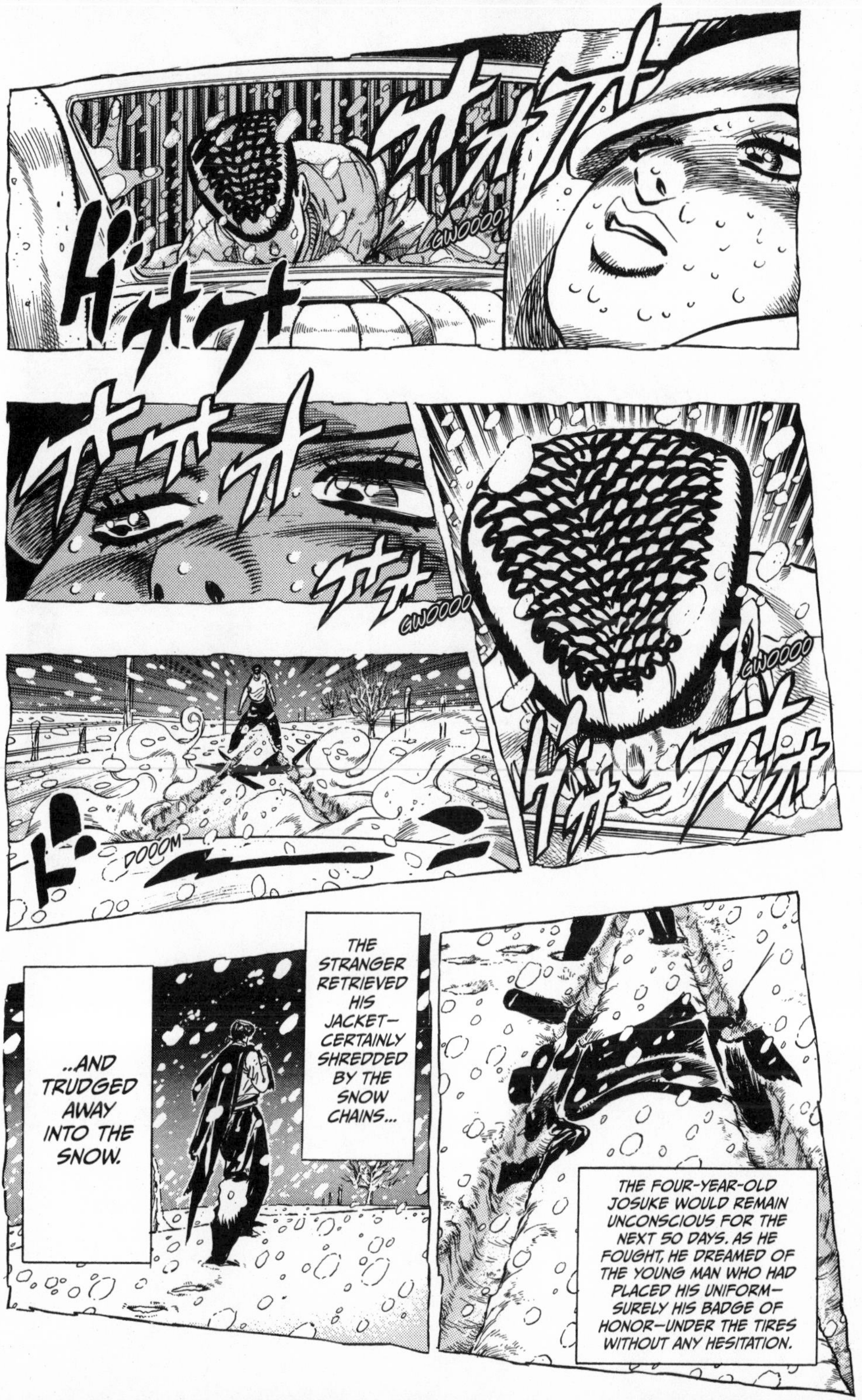
GWOOOO
GWOOOO
GWOOOO
DOOOM
THE FOUR-YEAR-OLD JOSUKE WOULD REMAIN UNCONSCIOUS FOR THE NEXT 50 DAYS. AS HE FOUGHT, HE DREAMED OF THE YOUNG MAN WHO HAD PLACED HIS UNIFORM—SURELY HIS BADGE OF HONOR—UNDER THE TIRES WITHOUT ANY HESITATION.
THE STRANGER RETRIEVED HIS JACKET—CERTAINLY SHREDDED BY THE SNOW CHAINS...
...AND TRUDGED AWAY INTO THE SNOW.

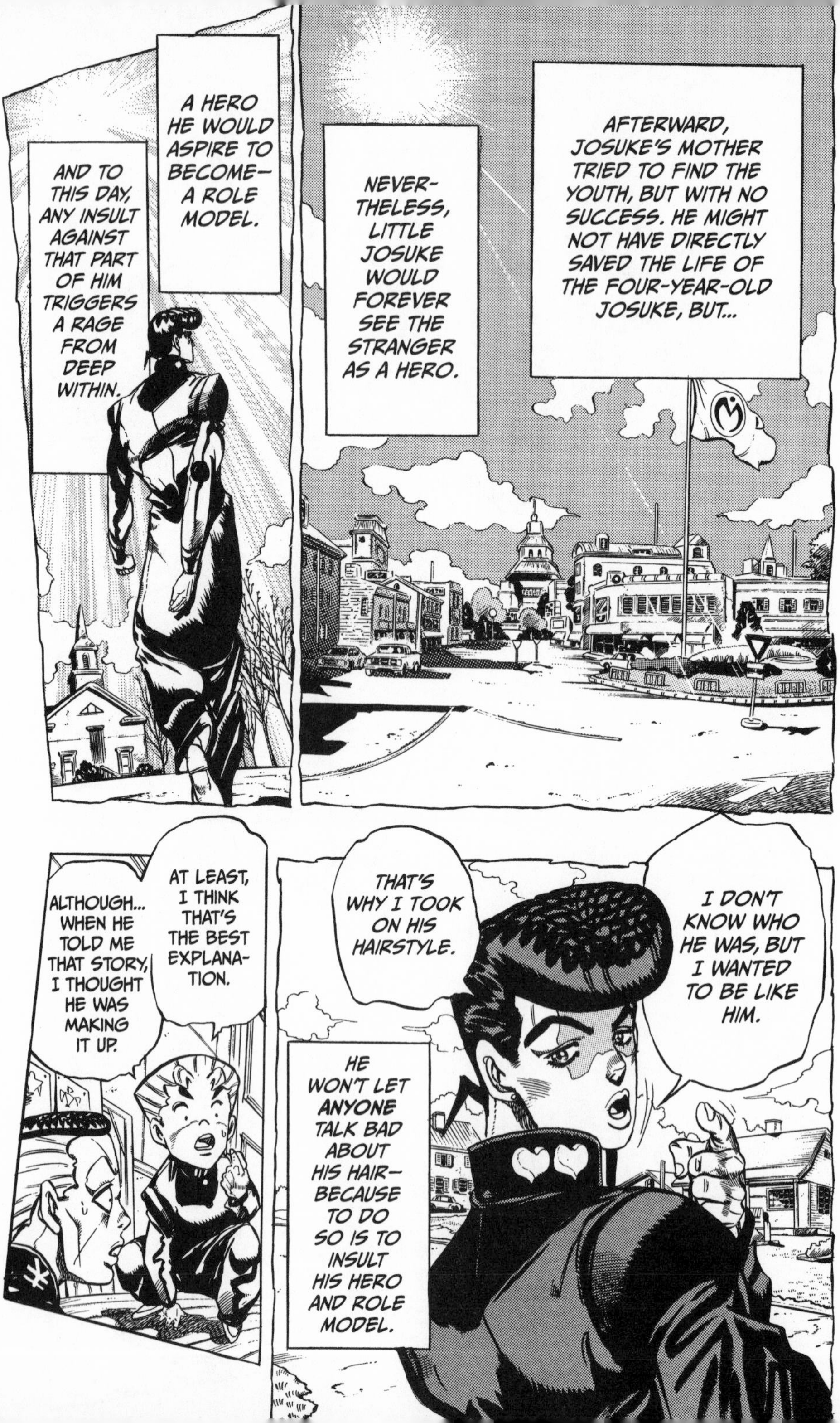
AFTERWARD, JOSUKE'S MOTHER TRIED TO FIND THE YOUTH, BUT WITH NO SUCCESS. HE MIGHT NOT HAVE DIRECTLY SAVED THE LIFE OF THE FOUR-YEAR-OLD JOSUKE, BUT...
NEVER-THELESS, LITTLE JOSUKE WOULD FOREVER SEE THE STRANGER AS A HERO.
A HERO HE WOULD ASPIRE TO BECOME—A ROLE MODEL.
AND TO THIS DAY, ANY INSULT AGAINST THAT PART OF HIM TRIGGERS A RAGE FROM DEEP WITHIN.
I DON'T KNOW WHO HE WAS, BUT I WANTED TO BE LIKE HIM.
THAT'S WHY I TOOK ON HIS HAIRSTYLE.
HE WON'T LET ANYONE TALK BAD ABOUT HIS HAIR—BECAUSE TO DO SO IS TO INSULT HIS HERO AND ROLE MODEL.
AT LEAST, I THINK THAT'S THE BEST EXPLANATION.
ALTHOUGH... WHEN HE TOLD ME THAT STORY, I THOUGHT HE WAS MAKING IT UP.

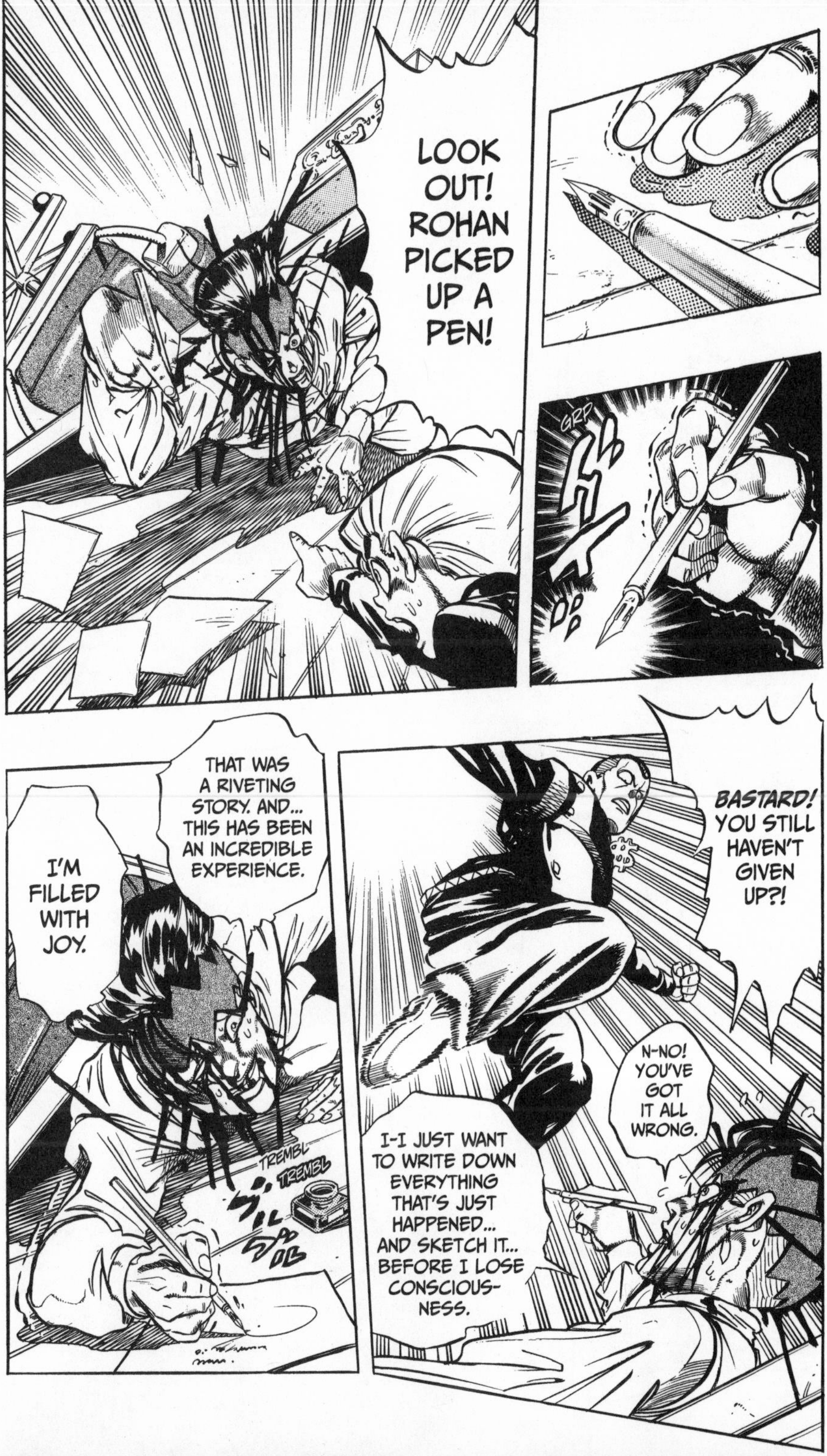
GRP
LOOK OUT! ROHAN PICKED UP A PEN!
BASTARD! YOU STILL HAVEN'T GIVEN UP?!
N-NO! YOU'VE GOT IT ALL WRONG.
I-I JUST WANT TO WRITE DOWN EVERYTHING THAT'S JUST HAPPENED... AND SKETCH IT... BEFORE I LOSE CONSCIOUS-NESS.
THAT WAS A RIVETING STORY. AND... THIS HAS BEEN AN INCREDIBLE EXPERIENCE.
I'M FILLED WITH JOY.
TREMBL
TREMBL

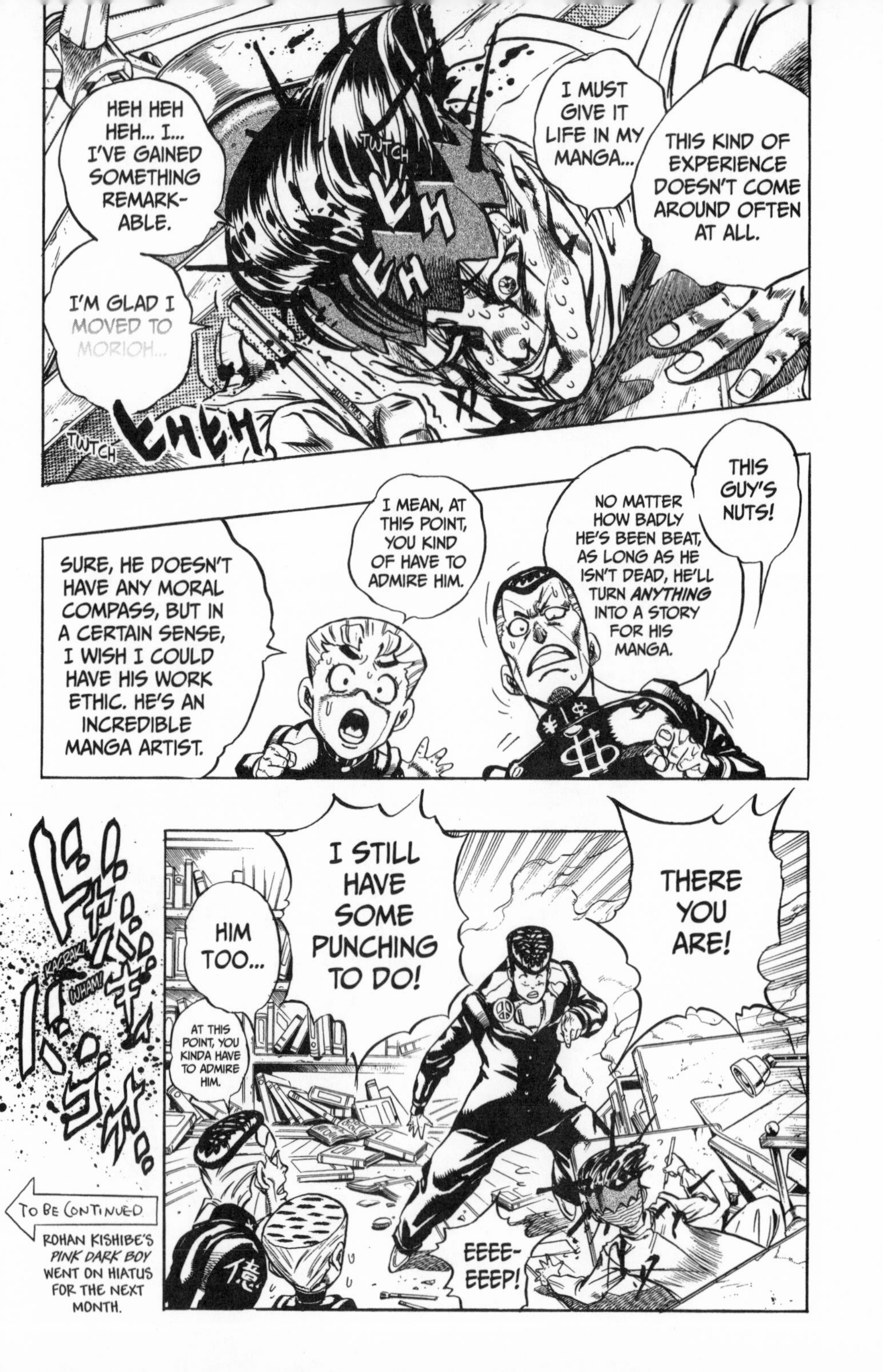
THIS KIND OF EXPERIENCE DOESN'T COME AROUND OFTEN AT ALL.
I MUST GIVE IT LIFE IN MY MANGA...
TWTCH
HEH HEH HEH... I... I'VE GAINED SOMETHING REMARKABLE.
I'M GLAD I MOVED TO MORIOH...
TWTCH
THIS GUY'S NUTS!
NO MATTER HOW BADLY HE'S BEEN BEAT, AS LONG AS HE ISN'T DEAD, HE'LL TURN *ANYTHING* INTO A STORY FOR HIS MANGA.
I MEAN, AT THIS POINT, YOU KIND OF HAVE TO ADMIRE HIM.
SURE, HE DOESN'T HAVE ANY MORAL COMPASS, BUT IN A CERTAIN SENSE, I WISH I COULD HAVE HIS WORK ETHIC. HE'S AN INCREDIBLE MANGA ARTIST.
THERE YOU ARE!
I STILL HAVE SOME PUNCHING TO DO!
HIM TOO...
AT THIS POINT, YOU KINDA HAVE TO ADMIRE HIM.
EEEE-EEEP!
KACRAK!
WHAM!
TO BE CONTINUED
ROHAN KISHIBE'S *PINK DARK BOY* WENT ON HIATUS FOR THE NEXT MONTH.

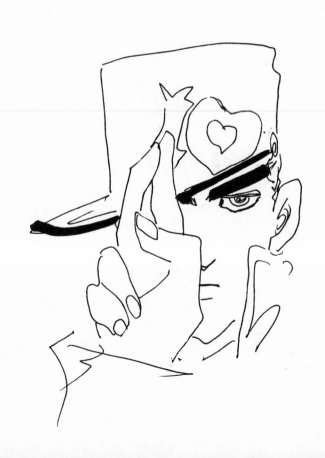

CHAPTER 60

LET'S GO HUNTING!, PART 1

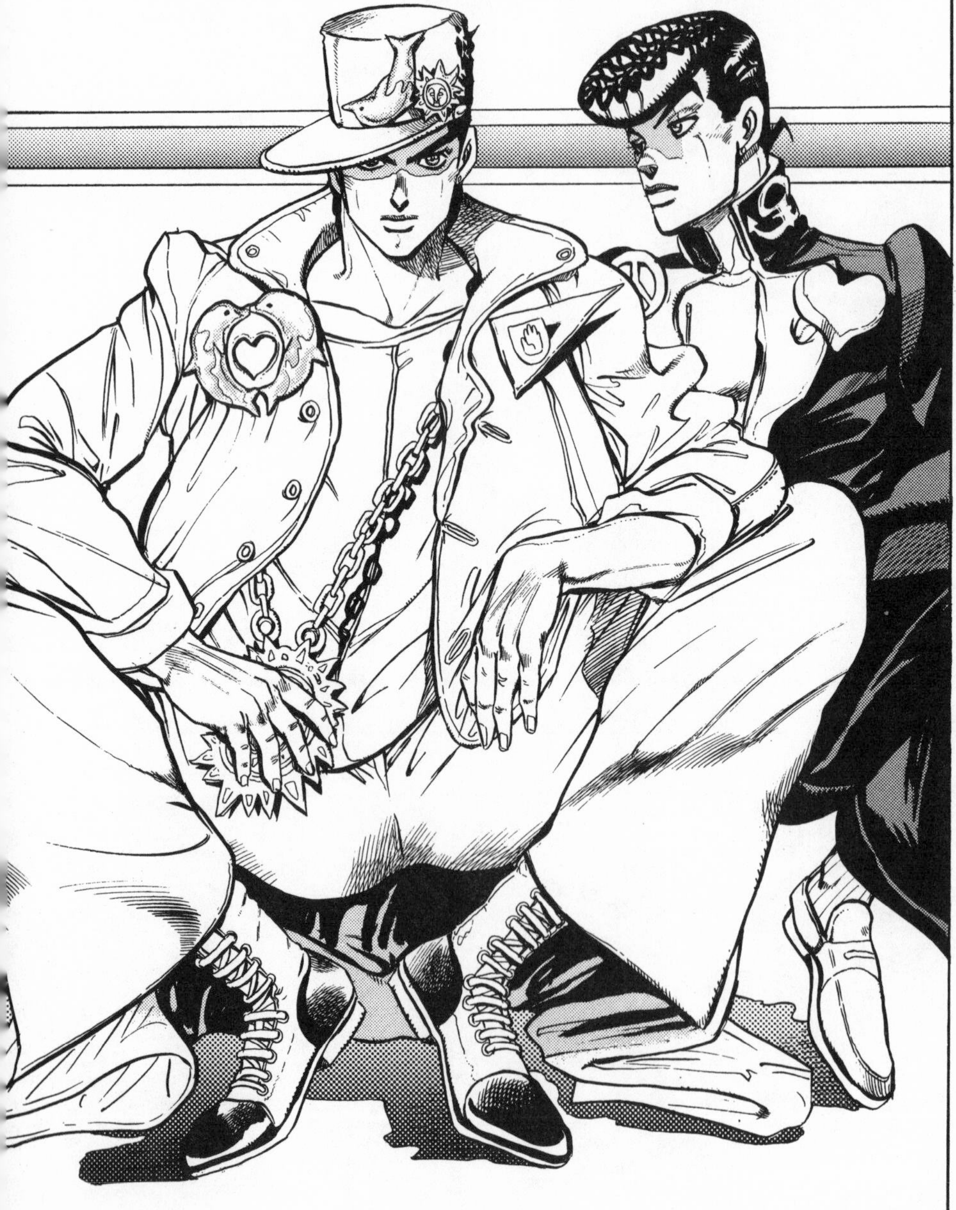

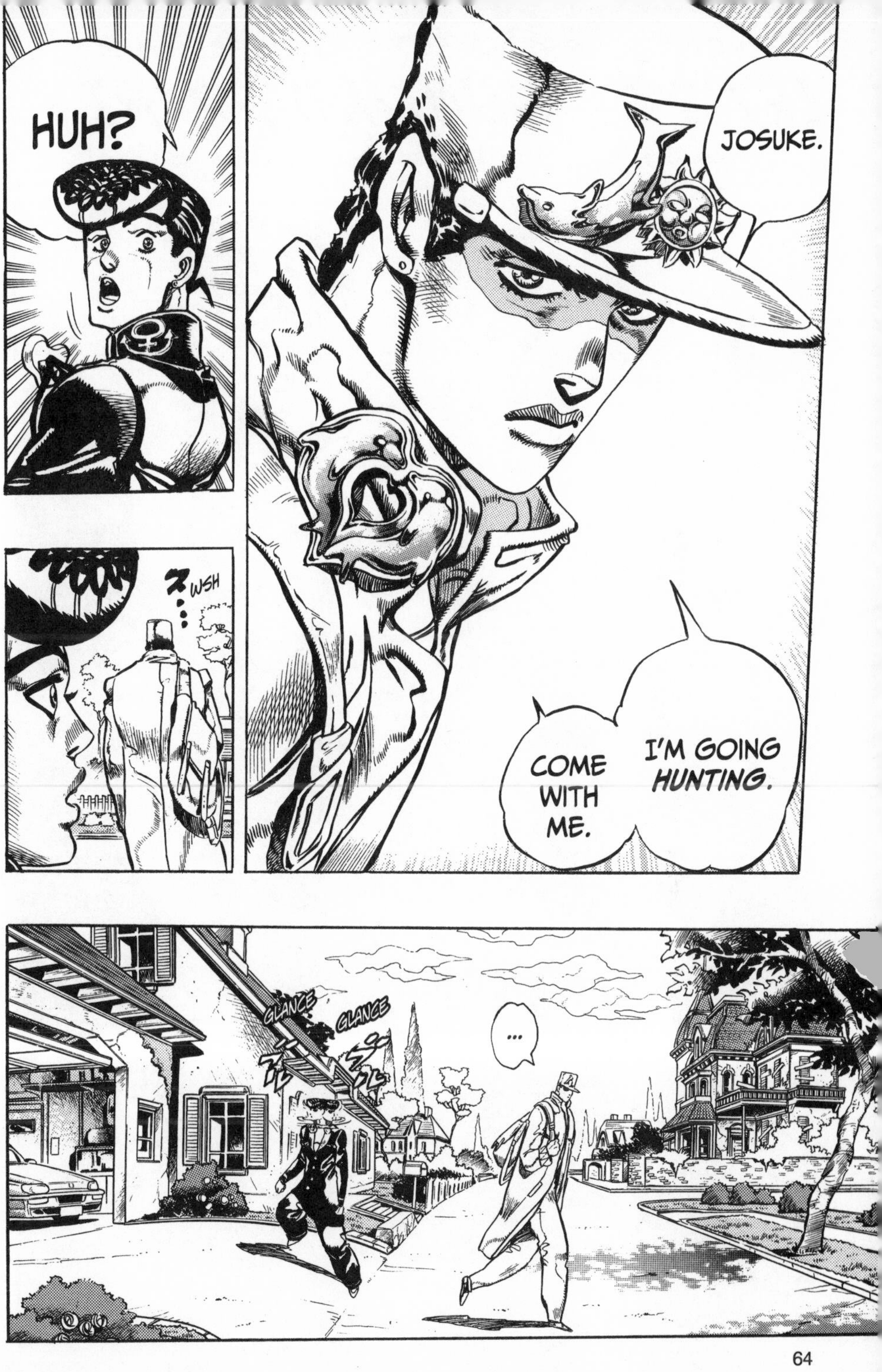
JOSUKE.
I'M GOING HUNTING.
COME WITH ME.
HUH?
WSH
...
GLANCE
GLANCE

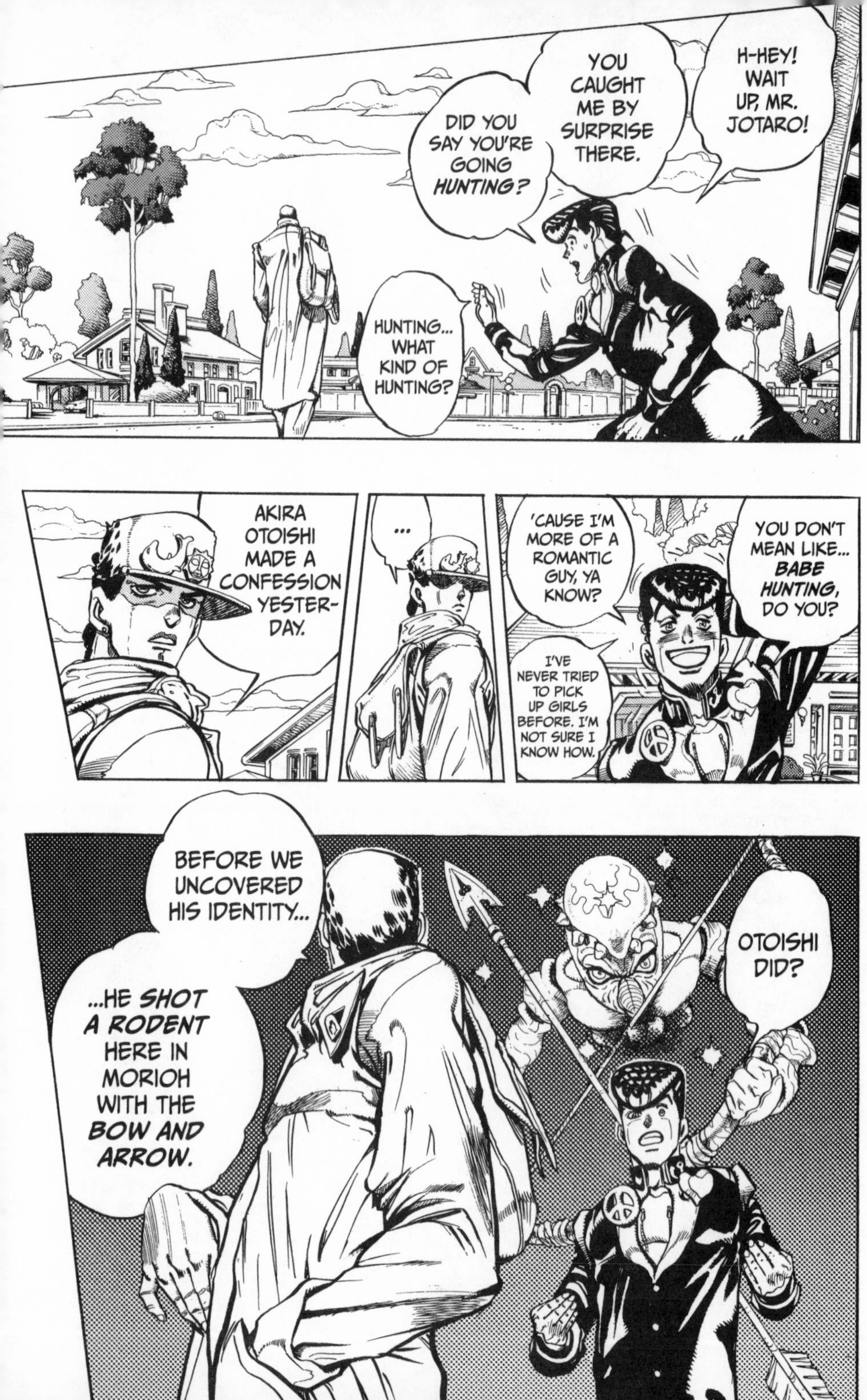
H-HEY! WAIT UP, MR. JOTARO!
YOU CAUGHT ME BY SURPRISE THERE.
DID YOU SAY YOU'RE GOING *HUNTING?*
HUNTING... WHAT KIND OF HUNTING?
YOU DON'T MEAN LIKE... *BABE HUNTING,* DO YOU?
'CAUSE I'M MORE OF A ROMANTIC GUY, YA KNOW?
I'VE NEVER TRIED TO PICK UP GIRLS BEFORE. I'M NOT SURE I KNOW HOW.
...
AKIRA OTOISHI MADE A CONFESSION YESTER-DAY.
OTOISHI DID?
BEFORE WE UNCOVERED HIS IDENTITY...
...HE *SHOT A RODENT* HERE IN MORIOH WITH THE *BOW AND ARROW.*

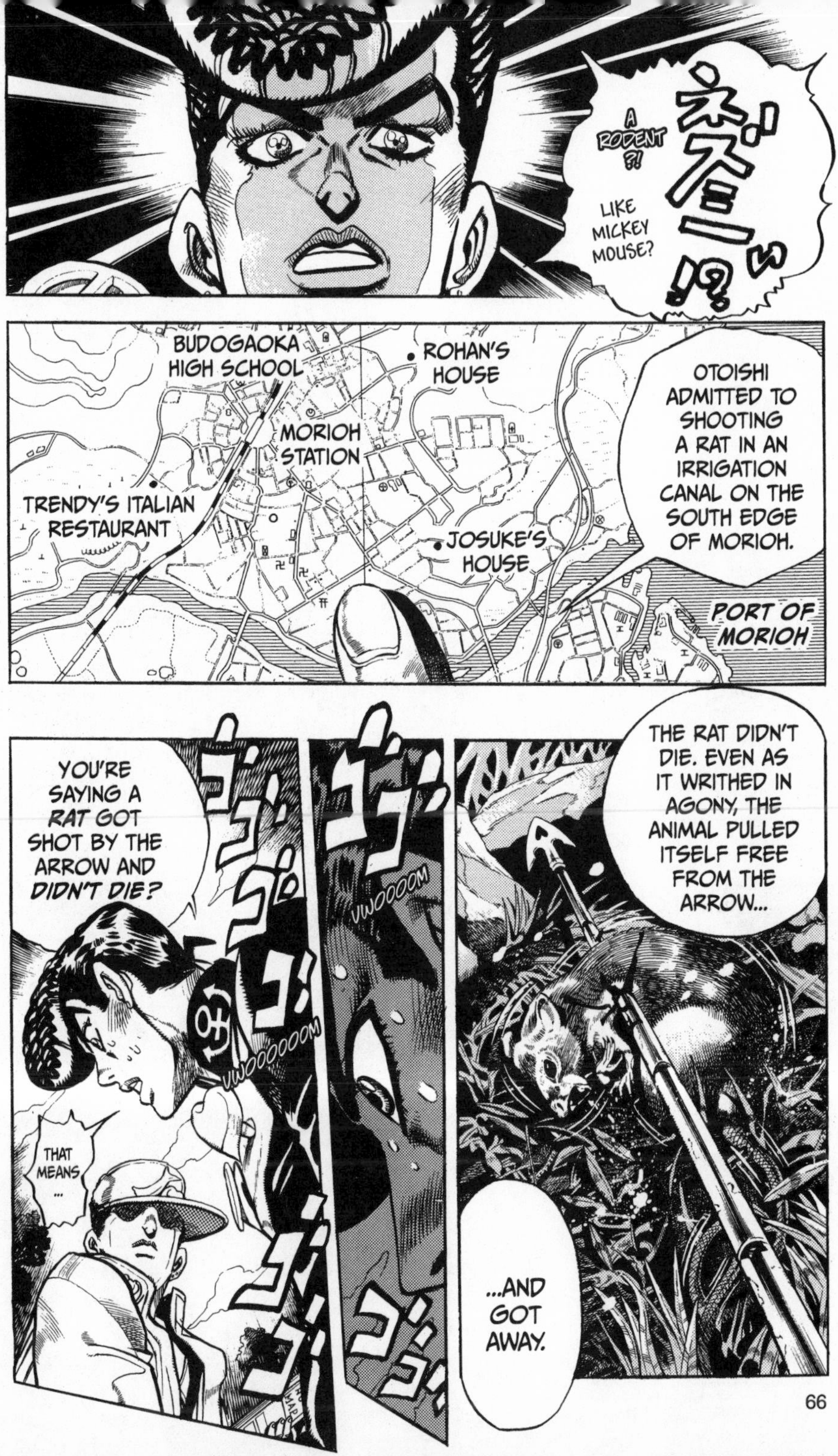
ネズミー!?
A RODENT?!
LIKE MICKEY MOUSE?
OTOISHI ADMITTED TO SHOOTING A RAT IN AN IRRIGATION CANAL ON THE SOUTH EDGE OF MORIOH.
PORT OF MORIOH
JOSUKE'S HOUSE
ROHAN'S HOUSE
MORIOH STATION
BUDOGAOKA HIGH SCHOOL
TRENDY'S ITALIAN RESTAURANT
THE RAT DIDN'T DIE. EVEN AS IT WRITHED IN AGONY, THE ANIMAL PULLED ITSELF FREE FROM THE ARROW...
...AND GOT AWAY.
VWOOOOM
YOU'RE SAYING A RAT GOT SHOT BY THE ARROW AND DIDN'T DIE?
VWOOOOOOM
THAT MEANS...

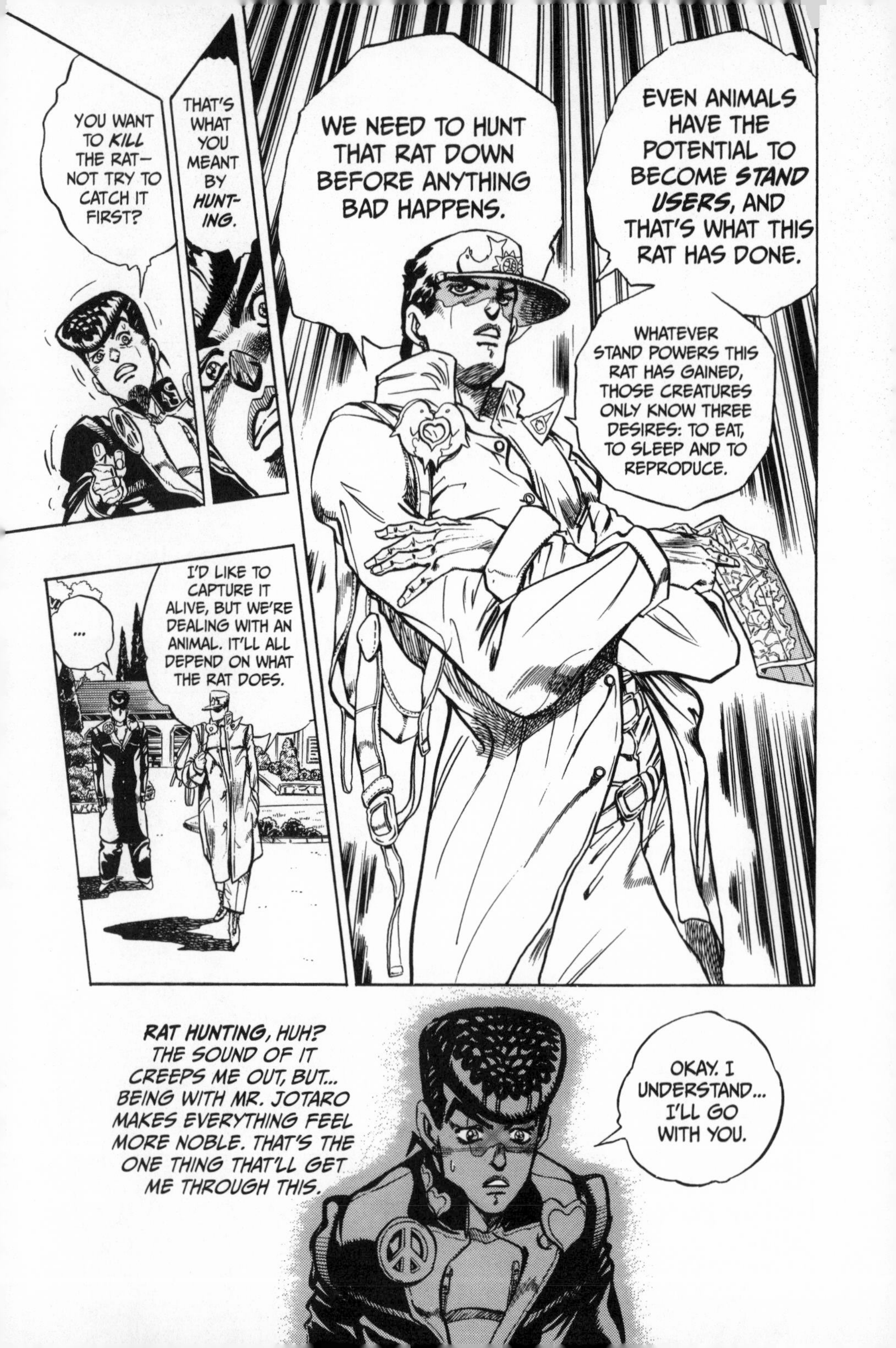
EVEN ANIMALS HAVE THE POTENTIAL TO BECOME STAND USERS, AND THAT'S WHAT THIS RAT HAS DONE.
WE NEED TO HUNT THAT RAT DOWN BEFORE ANYTHING BAD HAPPENS.
WHATEVER STAND POWERS THIS RAT HAS GAINED, THOSE CREATURES ONLY KNOW THREE DESIRES: TO EAT, TO SLEEP AND TO REPRODUCE.
THAT'S WHAT YOU MEANT BY HUNTING.
YOU WANT TO KILL THE RAT—NOT TRY TO CATCH IT FIRST?
I'D LIKE TO CAPTURE IT ALIVE, BUT WE'RE DEALING WITH AN ANIMAL. IT'LL ALL DEPEND ON WHAT THE RAT DOES.
...
OKAY. I UNDERSTAND... I'LL GO WITH YOU.
RAT HUNTING, HUH? THE SOUND OF IT CREEPS ME OUT, BUT... BEING WITH MR. JOTARO MAKES EVERYTHING FEEL MORE NOBLE. THAT'S THE ONE THING THAT'LL GET ME THROUGH THIS.

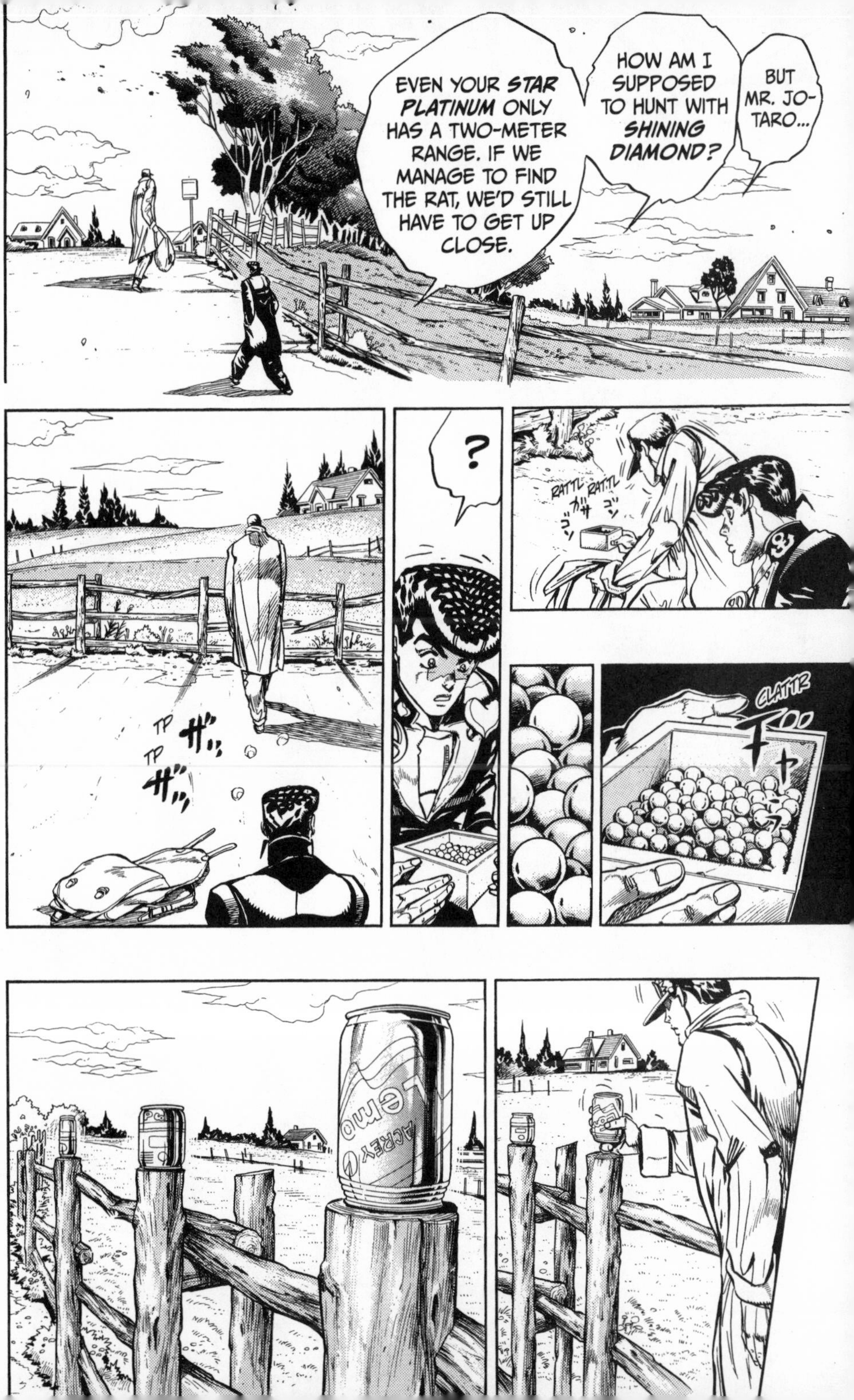
BUT MR. JO-TARO...
HOW AM I SUPPOSED TO HUNT WITH SHINING DIAMOND?
EVEN YOUR STAR PLATINUM ONLY HAS A TWO-METER RANGE. IF WE MANAGE TO FIND THE RAT, WE'D STILL HAVE TO GET UP CLOSE.
RATTL RATTL
CLATTR
?
TP
TP

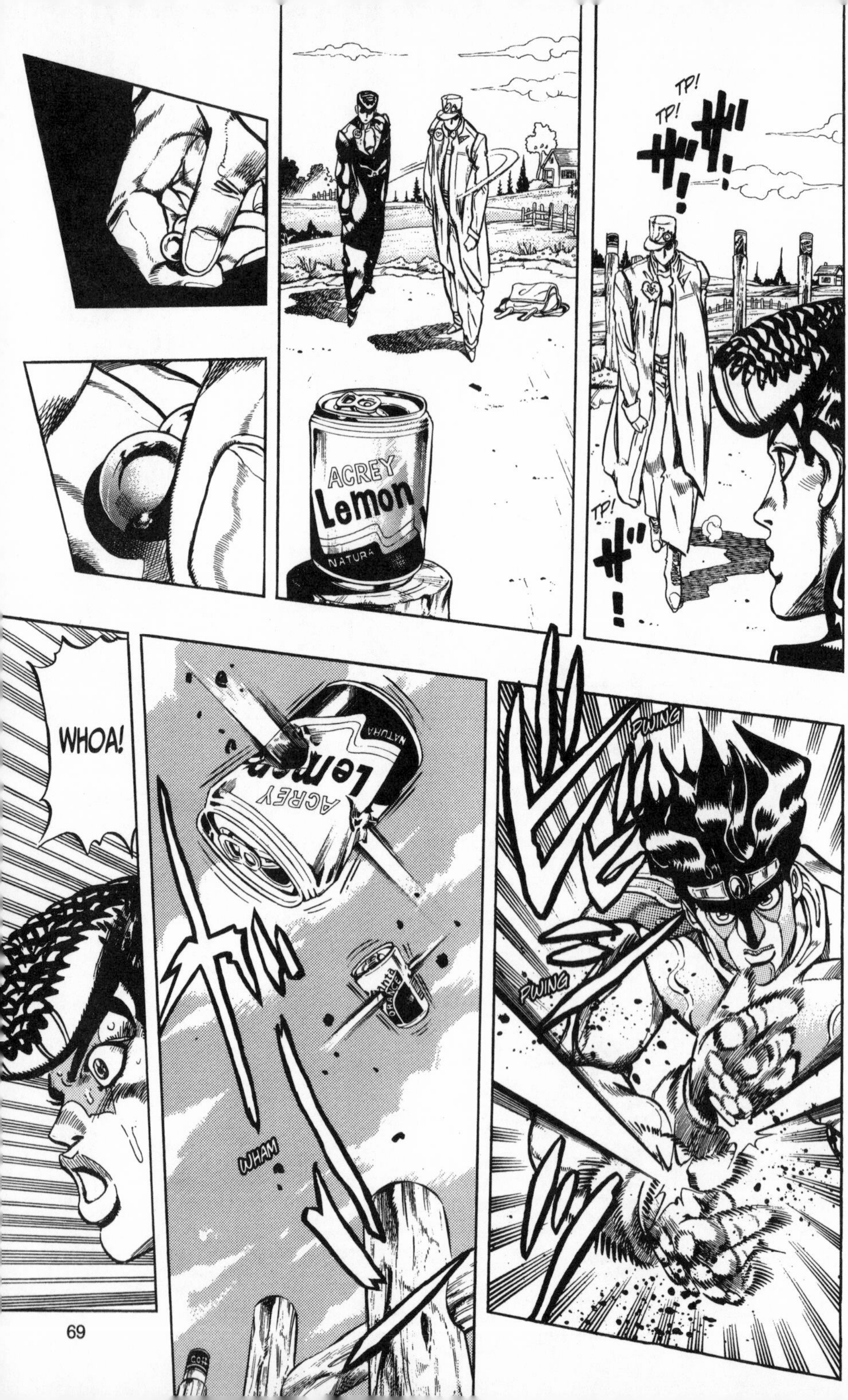
TP!
TP!
TP!
ACREY
Lemon
NATURA
PWING
PWING
WHAM
WHOA!

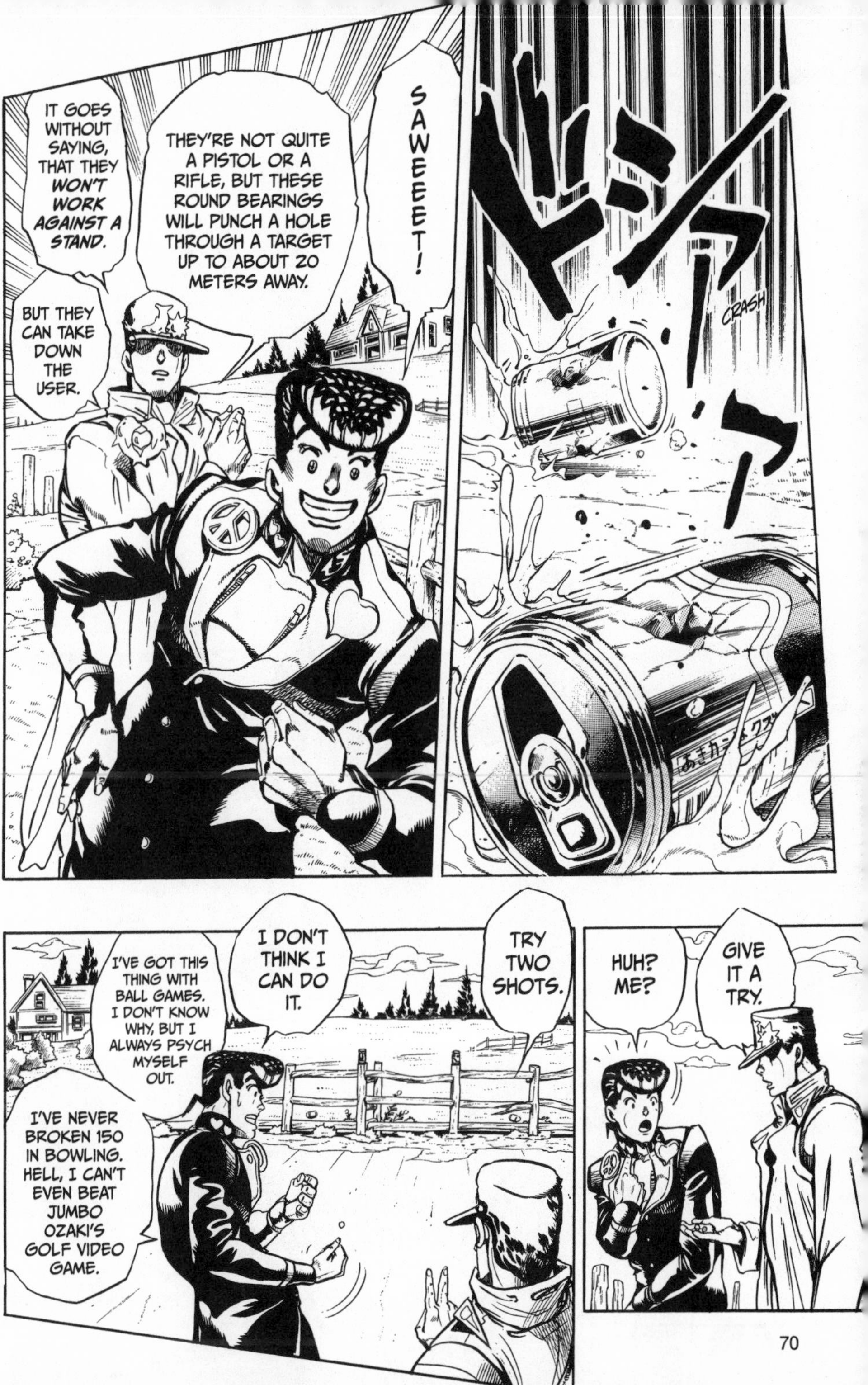
CRASH
SAWEEEET!
THEY'RE NOT QUITE A PISTOL OR A RIFLE, BUT THESE ROUND BEARINGS WILL PUNCH A HOLE THROUGH A TARGET UP TO ABOUT 20 METERS AWAY.
IT GOES WITHOUT SAYING, THAT THEY *WON'T WORK AGAINST A STAND.*
BUT THEY CAN TAKE DOWN THE USER.
GIVE IT A TRY.
HUH? ME?
TRY TWO SHOTS.
I DON'T THINK I CAN DO IT.
I'VE GOT THIS THING WITH BALL GAMES. I DON'T KNOW WHY, BUT I ALWAYS PSYCH MYSELF OUT.
I'VE NEVER BROKEN 150 IN BOWLING. HELL, I CAN'T EVEN BEAT JUMBO OZAKI'S GOLF VIDEO GAME.

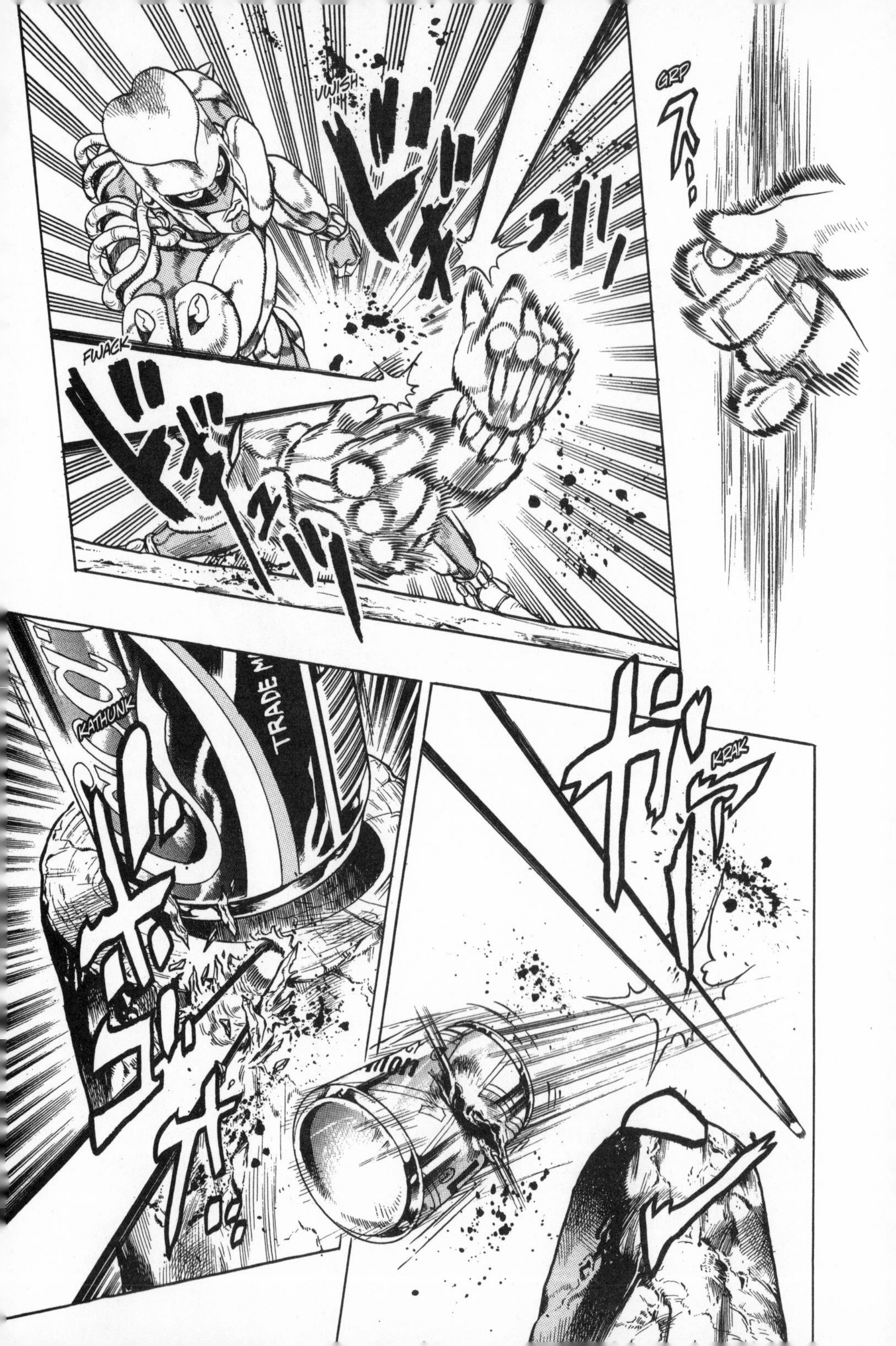
GRP
UWISH
FWACK
KRAK
KATHUNK

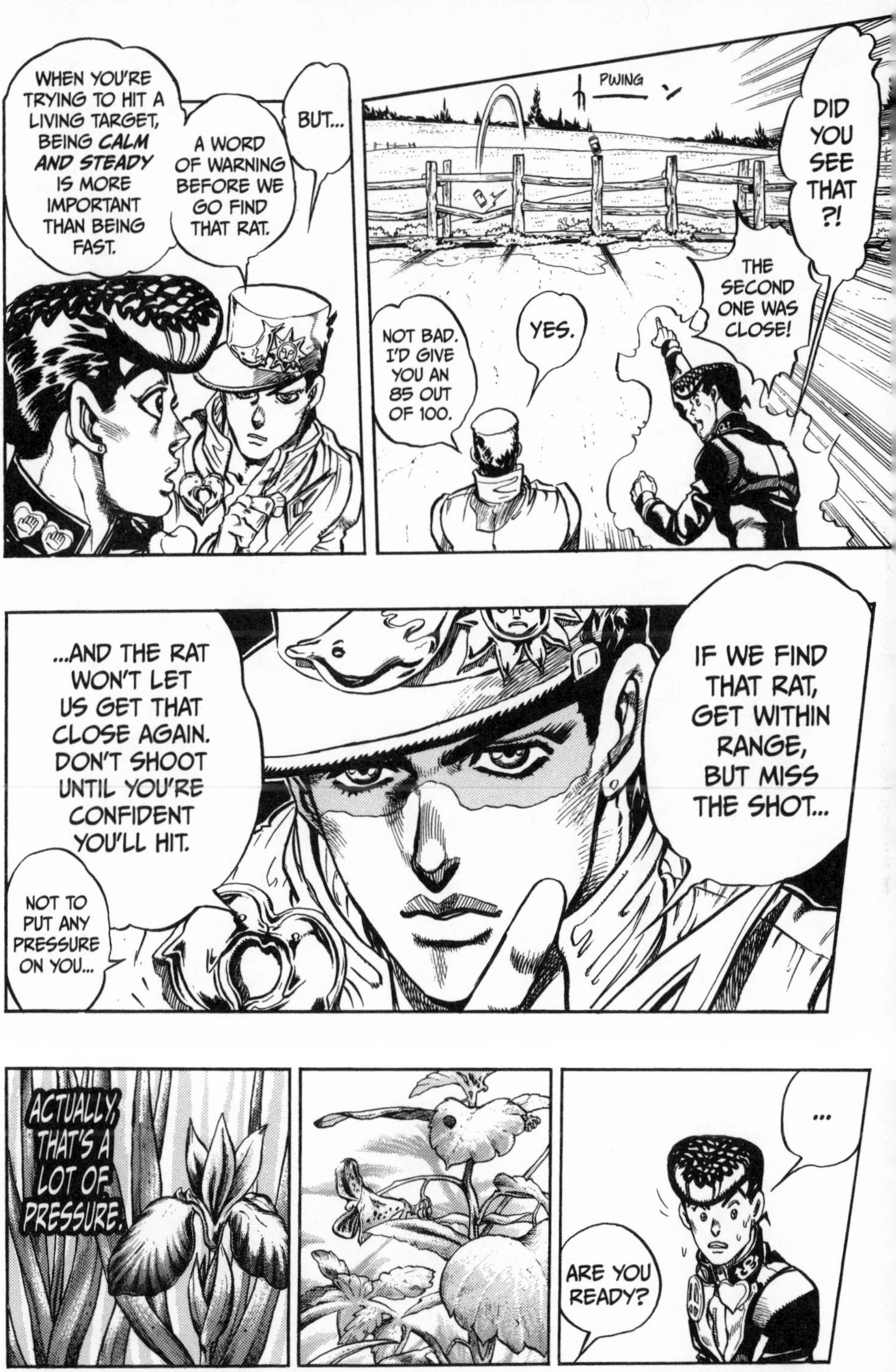
PWING
DID YOU SEE THAT?!
THE SECOND ONE WAS CLOSE!
YES.
NOT BAD. I'D GIVE YOU AN 85 OUT OF 100.
BUT...
A WORD OF WARNING BEFORE WE GO FIND THAT RAT.
WHEN YOU'RE TRYING TO HIT A LIVING TARGET, BEING CALM AND STEADY IS MORE IMPORTANT THAN BEING FAST.
IF WE FIND THAT RAT, GET WITHIN RANGE, BUT MISS THE SHOT...
...AND THE RAT WON'T LET US GET THAT CLOSE AGAIN. DON'T SHOOT UNTIL YOU'RE CONFIDENT YOU'LL HIT.
NOT TO PUT ANY PRESSURE ON YOU...
...
ARE YOU READY?
ACTUALLY, THAT'S A LOT OF PRESSURE.

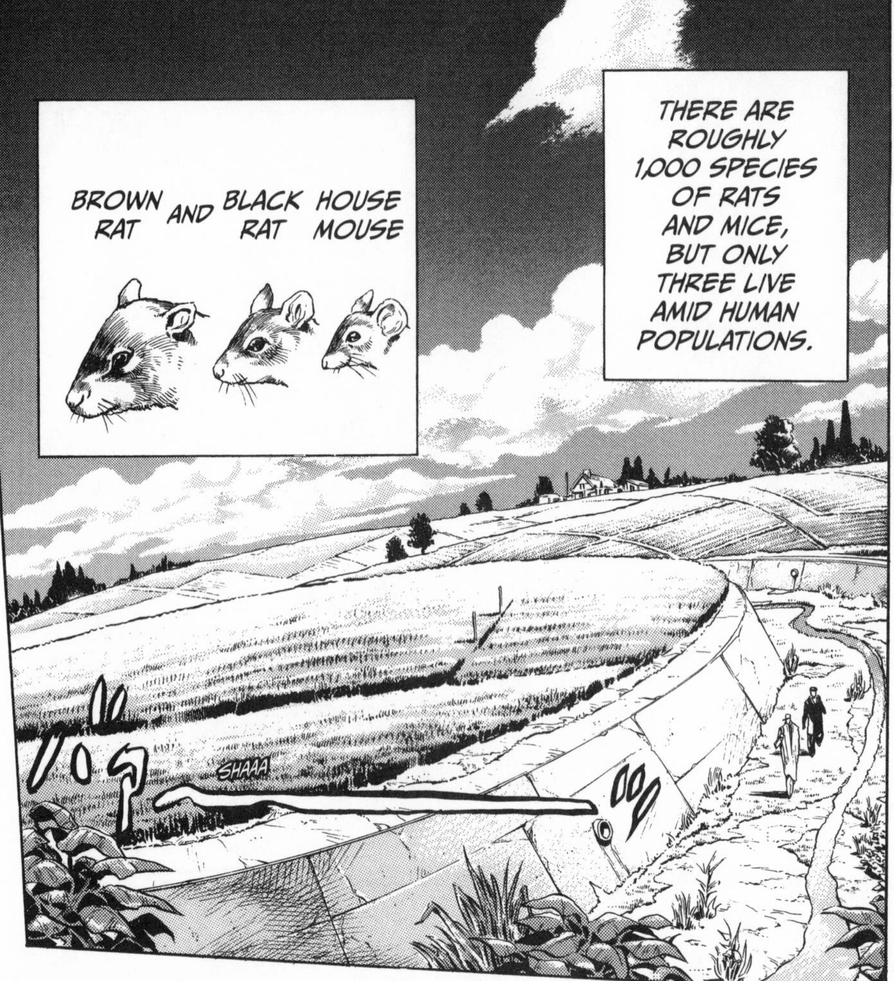
THERE ARE ROUGHLY 1,000 SPECIES OF RATS AND MICE, BUT ONLY THREE LIVE AMID HUMAN POPULATIONS.
BROWN RAT
AND
BLACK RAT
HOUSE MOUSE
SHAAA

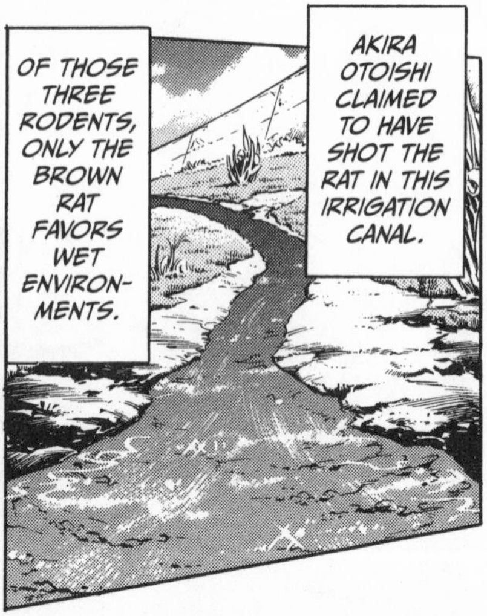
AKIRA OTOISHI CLAIMED TO HAVE SHOT THE RAT IN THIS IRRIGATION CANAL.
OF THOSE THREE RODENTS, ONLY THE BROWN RAT FAVORS WET ENVIRON-MENTS.

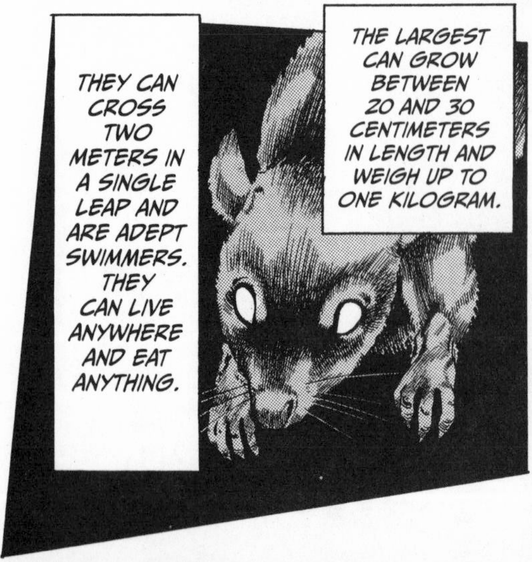
THE LARGEST CAN GROW BETWEEN 20 AND 30 CENTIMETERS IN LENGTH AND WEIGH UP TO ONE KILOGRAM.
THEY CAN CROSS TWO METERS IN A SINGLE LEAP AND ARE ADEPT SWIMMERS. THEY CAN LIVE ANYWHERE AND EAT ANYTHING.

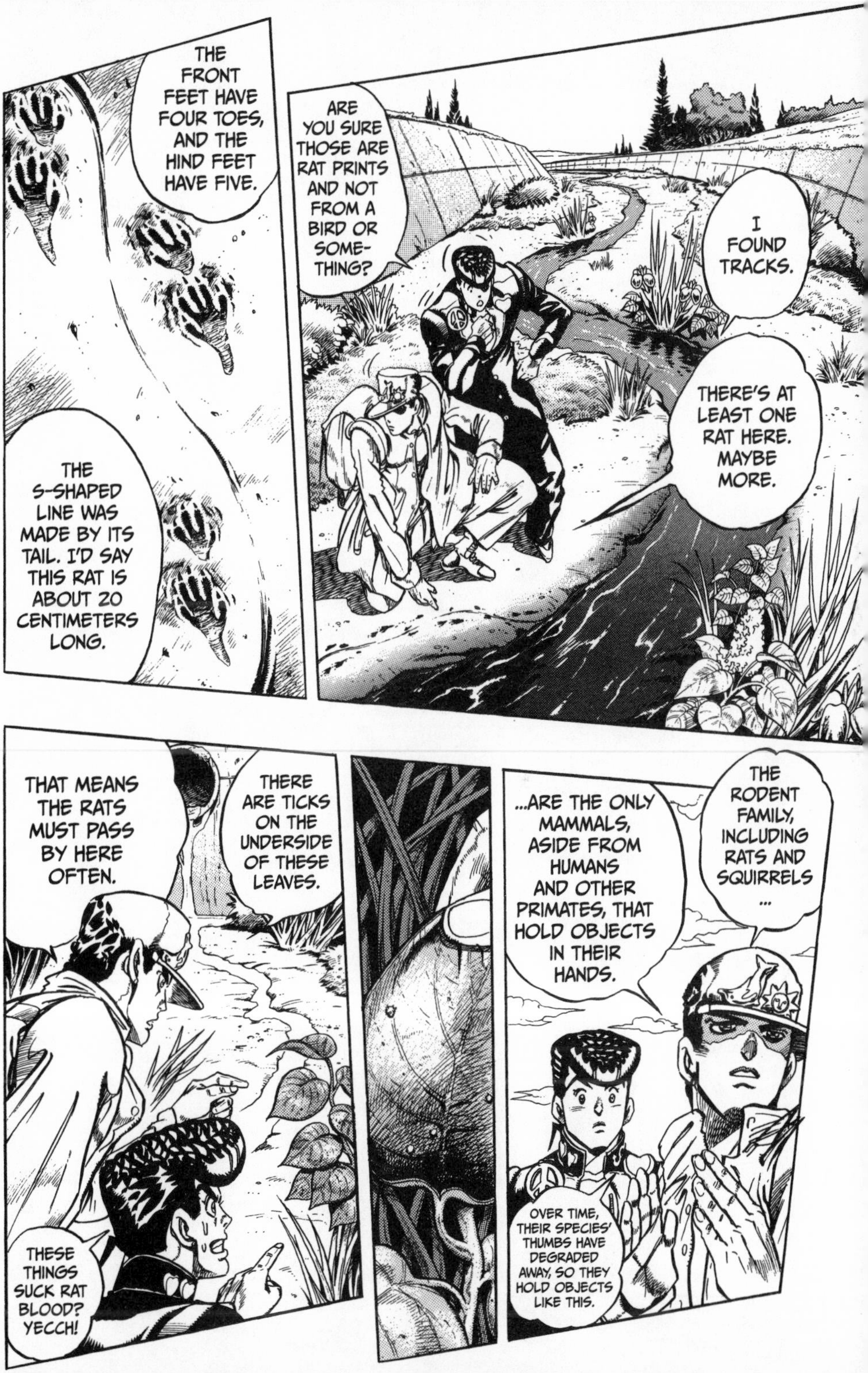
I FOUND TRACKS.
ARE YOU SURE THOSE ARE RAT PRINTS AND NOT FROM A BIRD OR SOME-THING?
THERE'S AT LEAST ONE RAT HERE. MAYBE MORE.
THE FRONT FEET HAVE FOUR TOES, AND THE HIND FEET HAVE FIVE.
THE S-SHAPED LINE WAS MADE BY ITS TAIL. I'D SAY THIS RAT IS ABOUT 20 CENTIMETERS LONG.
THE RODENT FAMILY, INCLUDING RATS AND SQUIRRELS ...
...ARE THE ONLY MAMMALS, ASIDE FROM HUMANS AND OTHER PRIMATES, THAT HOLD OBJECTS IN THEIR HANDS.
OVER TIME, THEIR SPECIES' THUMBS HAVE DEGRADED AWAY, SO THEY HOLD OBJECTS LIKE THIS.
THERE ARE TICKS ON THE UNDERSIDE OF THESE LEAVES.
THAT MEANS THE RATS MUST PASS BY HERE OFTEN.
THESE THINGS SUCK RAT BLOOD? YECCH!

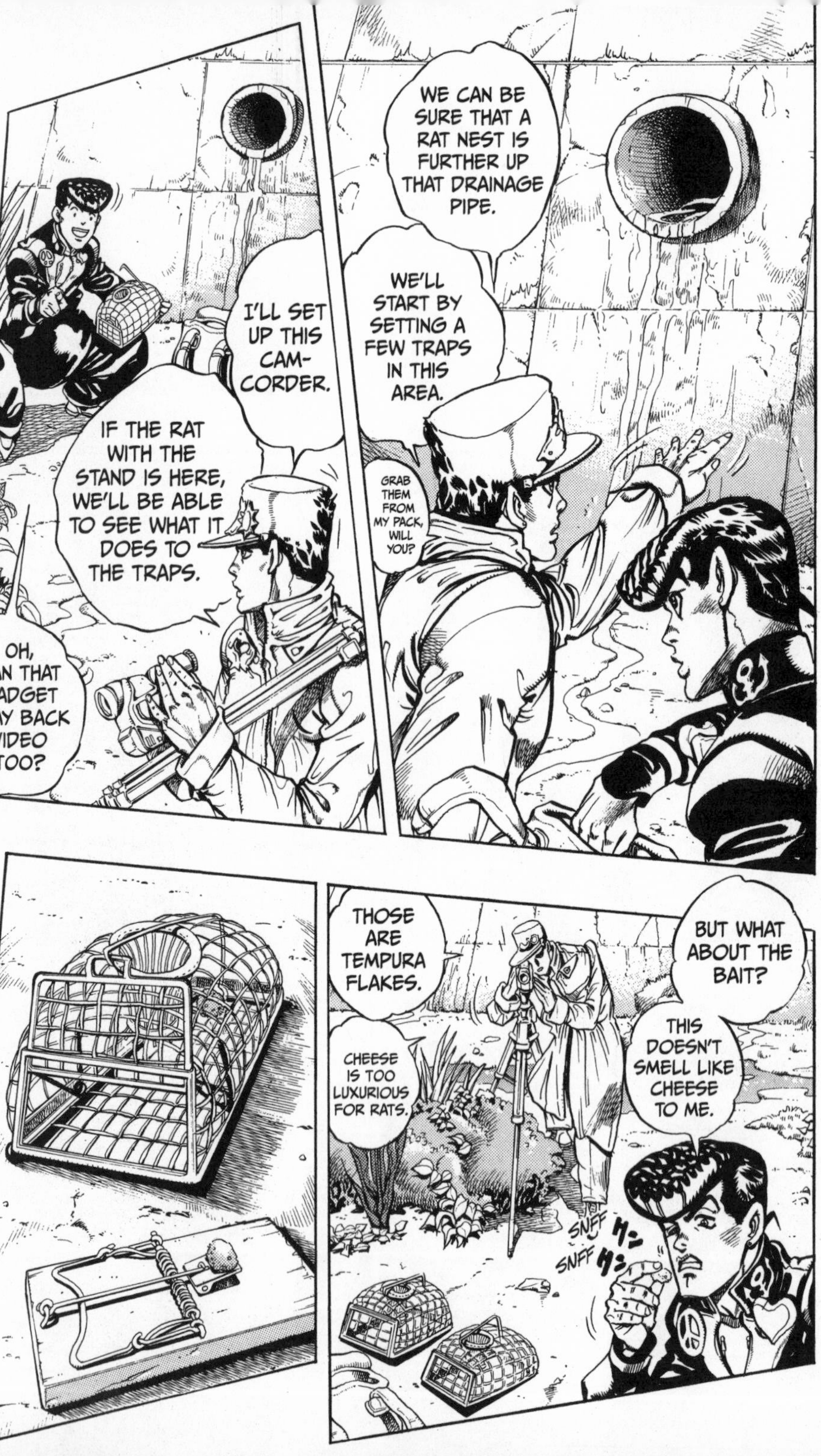
WE CAN BE SURE THAT A RAT NEST IS FURTHER UP THAT DRAINAGE PIPE.
WE'LL START BY SETTING A FEW TRAPS IN THIS AREA.
GRAB THEM FROM MY PACK, WILL YOU?
I'LL SET UP THIS CAM-CORDER.
IF THE RAT WITH THE STAND IS HERE, WE'LL BE ABLE TO SEE WHAT IT DOES TO THE TRAPS.
OH, CAN THAT GADGET PLAY BACK VIDEO TOO?
BUT WHAT ABOUT THE BAIT?
THIS DOESN'T SMELL LIKE CHEESE TO ME.
THOSE ARE TEMPURA FLAKES.
CHEESE IS TOO LUXURIOUS FOR RATS.
SNFF
SNFF

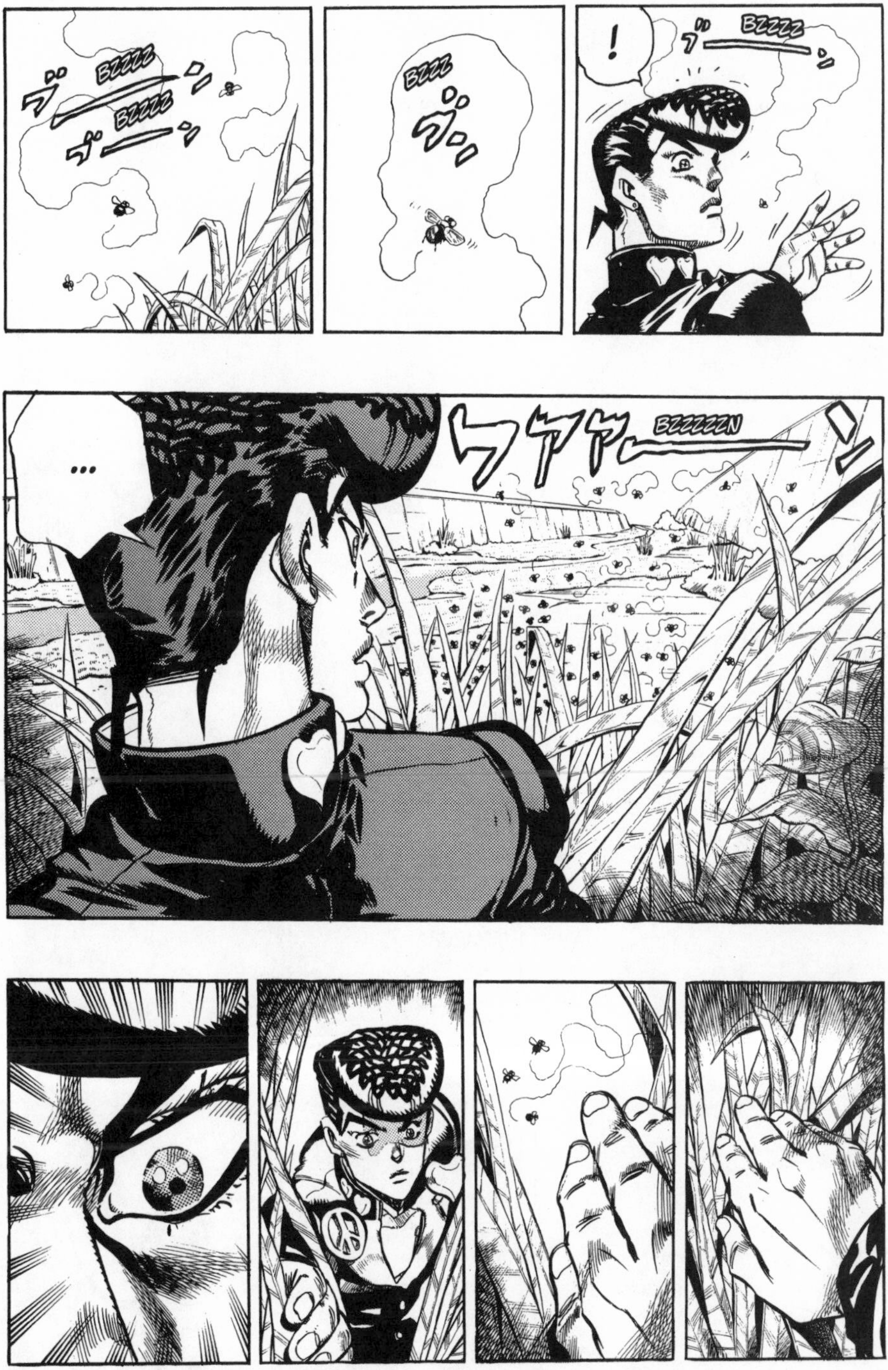
!
BZZZZ
BZZZ
BZZZZ
BZZZZ
BZZZZZN
...

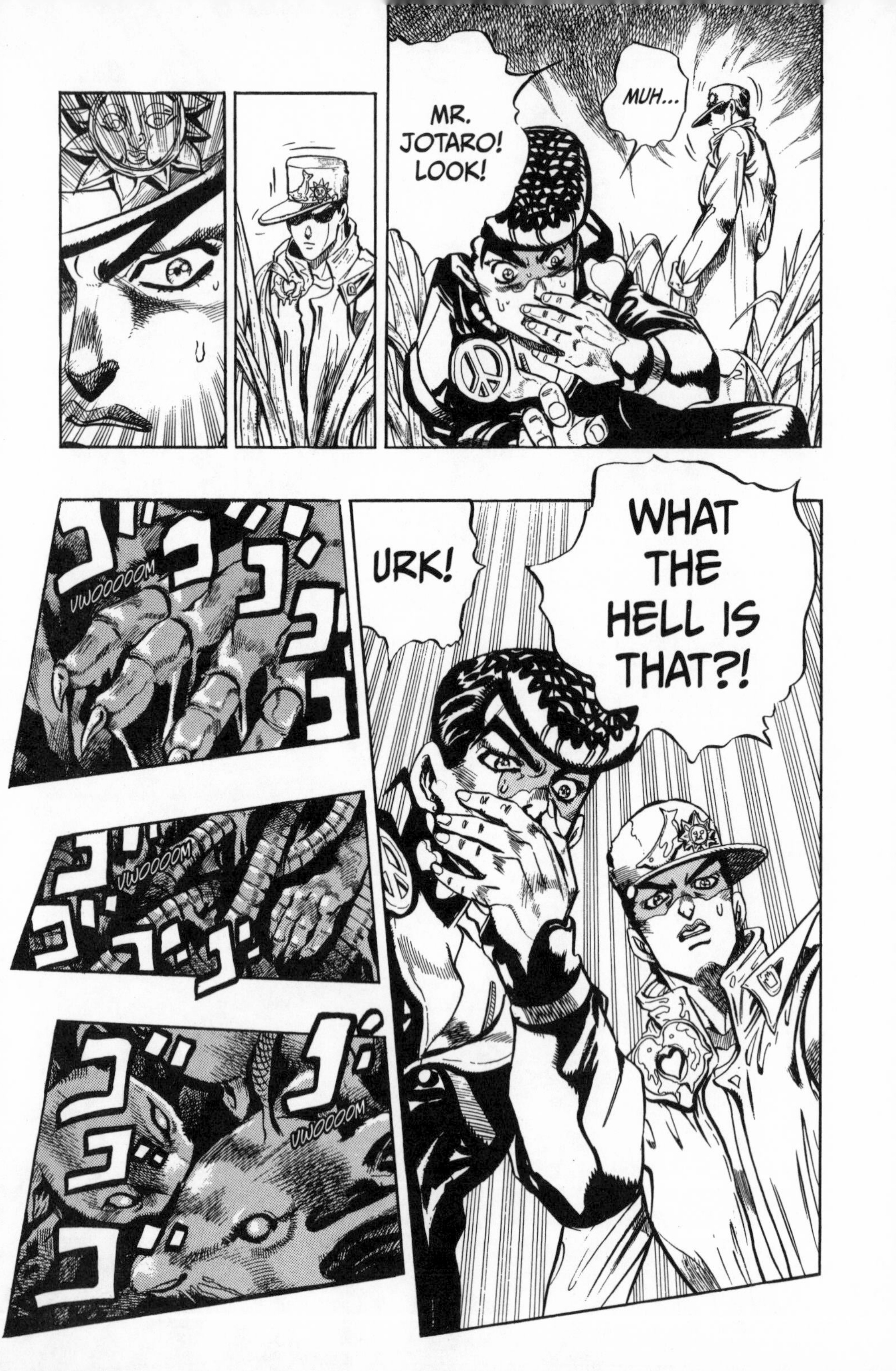
MUH...
MR. JOTARO! LOOK!
WHAT THE HELL IS THAT?!
URK!
VWOOOOOM
VWOOOOM
VWOOOOM

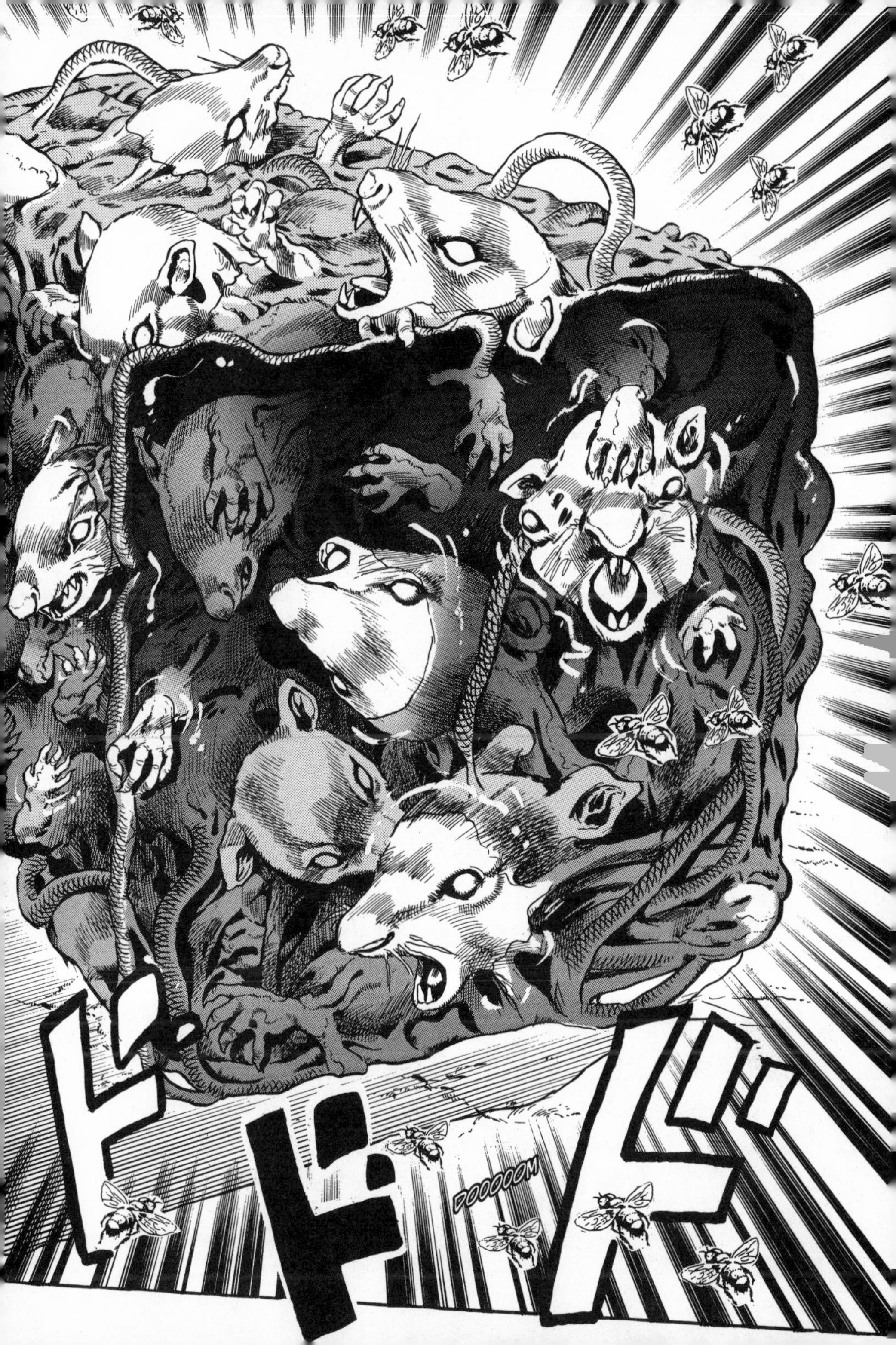
DOOOOOOM

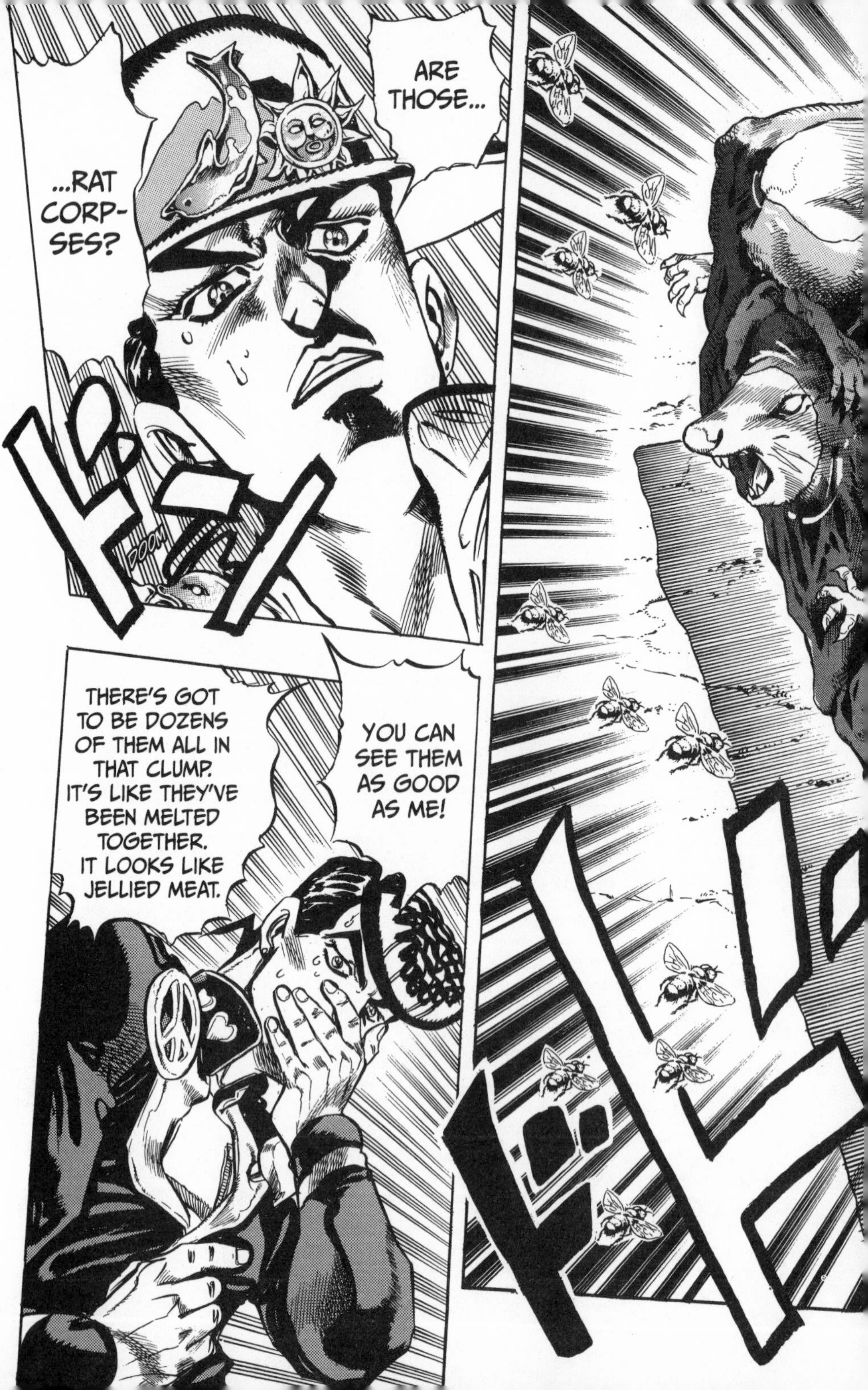
ARE THOSE...
...RAT CORPSES?
DOOM
YOU CAN SEE THEM AS GOOD AS ME!
THERE'S GOT TO BE DOZENS OF THEM ALL IN THAT CLUMP. IT'S LIKE THEY'VE BEEN MELTED TOGETHER. IT LOOKS LIKE JELLIED MEAT.

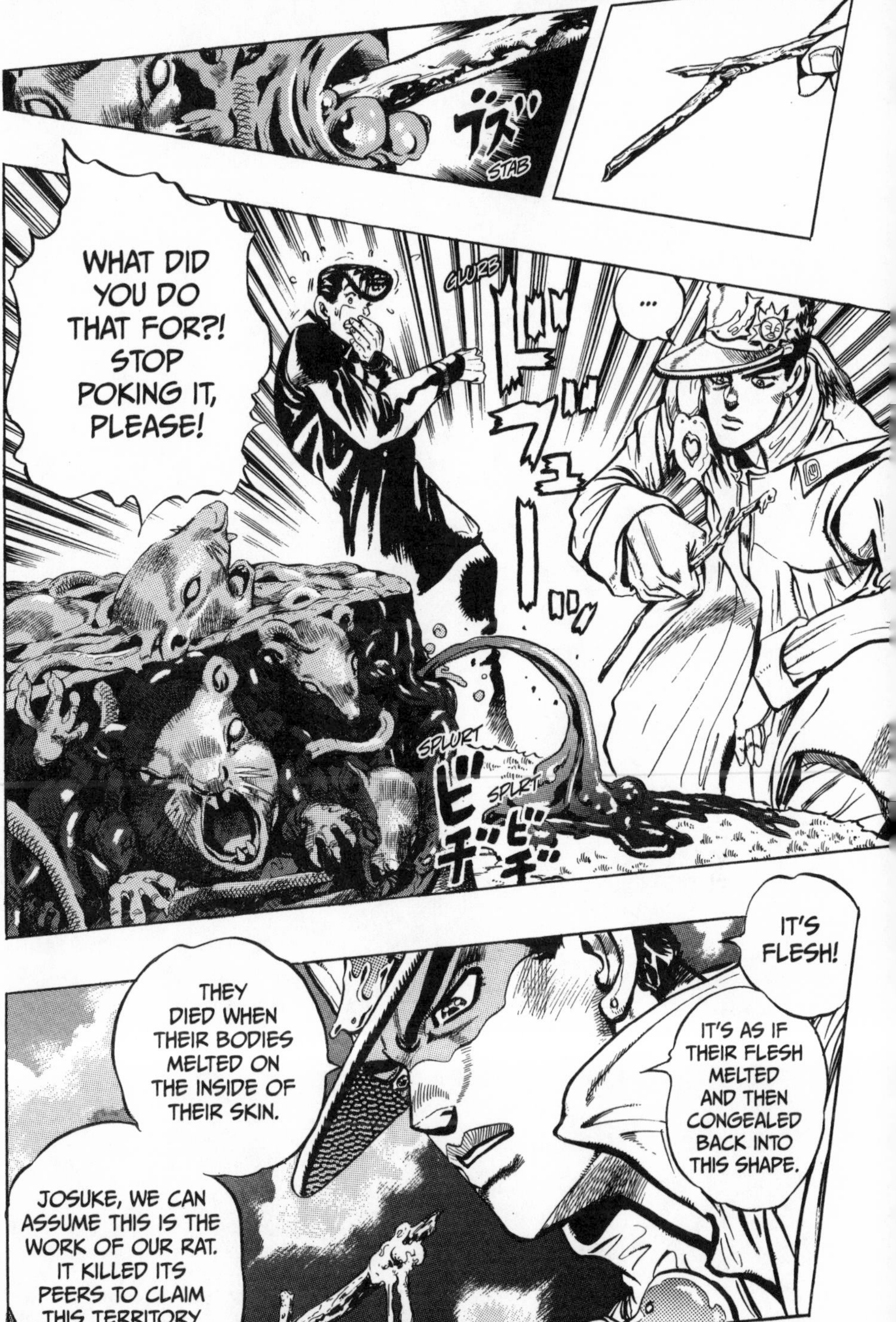
STAB
...
GLURB
WHAT DID YOU DO THAT FOR?! STOP POKING IT, PLEASE!
SPLURT
SPLRT
IT'S FLESH!
IT'S AS IF THEIR FLESH MELTED AND THEN CONGEALED BACK INTO THIS SHAPE.
THEY DIED WHEN THEIR BODIES MELTED ON THE INSIDE OF THEIR SKIN.
JOSUKE, WE CAN ASSUME THIS IS THE WORK OF OUR RAT. IT KILLED ITS PEERS TO CLAIM THIS TERRITORY FOR ITSELF.

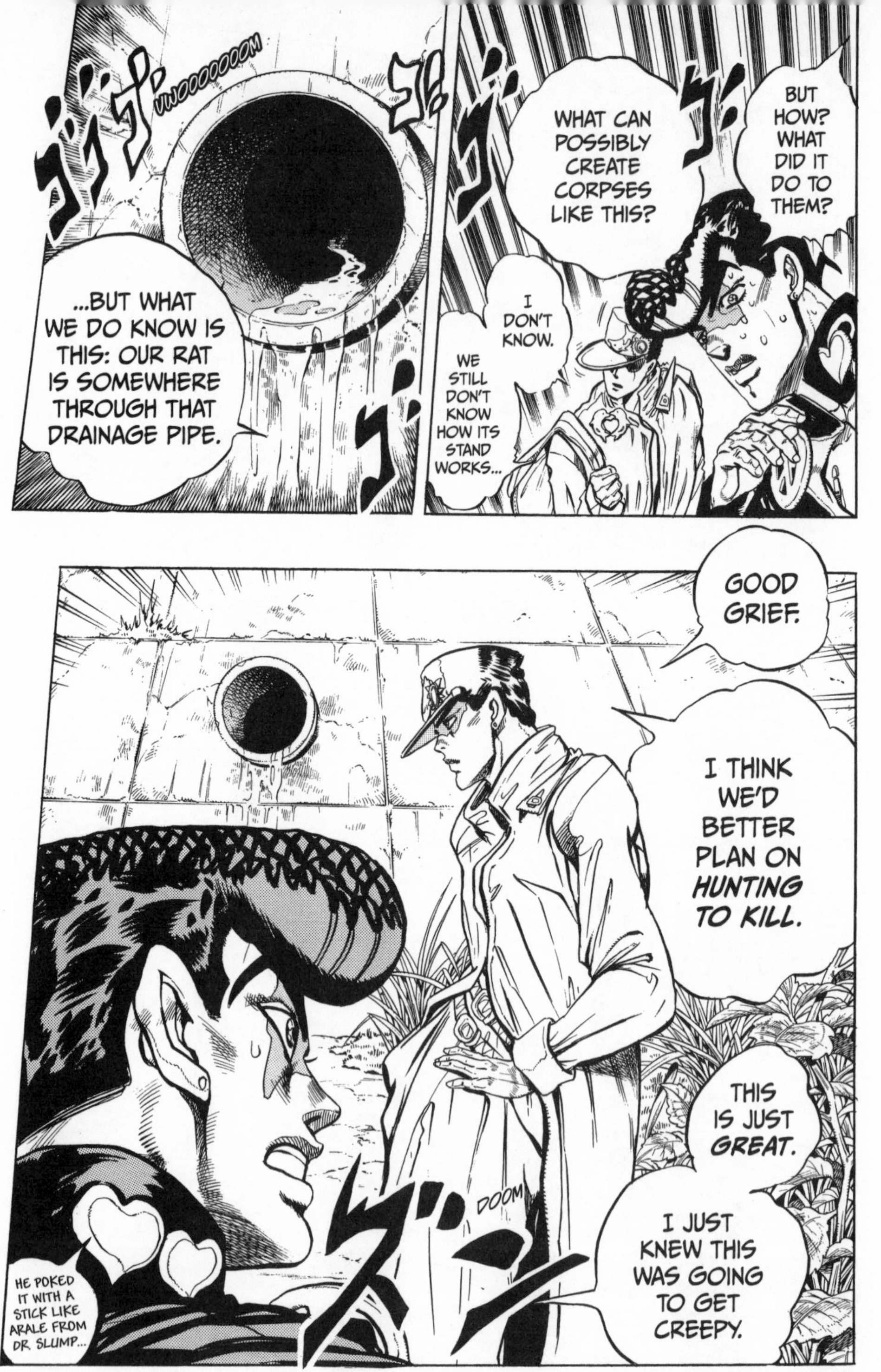
BUT HOW? WHAT DID IT DO TO THEM?
WHAT CAN POSSIBLY CREATE CORPSES LIKE THIS?
I DON'T KNOW.
WE STILL DON'T KNOW HOW ITS STAND WORKS...
VWOOOOOOOM
...BUT WHAT WE DO KNOW IS THIS: OUR RAT IS SOMEWHERE THROUGH THAT DRAINAGE PIPE.
GOOD GRIEF.
I THINK WE'D BETTER PLAN ON *HUNTING TO KILL*.
THIS IS JUST *GREAT*.
I JUST KNEW THIS WAS GOING TO GET CREEPY.
DOOM
HE POKED IT WITH A STICK LIKE ARALE FROM DR. SLUMP...

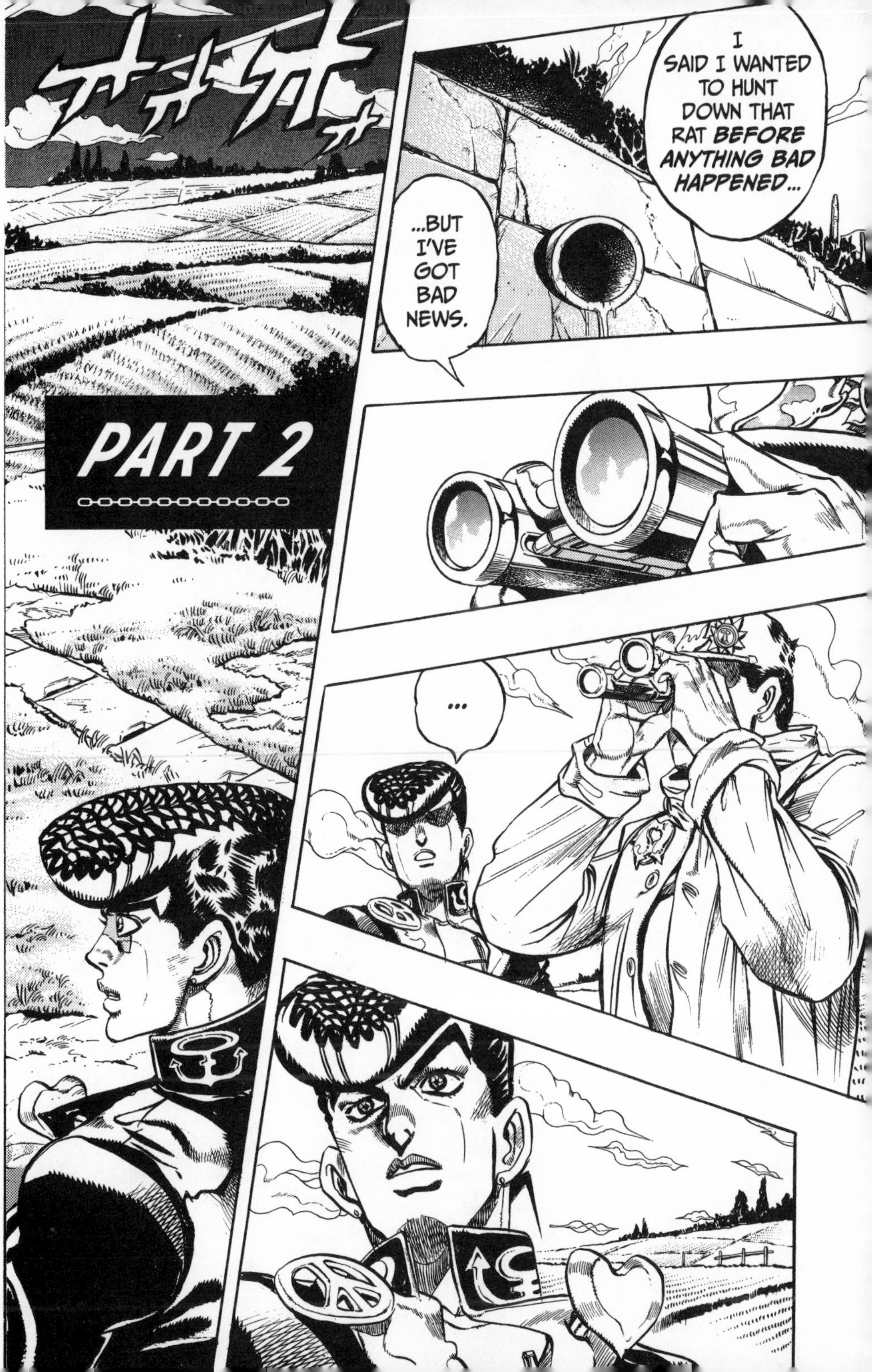
I SAID I WANTED TO HUNT DOWN THAT RAT BEFORE ANYTHING BAD HAPPENED...
...BUT I'VE GOT BAD NEWS.
...
PART 2

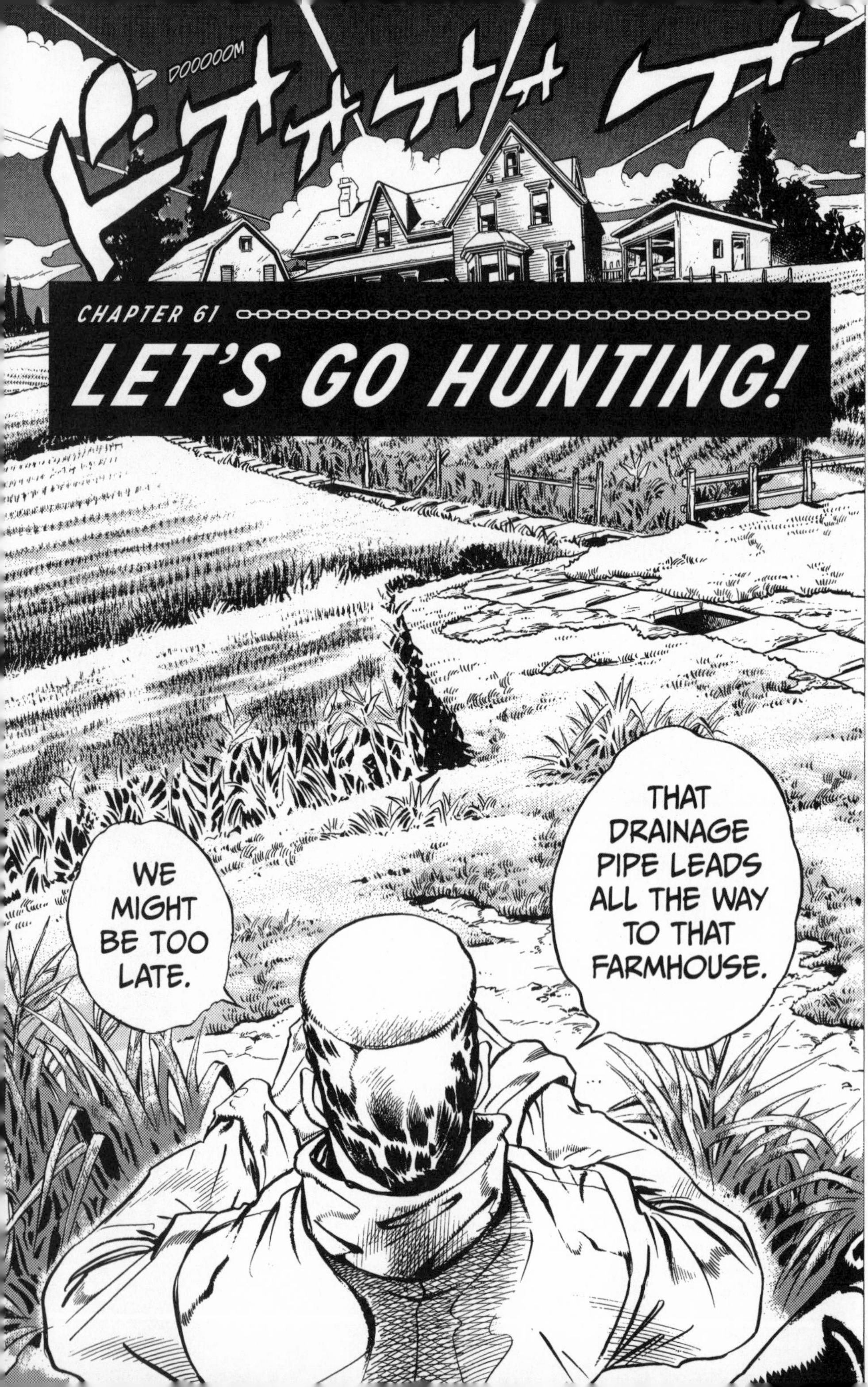
DOOOOOM
CHAPTER 61
LET'S GO HUNTING!
THAT DRAINAGE PIPE LEADS ALL THE WAY TO THAT FARMHOUSE.
...
WE MIGHT BE TOO LATE.

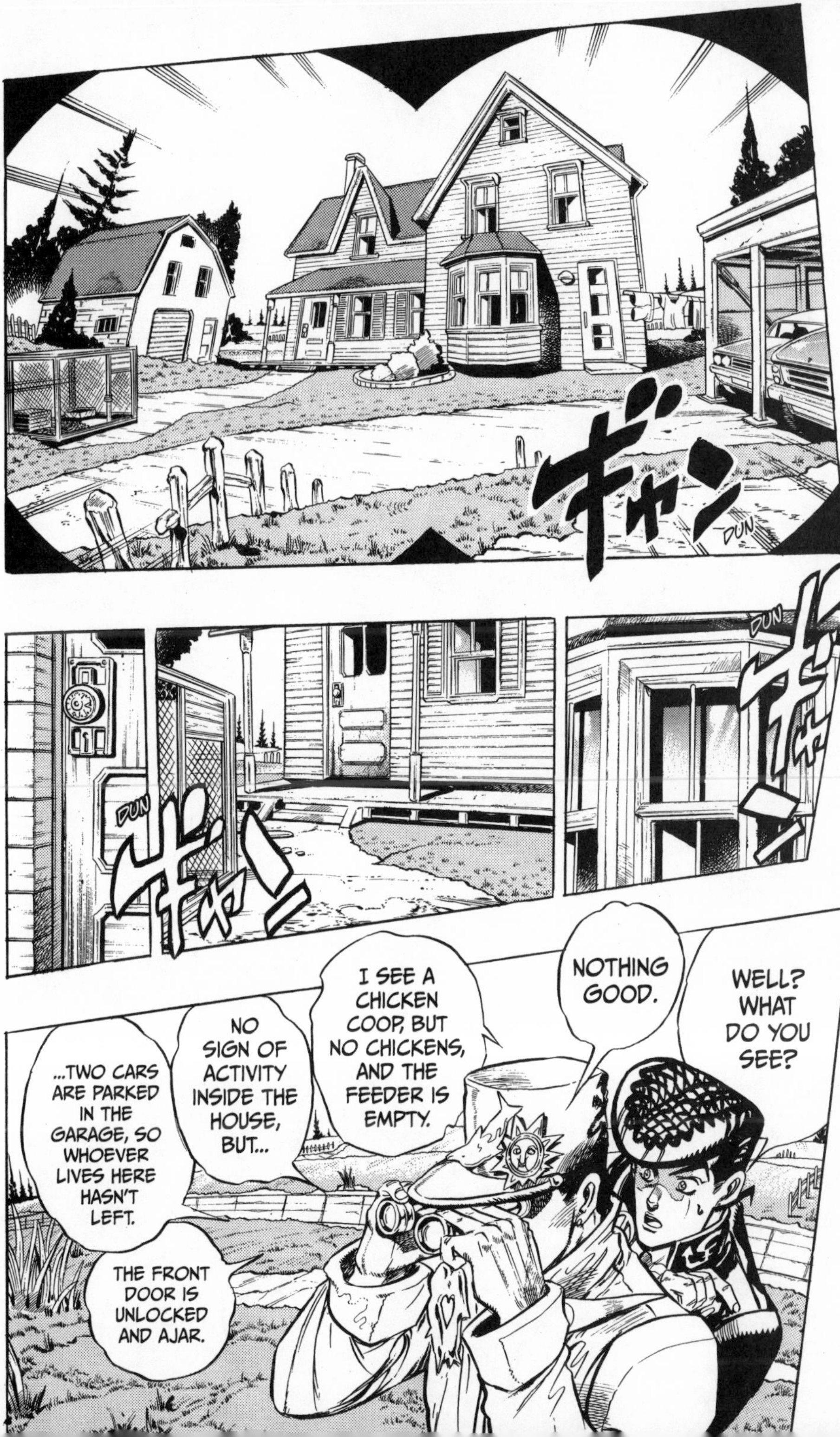
DUN
DUN
DUN
WELL? WHAT DO YOU SEE?
NOTHING GOOD.
I SEE A CHICKEN COOP, BUT NO CHICKENS, AND THE FEEDER IS EMPTY.
NO SIGN OF ACTIVITY INSIDE THE HOUSE, BUT...
...TWO CARS ARE PARKED IN THE GARAGE, SO WHOEVER LIVES HERE HASN'T LEFT.
THE FRONT DOOR IS UNLOCKED AND AJAR.

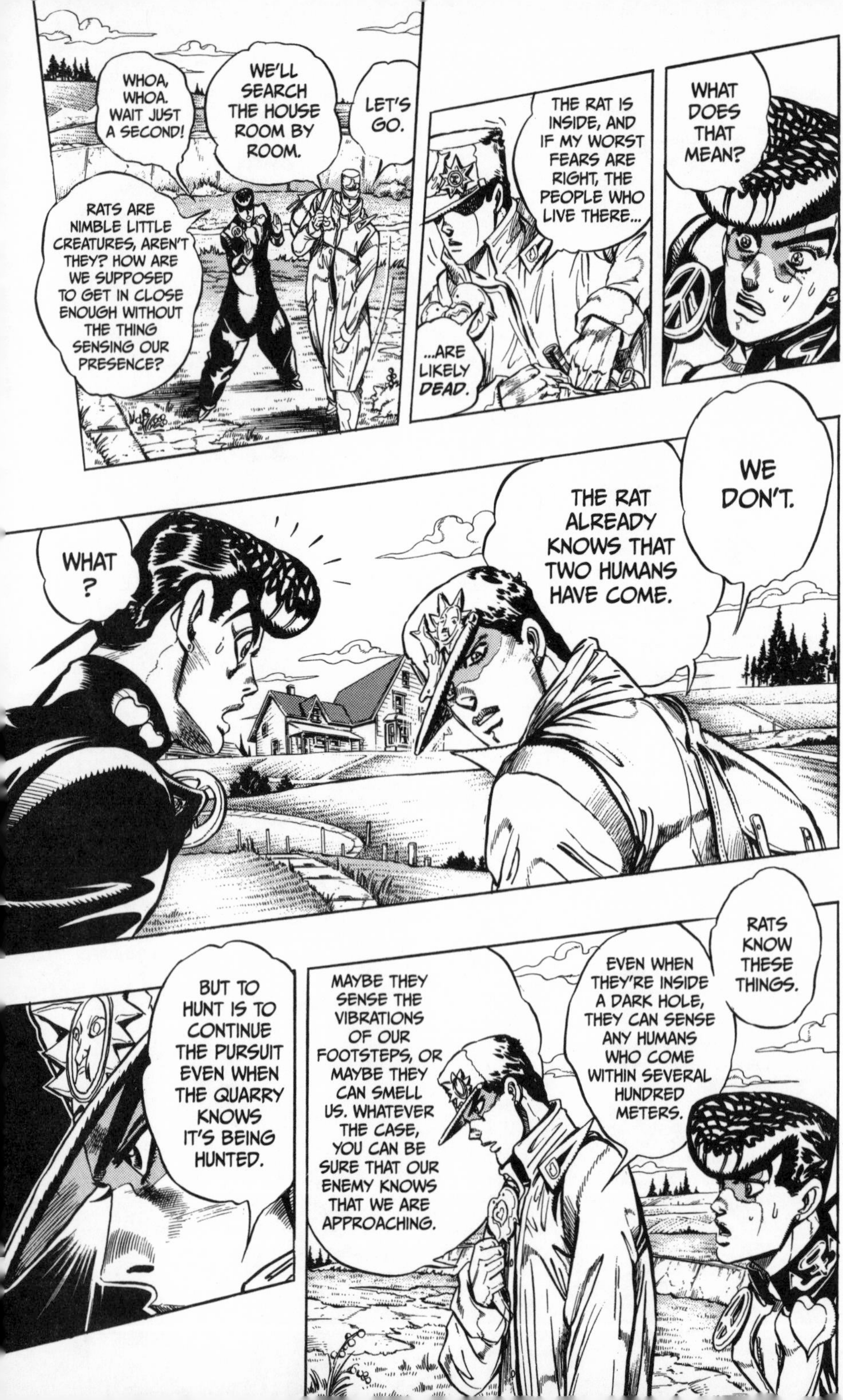
WHAT DOES THAT MEAN?
THE RAT IS INSIDE, AND IF MY WORST FEARS ARE RIGHT, THE PEOPLE WHO LIVE THERE...
...ARE LIKELY *DEAD*.
LET'S GO.
WE'LL SEARCH THE HOUSE ROOM BY ROOM.
WHOA, WHOA. WAIT JUST A SECOND!
RATS ARE NIMBLE LITTLE CREATURES, AREN'T THEY? HOW ARE WE SUPPOSED TO GET IN CLOSE ENOUGH WITHOUT THE THING SENSING OUR PRESENCE?
WE DON'T.
THE RAT ALREADY KNOWS THAT TWO HUMANS HAVE COME.
WHAT?
RATS KNOW THESE THINGS.
EVEN WHEN THEY'RE INSIDE A DARK HOLE, THEY CAN SENSE ANY HUMANS WHO COME WITHIN SEVERAL HUNDRED METERS.
MAYBE THEY SENSE THE VIBRATIONS OF OUR FOOTSTEPS, OR MAYBE THEY CAN SMELL US. WHATEVER THE CASE, YOU CAN BE SURE THAT OUR ENEMY KNOWS THAT WE ARE APPROACHING.
BUT TO HUNT IS TO CONTINUE THE PURSUIT EVEN WHEN THE QUARRY KNOWS IT'S BEING HUNTED.

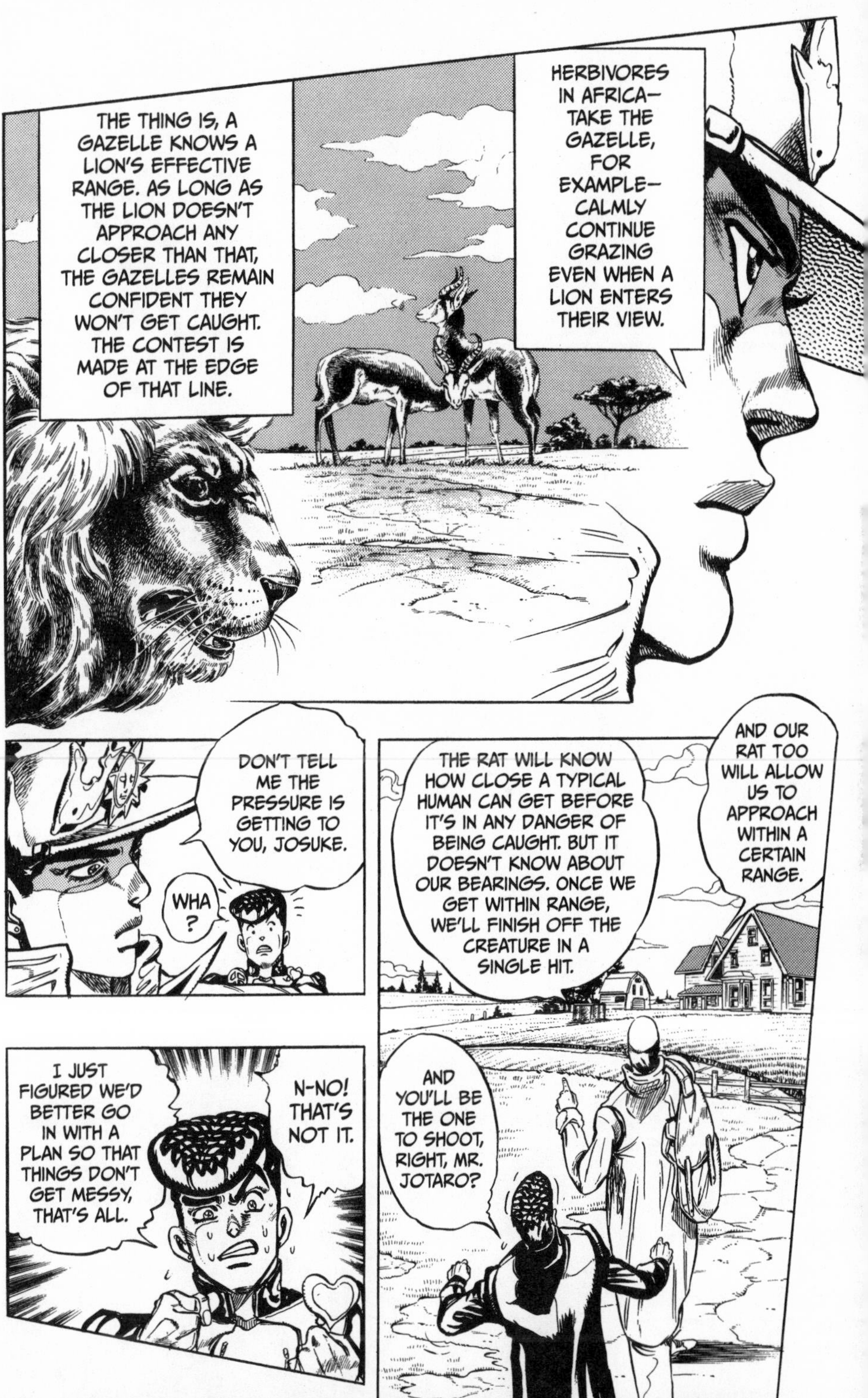
HERBIVORES IN AFRICA—TAKE THE GAZELLE, FOR EXAMPLE—CALMLY CONTINUE GRAZING EVEN WHEN A LION ENTERS THEIR VIEW.
THE THING IS, A GAZELLE KNOWS A LION'S EFFECTIVE RANGE. AS LONG AS THE LION DOESN'T APPROACH ANY CLOSER THAN THAT, THE GAZELLES REMAIN CONFIDENT THEY WON'T GET CAUGHT. THE CONTEST IS MADE AT THE EDGE OF THAT LINE.
AND OUR RAT TOO WILL ALLOW US TO APPROACH WITHIN A CERTAIN RANGE.
THE RAT WILL KNOW HOW CLOSE A TYPICAL HUMAN CAN GET BEFORE IT'S IN ANY DANGER OF BEING CAUGHT. BUT IT DOESN'T KNOW ABOUT OUR BEARINGS. ONCE WE GET WITHIN RANGE, WE'LL FINISH OFF THE CREATURE IN A SINGLE HIT.
AND YOU'LL BE THE ONE TO SHOOT, RIGHT, MR. JOTARO?
DON'T TELL ME THE PRESSURE IS GETTING TO YOU, JOSUKE.
WHA?
N-NO! THAT'S NOT IT.
I JUST FIGURED WE'D BETTER GO IN WITH A PLAN SO THAT THINGS DON'T GET MESSY, THAT'S ALL.

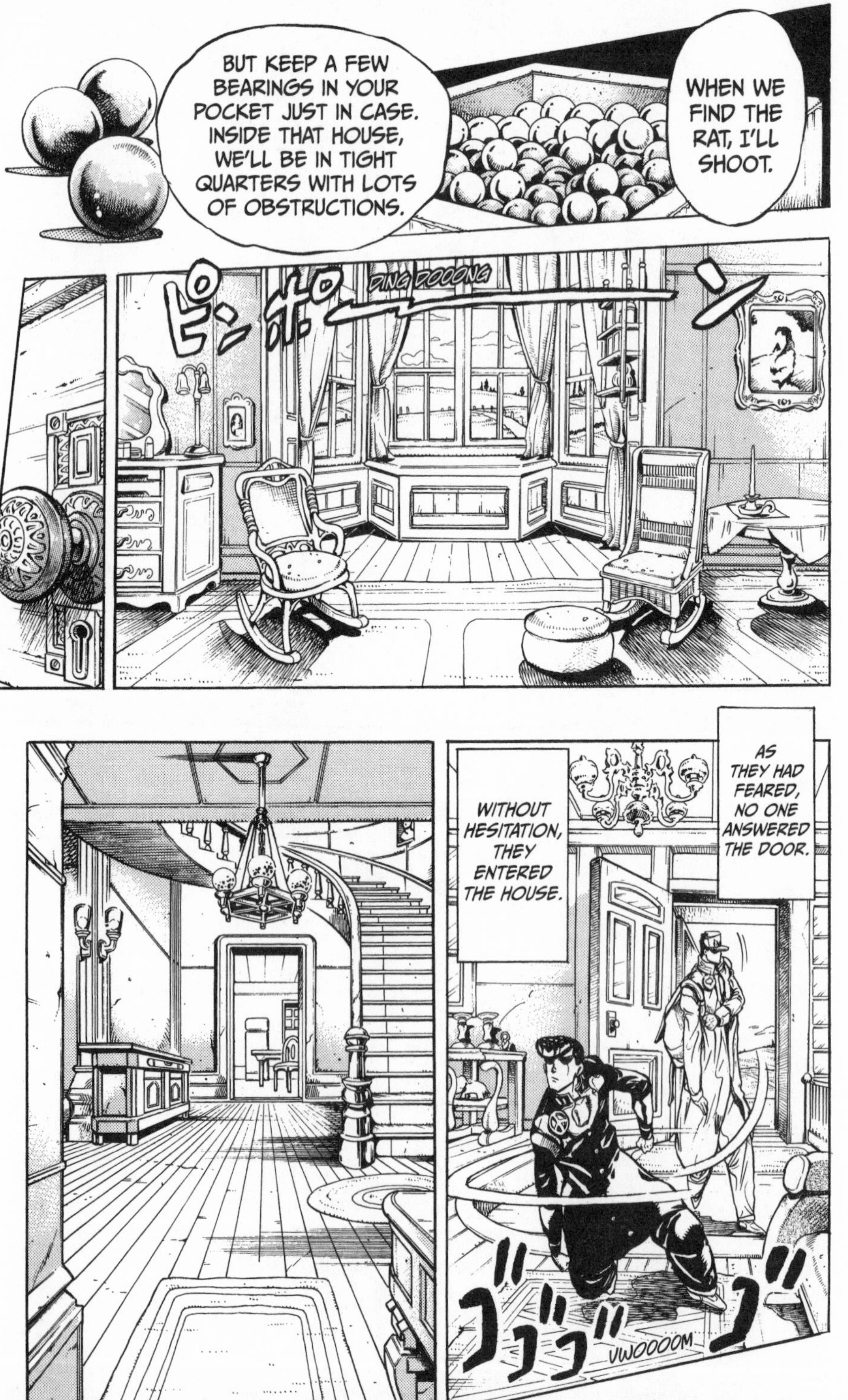
WHEN WE FIND THE RAT, I'LL SHOOT.
BUT KEEP A FEW BEARINGS IN YOUR POCKET JUST IN CASE. INSIDE THAT HOUSE, WE'LL BE IN TIGHT QUARTERS WITH LOTS OF OBSTRUCTIONS.
ピンポーン
DING DOOONG
AS THEY HAD FEARED, NO ONE ANSWERED THE DOOR.
WITHOUT HESITATION, THEY ENTERED THE HOUSE.
ゴゴゴゴ
VWOOOOM

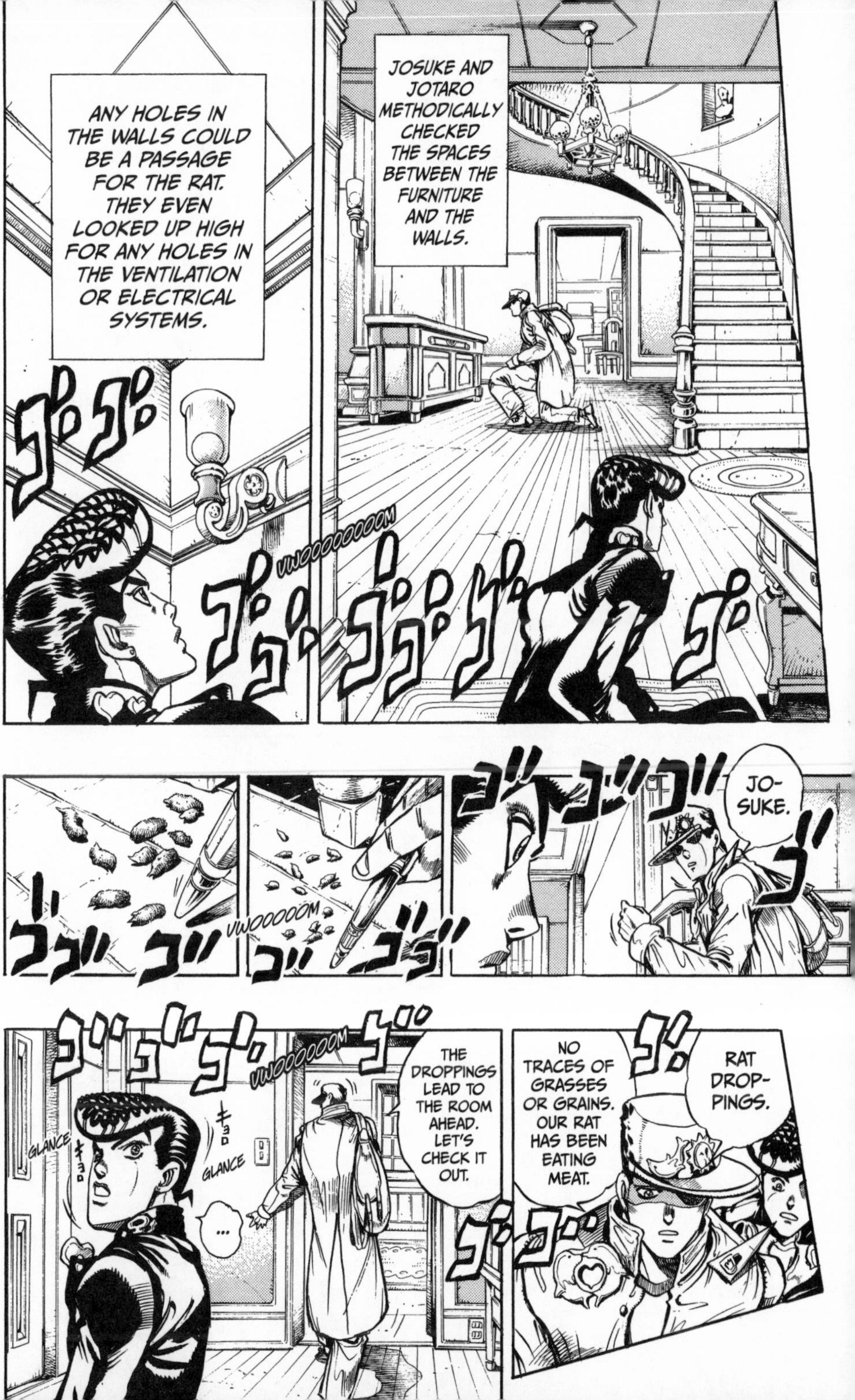
JOSUKE AND JOTARO METHODICALLY CHECKED THE SPACES BETWEEN THE FURNITURE AND THE WALLS.
ANY HOLES IN THE WALLS COULD BE A PASSAGE FOR THE RAT. THEY EVEN LOOKED UP HIGH FOR ANY HOLES IN THE VENTILATION OR ELECTRICAL SYSTEMS.
VWOOOOOOOOOM
JO-SUKE.
VWOOOOOM
RAT DROPPINGS.
NO TRACES OF GRASSES OR GRAINS. OUR RAT HAS BEEN EATING MEAT.
THE DROPPINGS LEAD TO THE ROOM AHEAD. LET'S CHECK IT OUT.
VWOOOOOOOM
GLANCE
GLANCE
...

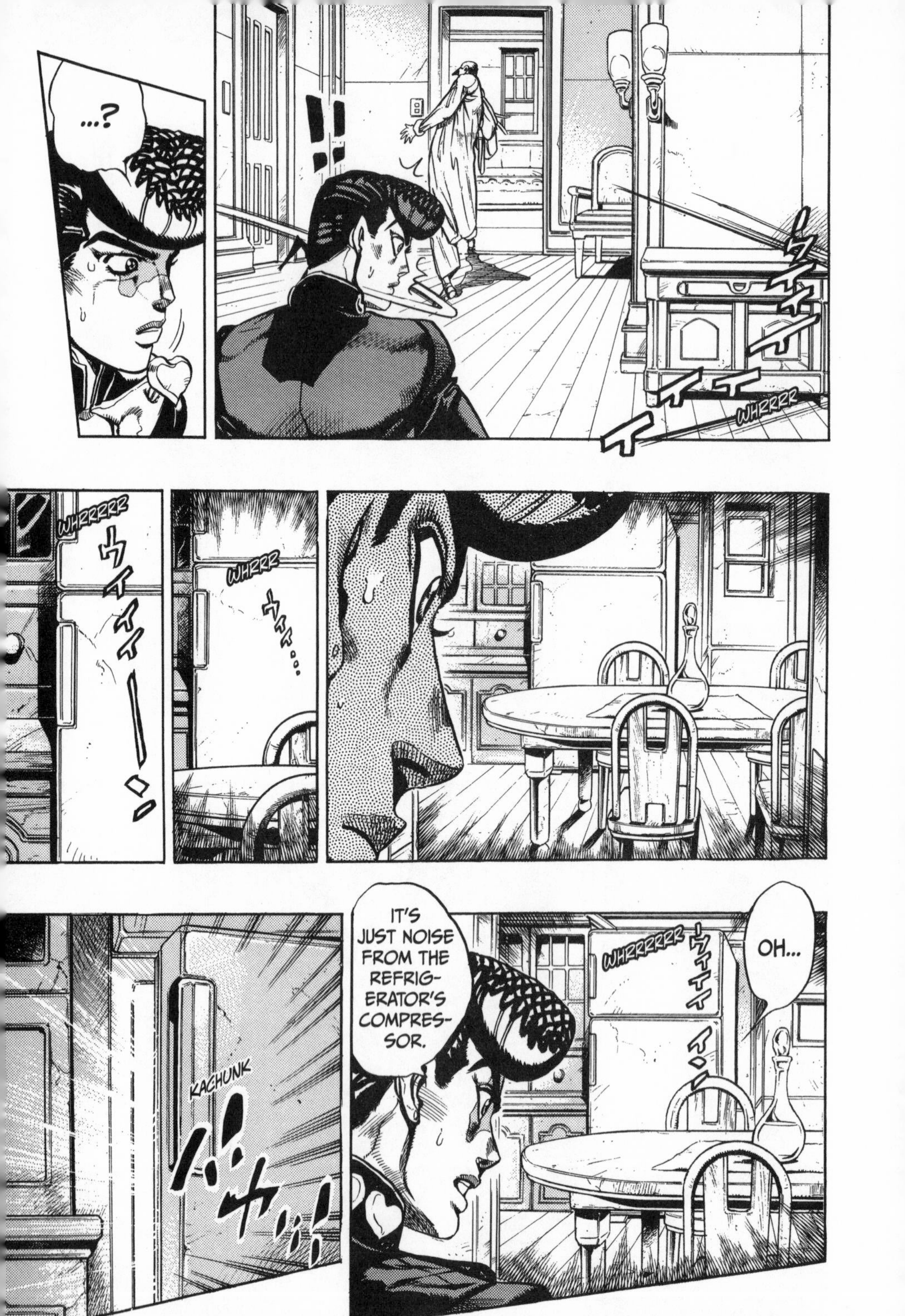
WHRRRR
...?
WHRRR
WHRRRRR
OH...
IT'S JUST NOISE FROM THE REFRIGERATOR'S COMPRESSOR.
WHRRRRRR
KACHUNK

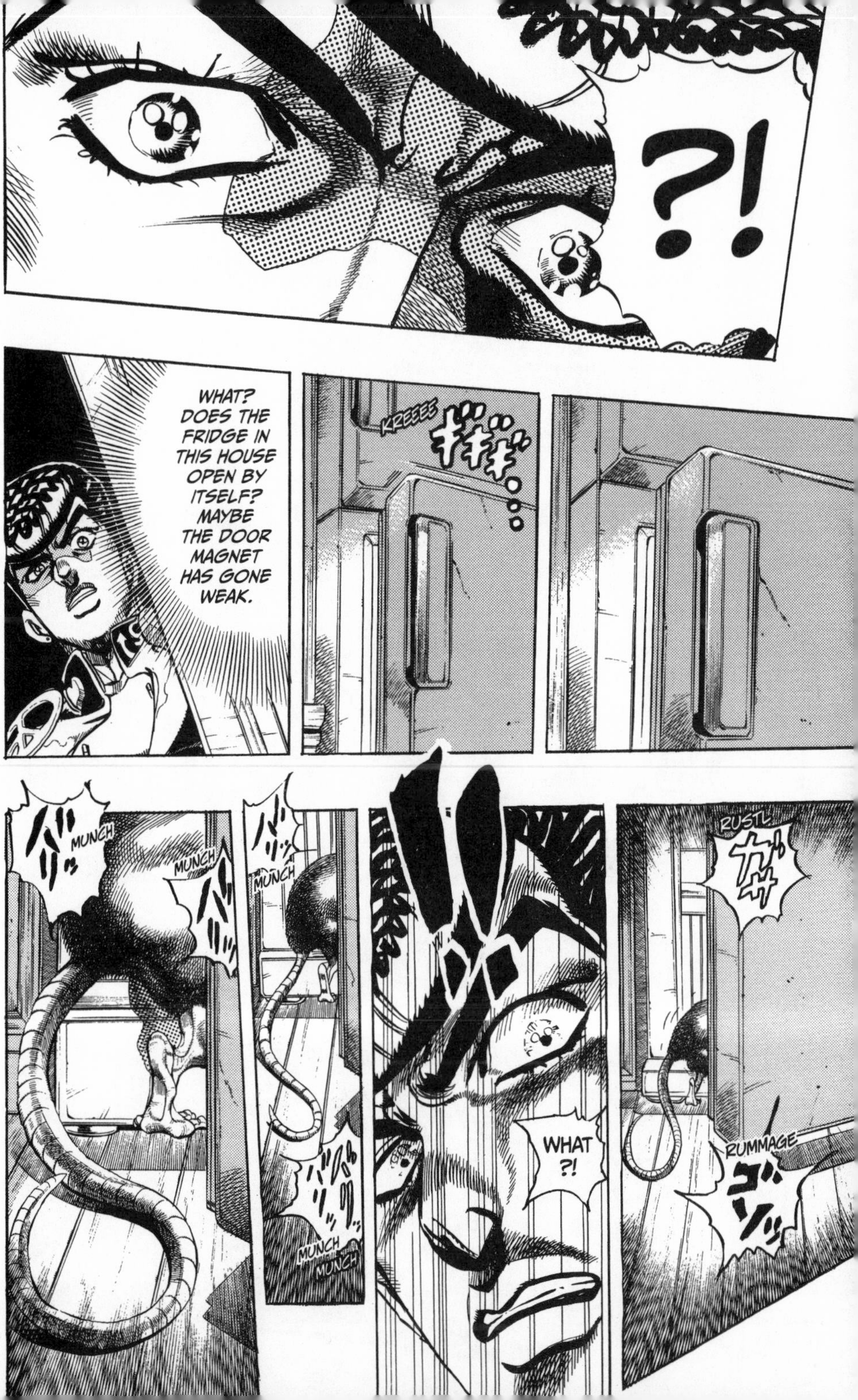

?!
KREEEE
ギギギ
WHAT? DOES THE FRIDGE IN THIS HOUSE OPEN BY ITSELF? MAYBE THE DOOR MAGNET HAS GONE WEAK.
RUSTL
カサ
RUMMAGE
ゴソッ
WHAT ?!
MUNCH
MUNCH MUNCH
MUNCH
MUNCH

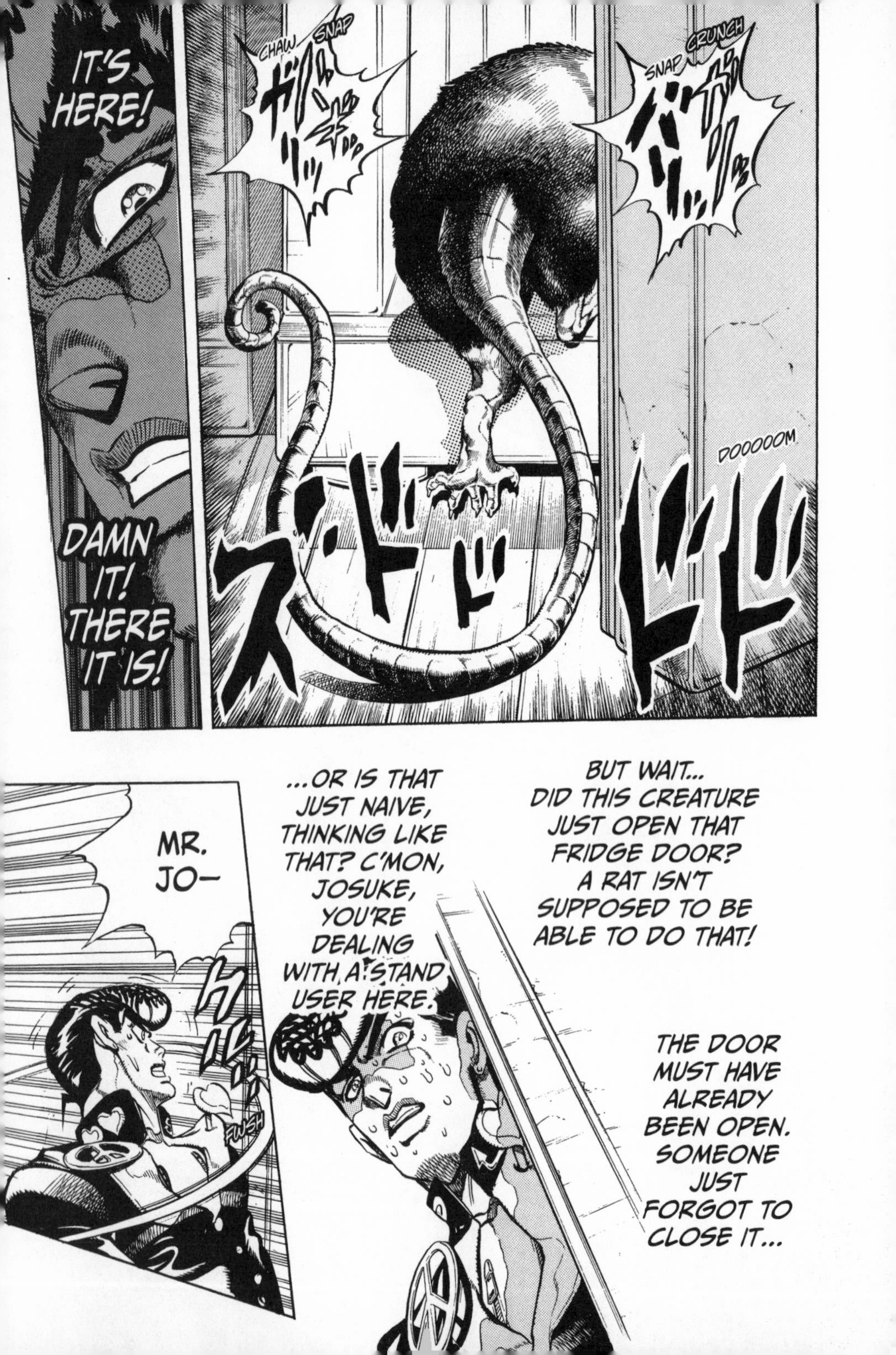
SNAP CRUNCH
CHAW SNAP
DOOOOOM
IT'S HERE!
DAMN IT! THERE IT IS!
BUT WAIT... DID THIS CREATURE JUST OPEN THAT FRIDGE DOOR? A RAT ISN'T SUPPOSED TO BE ABLE TO DO THAT!
THE DOOR MUST HAVE ALREADY BEEN OPEN. SOMEONE JUST FORGOT TO CLOSE IT...
...OR IS THAT JUST NAIVE, THINKING LIKE THAT? C'MON, JOSUKE, YOU'RE DEALING WITH A STAND USER HERE.
MR. JO—
FWSH

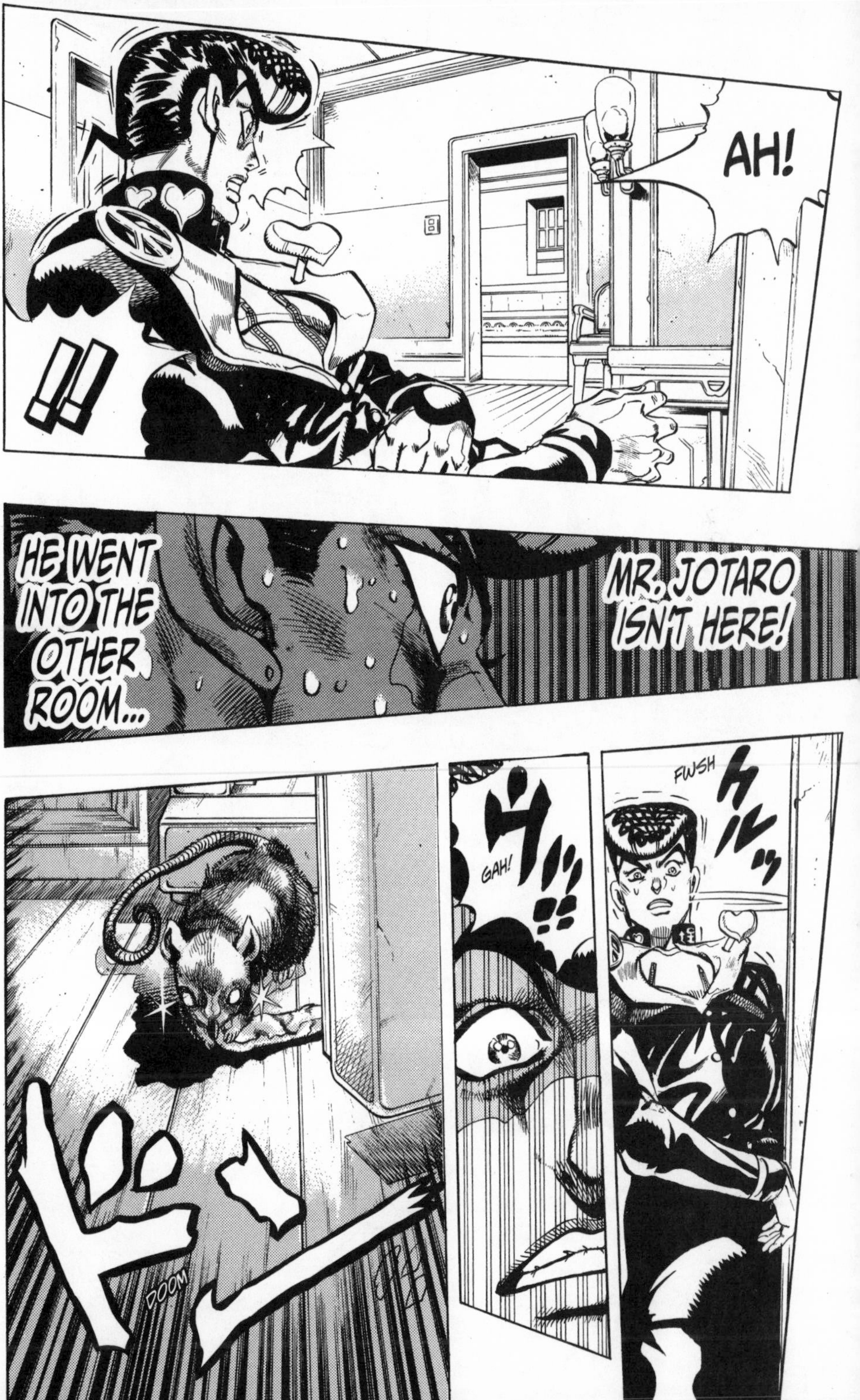
AH!
MR. JOTARO ISN'T HERE!
HE WENT INTO THE OTHER ROOM...
FWSH
GAH!
DOOM

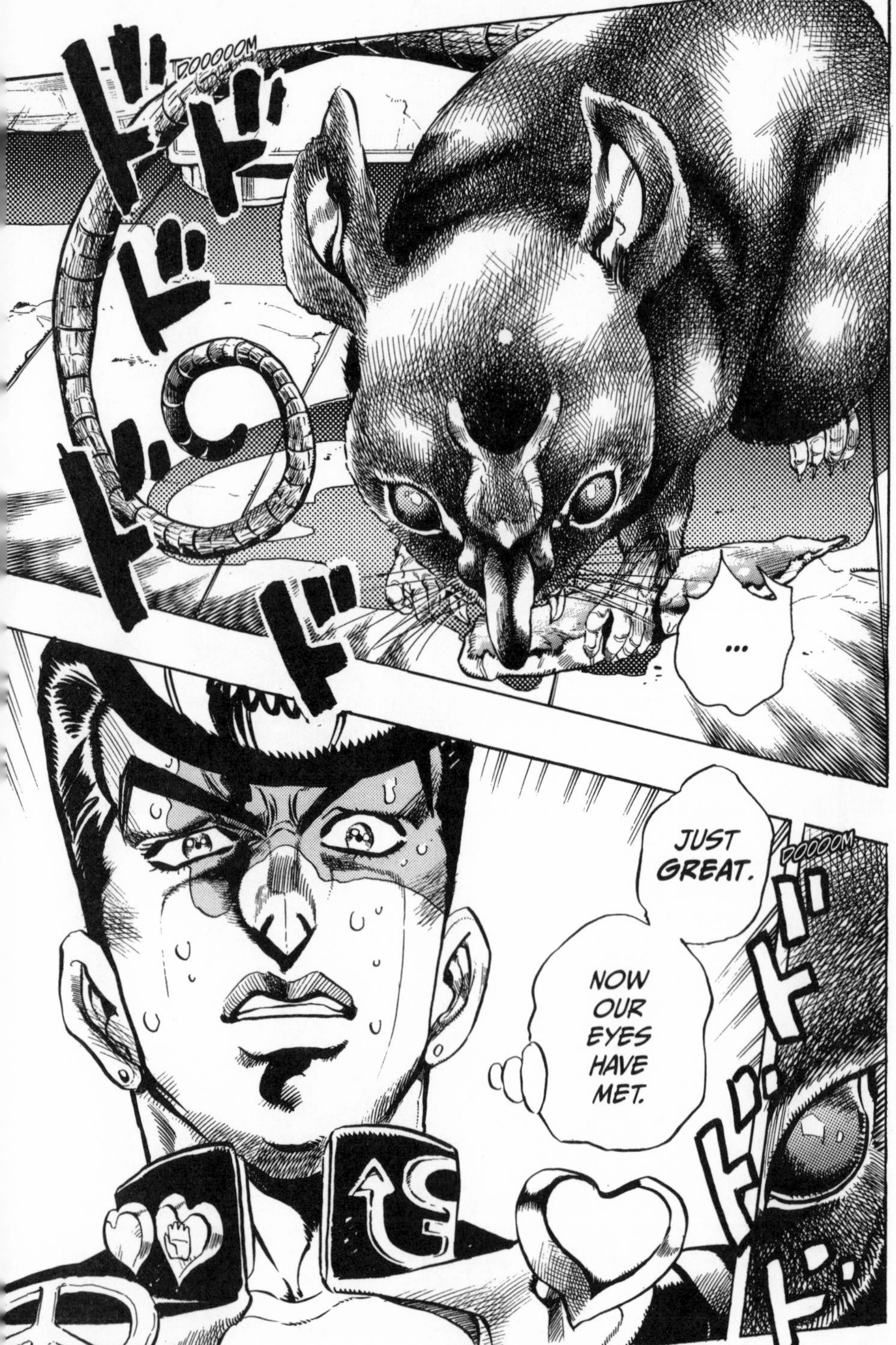
DOOOOOM
...
DOOOOM
JUST GREAT.
NOW OUR EYES HAVE MET.

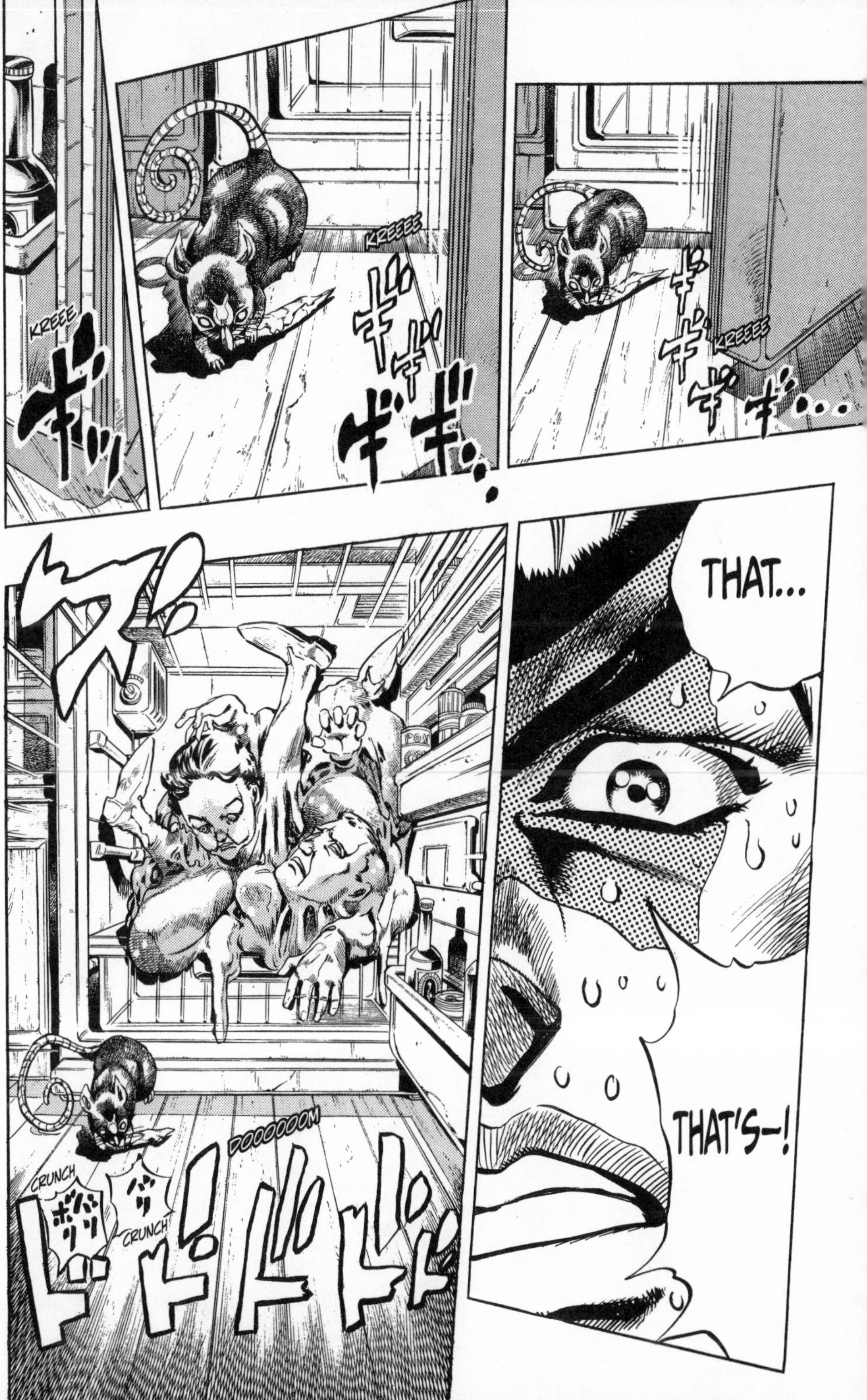

KREEEE
ギギギギ…
KREEEE
ギギギギ…
KREEE
ギッ
THAT...
THAT'S—!
DOOOOOOM
CRUNCH
CRUNCH
ドドドドド

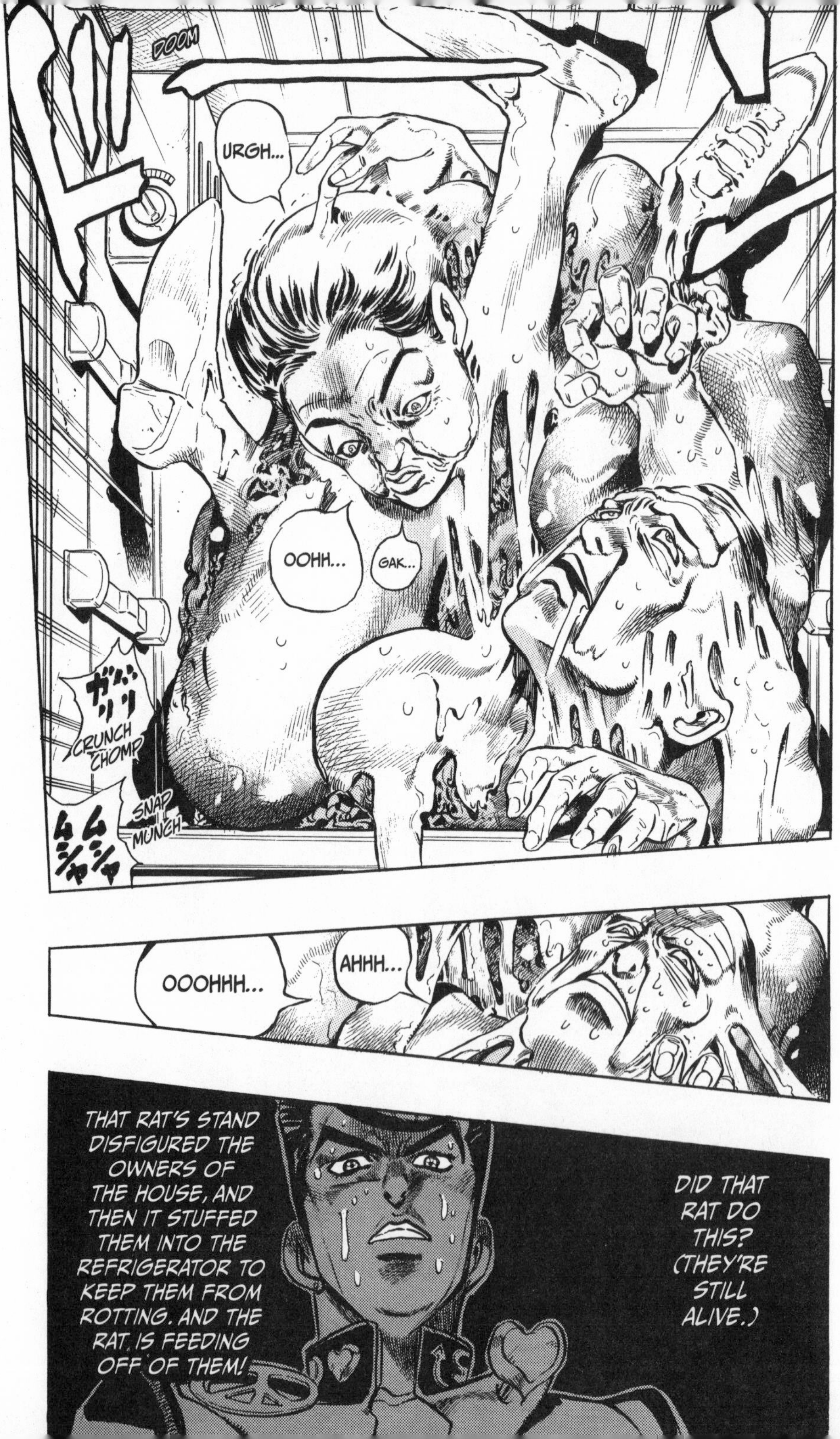
DOOM
URGH...
GAK...
OOHH...
CRUNCH CHOMP
SNAP MUNCH
ムシャムシャ
AHHH...
OOOHHH...
DID THAT RAT DO THIS? (THEY'RE STILL ALIVE.)
THAT RAT'S STAND DISFIGURED THE OWNERS OF THE HOUSE, AND THEN IT STUFFED THEM INTO THE REFRIGERATOR TO KEEP THEM FROM ROTTING. AND THE RAT IS FEEDING OFF OF THEM!

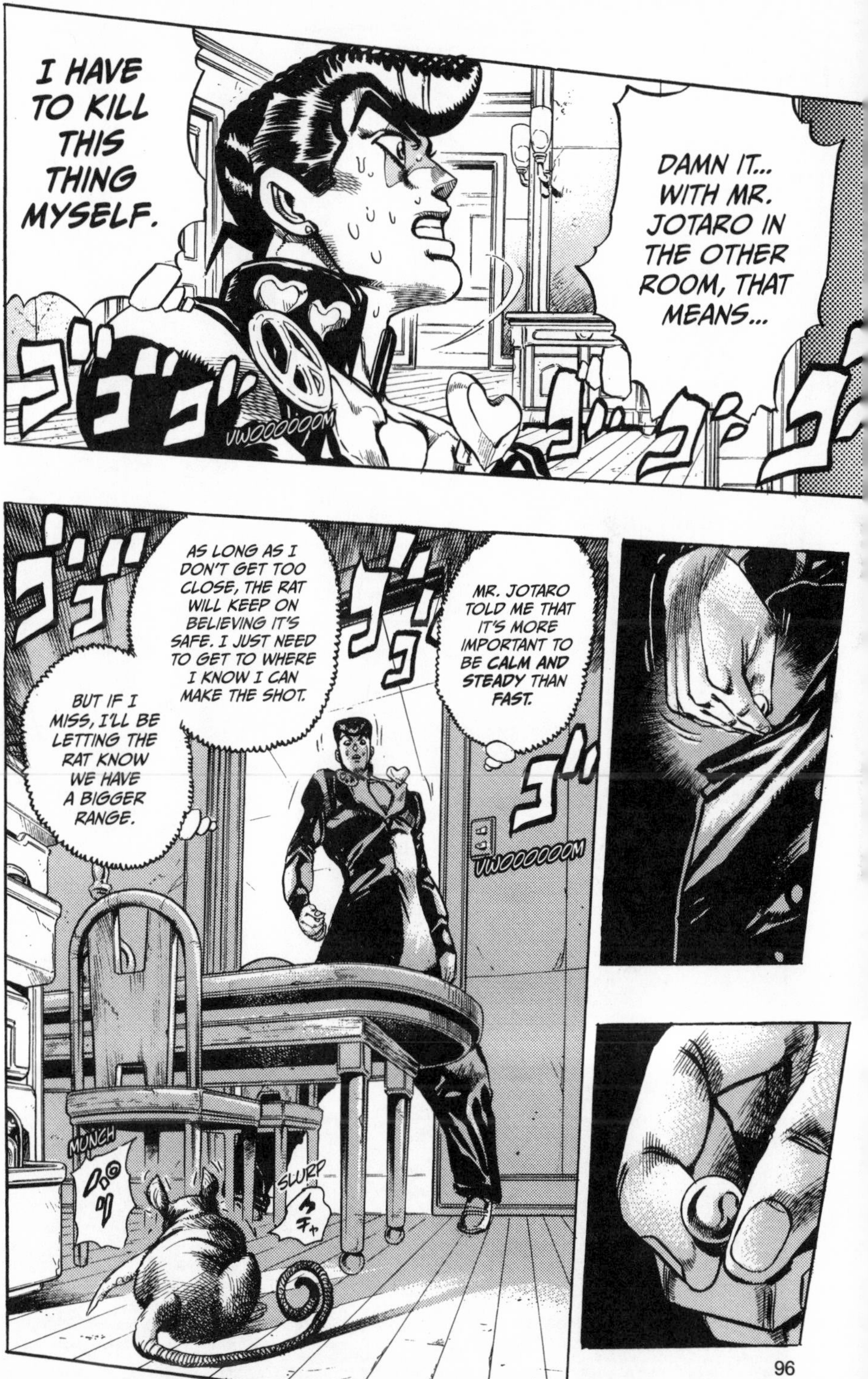
DAMN IT... WITH MR. JOTARO IN THE OTHER ROOM, THAT MEANS...
I HAVE TO KILL THIS THING MYSELF.
UWOOOOOOOM
MR. JOTARO TOLD ME THAT IT'S MORE IMPORTANT TO BE CALM AND STEADY THAN FAST.
AS LONG AS I DON'T GET TOO CLOSE, THE RAT WILL KEEP ON BELIEVING IT'S SAFE. I JUST NEED TO GET TO WHERE I KNOW I CAN MAKE THE SHOT.
BUT IF I MISS, I'LL BE LETTING THE RAT KNOW WE HAVE A BIGGER RANGE.
UWOOOOOOOM
SLURP
MUNCH

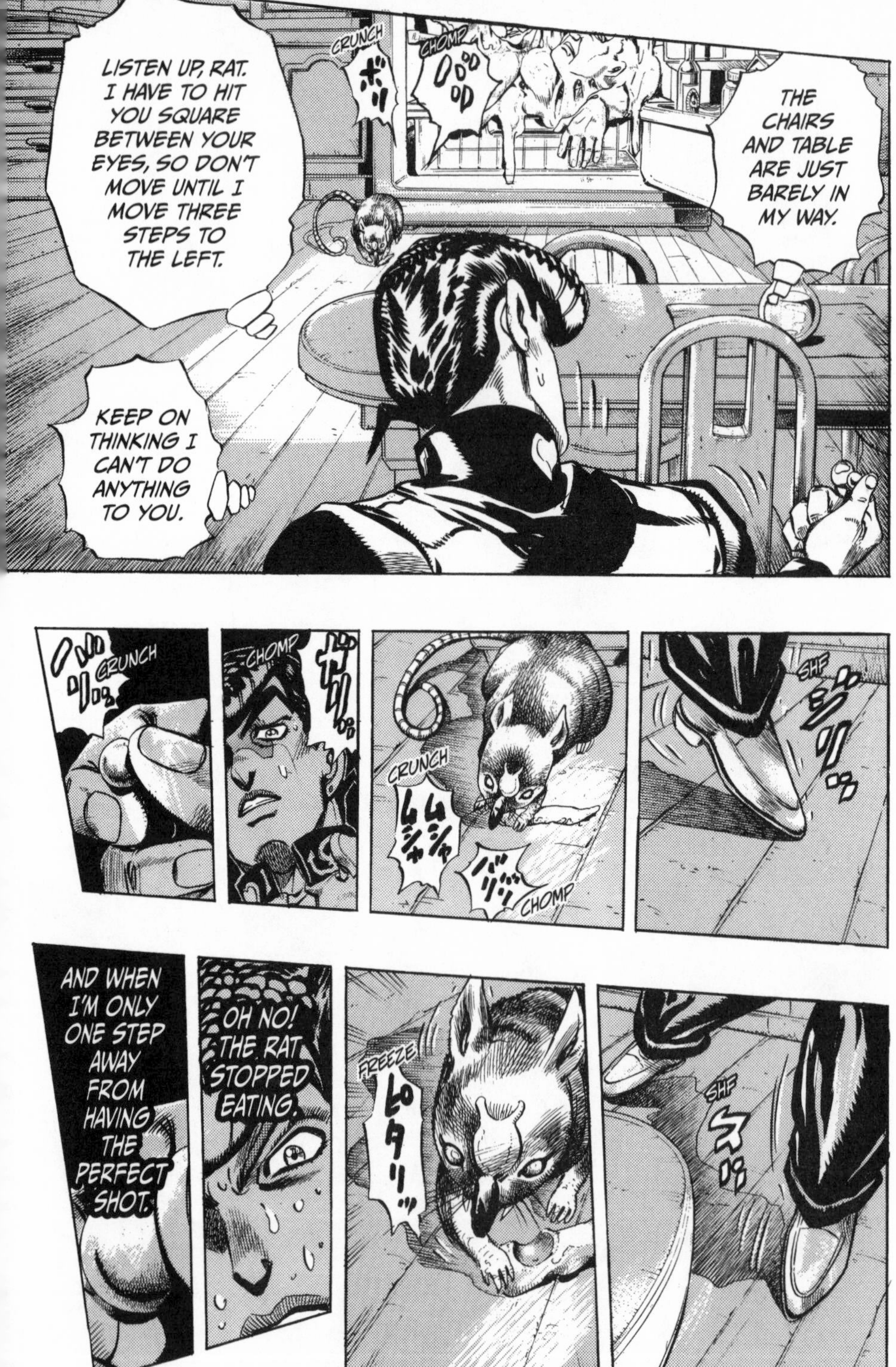
THE CHAIRS AND TABLE ARE JUST BARELY IN MY WAY.
CHOMP
CRUNCH
LISTEN UP, RAT. I HAVE TO HIT YOU SQUARE BETWEEN YOUR EYES, SO DON'T MOVE UNTIL I MOVE THREE STEPS TO THE LEFT.
KEEP ON THINKING I CAN'T DO ANYTHING TO YOU.
SHF
CRUNCH
CHOMP
CHOMP
CRUNCH
SHF
FREEZE
OH NO! THE RAT STOPPED EATING.
AND WHEN I'M ONLY ONE STEP AWAY FROM HAVING THE PERFECT SHOT.

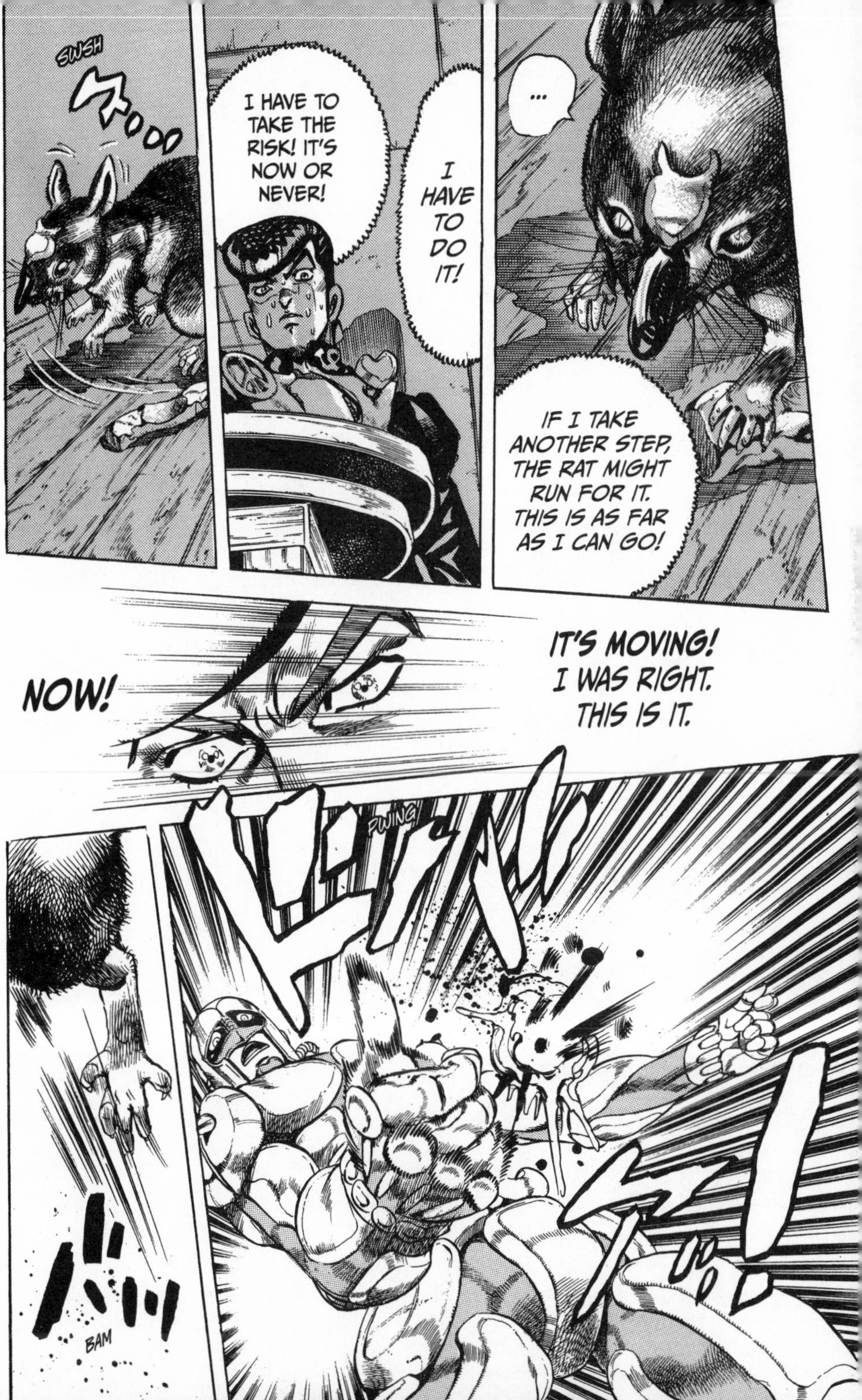
...
IF I TAKE ANOTHER STEP, THE RAT MIGHT RUN FOR IT. THIS IS AS FAR AS I CAN GO!
I HAVE TO DO IT!
I HAVE TO TAKE THE RISK! IT'S NOW OR NEVER!
SWSH
IT'S MOVING! I WAS RIGHT. THIS IS IT.
NOW!
PWING!
BAM

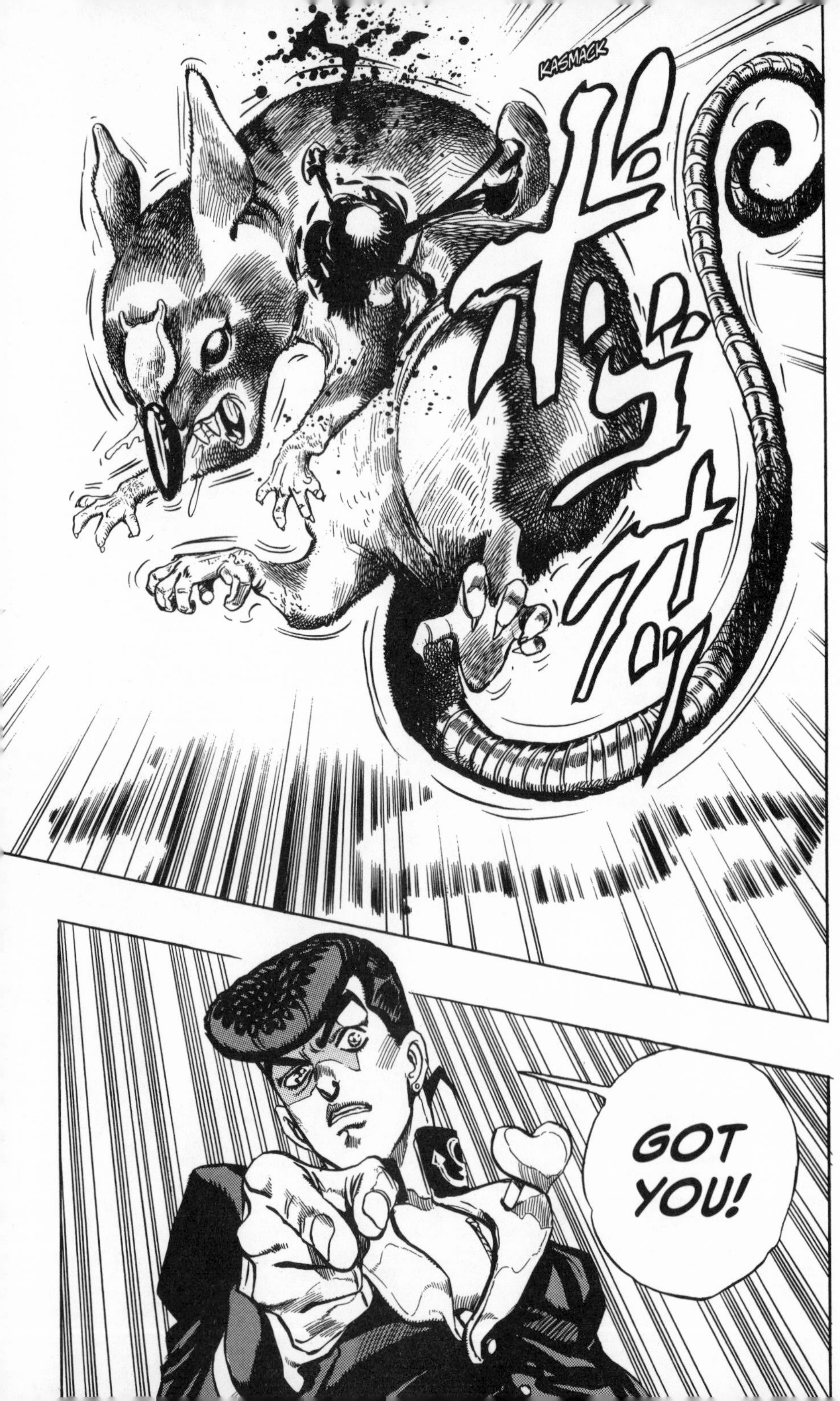
KASMACK
GOT YOU!

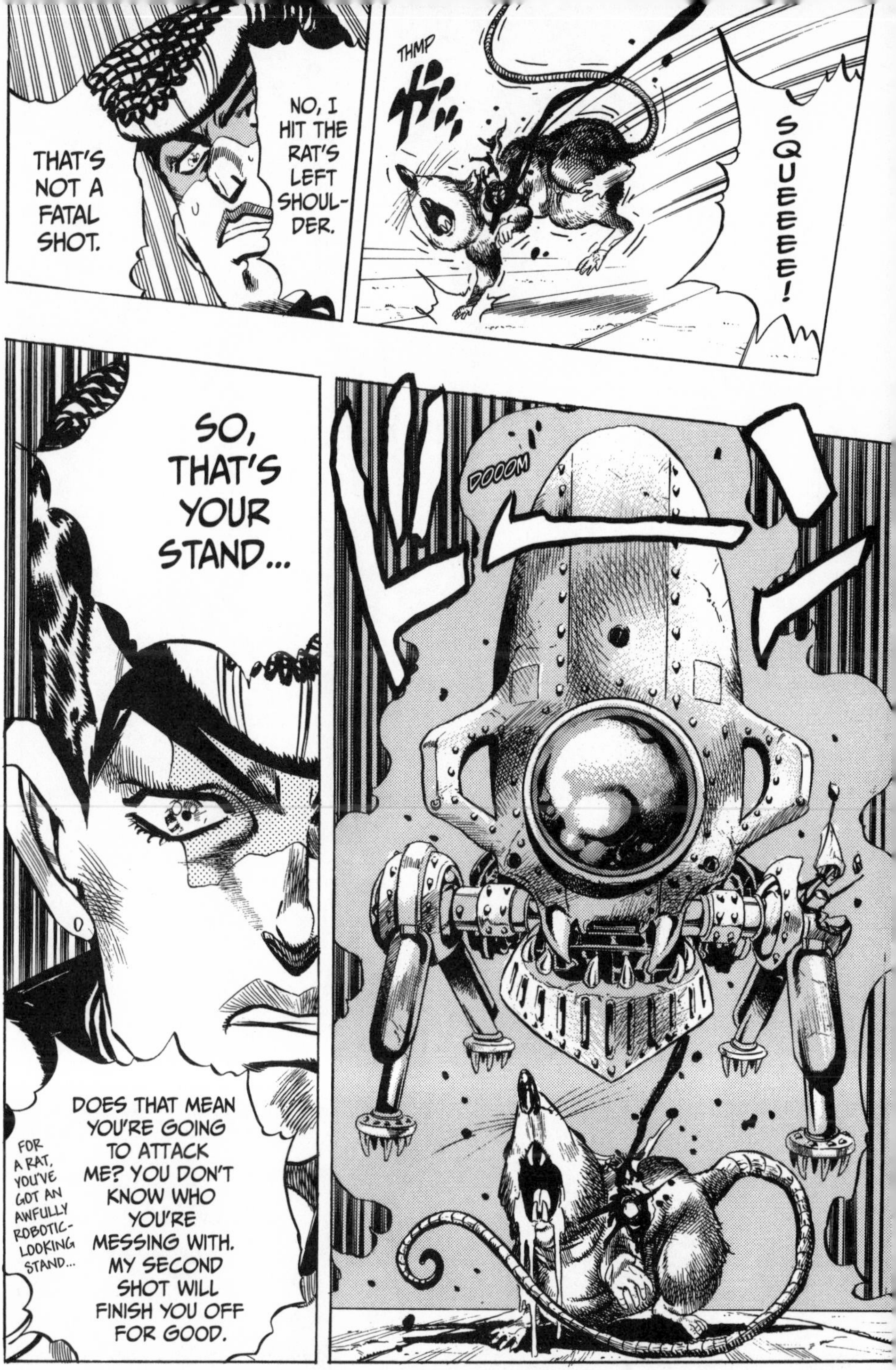
THMP
SQUEEEEE!
NO, I HIT THE RAT'S LEFT SHOULDER.
THAT'S NOT A FATAL SHOT.
DOOOM
SO, THAT'S YOUR STAND...
DOES THAT MEAN YOU'RE GOING TO ATTACK ME? YOU DON'T KNOW WHO YOU'RE MESSING WITH. MY SECOND SHOT WILL FINISH YOU OFF FOR GOOD.
FOR A RAT, YOU'VE GOT AN AWFULLY ROBOTIC-LOOKING STAND...

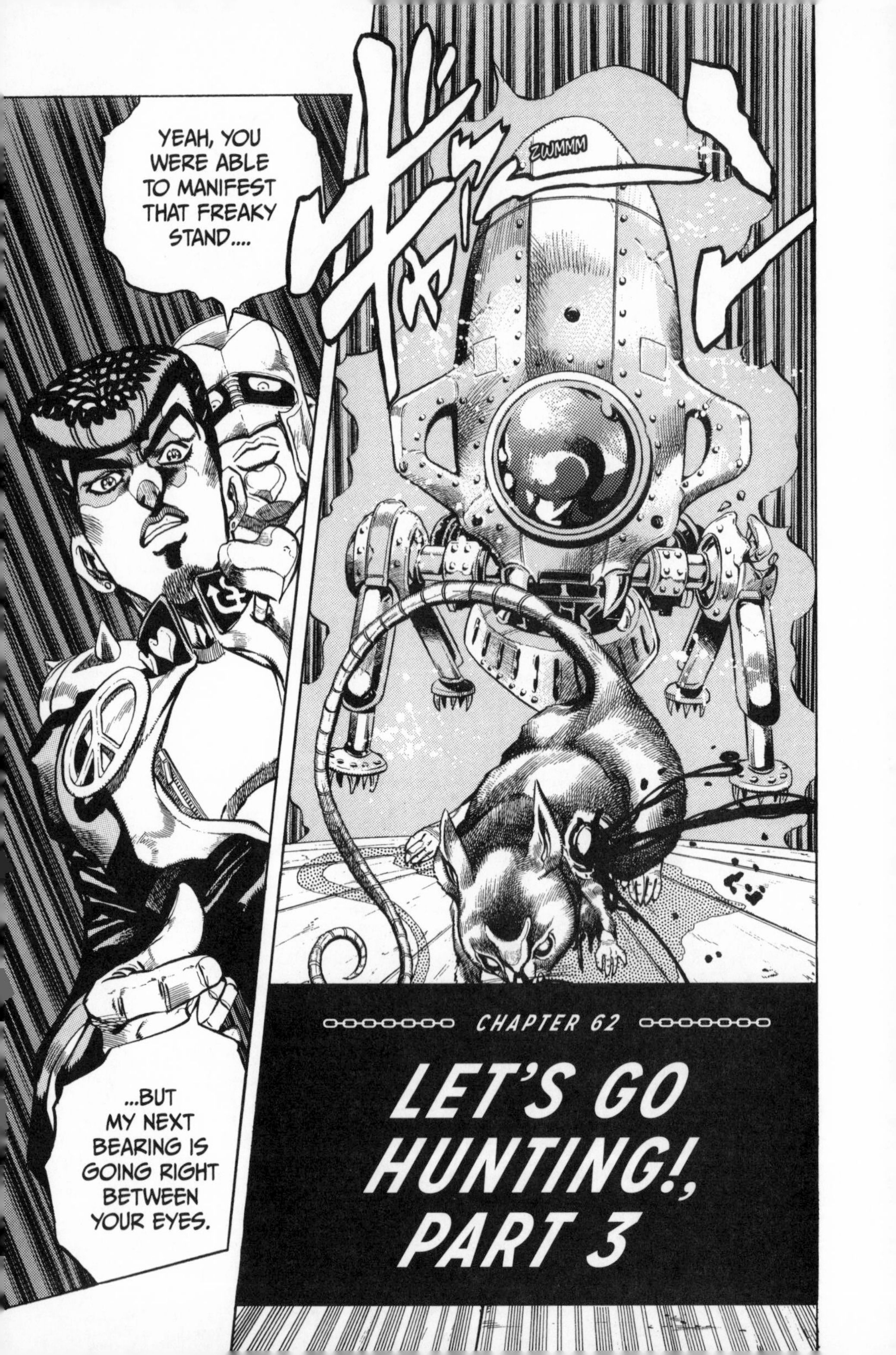
ZWMMM
CHAPTER 62
LET'S GO HUNTING!, PART 3
YEAH, YOU WERE ABLE TO MANIFEST THAT FREAKY STAND....
...BUT MY NEXT BEARING IS GOING RIGHT BETWEEN YOUR EYES.

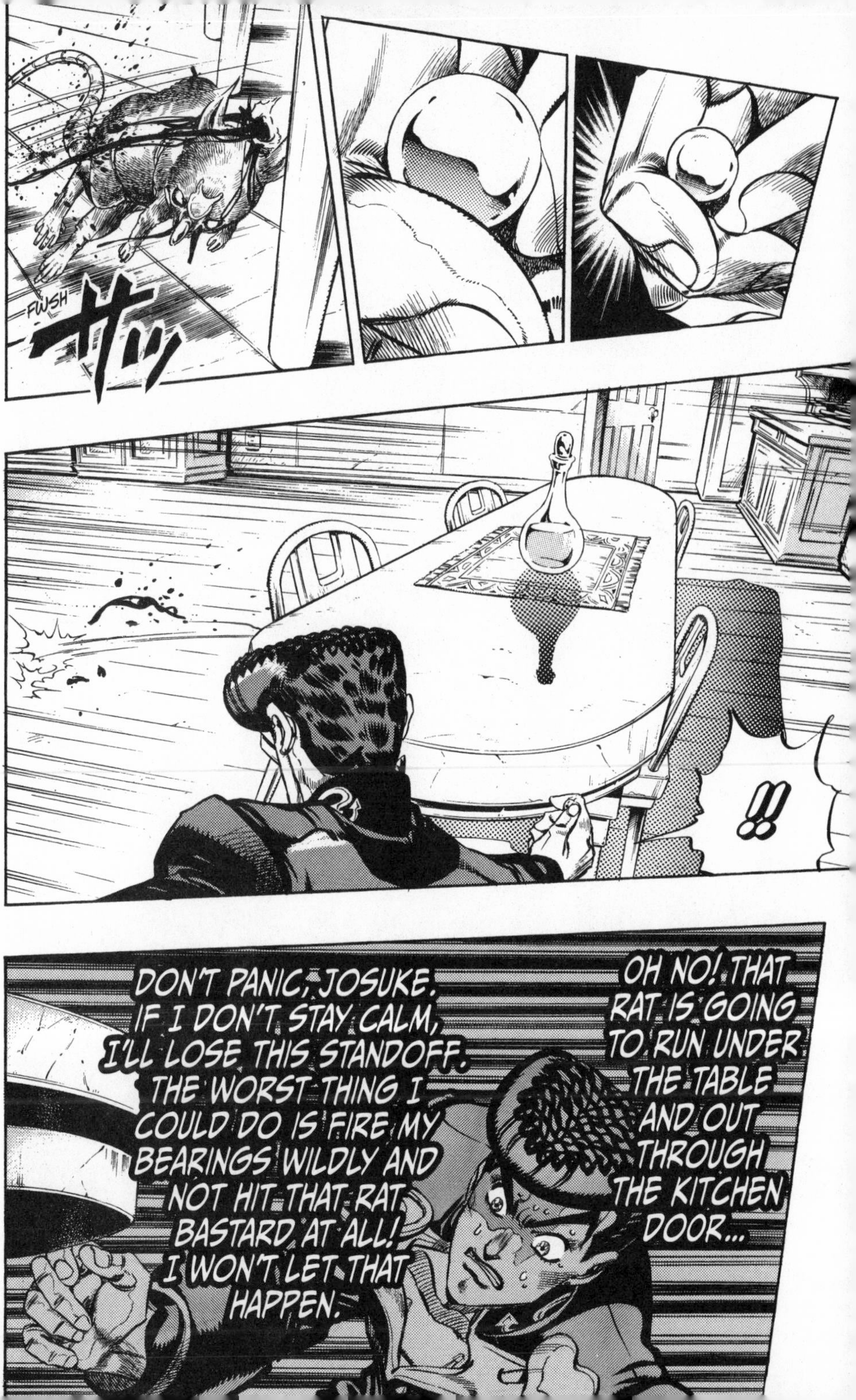
FWSH
サッ
!!
OH NO! THAT RAT IS GOING TO RUN UNDER THE TABLE AND OUT THROUGH THE KITCHEN DOOR...
DON'T PANIC, JOSUKE. IF I DON'T STAY CALM, I'LL LOSE THIS STANDOFF. THE WORST THING I COULD DO IS FIRE MY BEARINGS WILDLY AND NOT HIT THAT RAT BASTARD AT ALL! I WON'T LET THAT HAPPEN.

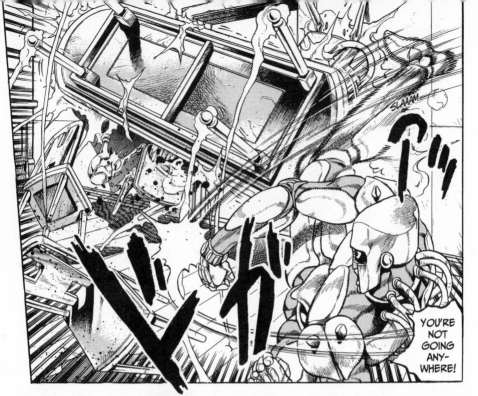

SLAAAM

YOU'RE
NOT
GOING
ANY-
WHERE!

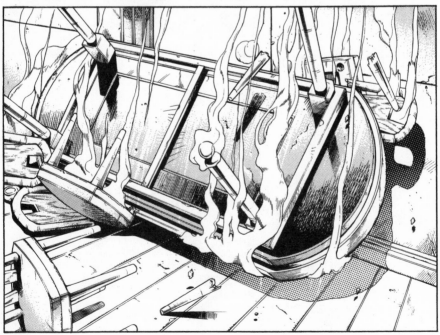

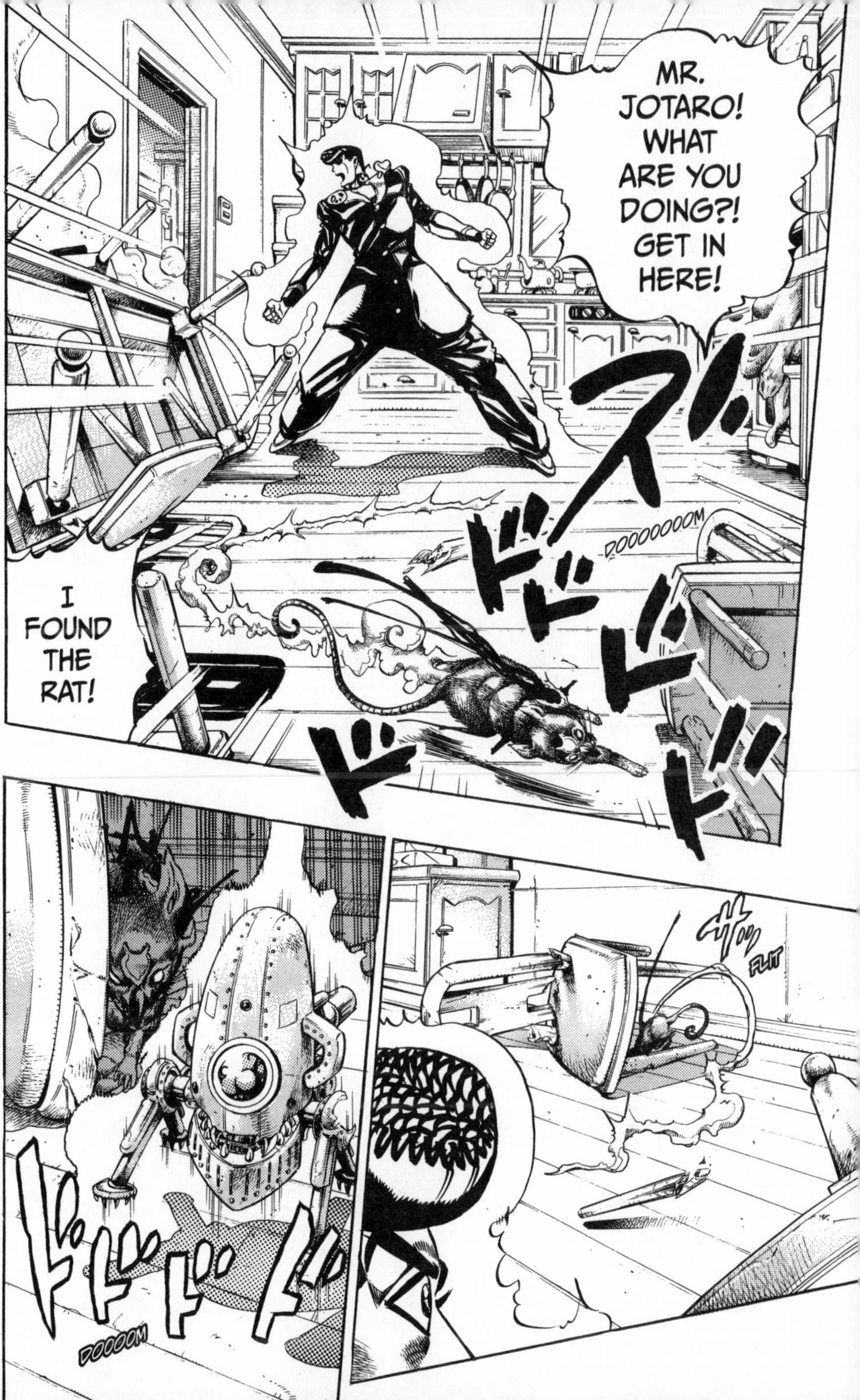
MR. JOTARO! WHAT ARE YOU DOING?! GET IN HERE!
I FOUND THE RAT!
DOOOOOOOM
FLIT
DOOOOM

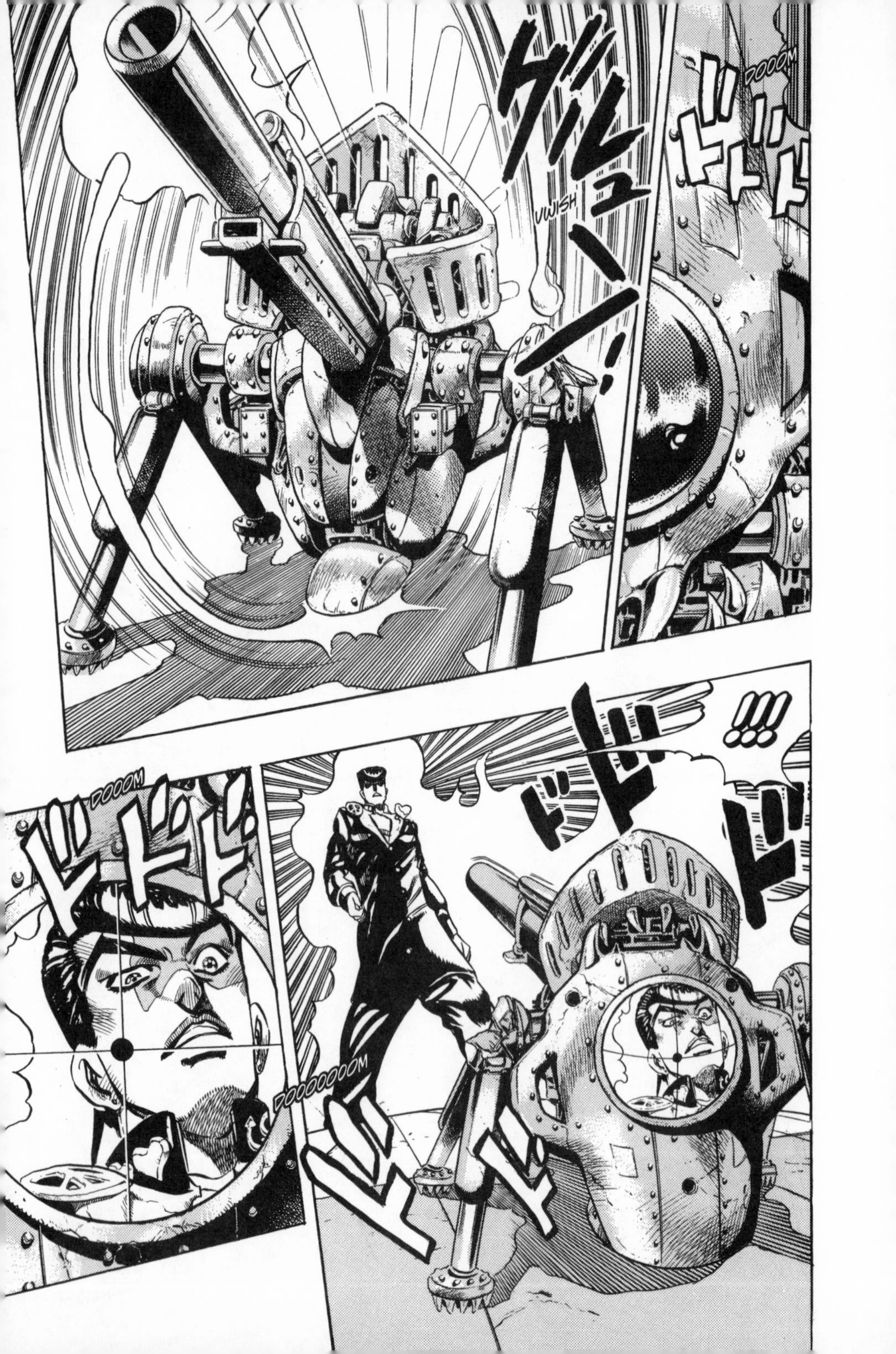
DOOOM
VWISH
!!!!
DOOOOOOOOM
DOOOM

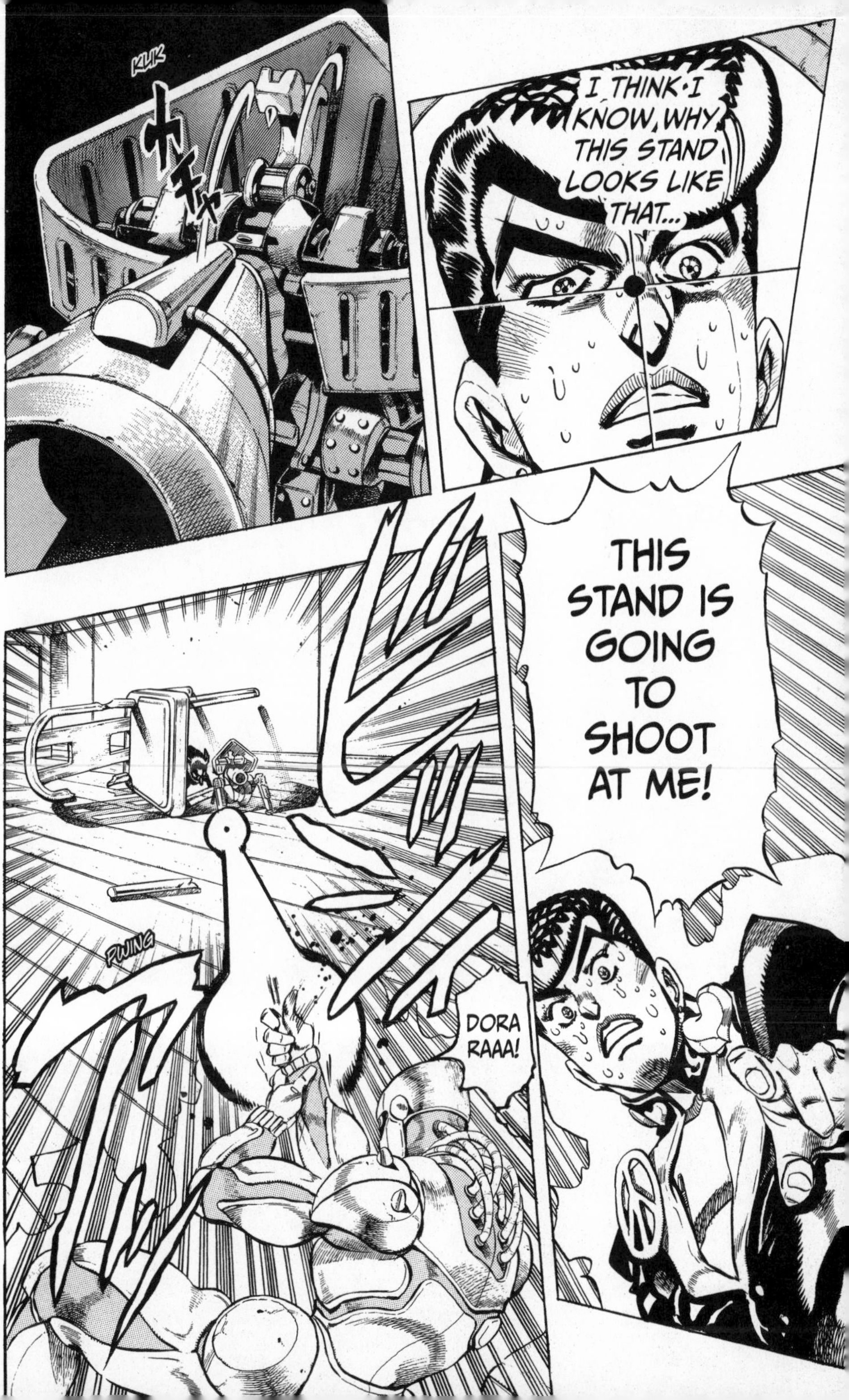
I THINK I KNOW WHY THIS STAND LOOKS LIKE THAT...
KUK
カチャ
THIS STAND IS GOING TO SHOOT AT ME!
PWING
DORA RAAA!

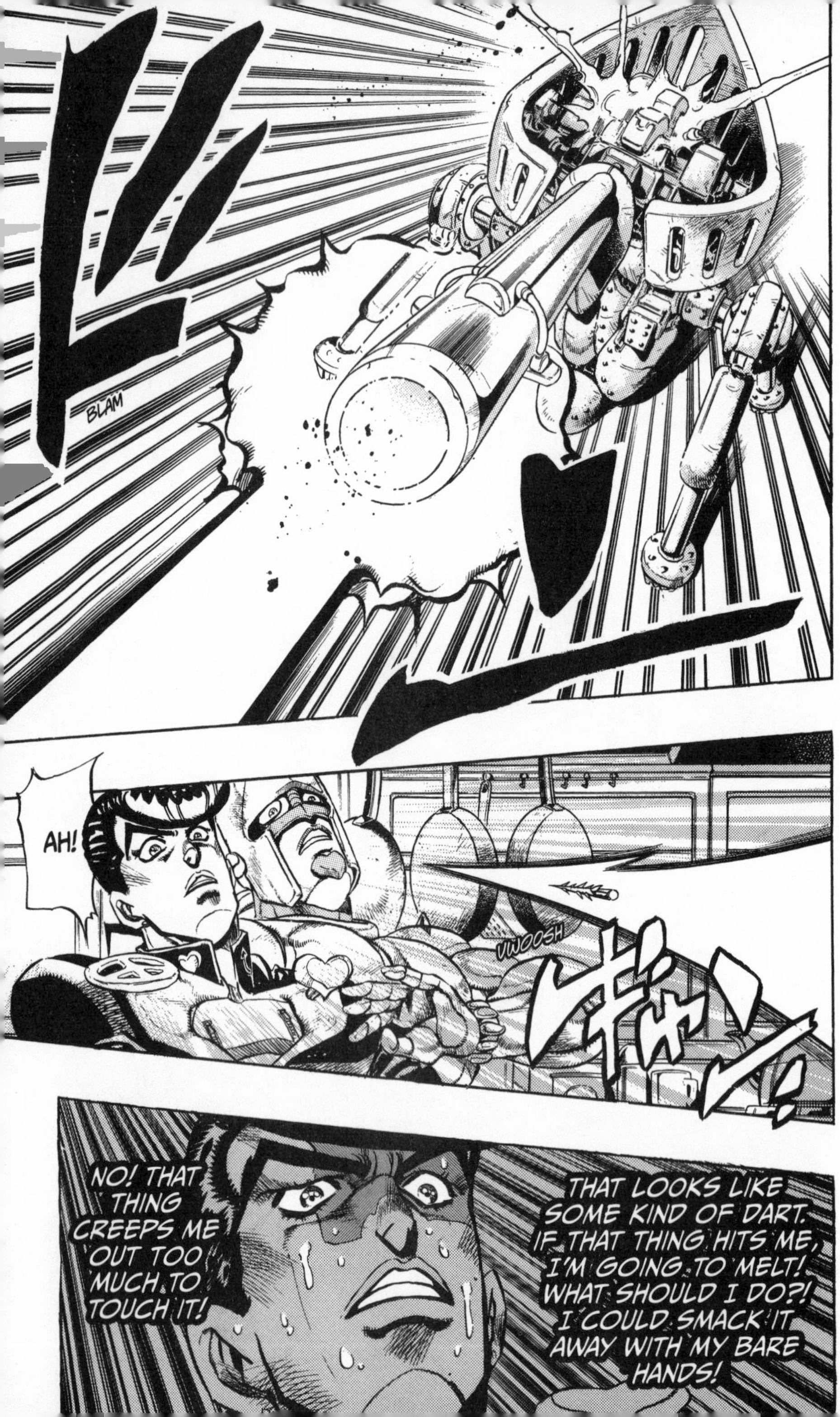
BLAM
AH!
WOOSH
THAT LOOKS LIKE SOME KIND OF DART. IF THAT THING HITS ME, I'M GOING TO MELT! WHAT SHOULD I DO?! I COULD SMACK IT AWAY WITH MY BARE HANDS!
NO! THAT THING CREEPS ME OUT TOO MUCH TO TOUCH IT!

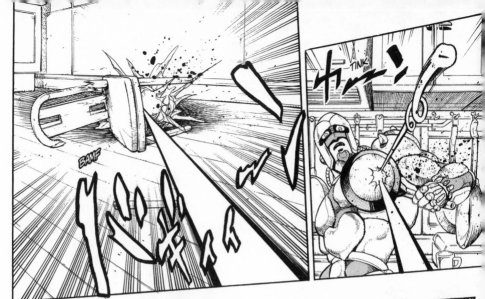

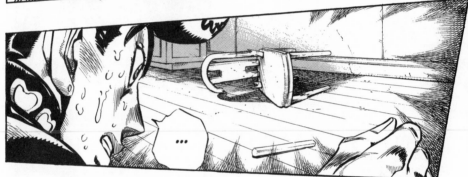

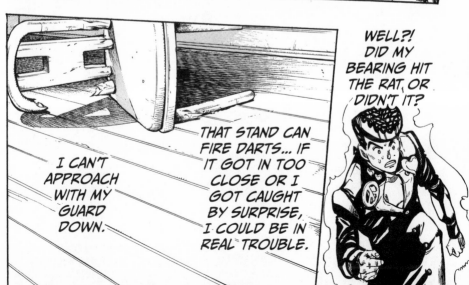

WELL?! DID MY BEARING HIT THE RAT, OR DIDN'T IT?

THAT STAND CAN FIRE DARTS... IF IT GOT IN TOO CLOSE OR I GOT CAUGHT BY SURPRISE, I COULD BE IN REAL TROUBLE.

I CAN'T APPROACH WITH MY GUARD DOWN.

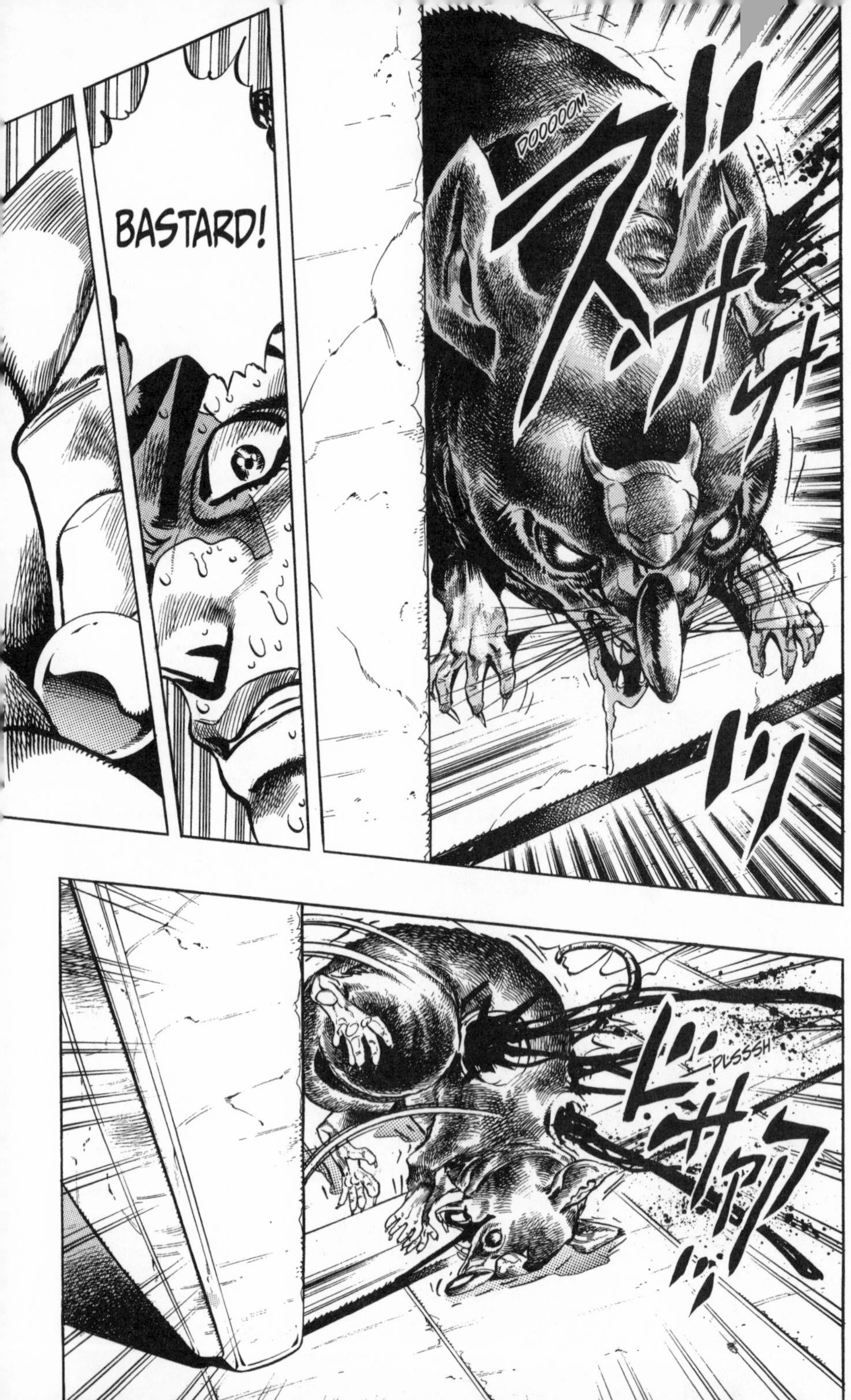
DOOOOOM
BASTARD!
PLSSSH

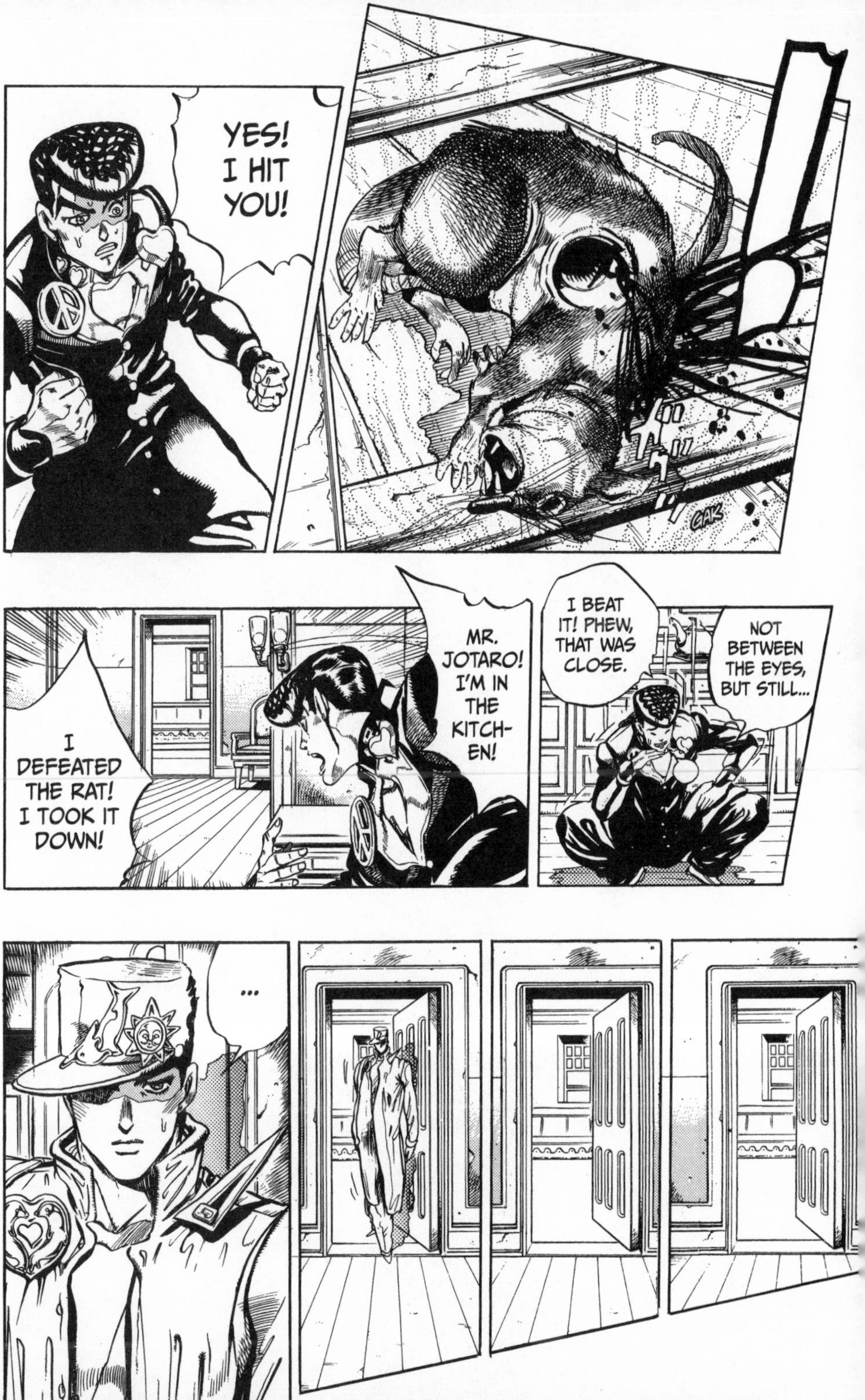
GAK
YES! I HIT YOU!
NOT BETWEEN THE EYES, BUT STILL...
I BEAT IT! PHEW, THAT WAS CLOSE.
MR. JOTARO! I'M IN THE KITCHEN!
I DEFEATED THE RAT! I TOOK IT DOWN!
...

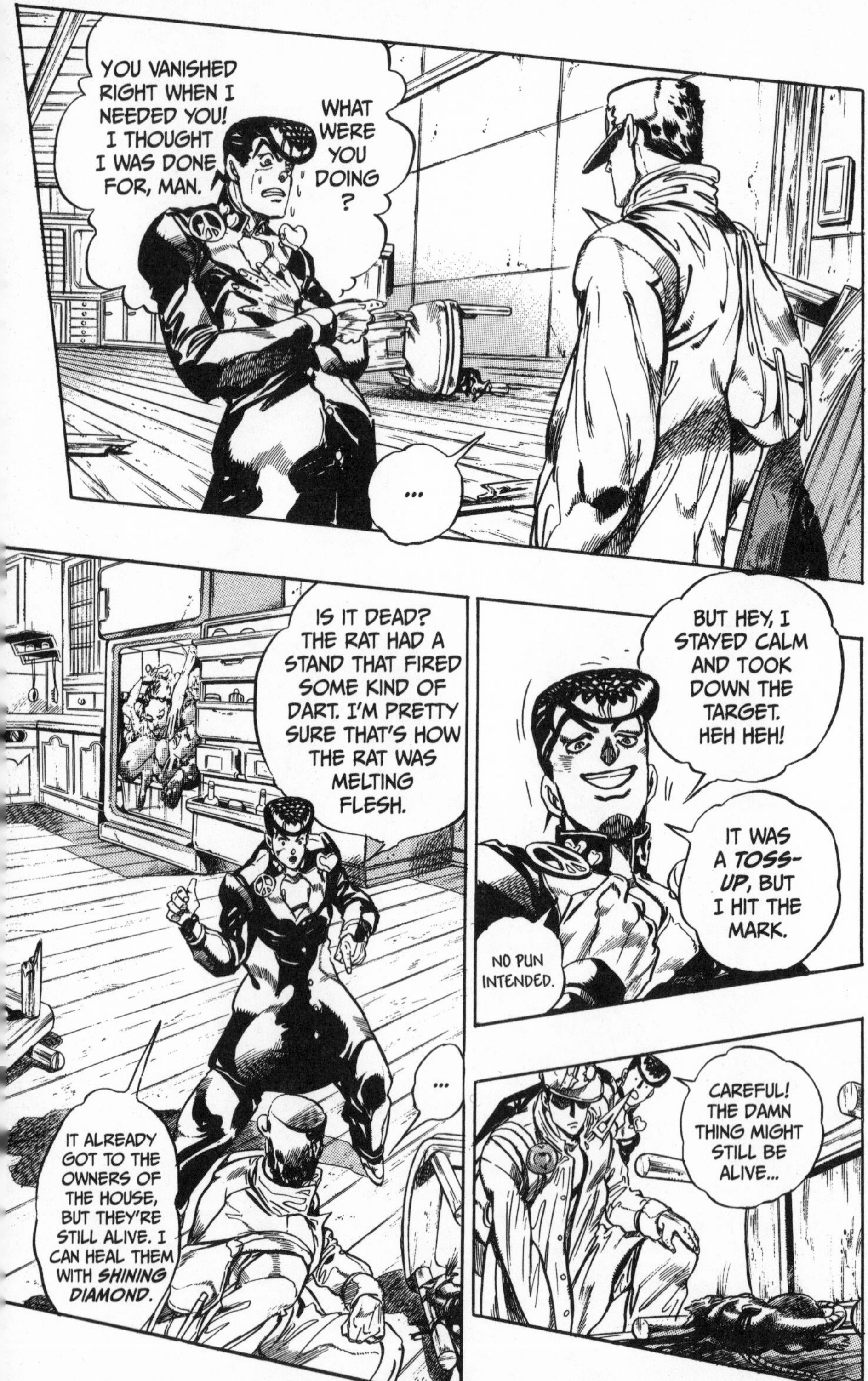
YOU VANISHED RIGHT WHEN I NEEDED YOU! I THOUGHT I WAS DONE FOR, MAN.
WHAT WERE YOU DOING?
...
BUT HEY, I STAYED CALM AND TOOK DOWN THE TARGET. HEH HEH!
IT WAS A *TOSS-UP*, BUT I HIT THE MARK.
NO PUN INTENDED.
CAREFUL! THE DAMN THING MIGHT STILL BE ALIVE...
IS IT DEAD? THE RAT HAD A STAND THAT FIRED SOME KIND OF DART. I'M PRETTY SURE THAT'S HOW THE RAT WAS MELTING FLESH.
...
IT ALREADY GOT TO THE OWNERS OF THE HOUSE, BUT THEY'RE STILL ALIVE. I CAN HEAL THEM WITH *SHINING DIAMOND*.

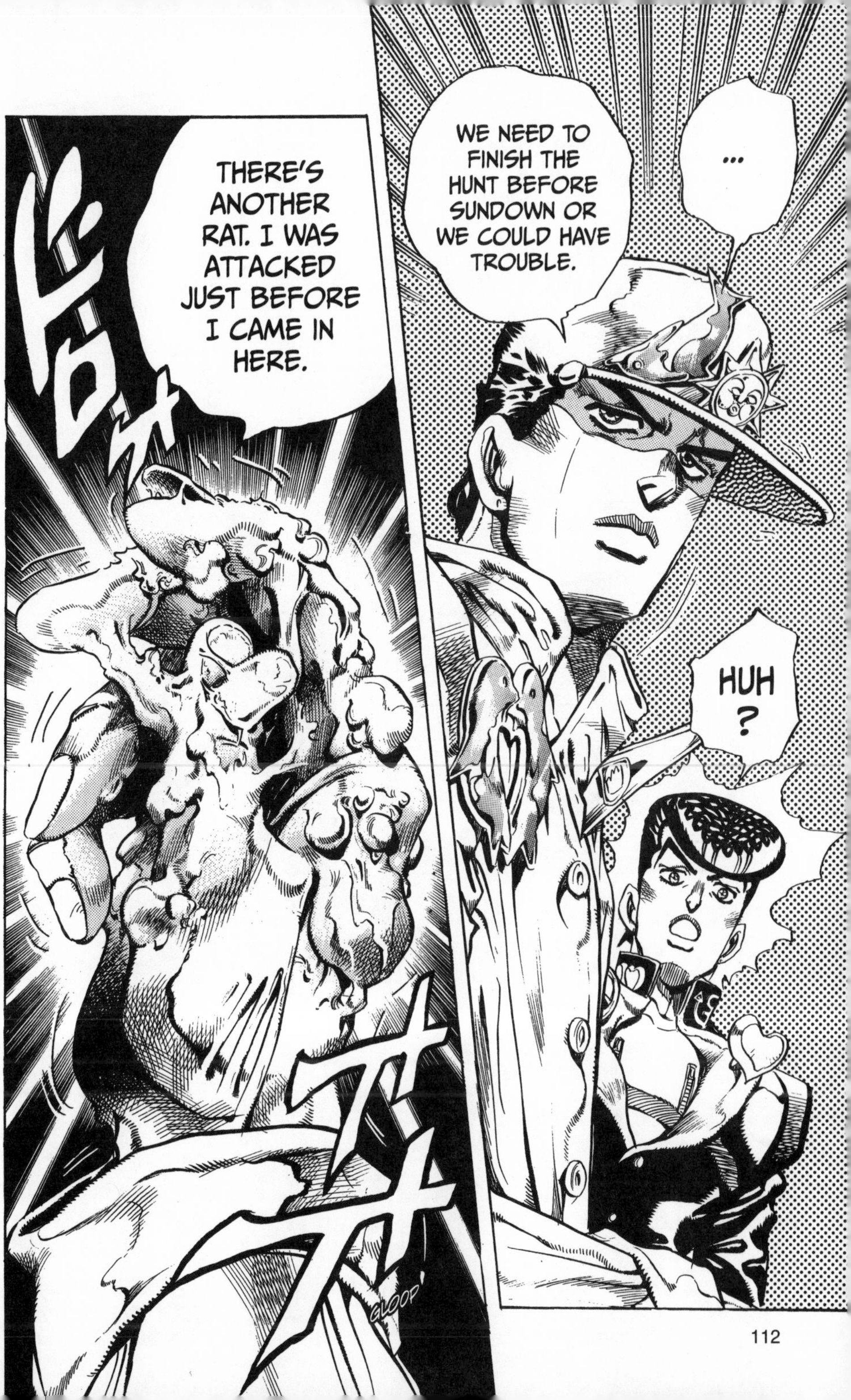
...
WE NEED TO FINISH THE HUNT BEFORE SUNDOWN OR WE COULD HAVE TROUBLE.
HUH?
THERE'S ANOTHER RAT. I WAS ATTACKED JUST BEFORE I CAME IN HERE.
GLOOP

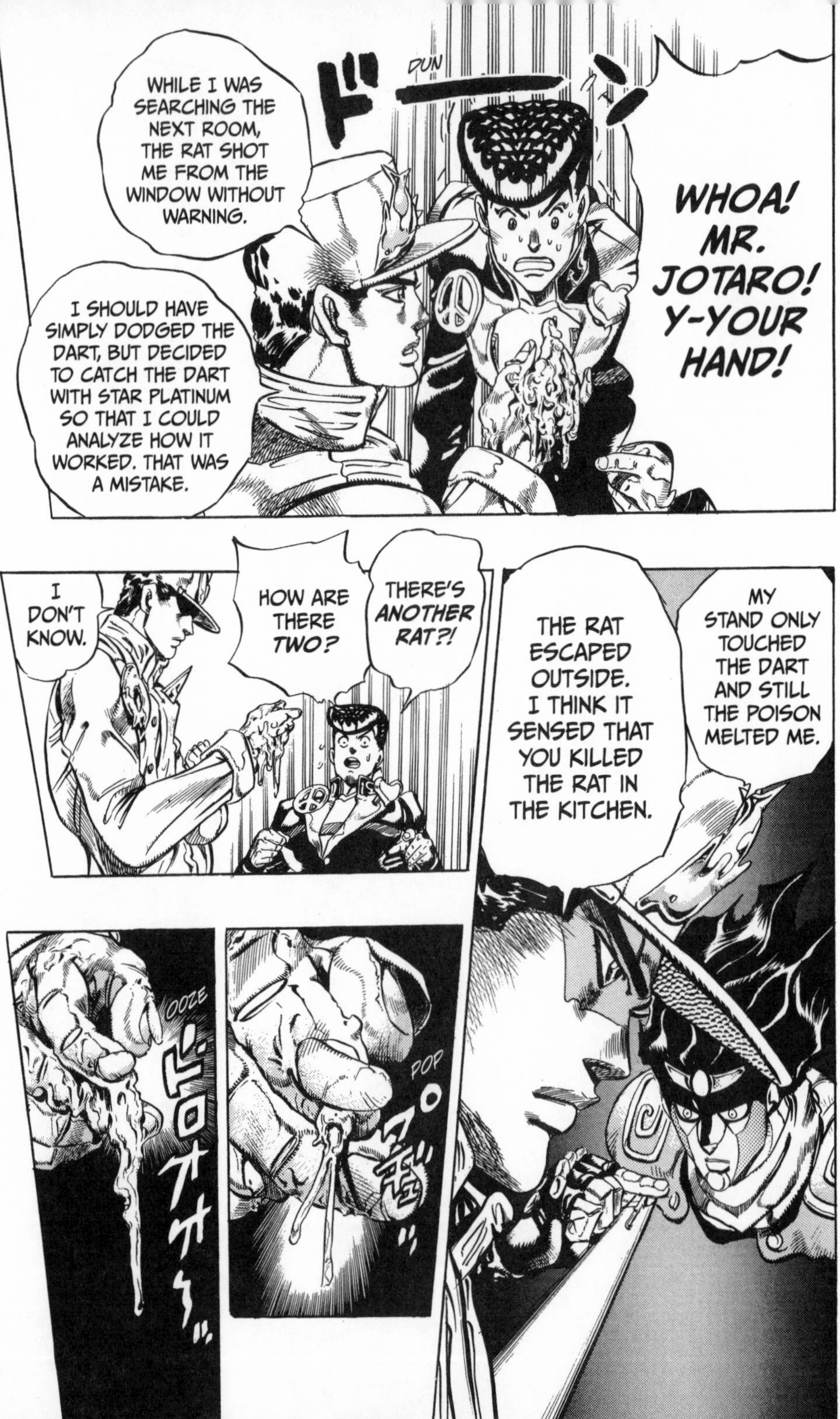
WHOA! MR. JOTARO! Y-YOUR HAND!
DUN
WHILE I WAS SEARCHING THE NEXT ROOM, THE RAT SHOT ME FROM THE WINDOW WITHOUT WARNING.
I SHOULD HAVE SIMPLY DODGED THE DART, BUT DECIDED TO CATCH THE DART WITH STAR PLATINUM SO THAT I COULD ANALYZE HOW IT WORKED. THAT WAS A MISTAKE.
MY STAND ONLY TOUCHED THE DART AND STILL THE POISON MELTED ME.
THE RAT ESCAPED OUTSIDE. I THINK IT SENSED THAT YOU KILLED THE RAT IN THE KITCHEN.
THERE'S *ANOTHER* RAT?!
HOW ARE THERE *TWO?*
I DON'T KNOW.
POP
OOZE

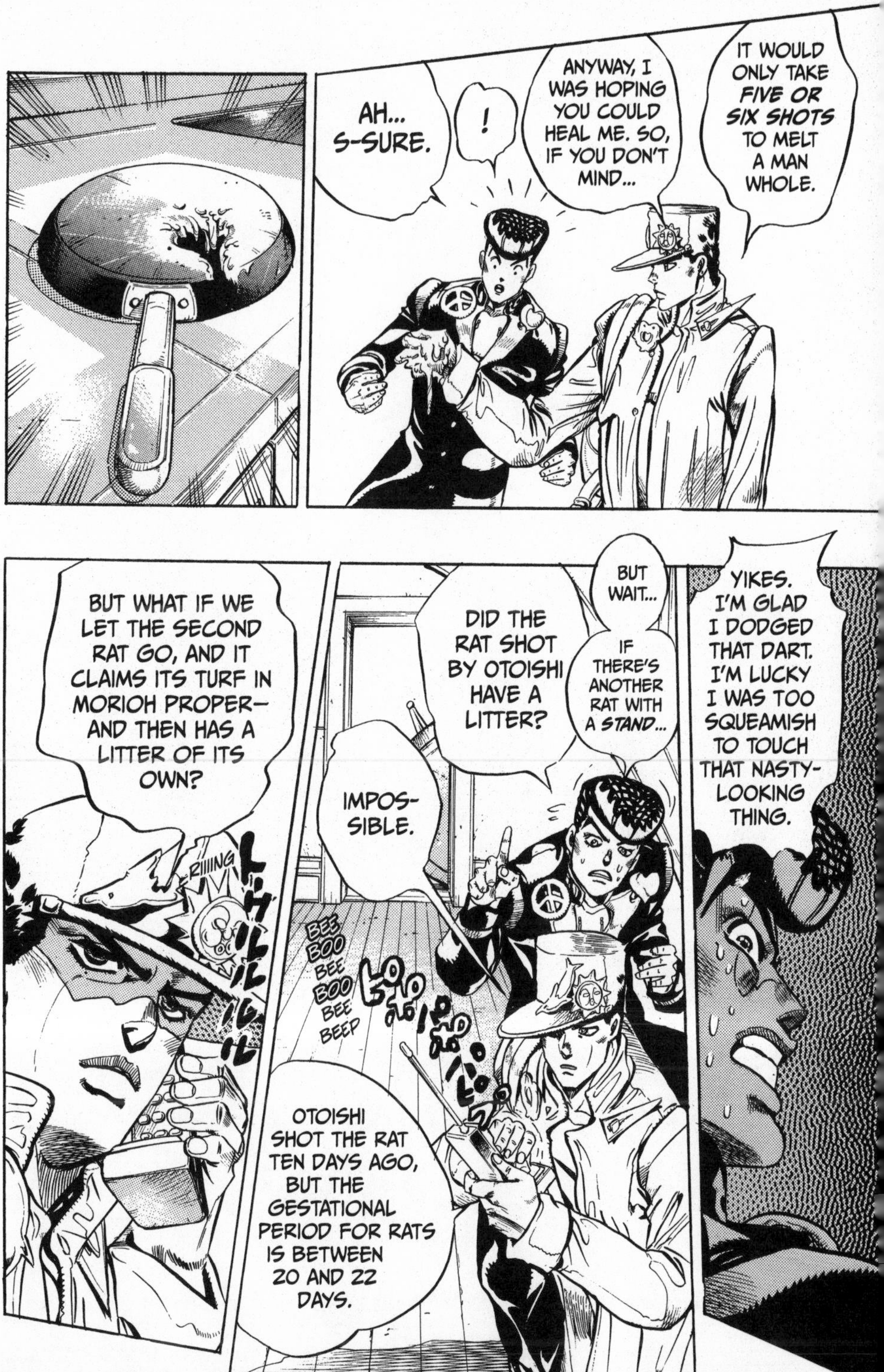
IT WOULD ONLY TAKE *FIVE OR SIX SHOTS* TO MELT A MAN WHOLE.
ANYWAY, I WAS HOPING YOU COULD HEAL ME. SO, IF YOU DON'T MIND...
!
AH... S-SURE.
YIKES. I'M GLAD I DODGED THAT DART. I'M LUCKY I WAS TOO SQUEAMISH TO TOUCH THAT NASTY-LOOKING THING.
BUT WAIT...
IF THERE'S ANOTHER RAT WITH A *STAND*...
DID THE RAT SHOT BY OTOISHI HAVE A LITTER?
IMPOSSIBLE.
BEE BOO BEE BOO BEE BEEP
OTOISHI SHOT THE RAT TEN DAYS AGO, BUT THE GESTATIONAL PERIOD FOR RATS IS BETWEEN 20 AND 22 DAYS.
BUT WHAT IF WE LET THE SECOND RAT GO, AND IT CLAIMS ITS TURF IN MORIOH PROPER—AND THEN HAS A LITTER OF ITS OWN?
RIIING

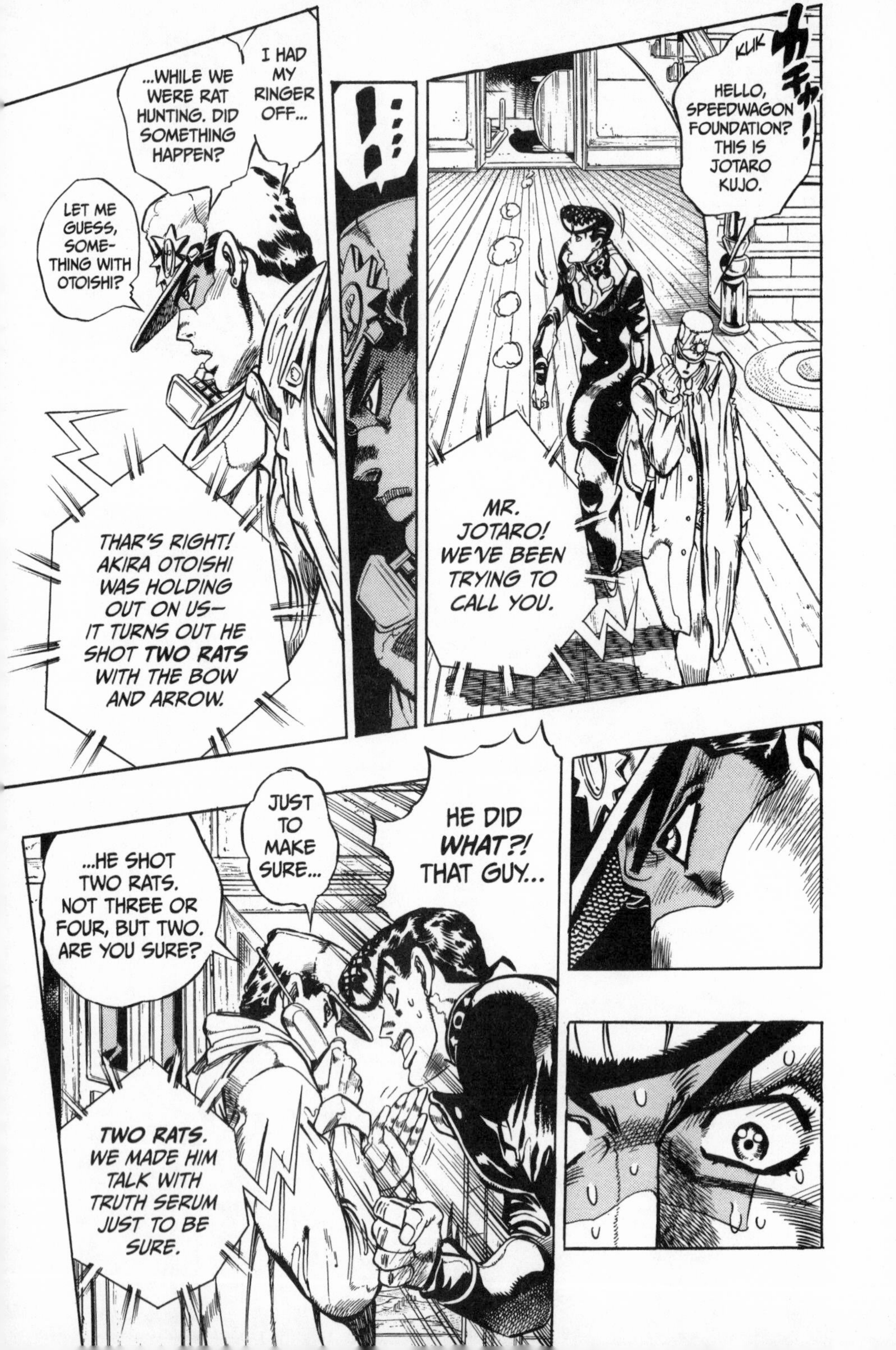
KUK
カチャ!!
HELLO, SPEEDWAGON FOUNDATION? THIS IS JOTARO KUJO.
MR. JOTARO! WE'VE BEEN TRYING TO CALL YOU.
!!
I HAD MY RINGER OFF...
...WHILE WE WERE RAT HUNTING. DID SOMETHING HAPPEN?
LET ME GUESS, SOMETHING WITH OTOISHI?
THAR'S RIGHT! AKIRA OTOISHI WAS HOLDING OUT ON US— IT TURNS OUT HE SHOT TWO RATS WITH THE BOW AND ARROW.
HE DID WHAT?! THAT GUY...
JUST TO MAKE SURE...
...HE SHOT TWO RATS. NOT THREE OR FOUR, BUT TWO. ARE YOU SURE?
TWO RATS. WE MADE HIM TALK WITH TRUTH SERUM JUST TO BE SURE.

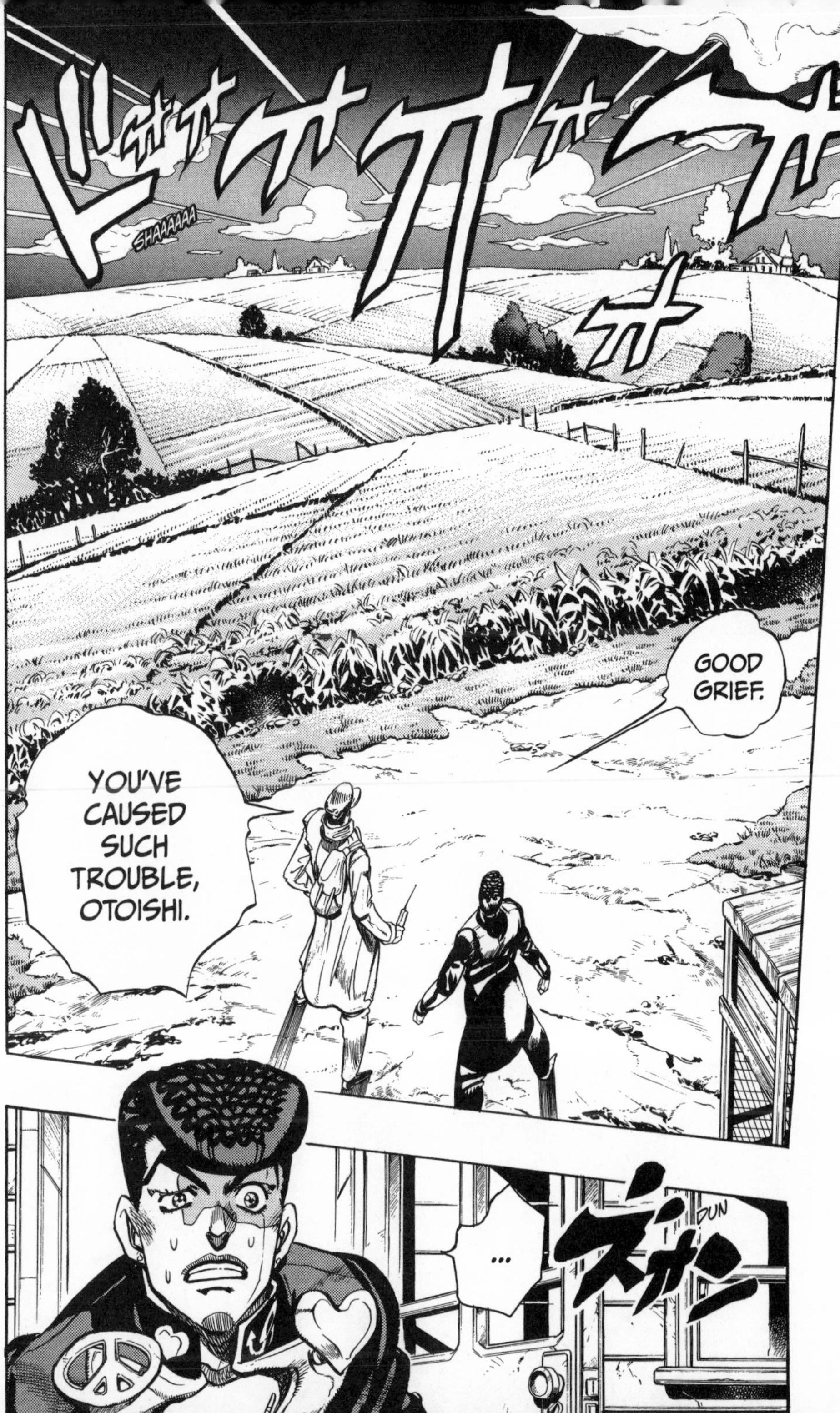
SHAAAAAA
GOOD GRIEF.
YOU'VE CAUSED SUCH TROUBLE, OTOISHI.
DUN
...

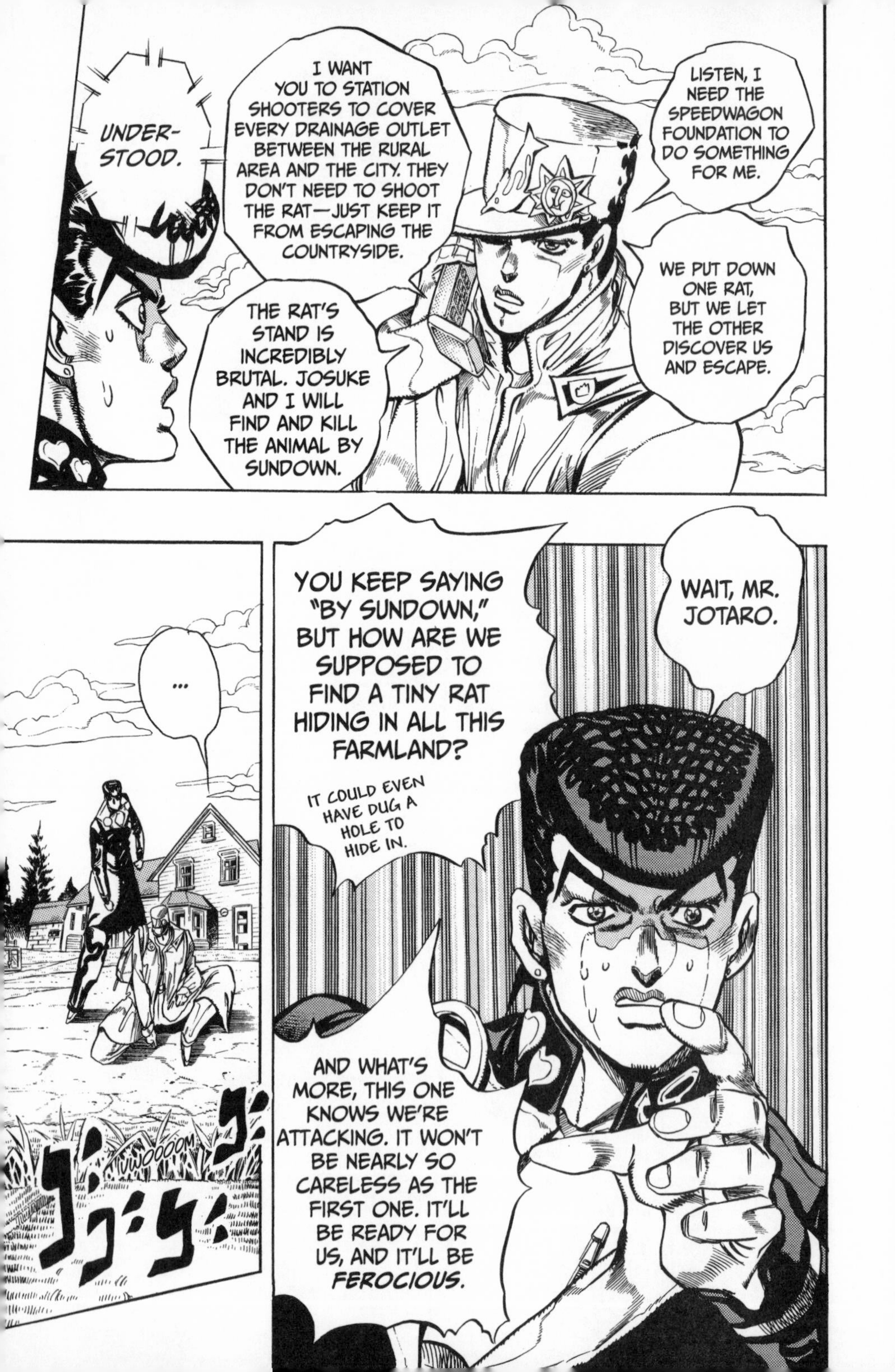
LISTEN, I NEED THE SPEEDWAGON FOUNDATION TO DO SOMETHING FOR ME.
WE PUT DOWN ONE RAT, BUT WE LET THE OTHER DISCOVER US AND ESCAPE.
I WANT YOU TO STATION SHOOTERS TO COVER EVERY DRAINAGE OUTLET BETWEEN THE RURAL AREA AND THE CITY. THEY DON'T NEED TO SHOOT THE RAT—JUST KEEP IT FROM ESCAPING THE COUNTRYSIDE.
THE RAT'S STAND IS INCREDIBLY BRUTAL. JOSUKE AND I WILL FIND AND KILL THE ANIMAL BY SUNDOWN.
UNDER-STOOD.
WAIT, MR. JOTARO.
YOU KEEP SAYING "BY SUNDOWN," BUT HOW ARE WE SUPPOSED TO FIND A TINY RAT HIDING IN ALL THIS FARMLAND?
IT COULD EVEN HAVE DUG A HOLE TO HIDE IN.
AND WHAT'S MORE, THIS ONE KNOWS WE'RE ATTACKING. IT WON'T BE NEARLY SO CARELESS AS THE FIRST ONE. IT'LL BE READY FOR US, AND IT'LL BE *FEROCIOUS*.
...
VWOOOOM

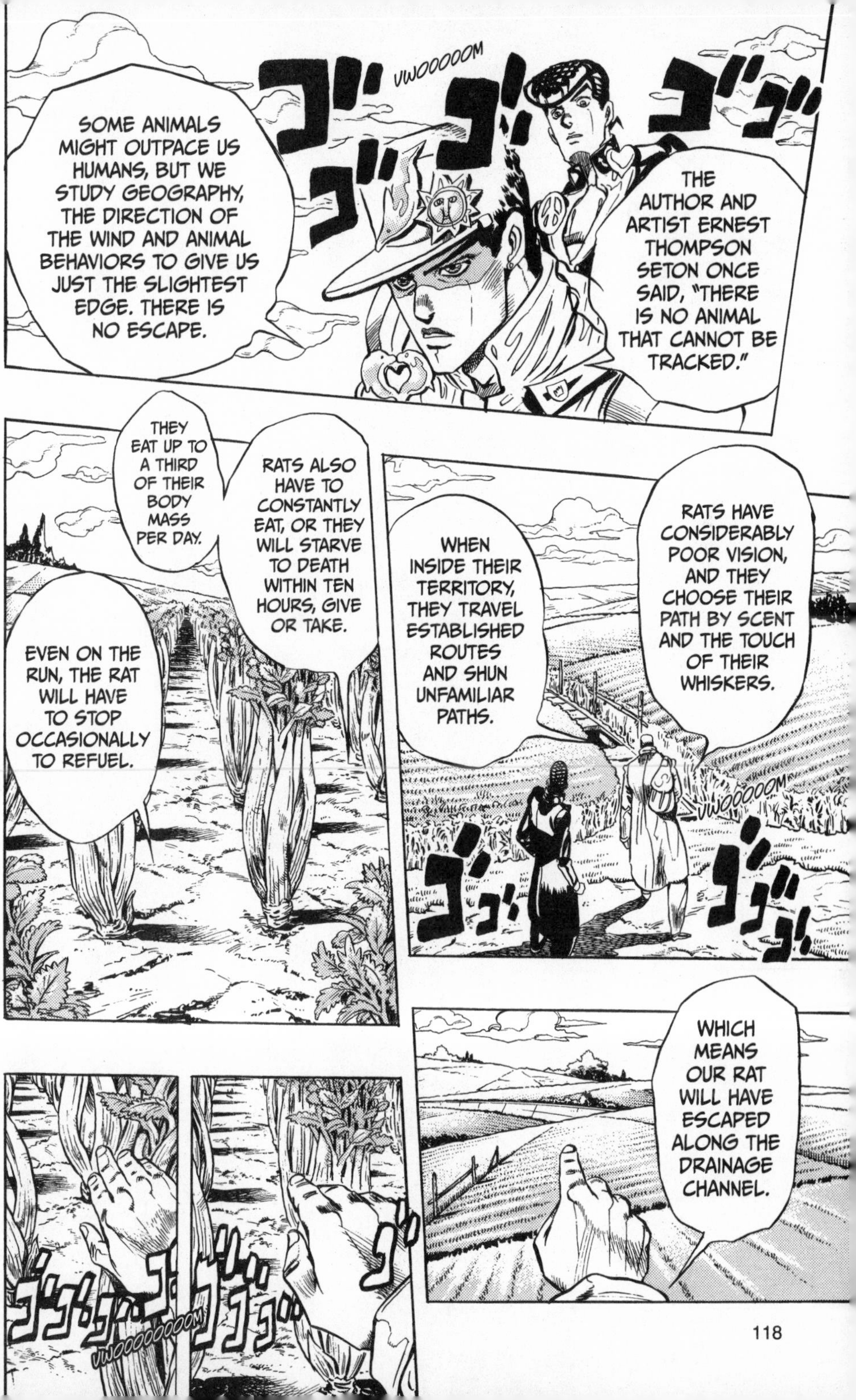
THE AUTHOR AND ARTIST ERNEST THOMPSON SETON ONCE SAID, "THERE IS NO ANIMAL THAT CANNOT BE TRACKED."
SOME ANIMALS MIGHT OUTPACE US HUMANS, BUT WE STUDY GEOGRAPHY, THE DIRECTION OF THE WIND AND ANIMAL BEHAVIORS TO GIVE US JUST THE SLIGHTEST EDGE. THERE IS NO ESCAPE.
VWOOOOOM
RATS HAVE CONSIDERABLY POOR VISION, AND THEY CHOOSE THEIR PATH BY SCENT AND THE TOUCH OF THEIR WHISKERS.
WHEN INSIDE THEIR TERRITORY, THEY TRAVEL ESTABLISHED ROUTES AND SHUN UNFAMILIAR PATHS.
VWOOOOOOM
RATS ALSO HAVE TO CONSTANTLY EAT, OR THEY WILL STARVE TO DEATH WITHIN TEN HOURS, GIVE OR TAKE.
THEY EAT UP TO A THIRD OF THEIR BODY MASS PER DAY.
EVEN ON THE RUN, THE RAT WILL HAVE TO STOP OCCASIONALLY TO REFUEL.
WHICH MEANS OUR RAT WILL HAVE ESCAPED ALONG THE DRAINAGE CHANNEL.
VWOOOOOOOOOM

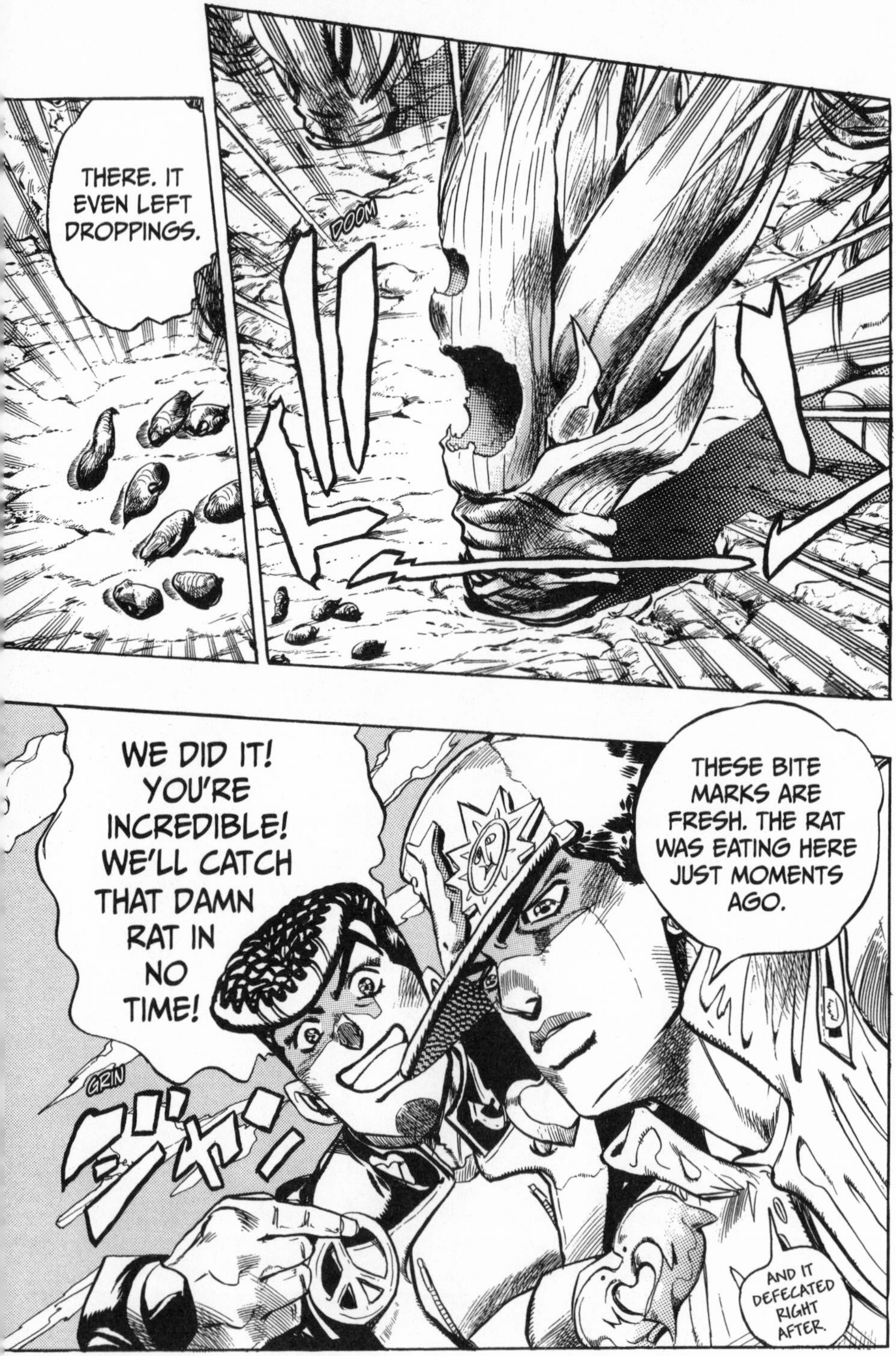
DOOM
THERE. IT EVEN LEFT DROPPINGS.
THESE BITE MARKS ARE FRESH. THE RAT WAS EATING HERE JUST MOMENTS AGO.
WE DID IT! YOU'RE INCREDIBLE! WE'LL CATCH THAT DAMN RAT IN NO TIME!
GRIN
AND IT DEFECATED RIGHT AFTER.

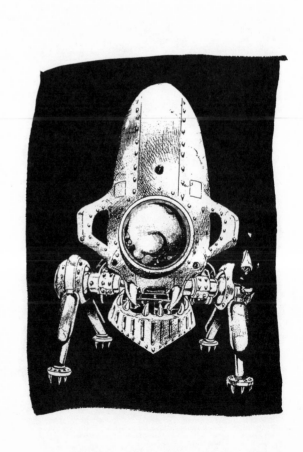

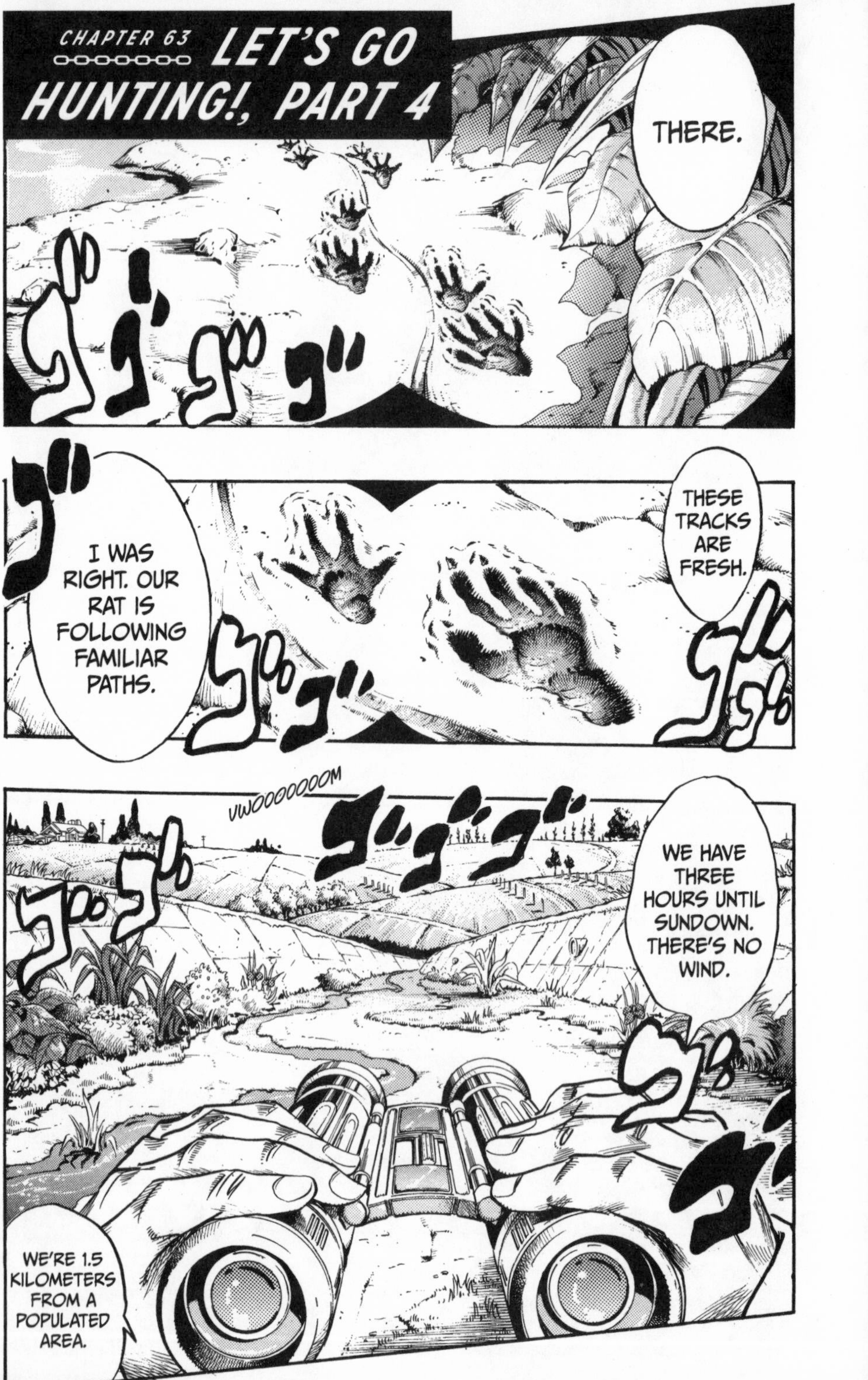
CHAPTER 63
LET'S GO HUNTING!, PART 4
THERE.
THESE TRACKS ARE FRESH.
I WAS RIGHT. OUR RAT IS FOLLOWING FAMILIAR PATHS.
VWOOOOOOOM
WE HAVE THREE HOURS UNTIL SUNDOWN. THERE'S NO WIND.
WE'RE 1.5 KILOMETERS FROM A POPULATED AREA.

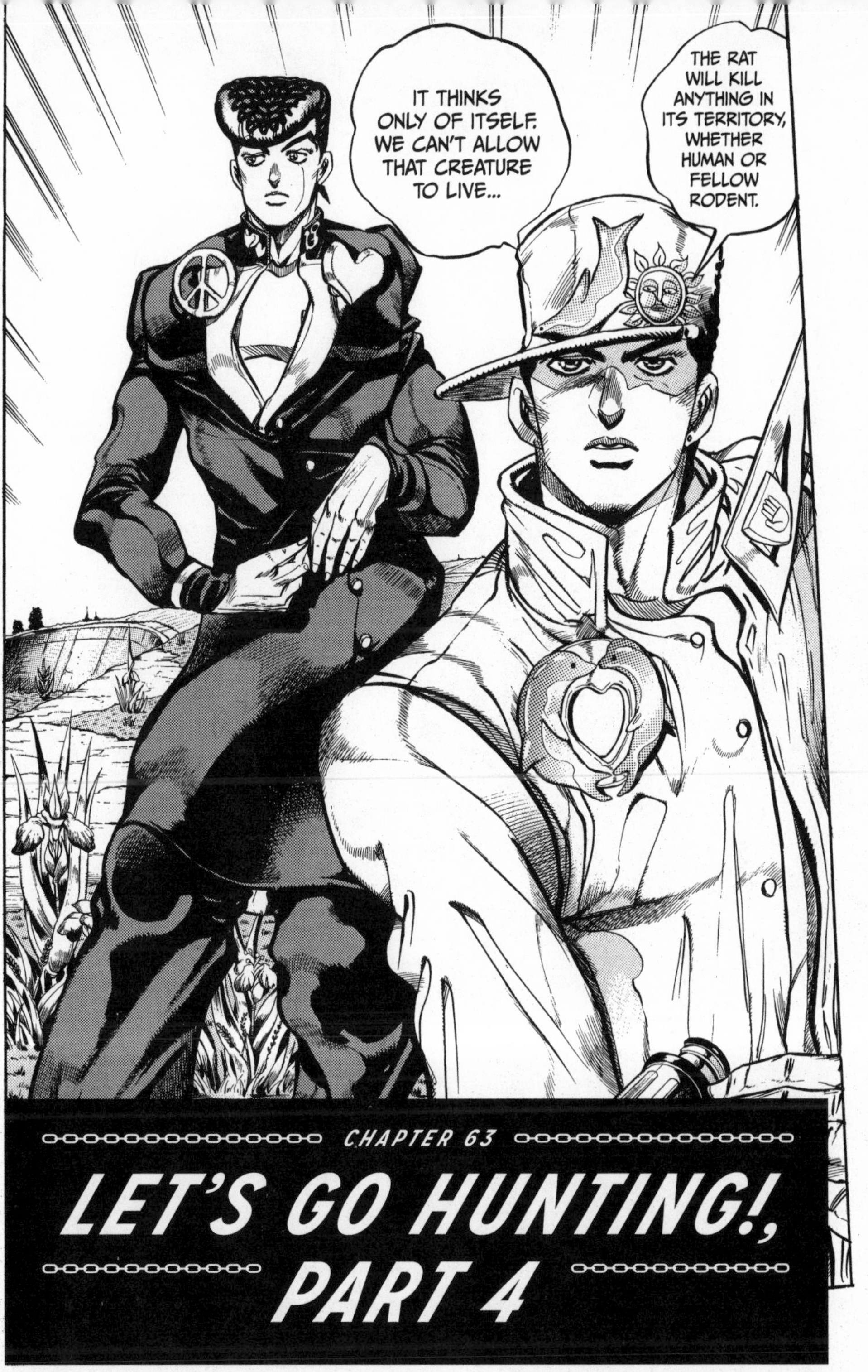
THE RAT WILL KILL ANYTHING IN ITS TERRITORY, WHETHER HUMAN OR FELLOW RODENT.
IT THINKS ONLY OF ITSELF. WE CAN'T ALLOW THAT CREATURE TO LIVE...

CHAPTER 63

LET'S GO HUNTING!, PART 4

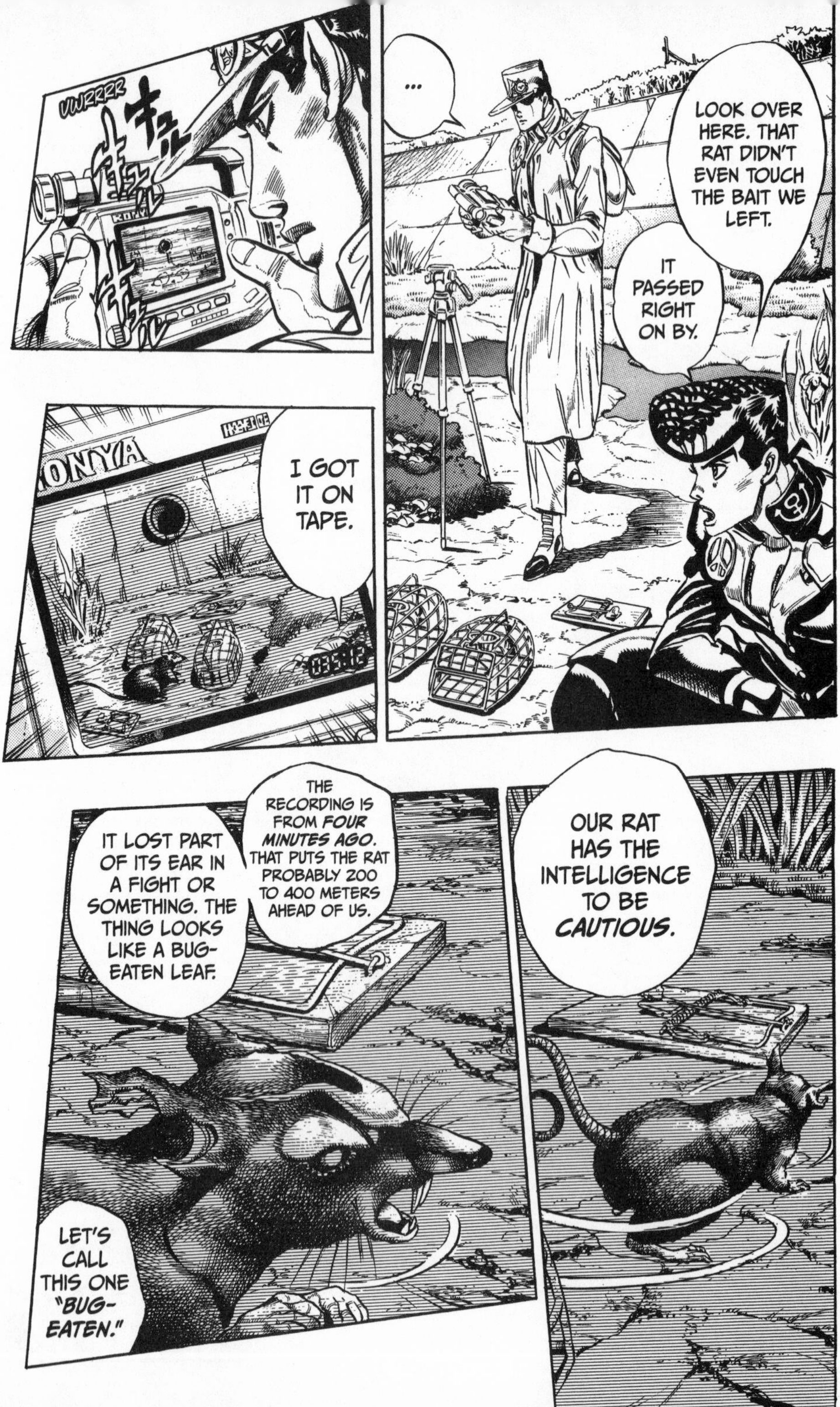
LOOK OVER HERE. THAT RAT DIDN'T EVEN TOUCH THE BAIT WE LEFT.
IT PASSED RIGHT ON BY.
...
UWRRRR
I GOT IT ON TAPE.
OUR RAT HAS THE INTELLIGENCE TO BE *CAUTIOUS.*
THE RECORDING IS FROM *FOUR MINUTES AGO.* THAT PUTS THE RAT PROBABLY 200 TO 400 METERS AHEAD OF US.
IT LOST PART OF ITS EAR IN A FIGHT OR SOMETHING. THE THING LOOKS LIKE A BUG-EATEN LEAF.
LET'S CALL THIS ONE *"BUG-EATEN."*

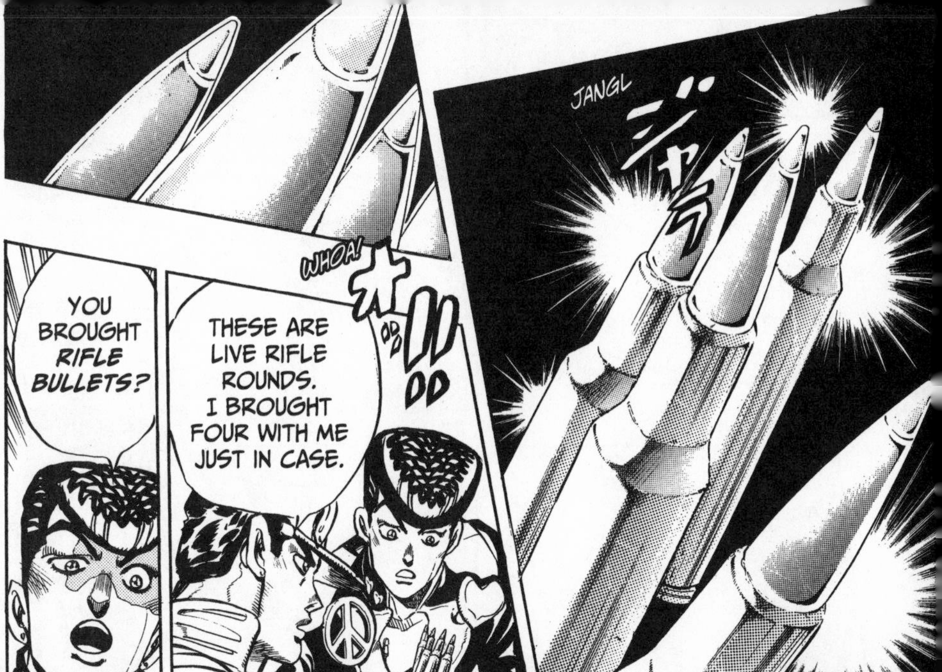
WHOA!
YOU BROUGHT RIFLE BULLETS?
THESE ARE LIVE RIFLE ROUNDS. I BROUGHT FOUR WITH ME JUST IN CASE.
JANGL
THE ROUND BEARINGS SIGNIFICANTLY LOSE ACCURACY AFTER 20 METERS DUE TO AIR RESISTANCE. BUT THESE BULLETS CAN STAY ON TARGET FOR MAYBE 50 TO 70 METERS.
WITH BUG-EATEN ON ITS GUARD, I DON'T IMAGINE THE CREATURE WILL LET US GET ANYWHERE NEAR OUR 20-METER FIRING DISTANCE.

NO MATTER HOW ACCURATE A SHOOTER'S AIM, BULLETS DO NOT FLY IN A STRAIGHT LINE. SKILLED SHARPSHOOTERS TAKE THESE DEVIATIONS INTO ACCOUNT WHEN CALCULATING THEIR SHOTS.

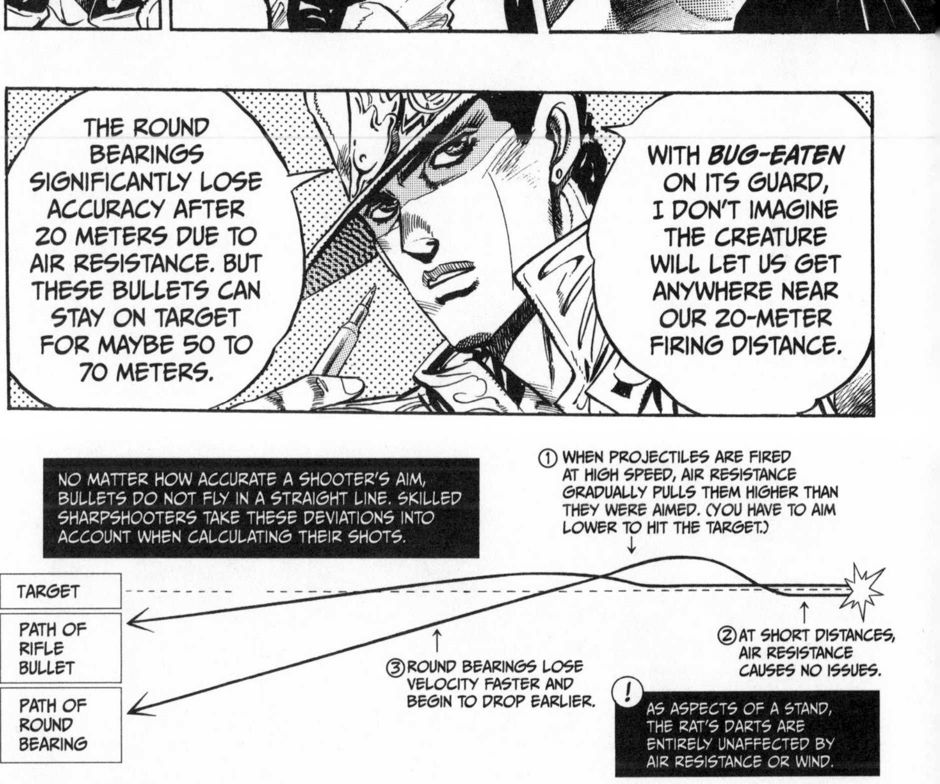
① WHEN PROJECTILES ARE FIRED AT HIGH SPEED, AIR RESISTANCE GRADUALLY PULLS THEM HIGHER THAN THEY WERE AIMED. (YOU HAVE TO AIM LOWER TO HIT THE TARGET.)
TARGET
PATH OF RIFLE BULLET
PATH OF ROUND BEARING
② AT SHORT DISTANCES, AIR RESISTANCE CAUSES NO ISSUES.
③ ROUND BEARINGS LOSE VELOCITY FASTER AND BEGIN TO DROP EARLIER.

!

AS ASPECTS OF A STAND, THE RAT'S DARTS ARE ENTIRELY UNAFFECTED BY AIR RESISTANCE OR WIND.

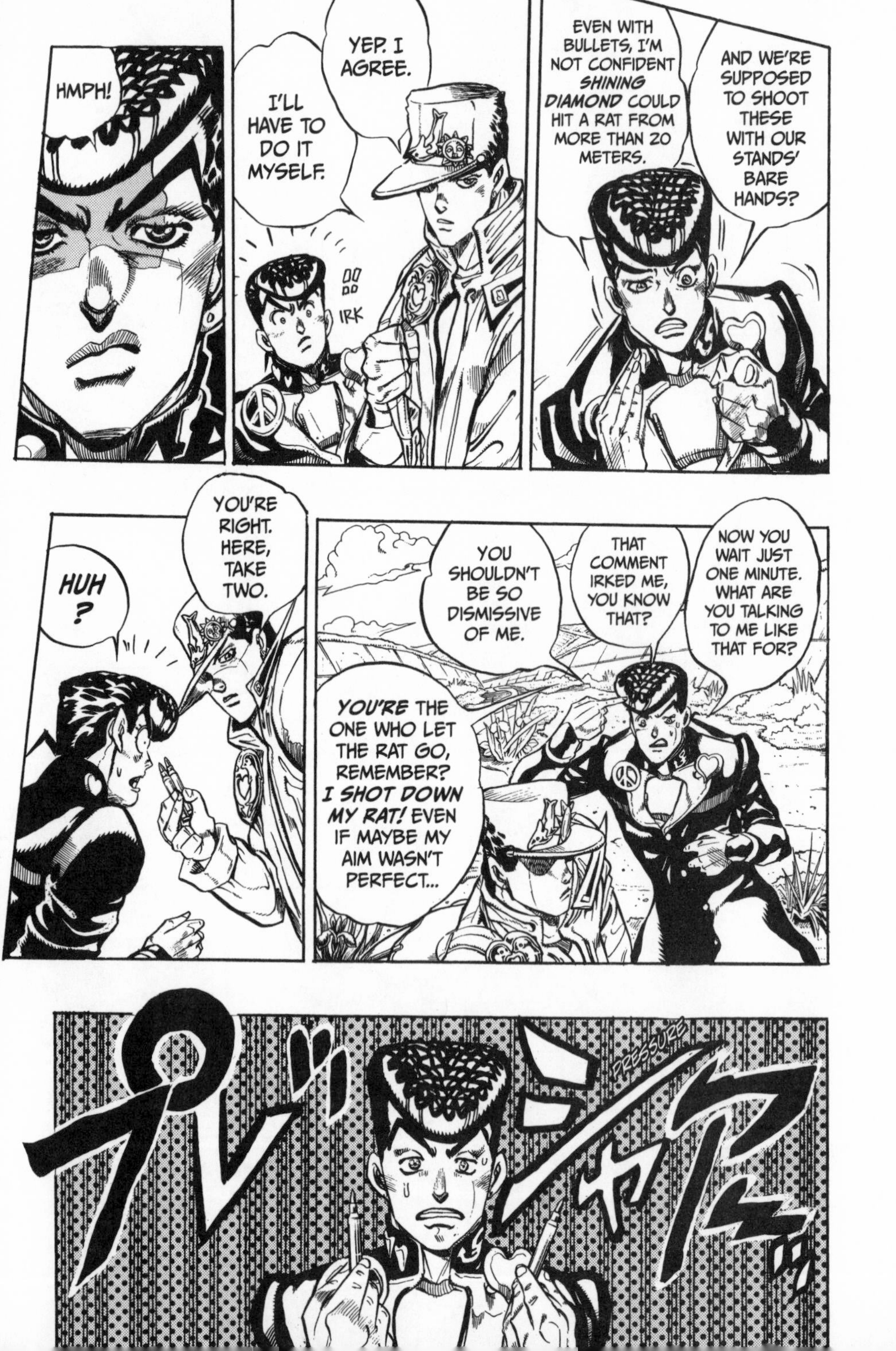
EVEN WITH BULLETS, I'M NOT CONFIDENT SHINING DIAMOND COULD HIT A RAT FROM MORE THAN 20 METERS.
AND WE'RE SUPPOSED TO SHOOT THESE WITH OUR STANDS' BARE HANDS?
YEP. I AGREE.
I'LL HAVE TO DO IT MYSELF.
IRK
HMPH!
NOW YOU WAIT JUST ONE MINUTE. WHAT ARE YOU TALKING TO ME LIKE THAT FOR?
THAT COMMENT IRKED ME, YOU KNOW THAT?
YOU SHOULDN'T BE SO DISMISSIVE OF ME.
YOU'RE THE ONE WHO LET THE RAT GO, REMEMBER? I SHOT DOWN MY RAT! EVEN IF MAYBE MY AIM WASN'T PERFECT...
YOU'RE RIGHT. HERE, TAKE TWO.
HUH?
PRESSURE

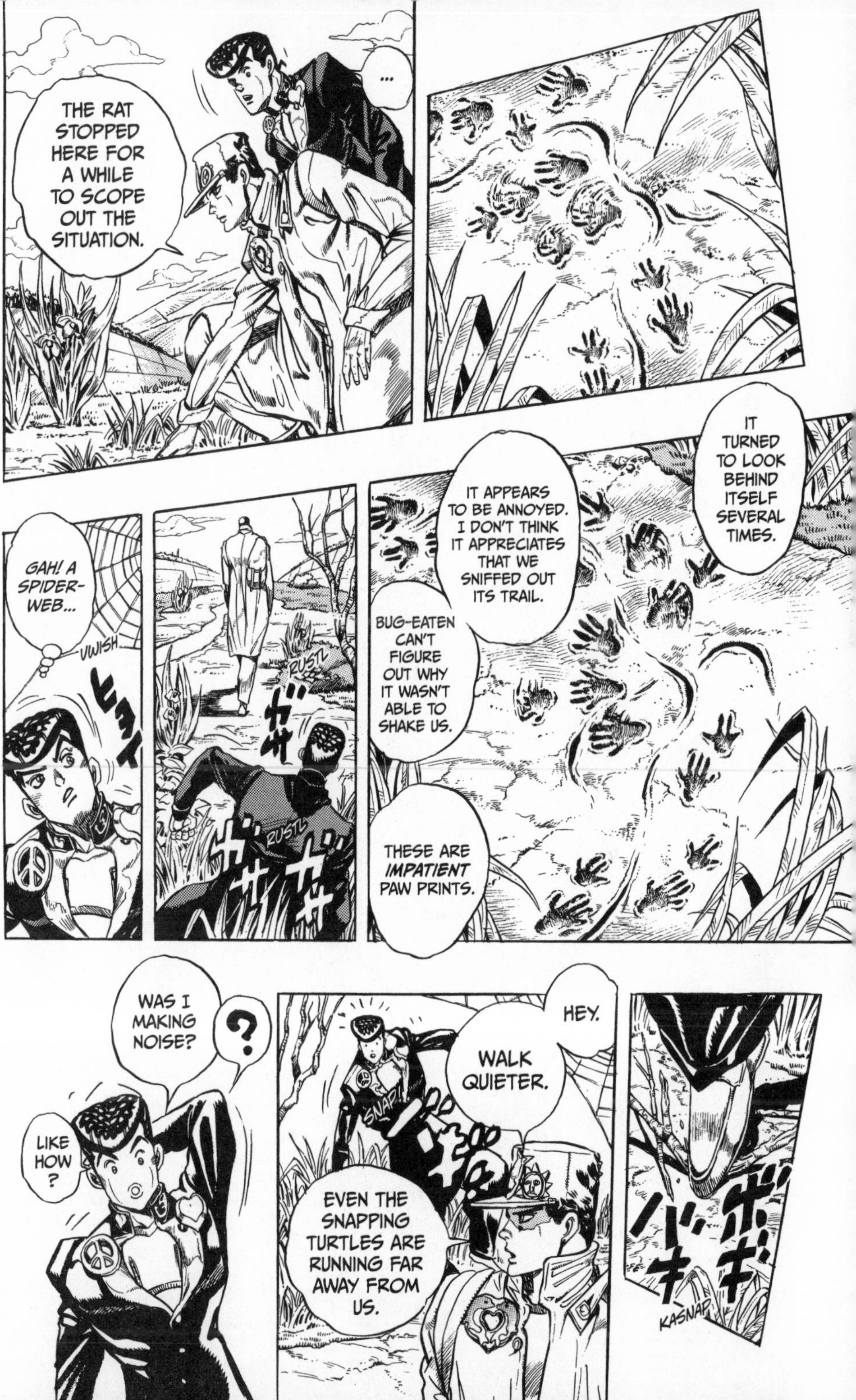
...
THE RAT STOPPED HERE FOR A WHILE TO SCOPE OUT THE SITUATION.
IT TURNED TO LOOK BEHIND ITSELF SEVERAL TIMES.
IT APPEARS TO BE ANNOYED. I DON'T THINK IT APPRECIATES THAT WE SNIFFED OUT ITS TRAIL.
BUG-EATEN CAN'T FIGURE OUT WHY IT WASN'T ABLE TO SHAKE US.
THESE ARE *IMPATIENT* PAW PRINTS.
RUSTL
RUSTL
GAH! A SPIDER-WEB...
VWISH
KASNAP
HEY.
WALK QUIETER.
SNAP!
EVEN THE SNAPPING TURTLES ARE RUNNING FAR AWAY FROM US.
WAS I MAKING NOISE?
?
LIKE HOW?

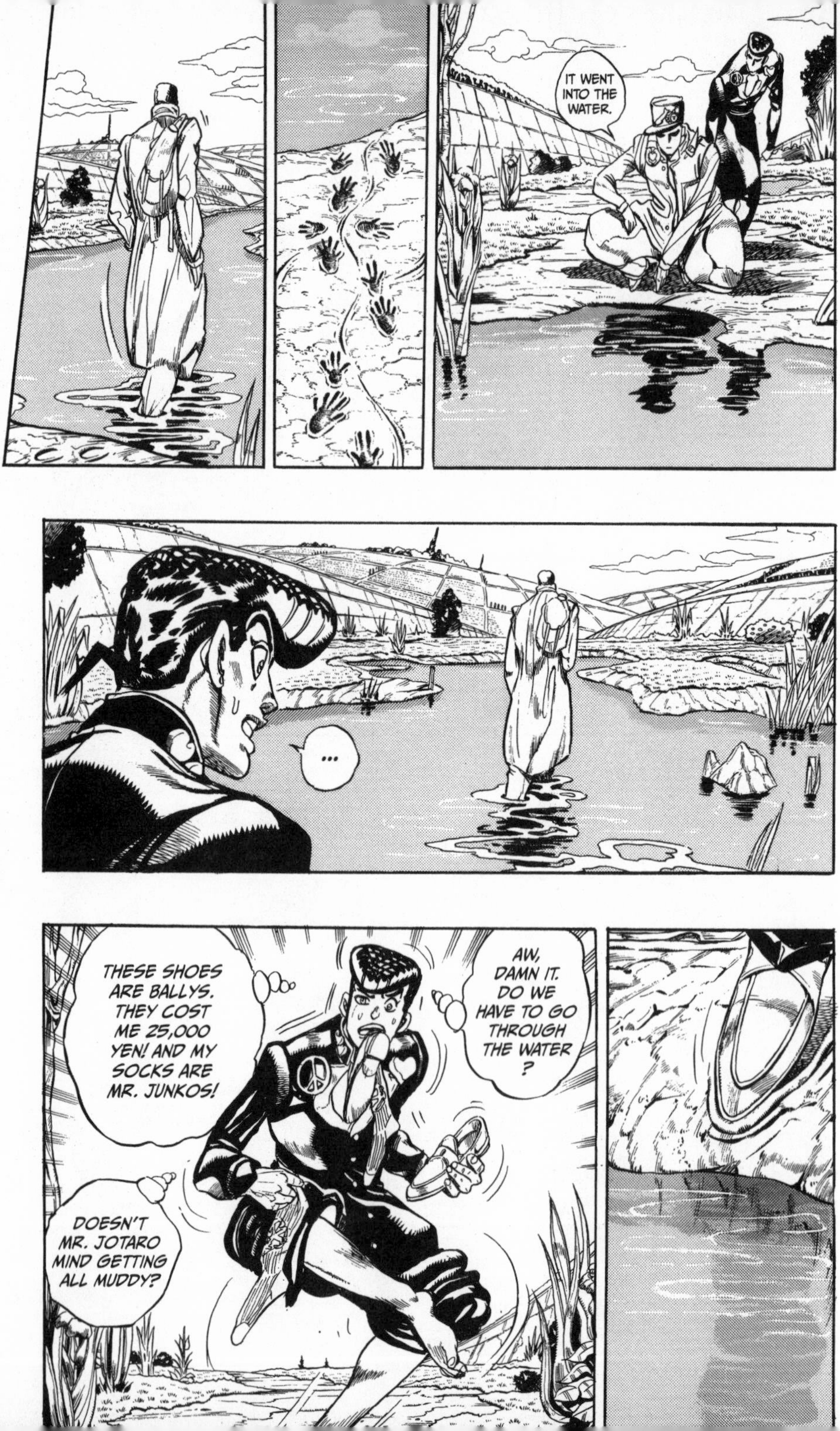
IT WENT INTO THE WATER.
...
AW, DAMN IT. DO WE HAVE TO GO THROUGH THE WATER ?
THESE SHOES ARE BALLYS. THEY COST ME 25,000 YEN! AND MY SOCKS ARE MR. JUNKOS!
DOESN'T MR. JOTARO MIND GETTING ALL MUDDY?

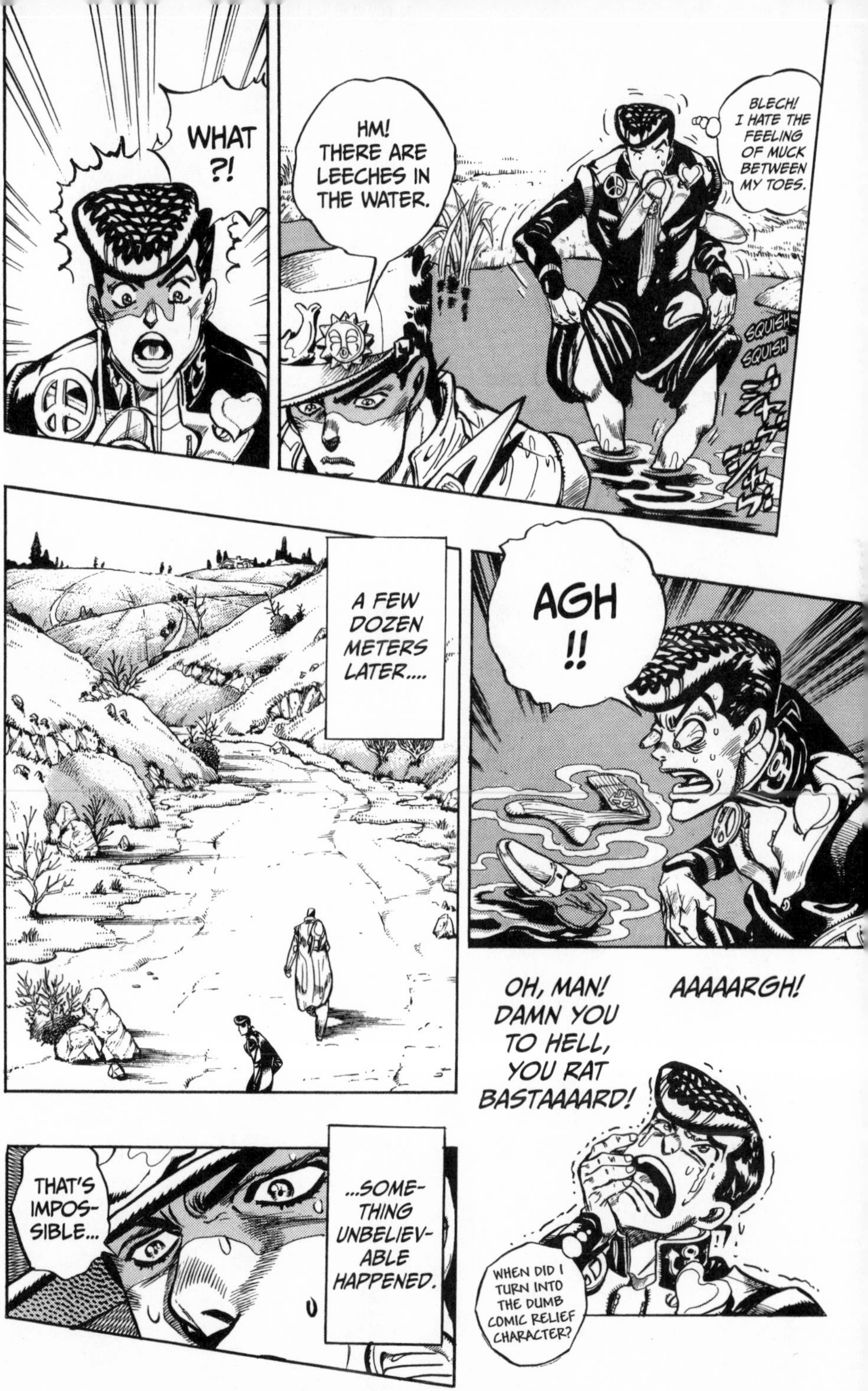
BLECH! I HATE THE FEELING OF MUCK BETWEEN MY TOES.
SQUISH SQUISH
HM! THERE ARE LEECHES IN THE WATER.
WHAT ?!
AGH !!
A FEW DOZEN METERS LATER....
AAAAARGH!
OH, MAN! DAMN YOU TO HELL, YOU RAT BASTAAAARD!
WHEN DID I TURN INTO THE DUMB COMIC RELIEF CHARACTER?
...SOME-THING UNBELIEV-ABLE HAPPENED.
THAT'S IMPOS-SIBLE...

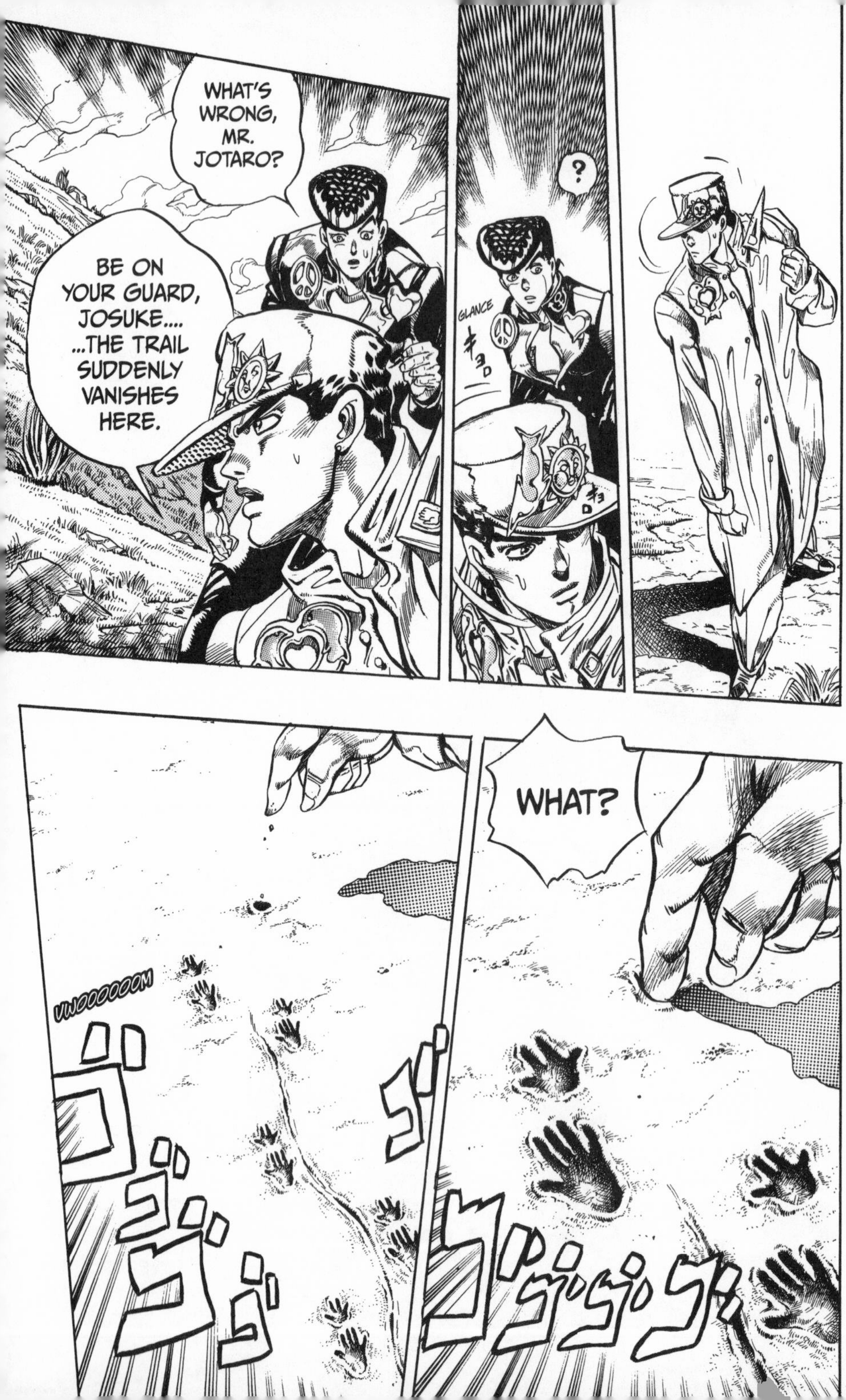
?
GLANCE
WHAT'S WRONG, MR. JOTARO?
BE ON YOUR GUARD, JOSUKE.... ...THE TRAIL SUDDENLY VANISHES HERE.
WHAT?
VWOOOOOOM

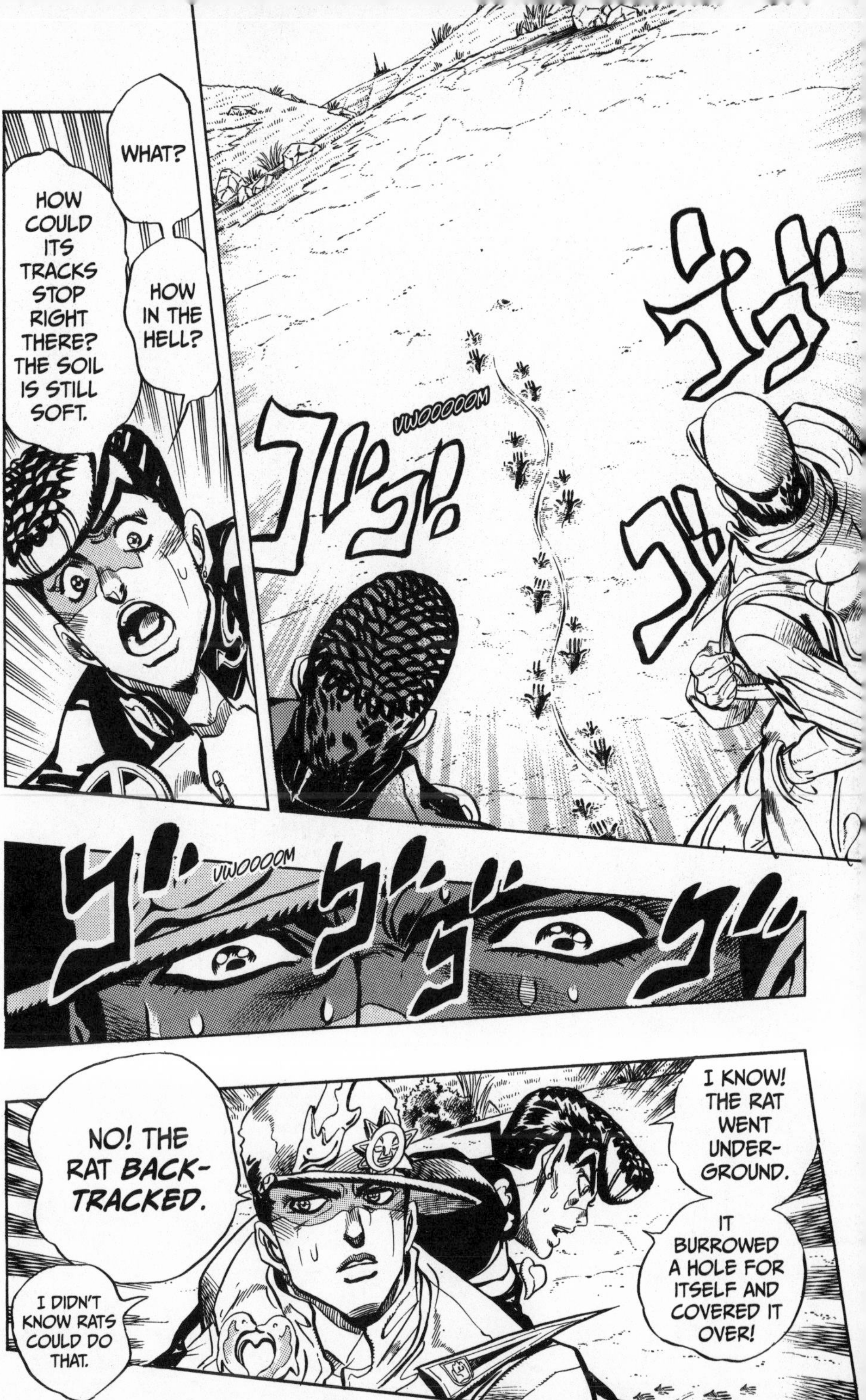
VWOOOOOM
WHAT?
HOW COULD ITS TRACKS STOP RIGHT THERE? THE SOIL IS STILL SOFT.
HOW IN THE HELL?
VWOOOOM
I KNOW! THE RAT WENT UNDER-GROUND.
IT BURROWED A HOLE FOR ITSELF AND COVERED IT OVER!
NO! THE RAT *BACK-TRACKED.*
I DIDN'T KNOW RATS COULD DO THAT.

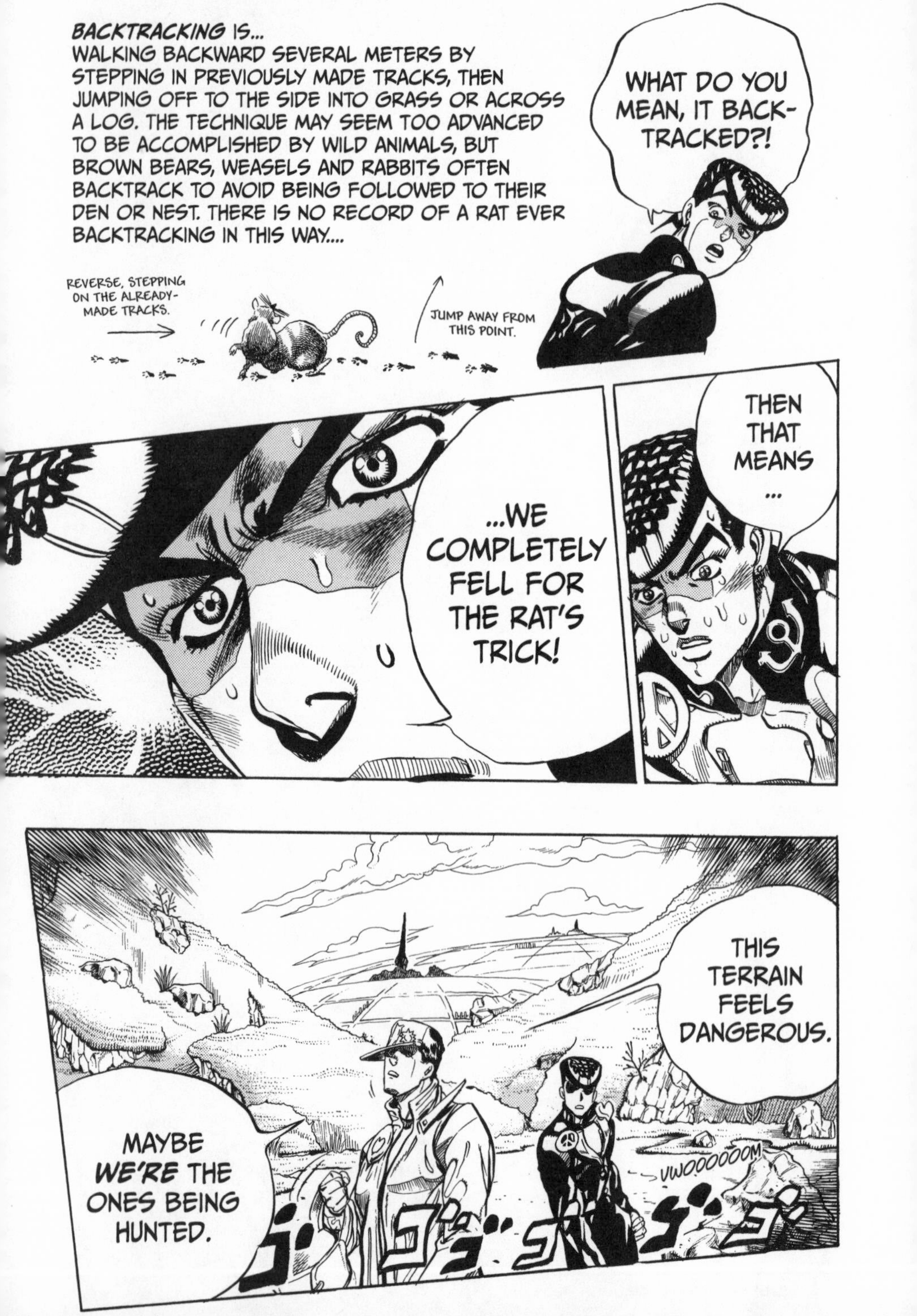
WHAT DO YOU MEAN, IT BACK-TRACKED?!
BACKTRACKING IS...
WALKING BACKWARD SEVERAL METERS BY STEPPING IN PREVIOUSLY MADE TRACKS, THEN JUMPING OFF TO THE SIDE INTO GRASS OR ACROSS A LOG. THE TECHNIQUE MAY SEEM TOO ADVANCED TO BE ACCOMPLISHED BY WILD ANIMALS, BUT BROWN BEARS, WEASELS AND RABBITS OFTEN BACKTRACK TO AVOID BEING FOLLOWED TO THEIR DEN OR NEST. THERE IS NO RECORD OF A RAT EVER BACKTRACKING IN THIS WAY....
JUMP AWAY FROM THIS POINT.
REVERSE, STEPPING ON THE ALREADY-MADE TRACKS.
THEN THAT MEANS ...
...WE COMPLETELY FELL FOR THE RAT'S TRICK!
THIS TERRAIN FEELS DANGEROUS.
VWOOOOOOM
MAYBE *WE'RE* THE ONES BEING HUNTED.

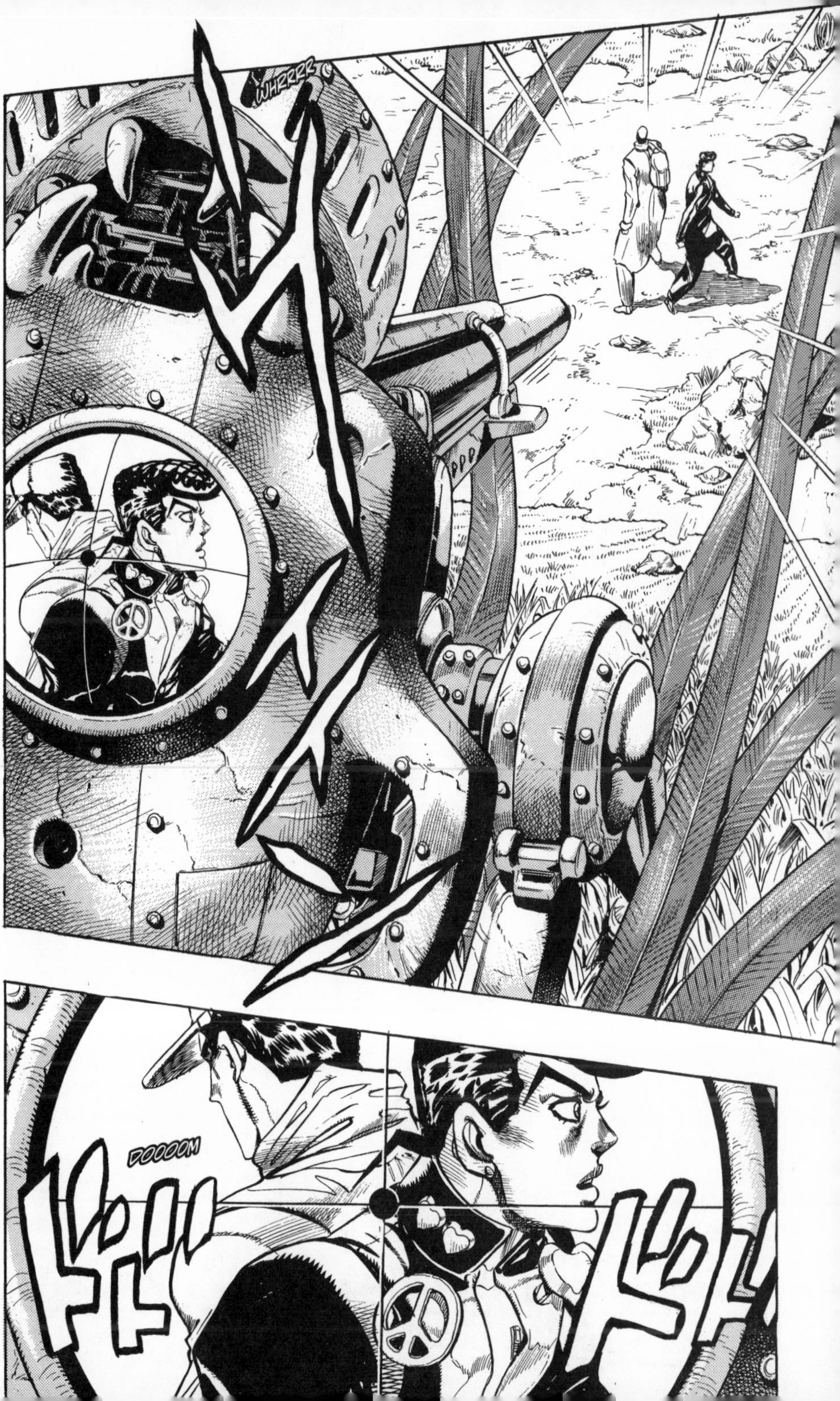
WHRRRR
DOOOOM

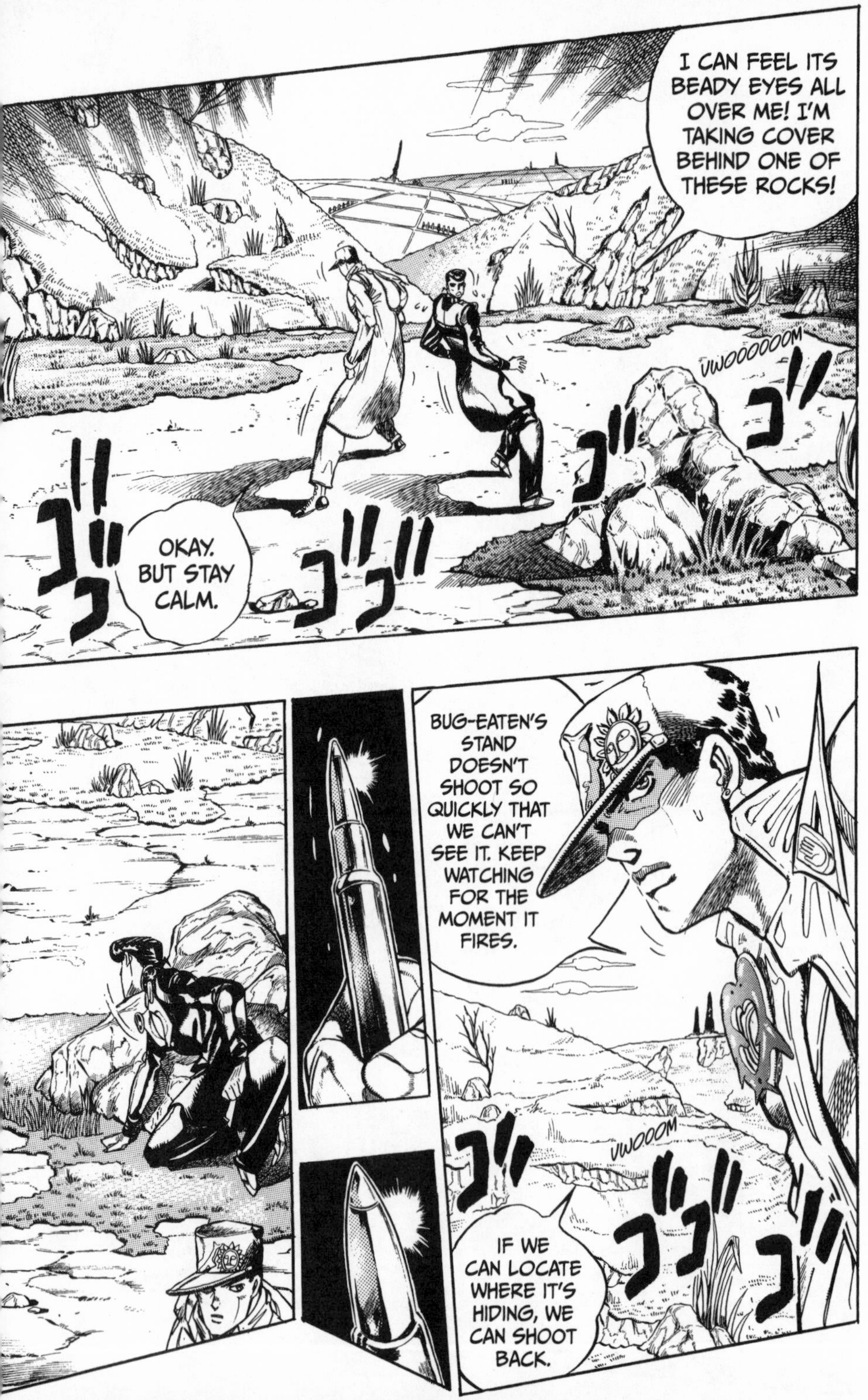
I CAN FEEL ITS BEADY EYES ALL OVER ME! I'M TAKING COVER BEHIND ONE OF THESE ROCKS!
VWOOOOOOM
OKAY. BUT STAY CALM.
BUG-EATEN'S STAND DOESN'T SHOOT SO QUICKLY THAT WE CAN'T SEE IT. KEEP WATCHING FOR THE MOMENT IT FIRES.
VWOOOM
IF WE CAN LOCATE WHERE IT'S HIDING, WE CAN SHOOT BACK.

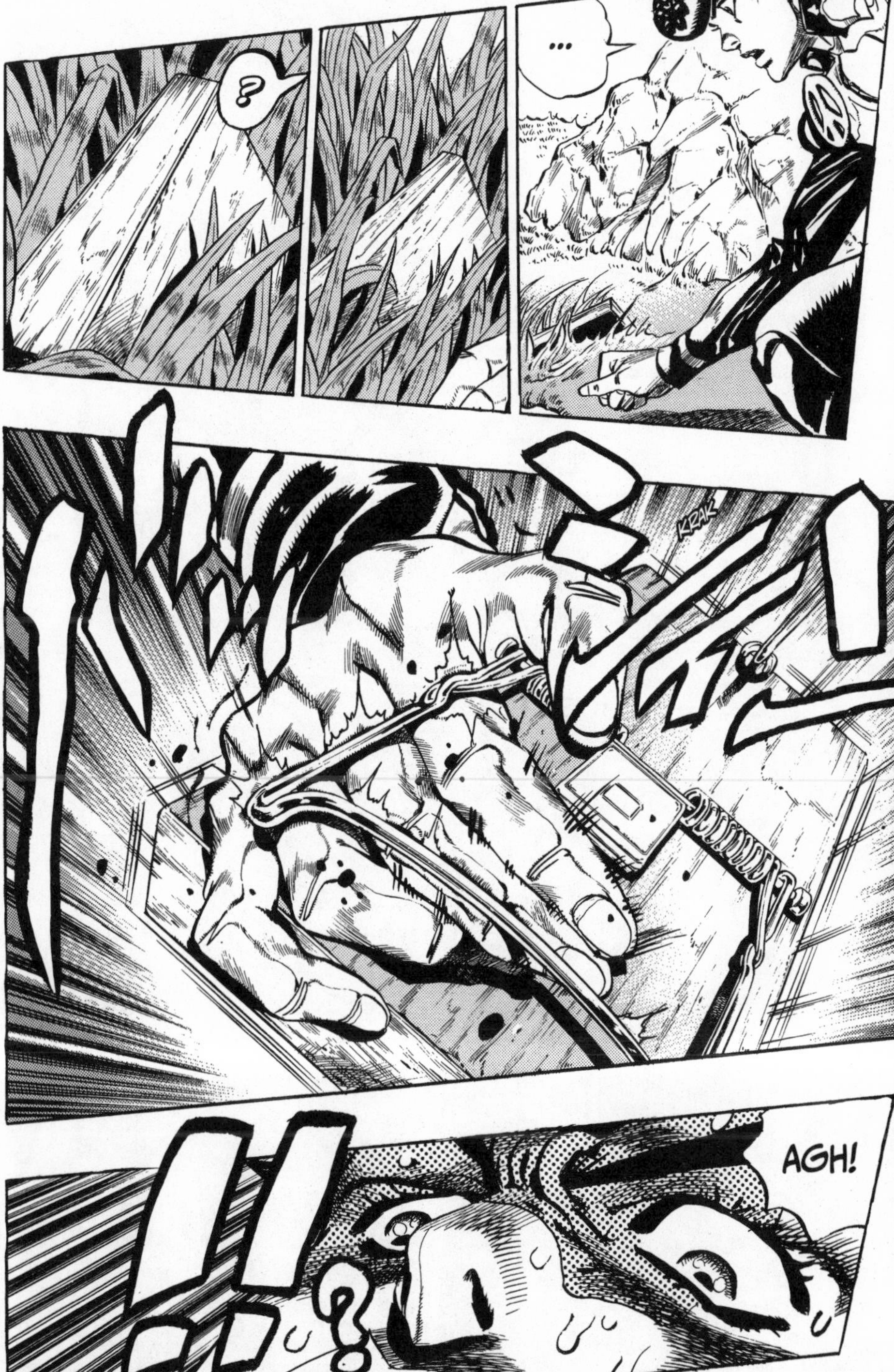
...
?
KRAK
AGH!

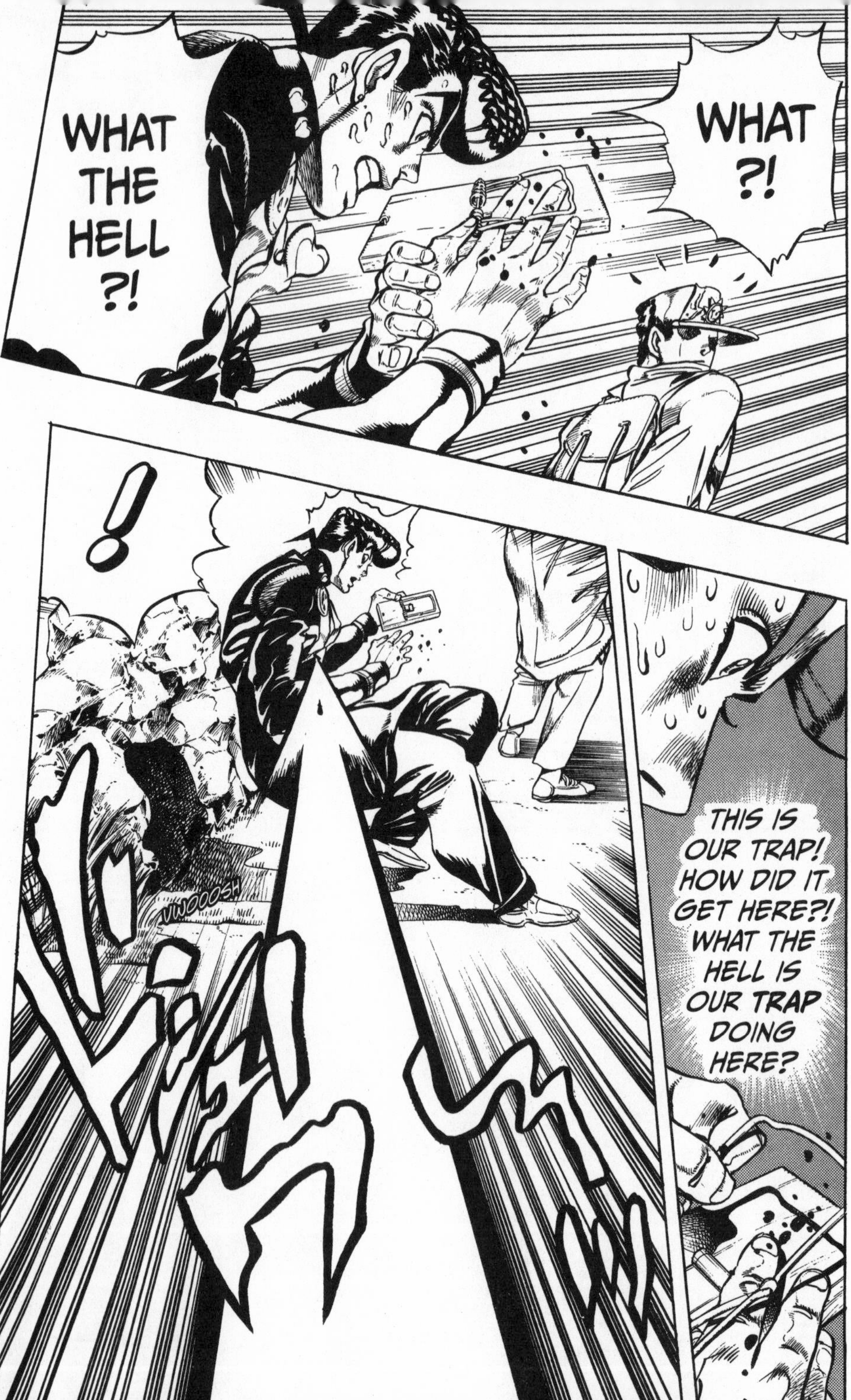
WHAT ?!
WHAT THE HELL ?!
THIS IS OUR TRAP! HOW DID IT GET HERE?! WHAT THE HELL IS OUR TRAP DOING HERE?
!
VWOOOSH

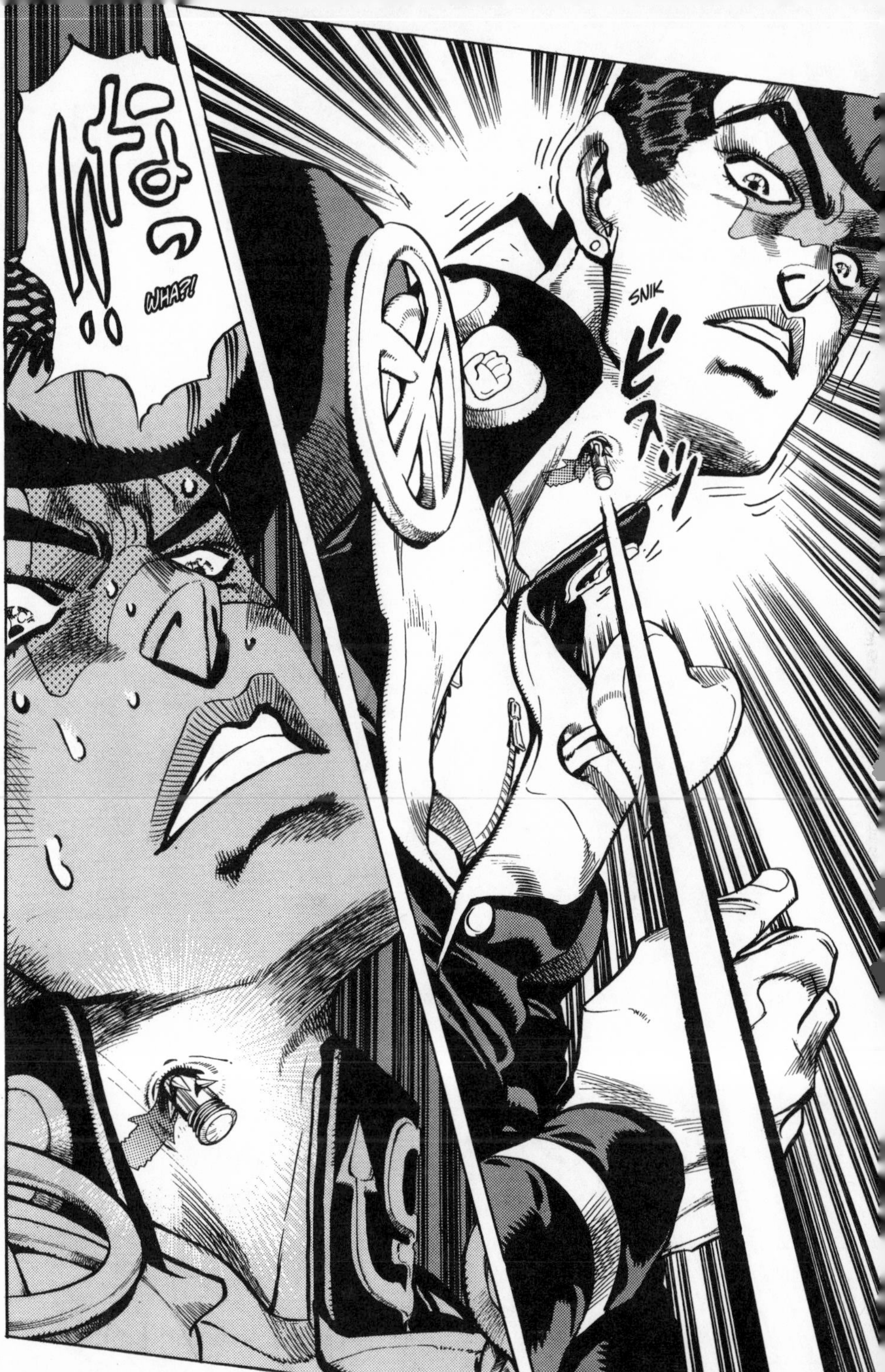
SNIK
ドスッ
なっ!!
WHA?!

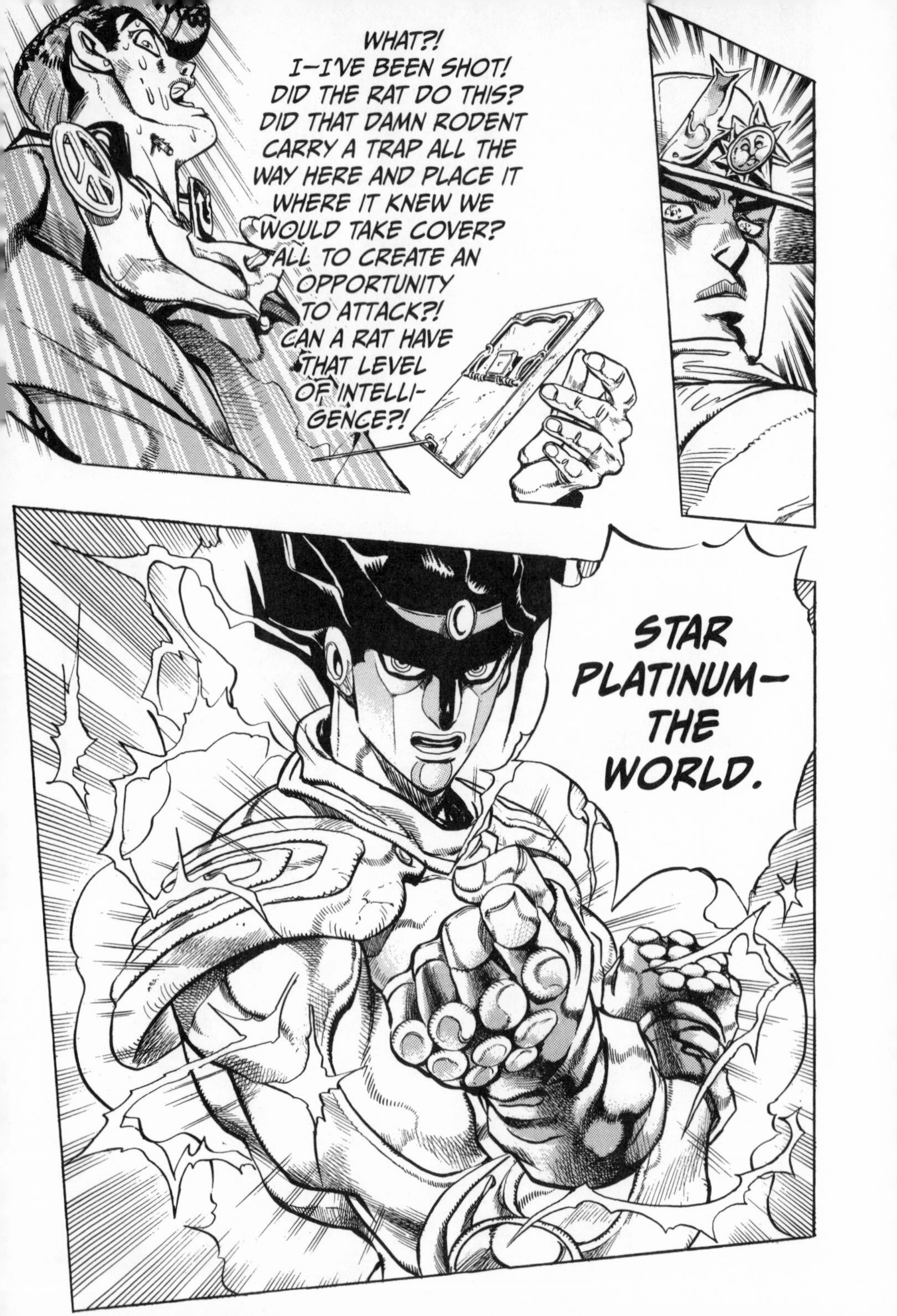
WHAT?! I-I'VE BEEN SHOT! DID THE RAT DO THIS? DID THAT DAMN RODENT CARRY A TRAP ALL THE WAY HERE AND PLACE IT WHERE IT KNEW WE WOULD TAKE COVER? ALL TO CREATE AN OPPORTUNITY TO ATTACK?! CAN A RAT HAVE THAT LEVEL OF INTELLI-GENCE?!
STAR PLATINUM-THE WORLD.

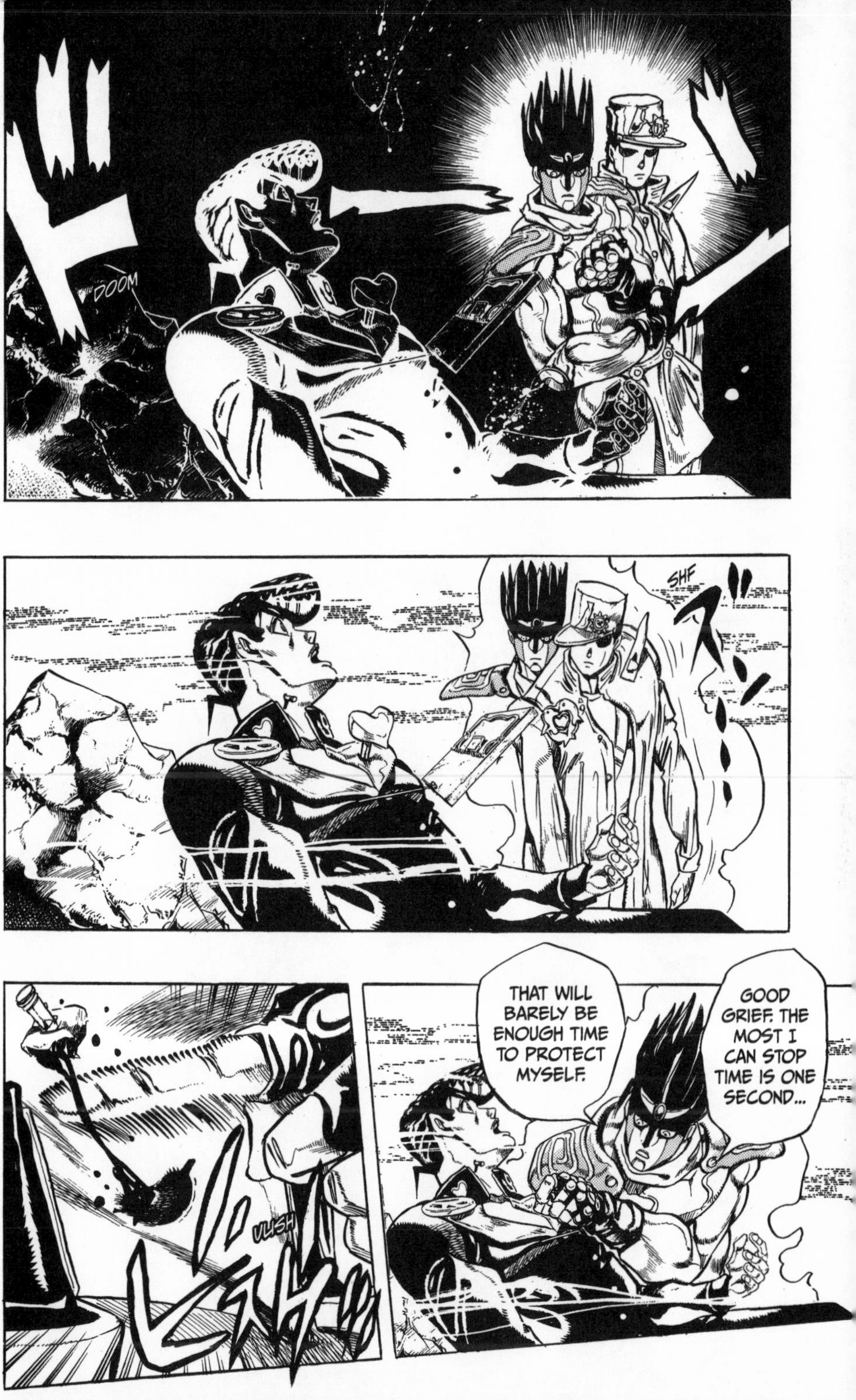
DOOM
SHF
GOOD GRIEF. THE MOST I CAN STOP TIME IS ONE SECOND...
THAT WILL BARELY BE ENOUGH TIME TO PROTECT MYSELF.
VLISH

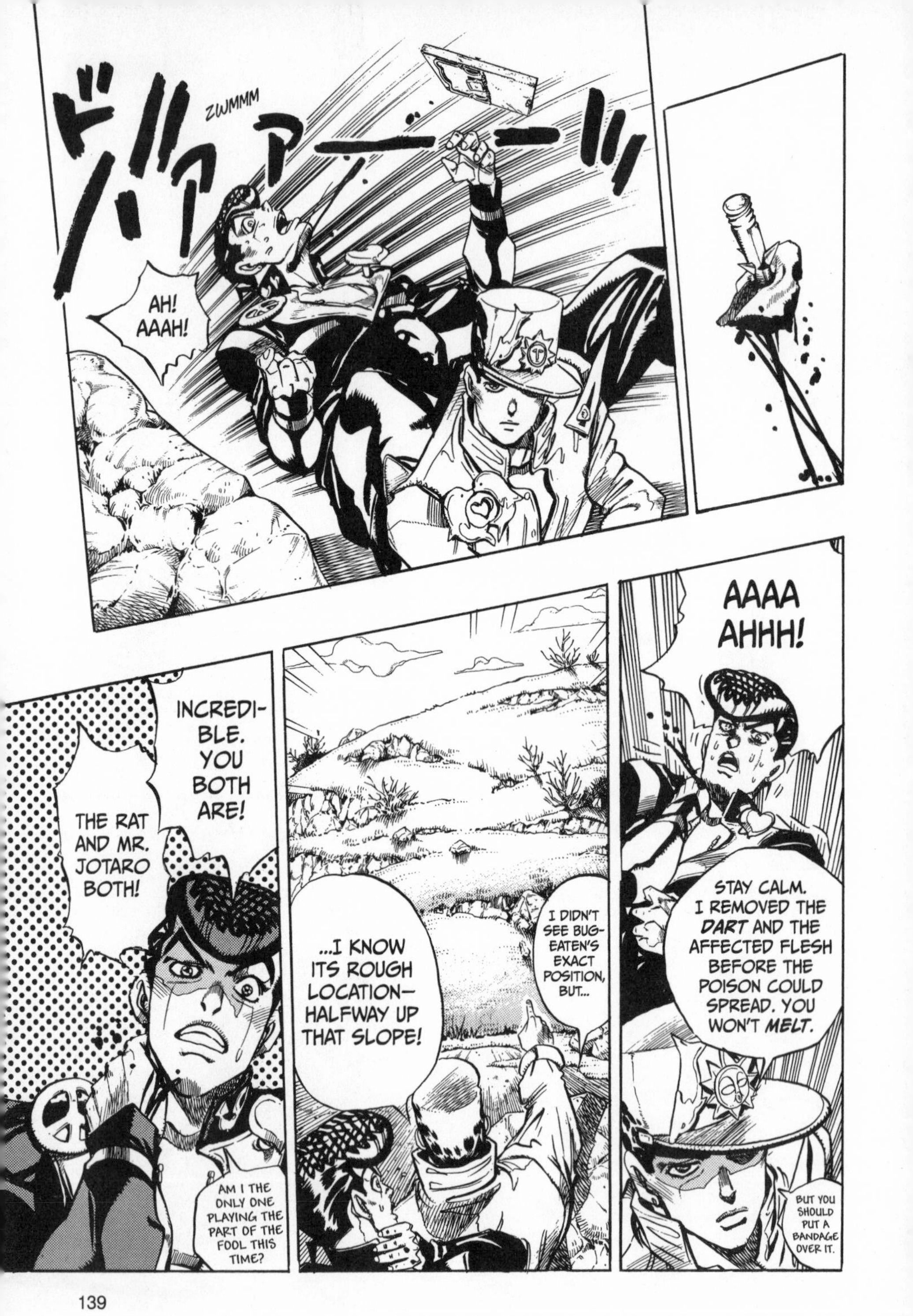
ZWMMM
ドバアアーーッ
AH! AAAH!
AAAA AHHH!
STAY CALM. I REMOVED THE DART AND THE AFFECTED FLESH BEFORE THE POISON COULD SPREAD. YOU WON'T MELT.
BUT YOU SHOULD PUT A BANDAGE OVER IT.
I DIDN'T SEE BUG-EATEN'S EXACT POSITION, BUT...
...I KNOW ITS ROUGH LOCATION— HALFWAY UP THAT SLOPE!
INCREDIBLE. YOU BOTH ARE!
THE RAT AND MR. JOTARO BOTH!
AM I THE ONLY ONE PLAYING THE PART OF THE FOOL THIS TIME?

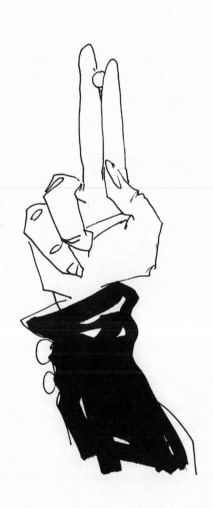

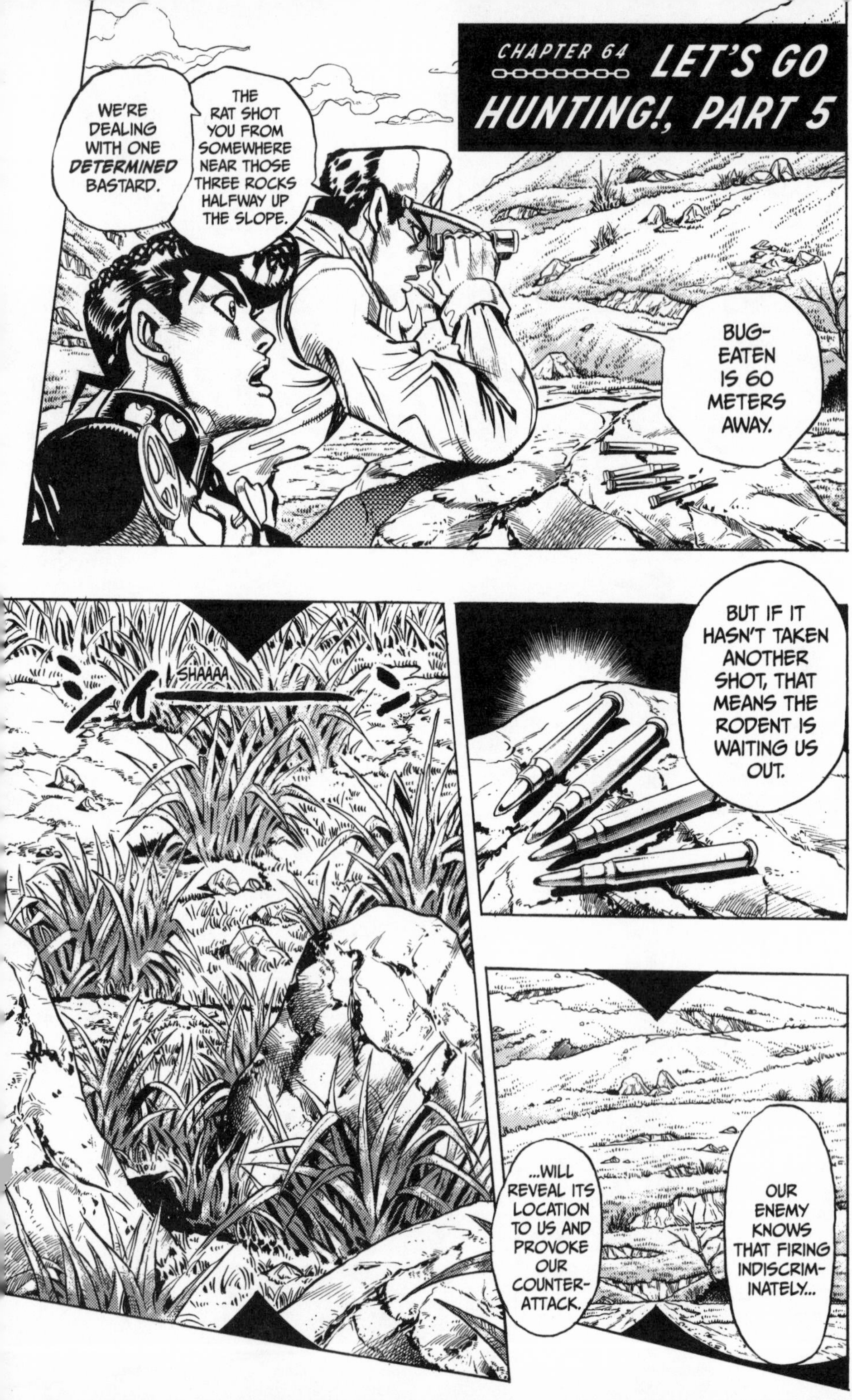
CHAPTER 64
LET'S GO HUNTING!, PART 5
BUG-EATEN IS 60 METERS AWAY.
THE RAT SHOT YOU FROM SOMEWHERE NEAR THOSE THREE ROCKS HALFWAY UP THE SLOPE.
WE'RE DEALING WITH ONE *DETERMINED* BASTARD.
BUT IF IT HASN'T TAKEN ANOTHER SHOT, THAT MEANS THE RODENT IS WAITING US OUT.
OUR ENEMY KNOWS THAT FIRING INDISCRIM-INATELY...
...WILL REVEAL ITS LOCATION TO US AND PROVOKE OUR COUNTER-ATTACK.
SHAAAA

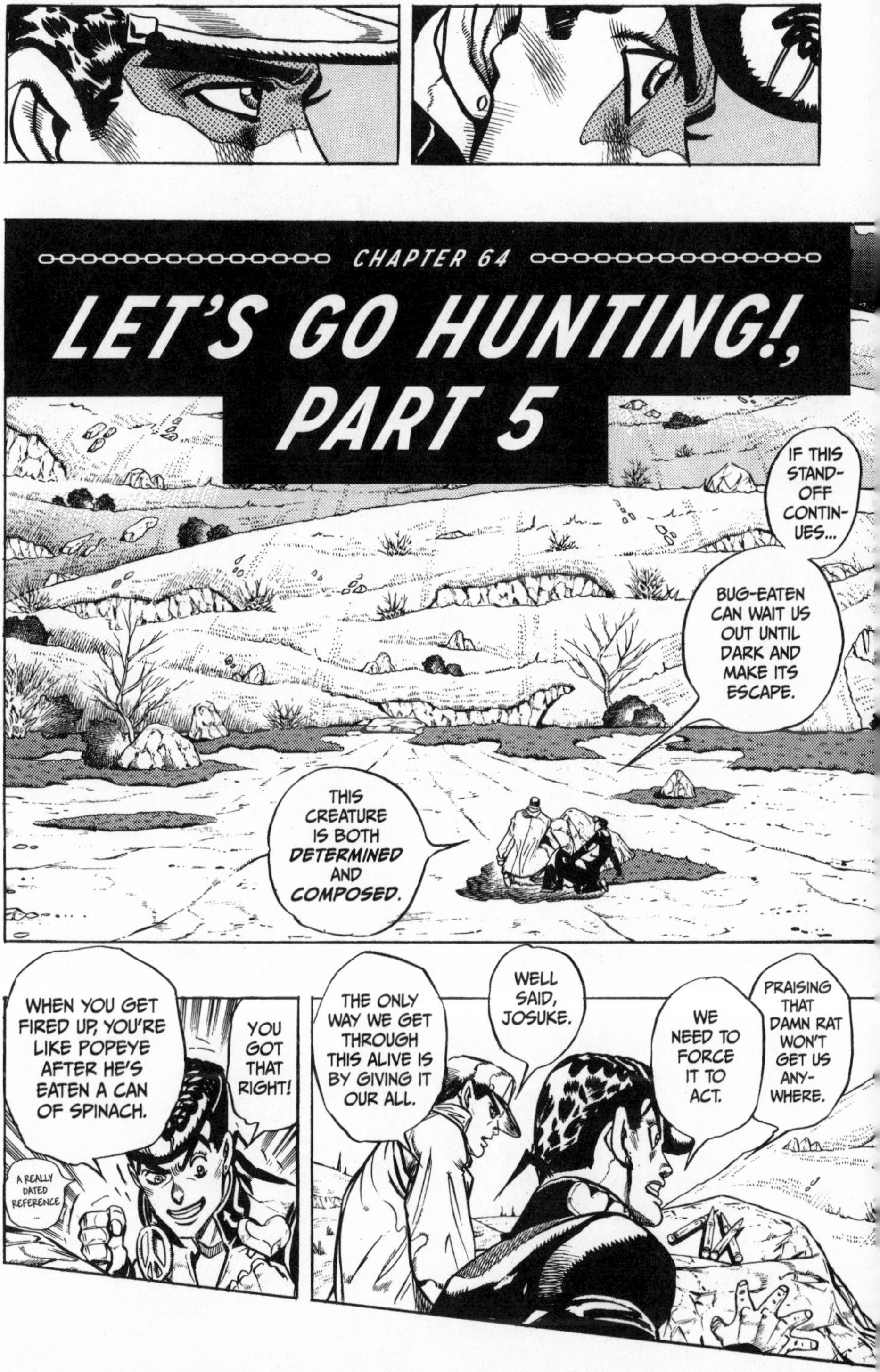
CHAPTER 64
LET'S GO HUNTING!, PART 5
IF THIS STAND-OFF CONTINUES...
BUG-EATEN CAN WAIT US OUT UNTIL DARK AND MAKE ITS ESCAPE.
THIS CREATURE IS BOTH DETERMINED AND COMPOSED.
PRAISING THAT DAMN RAT WON'T GET US ANYWHERE.
WE NEED TO FORCE IT TO ACT.
WELL SAID, JOSUKE.
THE ONLY WAY WE GET THROUGH THIS ALIVE IS BY GIVING IT OUR ALL.
YOU GOT THAT RIGHT!
WHEN YOU GET FIRED UP, YOU'RE LIKE POPEYE AFTER HE'S EATEN A CAN OF SPINACH.
A REALLY DATED REFERENCE...

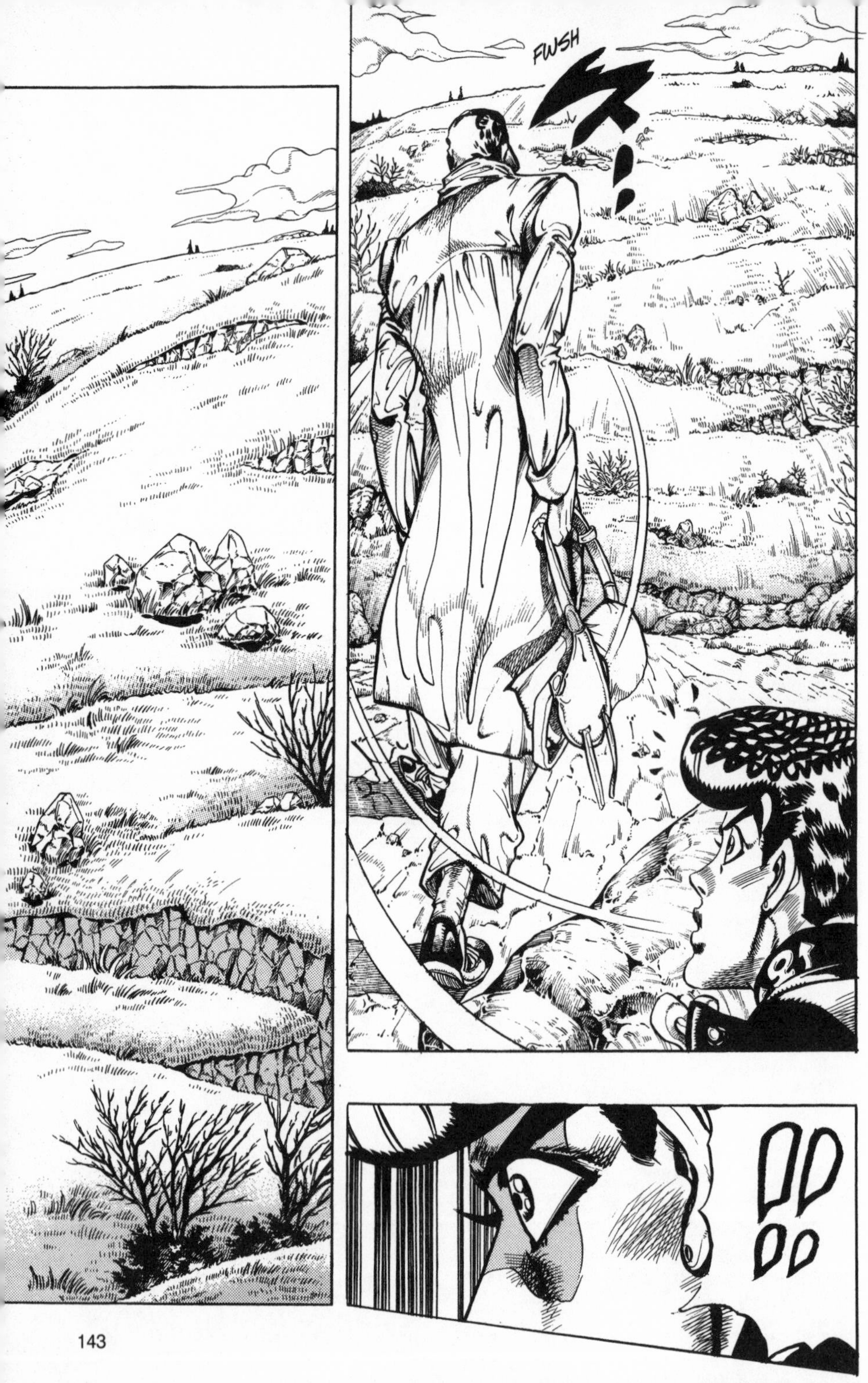
FWSH

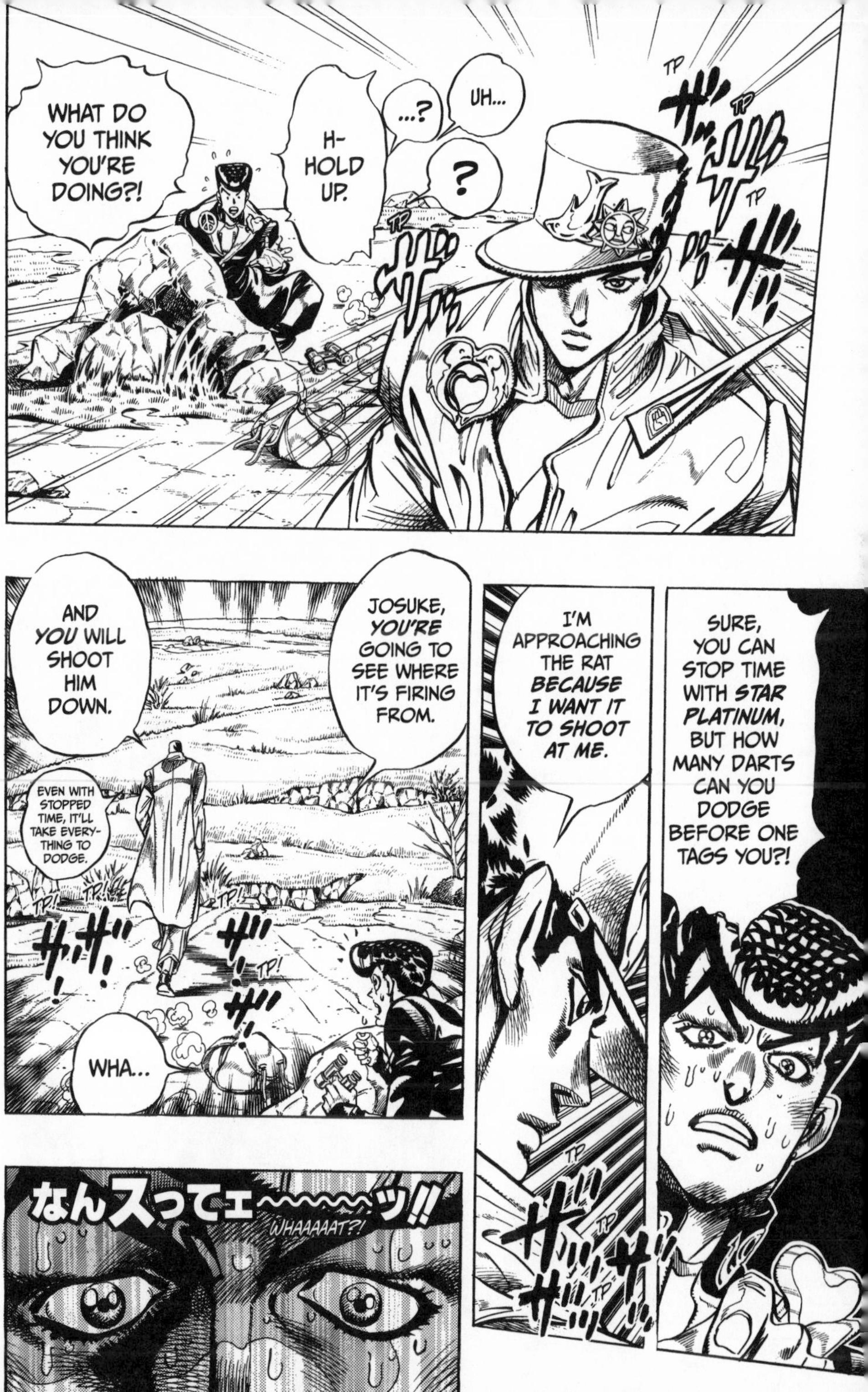

TP
UH...
?
...?
TP
H-
HOLD
UP.
WHAT DO YOU THINK YOU'RE DOING?!
SURE, YOU CAN STOP TIME WITH STAR PLATINUM, BUT HOW MANY DARTS CAN YOU DODGE BEFORE ONE TAGS YOU?!
I'M APPROACHING THE RAT BECAUSE I WANT IT TO SHOOT AT ME.
TP
TP
TP
JOSUKE, YOU'RE GOING TO SEE WHERE IT'S FIRING FROM.
AND YOU WILL SHOOT HIM DOWN.
EVEN WITH STOPPED TIME, IT'LL TAKE EVERY-THING TO DODGE.
TP!
TP!
TP!
TP!
WHA...
なんスってェ〜〜〜〜ッ!!
WHAAAAAT?!

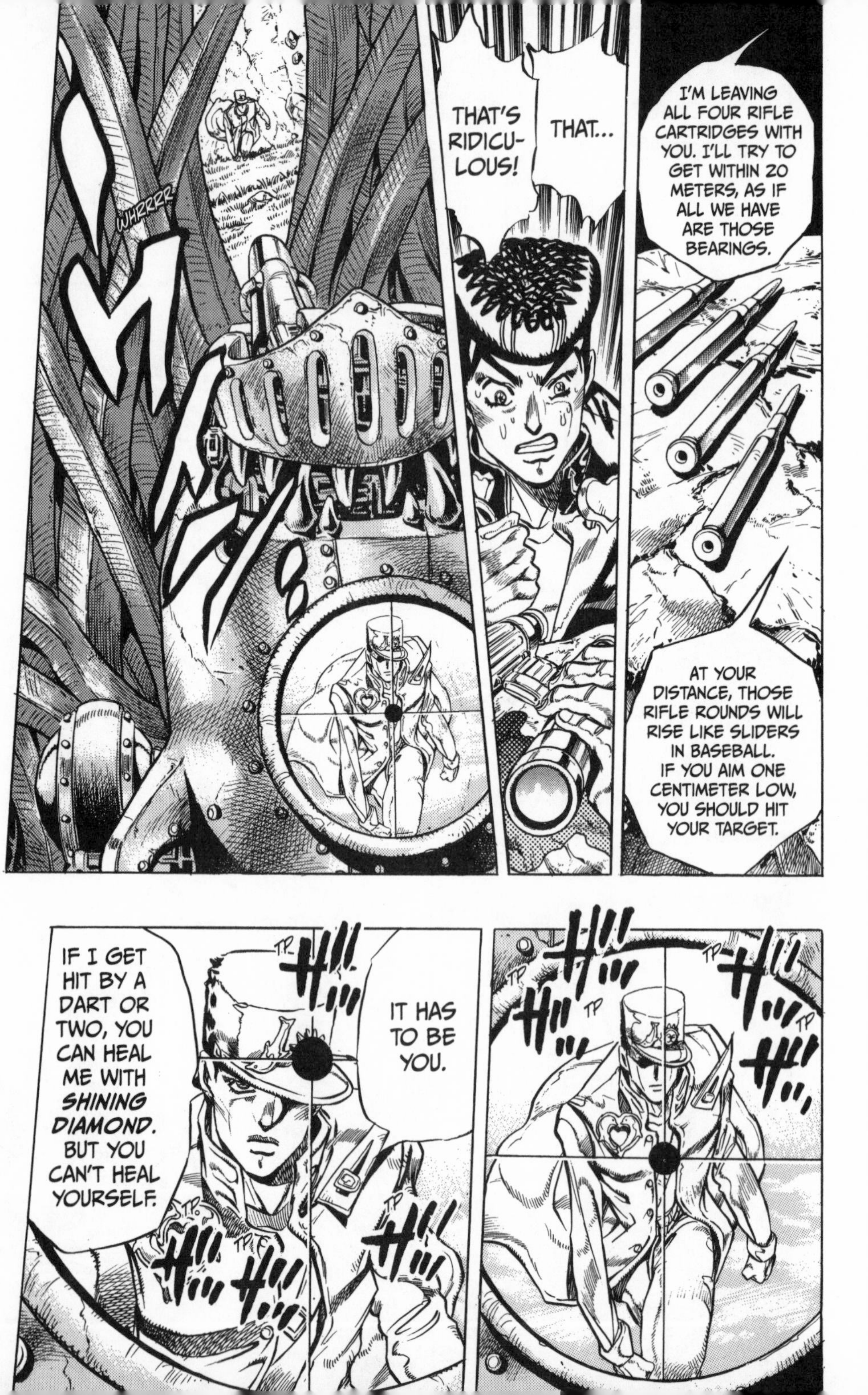
I'M LEAVING ALL FOUR RIFLE CARTRIDGES WITH YOU. I'LL TRY TO GET WITHIN 20 METERS, AS IF ALL WE HAVE ARE THOSE BEARINGS.
AT YOUR DISTANCE, THOSE RIFLE ROUNDS WILL RISE LIKE SLIDERS IN BASEBALL. IF YOU AIM ONE CENTIMETER LOW, YOU SHOULD HIT YOUR TARGET.
THAT...
THAT'S RIDICULOUS!
WHRRRR
TP
IT HAS TO BE YOU.
IF I GET HIT BY A DART OR TWO, YOU CAN HEAL ME WITH *SHINING DIAMOND*. BUT YOU CAN'T HEAL YOURSELF.
TP

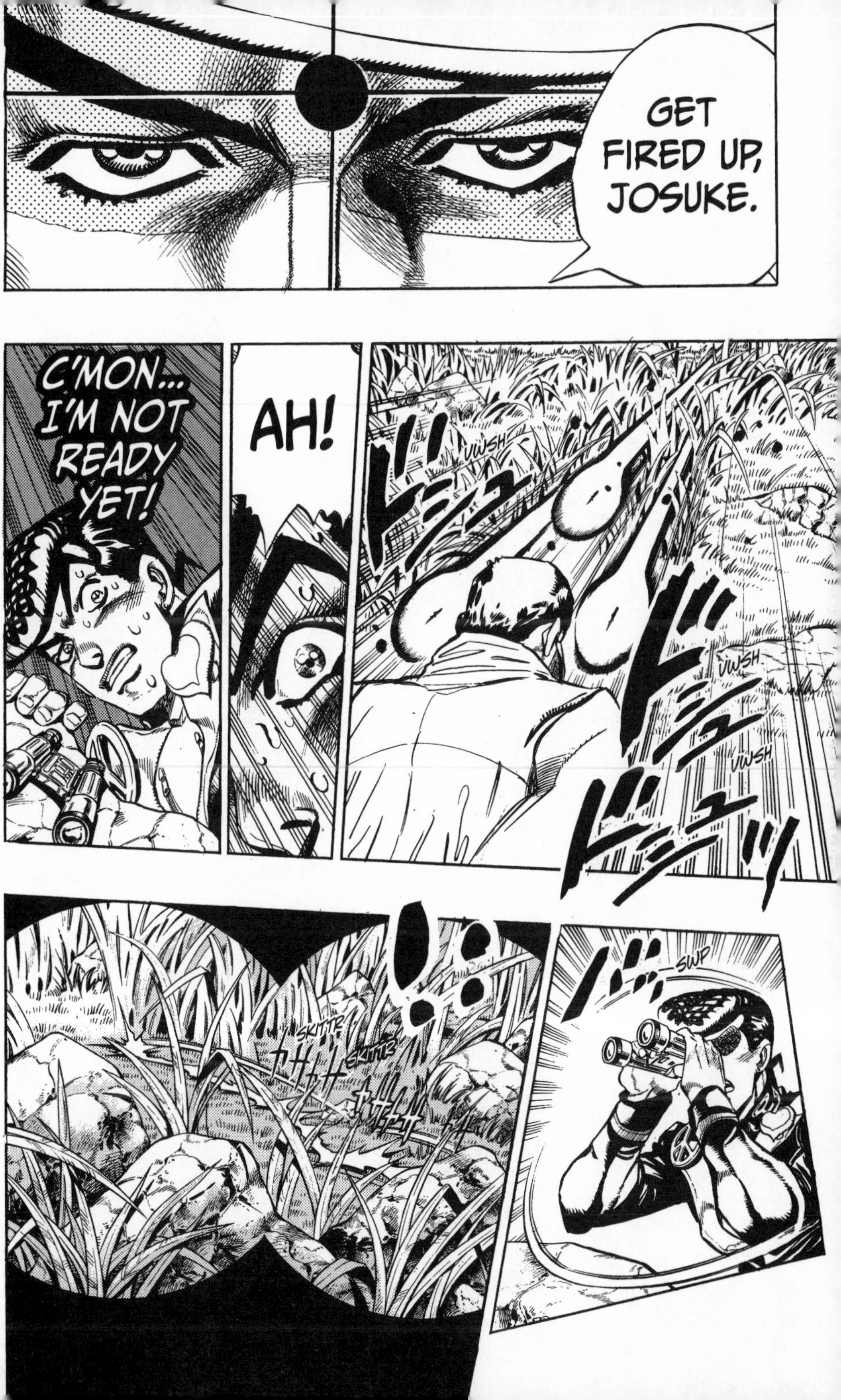
GET FIRED UP, JOSUKE.
VWSH
VWSH
VWSH
AH!
C'MON... I'M NOT READY YET!
SWP
SKITTR
SKITTR

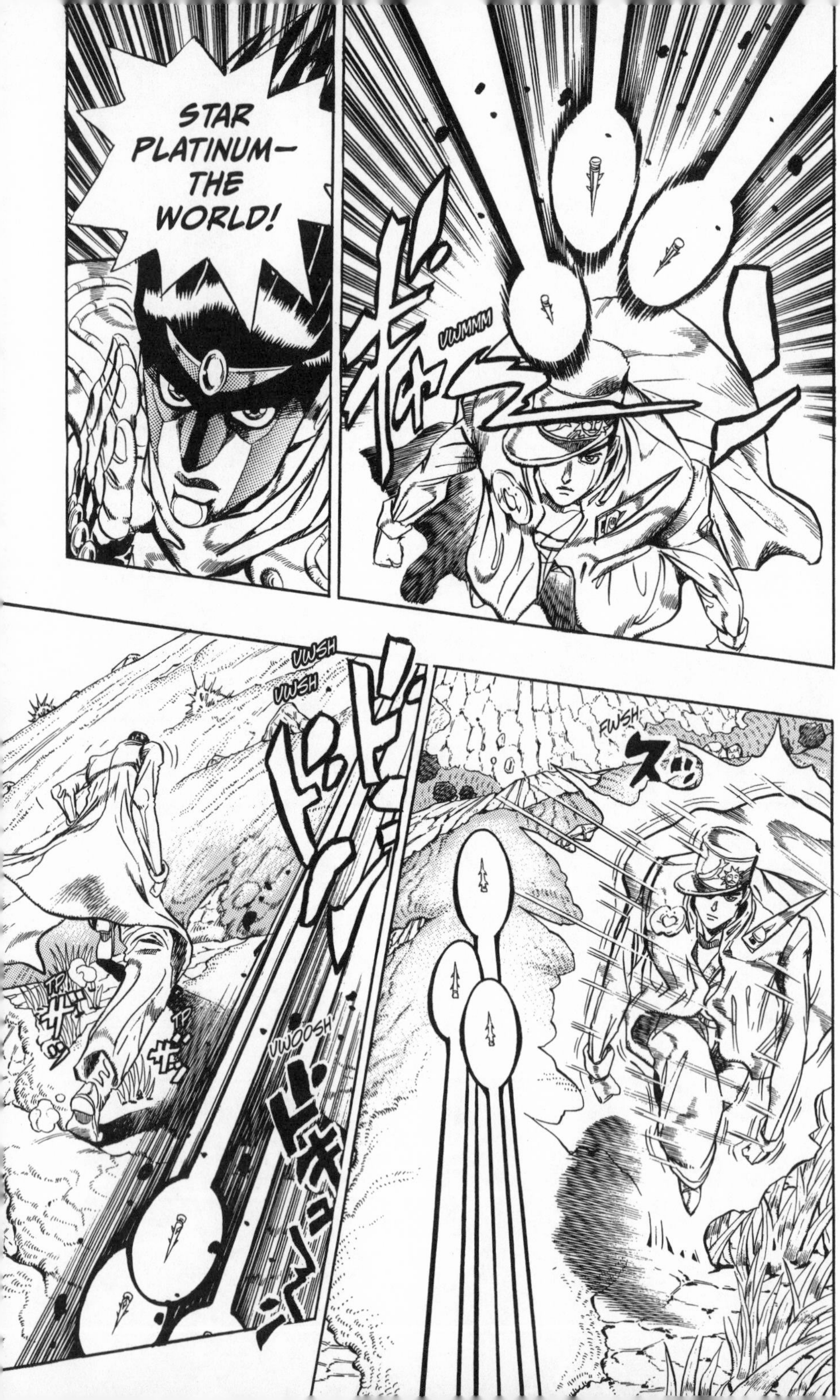
VWMMM
STAR PLATINUM—THE WORLD!
FWSH
VWSH
VWSH
TP
TP
VWOOSH

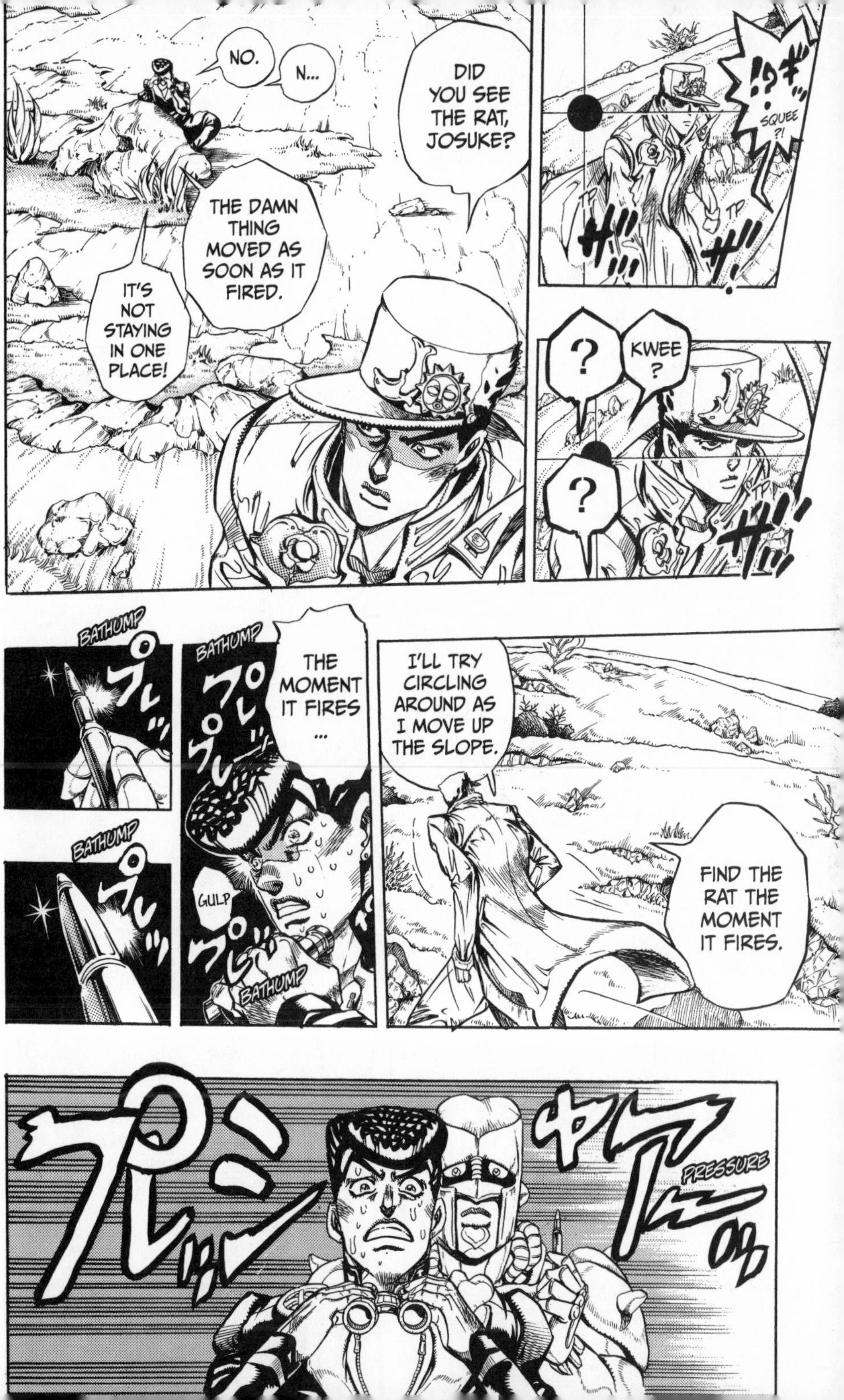
SQUEE ?!
TP
TP
?
KWEE ?
?
TP
DID YOU SEE THE RAT, JOSUKE?
N...
NO.
THE DAMN THING MOVED AS SOON AS IT FIRED.
IT'S NOT STAYING IN ONE PLACE!
I'LL TRY CIRCLING AROUND AS I MOVE UP THE SLOPE.
FIND THE RAT THE MOMENT IT FIRES.
THE MOMENT IT FIRES ...
BATHUMP
GULP
BATHUMP
BATHUMP
BATHUMP
PRESSURE

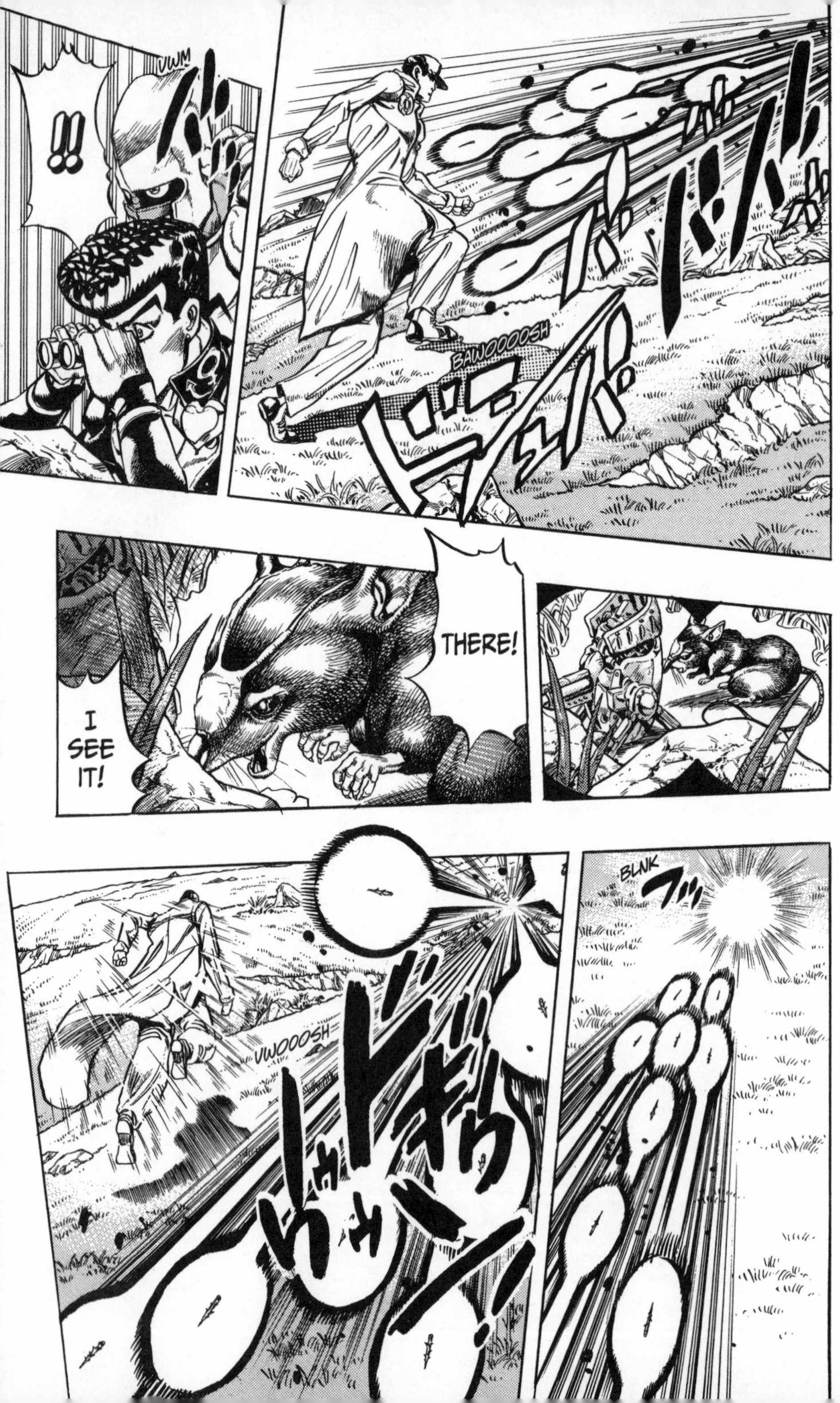
BAWOOOOSH
VWM
!!
THERE!
I SEE IT!
BLNK
VWOOOSH

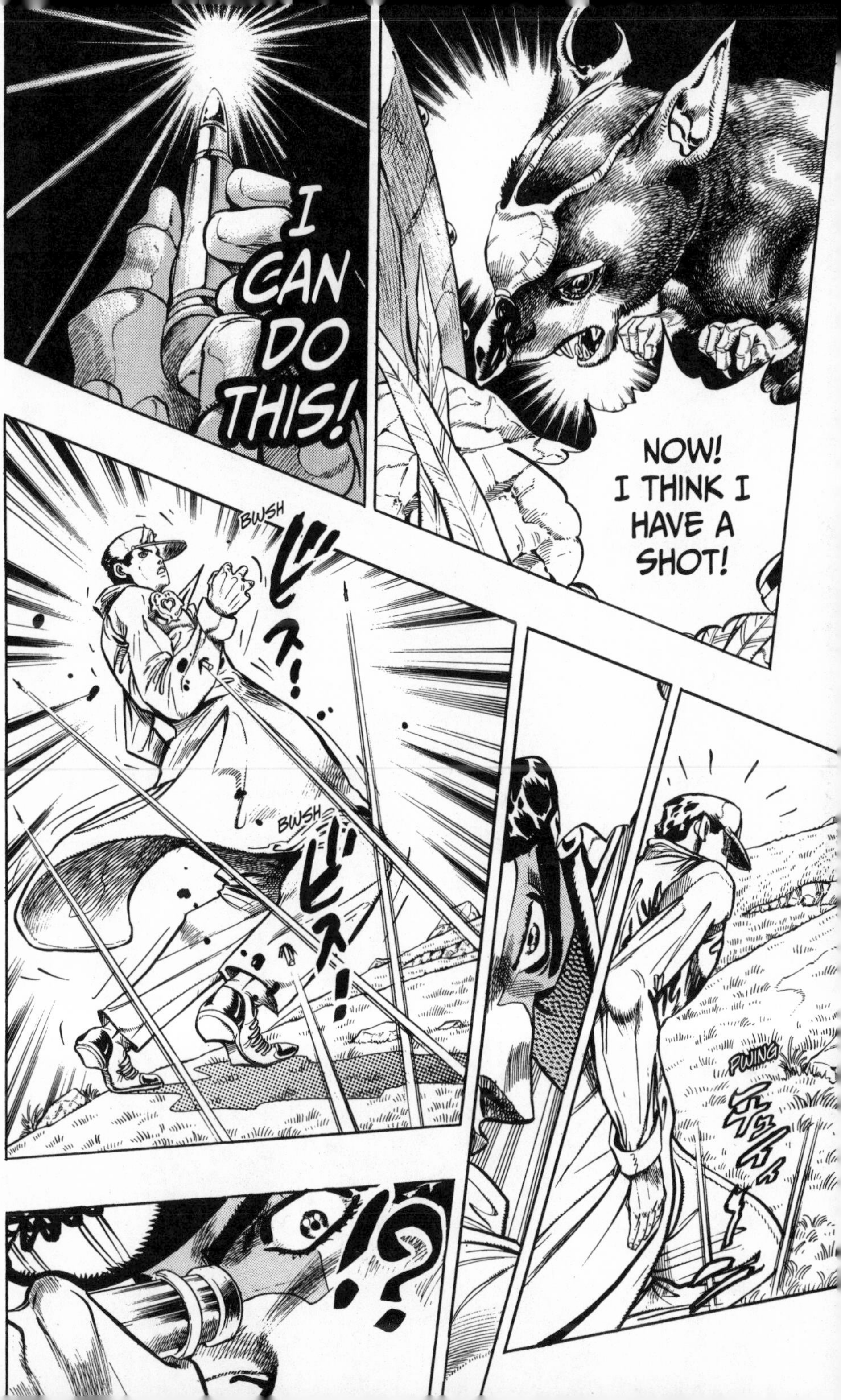
NOW! I THINK I HAVE A SHOT!
I CAN DO THIS!
PWING
BWSH
BWSH
!?

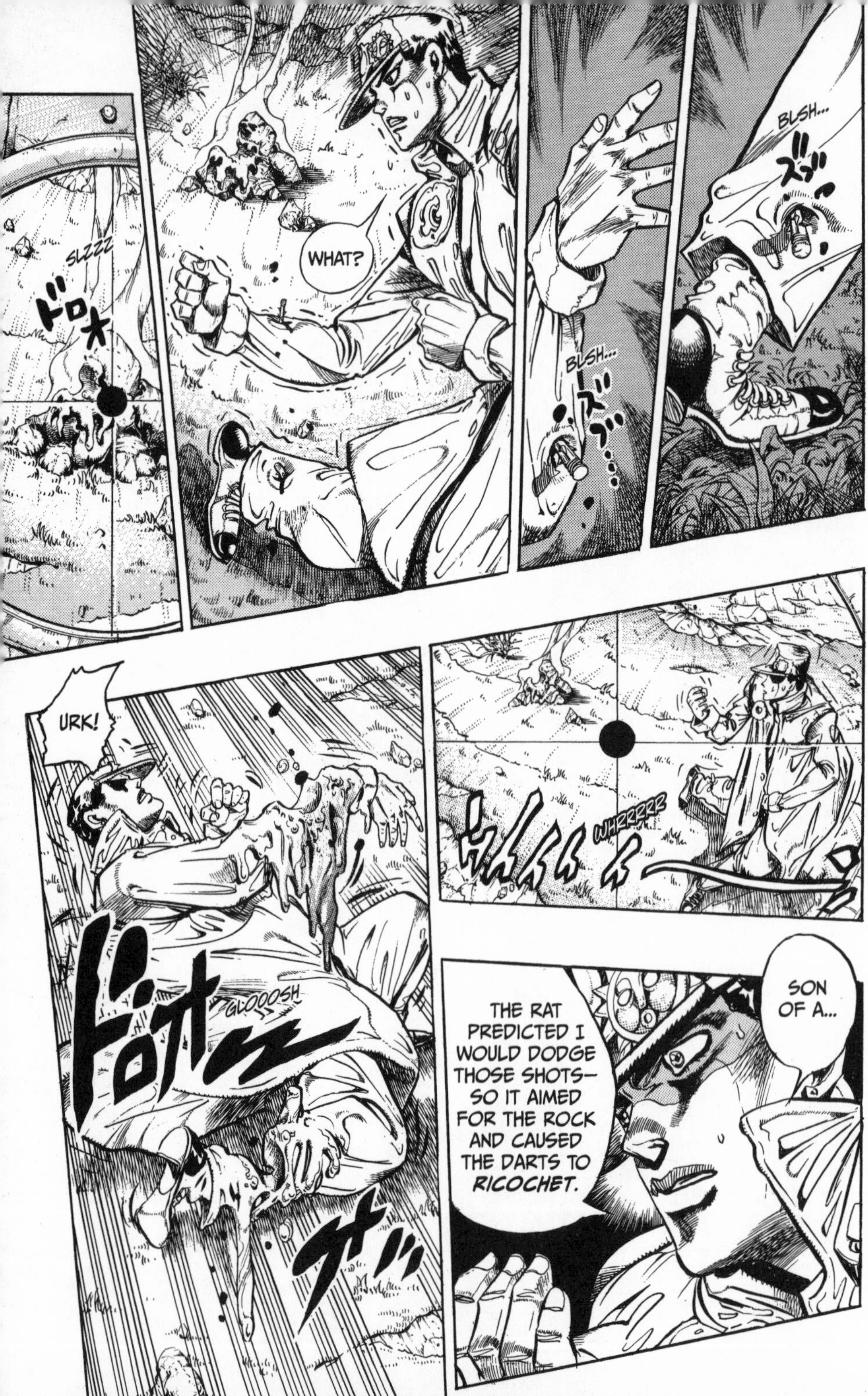
BLSH...
BLSH...
WHAT?
SLZZZ
WHRRRRR
SON OF A...
THE RAT PREDICTED I WOULD DODGE THOSE SHOTS— SO IT AIMED FOR THE ROCK AND CAUSED THE DARTS TO *RICOCHET*.
URK!
GLOOOSH

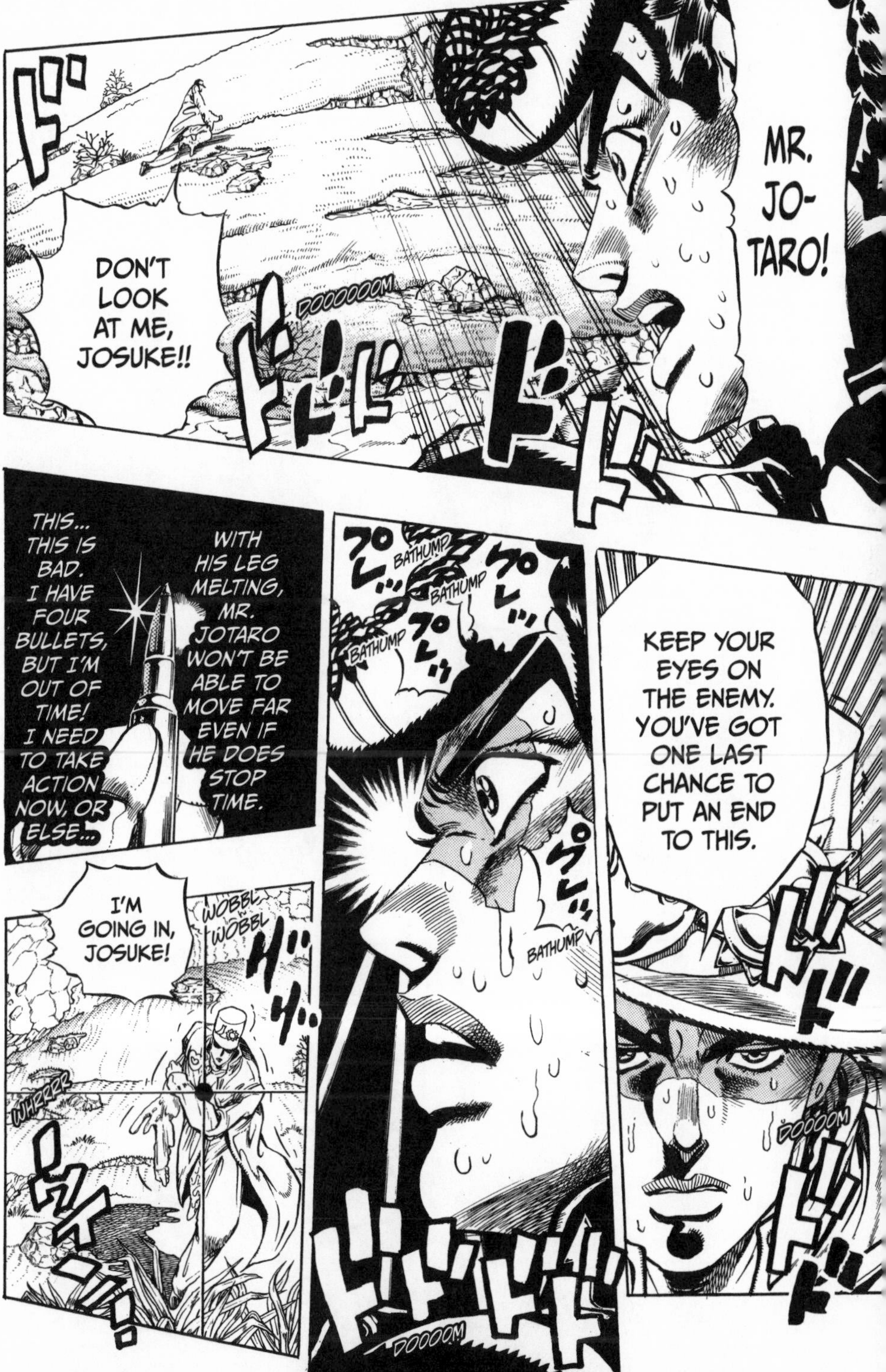
MR. JO-TARO!
DOOOOOOM
DON'T LOOK AT ME, JOSUKE!!
KEEP YOUR EYES ON THE ENEMY. YOU'VE GOT ONE LAST CHANCE TO PUT AN END TO THIS.
DOOOOM
BATHUMP
BATHUMP
BATHUMP
BATHUMP
DOOOOM
WITH HIS LEG MELTING, MR. JOTARO WON'T BE ABLE TO MOVE FAR EVEN IF HE DOES STOP TIME.
THIS... THIS IS BAD. I HAVE FOUR BULLETS, BUT I'M OUT OF TIME! I NEED TO TAKE ACTION NOW, OR ELSE...
I'M GOING IN, JOSUKE!
WOBBL WOBBL
WHRRRR

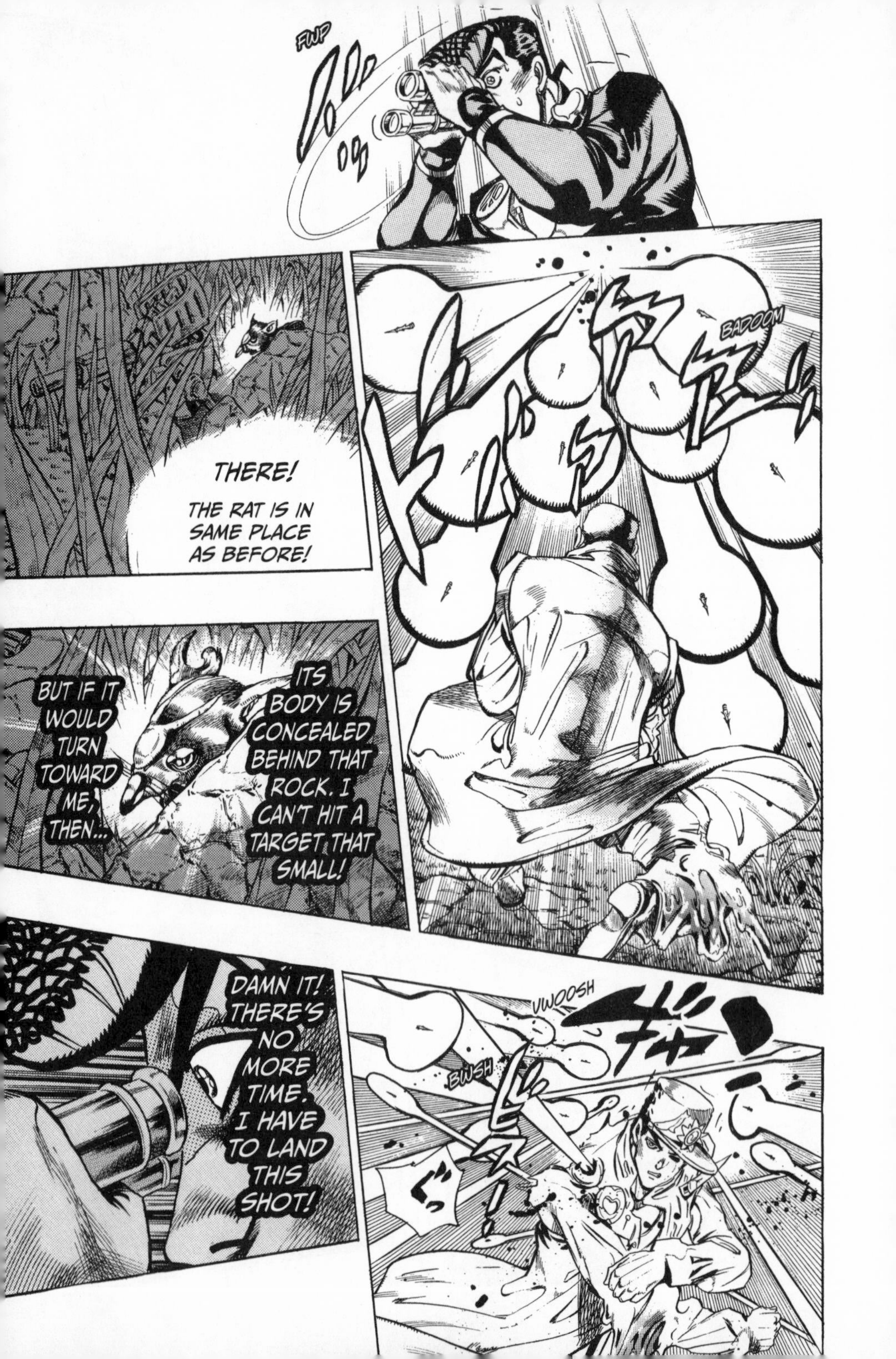
FWIP
BADOOM
THERE!
THE RAT IS IN SAME PLACE AS BEFORE!
ITS BODY IS CONCEALED BEHIND THAT ROCK. I CAN'T HIT A TARGET THAT SMALL!
BUT IF IT WOULD TURN TOWARD ME, THEN...
VWOOSH
BWSH
DAMN IT! THERE'S NO MORE TIME. I HAVE TO LAND THIS SHOT!

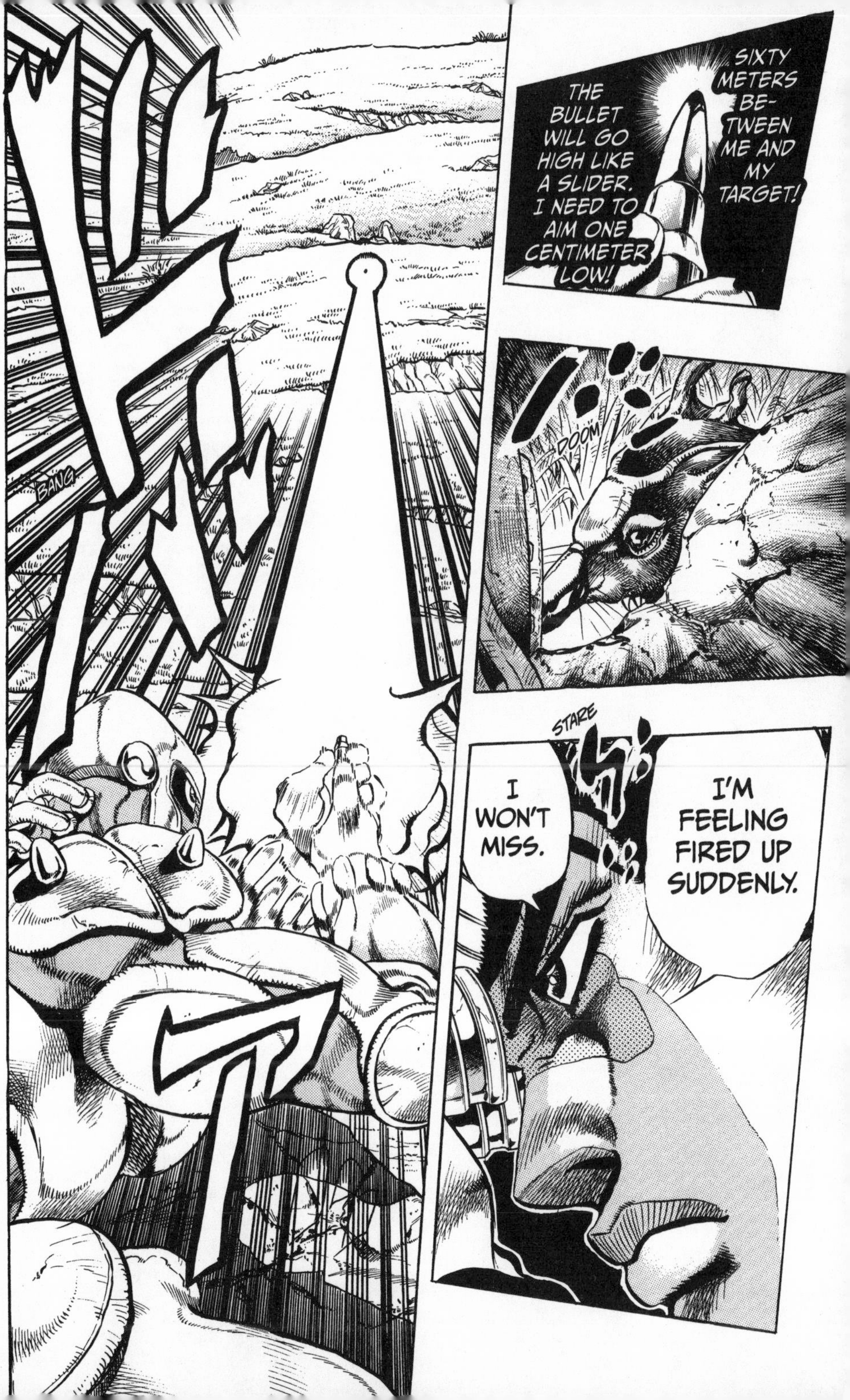
SIXTY METERS BE- TWEEN ME AND MY TARGET!
THE BULLET WILL GO HIGH LIKE A SLIDER. I NEED TO AIM ONE CENTIMETER LOW!
DOOM
STARE
I'M FEELING FIRED UP SUDDENLY.
I WON'T MISS.
BANG

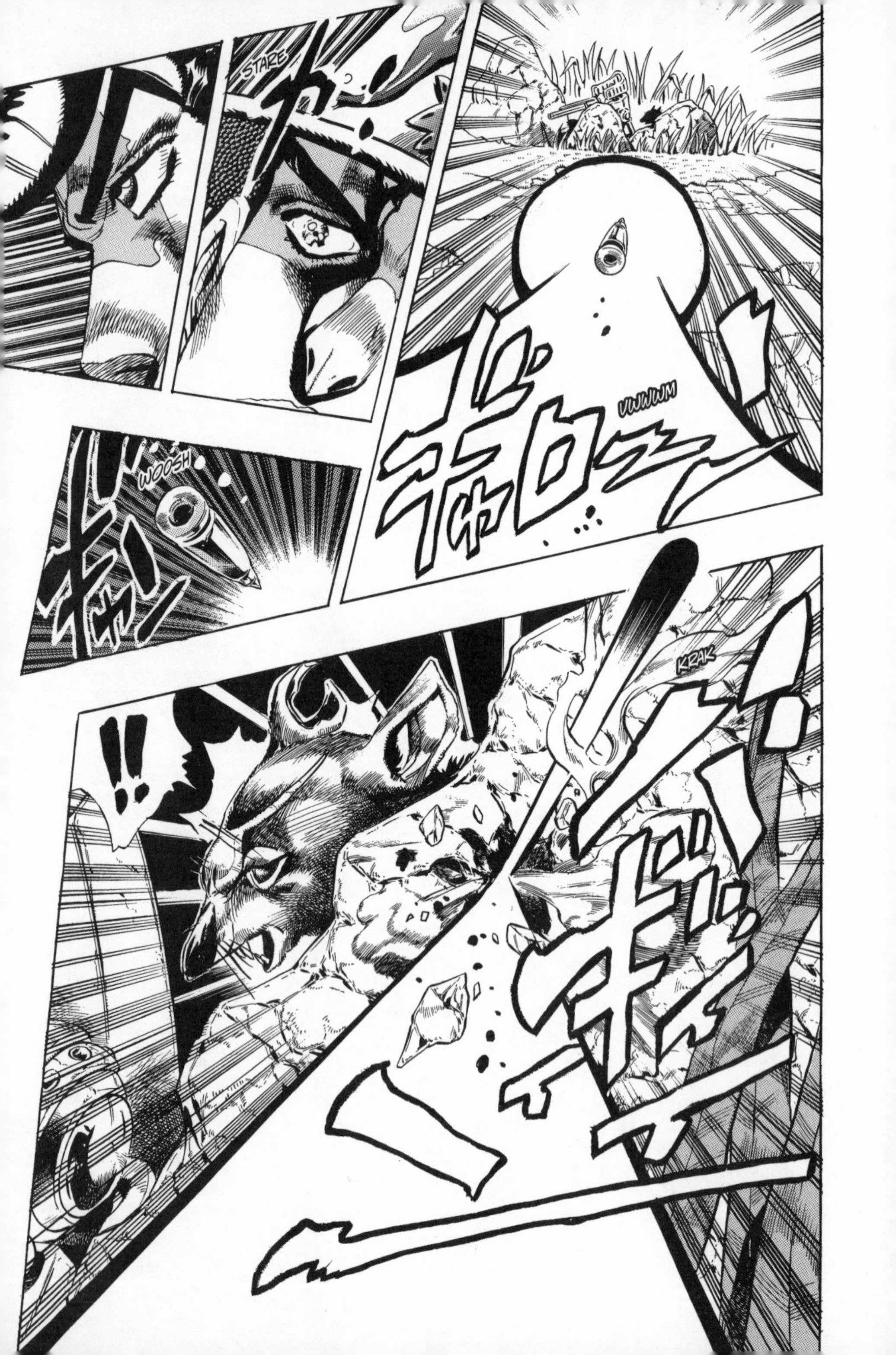
STARE
VWWWM
WOOSH
KRAK

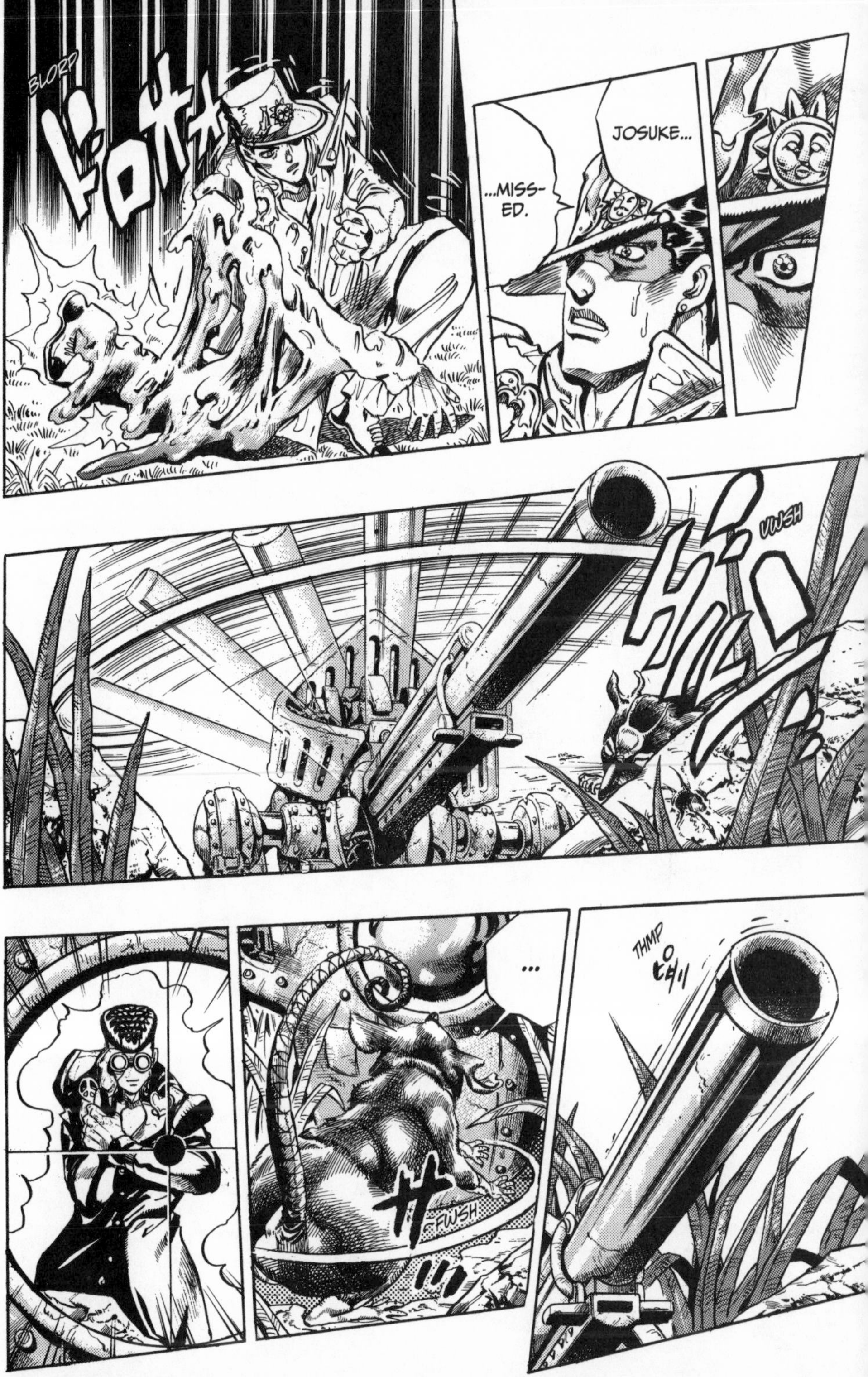
JOSUKE...
...MISS-ED.
BLORP
VWSH
THMP
...
FWSH

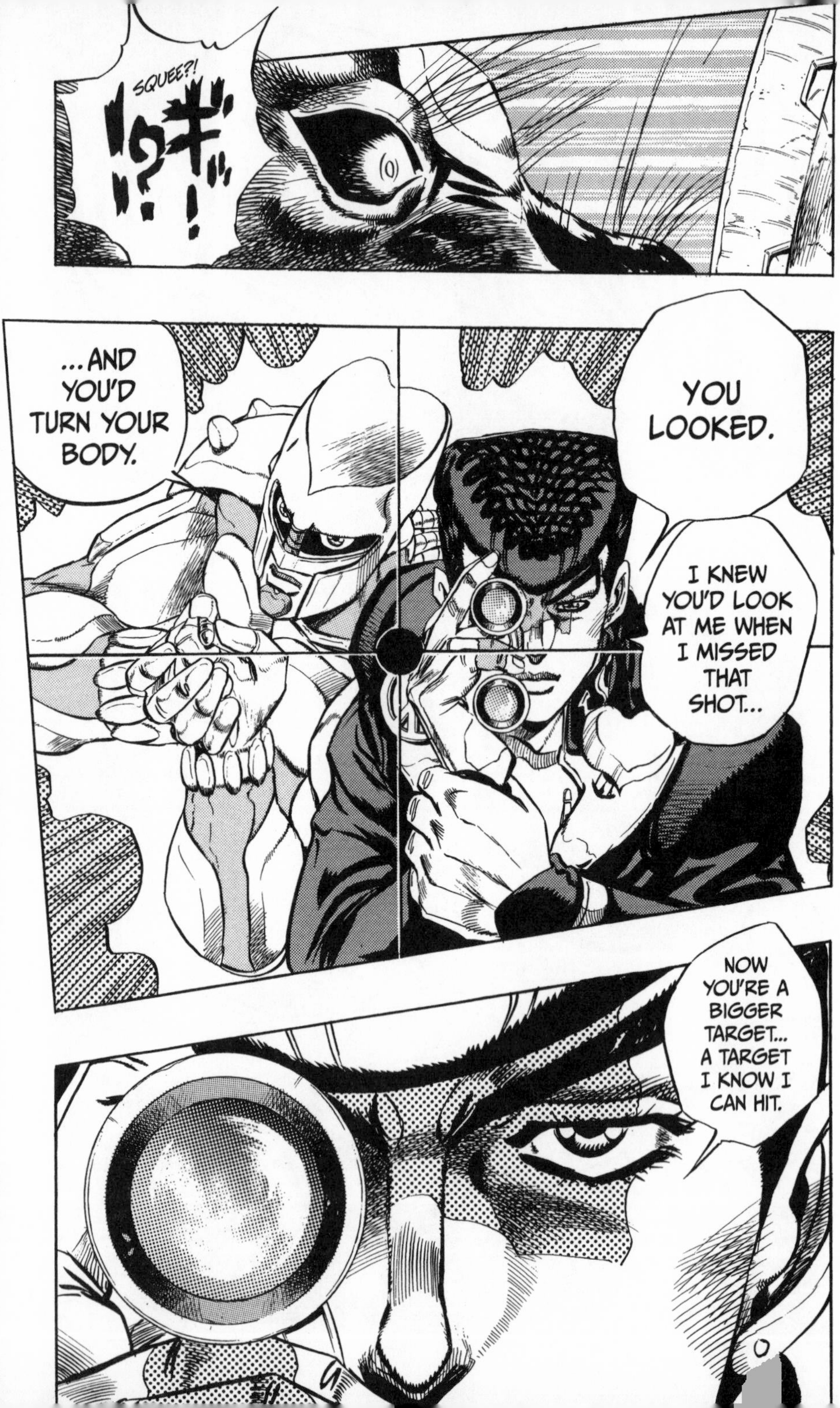
SQUEE?!
YOU LOOKED.
I KNEW YOU'D LOOK AT ME WHEN I MISSED THAT SHOT...
...AND YOU'D TURN YOUR BODY.
NOW YOU'RE A BIGGER TARGET... A TARGET I KNOW I CAN HIT.

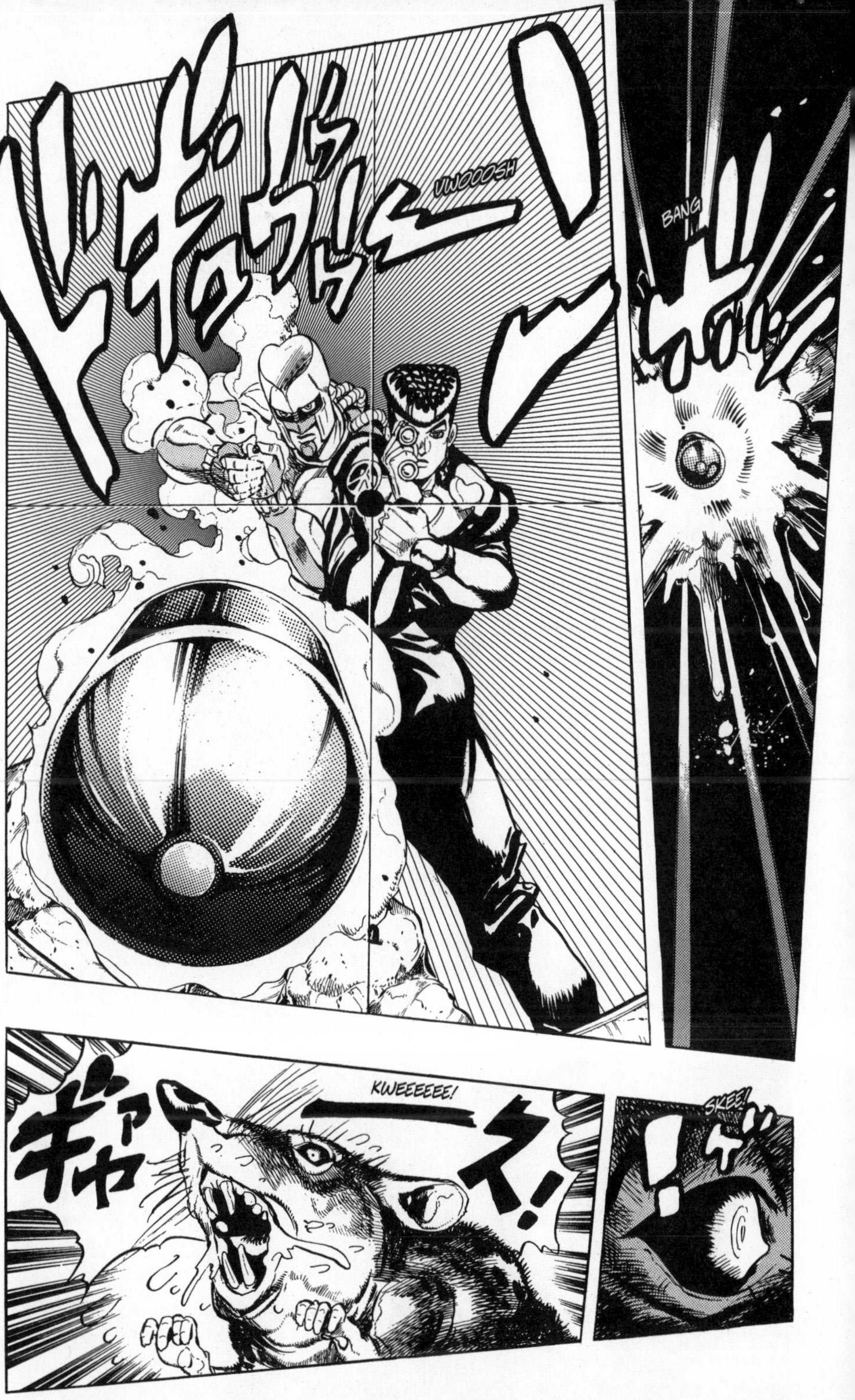
BANG
VWOOOSH
SKEE!
KWEEEEEE!

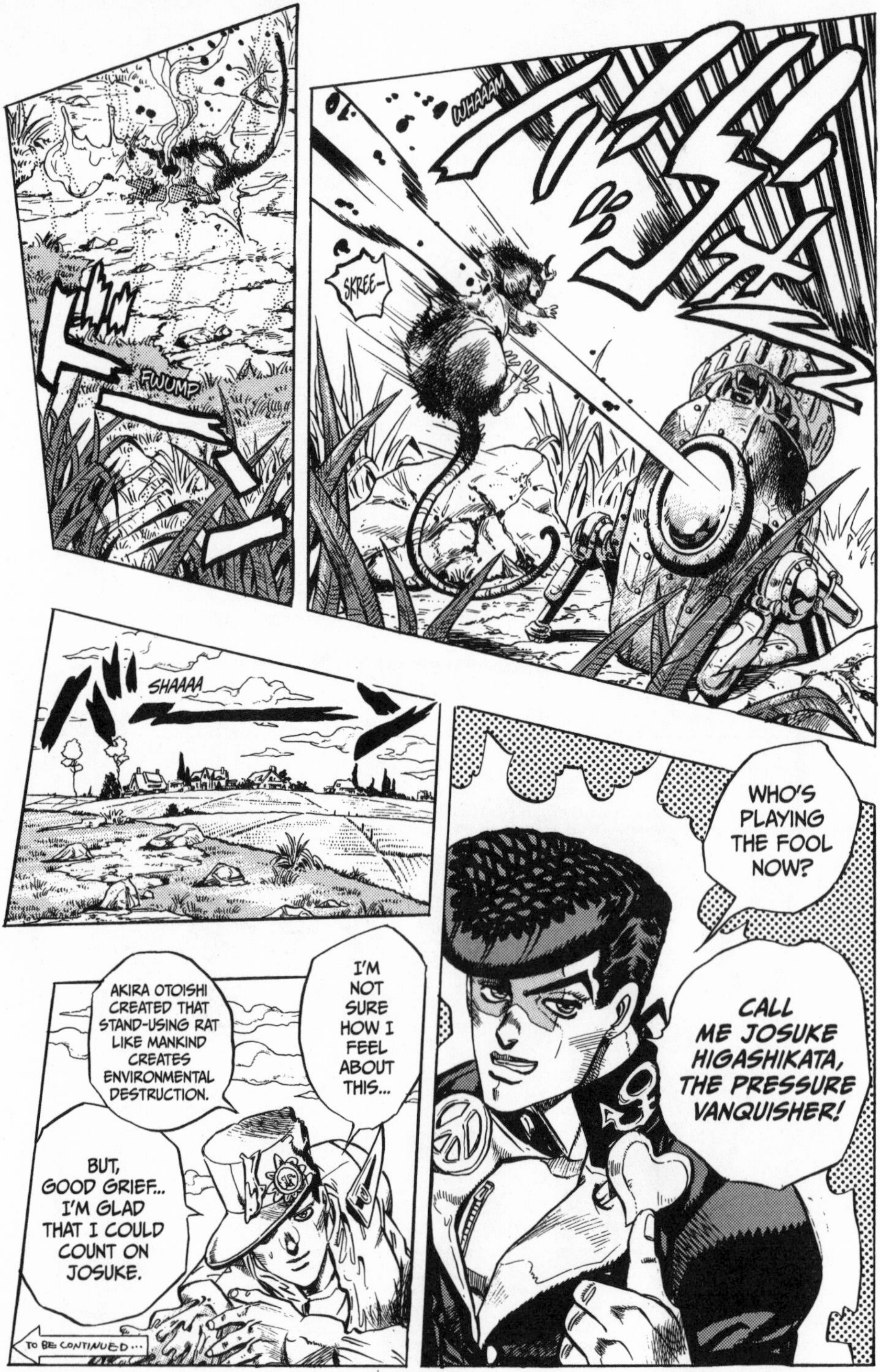
WHAAAM
SKREE-
FWUMP
WHO'S PLAYING THE FOOL NOW?
CALL ME JOSUKE HIGASHIKATA, THE PRESSURE VANQUISHER!
SHAAAA
I'M NOT SURE HOW I FEEL ABOUT THIS...
AKIRA OTOISHI CREATED THAT STAND-USING RAT LIKE MANKIND CREATES ENVIRONMENTAL DESTRUCTION.
BUT, GOOD GRIEF... I'M GLAD THAT I COULD COUNT ON JOSUKE.
TO BE CONTINUED...

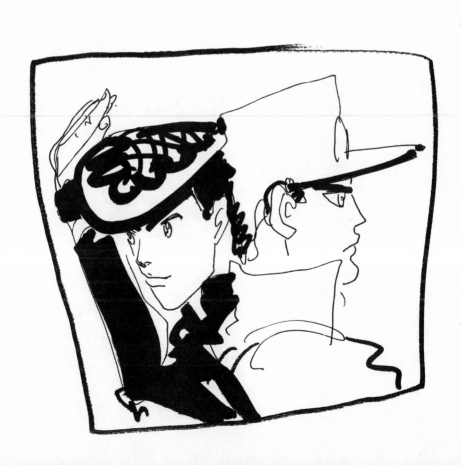

CHAPTER 65

ROHAN KISHIBE'S ADVENTURE, PART 1

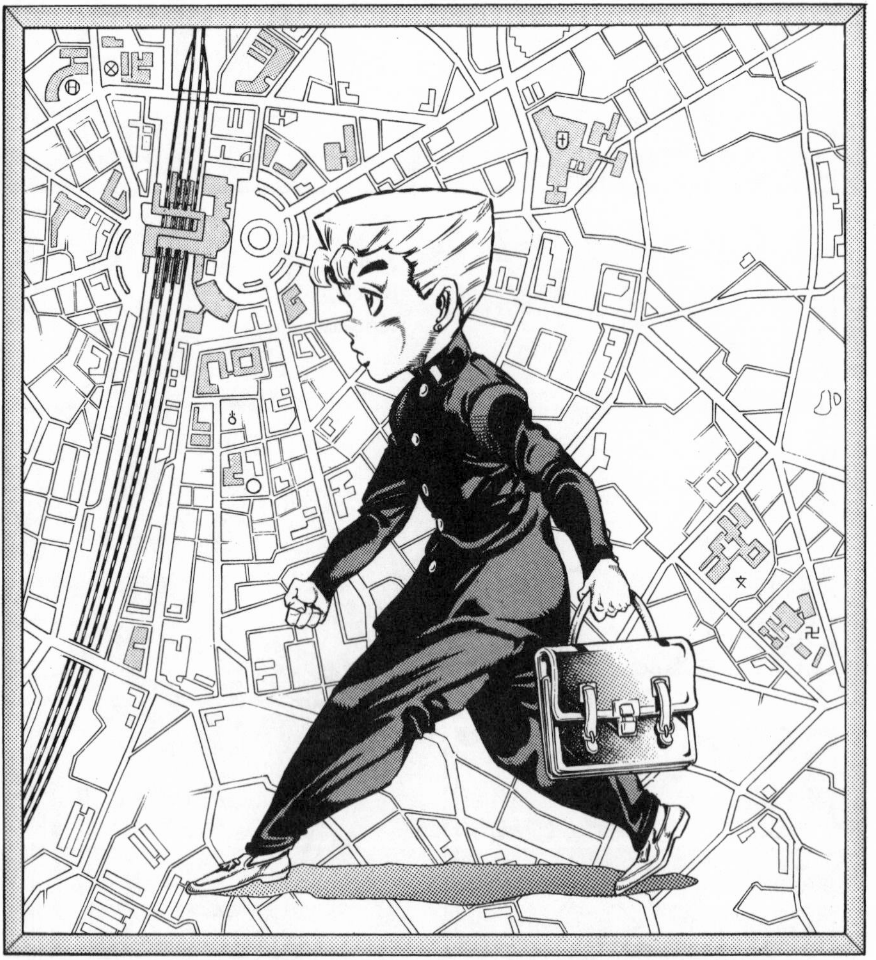

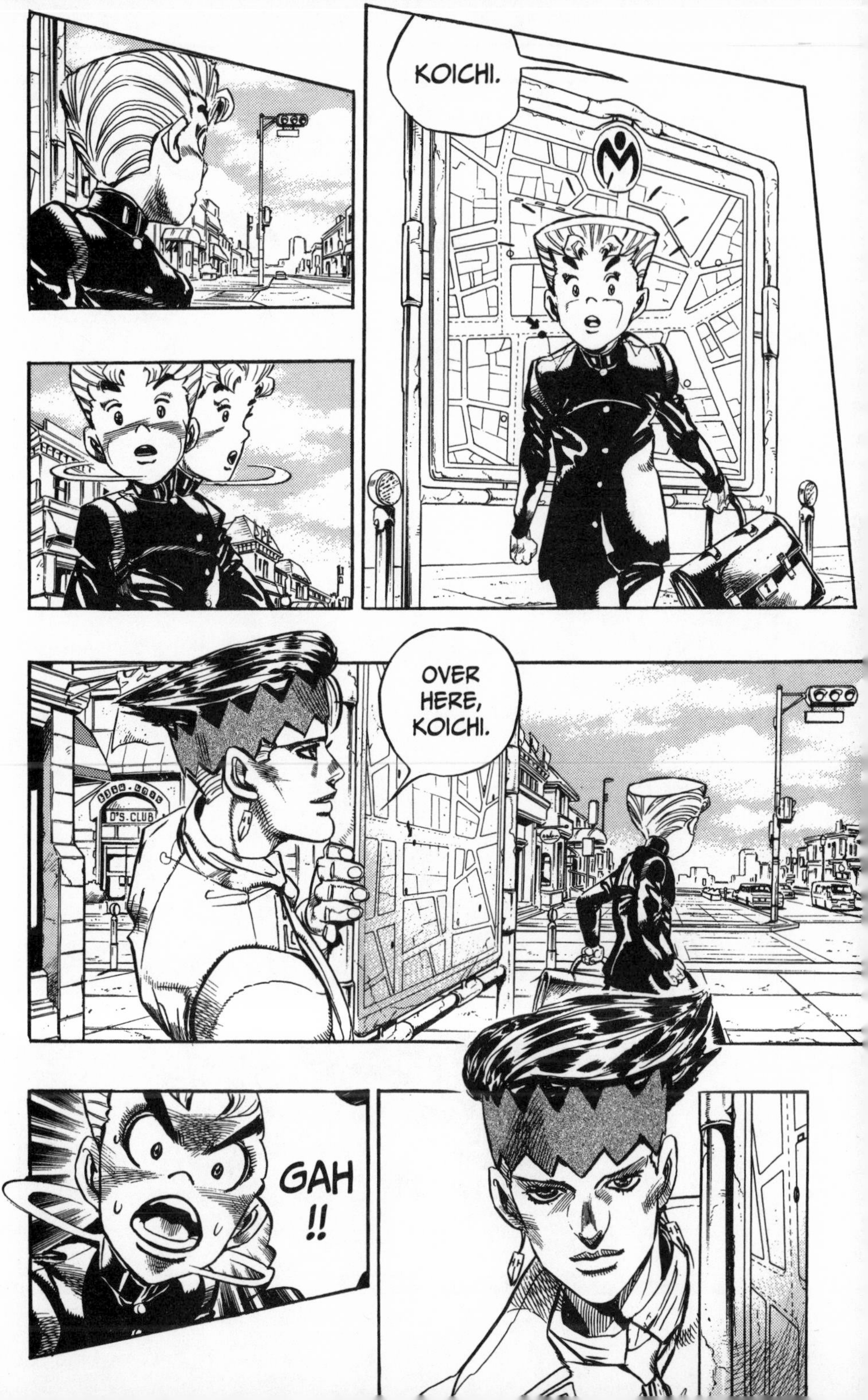
KOICHI.
OVER HERE, KOICHI.
GAH !!

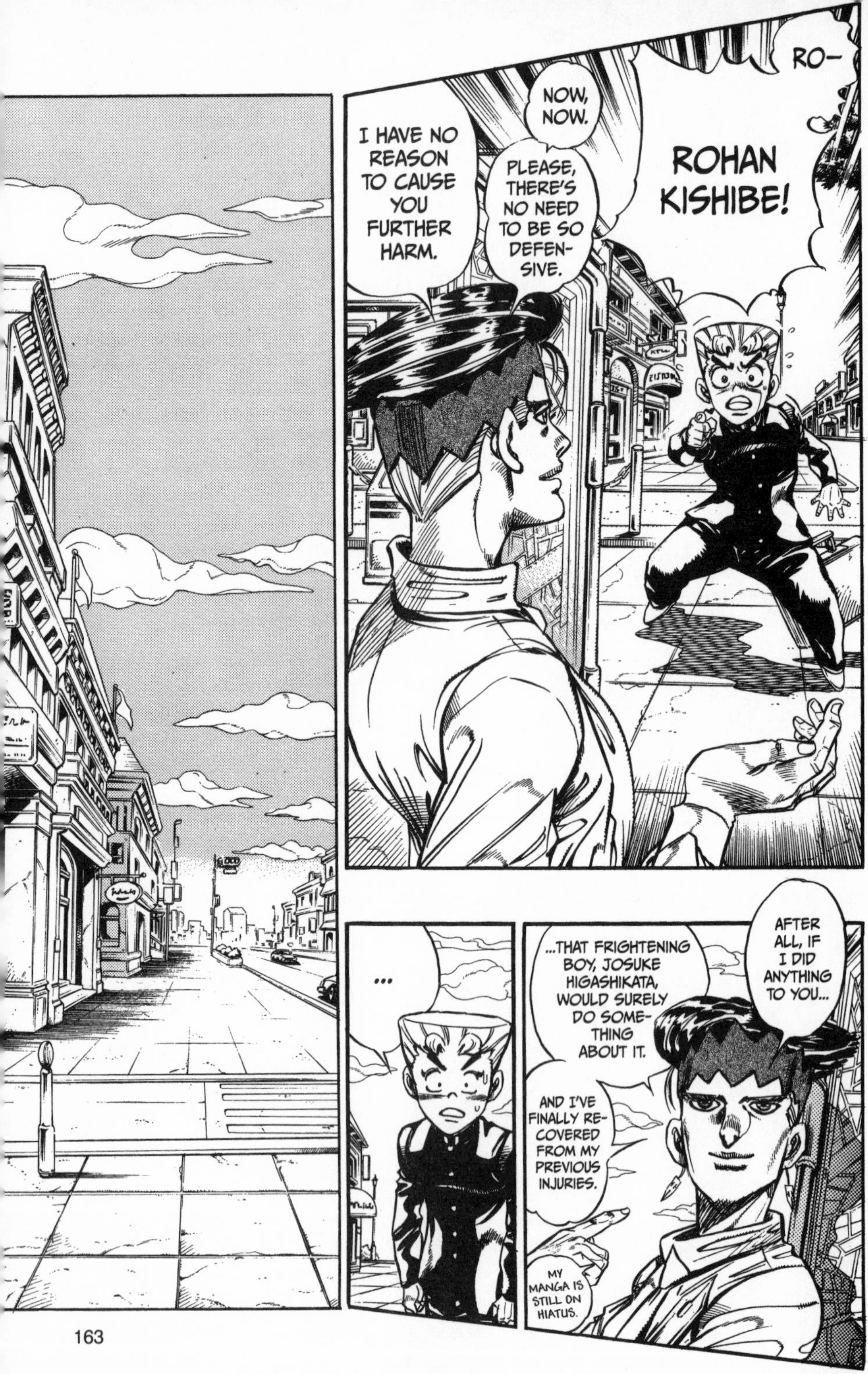
RO–
ROHAN KISHIBE!
NOW, NOW.
PLEASE, THERE'S NO NEED TO BE SO DEFENSIVE.
I HAVE NO REASON TO CAUSE YOU FURTHER HARM.
AFTER ALL, IF I DID ANYTHING TO YOU...
...THAT FRIGHTENING BOY, JOSUKE HIGASHIKATA, WOULD SURELY DO SOMETHING ABOUT IT.
AND I'VE FINALLY RECOVERED FROM MY PREVIOUS INJURIES.
MY MANGA IS STILL ON HIATUS.
...

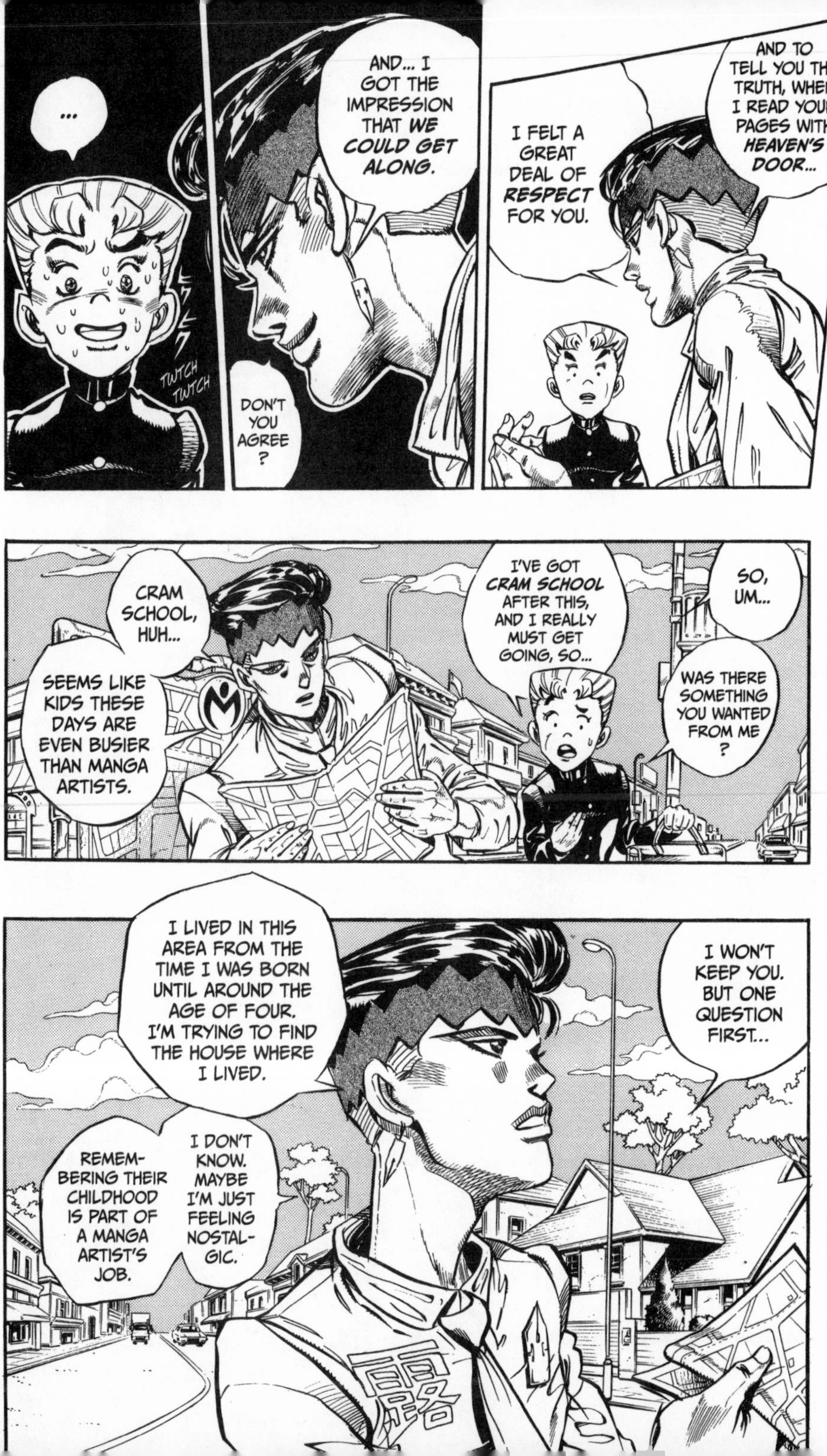
AND TO TELL YOU THE TRUTH, WHEN I READ YOUR PAGES WITH HEAVEN'S DOOR...
I FELT A GREAT DEAL OF RESPECT FOR YOU.
AND... I GOT THE IMPRESSION THAT WE COULD GET ALONG.
DON'T YOU AGREE?
...
TWITCH TWITCH
SO, UM...
WAS THERE SOMETHING YOU WANTED FROM ME?
I'VE GOT CRAM SCHOOL AFTER THIS, AND I REALLY MUST GET GOING, SO...
CRAM SCHOOL, HUH...
SEEMS LIKE KIDS THESE DAYS ARE EVEN BUSIER THAN MANGA ARTISTS.
I WON'T KEEP YOU. BUT ONE QUESTION FIRST...
I LIVED IN THIS AREA FROM THE TIME I WAS BORN UNTIL AROUND THE AGE OF FOUR. I'M TRYING TO FIND THE HOUSE WHERE I LIVED.
I DON'T KNOW. MAYBE I'M JUST FEELING NOSTAL-GIC.
REMEM-BERING THEIR CHILDHOOD IS PART OF A MANGA ARTIST'S JOB.

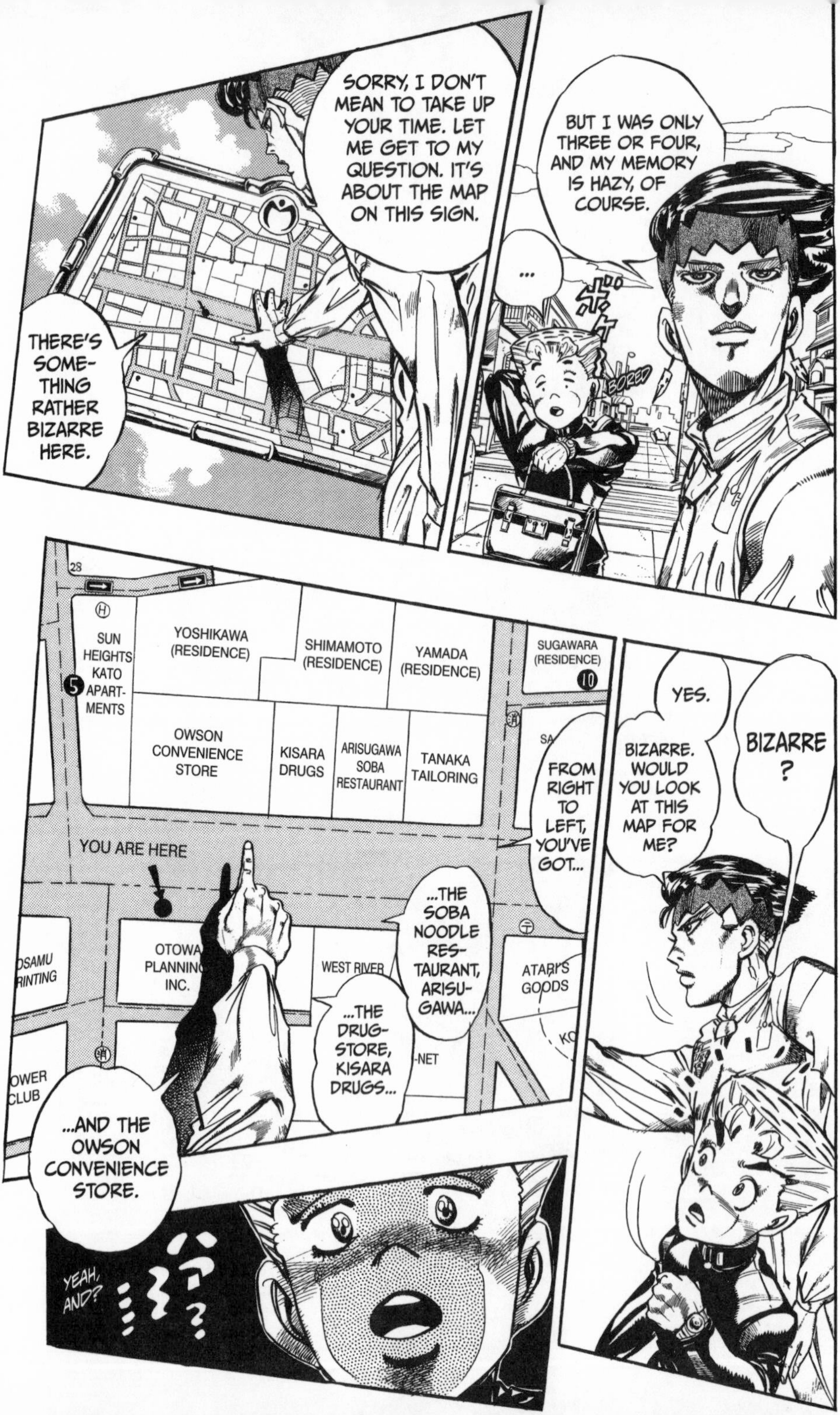
BUT I WAS ONLY THREE OR FOUR, AND MY MEMORY IS HAZY, OF COURSE.
...
BORED
SORRY, I DON'T MEAN TO TAKE UP YOUR TIME. LET ME GET TO MY QUESTION. IT'S ABOUT THE MAP ON THIS SIGN.
THERE'S SOME-THING RATHER BIZARRE HERE.
BIZARRE?
YES.
BIZARRE. WOULD YOU LOOK AT THIS MAP FOR ME?
28
SUN HEIGHTS KATO APART-MENTS
YOSHIKAWA (RESIDENCE)
SHIMAMOTO (RESIDENCE)
YAMADA (RESIDENCE)
SUGAWARA (RESIDENCE)
OWSON CONVENIENCE STORE
KISARA DRUGS
ARISUGAWA SOBA RESTAURANT
TANAKA TAILORING
YOU ARE HERE
OTOWA PLANNING INC.
WEST RIVER
ATARI'S GOODS
-NET
FROM RIGHT TO LEFT, YOU'VE GOT...
...THE SOBA NOODLE RES-TAURANT, ARISU-GAWA...
...THE DRUG-STORE, KISARA DRUGS...
...AND THE OWSON CONVENIENCE STORE.
YEAH, AND?

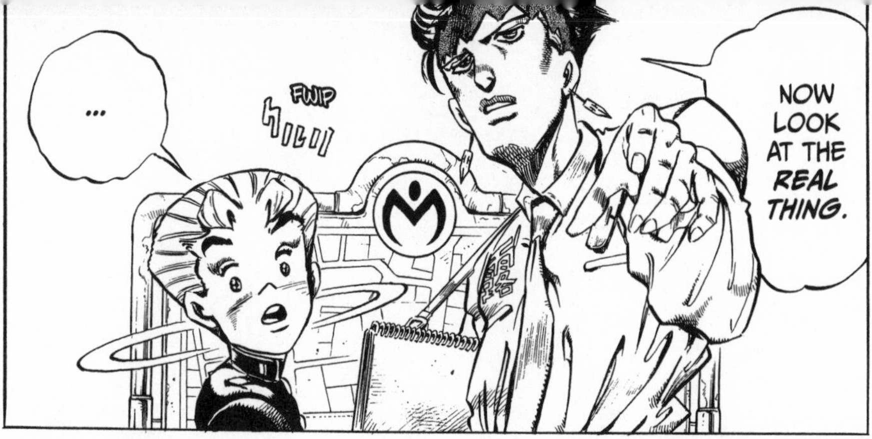
NOW LOOK AT THE REAL THING.
FWIP
...

SHIRT: RO (FROM ROHAN)

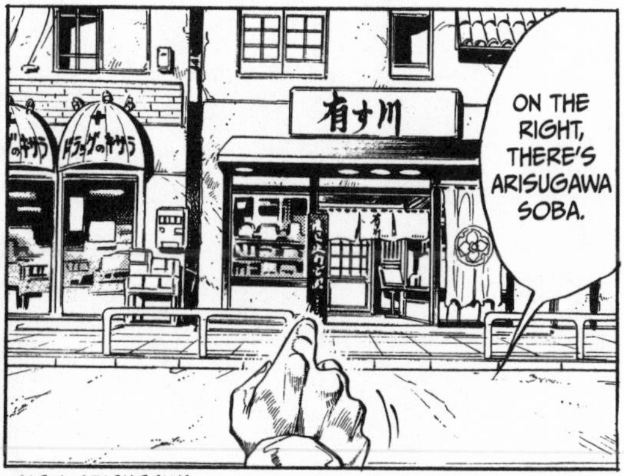
有す川
ON THE RIGHT, THERE'S ARISUGAWA SOBA.

SIGN: ARISUGAWA

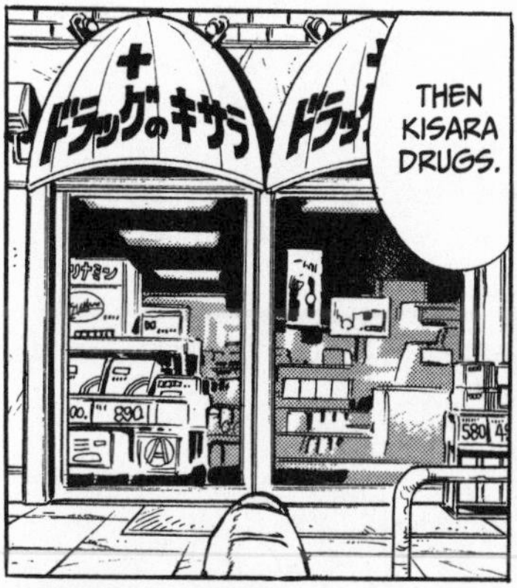
ドラッグのキサラ
THEN KISARA DRUGS.

SIGN: KISARA DRUGS

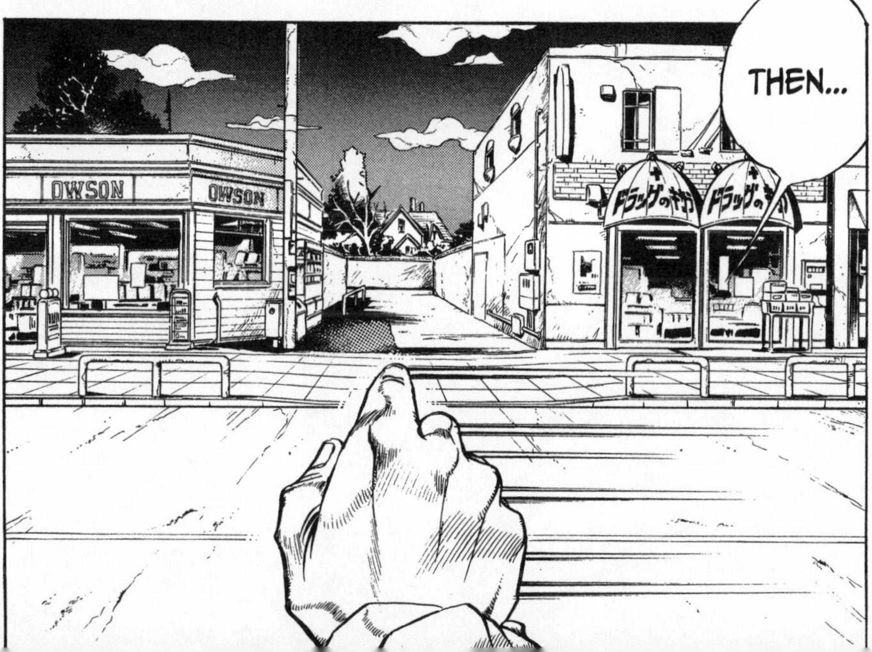
THEN...
OWSON
OWSON

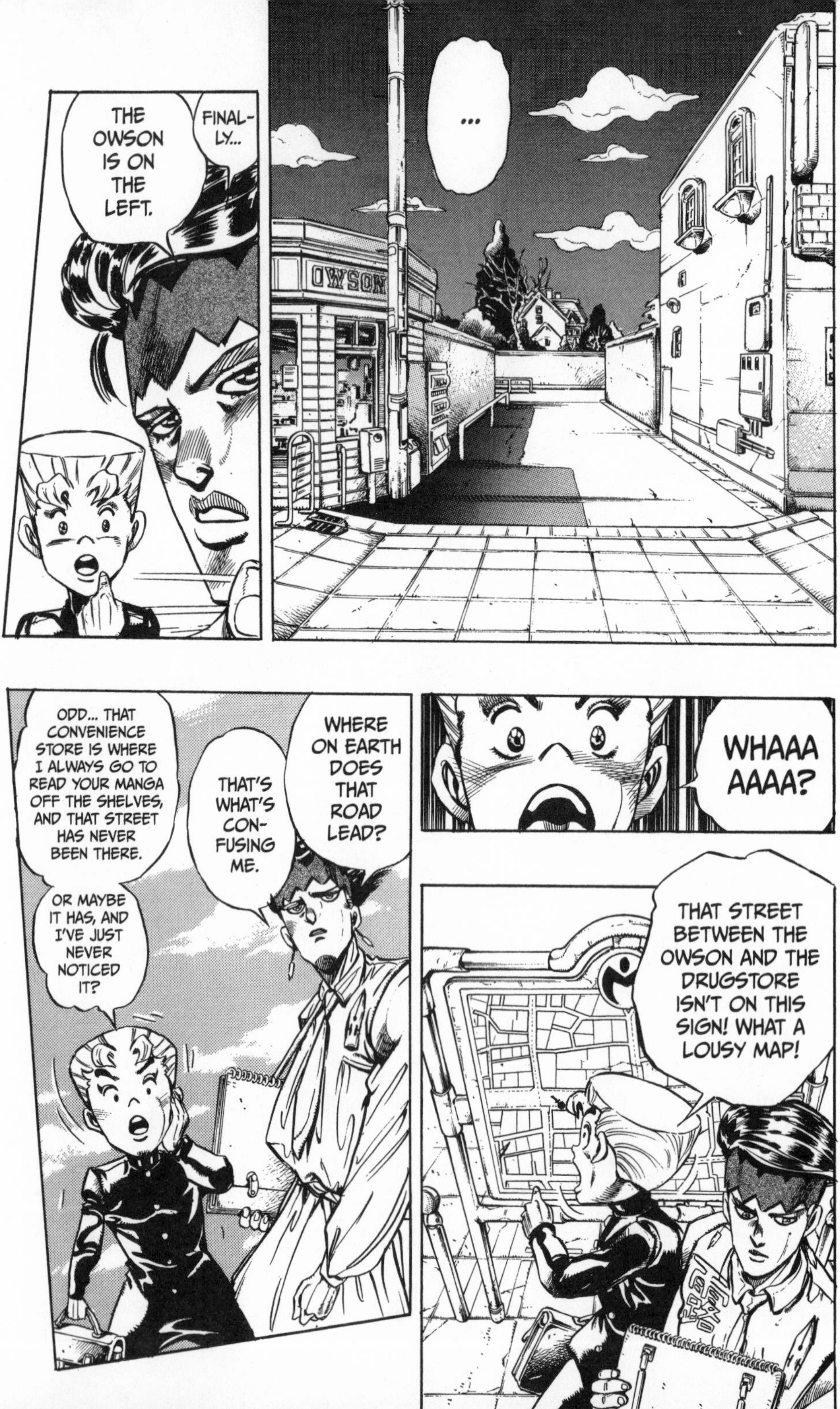
...
OWSON
FINAL-LY...
THE OWSON IS ON THE LEFT.
WHAAA AAAA?
THAT STREET BETWEEN THE OWSON AND THE DRUGSTORE ISN'T ON THIS SIGN! WHAT A LOUSY MAP!
WHERE ON EARTH DOES THAT ROAD LEAD?
THAT'S WHAT'S CON-FUSING ME.
ODD... THAT CONVENIENCE STORE IS WHERE I ALWAYS GO TO READ YOUR MANGA OFF THE SHELVES, AND THAT STREET HAS NEVER BEEN THERE.
OR MAYBE IT HAS, AND I'VE JUST NEVER NOTICED IT?

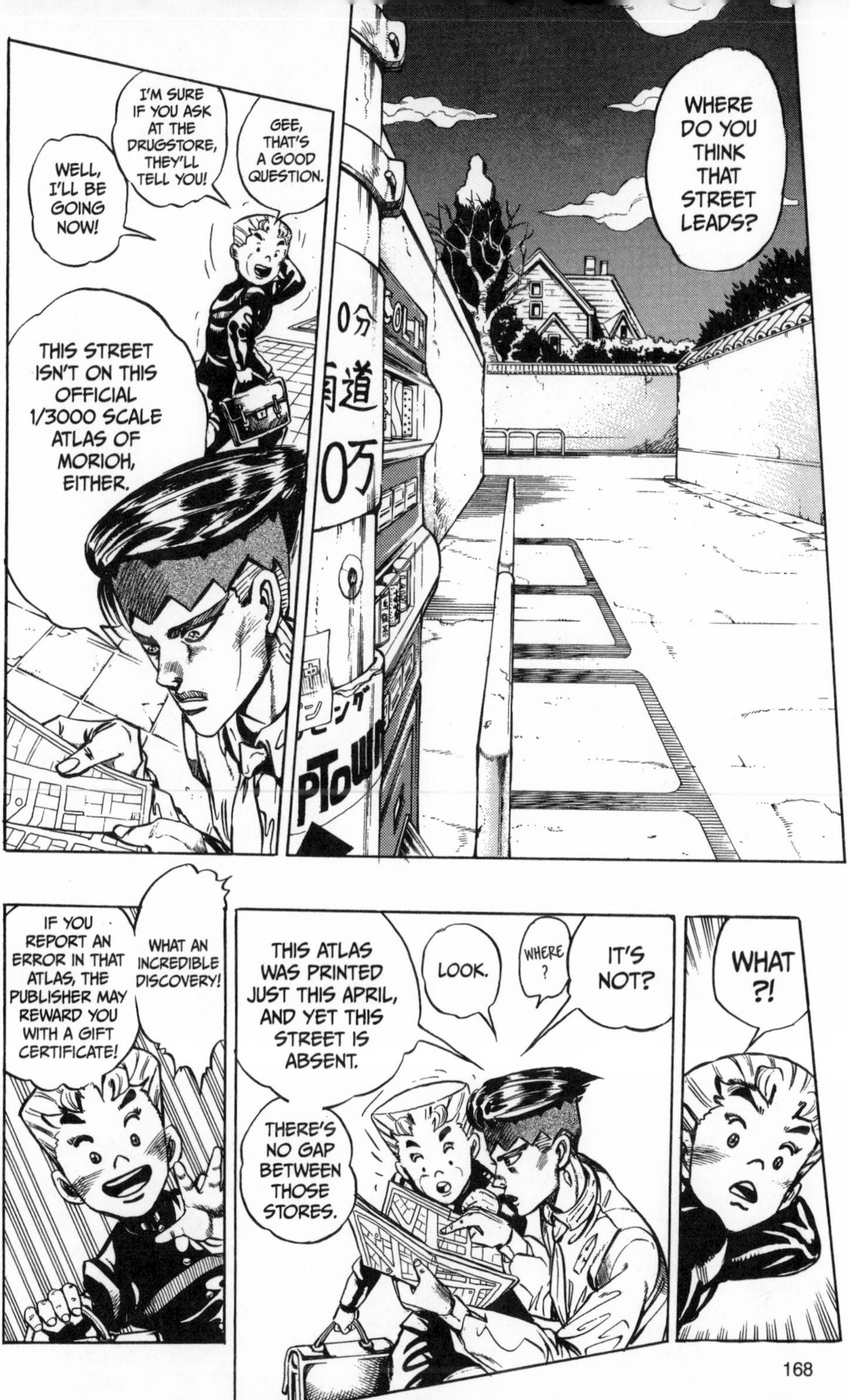
WHERE DO YOU THINK THAT STREET LEADS?
GEE, THAT'S A GOOD QUESTION.
I'M SURE IF YOU ASK AT THE DRUGSTORE, THEY'LL TELL YOU!
WELL, I'LL BE GOING NOW!
THIS STREET ISN'T ON THIS OFFICIAL 1/3000 SCALE ATLAS OF MORIOH, EITHER.
WHAT?!
IT'S NOT?
WHERE?
LOOK.
THIS ATLAS WAS PRINTED JUST THIS APRIL, AND YET THIS STREET IS ABSENT.
THERE'S NO GAP BETWEEN THOSE STORES.
WHAT AN INCREDIBLE DISCOVERY!
IF YOU REPORT AN ERROR IN THAT ATLAS, THE PUBLISHER MAY REWARD YOU WITH A GIFT CERTIFICATE!

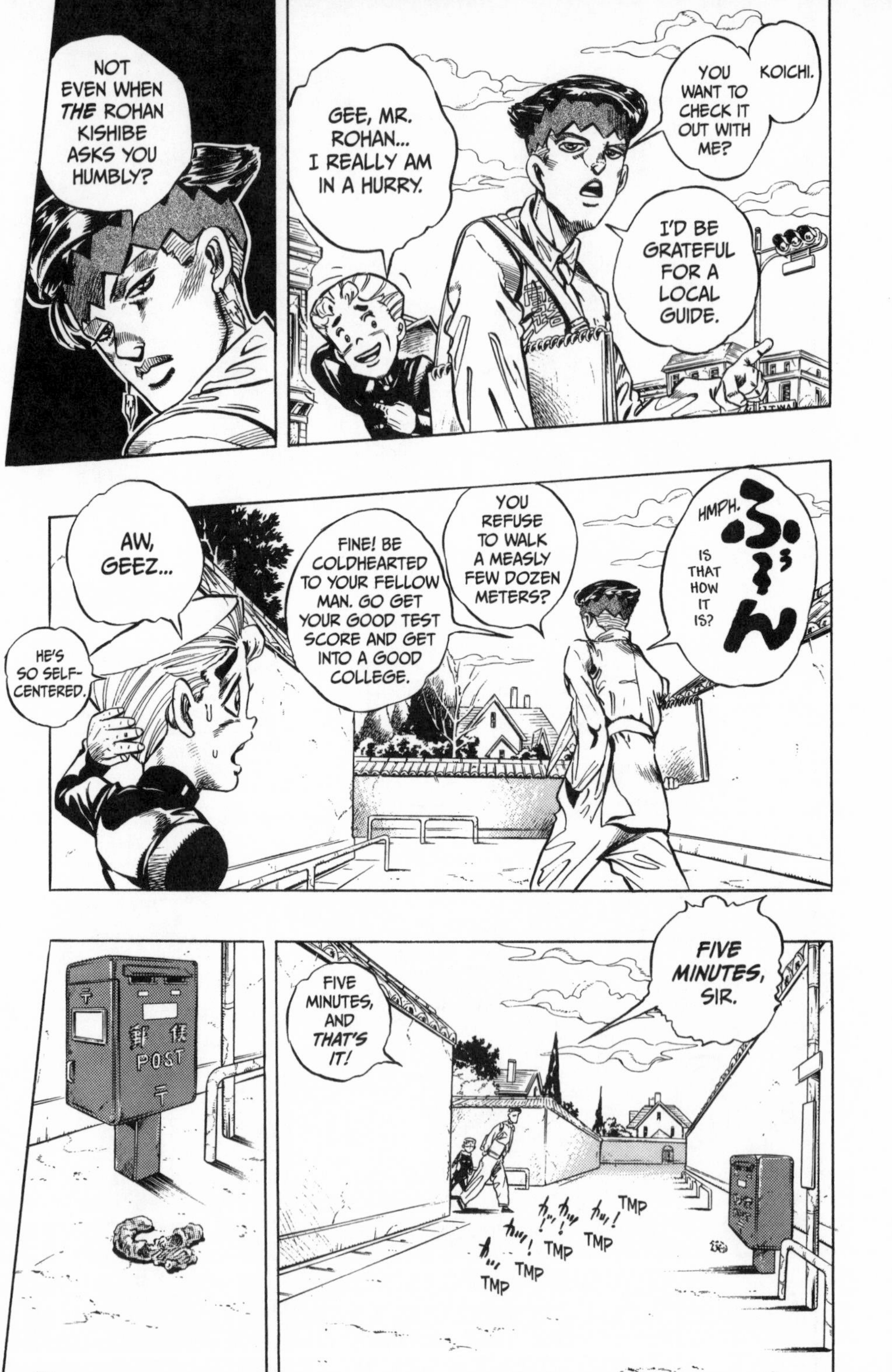
KOICHI.
YOU WANT TO CHECK IT OUT WITH ME?
I'D BE GRATEFUL FOR A LOCAL GUIDE.
GEE, MR. ROHAN... I REALLY AM IN A HURRY.
NOT EVEN WHEN *THE* ROHAN KISHIBE ASKS YOU HUMBLY?
HMPH.
IS THAT HOW IT IS?
YOU REFUSE TO WALK A MEASLY FEW DOZEN METERS?
FINE! BE COLDHEARTED TO YOUR FELLOW MAN. GO GET YOUR GOOD TEST SCORE AND GET INTO A GOOD COLLEGE.
AW, GEEZ...
HE'S SO SELF-CENTERED.
FIVE MINUTES, SIR.
FIVE MINUTES, AND *THAT'S* IT!
TMP TMP TMP TMP TMP
POST

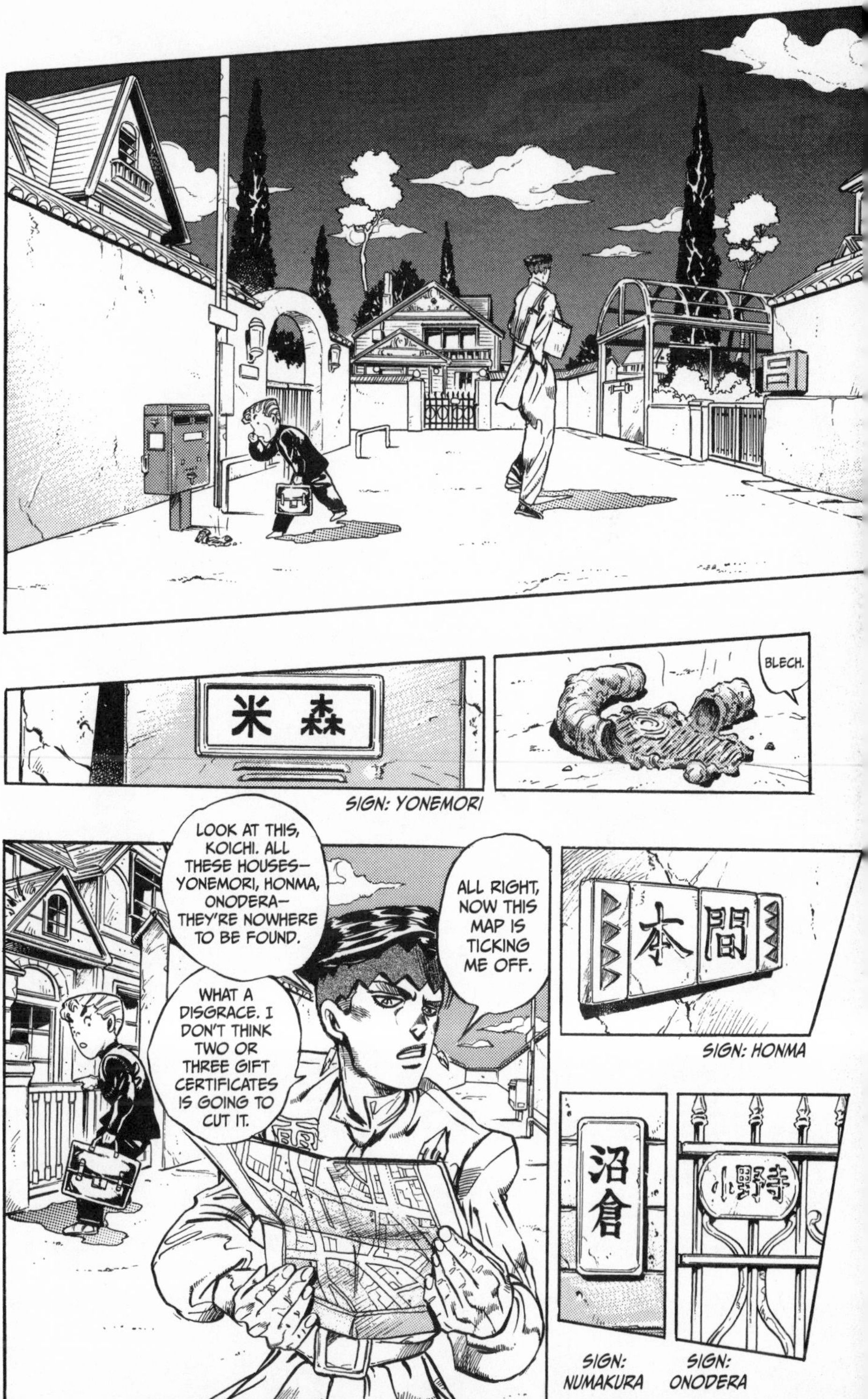
BLECH.
米森
SIGN: YONEMORI
本間
SIGN: HONMA
小野寺
SIGN: ONODERA
沼倉
SIGN: NUMAKURA
ALL RIGHT, NOW THIS MAP IS TICKING ME OFF.
LOOK AT THIS, KOICHI. ALL THESE HOUSES—YONEMORI, HONMA, ONODERA—THEY'RE NOWHERE TO BE FOUND.
WHAT A DISGRACE. I DON'T THINK TWO OR THREE GIFT CERTIFICATES IS GOING TO CUT IT.

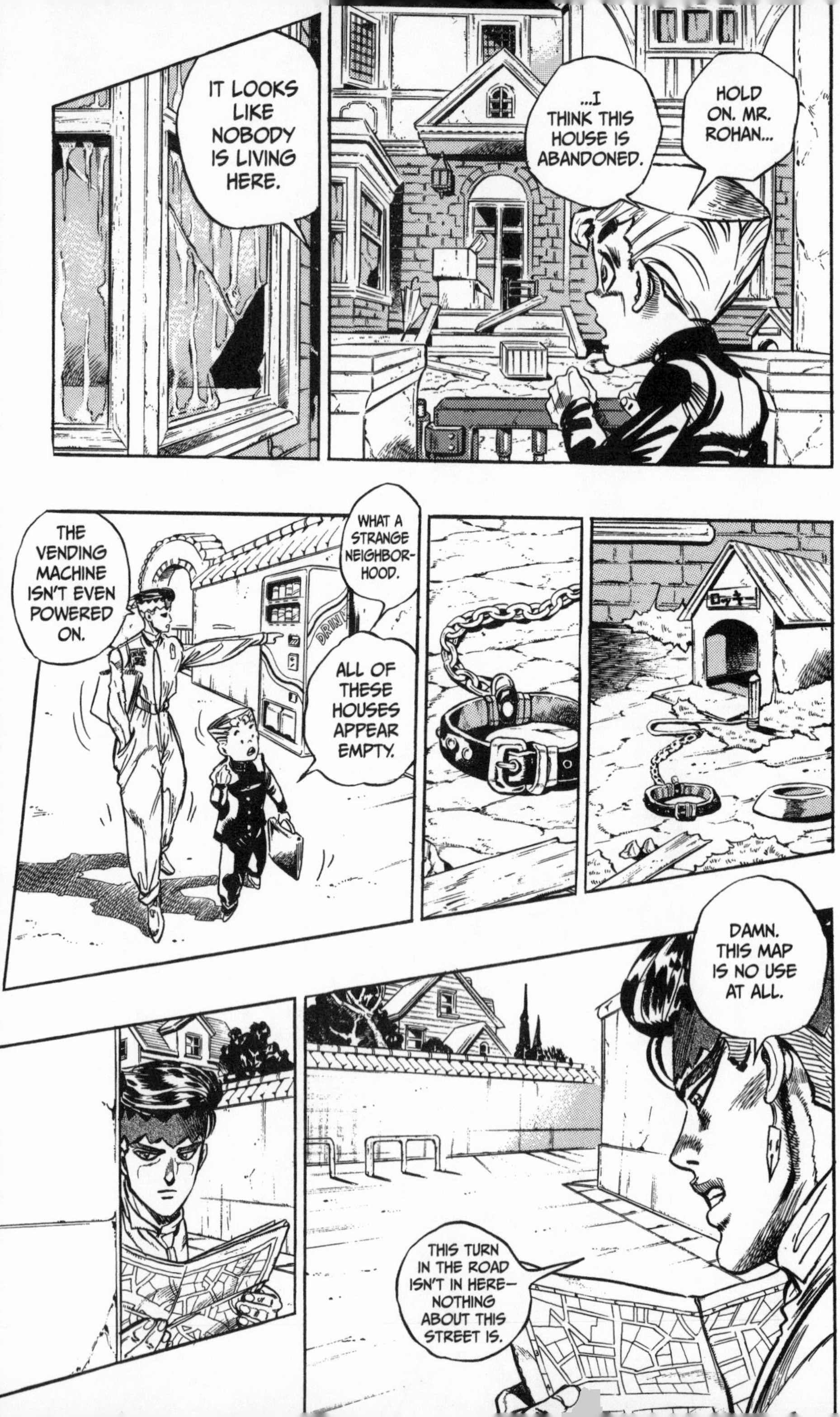
HOLD ON. MR. ROHAN...
...I THINK THIS HOUSE IS ABANDONED.
IT LOOKS LIKE NOBODY IS LIVING HERE.
ロッキー
WHAT A STRANGE NEIGHBOR-HOOD.
ALL OF THESE HOUSES APPEAR EMPTY.
THE VENDING MACHINE ISN'T EVEN POWERED ON.
DAMN. THIS MAP IS NO USE AT ALL.
THIS TURN IN THE ROAD ISN'T IN HERE—NOTHING ABOUT THIS STREET IS.

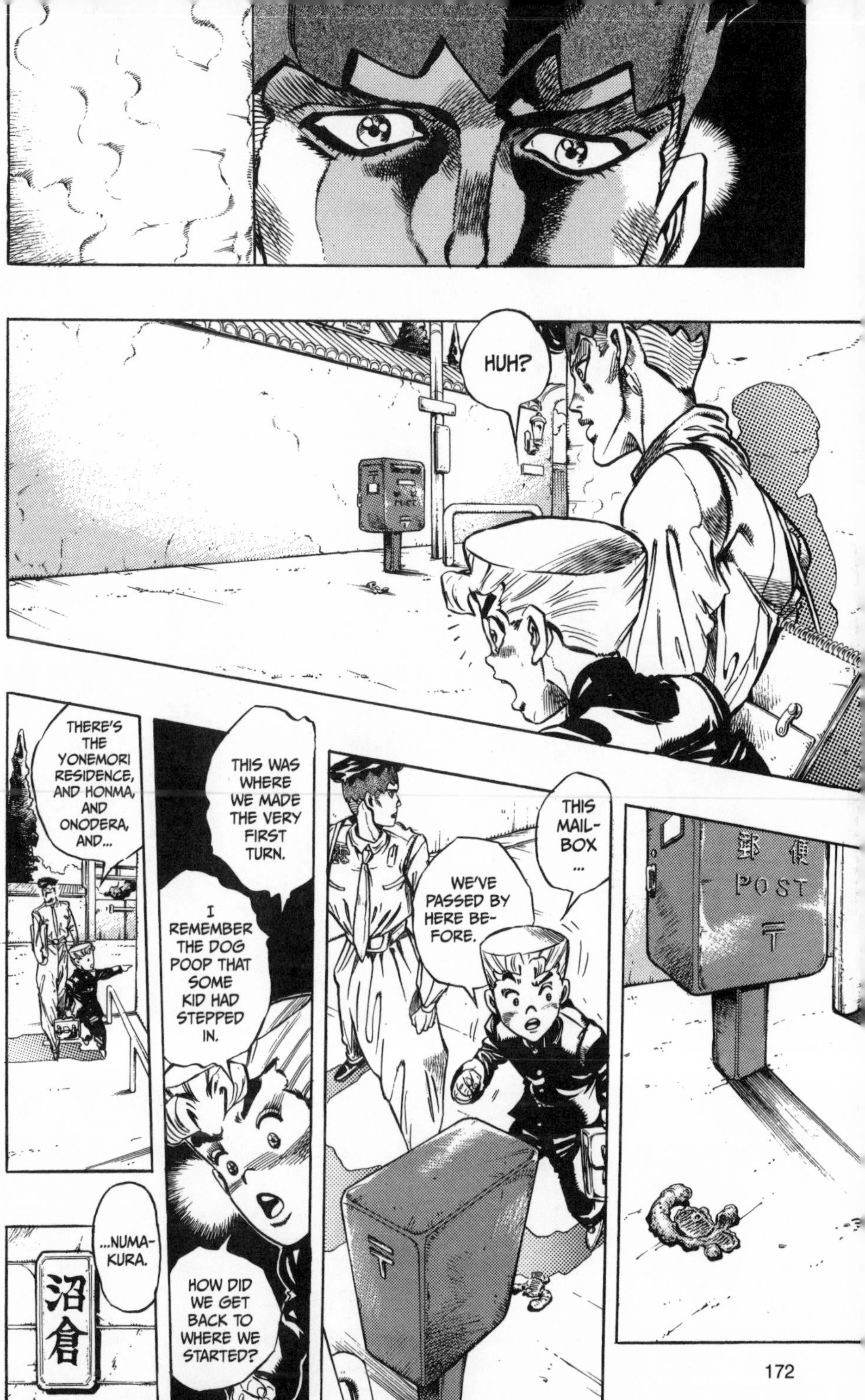
HUH?
THIS MAIL-BOX ...
WE'VE PASSED BY HERE BE-FORE.
THIS WAS WHERE WE MADE THE VERY FIRST TURN.
I REMEMBER THE DOG POOP THAT SOME KID HAD STEPPED IN.
HOW DID WE GET BACK TO WHERE WE STARTED?
THERE'S THE YONEMORI RESIDENCE, AND HONMA, AND ONODERA, AND...
...NUMA-KURA.
沼倉
POST

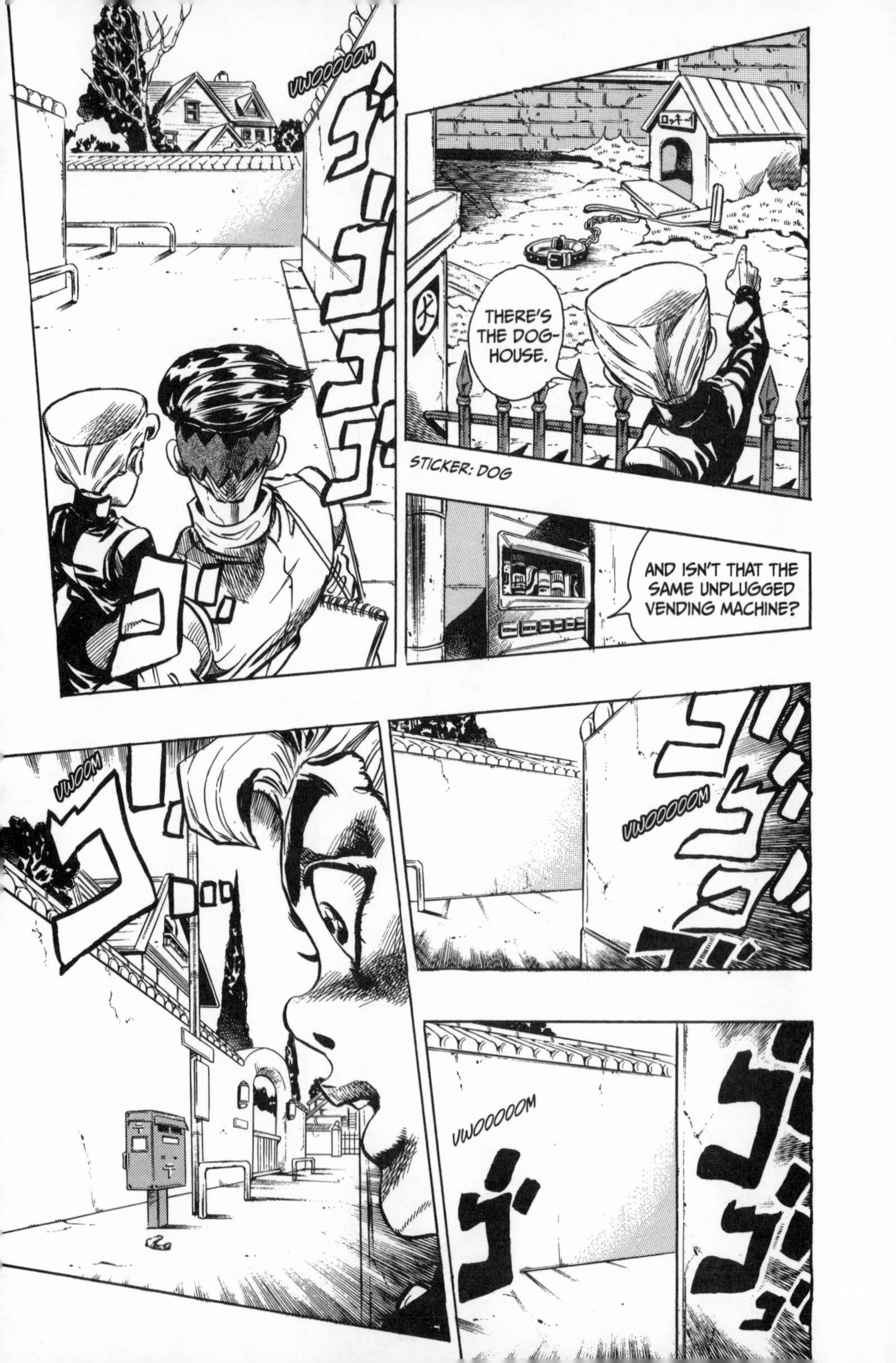
THERE'S THE DOG-HOUSE.
STICKER: DOG
AND ISN'T THAT THE SAME UNPLUGGED VENDING MACHINE?
VWOOOOOM
VWOOOOOM
VWOOOOOM
VWOOM

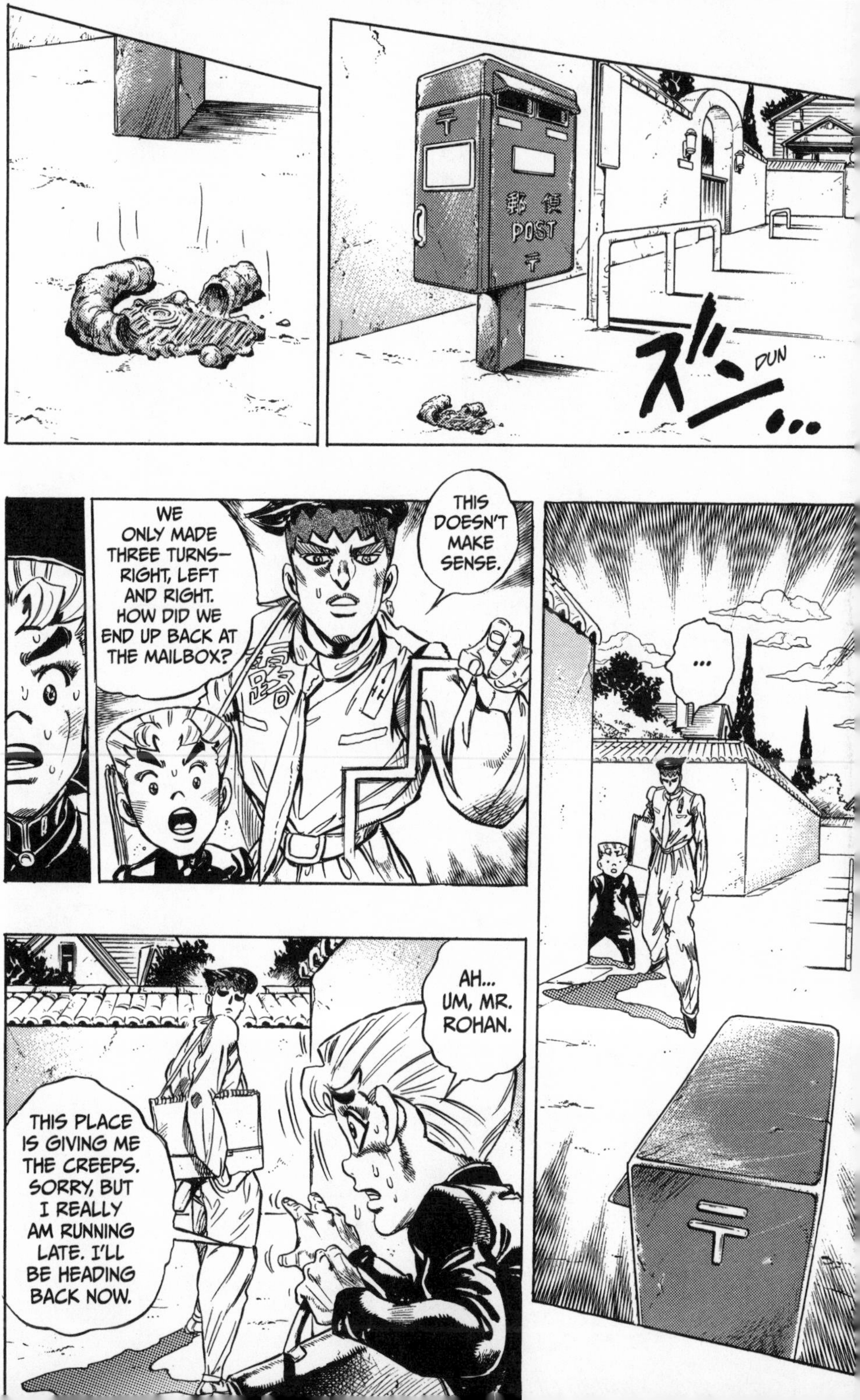

郵便
POST
DUN
...
THIS DOESN'T MAKE SENSE.
WE ONLY MADE THREE TURNS—RIGHT, LEFT AND RIGHT. HOW DID WE END UP BACK AT THE MAILBOX?
AH... UM, MR. ROHAN.
THIS PLACE IS GIVING ME THE CREEPS. SORRY, BUT I REALLY AM RUNNING LATE. I'LL BE HEADING BACK NOW.

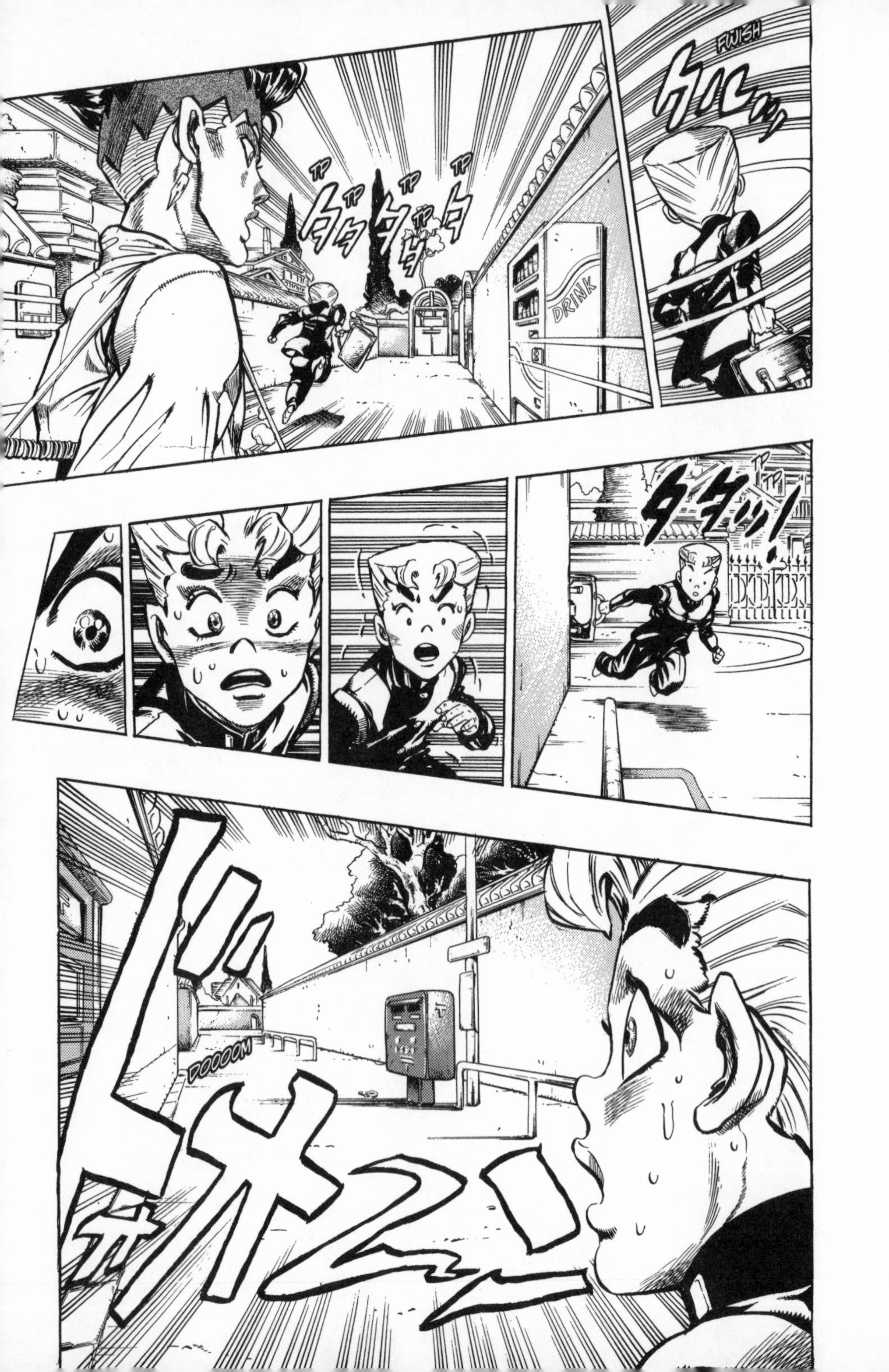
FWISH
TP TP TP TP TP
TP TP
DOOOOM

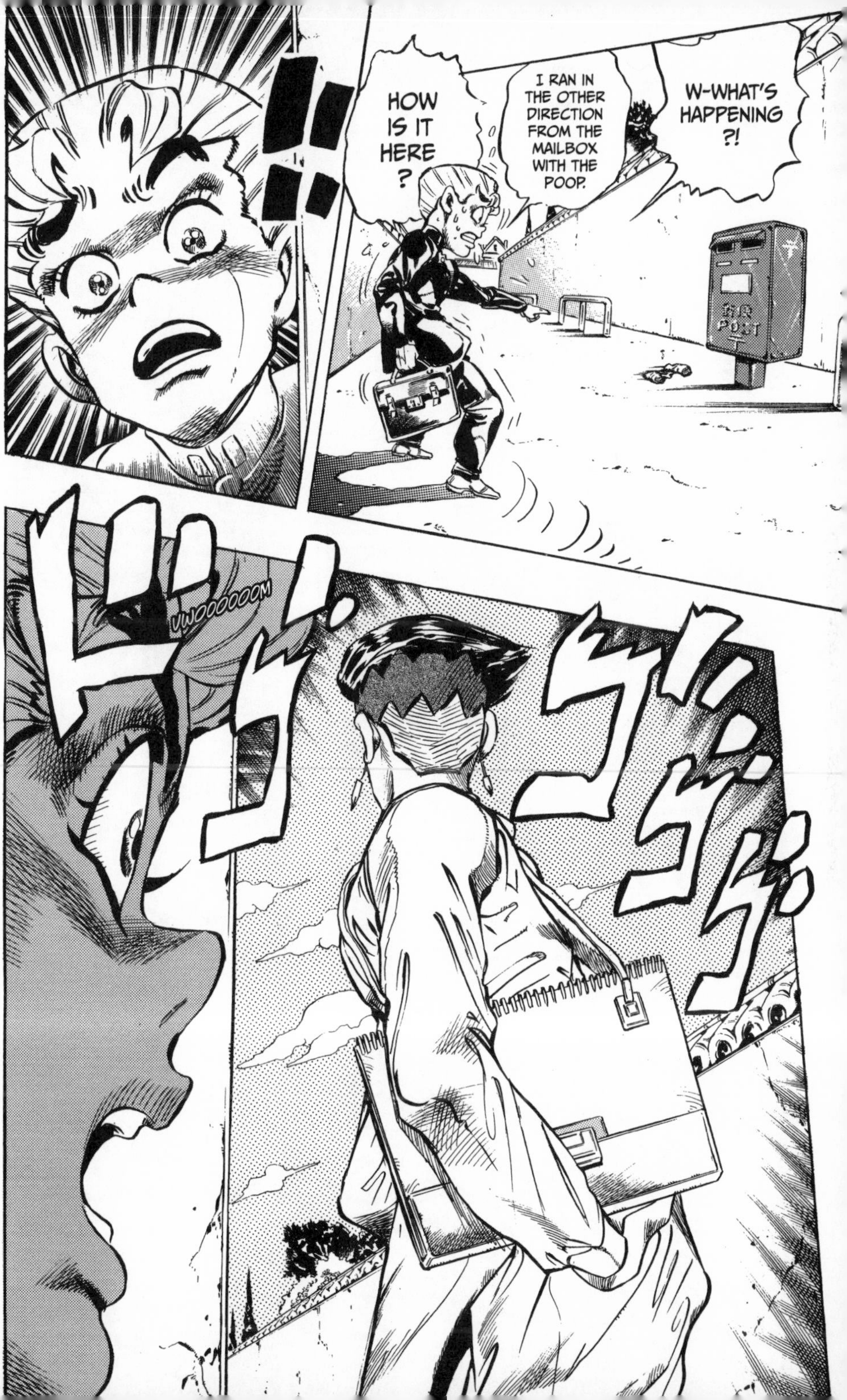
W-WHAT'S HAPPENING ?!
I RAN IN THE OTHER DIRECTION FROM THE MAILBOX WITH THE POOP.
HOW IS IT HERE ?
POST
UWOOOOOOM

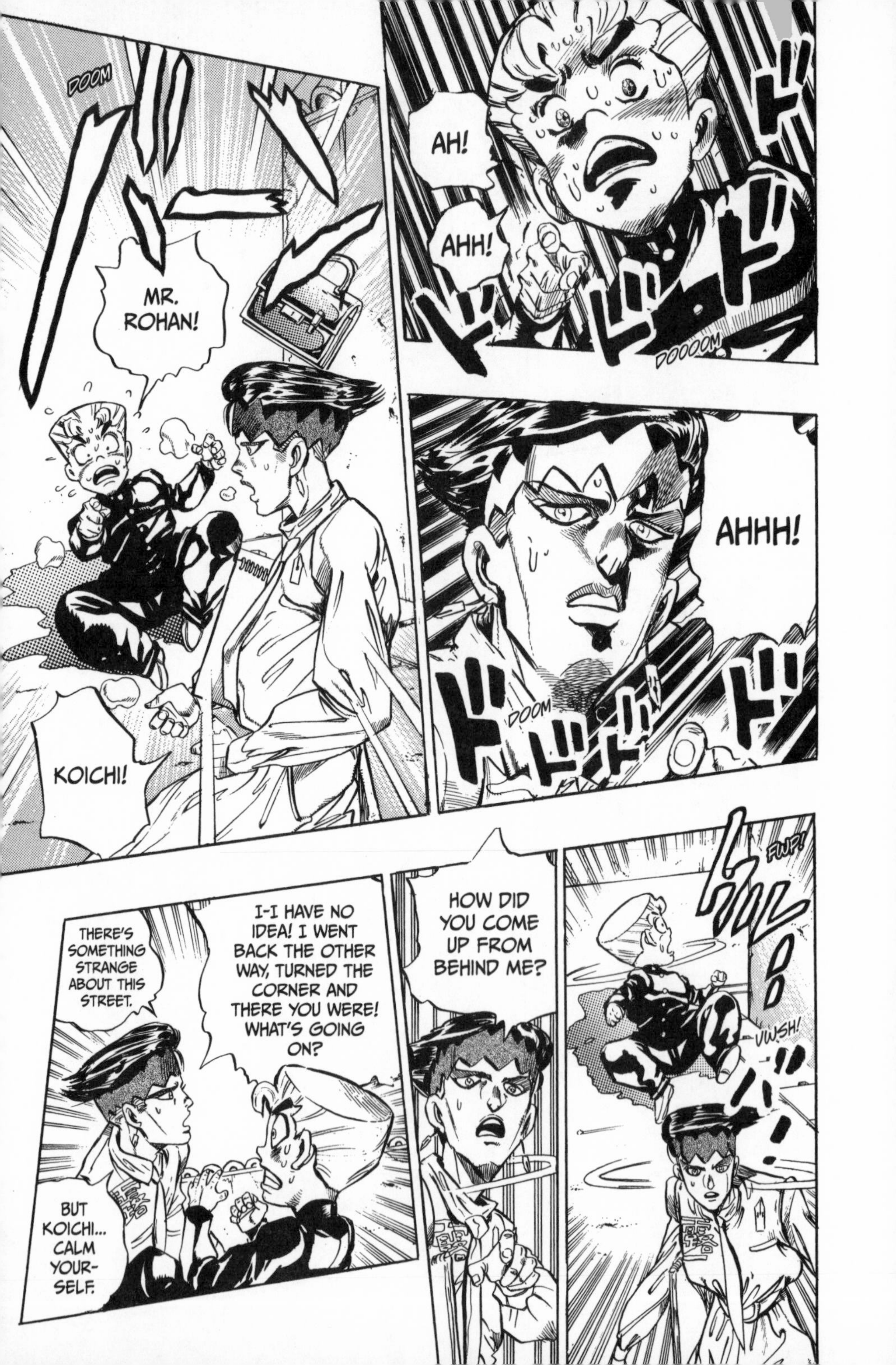
AH!
AHH!
DOOOOM
AHHH!
DOOM
DOOM
MR. ROHAN!
KOICHI!
FWIP!
VWSH!
HOW DID YOU COME UP FROM BEHIND ME?
I-I HAVE NO IDEA! I WENT BACK THE OTHER WAY, TURNED THE CORNER AND THERE YOU WERE! WHAT'S GOING ON?
THERE'S SOMETHING STRANGE ABOUT THIS STREET.
BUT KOICHI... CALM YOUR-SELF.

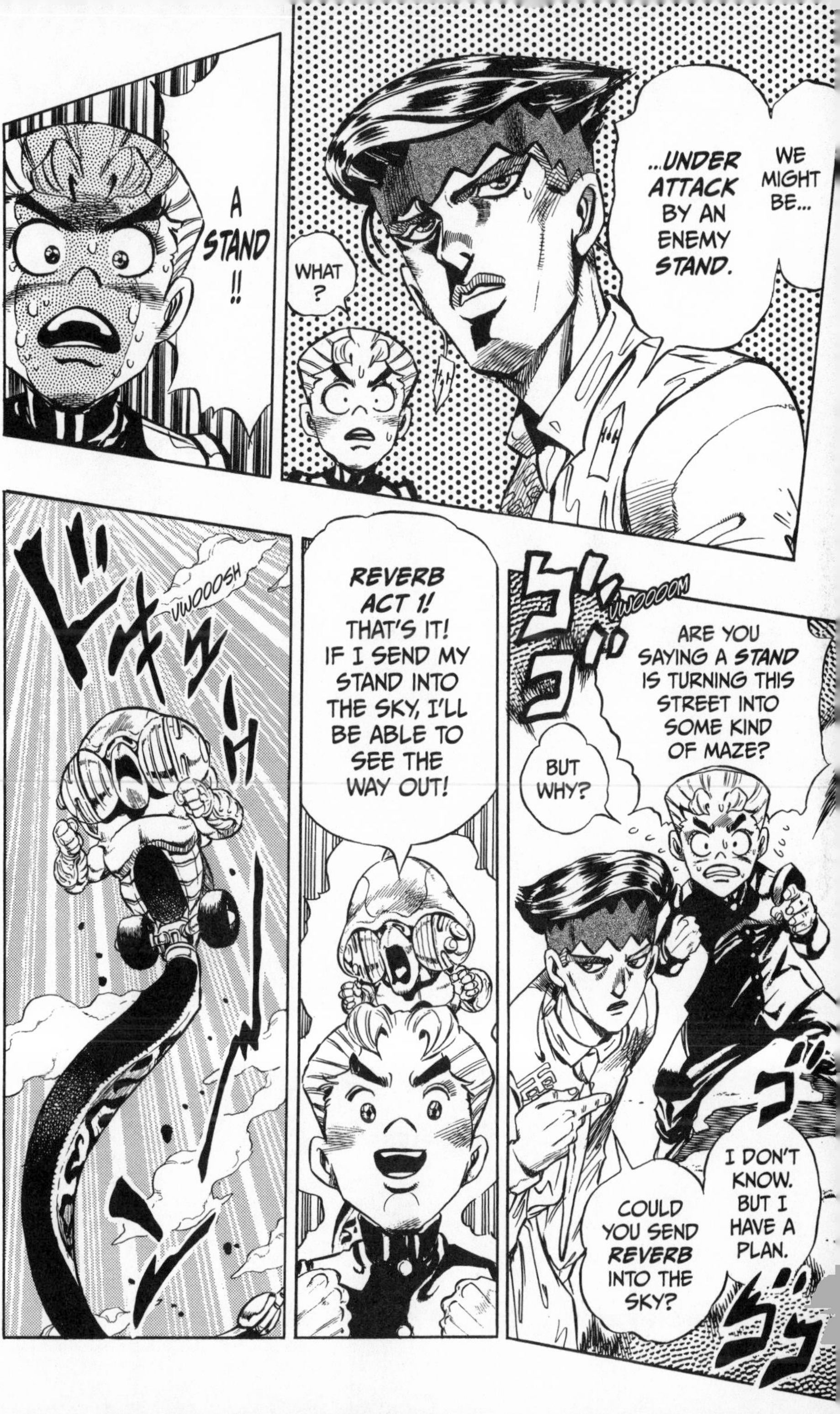
WE MIGHT BE...
...UNDER ATTACK BY AN ENEMY STAND.
WHAT?
A STAND!!
VWOOOOM
ARE YOU SAYING A STAND IS TURNING THIS STREET INTO SOME KIND OF MAZE?
BUT WHY?
I DON'T KNOW. BUT I HAVE A PLAN.
COULD YOU SEND REVERB INTO THE SKY?
REVERB ACT 1! THAT'S IT! IF I SEND MY STAND INTO THE SKY, I'LL BE ABLE TO SEE THE WAY OUT!
VWOOOSH

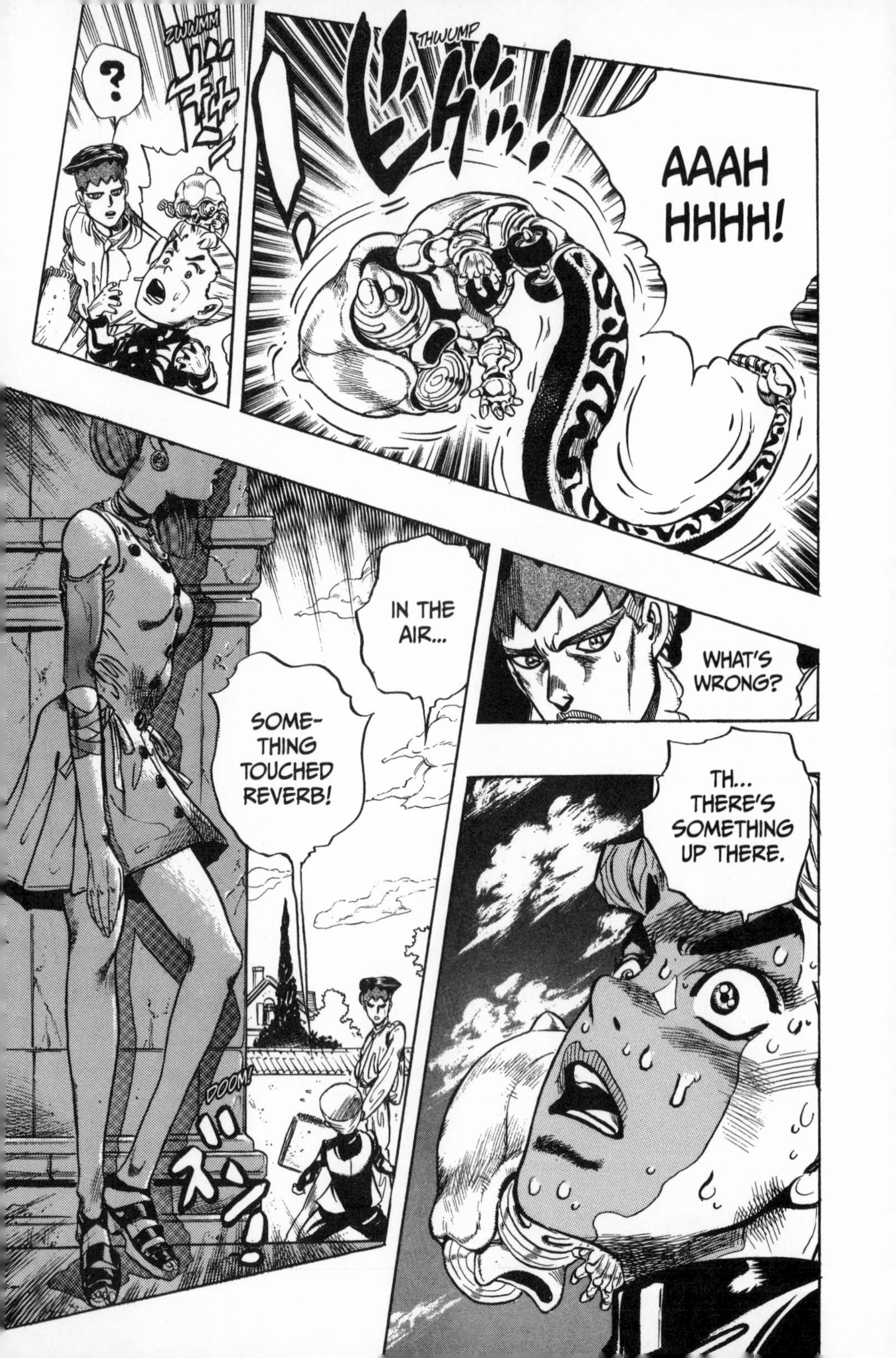
THWUMP
AAAH HHHH!
ZWWMM
?
WHAT'S WRONG?
TH... THERE'S SOMETHING UP THERE.
IN THE AIR...
SOME-THING TOUCHED REVERB!
DOOM

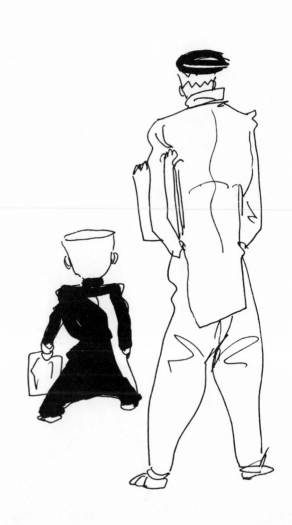

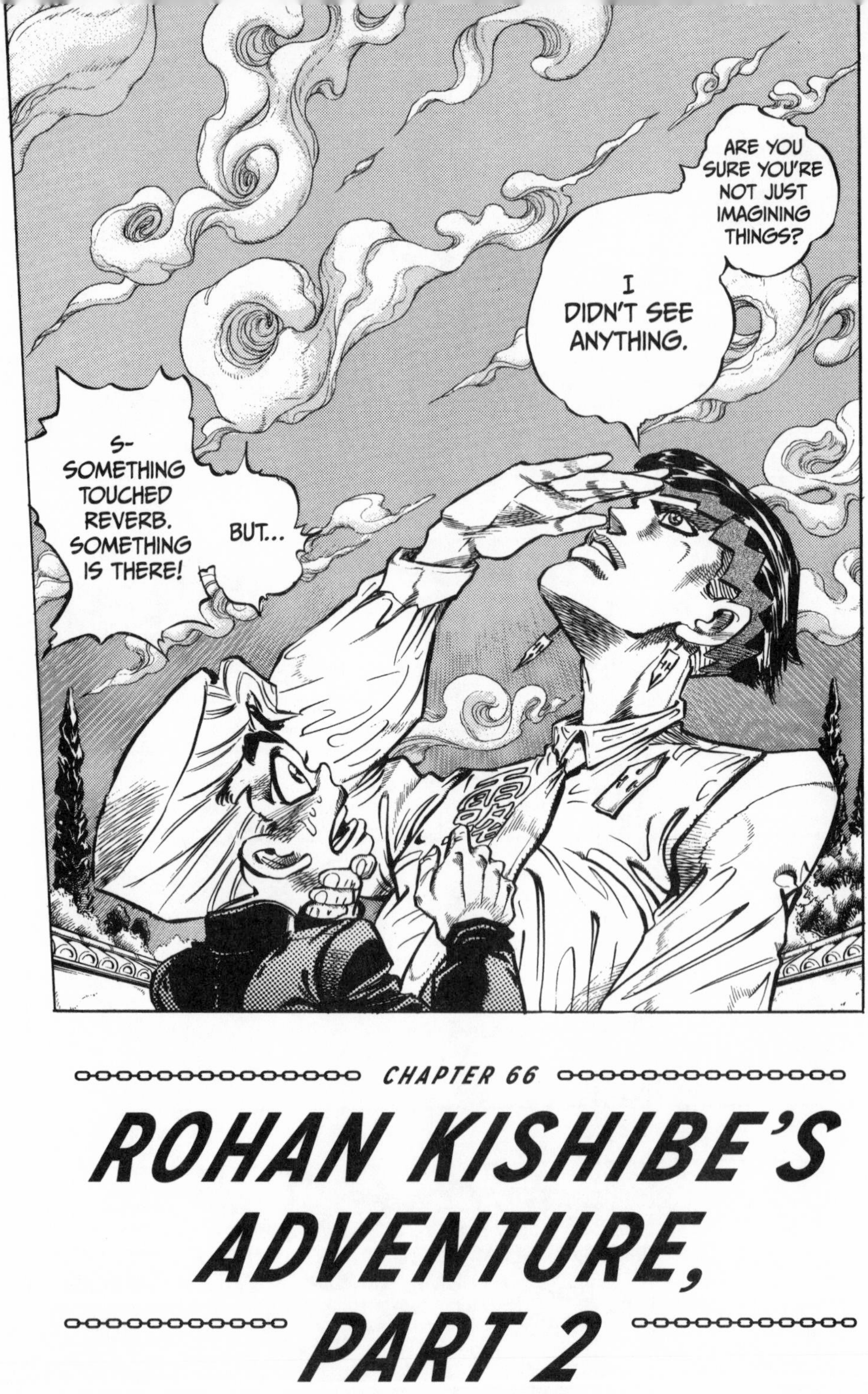
ARE YOU SURE YOU'RE NOT JUST IMAGINING THINGS?
I DIDN'T SEE ANYTHING.
BUT...
S-SOMETHING TOUCHED REVERB. SOMETHING IS THERE!

CHAPTER 66

ROHAN KISHIBE'S ADVENTURE, PART 2

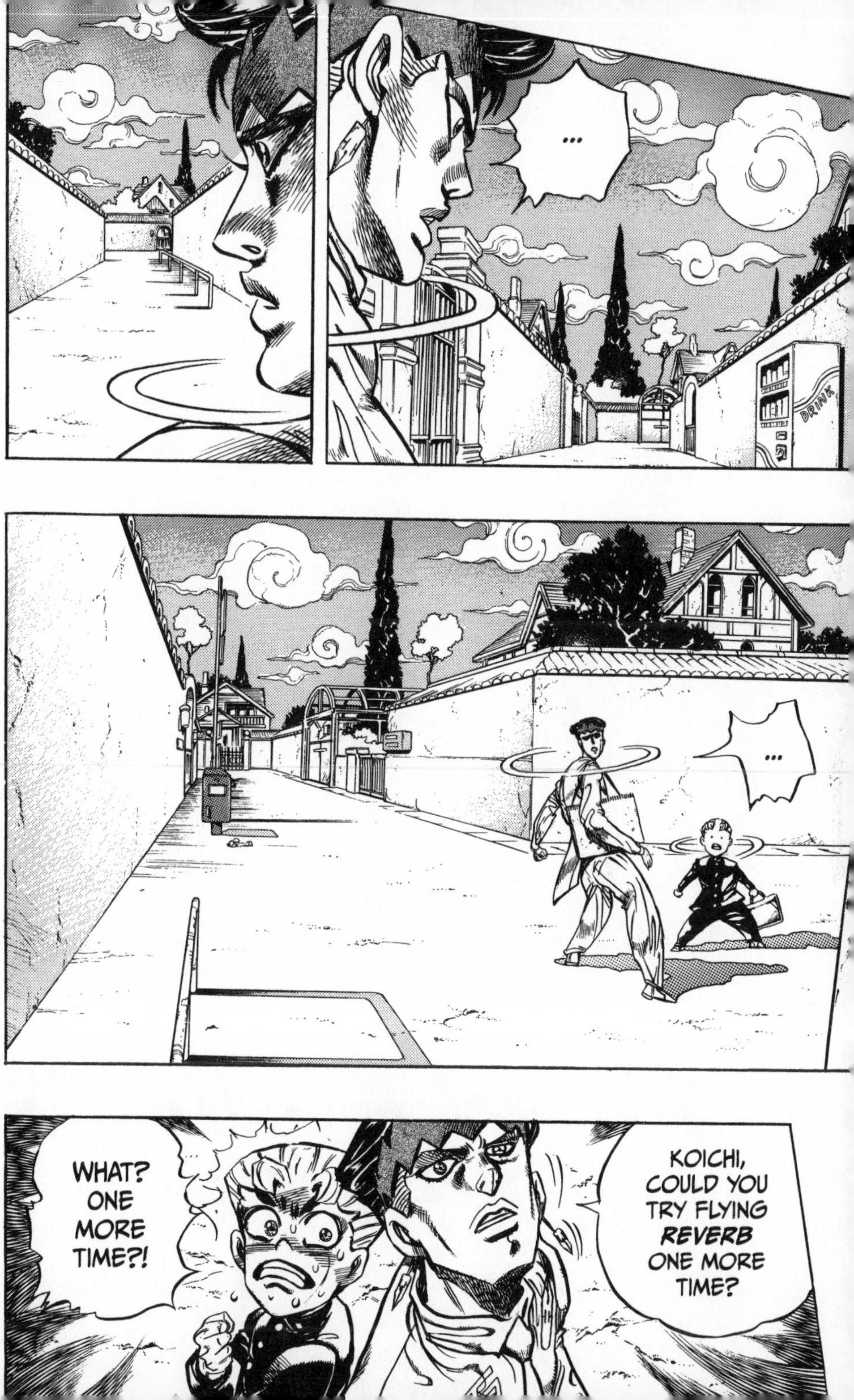
...
...
KOICHI, COULD YOU TRY FLYING REVERB ONE MORE TIME?
WHAT? ONE MORE TIME?!

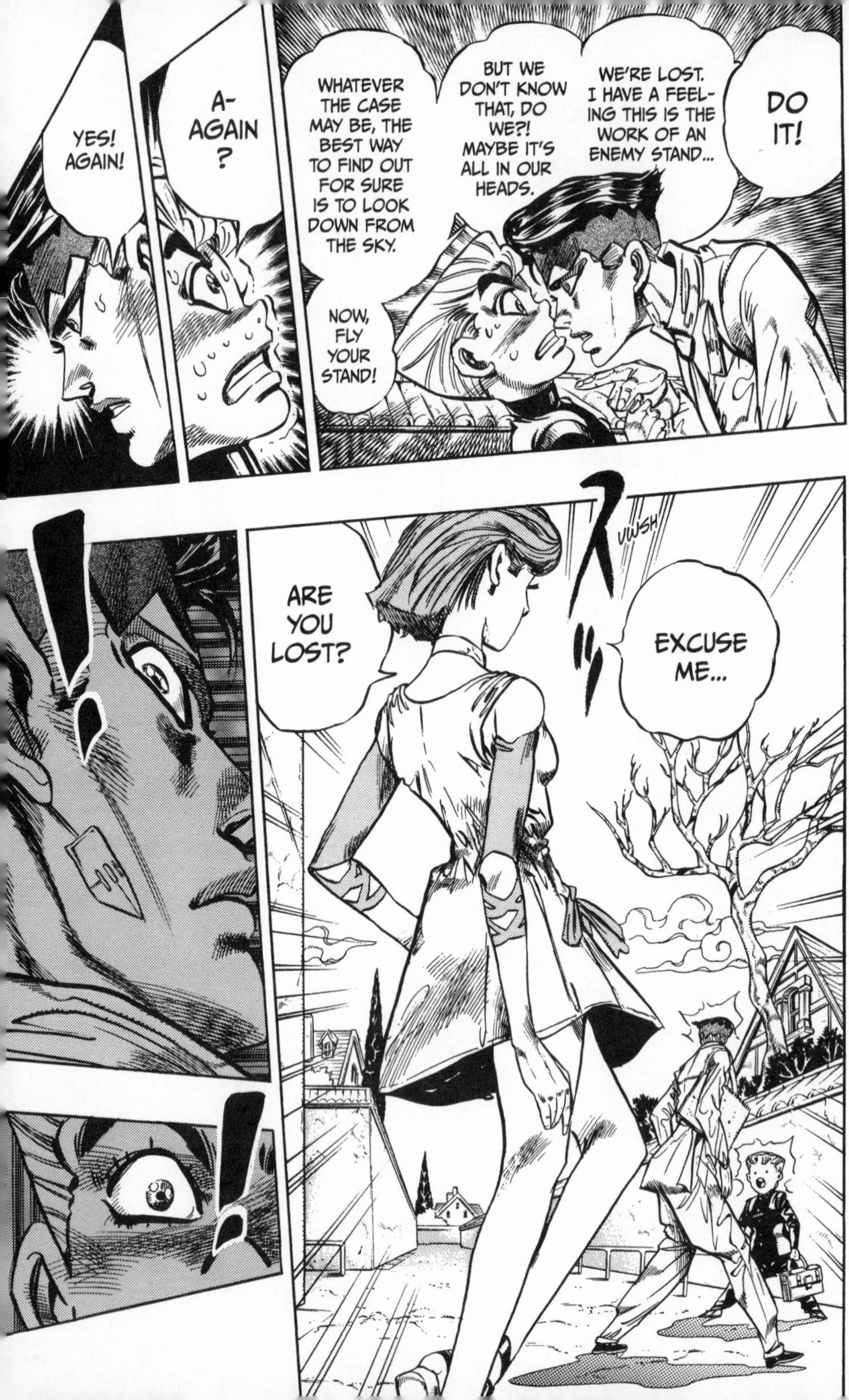

DO IT!
WE'RE LOST. I HAVE A FEELING THIS IS THE WORK OF AN ENEMY STAND...
BUT WE DON'T KNOW THAT, DO WE?! MAYBE IT'S ALL IN OUR HEADS.
WHATEVER THE CASE MAY BE, THE BEST WAY TO FIND OUT FOR SURE IS TO LOOK DOWN FROM THE SKY.
NOW, FLY YOUR STAND!
A-AGAIN?
YES! AGAIN!
VWSH
EXCUSE ME...
ARE YOU LOST?

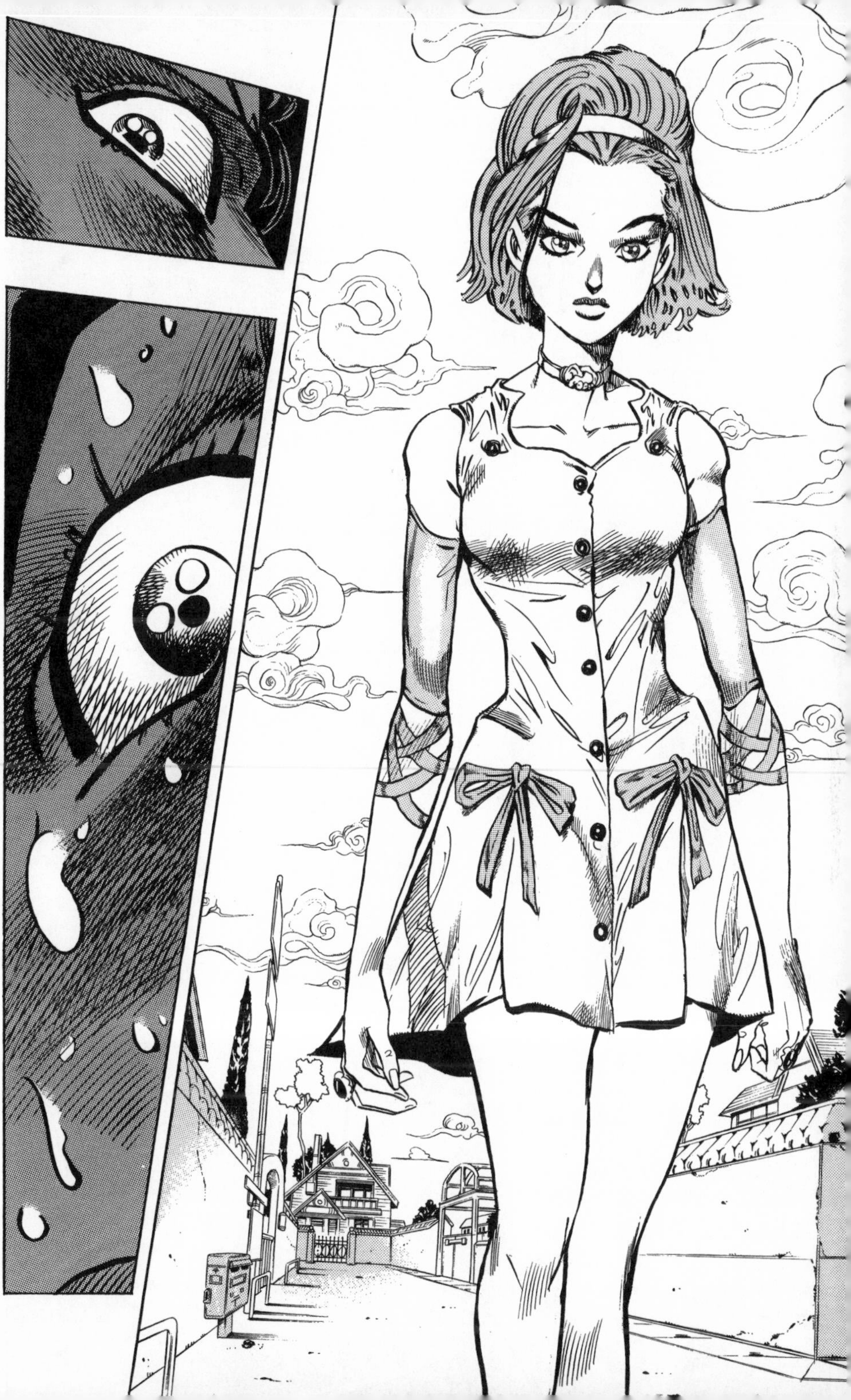

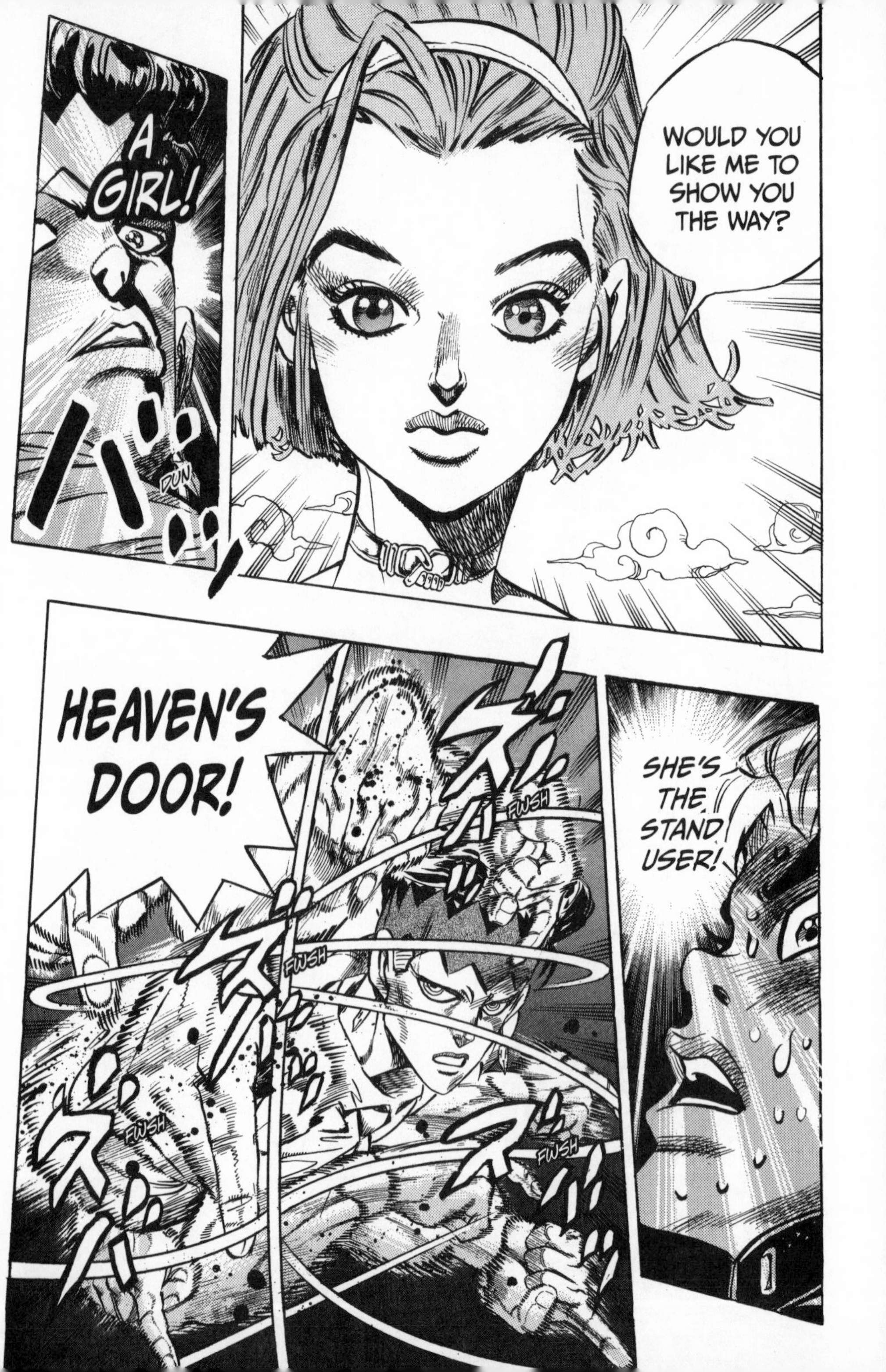
WOULD YOU LIKE ME TO SHOW YOU THE WAY?
A GIRL!
DUN
SHE'S THE STAND USER!
HEAVEN'S DOOR!
FWSH
FWSH
FWSH
FWSH

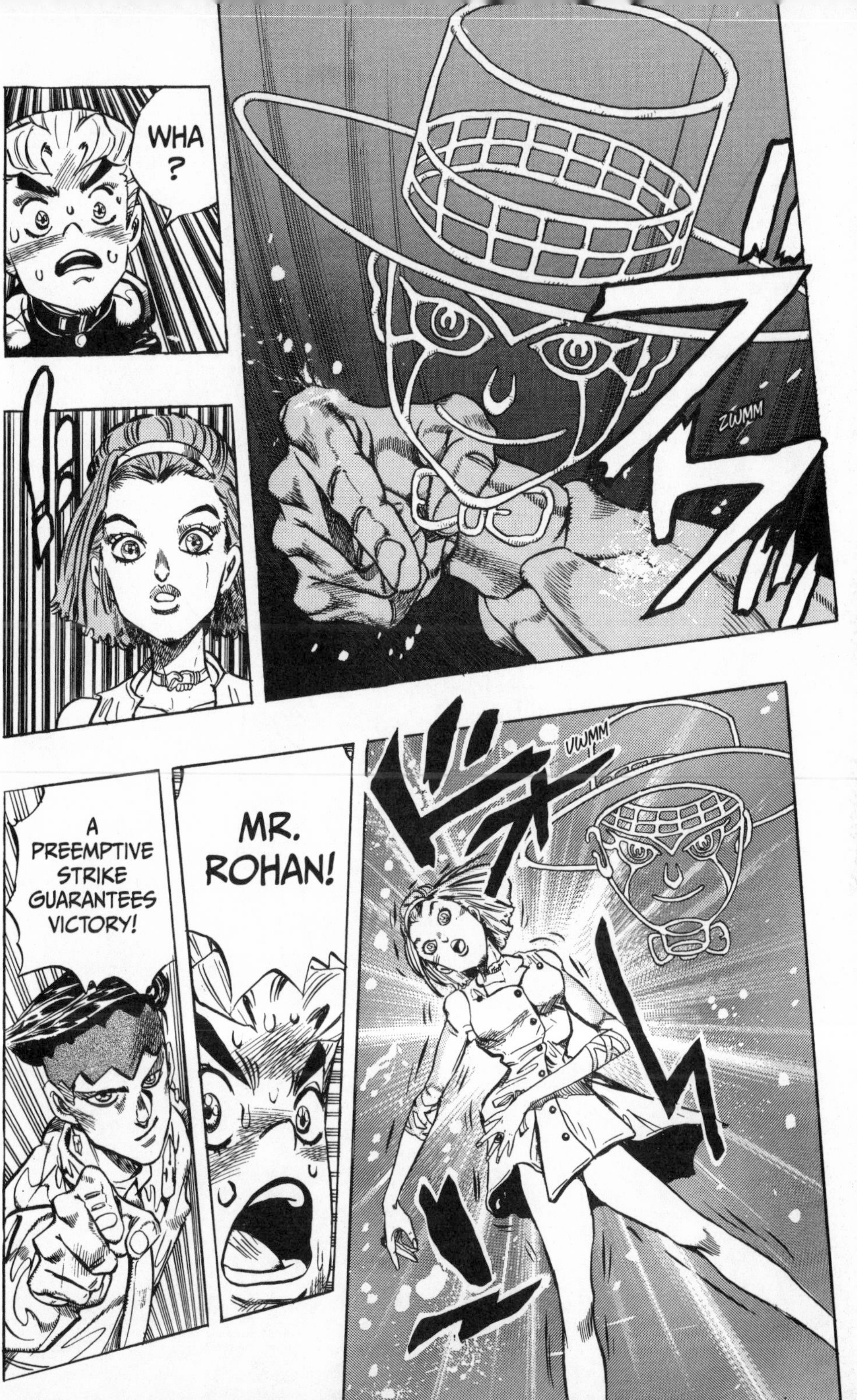
ZWMM
WHA ?
UWMM
MR. ROHAN!
A PREEMPTIVE STRIKE GUARANTEES VICTORY!

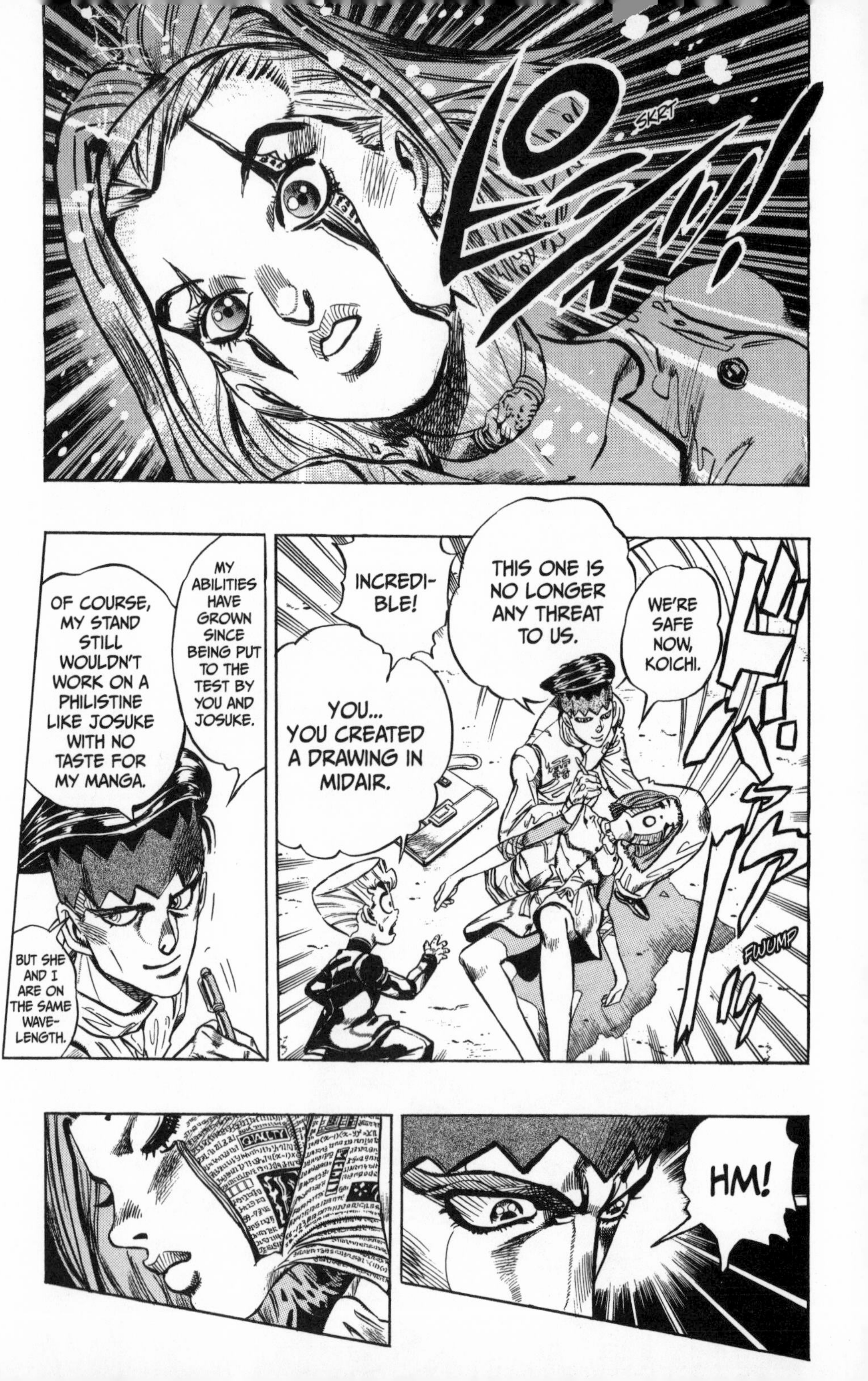
SKRT
WE'RE SAFE NOW, KOICHI.
THIS ONE IS NO LONGER ANY THREAT TO US.
INCREDI-BLE!
YOU... YOU CREATED A DRAWING IN MIDAIR.
FWUMP
MY ABILITIES HAVE GROWN SINCE BEING PUT TO THE TEST BY YOU AND JOSUKE.
OF COURSE, MY STAND STILL WOULDN'T WORK ON A PHILISTINE LIKE JOSUKE WITH NO TASTE FOR MY MANGA.
BUT SHE AND I ARE ON THE SAME WAVE-LENGTH.
HM!

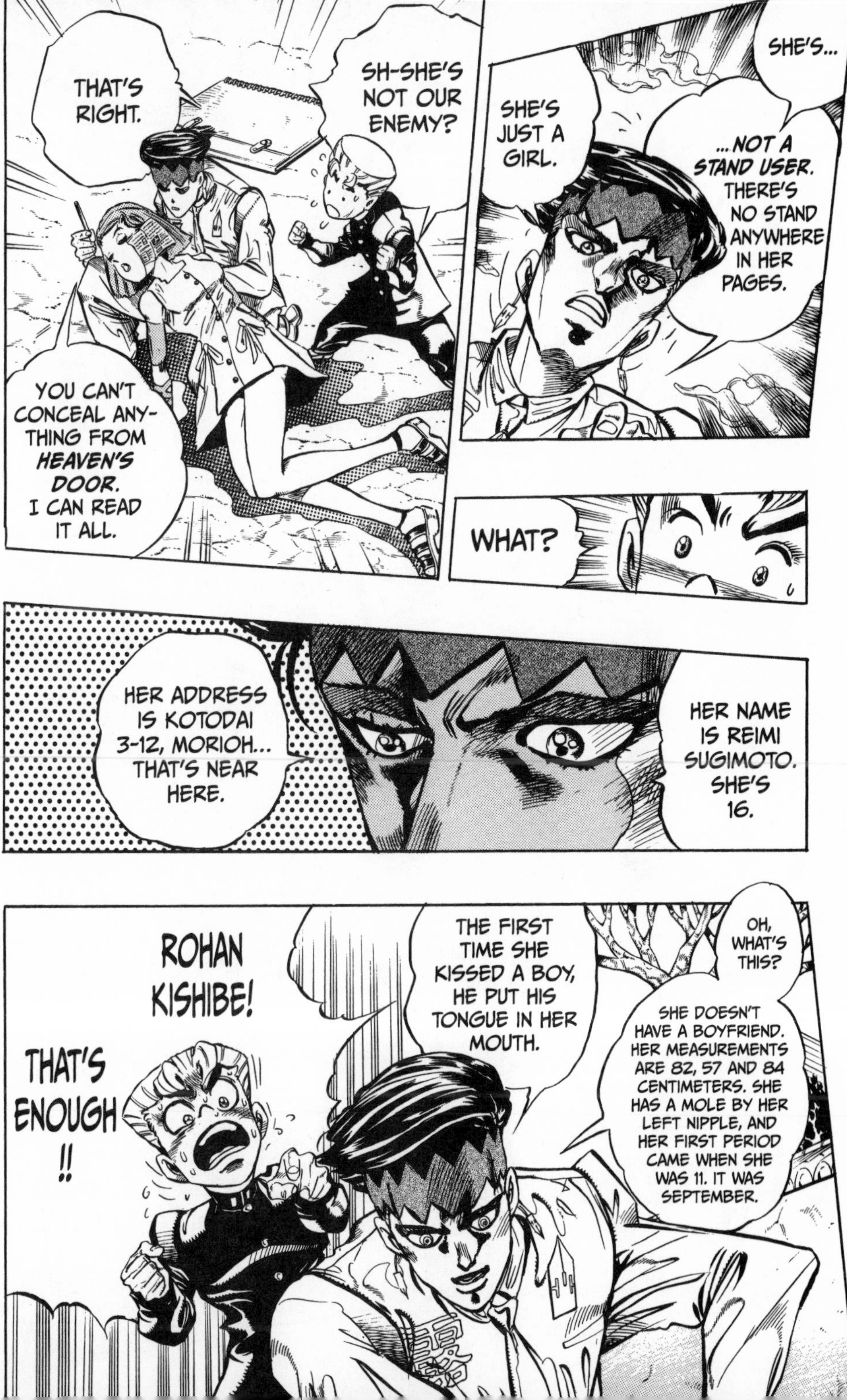
SHE'S...
...NOT A STAND USER. THERE'S NO STAND ANYWHERE IN HER PAGES.
SHE'S JUST A GIRL.
WHAT?
SH-SHE'S NOT OUR ENEMY?
THAT'S RIGHT.
YOU CAN'T CONCEAL ANYTHING FROM HEAVEN'S DOOR. I CAN READ IT ALL.
HER NAME IS REIMI SUGIMOTO. SHE'S 16.
HER ADDRESS IS KOTODAI 3-12, MORIOH... THAT'S NEAR HERE.
OH, WHAT'S THIS?
SHE DOESN'T HAVE A BOYFRIEND. HER MEASUREMENTS ARE 82, 57 AND 84 CENTIMETERS. SHE HAS A MOLE BY HER LEFT NIPPLE, AND HER FIRST PERIOD CAME WHEN SHE WAS 11. IT WAS SEPTEMBER.
THE FIRST TIME SHE KISSED A BOY, HE PUT HIS TONGUE IN HER MOUTH.
ROHAN KISHIBE!
THAT'S ENOUGH!!

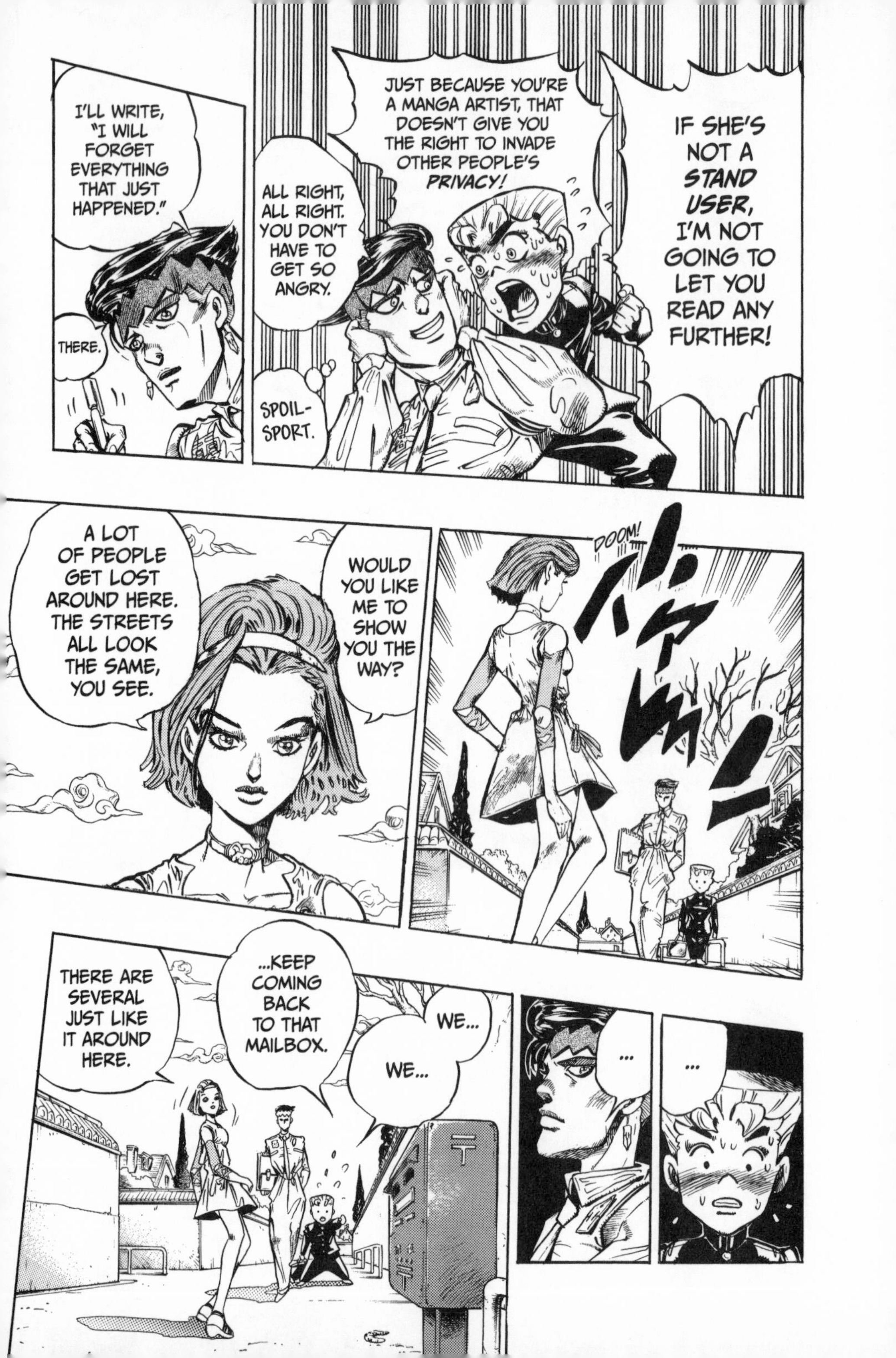
JUST BECAUSE YOU'RE A MANGA ARTIST, THAT DOESN'T GIVE YOU THE RIGHT TO INVADE OTHER PEOPLE'S *PRIVACY!*
IF SHE'S NOT A ***STAND USER,*** I'M NOT GOING TO LET YOU READ ANY FURTHER!
ALL RIGHT, ALL RIGHT. YOU DON'T HAVE TO GET SO ANGRY.
SPOIL-SPORT.
I'LL WRITE, "I WILL FORGET EVERYTHING THAT JUST HAPPENED."
THERE.
DOOM!
A LOT OF PEOPLE GET LOST AROUND HERE. THE STREETS ALL LOOK THE SAME, YOU SEE.
WOULD YOU LIKE ME TO SHOW YOU THE WAY?
...
...
WE...
WE...
...KEEP COMING BACK TO THAT MAILBOX.
THERE ARE SEVERAL JUST LIKE IT AROUND HERE.

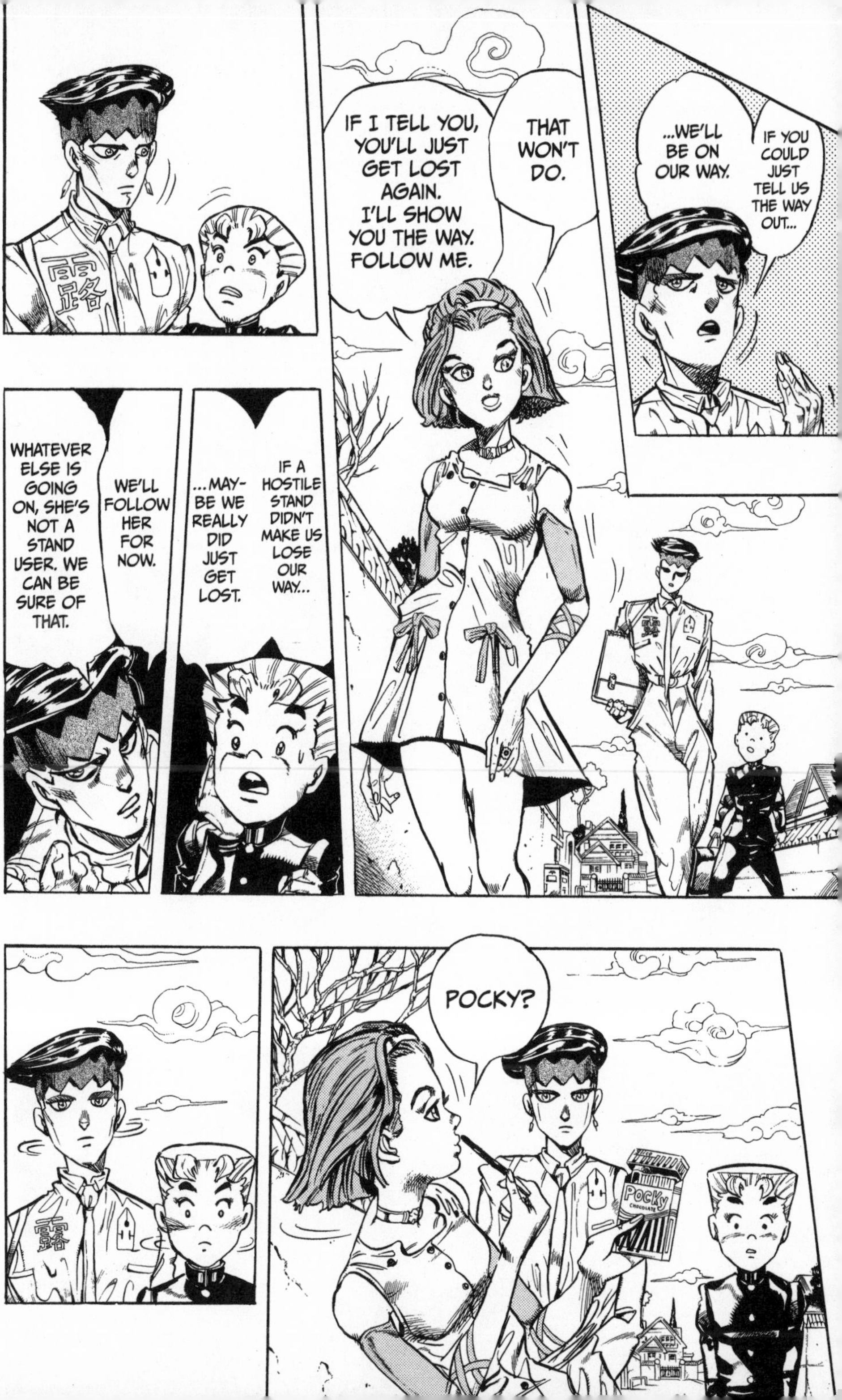
IF YOU COULD JUST TELL US THE WAY OUT...
...WE'LL BE ON OUR WAY.
THAT WON'T DO.
IF I TELL YOU, YOU'LL JUST GET LOST AGAIN. I'LL SHOW YOU THE WAY. FOLLOW ME.
IF A HOSTILE STAND DIDN'T MAKE US LOSE OUR WAY...
...MAY-BE WE REALLY DID JUST GET LOST.
WE'LL FOLLOW HER FOR NOW.
WHATEVER ELSE IS GOING ON, SHE'S NOT A STAND USER. WE CAN BE SURE OF THAT.
POCKY?
POCKY
CHOCOLATE

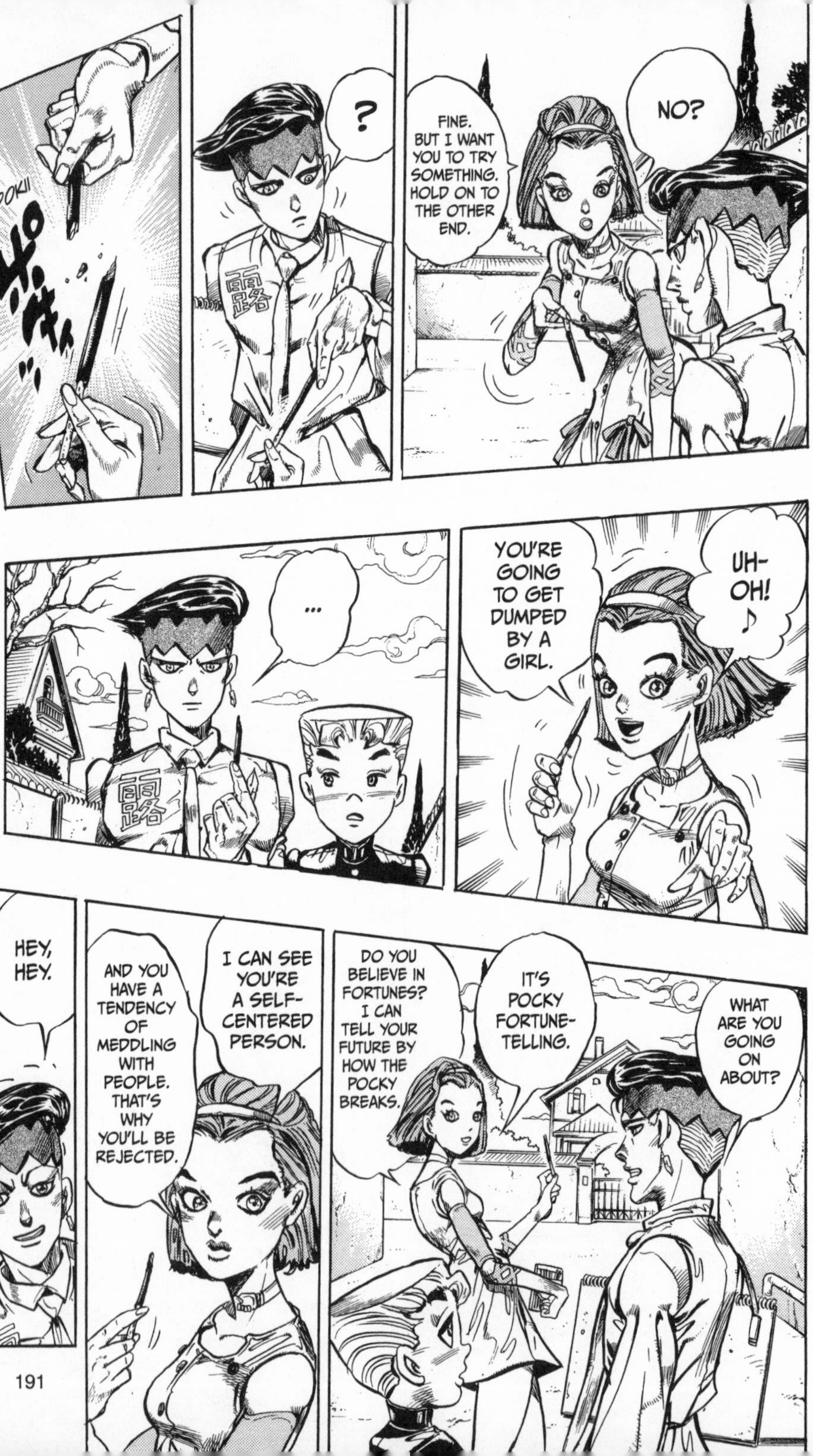
NO?
FINE. BUT I WANT YOU TO TRY SOMETHING. HOLD ON TO THE OTHER END.
?
POKII
UH-OH! ♪
YOU'RE GOING TO GET DUMPED BY A GIRL.
...
WHAT ARE YOU GOING ON ABOUT?
IT'S POCKY FORTUNE-TELLING.
DO YOU BELIEVE IN FORTUNES? I CAN TELL YOUR FUTURE BY HOW THE POCKY BREAKS.
I CAN SEE YOU'RE A SELF-CENTERED PERSON.
AND YOU HAVE A TENDENCY OF MEDDLING WITH PEOPLE. THAT'S WHY YOU'LL BE REJECTED.
HEY, HEY.

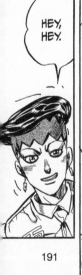

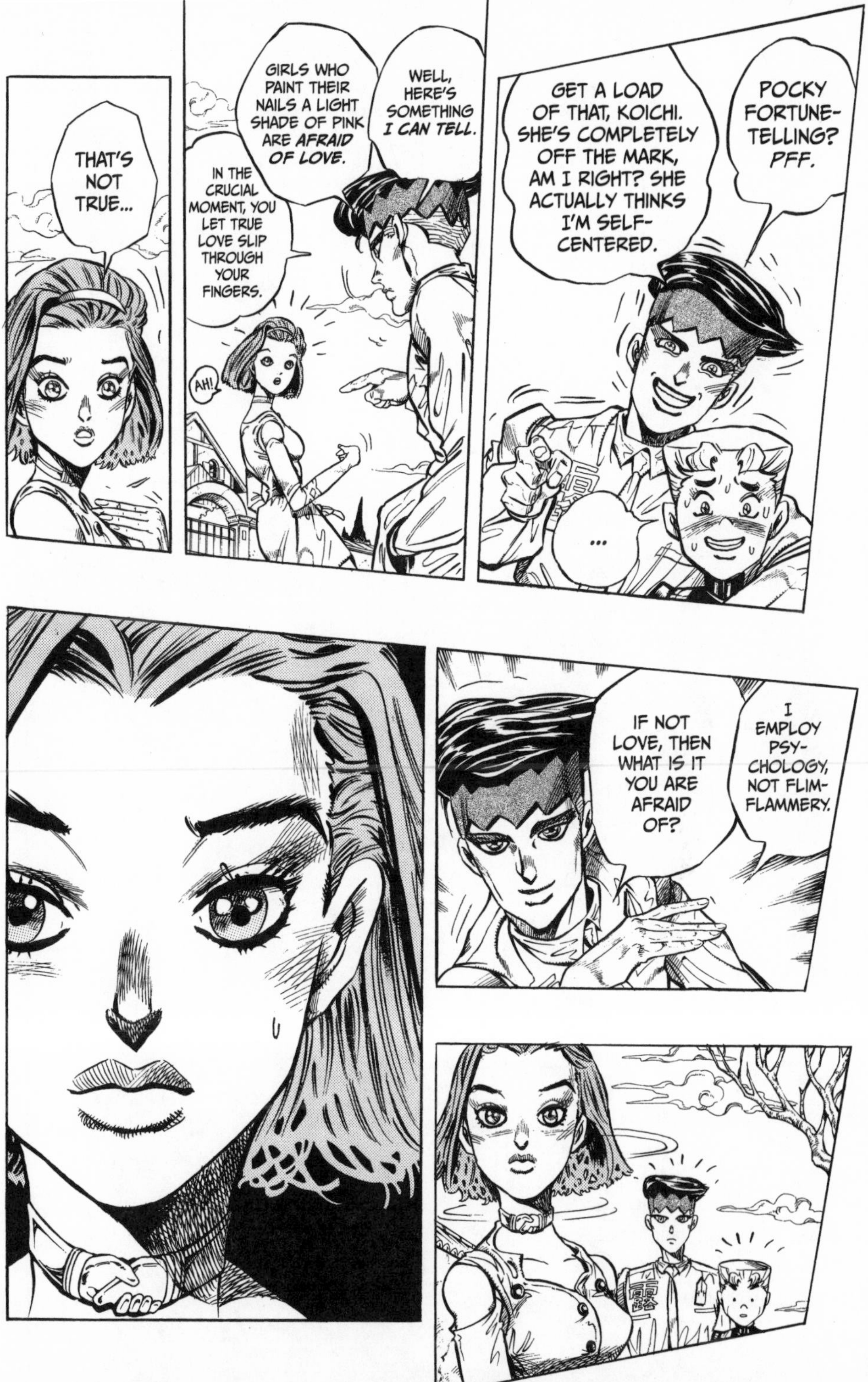
POCKY FORTUNE-TELLING? PFF.
GET A LOAD OF THAT, KOICHI. SHE'S COMPLETELY OFF THE MARK, AM I RIGHT? SHE ACTUALLY THINKS I'M SELF-CENTERED.
...
WELL, HERE'S SOMETHING I CAN TELL.
GIRLS WHO PAINT THEIR NAILS A LIGHT SHADE OF PINK ARE AFRAID OF LOVE.
IN THE CRUCIAL MOMENT, YOU LET TRUE LOVE SLIP THROUGH YOUR FINGERS.
AH!
THAT'S NOT TRUE...
I EMPLOY PSYCHOLOGY, NOT FLIMFLAMMERY.
IF NOT LOVE, THEN WHAT IS IT YOU ARE AFRAID OF?

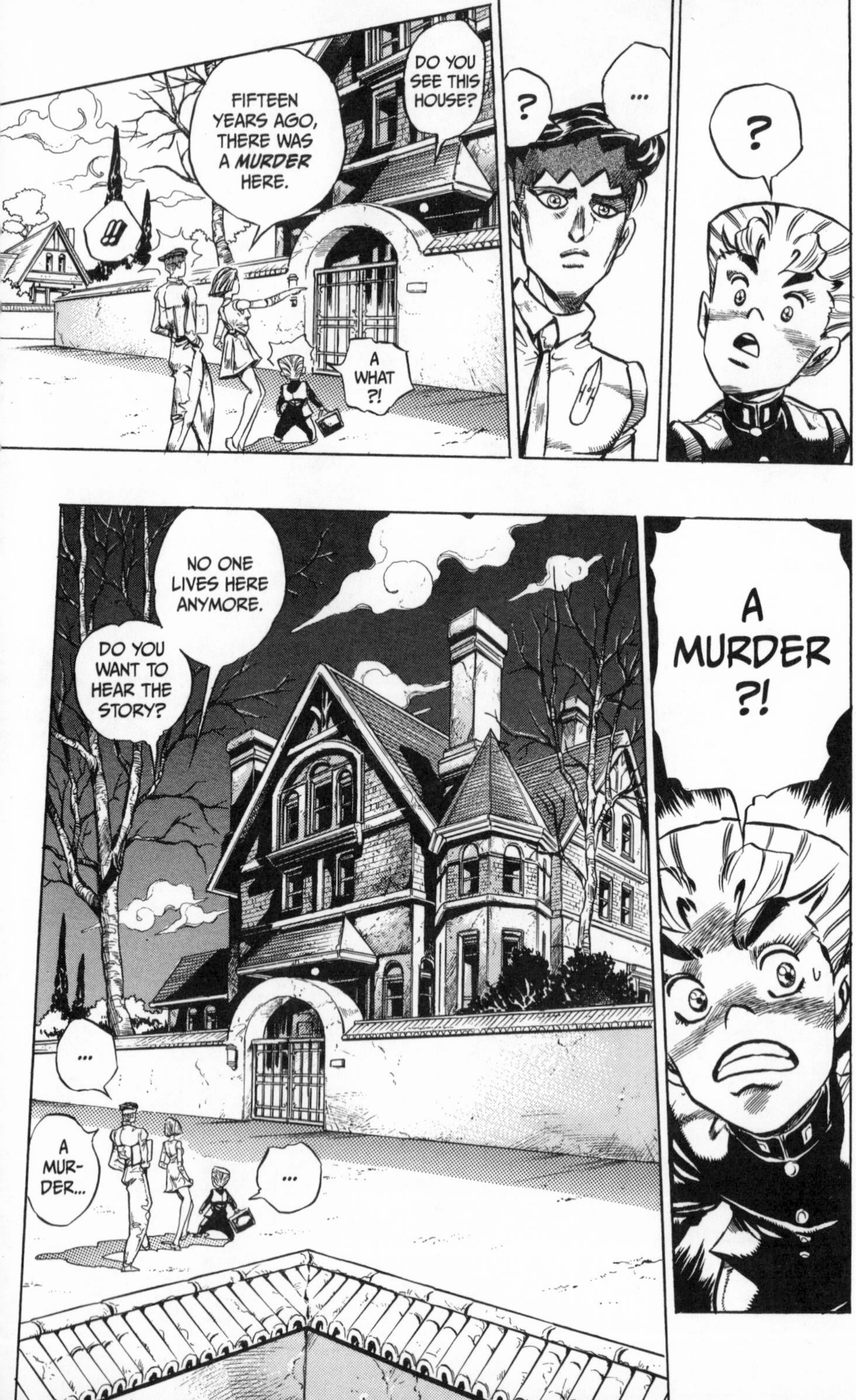
?
...
?
DO YOU SEE THIS HOUSE?
FIFTEEN YEARS AGO, THERE WAS A *MURDER* HERE.
!!
A WHAT ?!
A MURDER ?!
NO ONE LIVES HERE ANYMORE.
DO YOU WANT TO HEAR THE STORY?
...
...
A MUR-DER...

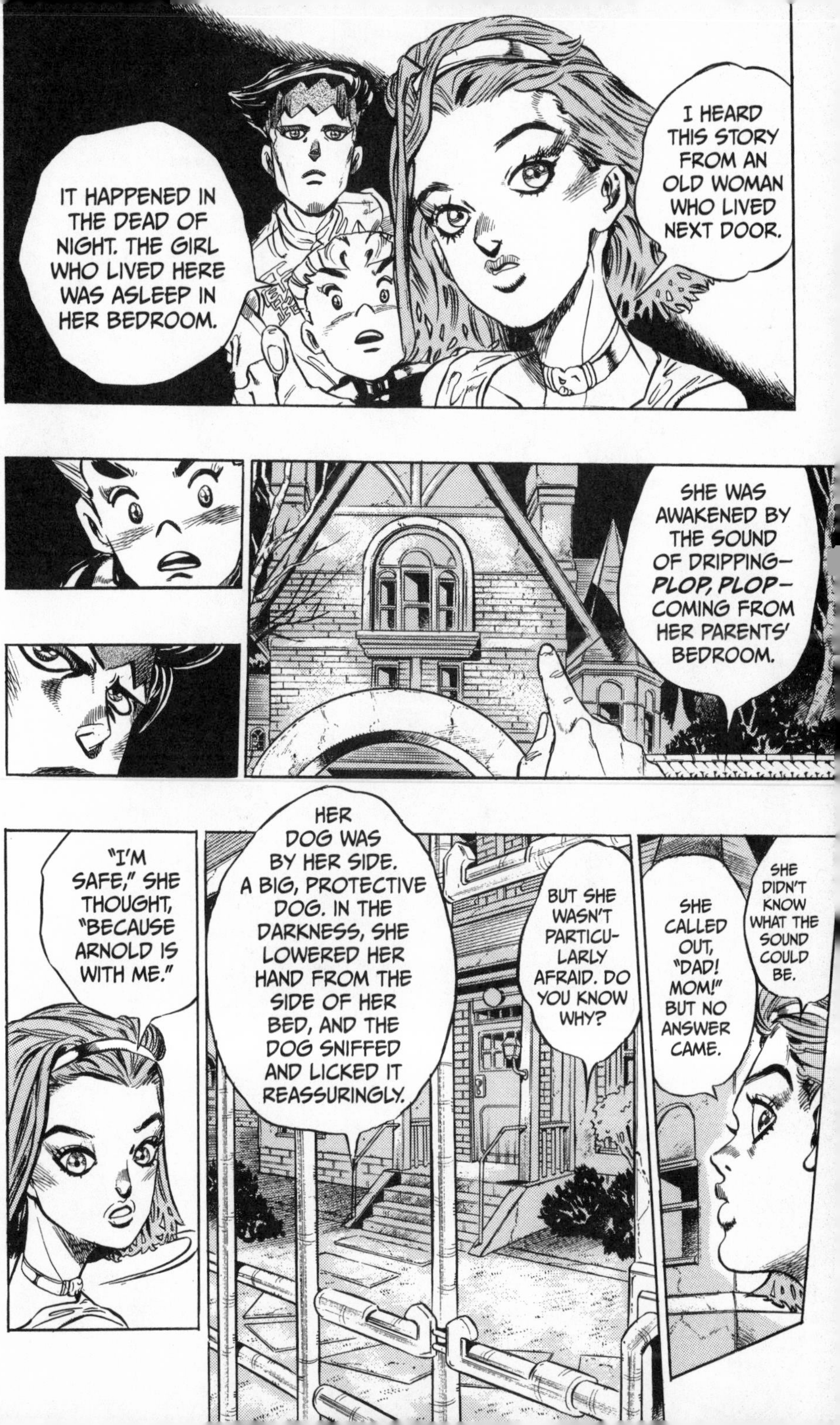
I HEARD THIS STORY FROM AN OLD WOMAN WHO LIVED NEXT DOOR.
IT HAPPENED IN THE DEAD OF NIGHT. THE GIRL WHO LIVED HERE WAS ASLEEP IN HER BEDROOM.
SHE WAS AWAKENED BY THE SOUND OF DRIPPING—*PLOP, PLOP*—COMING FROM HER PARENTS' BEDROOM.
SHE DIDN'T KNOW WHAT THE SOUND COULD BE.
SHE CALLED OUT, "DAD! MOM!" BUT NO ANSWER CAME.
BUT SHE WASN'T PARTICU-LARLY AFRAID. DO YOU KNOW WHY?
HER DOG WAS BY HER SIDE. A BIG, PROTECTIVE DOG. IN THE DARKNESS, SHE LOWERED HER HAND FROM THE SIDE OF HER BED, AND THE DOG SNIFFED AND LICKED IT REASSURINGLY.
"I'M SAFE," SHE THOUGHT, "BECAUSE ARNOLD IS WITH ME."

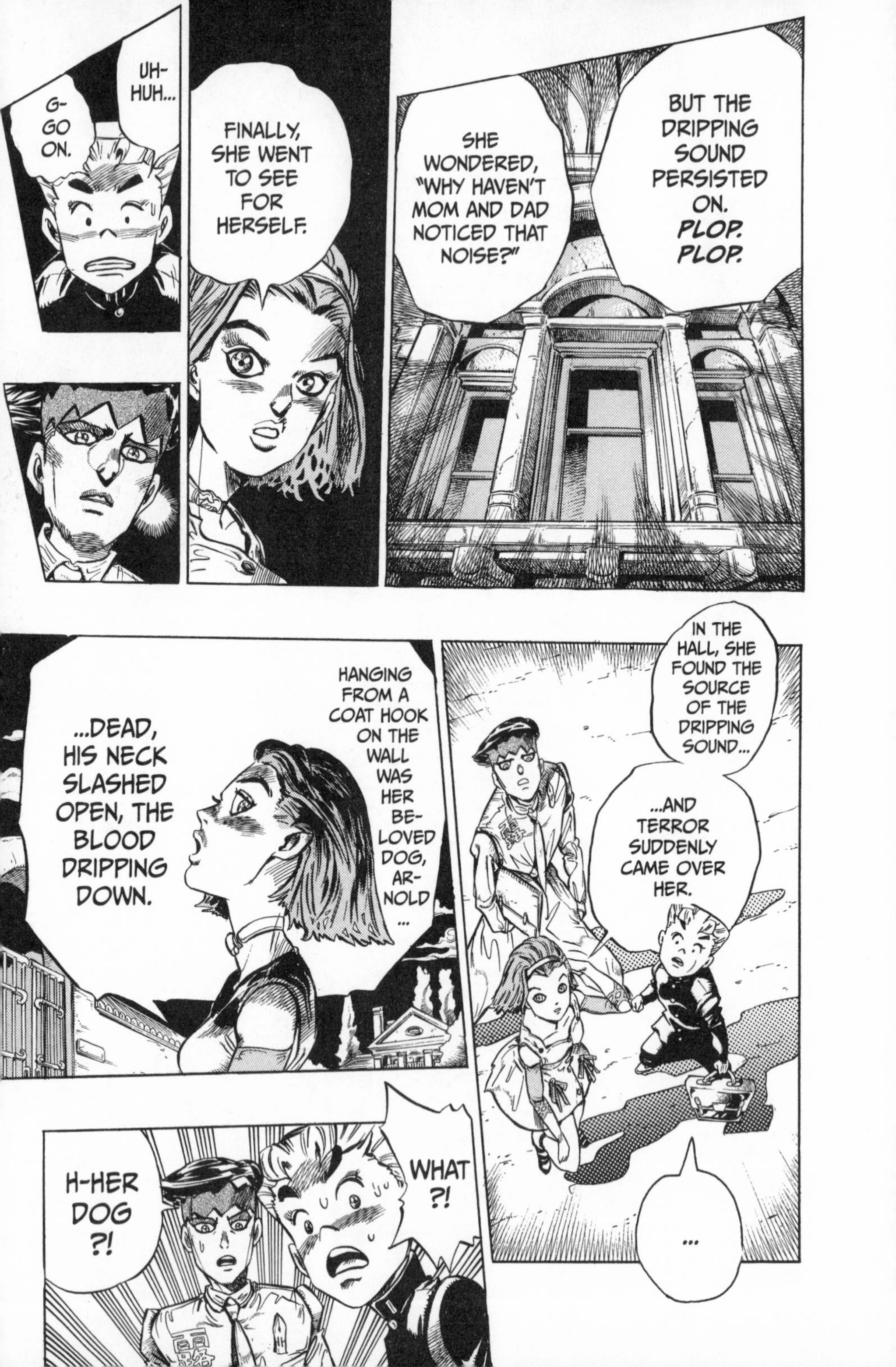
BUT THE DRIPPING SOUND PERSISTED ON. *PLOP. PLOP.*
SHE WONDERED, "WHY HAVEN'T MOM AND DAD NOTICED THAT NOISE?"
FINALLY, SHE WENT TO SEE FOR HERSELF.
UH-HUH...
G-GO ON.
IN THE HALL, SHE FOUND THE SOURCE OF THE DRIPPING SOUND...
...AND TERROR SUDDENLY CAME OVER HER.
...
HANGING FROM A COAT HOOK ON THE WALL WAS HER BE-LOVED DOG, AR-NOLD...
...DEAD, HIS NECK SLASHED OPEN, THE BLOOD DRIPPING DOWN.
WHAT?!
H-HER DOG?!

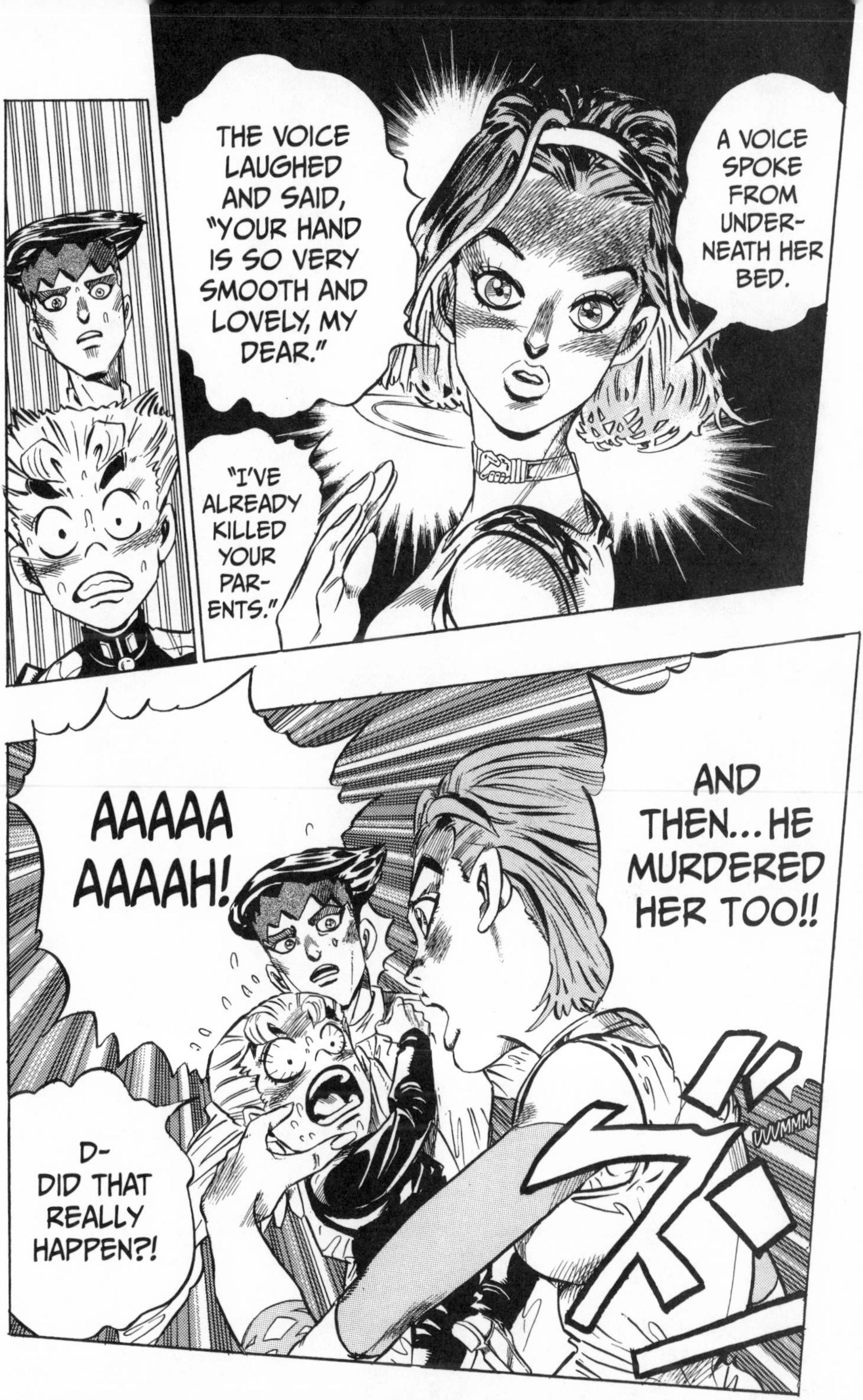
A VOICE SPOKE FROM UNDERNEATH HER BED.
THE VOICE LAUGHED AND SAID, "YOUR HAND IS SO VERY SMOOTH AND LOVELY, MY DEAR."
"I'VE ALREADY KILLED YOUR PARENTS."
AND THEN... HE MURDERED HER TOO!!
AAAAA AAAAH!
VVVMMM
D- DID THAT REALLY HAPPEN?!

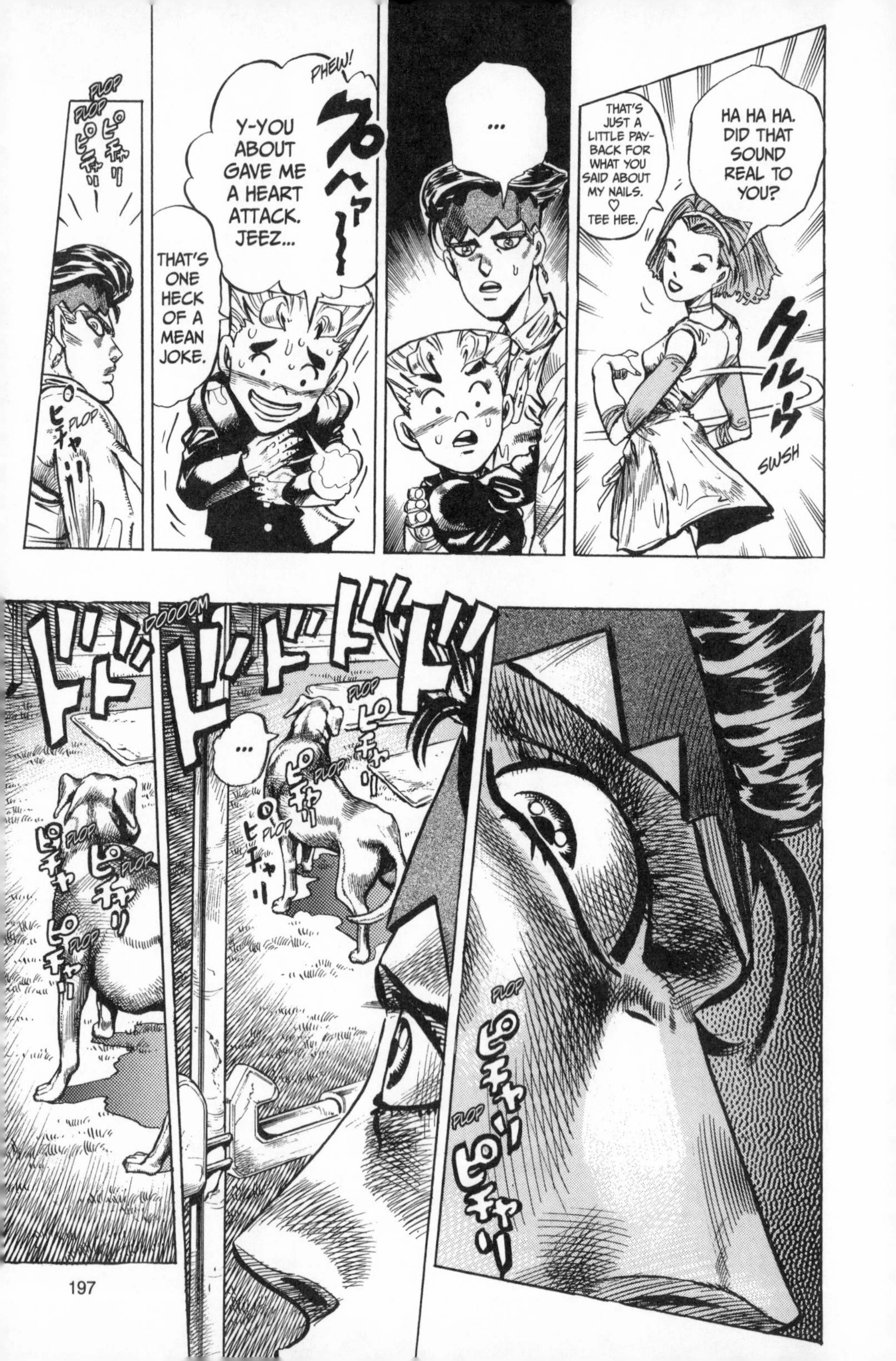
HA HA HA. DID THAT SOUND REAL TO YOU?
THAT'S JUST A LITTLE PAY-BACK FOR WHAT YOU SAID ABOUT MY NAILS. ♡ TEE HEE.
SWSH
...
PHEW!
Y-YOU ABOUT GAVE ME A HEART ATTACK. JEEZ...
THAT'S ONE HECK OF A MEAN JOKE.
PLOP PLOP
PLOP
PLOP
PLOP
DOOOOM
PLOP
...
PLOP
PLOP
PLOP
PLOP
PLOP

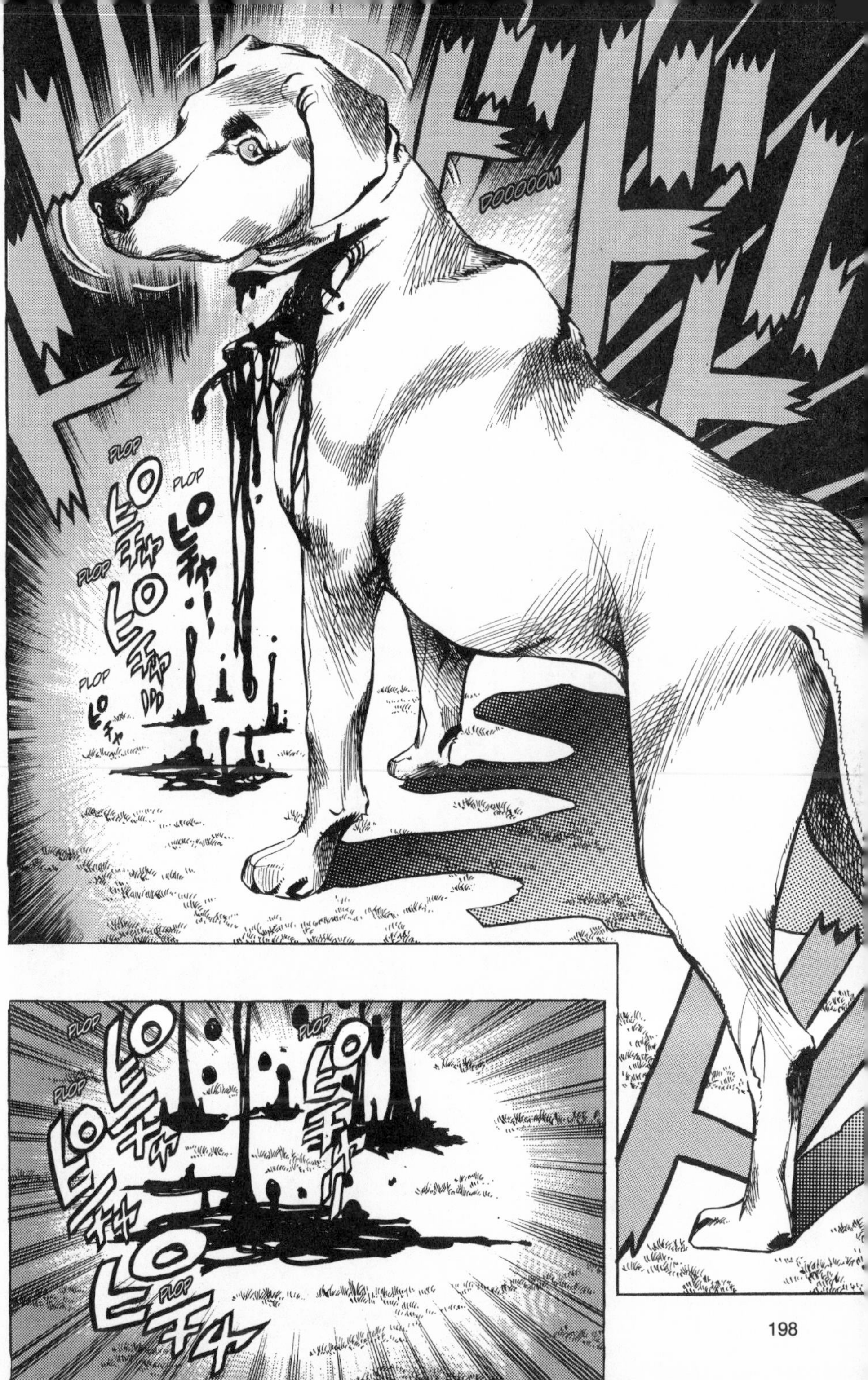
DOOOOOM
PLOP
PLOP
PLOP
PLOP
PLOP
PLOP
PLOP
PLOP

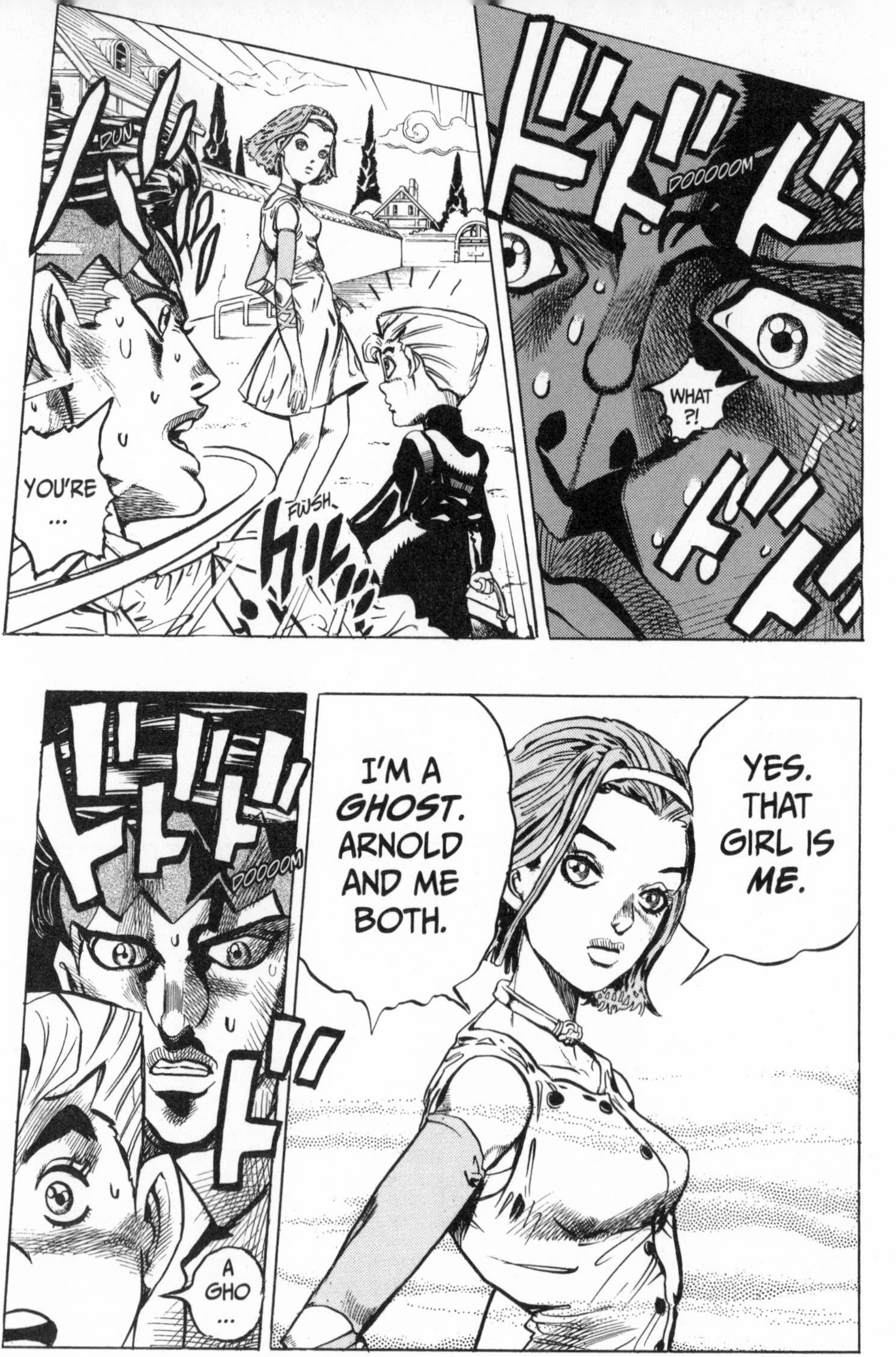

DOOOOOM
WHAT ?!
DUN
YOU'RE ...
FWSH
YES. THAT GIRL IS ME.
I'M A GHOST. ARNOLD AND ME BOTH.
DOOOOM
A GHO ...

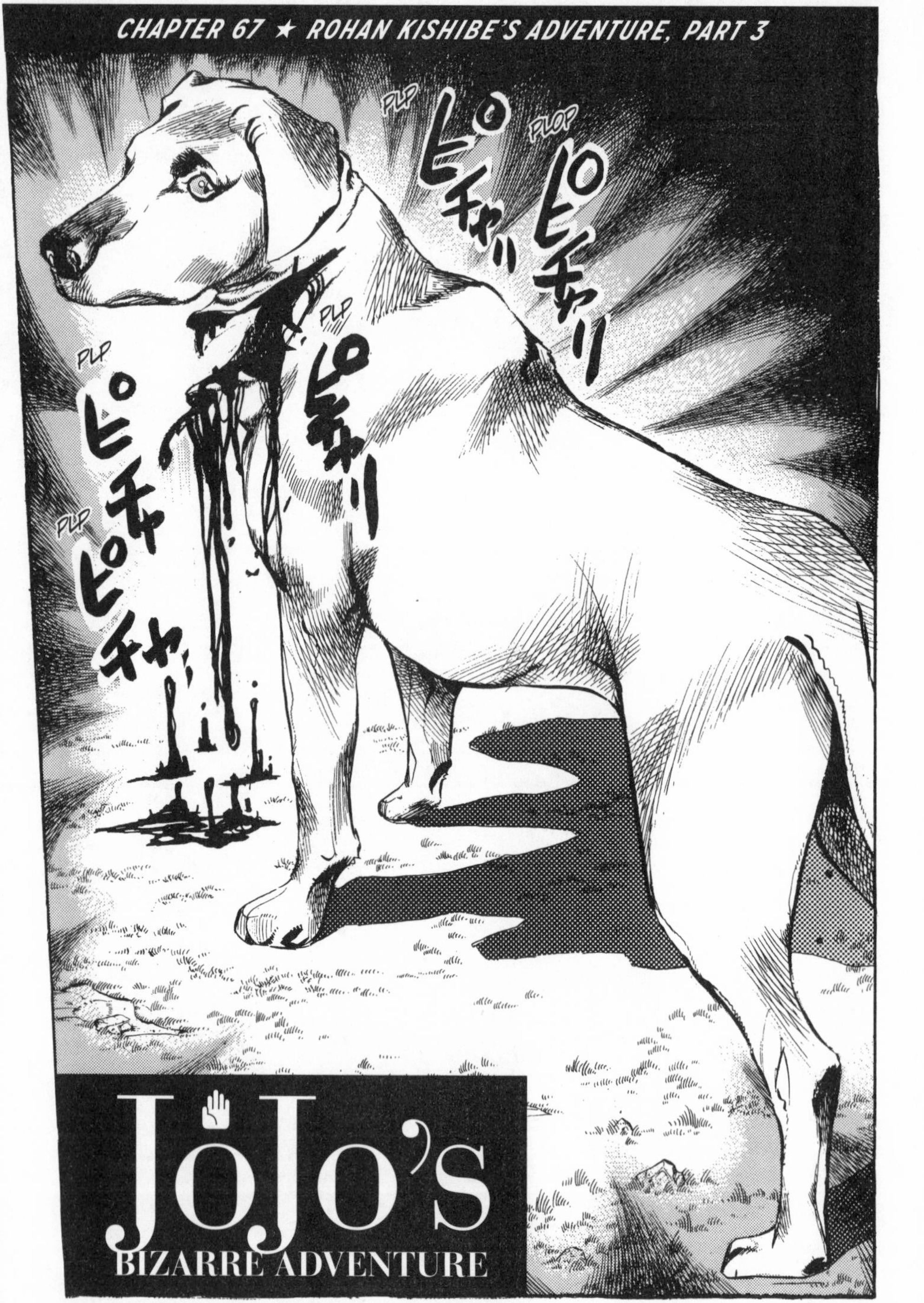
CHAPTER 67 ★ ROHAN KISHIBE'S ADVENTURE, PART 3
PLOP
ピチャリ
PLP
ピチャリ
PLP
ピチャリ
PLP
ピチャ
PLP
ピチャッ
JoJo's
BIZARRE ADVENTURE

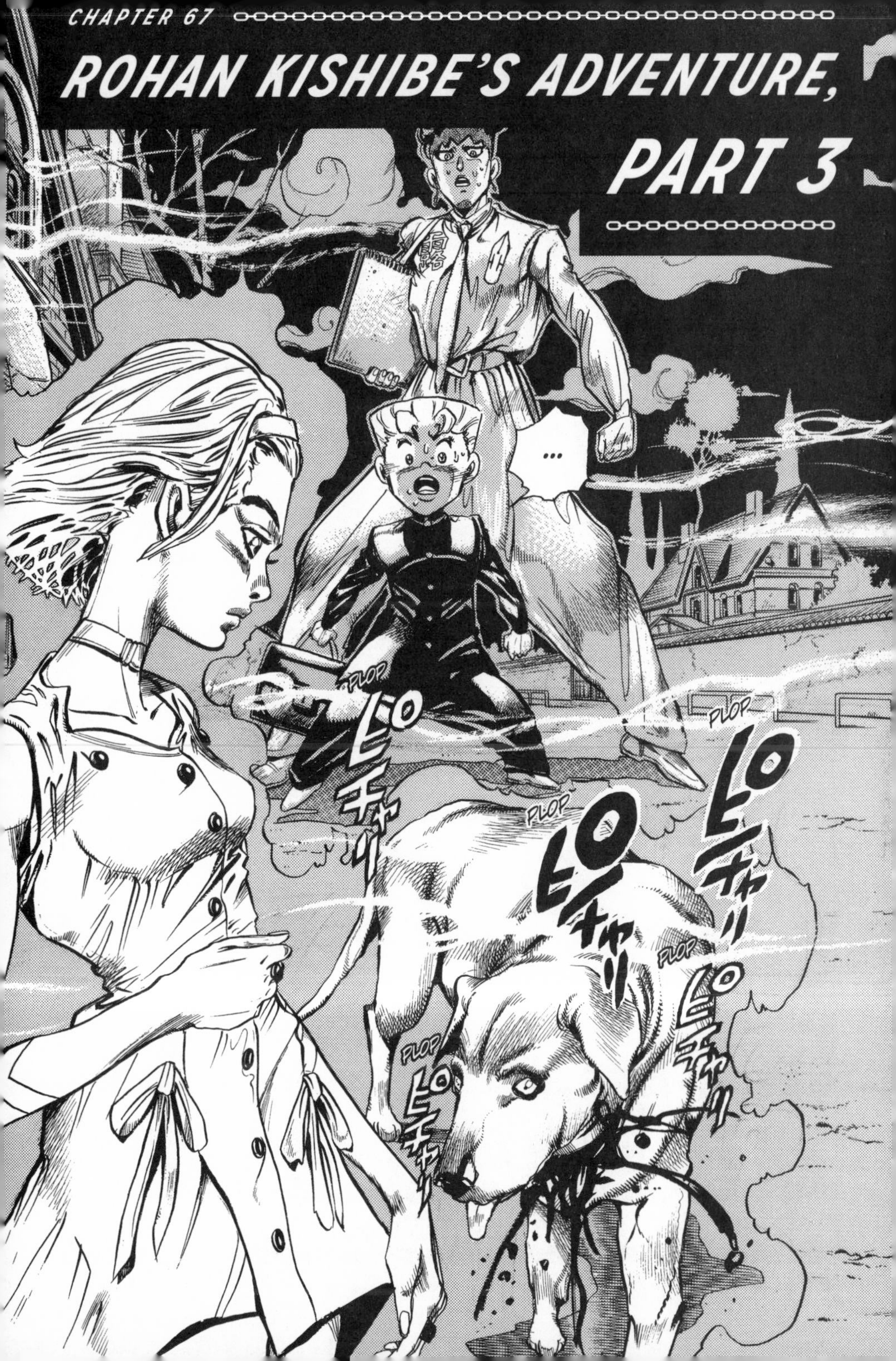

CHAPTER 67
ROHAN KISHIBE'S ADVENTURE, PART 3
...
PLOP
PLOP
PLOP
PLOP
PLOP

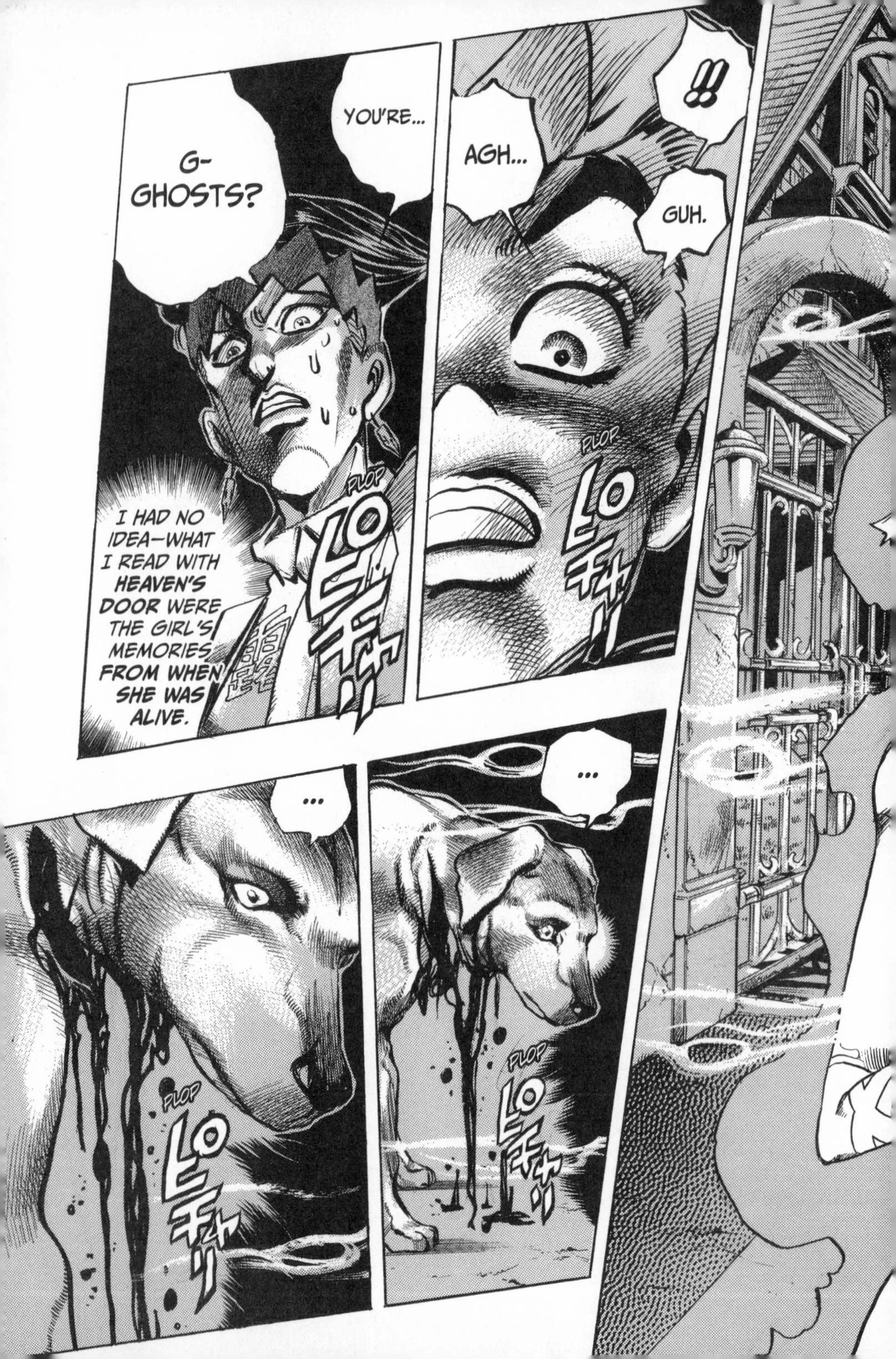
!!
AGH...
GUH.
PLOP
YOU'RE...
G-GHOSTS?
PLOP
I HAD NO IDEA—WHAT I READ WITH **HEAVEN'S DOOR** WERE THE GIRL'S MEMORIES FROM WHEN SHE WAS ALIVE.
...
PLOP
...
PLOP

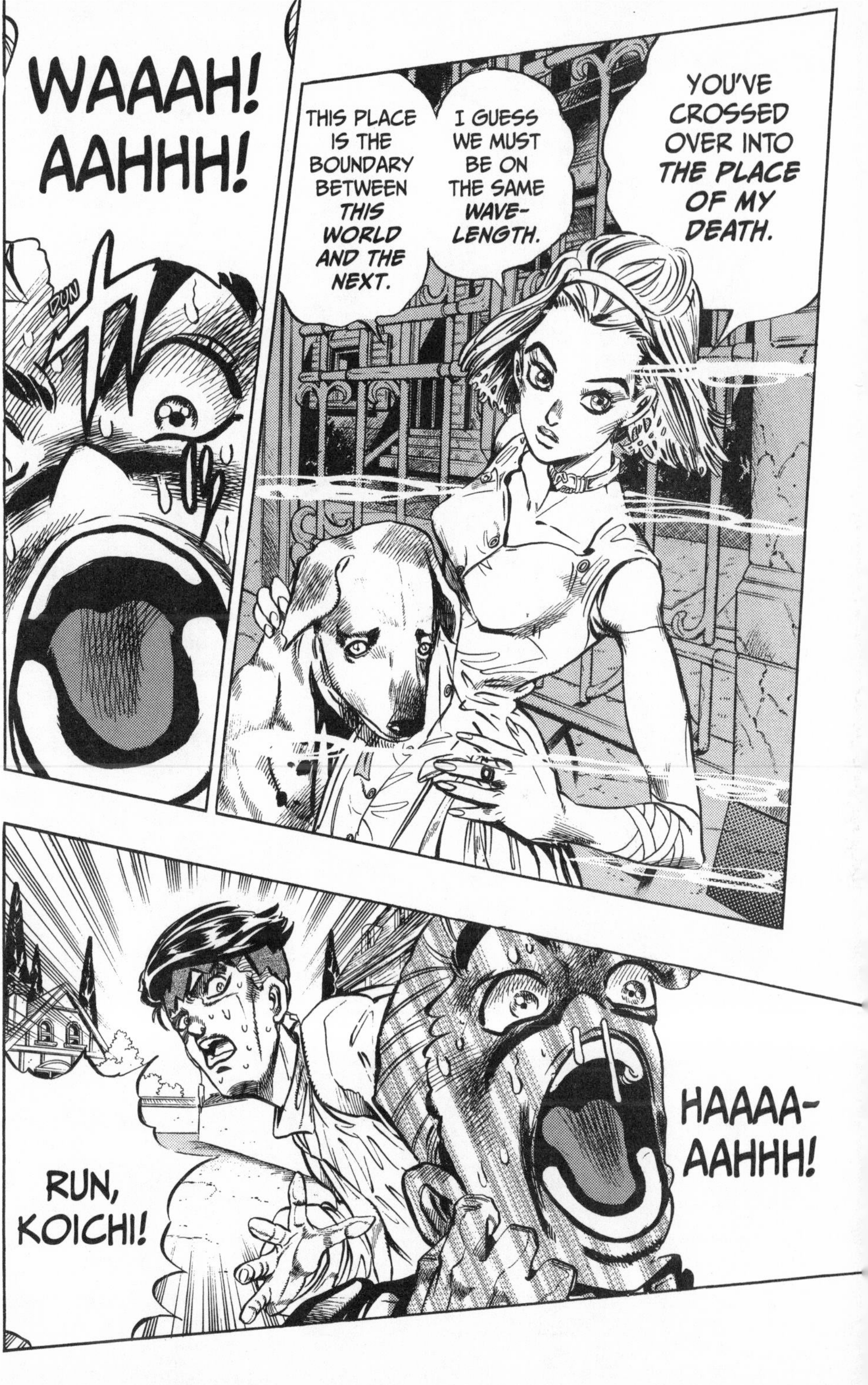
YOU'VE CROSSED OVER INTO THE PLACE OF MY DEATH.
I GUESS WE MUST BE ON THE SAME WAVE-LENGTH.
THIS PLACE IS THE BOUNDARY BETWEEN THIS WORLD AND THE NEXT.
WAAAH! AAHHH!
DUN
HAAAA-AAHHH!
RUN, KOICHI!

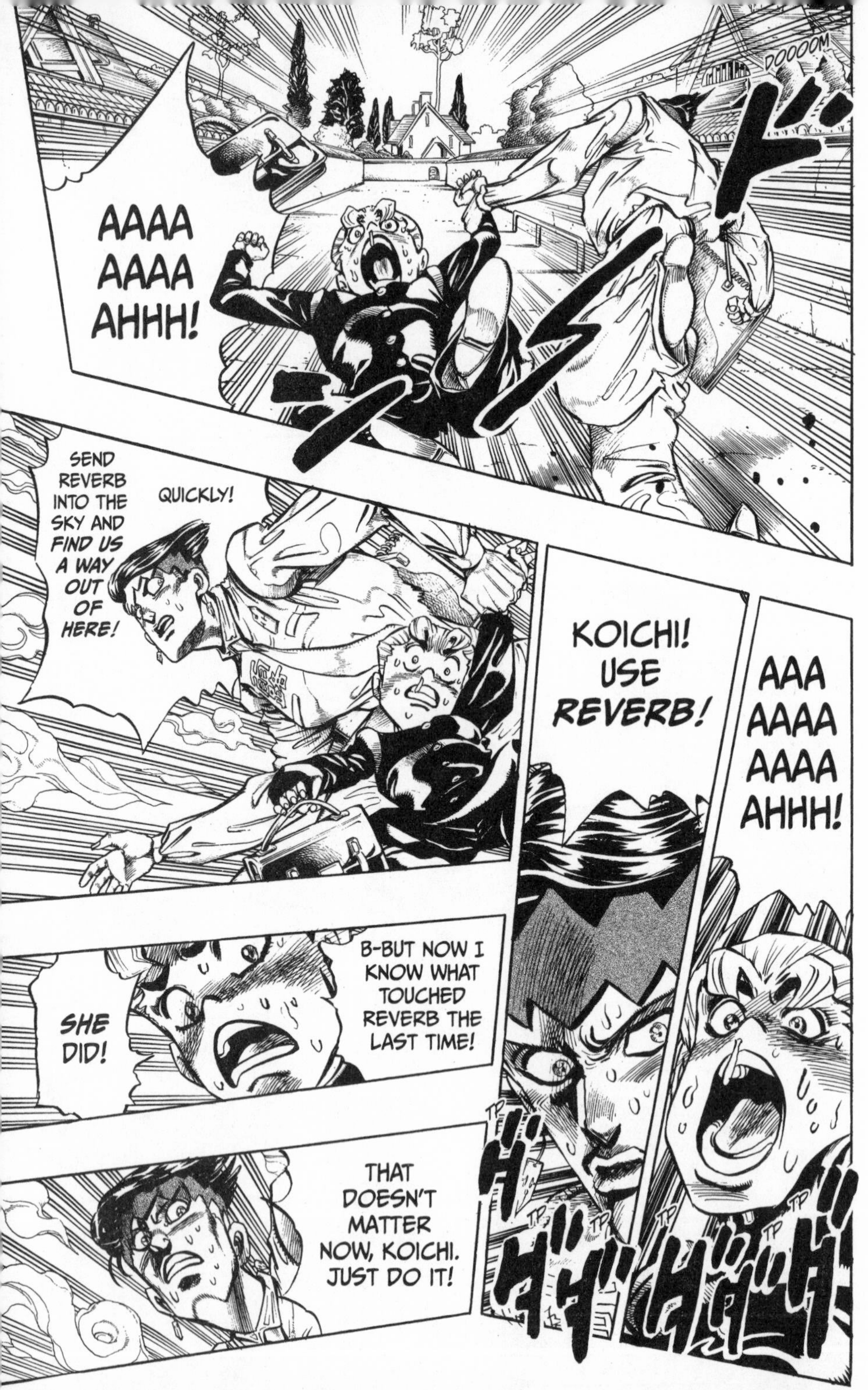
DOOOOM
AAAA AAAA AHHH!
AAA AAAA AAAA AHHH!
KOICHI! USE REVERB!
TP TP TP TP TP
SEND REVERB INTO THE SKY AND FIND US A WAY OUT OF HERE!
QUICKLY!
B-BUT NOW I KNOW WHAT TOUCHED REVERB THE LAST TIME!
SHE DID!
THAT DOESN'T MATTER NOW, KOICHI. JUST DO IT!

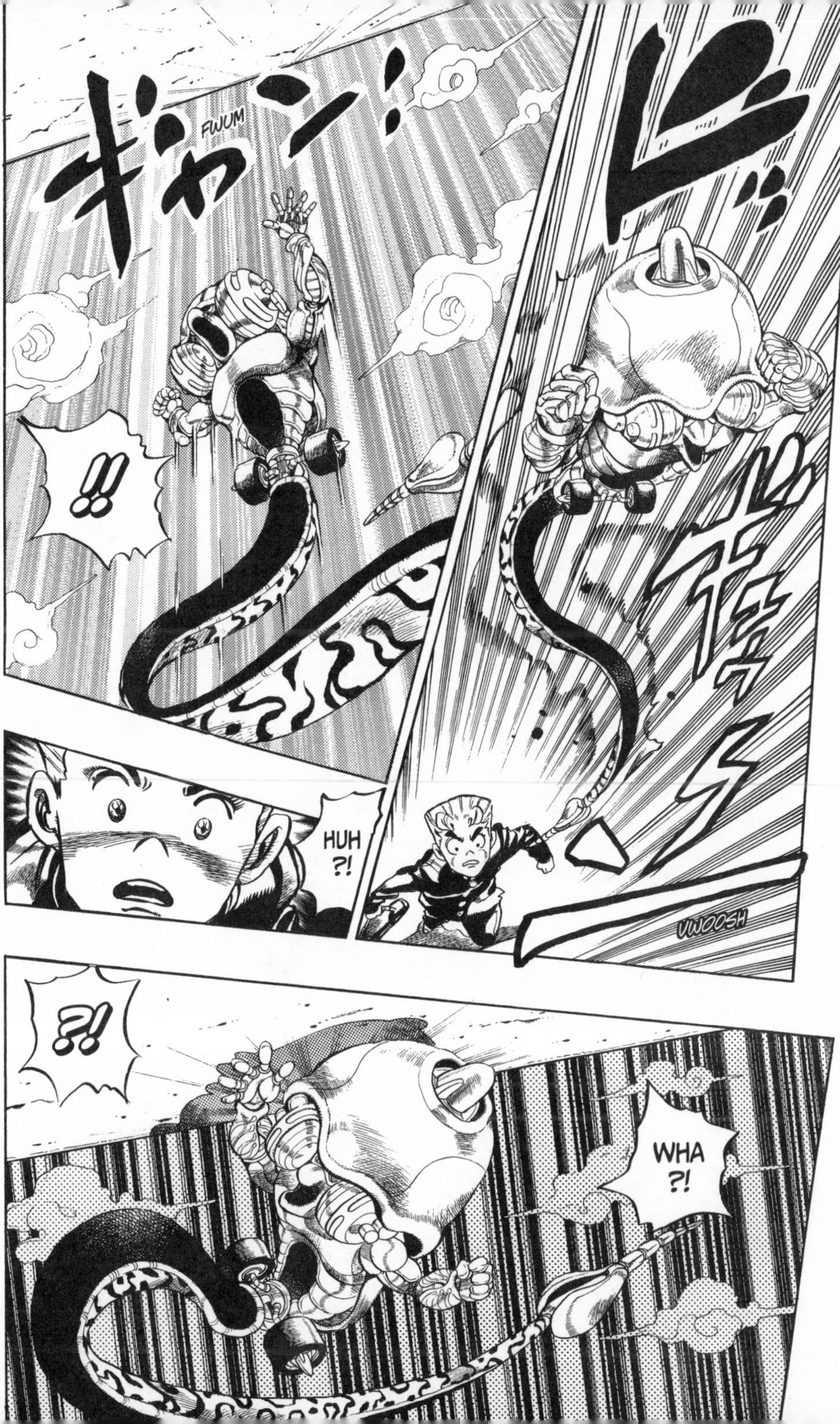

VWOOSH
FWUM
!!
HUH ?!
WHA ?!
?!

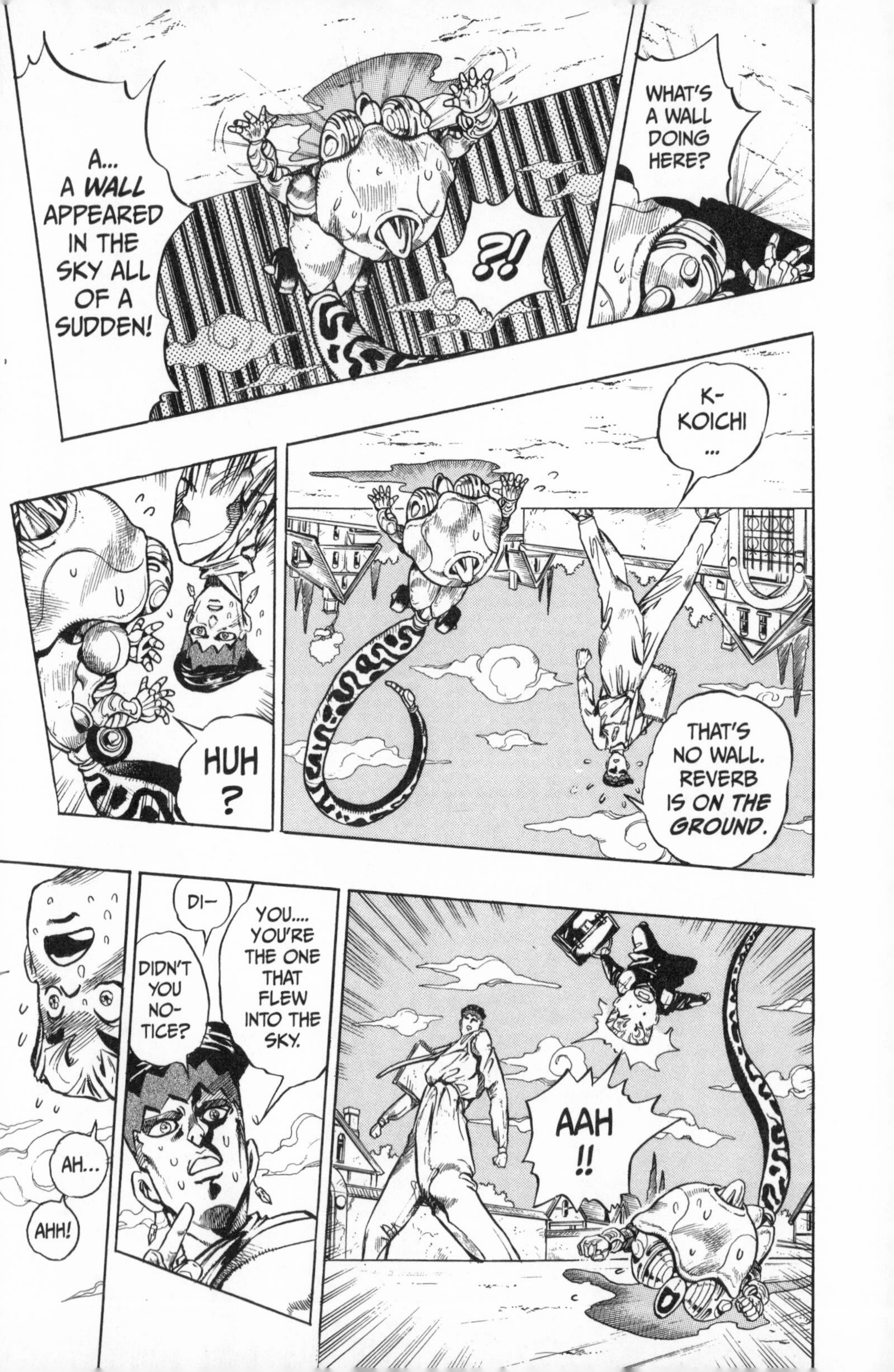
WHAT'S A WALL DOING HERE?
A... A WALL APPEARED IN THE SKY ALL OF A SUDDEN!
?!
K-KOICHI ...
THAT'S NO WALL. REVERB IS ON THE GROUND.
HUH ?
AAH !!
YOU.... YOU'RE THE ONE THAT FLEW INTO THE SKY.
DI–
DIDN'T YOU NO-TICE?
AH...
AHH!

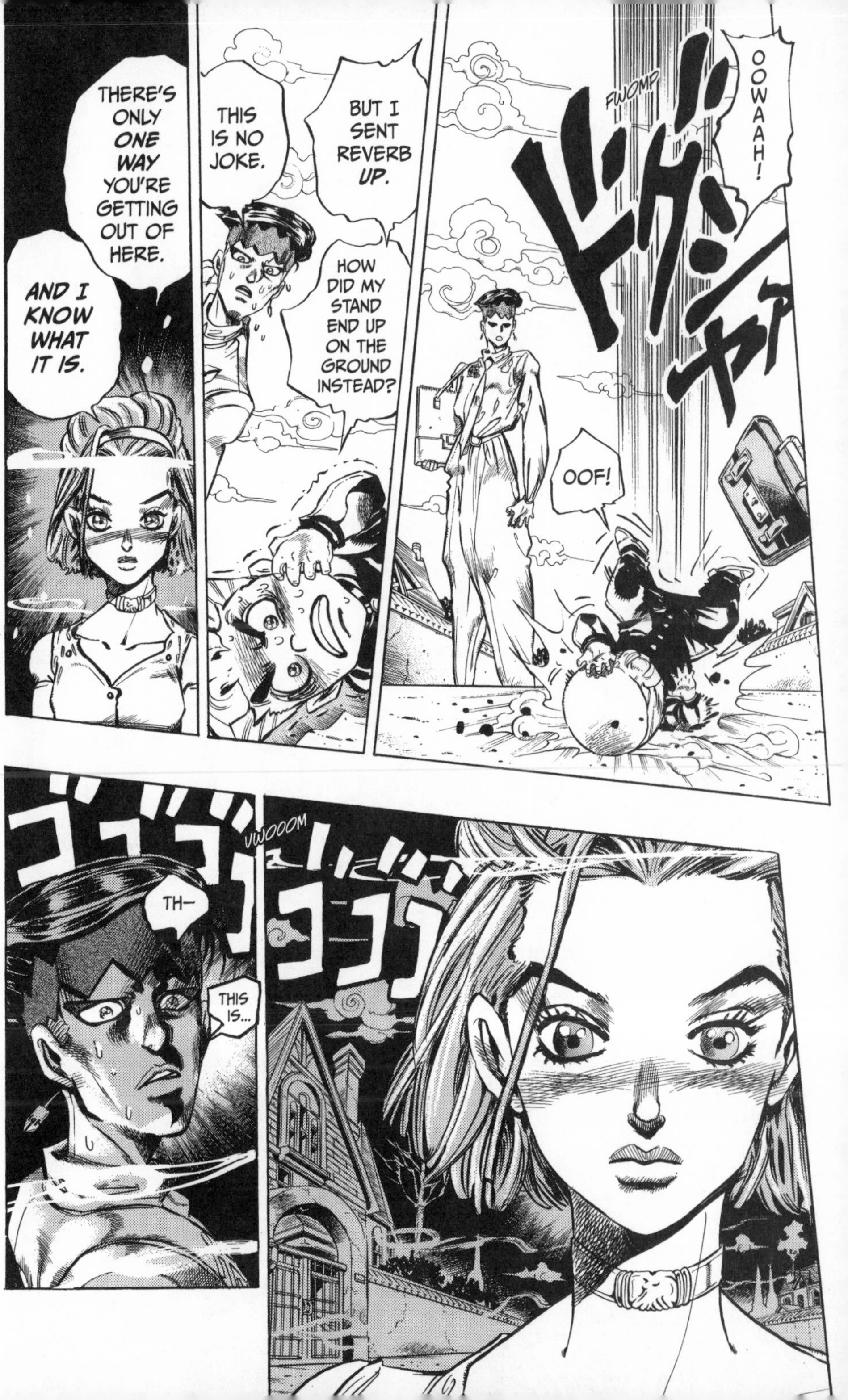
OOWAAAH!
FWOMP
OOF!
BUT I SENT REVERB UP.
THIS IS NO JOKE.
HOW DID MY STAND END UP ON THE GROUND INSTEAD?
THERE'S ONLY ONE WAY YOU'RE GETTING OUT OF HERE.
AND I KNOW WHAT IT IS.
VWOOOM
TH—
THIS IS...

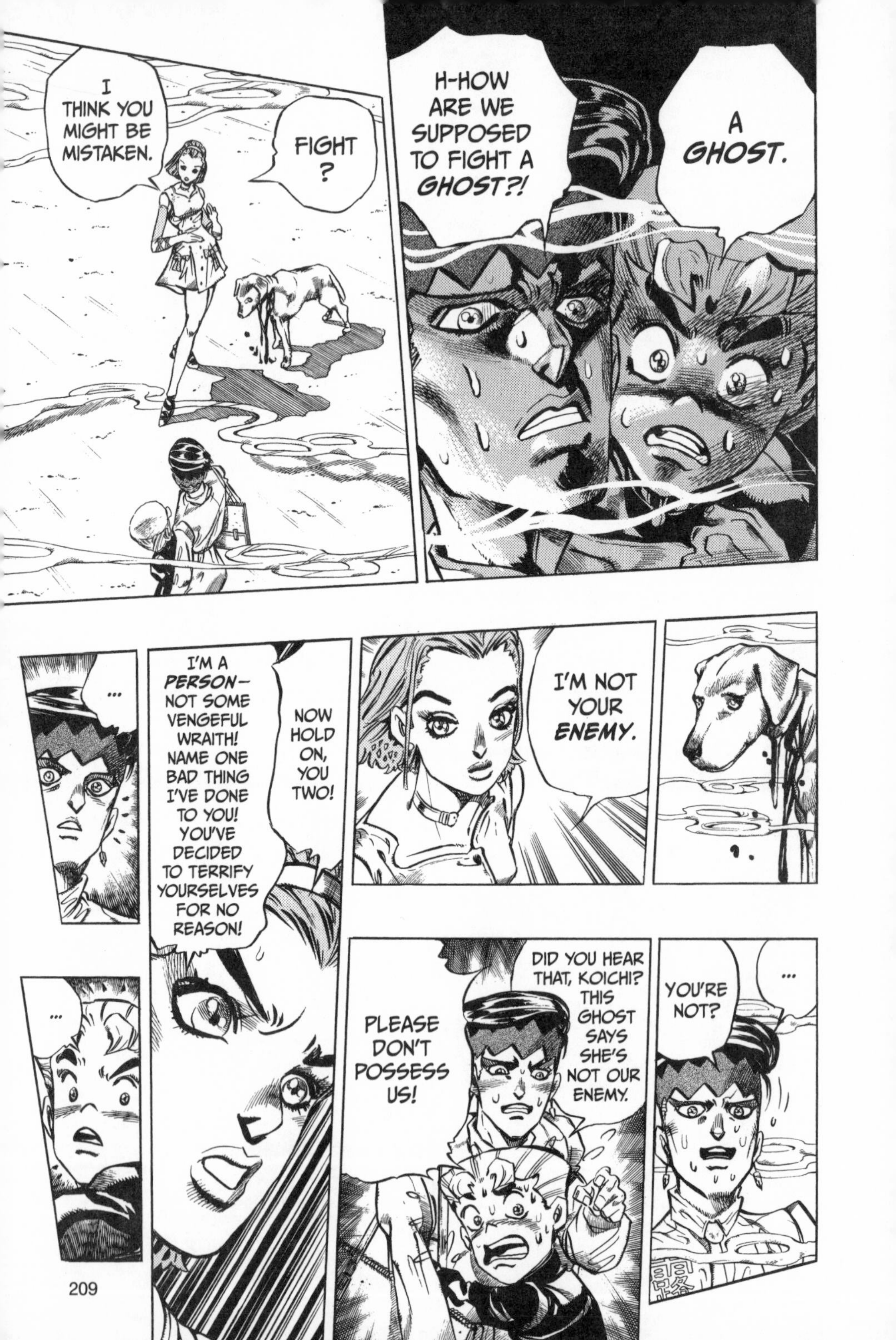
A GHOST.
H-HOW ARE WE SUPPOSED TO FIGHT A GHOST?!
FIGHT?
I THINK YOU MIGHT BE MISTAKEN.
I'M NOT YOUR ENEMY.
...
YOU'RE NOT?
DID YOU HEAR THAT, KOICHI? THIS GHOST SAYS SHE'S NOT OUR ENEMY.
PLEASE DON'T POSSESS US!
NOW HOLD ON, YOU TWO!
I'M A PERSON— NOT SOME VENGEFUL WRAITH! NAME ONE BAD THING I'VE DONE TO YOU! YOU'VE DECIDED TO TERRIFY YOURSELVES FOR NO REASON!
...
...

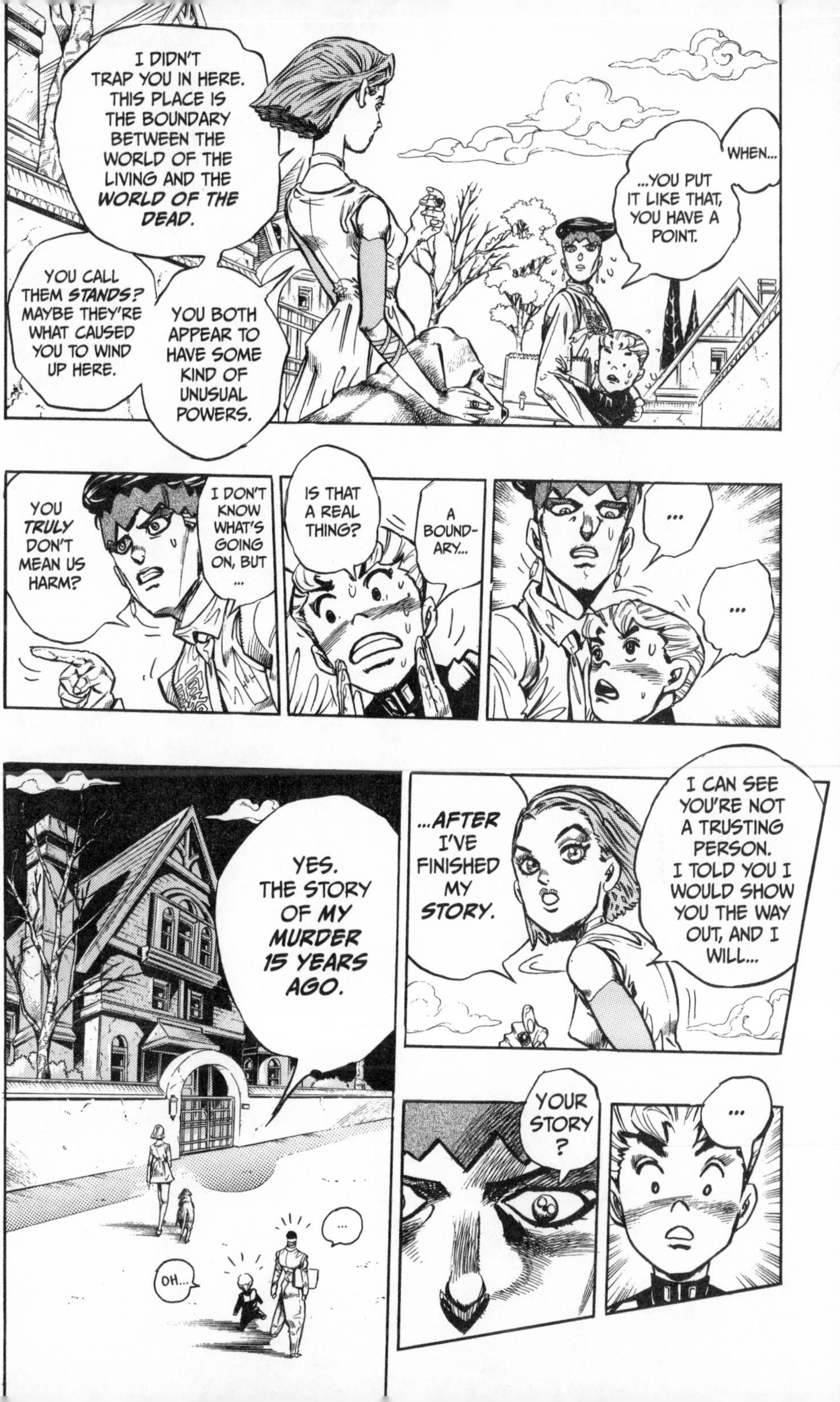
WHEN...
...YOU PUT IT LIKE THAT, YOU HAVE A POINT.
I DIDN'T TRAP YOU IN HERE. THIS PLACE IS THE BOUNDARY BETWEEN THE WORLD OF THE LIVING AND THE *WORLD OF THE DEAD*.
YOU BOTH APPEAR TO HAVE SOME KIND OF UNUSUAL POWERS.
YOU CALL THEM *STANDS?* MAYBE THEY'RE WHAT CAUSED YOU TO WIND UP HERE.
...
...
A BOUNDARY...
IS THAT A REAL THING?
I DON'T KNOW WHAT'S GOING ON, BUT...
YOU *TRULY* DON'T MEAN US HARM?
I CAN SEE YOU'RE NOT A TRUSTING PERSON. I TOLD YOU I WOULD SHOW YOU THE WAY OUT, AND I WILL...
...AFTER I'VE FINISHED MY *STORY*.
...
YOUR STORY?
YES. THE STORY OF *MY MURDER 15 YEARS AGO*.
...
OH...

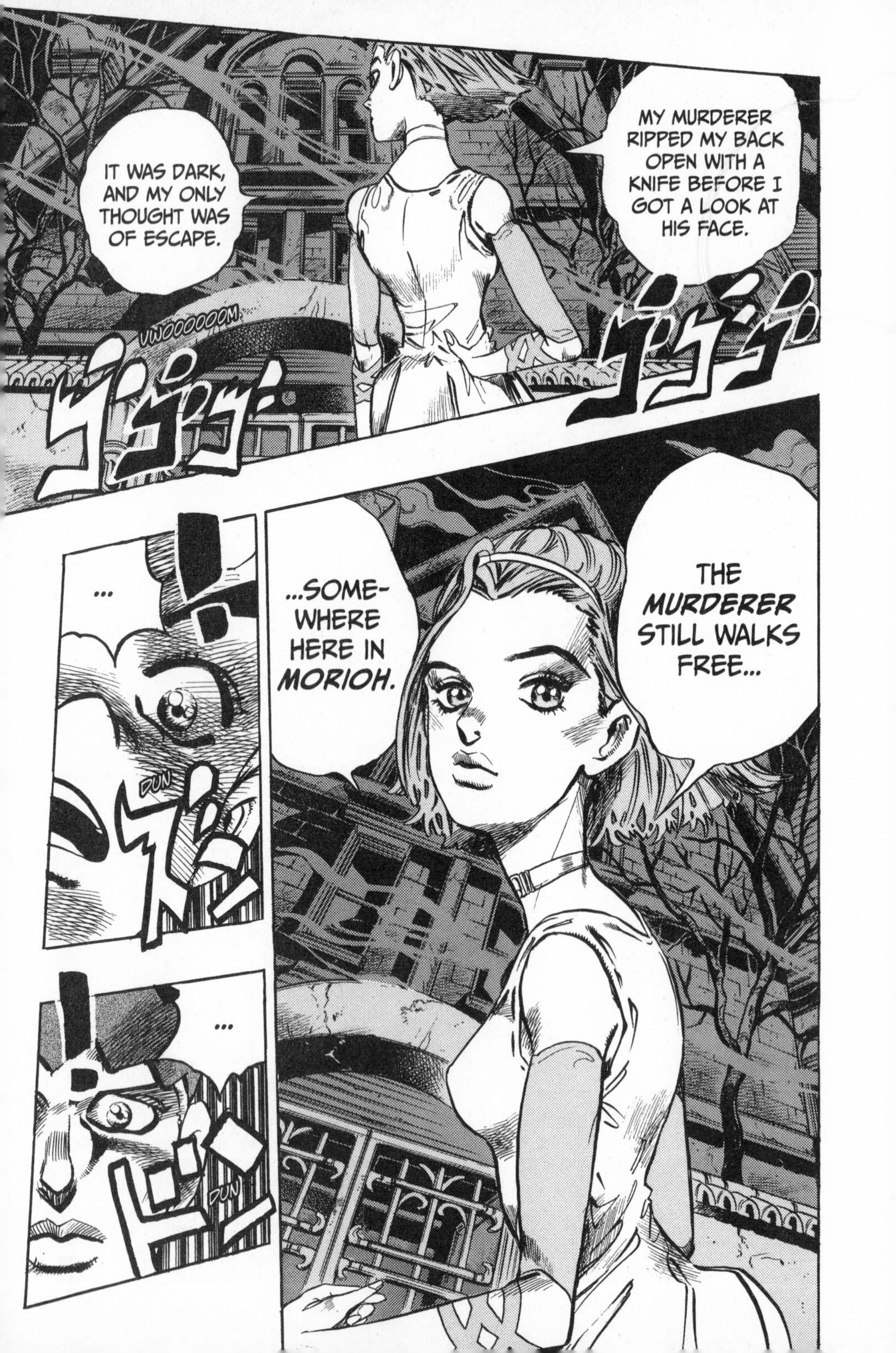
MY MURDERER RIPPED MY BACK OPEN WITH A KNIFE BEFORE I GOT A LOOK AT HIS FACE.
IT WAS DARK, AND MY ONLY THOUGHT WAS OF ESCAPE.
VWOOOOOOM
THE MURDERER STILL WALKS FREE...
...SOME-WHERE HERE IN MORIOH.
...
DUN
...
DUN

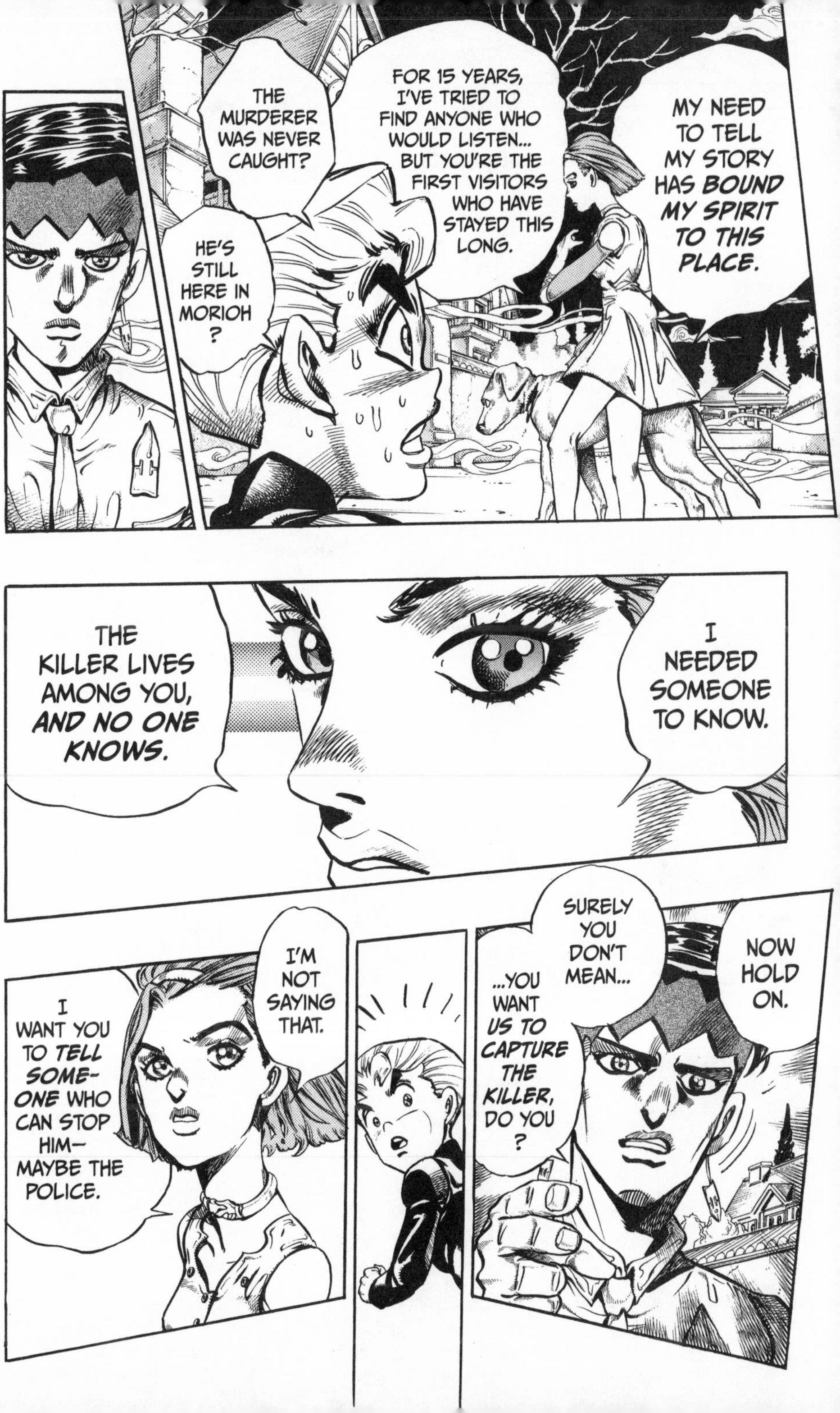
MY NEED TO TELL MY STORY HAS *BOUND MY SPIRIT TO THIS PLACE.*
FOR 15 YEARS, I'VE TRIED TO FIND ANYONE WHO WOULD LISTEN... BUT YOU'RE THE FIRST VISITORS WHO HAVE STAYED THIS LONG.
THE MURDERER WAS NEVER CAUGHT?
HE'S STILL HERE IN MORIOH?
I NEEDED SOMEONE TO KNOW.
THE KILLER LIVES AMONG YOU, *AND NO ONE KNOWS.*
NOW HOLD ON.
SURELY YOU DON'T MEAN...
...YOU WANT *US TO CAPTURE THE KILLER,* DO YOU?
I'M NOT SAYING THAT.
I WANT YOU TO *TELL SOMEONE* WHO CAN STOP HIM—MAYBE THE POLICE.

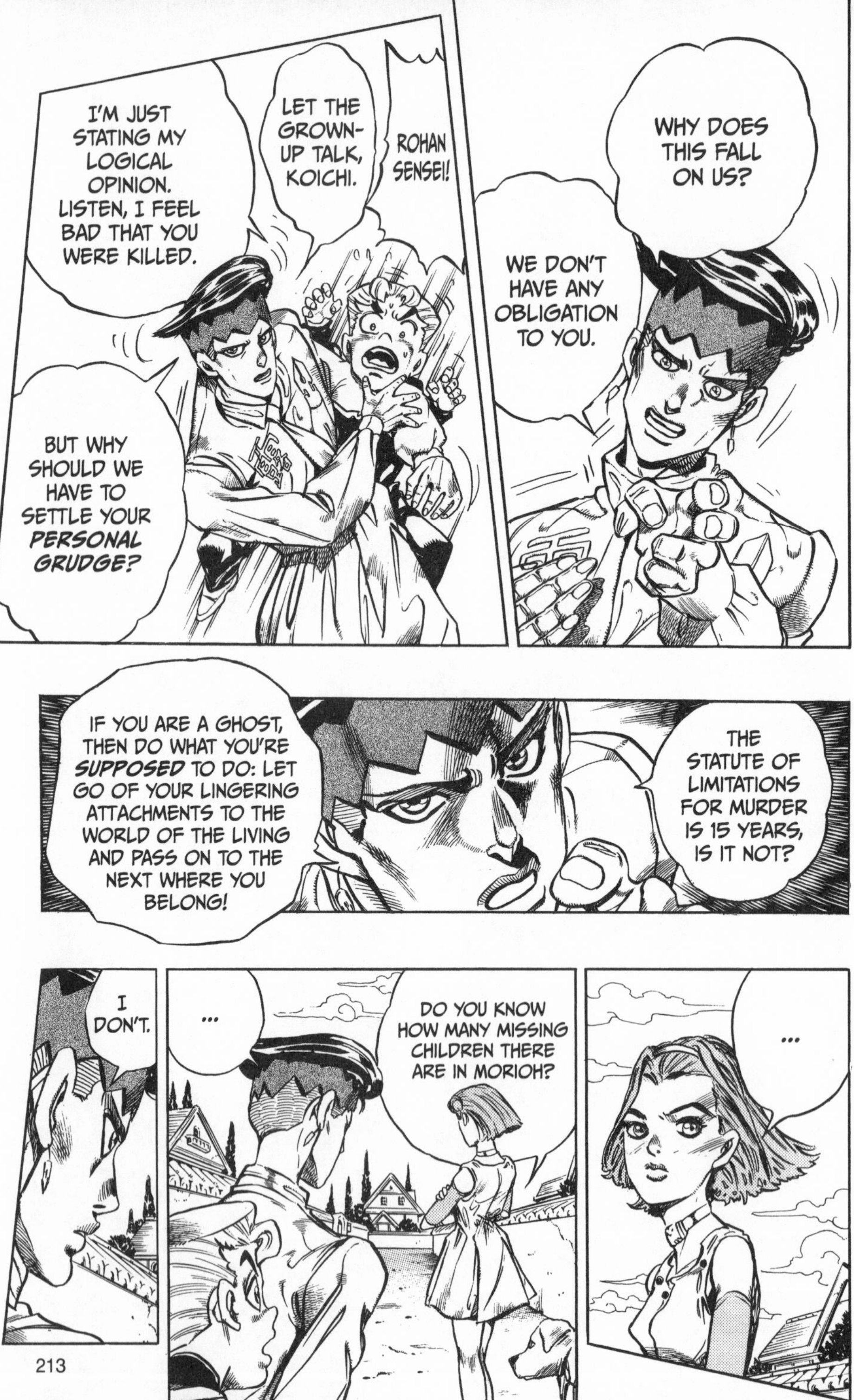
WHY DOES THIS FALL ON US?
WE DON'T HAVE ANY OBLIGATION TO YOU.
ROHAN SENSEI!
LET THE GROWN-UP TALK, KOICHI.
I'M JUST STATING MY LOGICAL OPINION. LISTEN, I FEEL BAD THAT YOU WERE KILLED.
BUT WHY SHOULD WE HAVE TO SETTLE YOUR *PERSONAL GRUDGE?*
THE STATUTE OF LIMITATIONS FOR MURDER IS 15 YEARS, IS IT NOT?
IF YOU ARE A GHOST, THEN DO WHAT YOU'RE *SUPPOSED* TO DO: LET GO OF YOUR LINGERING ATTACHMENTS TO THE WORLD OF THE LIVING AND PASS ON TO THE NEXT WHERE YOU BELONG!
...
DO YOU KNOW HOW MANY MISSING CHILDREN THERE ARE IN MORIOH?
...
I DON'T.

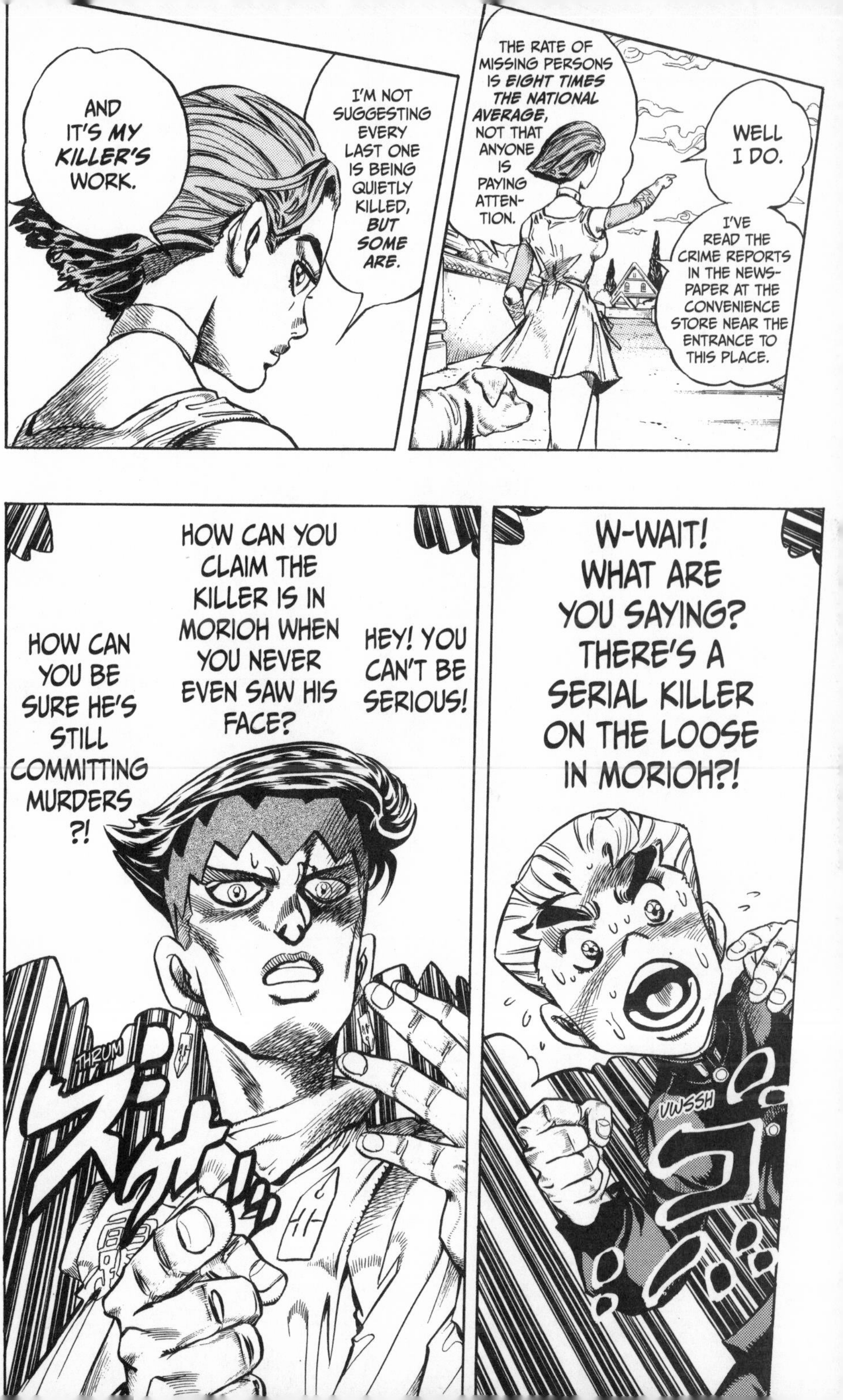
THE RATE OF MISSING PERSONS IS EIGHT TIMES THE NATIONAL AVERAGE, NOT THAT ANYONE IS PAYING ATTENTION.
WELL I DO.
I'VE READ THE CRIME REPORTS IN THE NEWS-PAPER AT THE CONVENIENCE STORE NEAR THE ENTRANCE TO THIS PLACE.
I'M NOT SUGGESTING EVERY LAST ONE IS BEING QUIETLY KILLED, BUT SOME ARE.
AND IT'S MY KILLER'S WORK.
W-WAIT! WHAT ARE YOU SAYING? THERE'S A SERIAL KILLER ON THE LOOSE IN MORIOH?!
VWSSH
HEY! YOU CAN'T BE SERIOUS!
HOW CAN YOU CLAIM THE KILLER IS IN MORIOH WHEN YOU NEVER EVEN SAW HIS FACE?
HOW CAN YOU BE SURE HE'S STILL COMMITTING MURDERS?!
THRUM

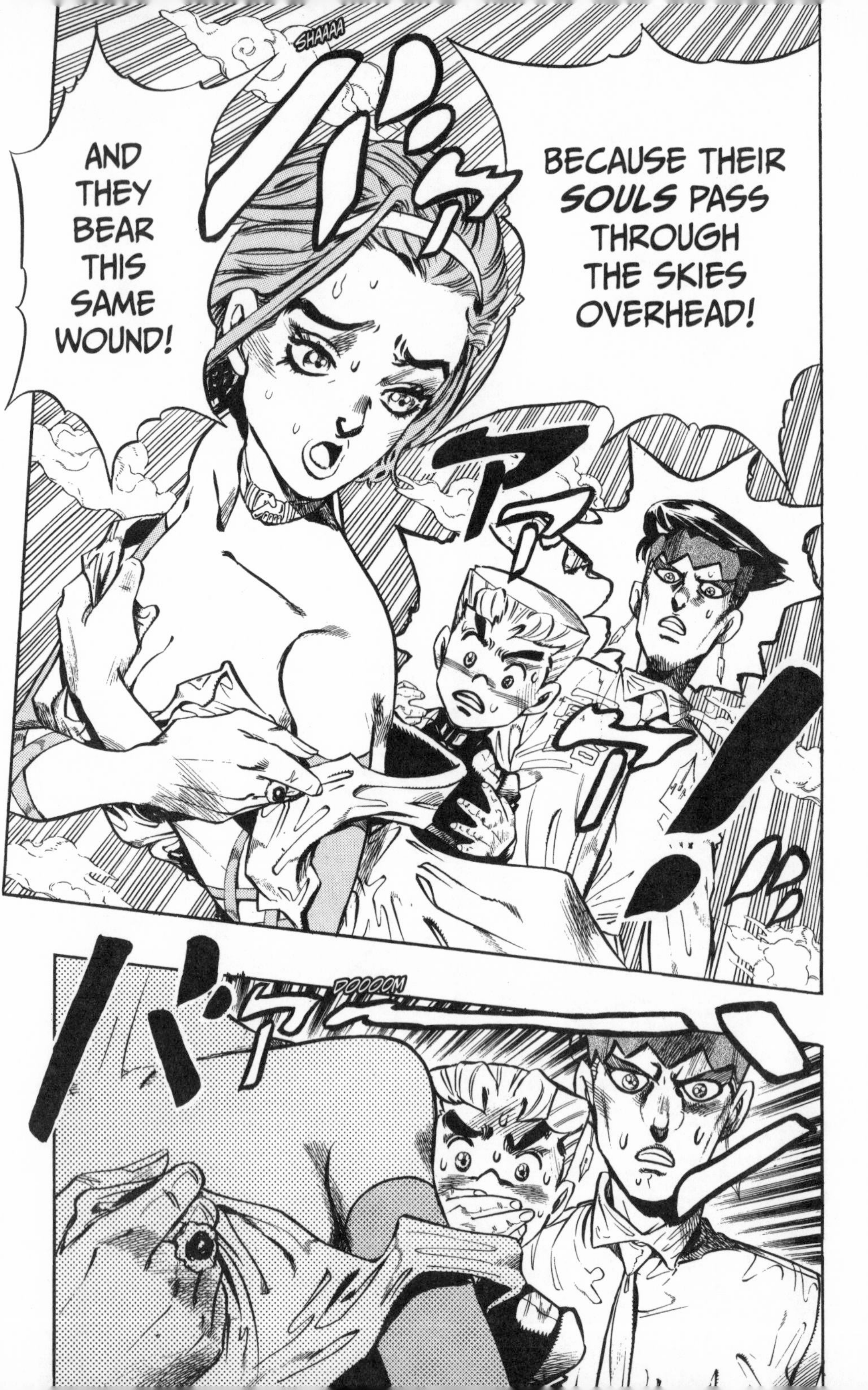
SHAAAA
BECAUSE THEIR SOULS PASS THROUGH THE SKIES OVERHEAD!
AND THEY BEAR THIS SAME WOUND!
DOOOOM

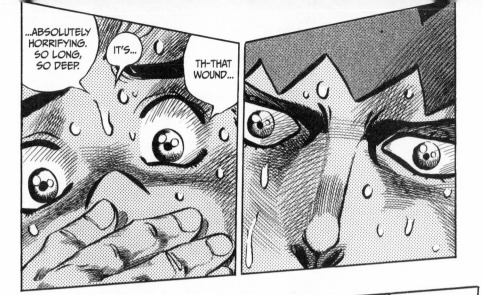

...ABSOLUTELY HORRIFYING. SO LONG, SO DEEP.

IT'S...

TH-THAT WOUND...

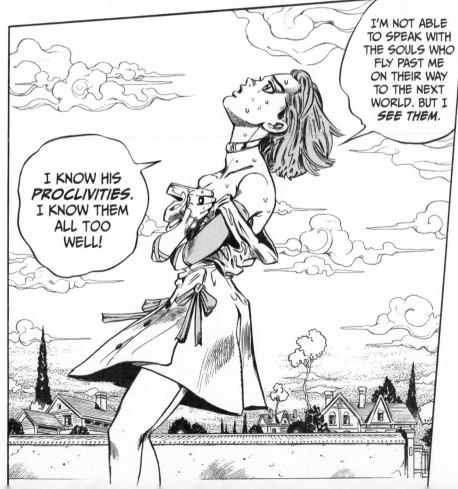

I'M NOT ABLE TO SPEAK WITH THE SOULS WHO FLY PAST ME ON THEIR WAY TO THE NEXT WORLD. BUT I *SEE THEM*.

I KNOW HIS *PROCLIVITIES.* I KNOW THEM ALL TOO WELL!

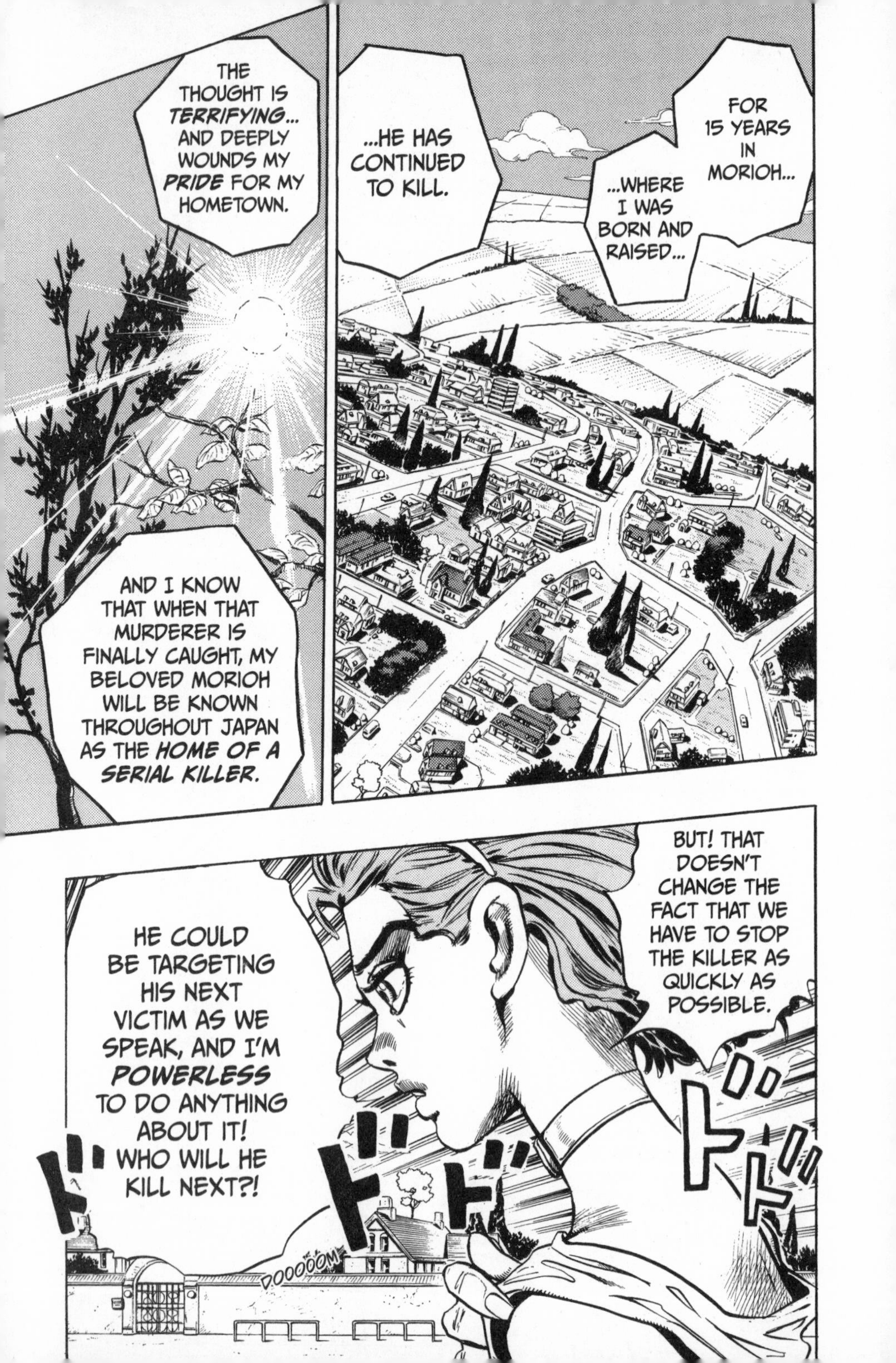
FOR 15 YEARS IN MORIOH...
...WHERE I WAS BORN AND RAISED...
...HE HAS CONTINUED TO KILL.
THE THOUGHT IS TERRIFYING... AND DEEPLY WOUNDS MY PRIDE FOR MY HOMETOWN.
AND I KNOW THAT WHEN THAT MURDERER IS FINALLY CAUGHT, MY BELOVED MORIOH WILL BE KNOWN THROUGHOUT JAPAN AS THE HOME OF A SERIAL KILLER.
BUT! THAT DOESN'T CHANGE THE FACT THAT WE HAVE TO STOP THE KILLER AS QUICKLY AS POSSIBLE.
HE COULD BE TARGETING HIS NEXT VICTIM AS WE SPEAK, AND I'M POWERLESS TO DO ANYTHING ABOUT IT! WHO WILL HE KILL NEXT?!
DOOOOOM

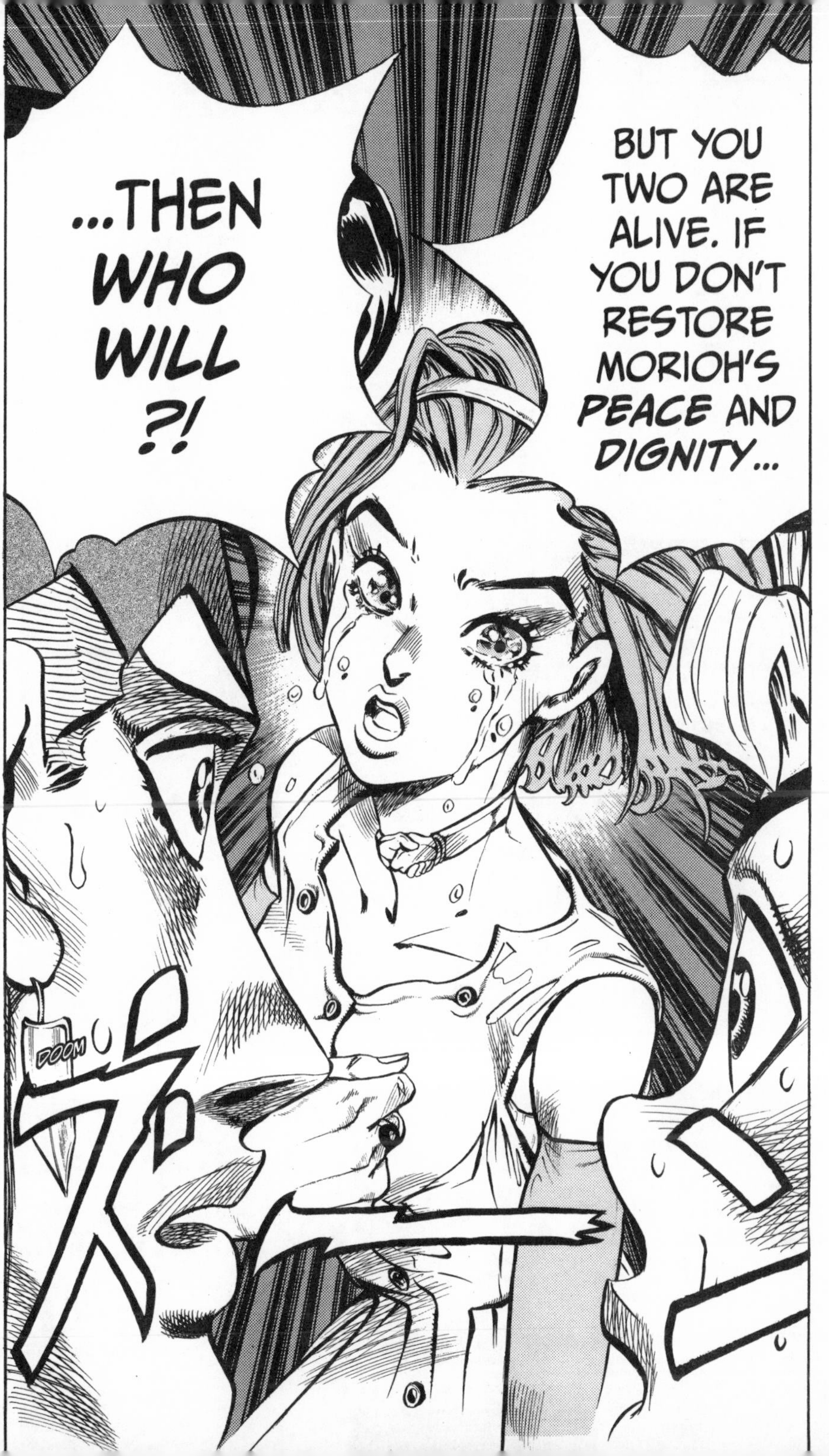
BUT YOU TWO ARE ALIVE. IF YOU DON'T RESTORE MORIOH'S PEACE AND DIGNITY...
...THEN WHO WILL ?!
DOOM

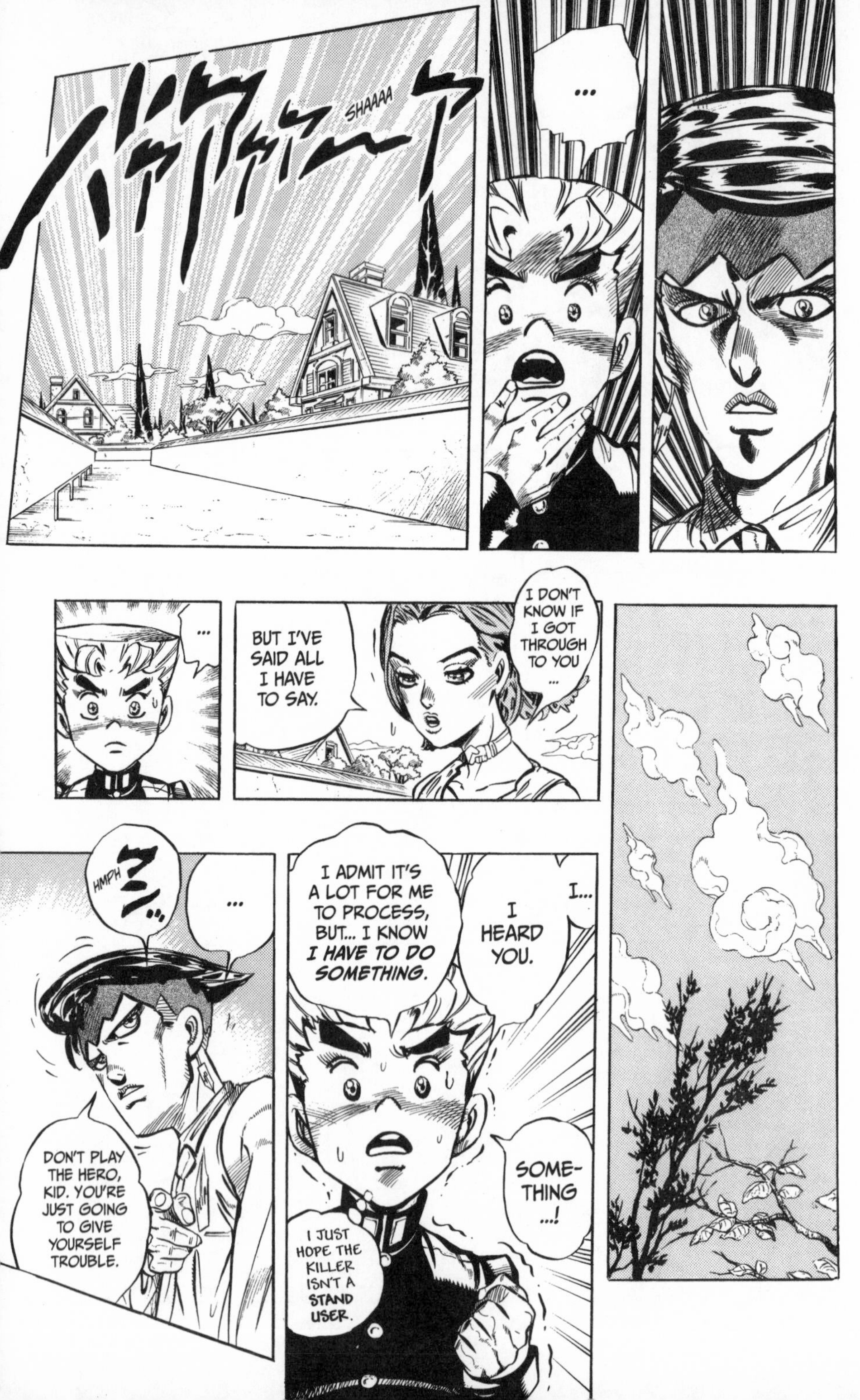
...
SHAAAA
I DON'T KNOW IF I GOT THROUGH TO YOU ...
BUT I'VE SAID ALL I HAVE TO SAY.
...
I... I HEARD YOU.
I ADMIT IT'S A LOT FOR ME TO PROCESS, BUT... I KNOW *I HAVE TO DO SOMETHING.*
SOME-THING ...!
I JUST HOPE THE KILLER ISN'T A **STAND USER.**
HMPH
...
DON'T PLAY THE HERO, KID. YOU'RE JUST GOING TO GIVE YOURSELF TROUBLE.

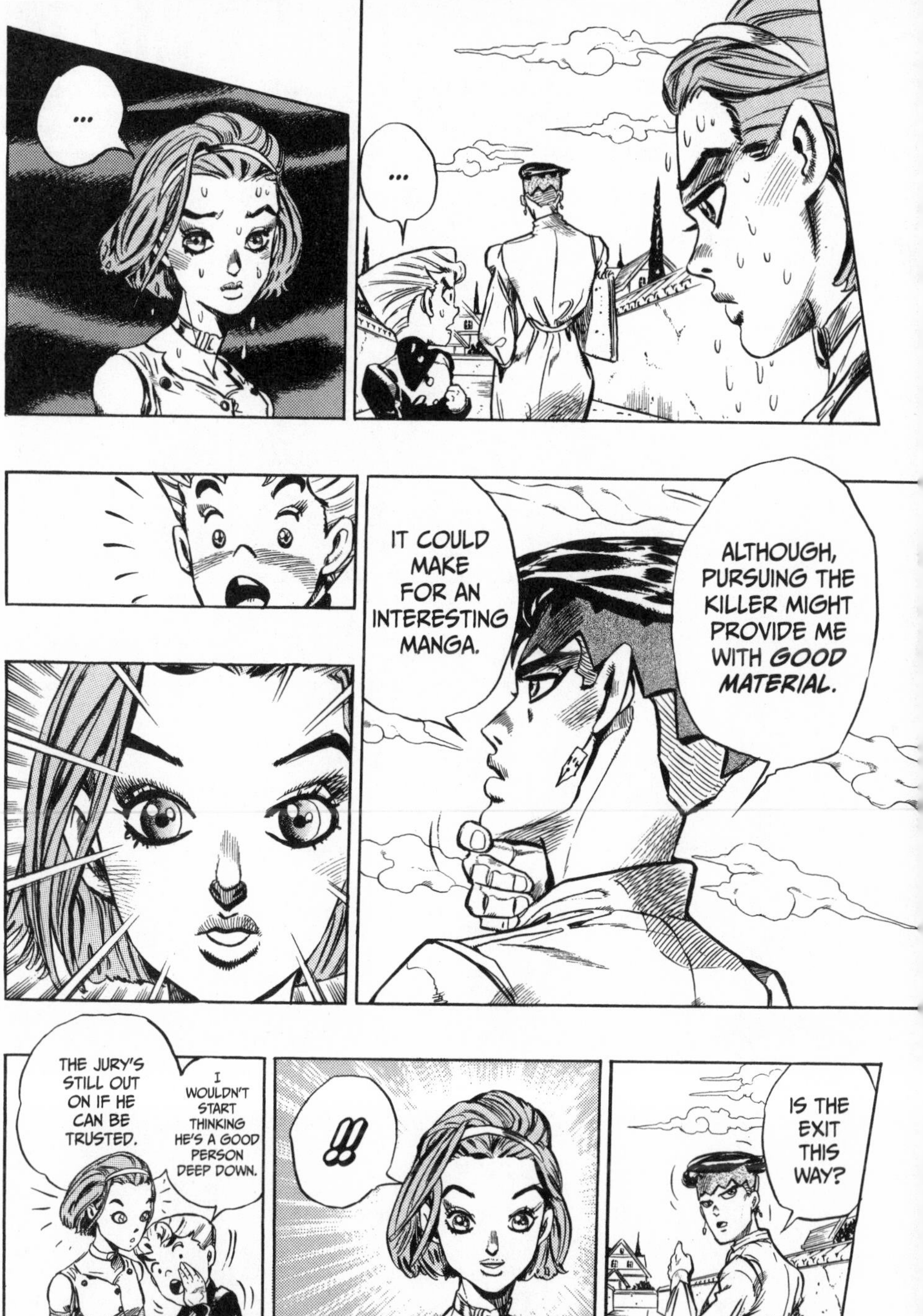
...
...
ALTHOUGH, PURSUING THE KILLER MIGHT PROVIDE ME WITH *GOOD MATERIAL*.
IT COULD MAKE FOR AN INTERESTING MANGA.
IS THE EXIT THIS WAY?
!!
THE JURY'S STILL OUT ON IF HE CAN BE TRUSTED.
I WOULDN'T START THINKING HE'S A GOOD PERSON DEEP DOWN.

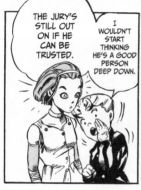

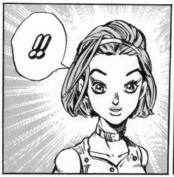

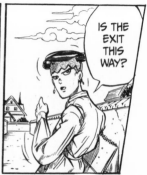

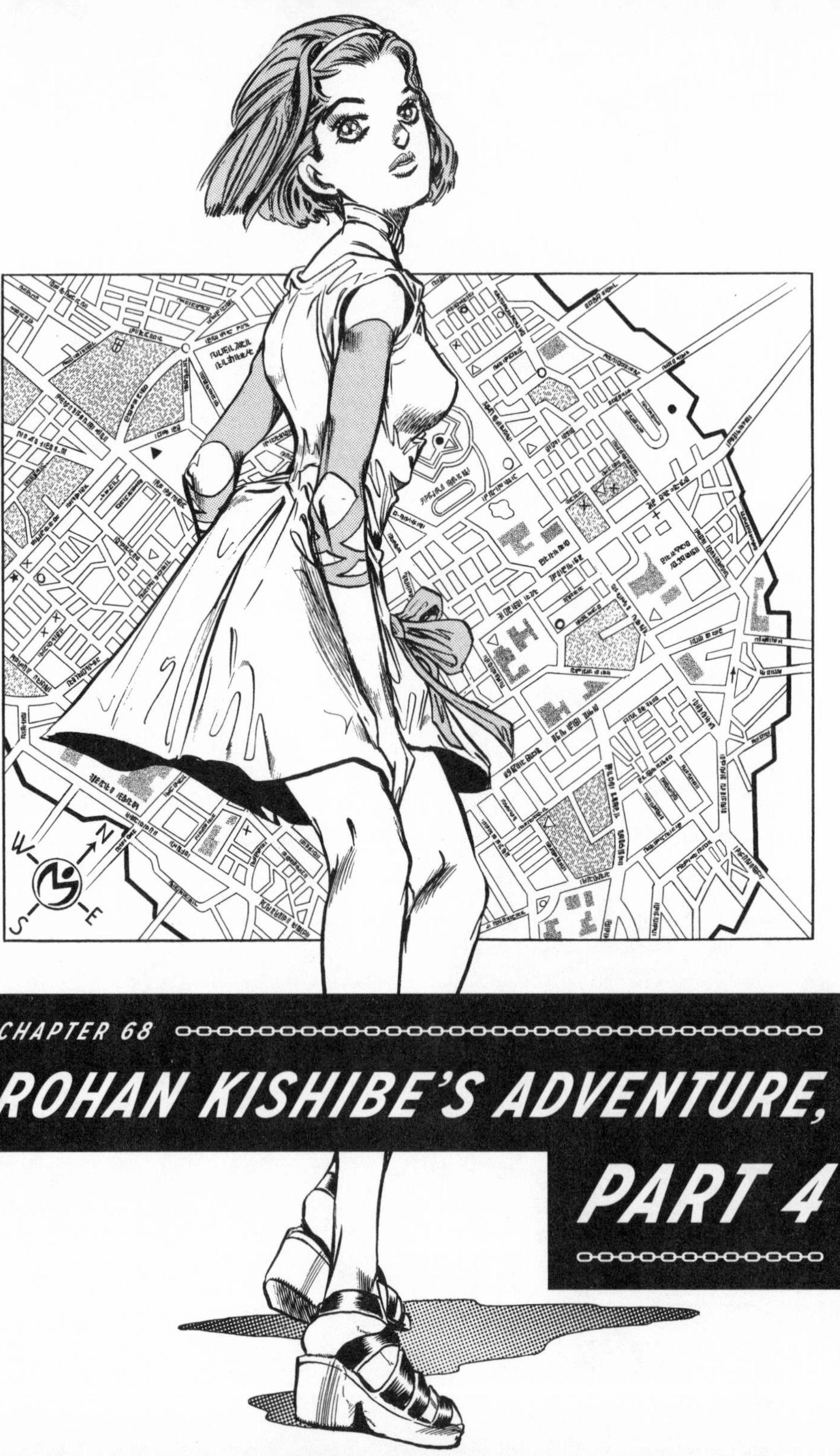
N
W
S
E

CHAPTER 68

ROHAN KISHIBE'S ADVENTURE, PART 4

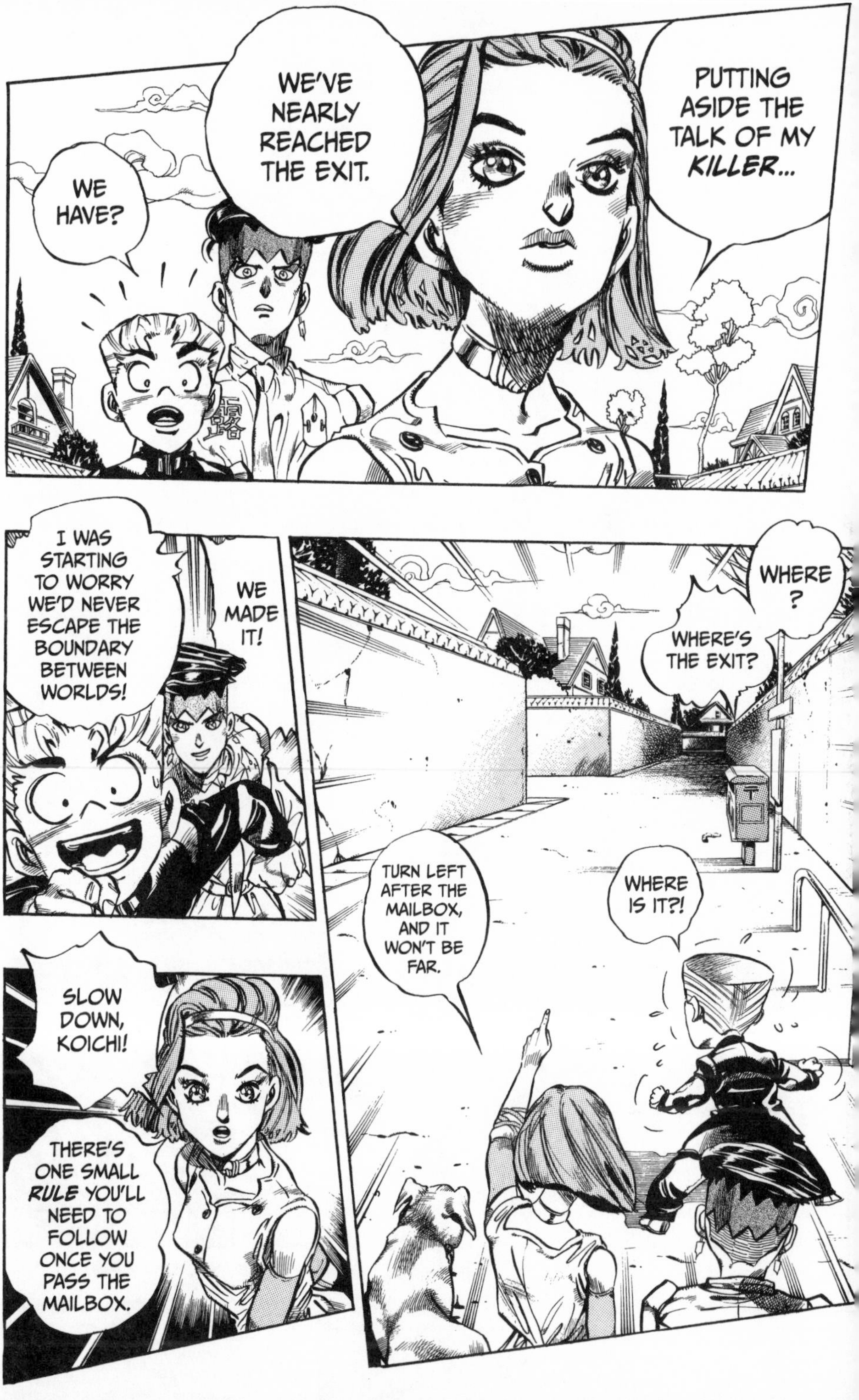
PUTTING ASIDE THE TALK OF MY *KILLER*...
WE'VE NEARLY REACHED THE EXIT.
WE HAVE?
WHERE?
WHERE'S THE EXIT?
WHERE IS IT?!
TURN LEFT AFTER THE MAILBOX, AND IT WON'T BE FAR.
WE MADE IT!
I WAS STARTING TO WORRY WE'D NEVER ESCAPE THE BOUNDARY BETWEEN WORLDS!
SLOW DOWN, KOICHI!
THERE'S ONE SMALL *RULE* YOU'LL NEED TO FOLLOW ONCE YOU PASS THE MAILBOX.

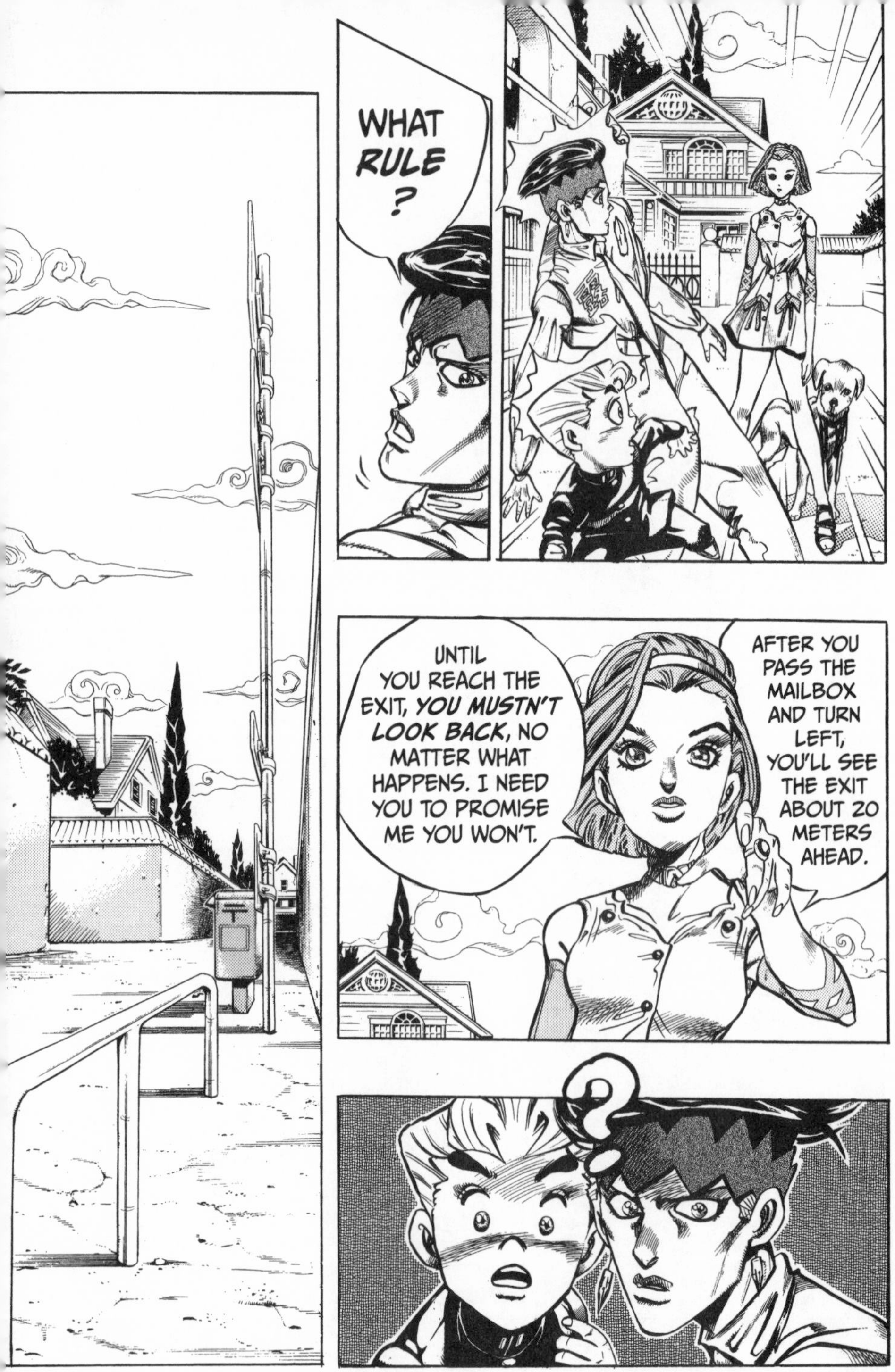

WHAT RULE ?
AFTER YOU PASS THE MAILBOX AND TURN LEFT, YOU'LL SEE THE EXIT ABOUT 20 METERS AHEAD.
UNTIL YOU REACH THE EXIT, YOU MUSTN'T LOOK BACK, NO MATTER WHAT HAPPENS. I NEED YOU TO PROMISE ME YOU WON'T.
?

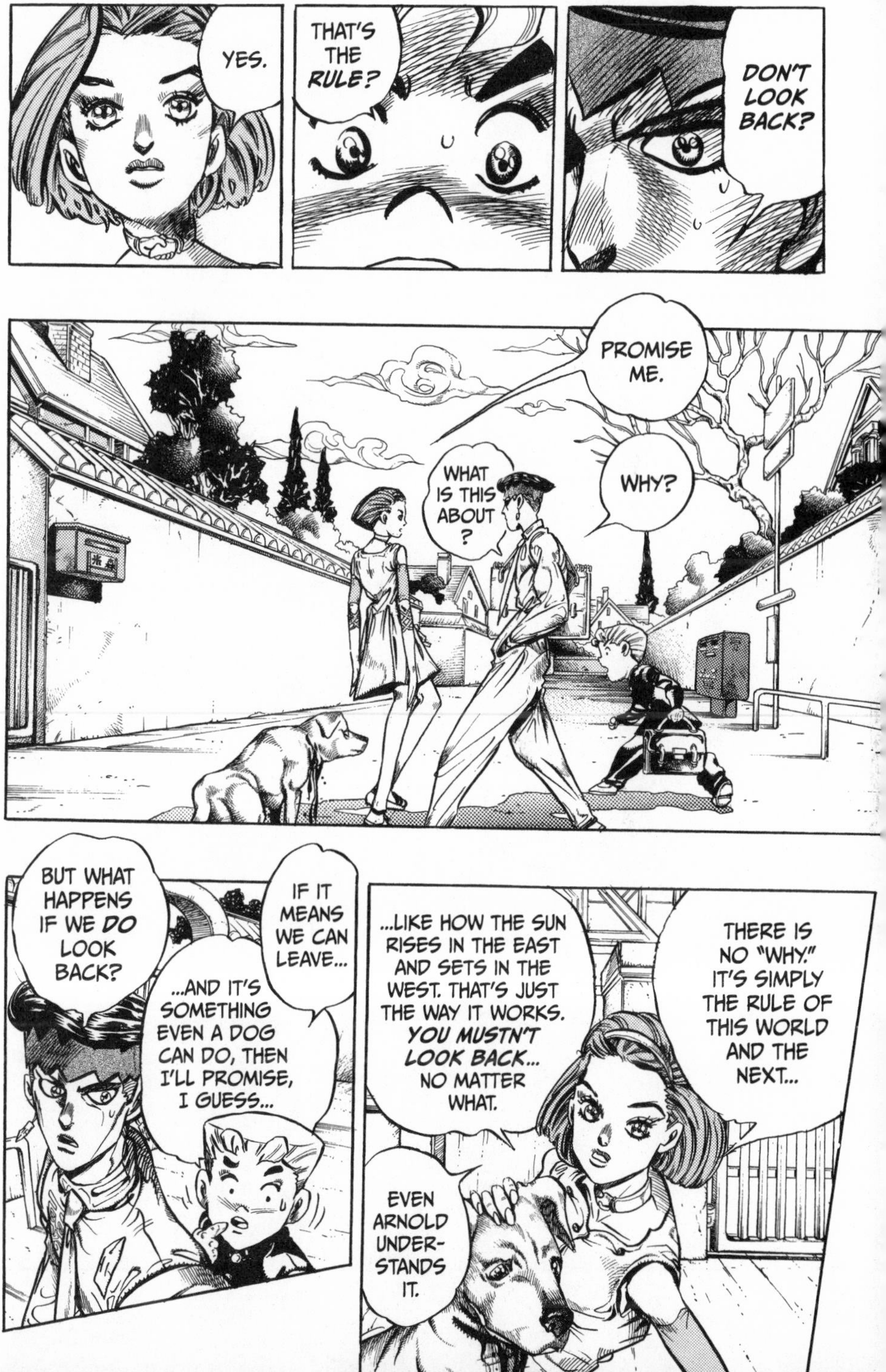
DON'T LOOK BACK?
THAT'S THE *RULE?*
YES.
PROMISE ME.
WHY?
WHAT IS THIS ABOUT?
THERE IS NO "WHY." IT'S SIMPLY THE RULE OF THIS WORLD AND THE NEXT...
...LIKE HOW THE SUN RISES IN THE EAST AND SETS IN THE WEST. THAT'S JUST THE WAY IT WORKS. *YOU MUSTN'T LOOK BACK...* NO MATTER WHAT.
EVEN ARNOLD UNDER-STANDS IT.
IF IT MEANS WE CAN LEAVE...
BUT WHAT HAPPENS IF WE *DO* LOOK BACK?
...AND IT'S SOMETHING EVEN A DOG CAN DO, THEN I'LL PROMISE, I GUESS...

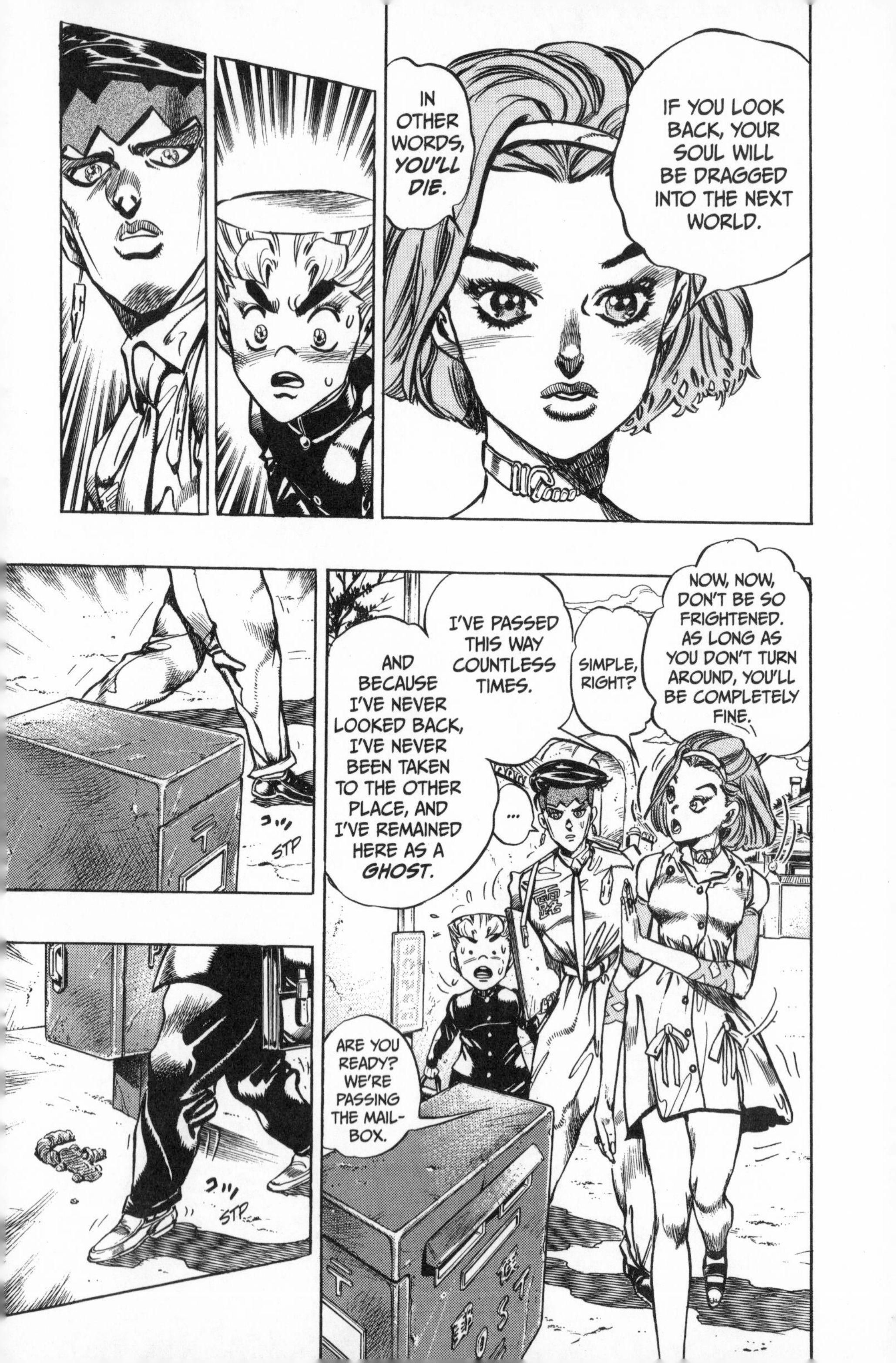
IF YOU LOOK BACK, YOUR SOUL WILL BE DRAGGED INTO THE NEXT WORLD.
IN OTHER WORDS, *YOU'LL DIE*.
NOW, NOW, DON'T BE SO FRIGHTENED. AS LONG AS YOU DON'T TURN AROUND, YOU'LL BE COMPLETELY FINE.
SIMPLE, RIGHT?
I'VE PASSED THIS WAY COUNTLESS TIMES.
AND BECAUSE I'VE NEVER LOOKED BACK, I'VE NEVER BEEN TAKEN TO THE OTHER PLACE, AND I'VE REMAINED HERE AS A *GHOST*.
...
ARE YOU READY? WE'RE PASSING THE MAIL-BOX.
コツ
STP
コツ
STP

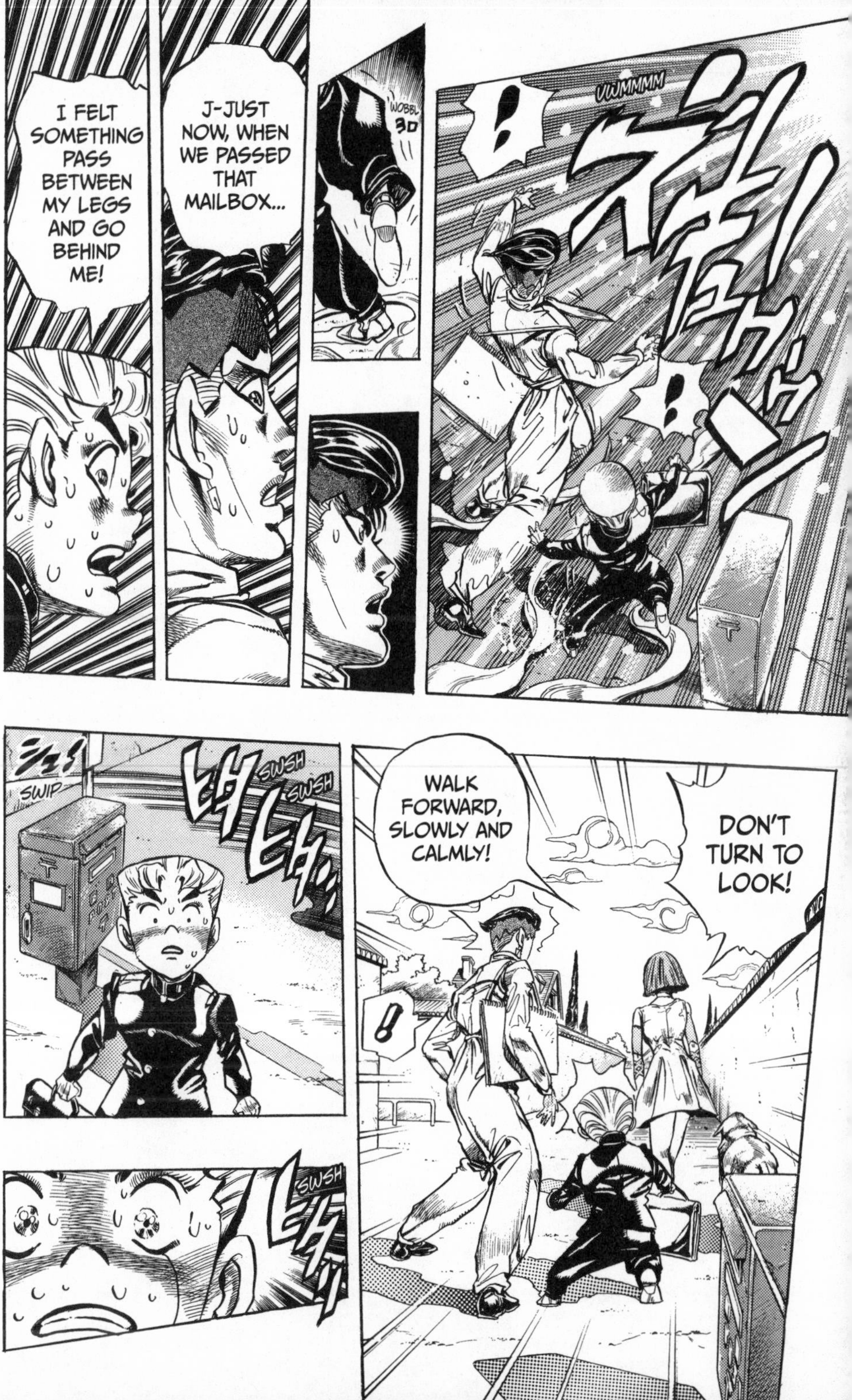

UWMMMM
!
!
WOBBL
J-JUST NOW, WHEN WE PASSED THAT MAILBOX...
I FELT SOMETHING PASS BETWEEN MY LEGS AND GO BEHIND ME!
DON'T TURN TO LOOK!
WALK FORWARD, SLOWLY AND CALMLY!
!
SWSH
SWSH
SWIP
SWSH

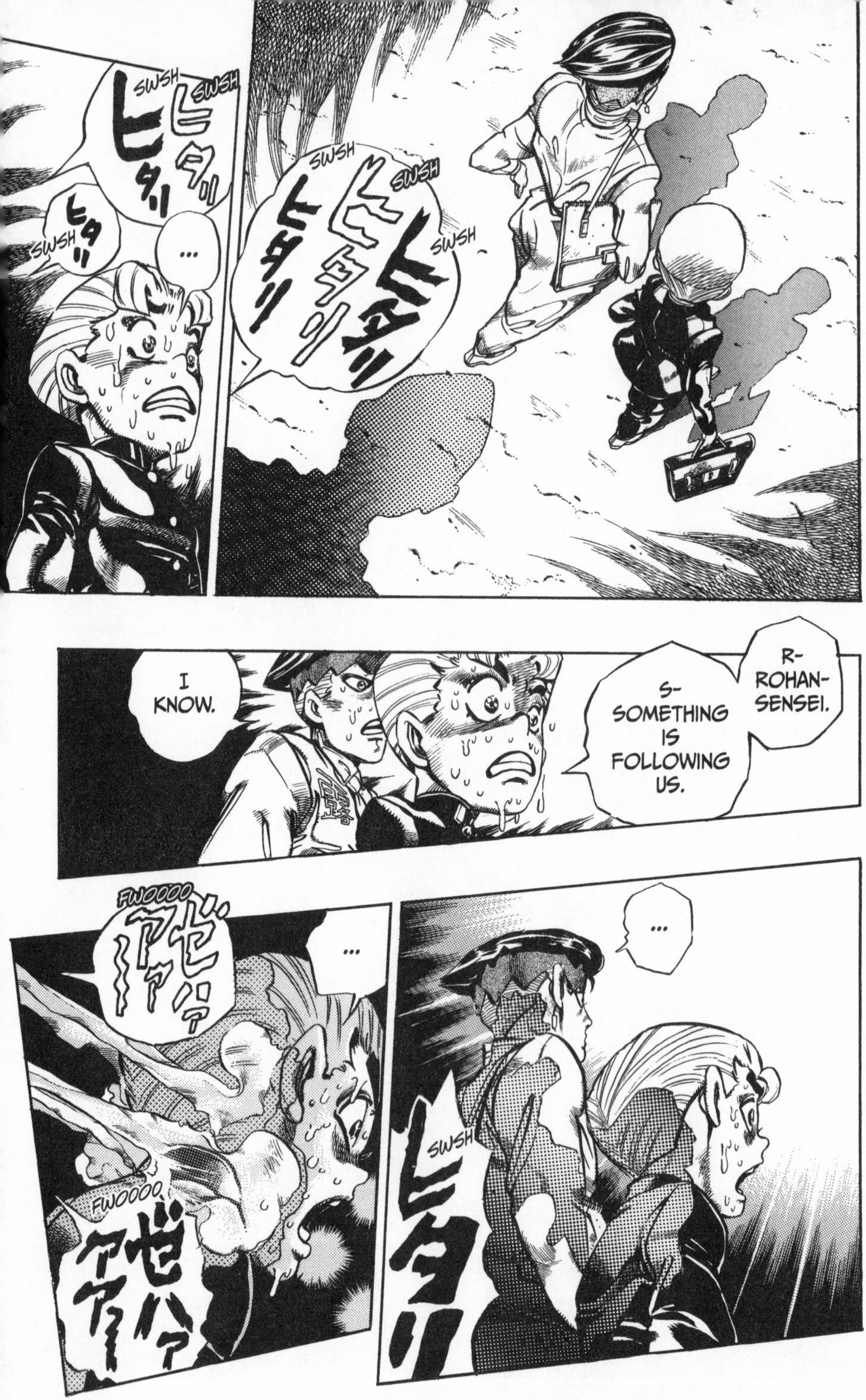
SWSH SWSH SWSH
ヒタッ ヒタッ ヒタッ
SWSH SWSH
ヒタッ ヒタッ
SWSH
ヒタッ
...
R-ROHAN-SENSEI.
S-SOMETHING IS FOLLOWING US.
I KNOW.
...
SWSH
ヒタッ
...
FWOOOO
ゼハァ~
FWOOOO
ゼハァアァ~

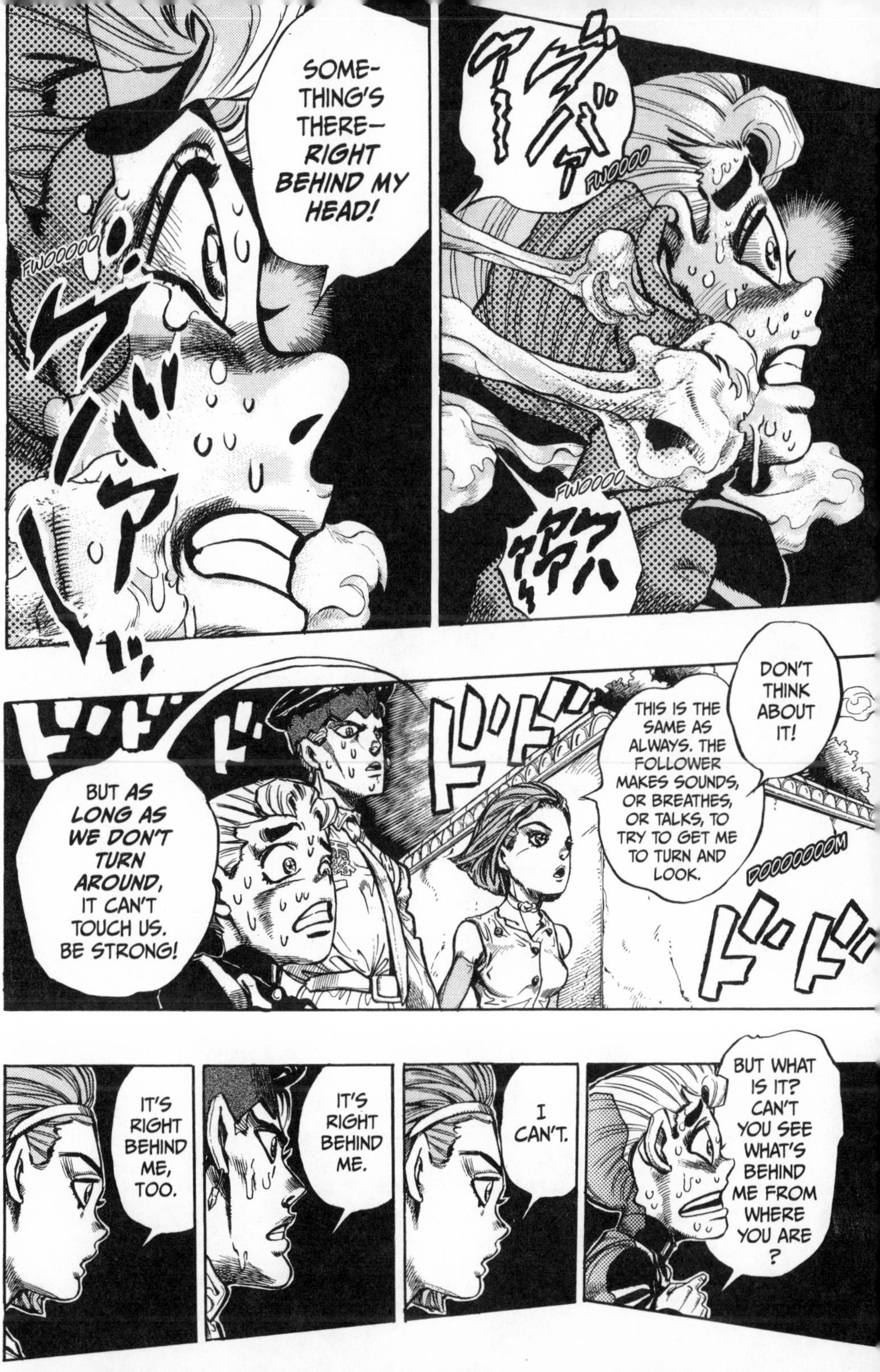
FWOOOO
FWOOOO
SOMETHING'S THERE—RIGHT BEHIND MY HEAD!
FWOOOOOO
DON'T THINK ABOUT IT!
THIS IS THE SAME AS ALWAYS. THE FOLLOWER MAKES SOUNDS, OR BREATHES, OR TALKS, TO TRY TO GET ME TO TURN AND LOOK.
DOOOOOOOM
BUT AS LONG AS WE DON'T TURN AROUND, IT CAN'T TOUCH US. BE STRONG!
BUT WHAT IS IT? CAN'T YOU SEE WHAT'S BEHIND ME FROM WHERE YOU ARE?
I CAN'T.
IT'S RIGHT BEHIND ME.
IT'S RIGHT BEHIND ME, TOO.

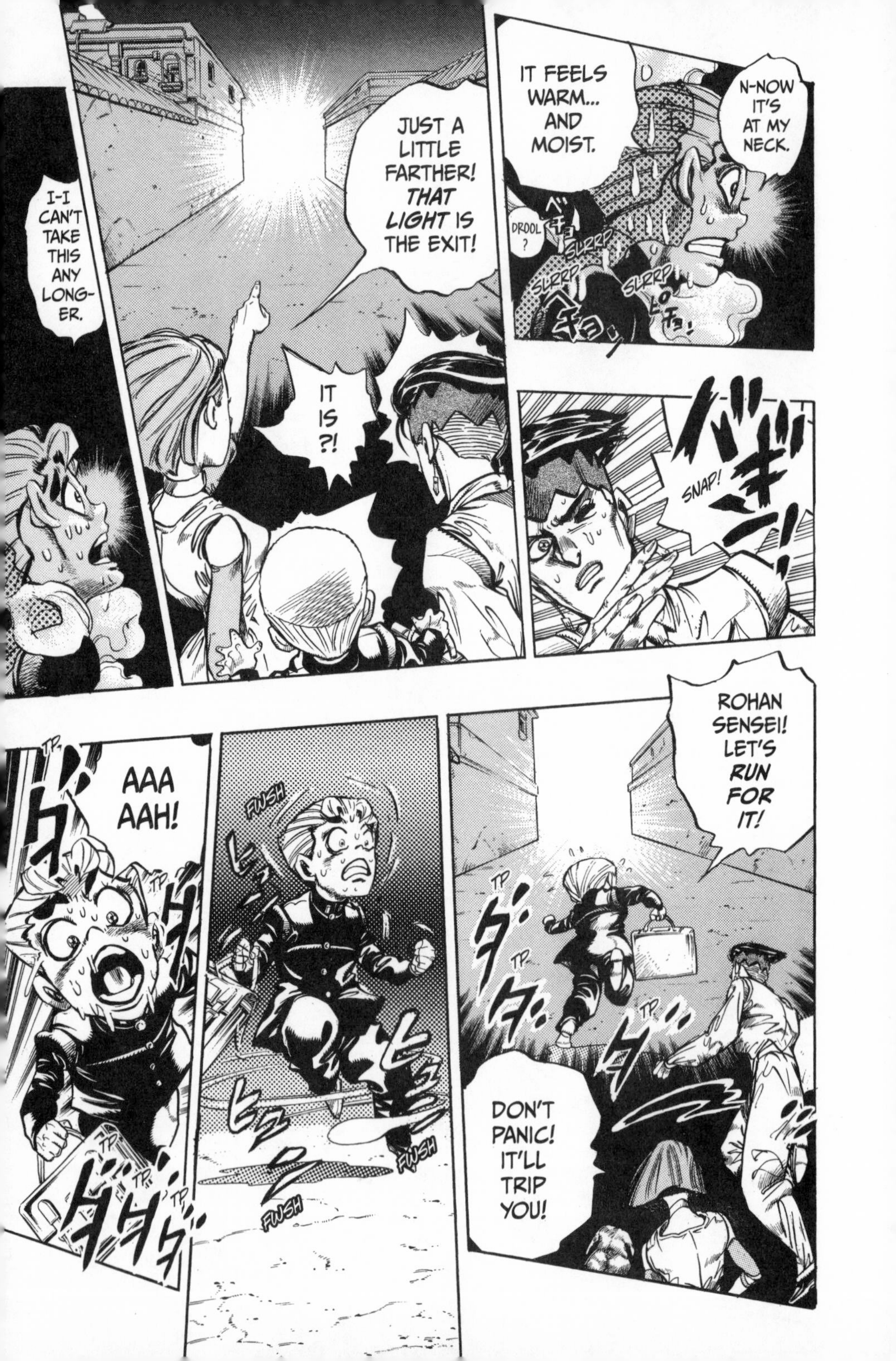
N-NOW IT'S AT MY NECK.
IT FEELS WARM... AND MOIST.
DROOL ?
SLURRP
SLURRP
SLURRP
SNAP!
JUST A LITTLE FARTHER! *THAT LIGHT* IS THE EXIT!
IT IS?!
I-I CAN'T TAKE THIS ANY LONGER.
ROHAN SENSEI! LET'S *RUN* FOR IT!
TP
TP
TP
DON'T PANIC! IT'LL TRIP YOU!
FWSH
FWSH
FWSH
AAA AAH!
TP
TP
TP
TP
TP

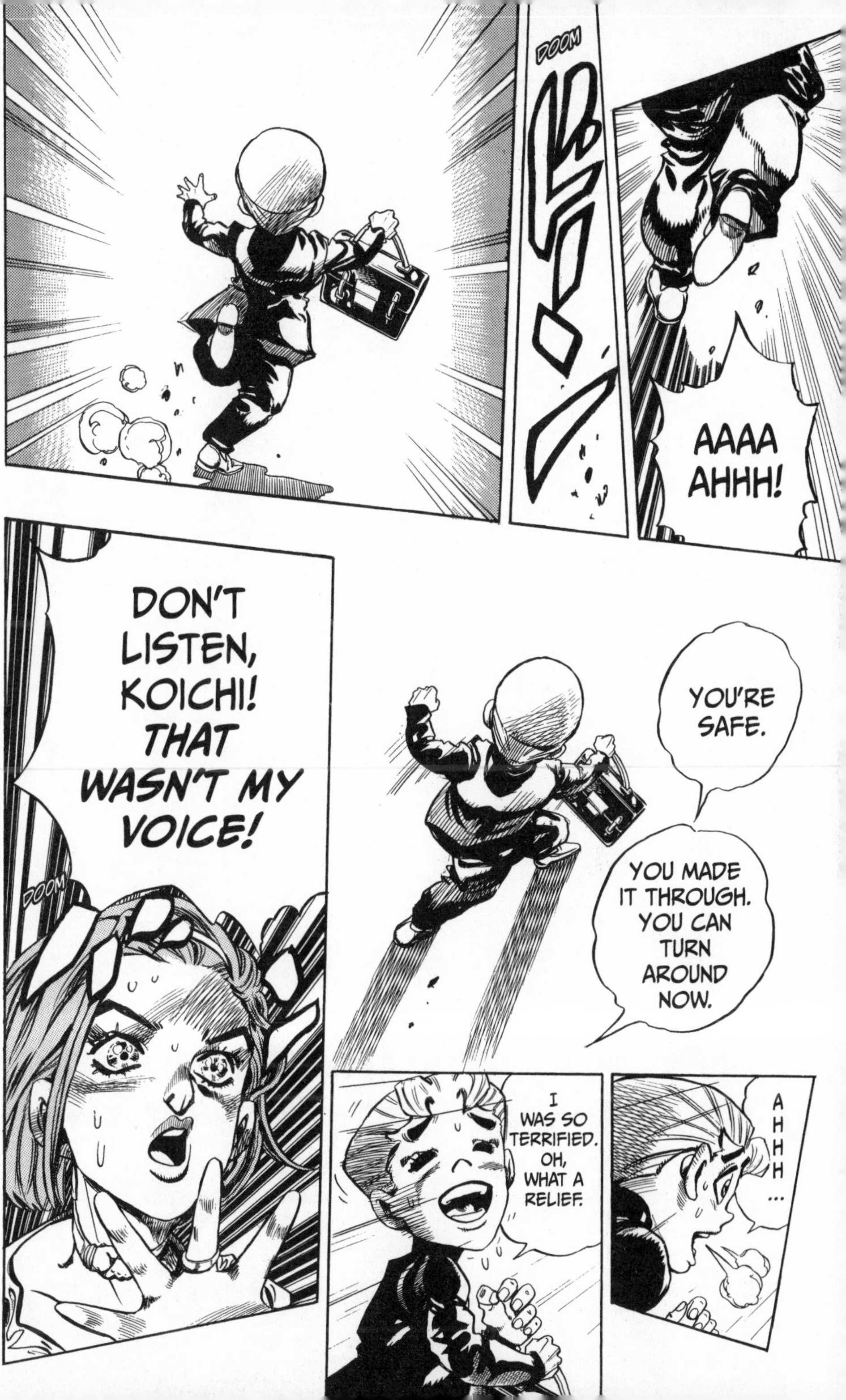
AAAA AHHH!
DOOM
YOU'RE SAFE.
YOU MADE IT THROUGH. YOU CAN TURN AROUND NOW.
AHHH...
I WAS SO TERRIFIED. OH, WHAT A RELIEF.
DON'T LISTEN, KOICHI! THAT WASN'T MY VOICE!
DOOM

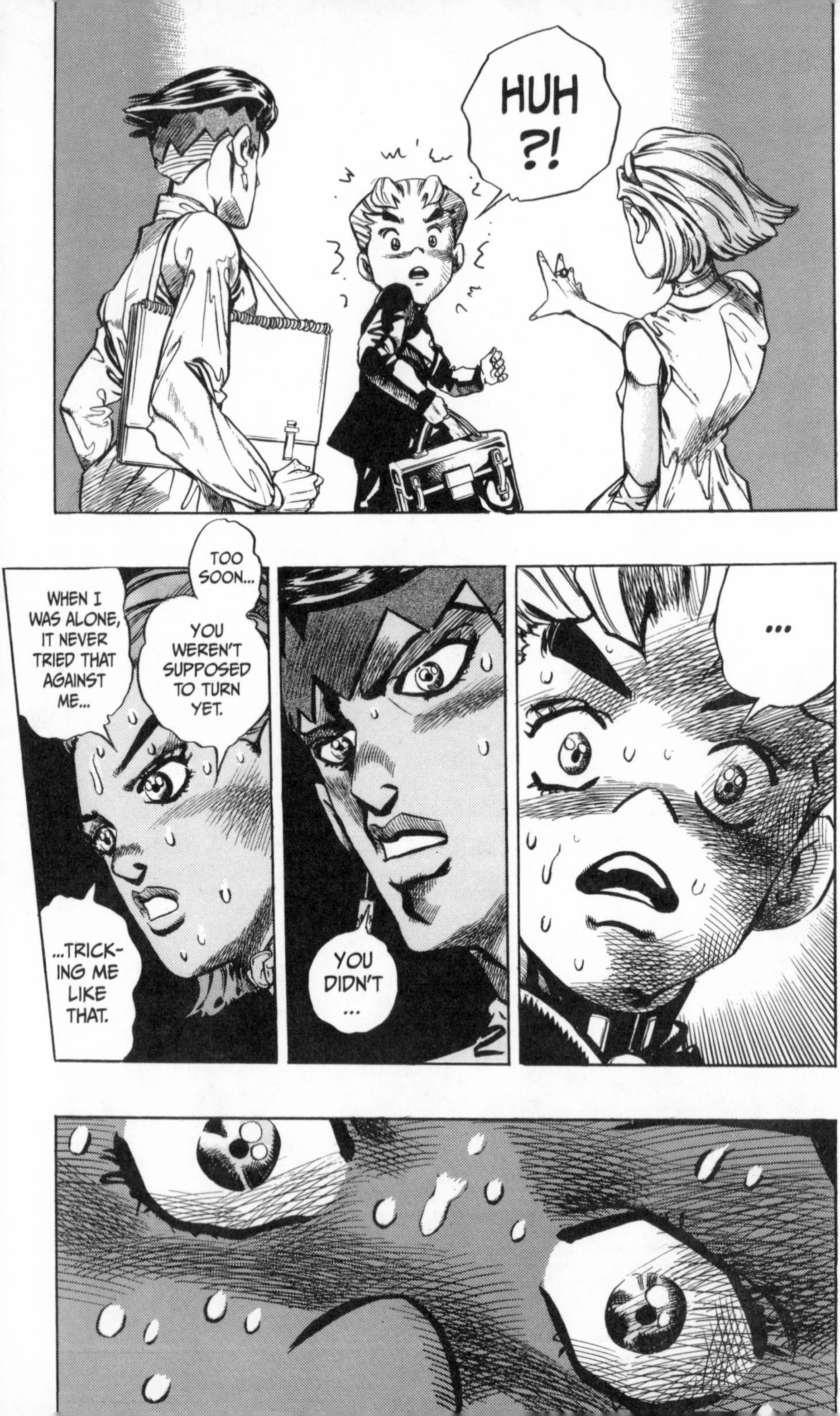
HUH ?!
...
YOU DIDN'T ...
TOO SOON...
YOU WEREN'T SUPPOSED TO TURN YET.
WHEN I WAS ALONE, IT NEVER TRIED THAT AGAINST ME...
...TRICKING ME LIKE THAT.

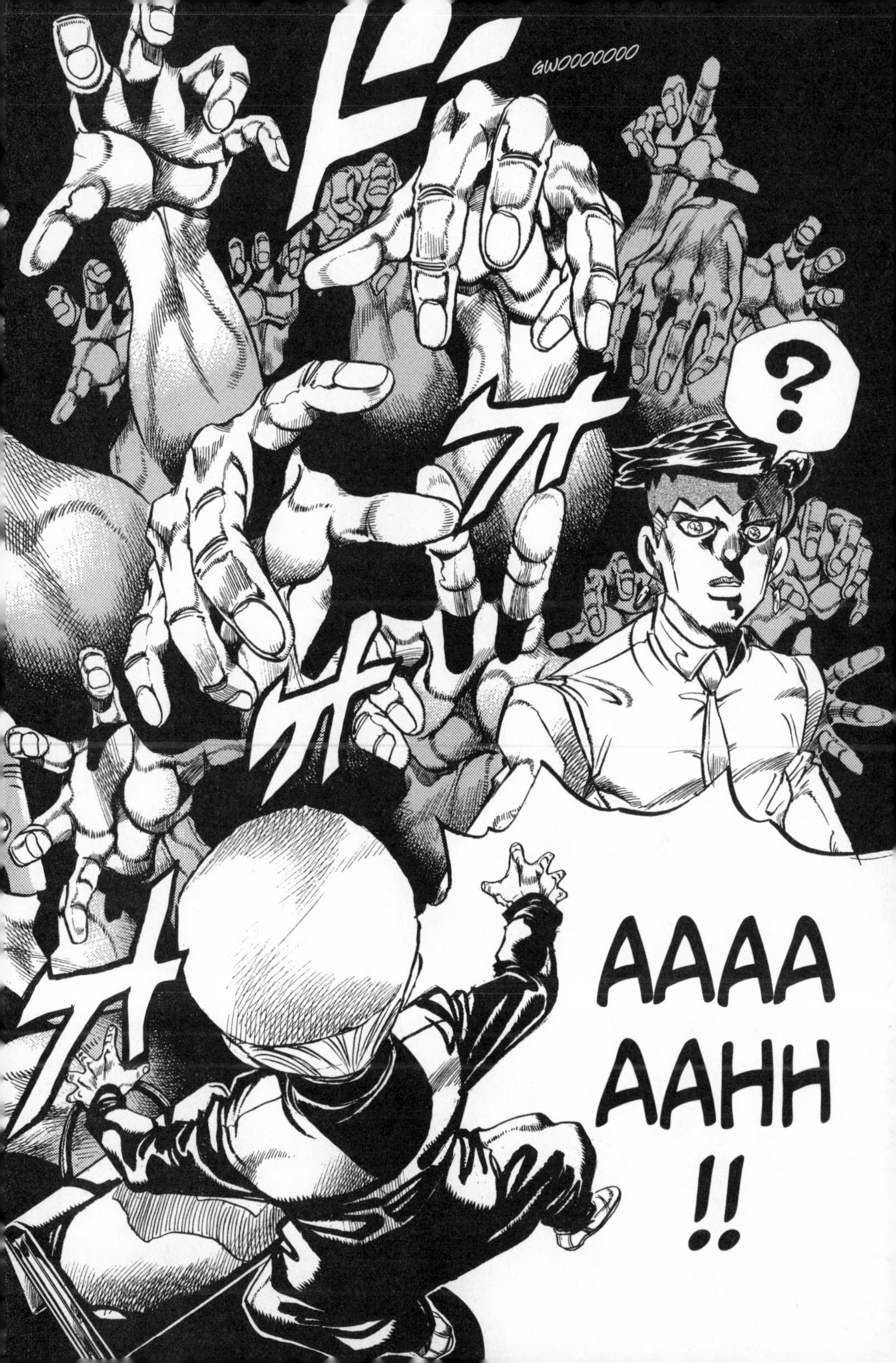
GWOOOOOOO
?
AAAA
AAHH
!!

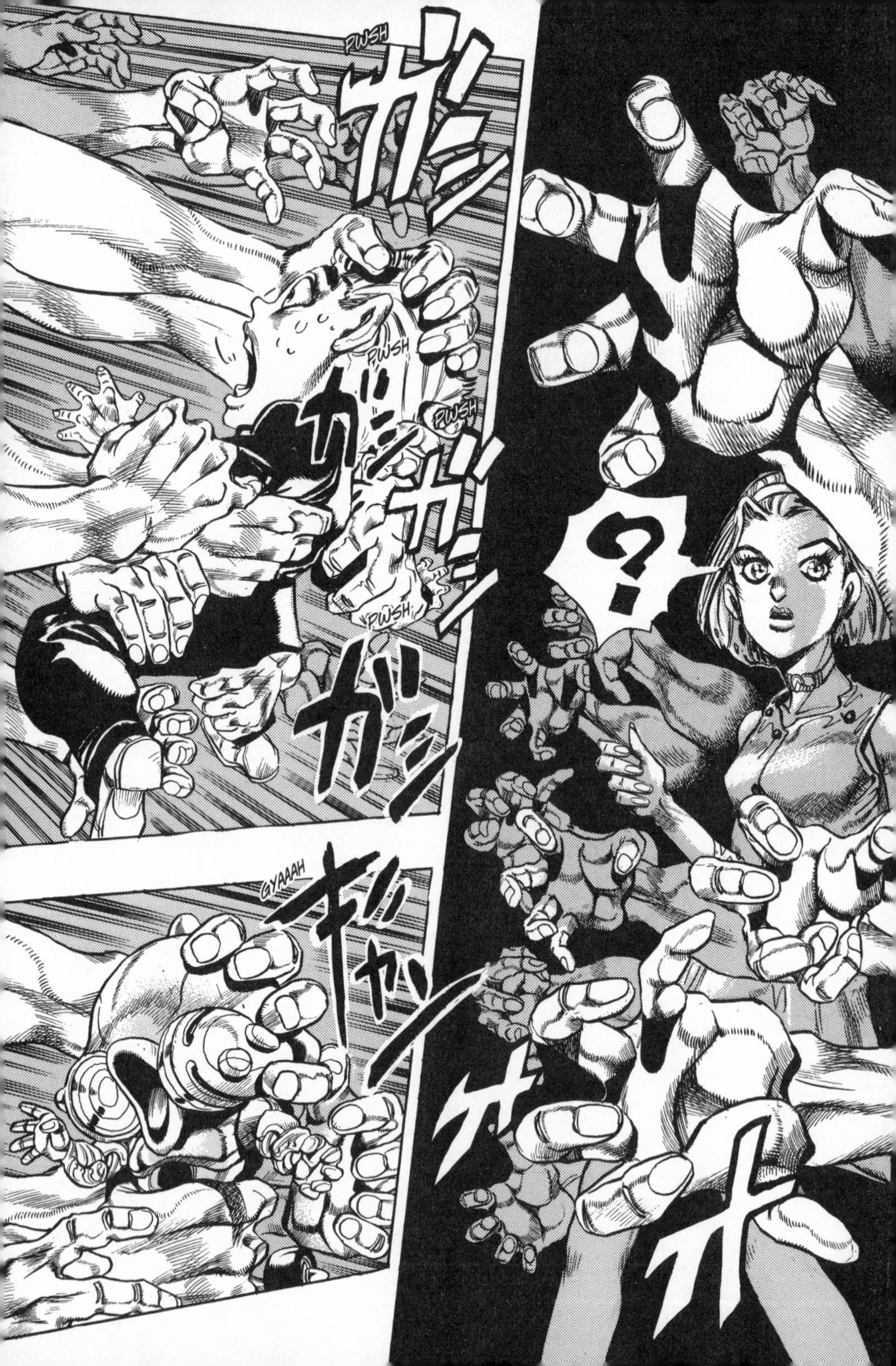
?
PWSH
PWSH
PWSH
PWSH
GYAAAH

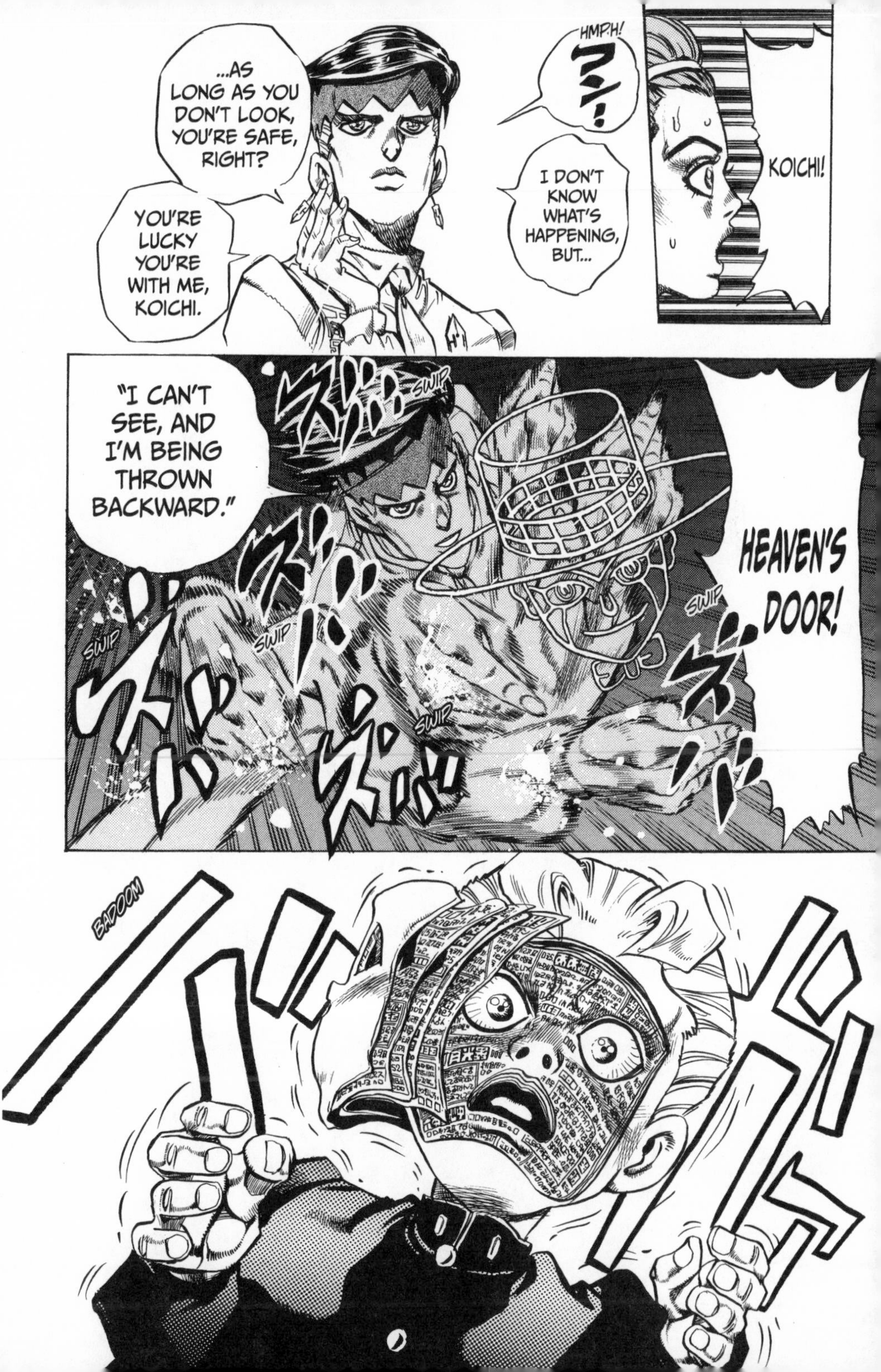
KOICHI!
HMPH!
I DON'T KNOW WHAT'S HAPPENING, BUT...
...AS LONG AS YOU DON'T LOOK, YOU'RE SAFE, RIGHT?
YOU'RE LUCKY YOU'RE WITH ME, KOICHI.
HEAVEN'S DOOR!
SWIP
SWIP
"I CAN'T SEE, AND I'M BEING THROWN BACKWARD."
SWIP
SWIP
SWIP
BADOOM

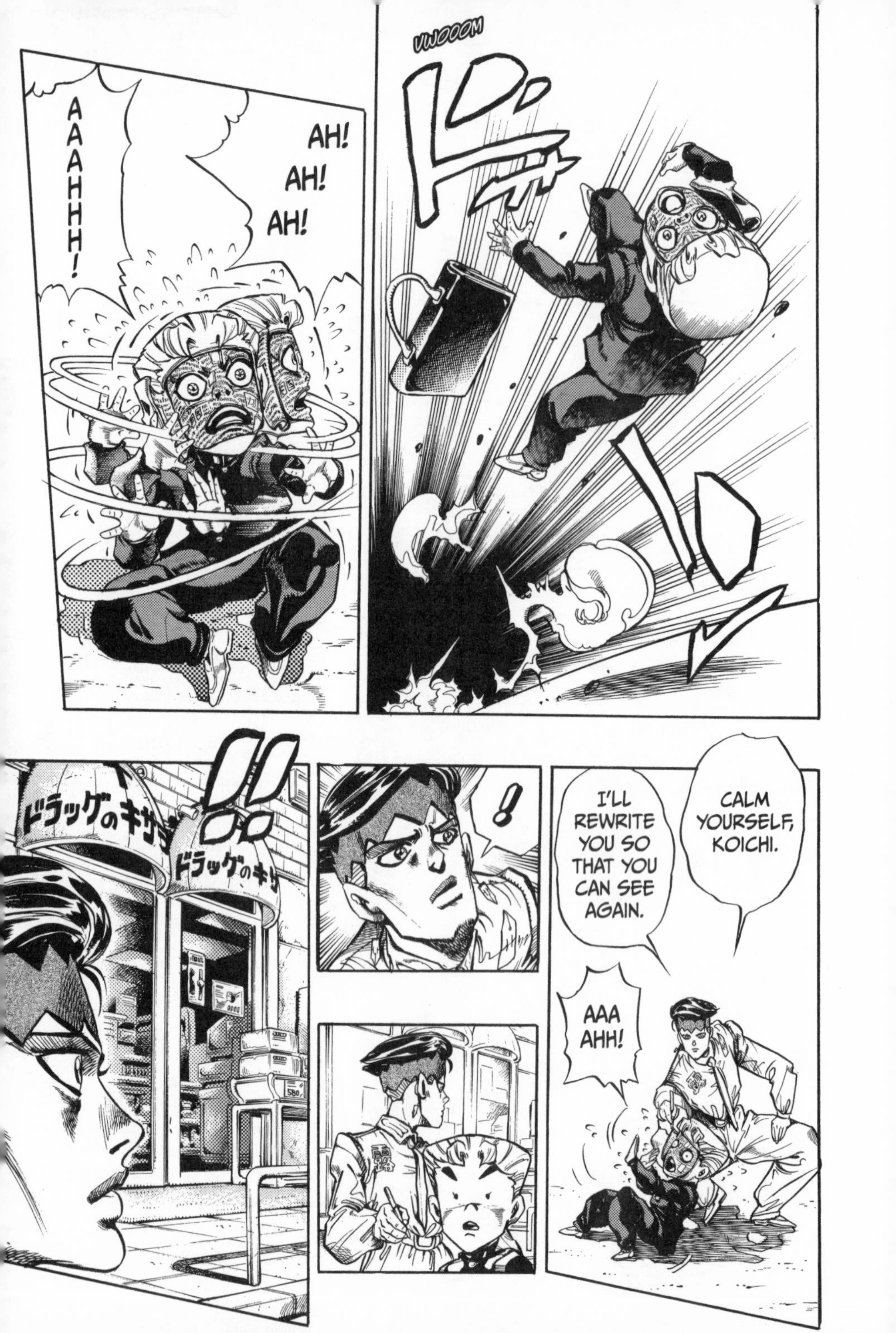
VWOOOM
AAAAHHH!
AH!
AH!
AH!
CALM YOURSELF, KOICHI.
I'LL REWRITE YOU SO THAT YOU CAN SEE AGAIN.
AAA AHH!
!
ドラッグのキサ
ドラッグのキ

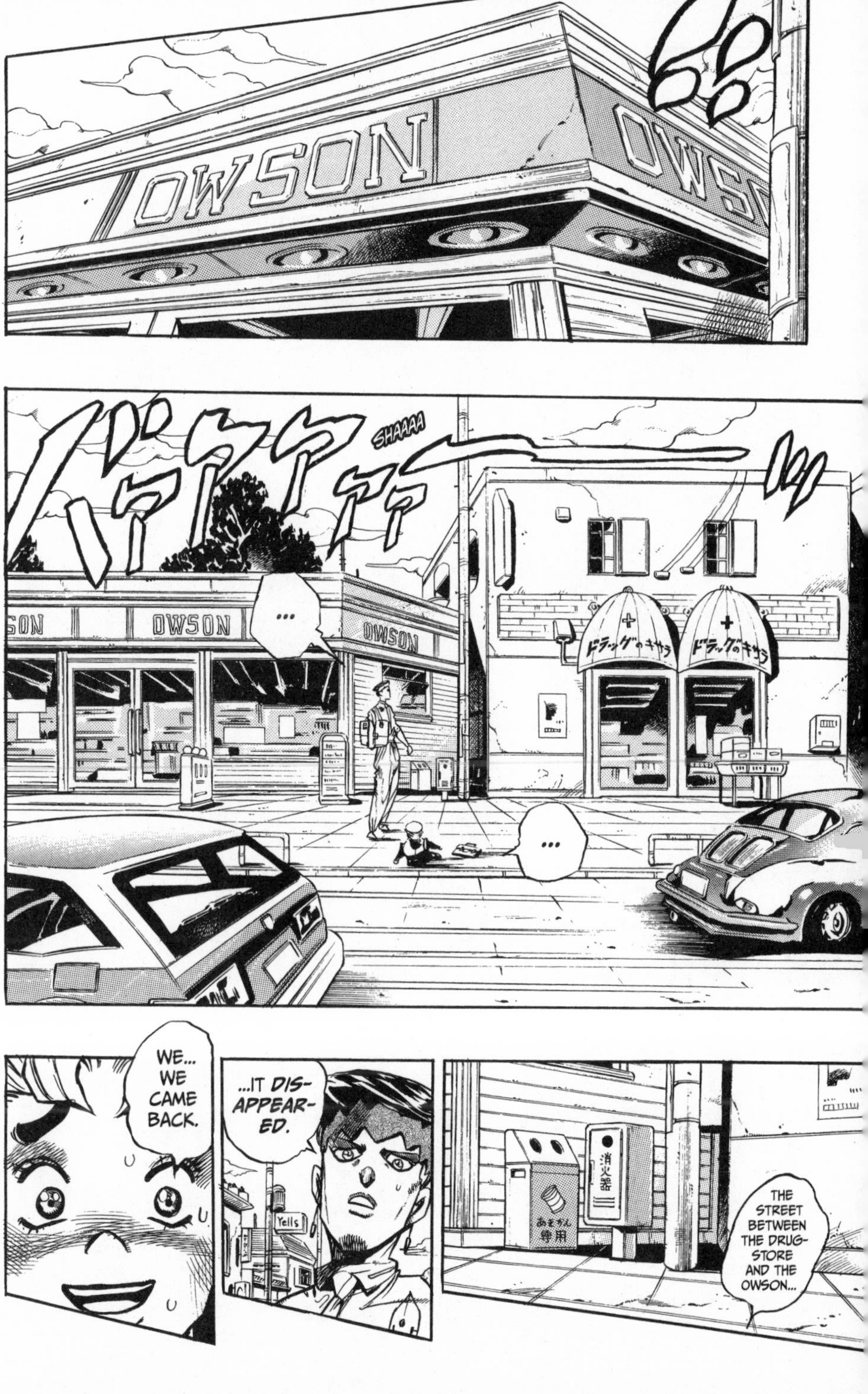
OWSON
OWSO
SHAAAA
OWSON
OWSON
...
ドラッグのキサラ
ドラッグのキサラ
...
THE STREET BETWEEN THE DRUG-STORE AND THE OWSON...
消火器
あきかん専用
...IT DIS-APPEAR-ED.
Yells
WE... WE CAME BACK.

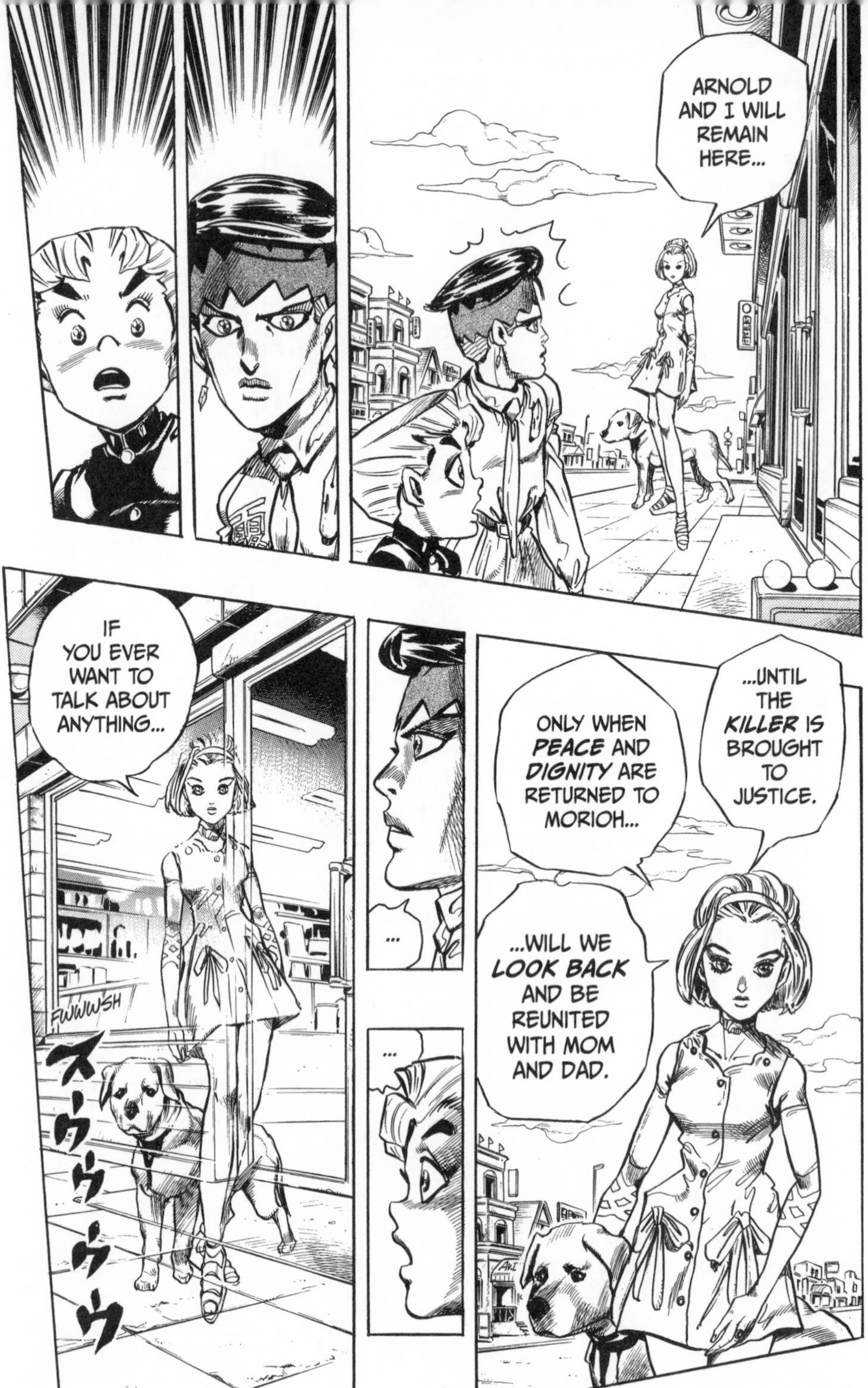
ARNOLD AND I WILL REMAIN HERE...
...UNTIL THE KILLER IS BROUGHT TO JUSTICE.
ONLY WHEN PEACE AND DIGNITY ARE RETURNED TO MORIOH...
...WILL WE LOOK BACK AND BE REUNITED WITH MOM AND DAD.
...
...
IF YOU EVER WANT TO TALK ABOUT ANYTHING...
FWWWSH
スーウウウウ

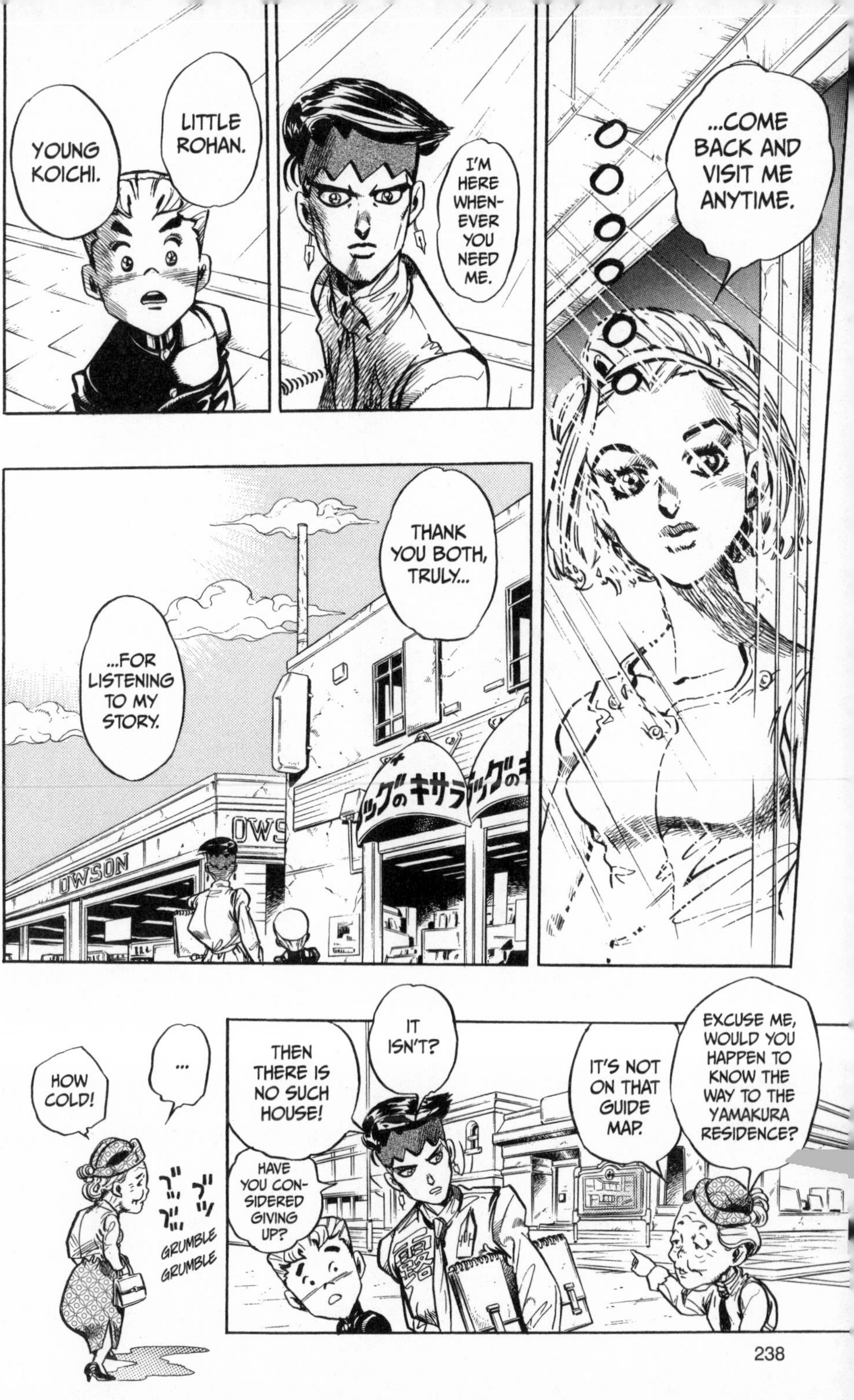

...COME BACK AND VISIT ME ANYTIME.
I'M HERE WHENEVER YOU NEED ME.
LITTLE ROHAN.
YOUNG KOICHI.
THANK YOU BOTH, TRULY...
...FOR LISTENING TO MY STORY.
EXCUSE ME, WOULD YOU HAPPEN TO KNOW THE WAY TO THE YAMAKURA RESIDENCE?
IT'S NOT ON THAT GUIDE MAP.
IT ISN'T?
THEN THERE IS NO SUCH HOUSE!
HAVE YOU CONSIDERED GIVING UP?
...
HOW COLD!
ブツブツ
GRUMBLE GRUMBLE

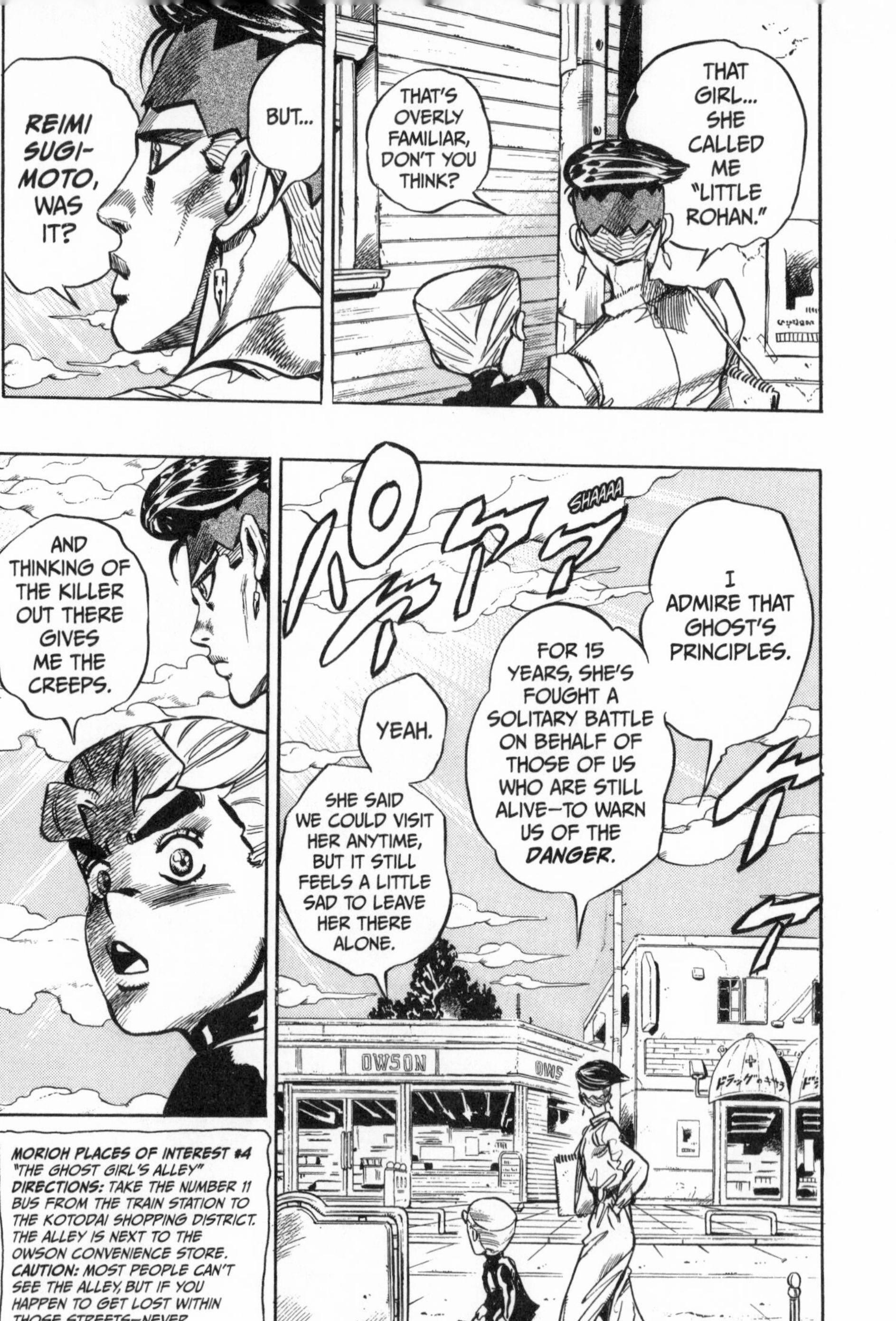
THAT GIRL... SHE CALLED ME "LITTLE ROHAN."
THAT'S OVERLY FAMILIAR, DON'T YOU THINK?
BUT...
REIMI SUGIMOTO, WAS IT?
SHAAAA
I ADMIRE THAT GHOST'S PRINCIPLES.
FOR 15 YEARS, SHE'S FOUGHT A SOLITARY BATTLE ON BEHALF OF THOSE OF US WHO ARE STILL ALIVE—TO WARN US OF THE DANGER.
YEAH.
SHE SAID WE COULD VISIT HER ANYTIME, BUT IT STILL FEELS A LITTLE SAD TO LEAVE HER THERE ALONE.
OWSON
AND THINKING OF THE KILLER OUT THERE GIVES ME THE CREEPS.
MORIOH PLACES OF INTEREST #4 "THE GHOST GIRL'S ALLEY" DIRECTIONS: TAKE THE NUMBER 11 BUS FROM THE TRAIN STATION TO THE KOTODAI SHOPPING DISTRICT. THE ALLEY IS NEXT TO THE OWSON CONVENIENCE STORE. CAUTION: MOST PEOPLE CAN'T SEE THE ALLEY, BUT IF YOU HAPPEN TO GET LOST WITHIN THOSE STREETS—NEVER LOOK BACK.

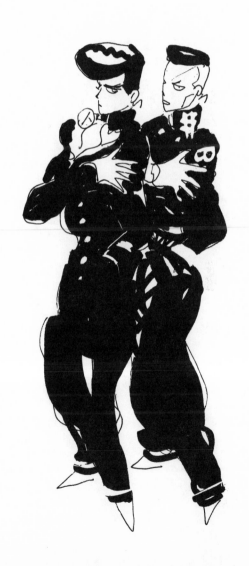

CHAPTER 69

ROHAN KISHIBE'S ADVENTURE, PART 5

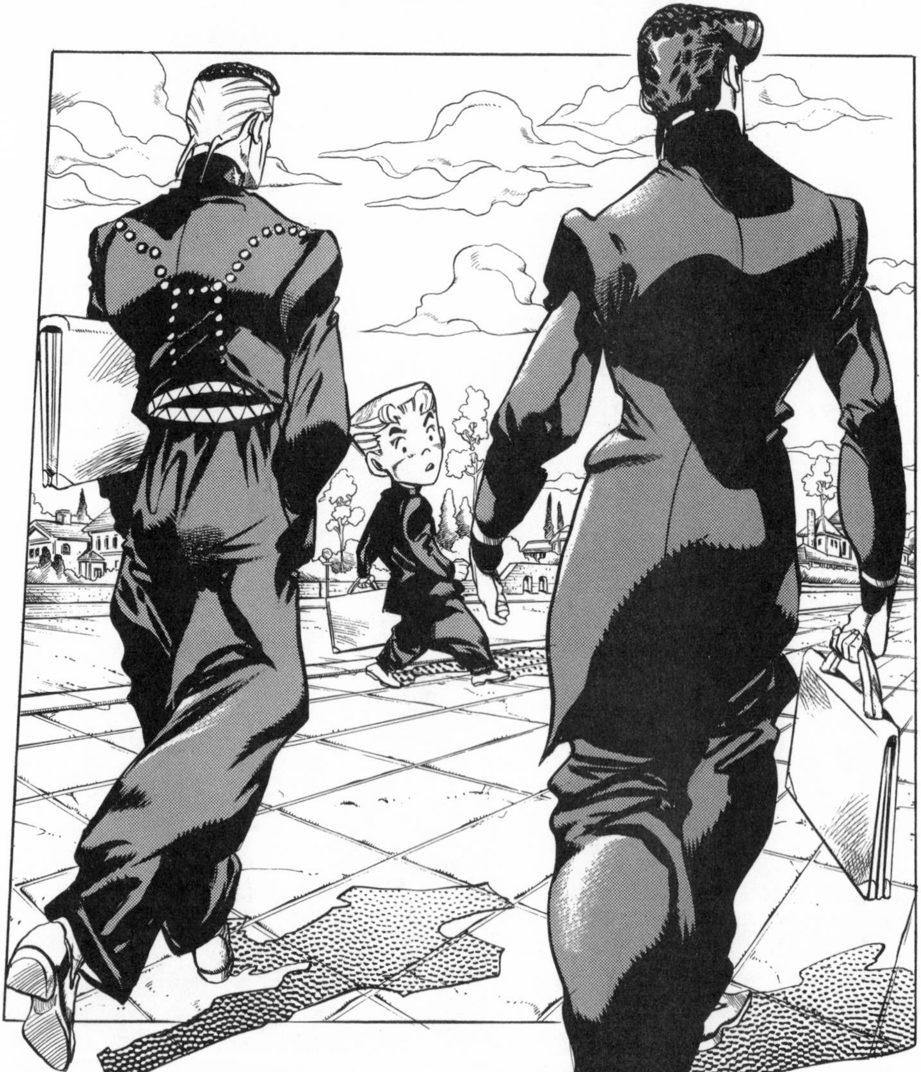

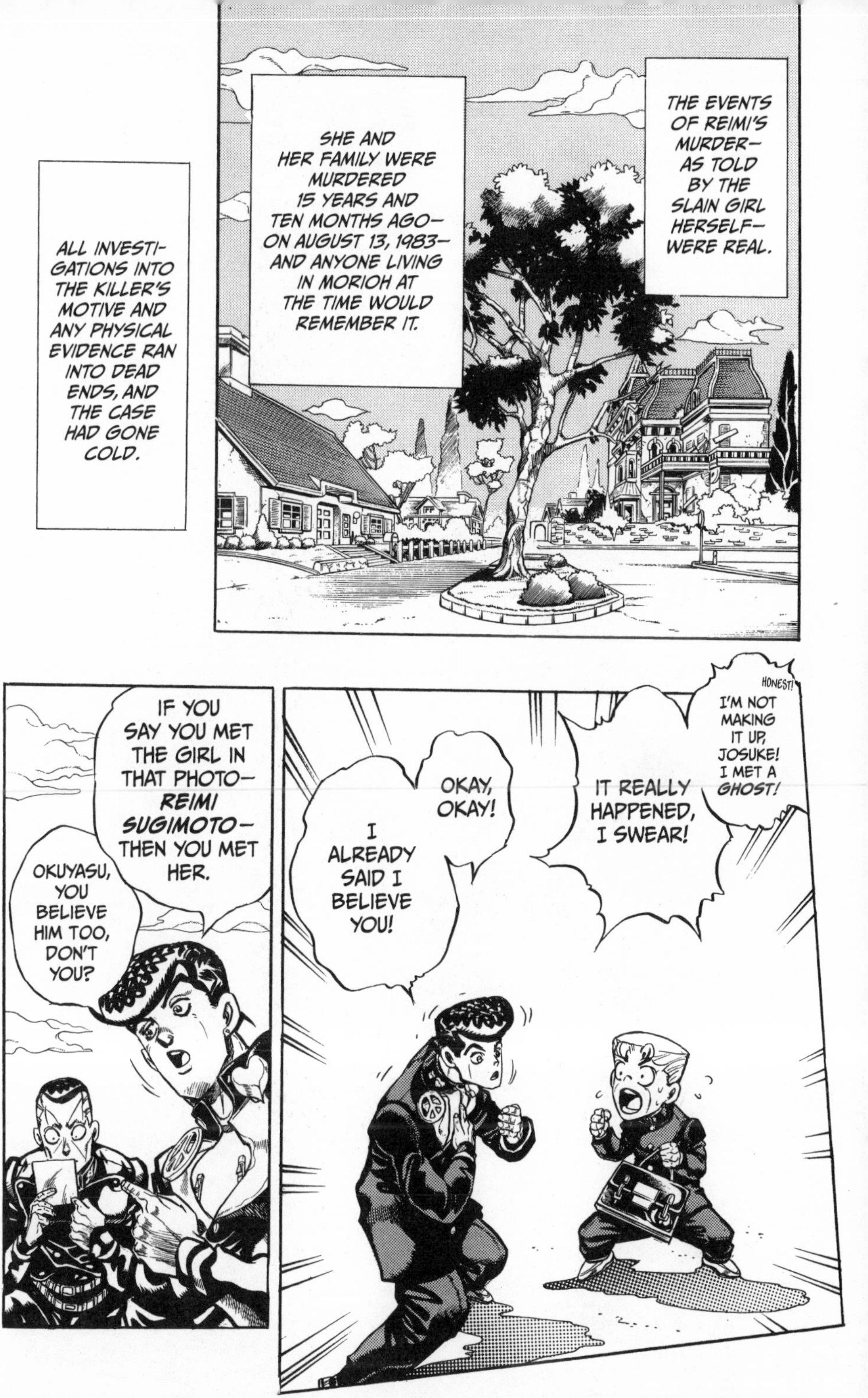
THE EVENTS OF REIMI'S MURDER—AS TOLD BY THE SLAIN GIRL HERSELF—WERE REAL.
SHE AND HER FAMILY WERE MURDERED 15 YEARS AND TEN MONTHS AGO—ON AUGUST 13, 1983—AND ANYONE LIVING IN MORIOH AT THE TIME WOULD REMEMBER IT.
ALL INVESTIGATIONS INTO THE KILLER'S MOTIVE AND ANY PHYSICAL EVIDENCE RAN INTO DEAD ENDS, AND THE CASE HAD GONE COLD.
HONEST!
I'M NOT MAKING IT UP, JOSUKE! I MET A GHOST!
IT REALLY HAPPENED, I SWEAR!
OKAY, OKAY!
I ALREADY SAID I BELIEVE YOU!
IF YOU SAY YOU MET THE GIRL IN THAT PHOTO—REIMI SUGIMOTO—THEN YOU MET HER.
OKUYASU, YOU BELIEVE HIM TOO, DON'T YOU?

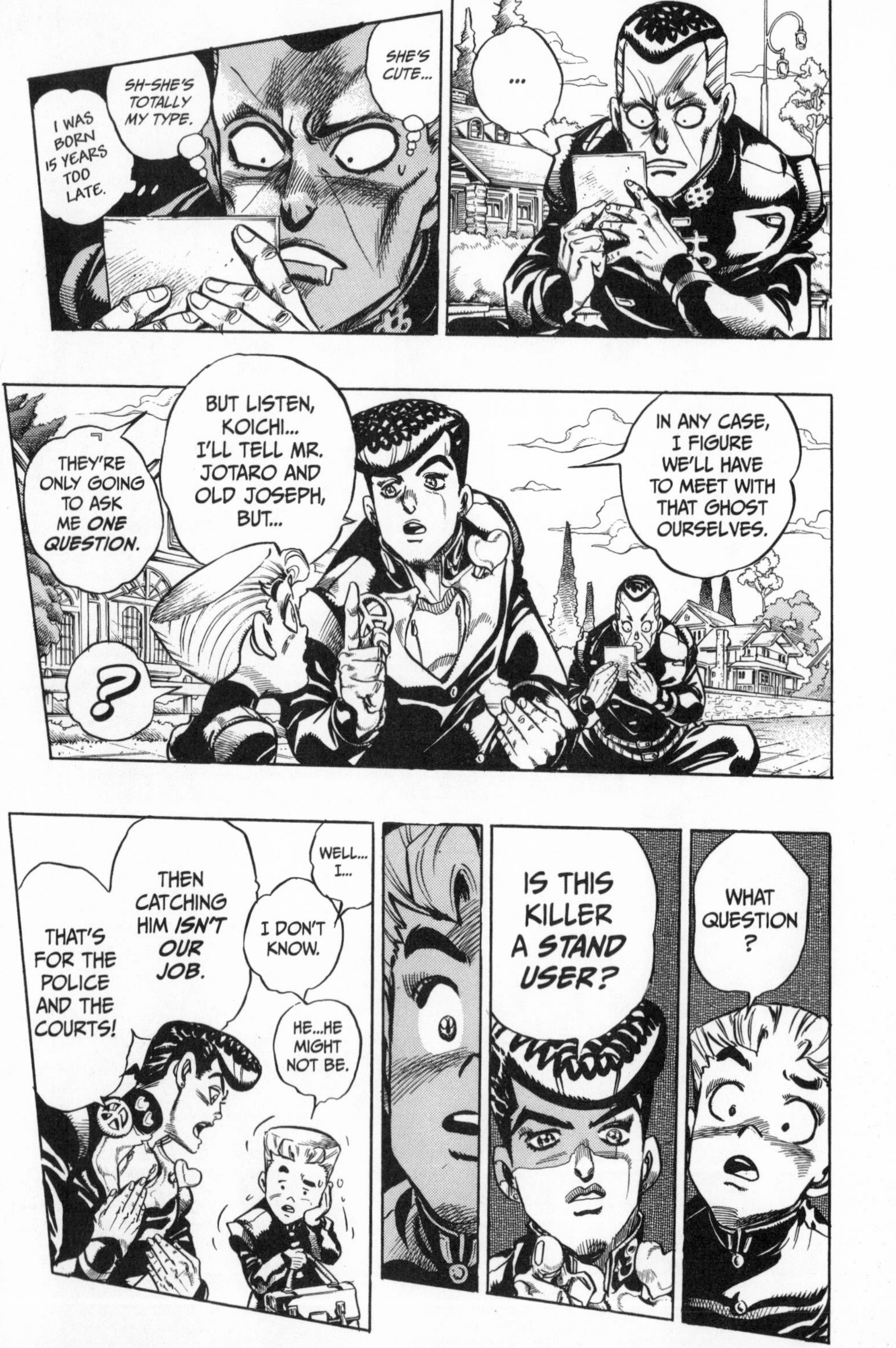
...
SHE'S CUTE...
SH-SHE'S TOTALLY MY TYPE.
I WAS BORN 15 YEARS TOO LATE.
IN ANY CASE, I FIGURE WE'LL HAVE TO MEET WITH THAT GHOST OURSELVES.
BUT LISTEN, KOICHI... I'LL TELL MR. JOTARO AND OLD JOSEPH, BUT...
THEY'RE ONLY GOING TO ASK ME *ONE QUESTION*.
?
WHAT QUESTION ?
IS THIS KILLER A *STAND USER?*
WELL... I...
I DON'T KNOW.
HE...HE MIGHT NOT BE.
THEN CATCHING HIM *ISN'T OUR JOB*.
THAT'S FOR THE POLICE AND THE COURTS!

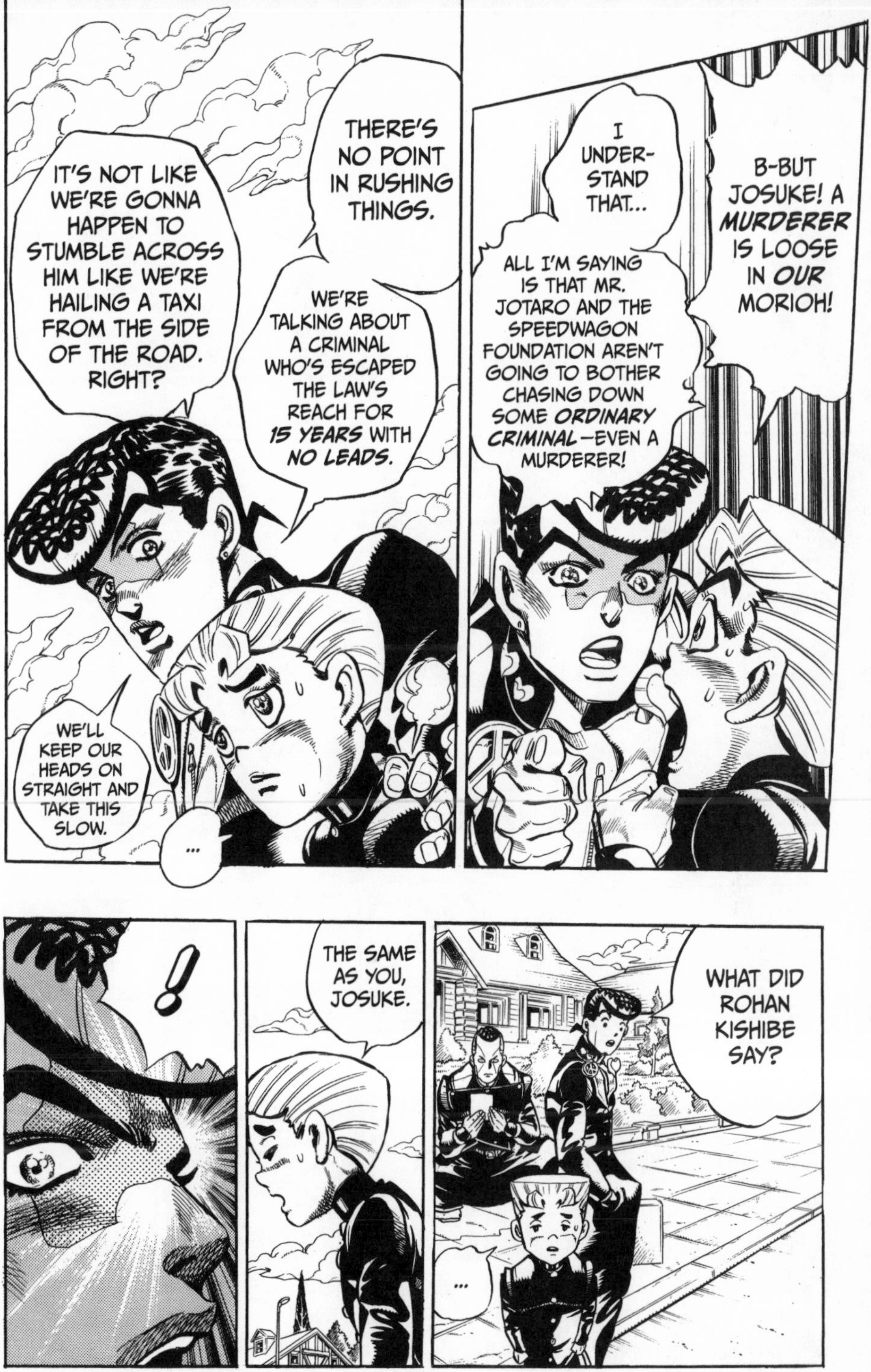
B-BUT JOSUKE! A *MURDERER* IS LOOSE IN *OUR* MORIOH!
I UNDER-STAND THAT...
ALL I'M SAYING IS THAT MR. JOTARO AND THE SPEEDWAGON FOUNDATION AREN'T GOING TO BOTHER CHASING DOWN SOME *ORDINARY CRIMINAL*—EVEN A MURDERER!
THERE'S NO POINT IN RUSHING THINGS.
IT'S NOT LIKE WE'RE GONNA HAPPEN TO STUMBLE ACROSS HIM LIKE WE'RE HAILING A TAXI FROM THE SIDE OF THE ROAD. RIGHT?
WE'RE TALKING ABOUT A CRIMINAL WHO'S ESCAPED THE LAW'S REACH FOR *15 YEARS* WITH *NO LEADS*.
WE'LL KEEP OUR HEADS ON STRAIGHT AND TAKE THIS SLOW.
...
WHAT DID ROHAN KISHIBE SAY?
...
THE SAME AS YOU, JOSUKE.
!

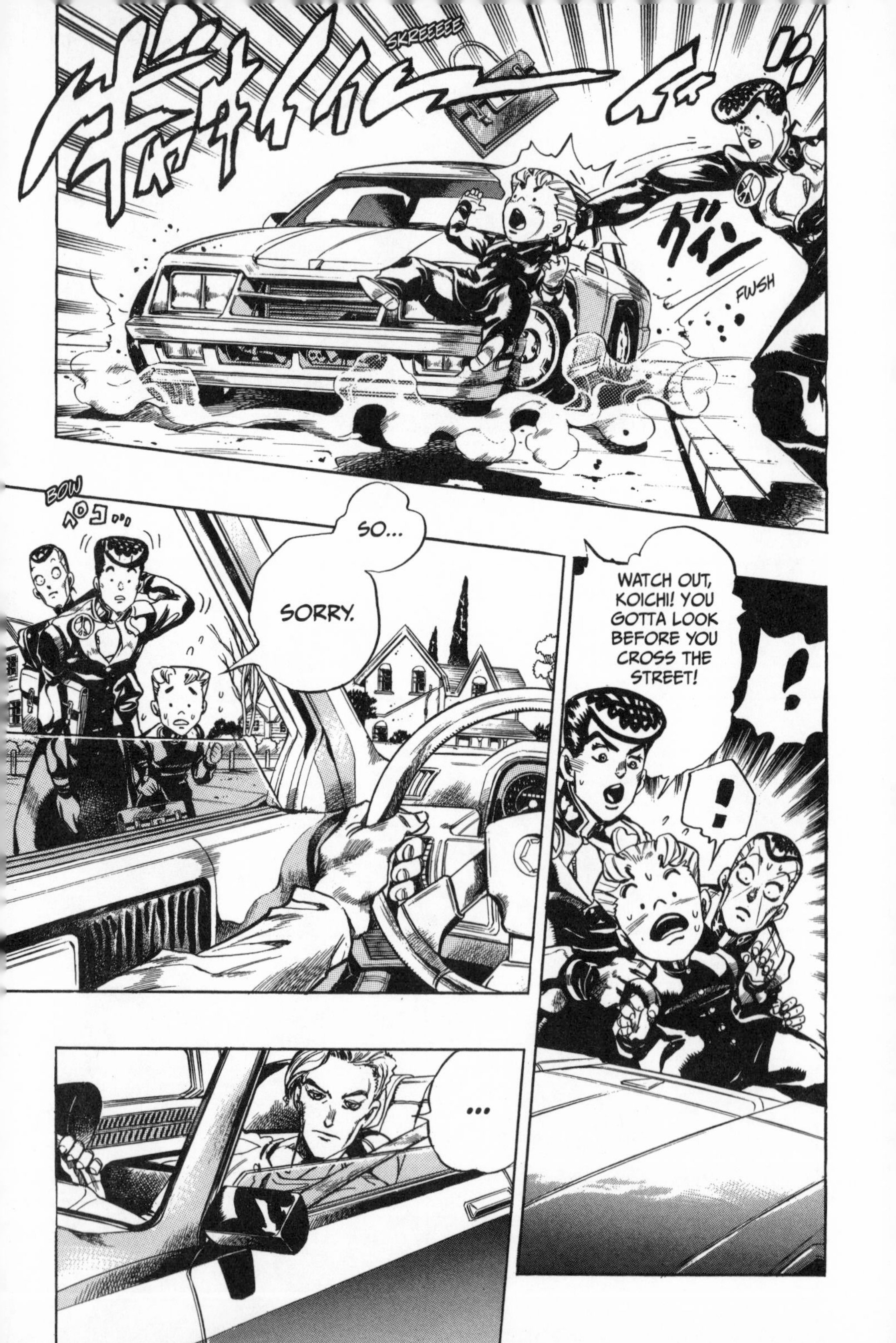
SKREEEEE
グイン
FWSH
WATCH OUT, KOICHI! YOU GOTTA LOOK BEFORE YOU CROSS THE STREET!
!
!
BOW
ペコッ
SO...
SORRY.
...

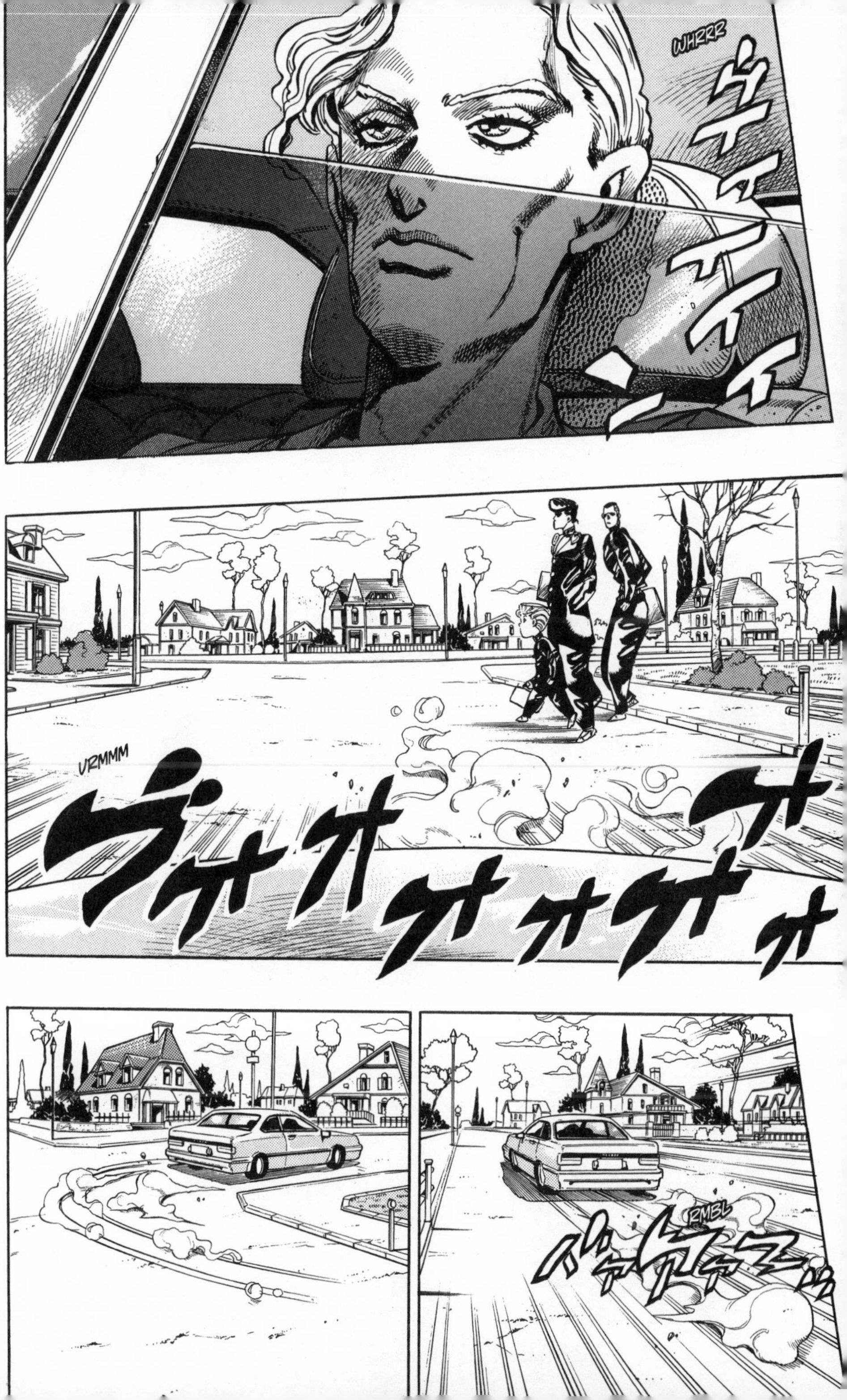
WHRRR
VRMMM
RMBL

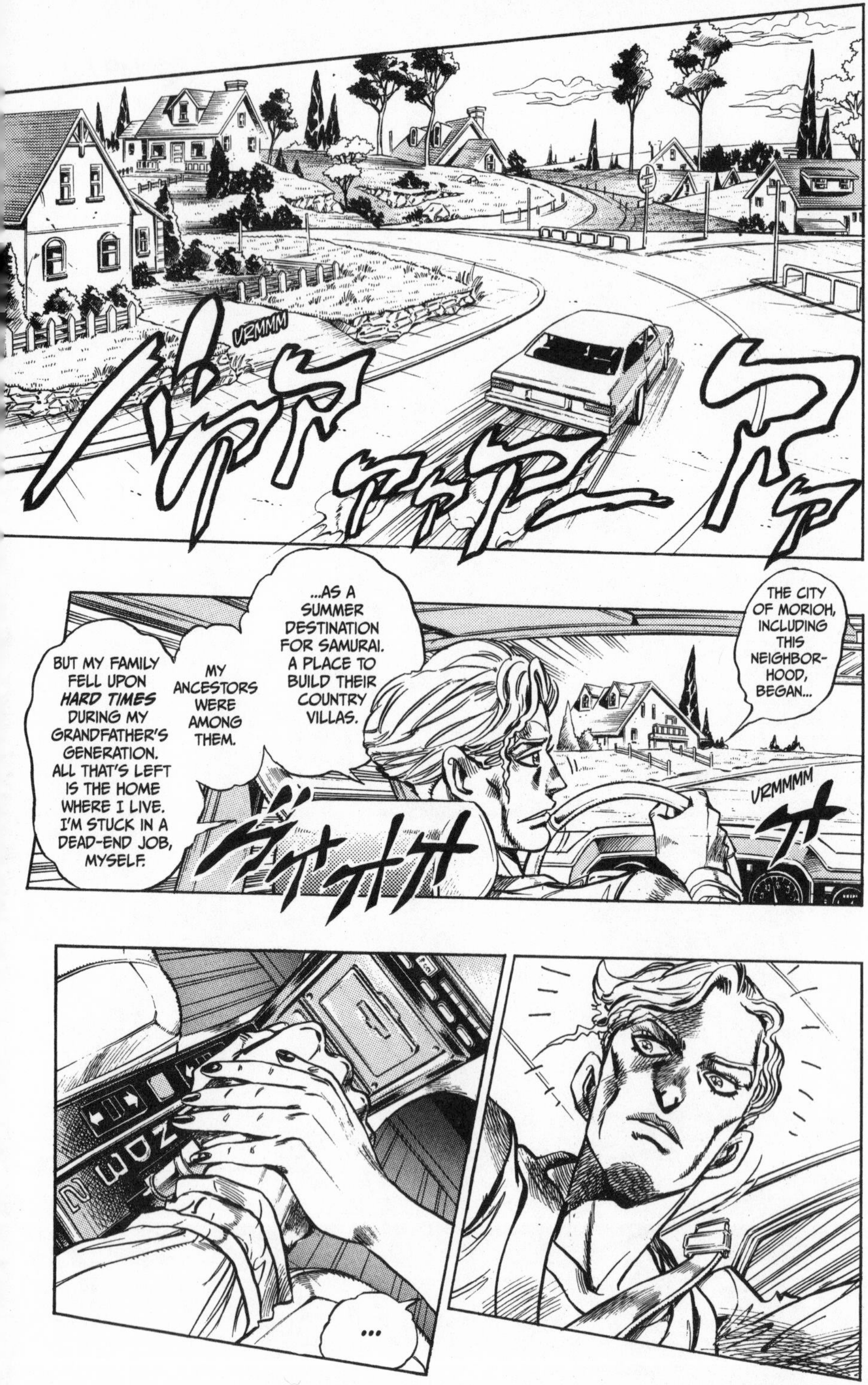
URMMM
THE CITY OF MORIOH, INCLUDING THIS NEIGHBORHOOD, BEGAN...
...AS A SUMMER DESTINATION FOR SAMURAI. A PLACE TO BUILD THEIR COUNTRY VILLAS.
MY ANCESTORS WERE AMONG THEM.
BUT MY FAMILY FELL UPON *HARD TIMES* DURING MY GRANDFATHER'S GENERATION. ALL THAT'S LEFT IS THE HOME WHERE I LIVE. I'M STUCK IN A DEAD-END JOB, MYSELF.
URMMMM
...

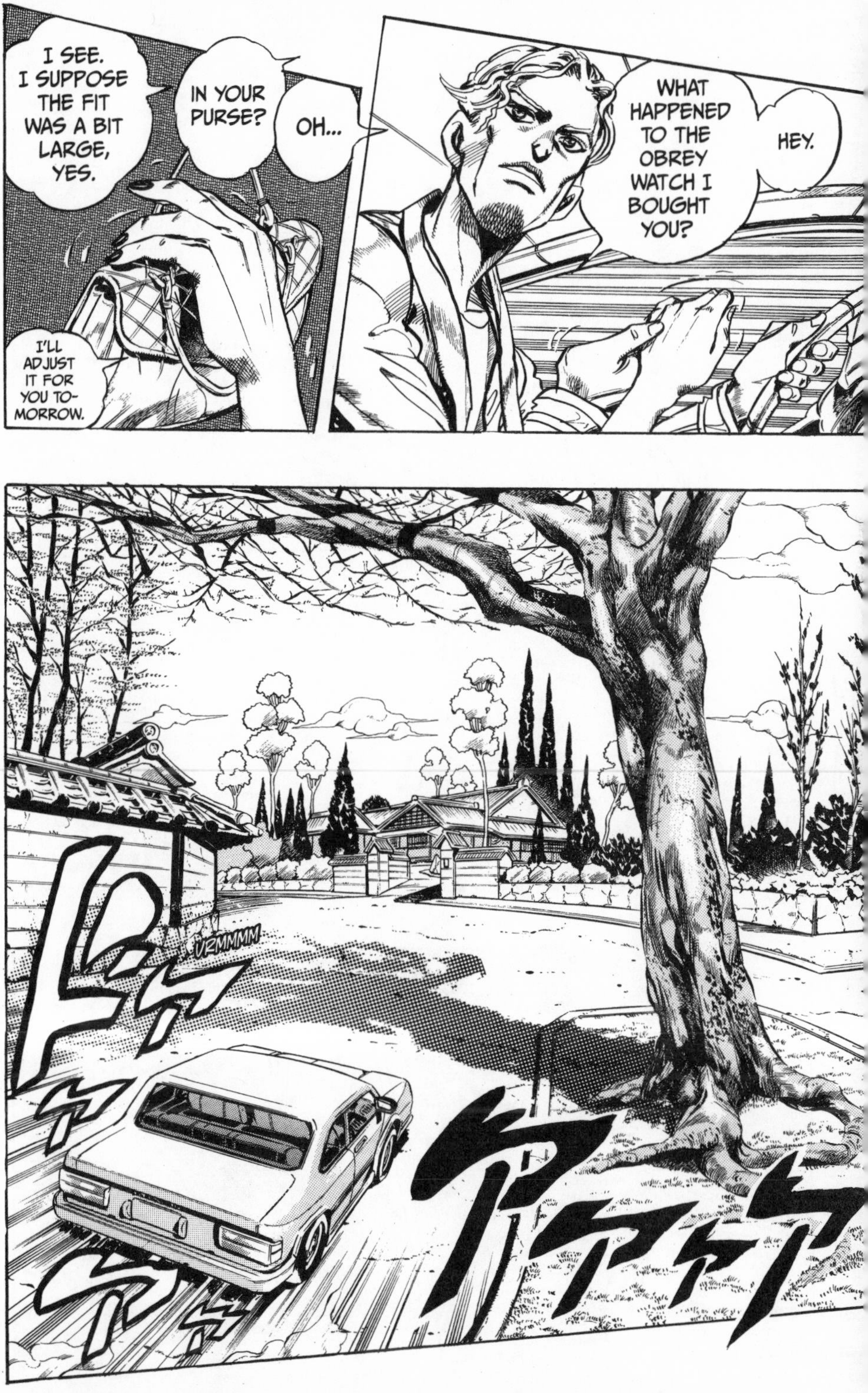
HEY.
WHAT HAPPENED TO THE OBREY WATCH I BOUGHT YOU?
OH...
IN YOUR PURSE?
I SEE. I SUPPOSE THE FIT WAS A BIT LARGE, YES.
I'LL ADJUST IT FOR YOU TO-MORROW.
URMMMM

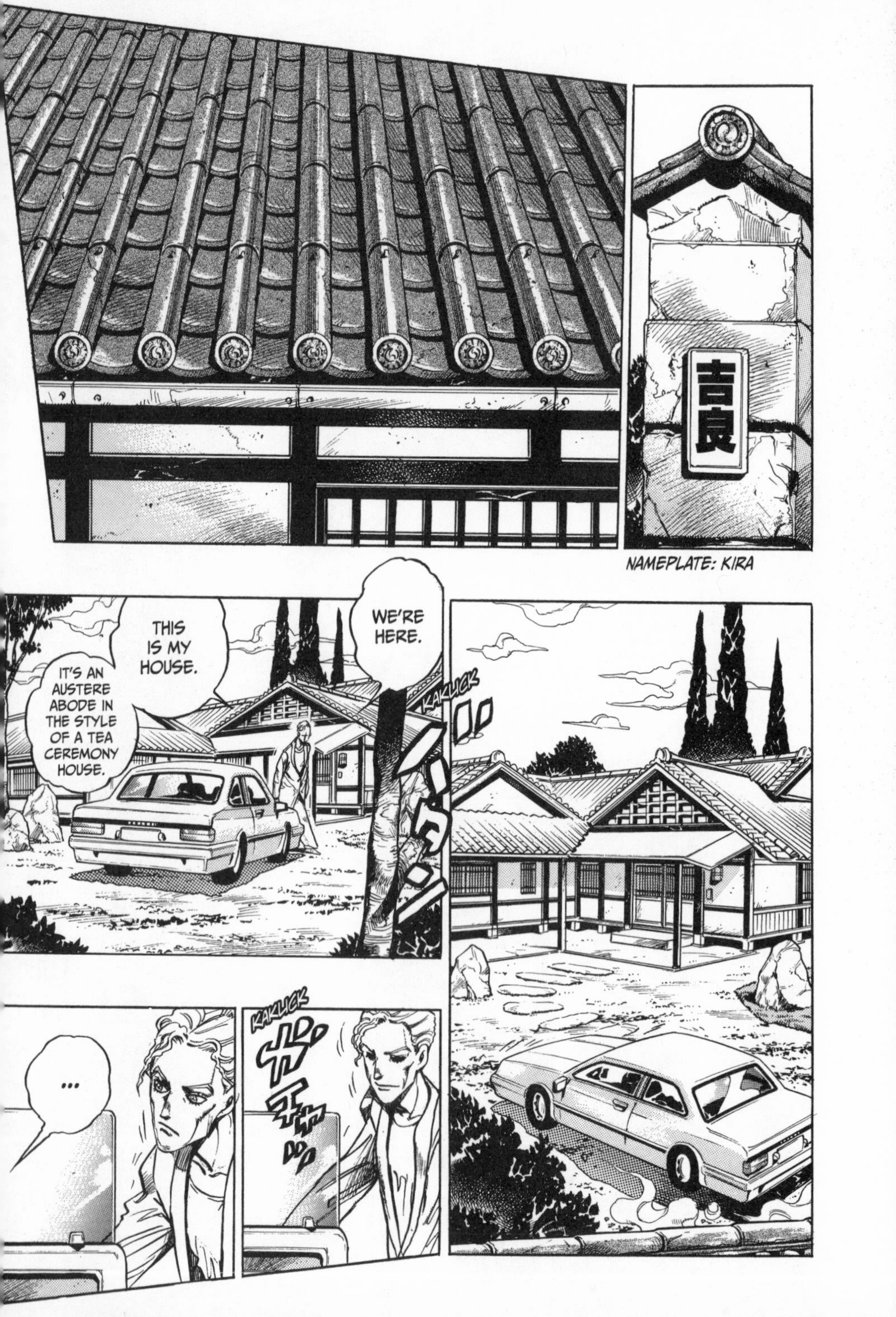

吉良
NAMEPLATE: KIRA
WE'RE HERE.
THIS IS MY HOUSE.
IT'S AN AUSTERE ABODE IN THE STYLE OF A TEA CEREMONY HOUSE.
KAKUCK
KAKUCK
...

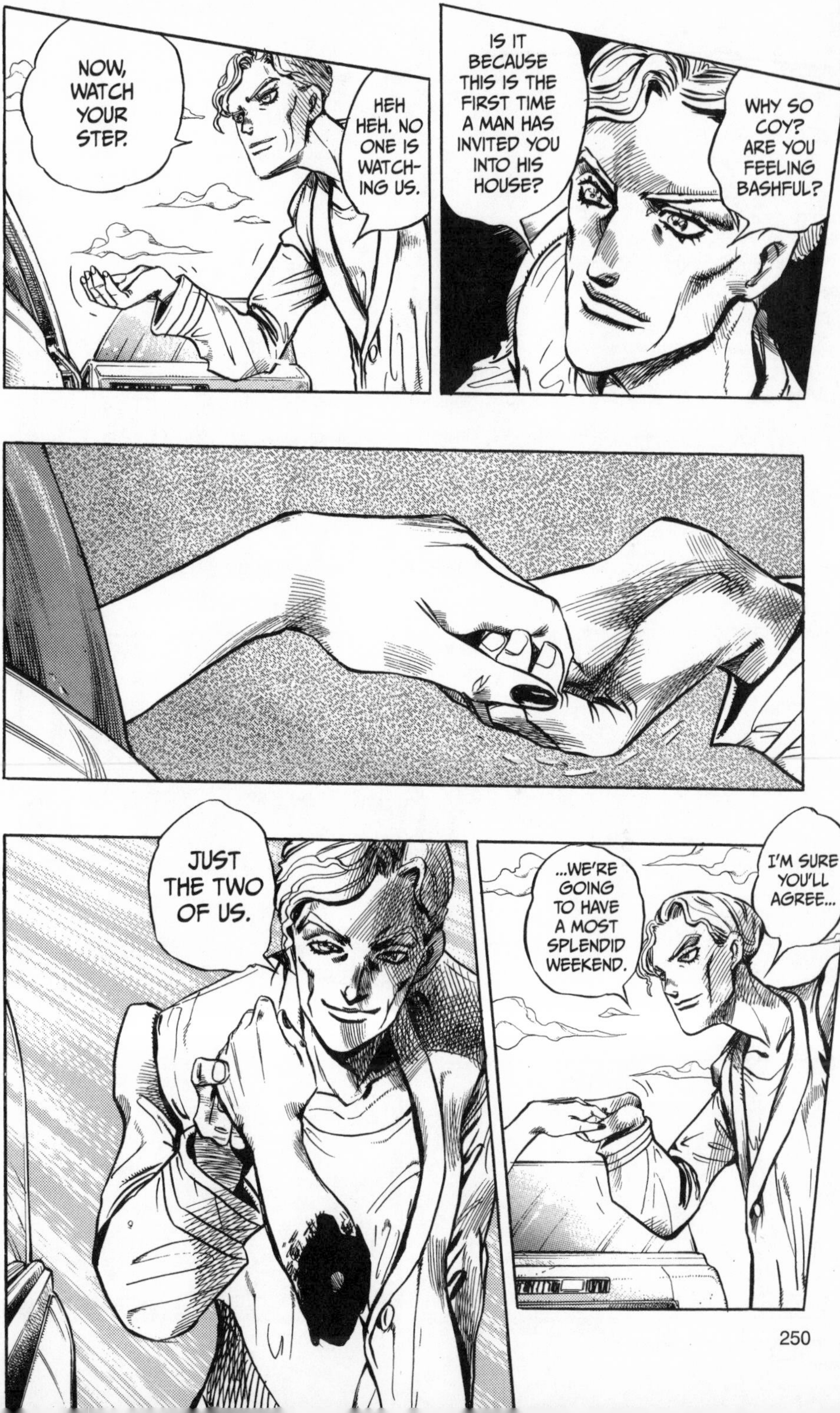
WHY SO COY? ARE YOU FEELING BASHFUL?
IS IT BECAUSE THIS IS THE FIRST TIME A MAN HAS INVITED YOU INTO HIS HOUSE?
HEH HEH. NO ONE IS WATCHING US.
NOW, WATCH YOUR STEP.
I'M SURE YOU'LL AGREE...
...WE'RE GOING TO HAVE A MOST SPLENDID WEEKEND.
JUST THE TWO OF US.

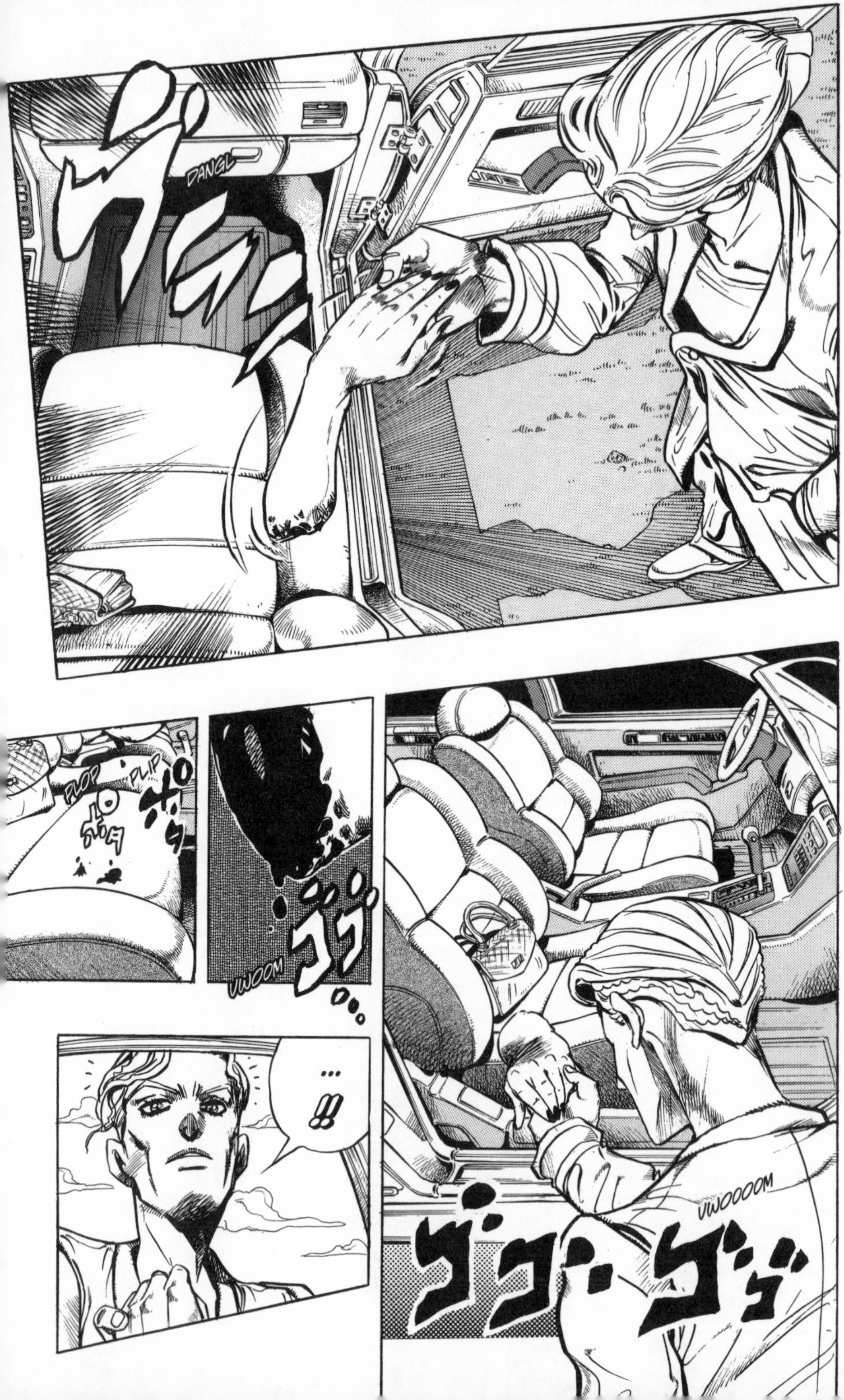
DANGL
VWOOOOM
VWOOM
PLIP
PLOP
...!!

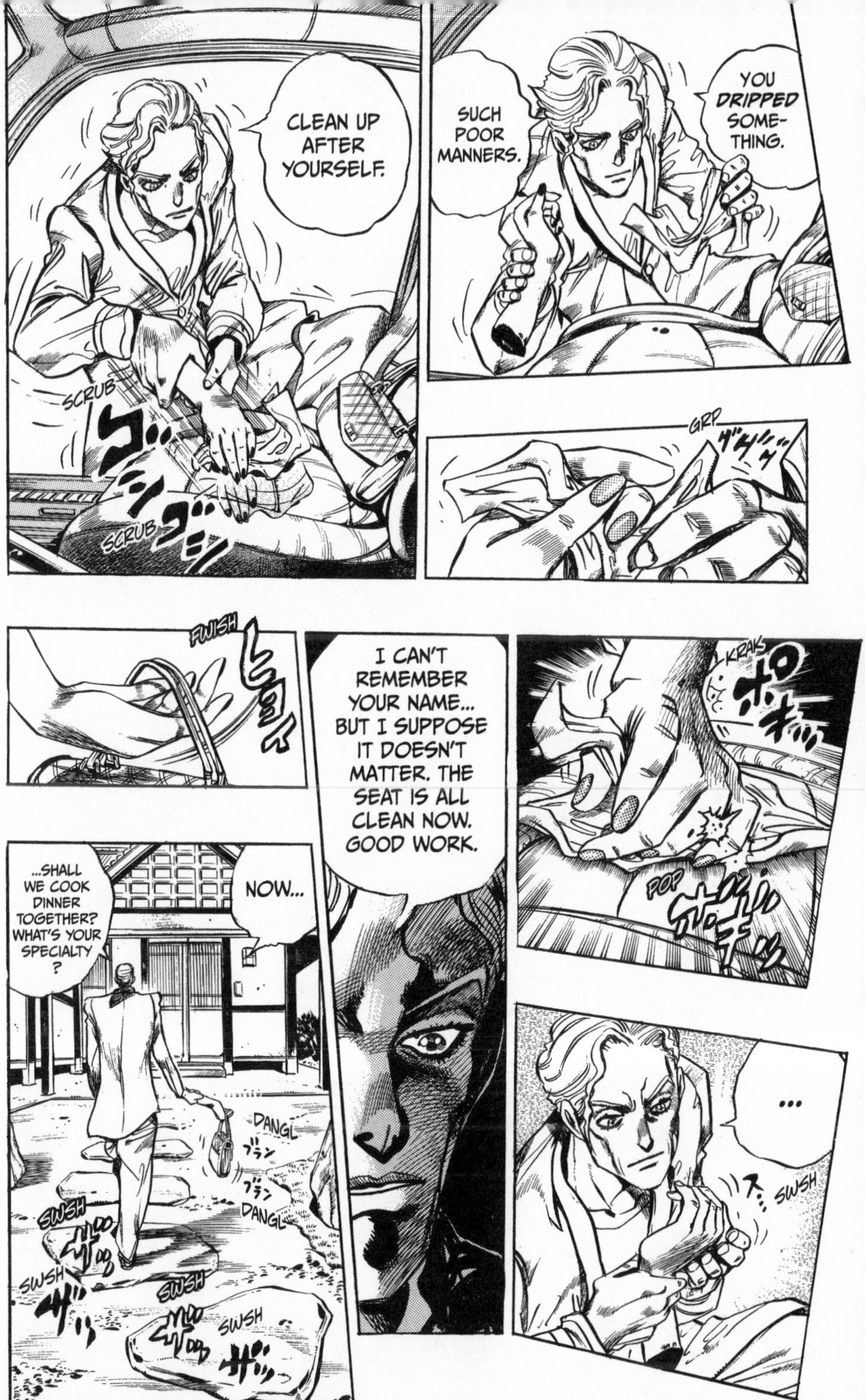

YOU DRIPPED SOMETHING.
SUCH POOR MANNERS.
GRP
CLEAN UP AFTER YOURSELF.
SCRUB
SCRUB
KRAK
POP
...
SWSH
I CAN'T REMEMBER YOUR NAME... BUT I SUPPOSE IT DOESN'T MATTER. THE SEAT IS ALL CLEAN NOW. GOOD WORK.
FWISH
NOW...
...SHALL WE COOK DINNER TOGETHER? WHAT'S YOUR SPECIALTY?
DANGL
ブラン
ブラン
DANGL
SWSH
SWSH
SWSH
SWSH

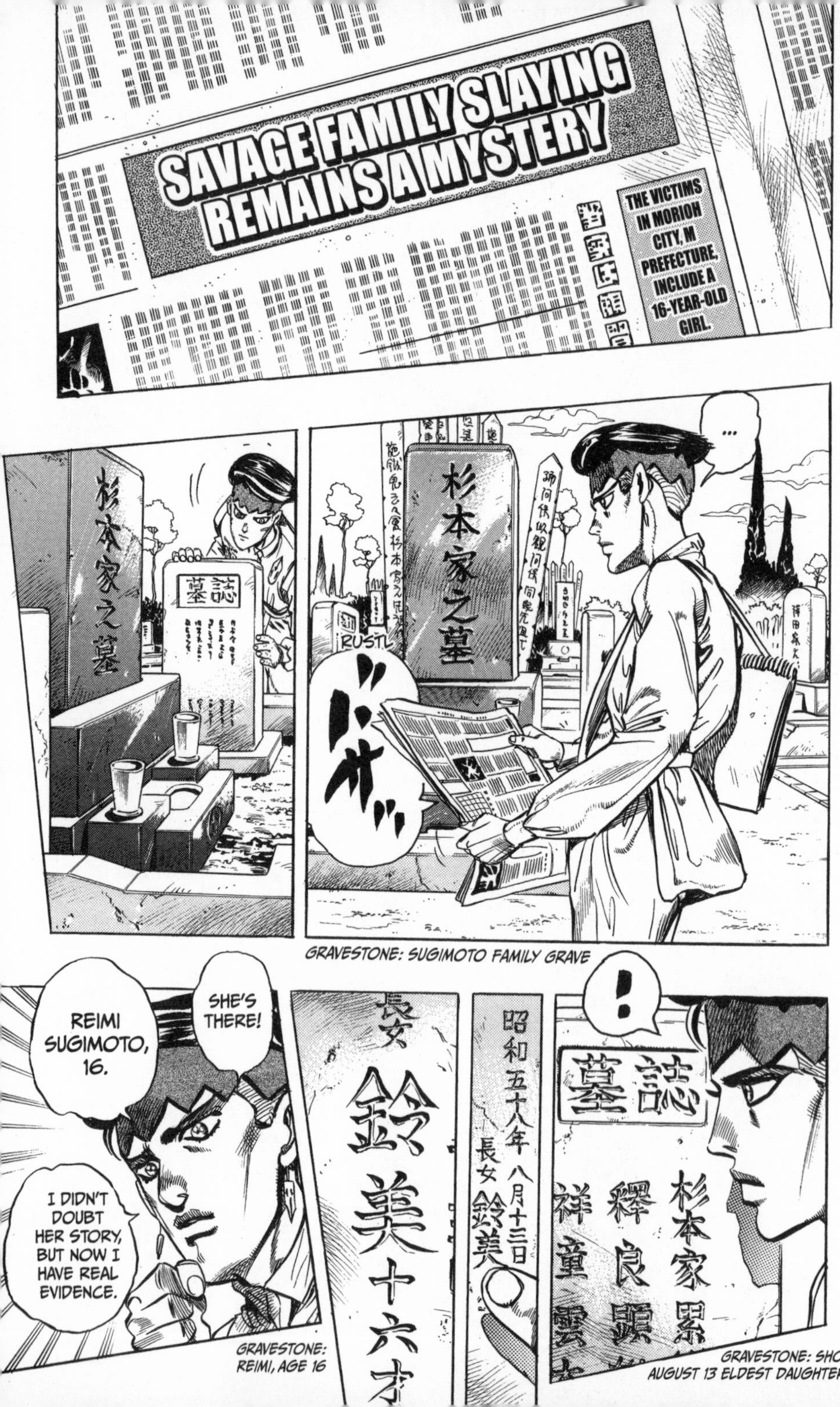
SAVAGE FAMILY SLAYING REMAINS A MYSTERY
THE VICTIMS IN MORIOH CITY, M PREFECTURE, INCLUDE A 16-YEAR-OLD GIRL.
...
杉本家之墓
RUSTL
GRAVESTONE: SUGIMOTO FAMILY GRAVE
!
GRAVESTONE: SHOWA 58, AUGUST 13 ELDEST DAUGHTER: REIMI
GRAVESTONE: REIMI, AGE 16
SHE'S THERE!
REIMI SUGIMOTO, 16.
I DIDN'T DOUBT HER STORY, BUT NOW I HAVE REAL EVIDENCE.

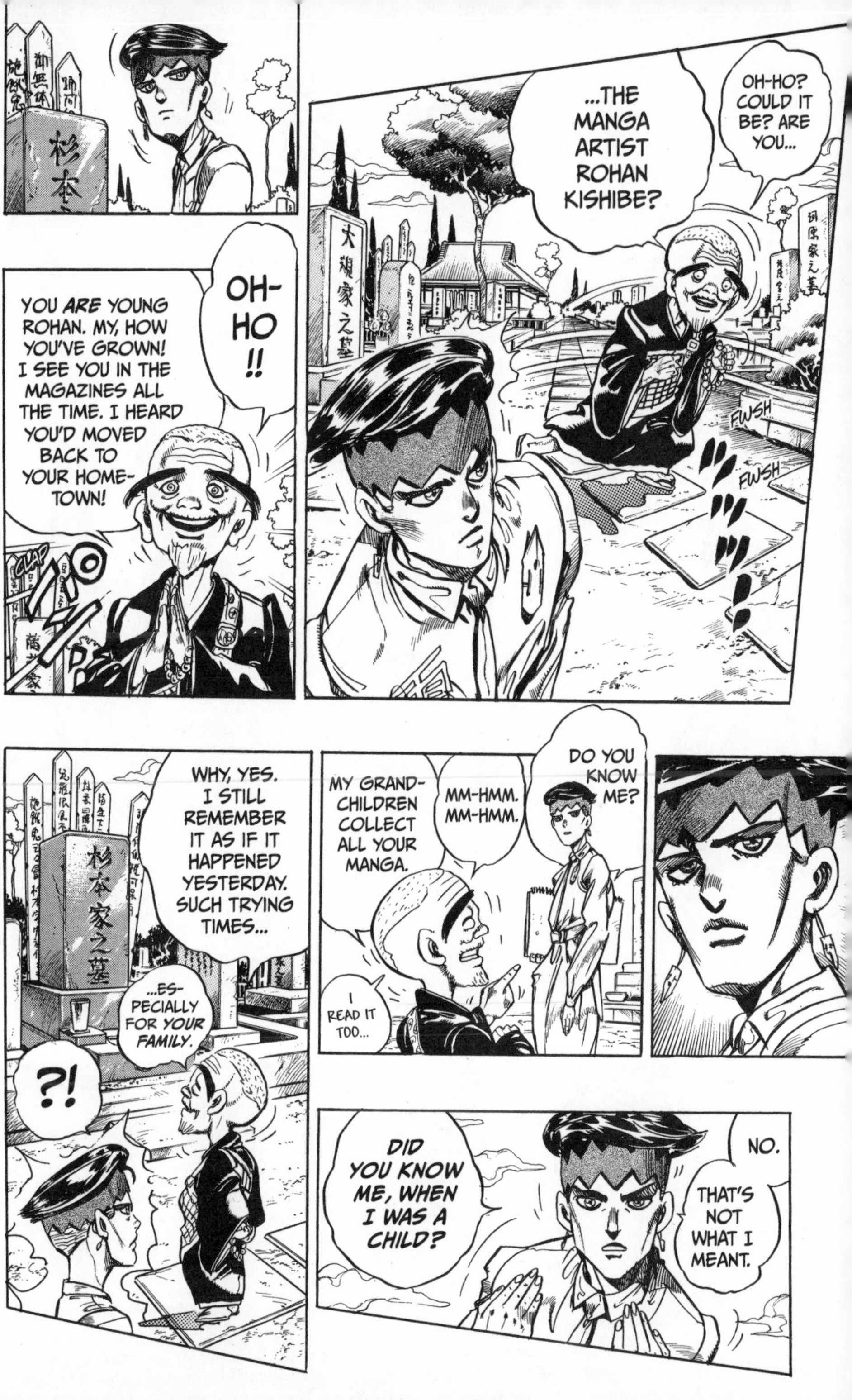
OH-HO? COULD IT BE? ARE YOU...
...THE MANGA ARTIST ROHAN KISHIBE?
FWSH
FWSH
OH-HO !!
YOU ARE YOUNG ROHAN. MY, HOW YOU'VE GROWN! I SEE YOU IN THE MAGAZINES ALL THE TIME. I HEARD YOU'D MOVED BACK TO YOUR HOME-TOWN!
CLAP
DO YOU KNOW ME?
MM-HMM. MM-HMM.
MY GRAND-CHILDREN COLLECT ALL YOUR MANGA.
I READ IT TOO...
NO.
THAT'S NOT WHAT I MEANT.
DID YOU KNOW ME, WHEN I WAS A CHILD?
WHY, YES. I STILL REMEMBER IT AS IF IT HAPPENED YESTERDAY. SUCH TRYING TIMES...
...ES-PECIALLY FOR YOUR FAMILY.
?!

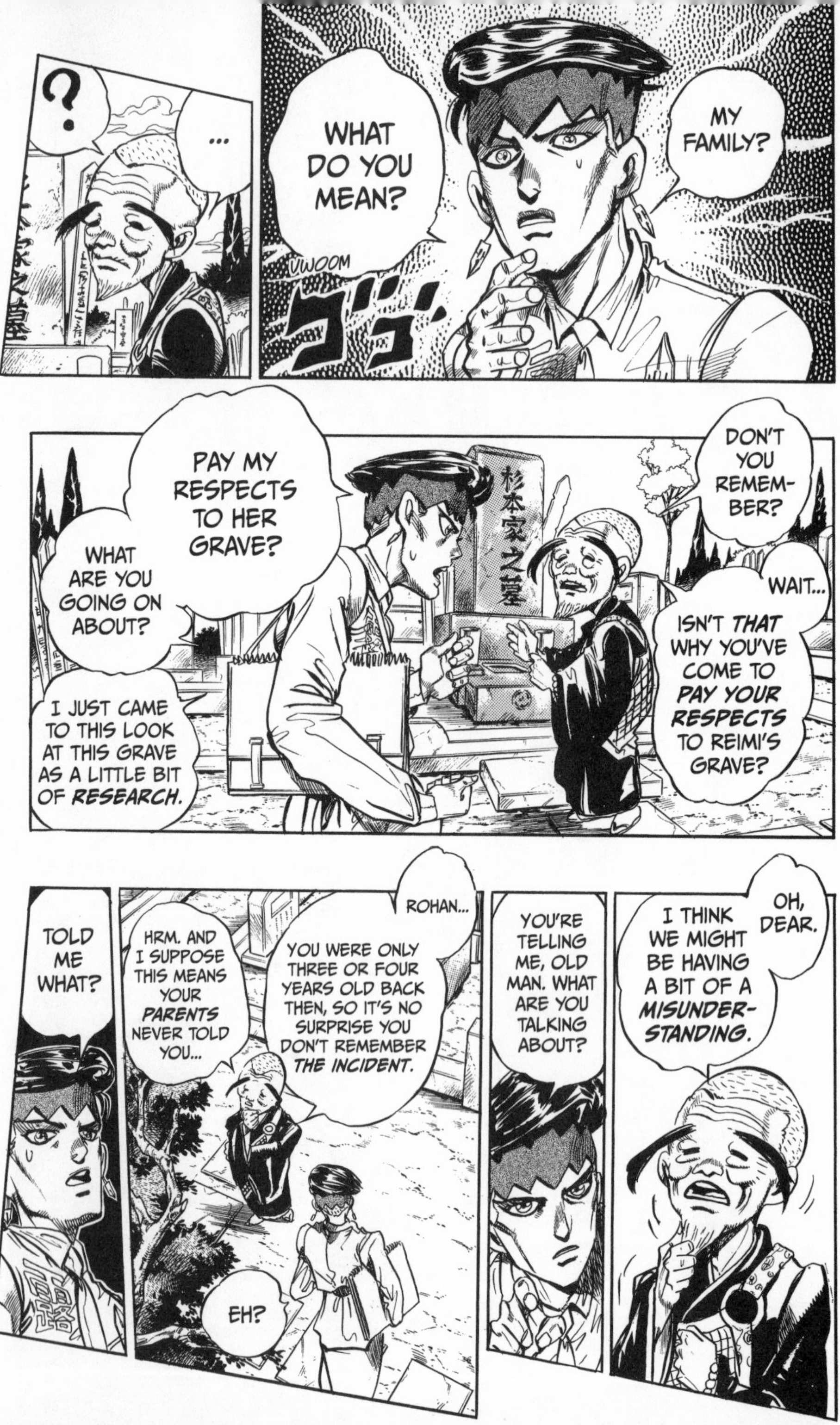

MY FAMILY?
WHAT DO YOU MEAN?
UWOOM
ゴゴ
...
?
DON'T YOU REMEMBER?
WAIT...
ISN'T *THAT* WHY YOU'VE COME TO *PAY YOUR RESPECTS* TO REIMI'S GRAVE?
杉本家之墓
PAY MY RESPECTS TO HER GRAVE?
WHAT ARE YOU GOING ON ABOUT?
I JUST CAME TO THIS LOOK AT THIS GRAVE AS A LITTLE BIT OF *RESEARCH*.
OH, DEAR.
I THINK WE MIGHT BE HAVING A BIT OF A *MISUNDERSTANDING*.
YOU'RE TELLING ME, OLD MAN. WHAT ARE YOU TALKING ABOUT?
ROHAN...
YOU WERE ONLY THREE OR FOUR YEARS OLD BACK THEN, SO IT'S NO SURPRISE YOU DON'T REMEMBER *THE INCIDENT*.
HRM. AND I SUPPOSE THIS MEANS YOUR *PARENTS* NEVER TOLD YOU...
EH?
TOLD ME WHAT?

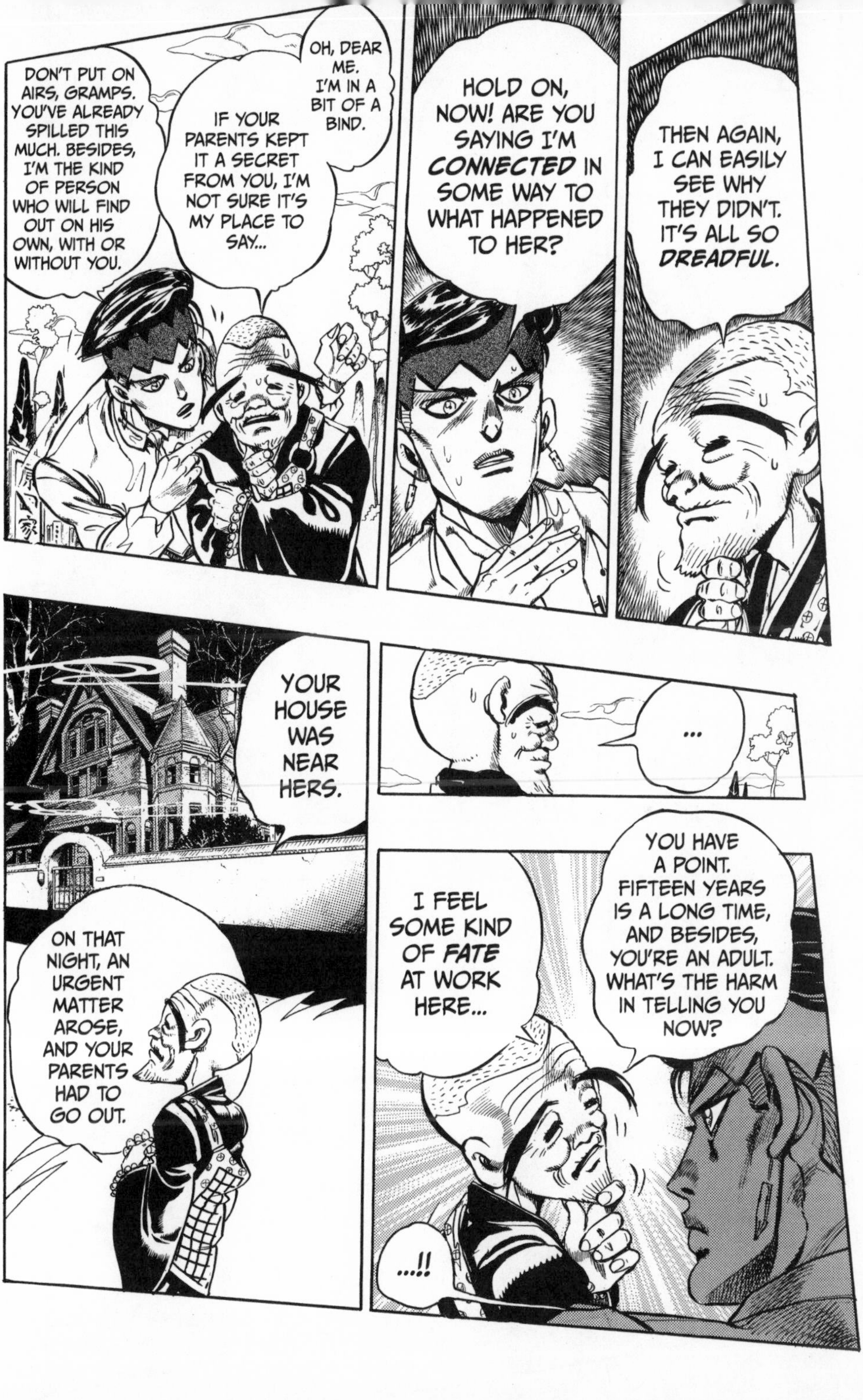
THEN AGAIN, I CAN EASILY SEE WHY THEY DIDN'T. IT'S ALL SO *DREADFUL*.
HOLD ON, NOW! ARE YOU SAYING I'M *CONNECTED* IN SOME WAY TO WHAT HAPPENED TO HER?
OH, DEAR ME. I'M IN A BIT OF A BIND.
IF YOUR PARENTS KEPT IT A SECRET FROM YOU, I'M NOT SURE IT'S MY PLACE TO SAY...
DON'T PUT ON AIRS, GRAMPS. YOU'VE ALREADY SPILLED THIS MUCH. BESIDES, I'M THE KIND OF PERSON WHO WILL FIND OUT ON HIS OWN, WITH OR WITHOUT YOU.
...
YOU HAVE A POINT. FIFTEEN YEARS IS A LONG TIME, AND BESIDES, YOU'RE AN ADULT. WHAT'S THE HARM IN TELLING YOU NOW?
I FEEL SOME KIND OF *FATE* AT WORK HERE...
...!!
YOUR HOUSE WAS NEAR HERS.
ON THAT NIGHT, AN URGENT MATTER AROSE, AND YOUR PARENTS HAD TO GO OUT.

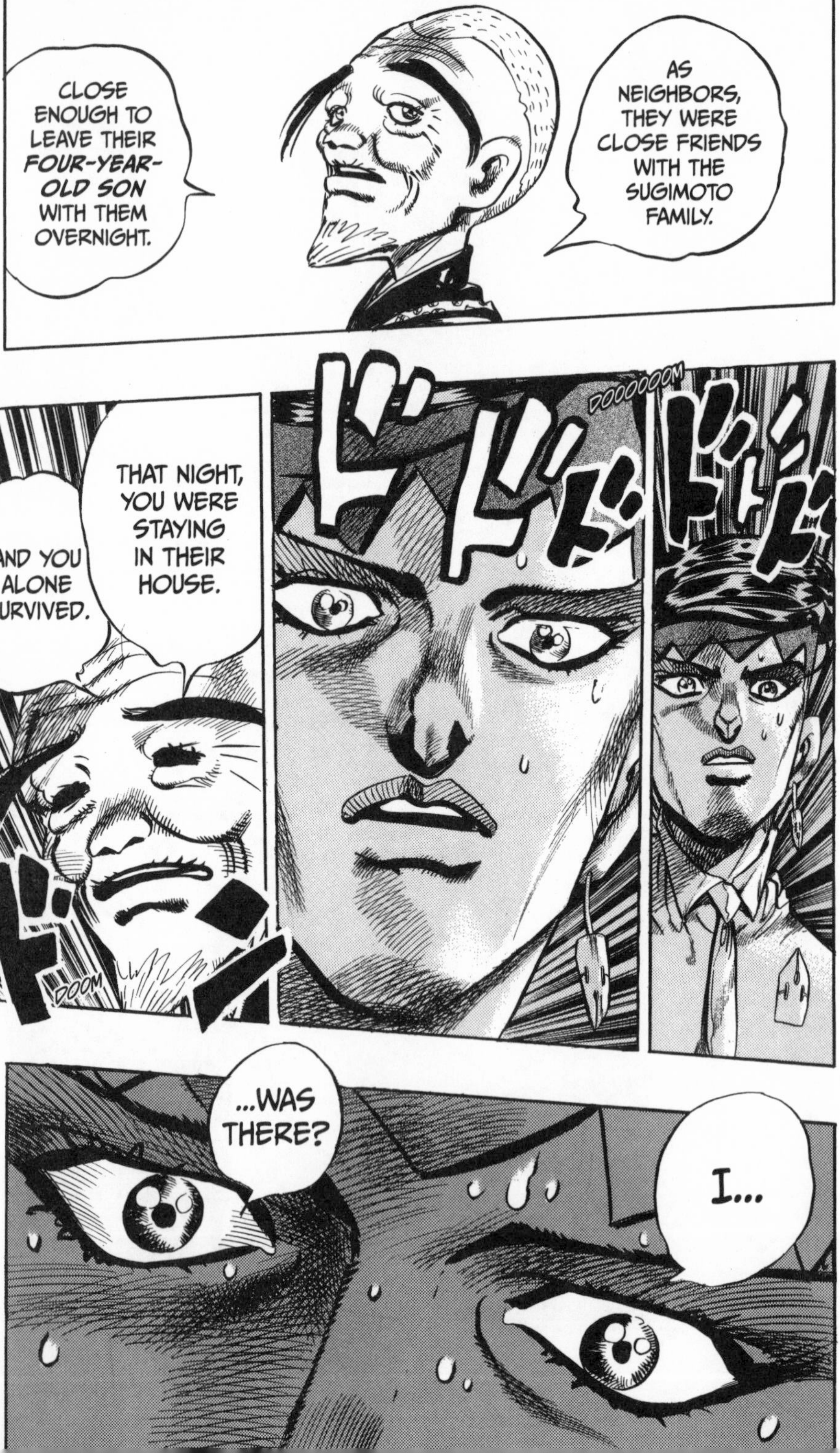
AS NEIGHBORS, THEY WERE CLOSE FRIENDS WITH THE SUGIMOTO FAMILY.
CLOSE ENOUGH TO LEAVE THEIR *FOUR-YEAR-OLD SON* WITH THEM OVERNIGHT.
DOOOOOOOM
THAT NIGHT, YOU WERE STAYING IN THEIR HOUSE.
AND YOU ALONE SURVIVED.
DOOM
I...
...WAS THERE?

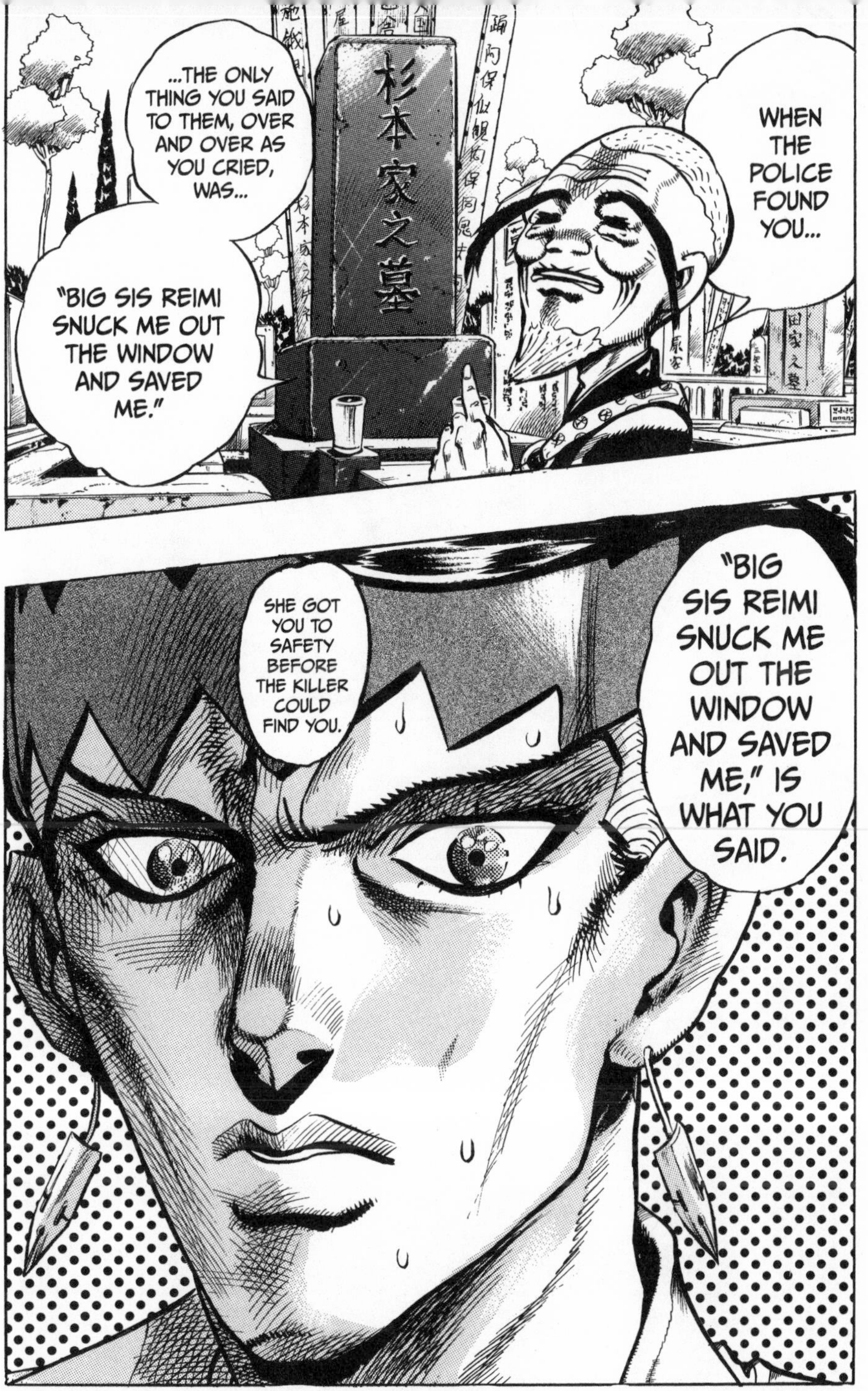
WHEN THE POLICE FOUND YOU...
...THE ONLY THING YOU SAID TO THEM, OVER AND OVER AS YOU CRIED, WAS...
杉本家之墓
"BIG SIS REIMI SNUCK ME OUT THE WINDOW AND SAVED ME."
"BIG SIS REIMI SNUCK ME OUT THE WINDOW AND SAVED ME," IS WHAT YOU SAID.
SHE GOT YOU TO SAFETY BEFORE THE KILLER COULD FIND YOU.

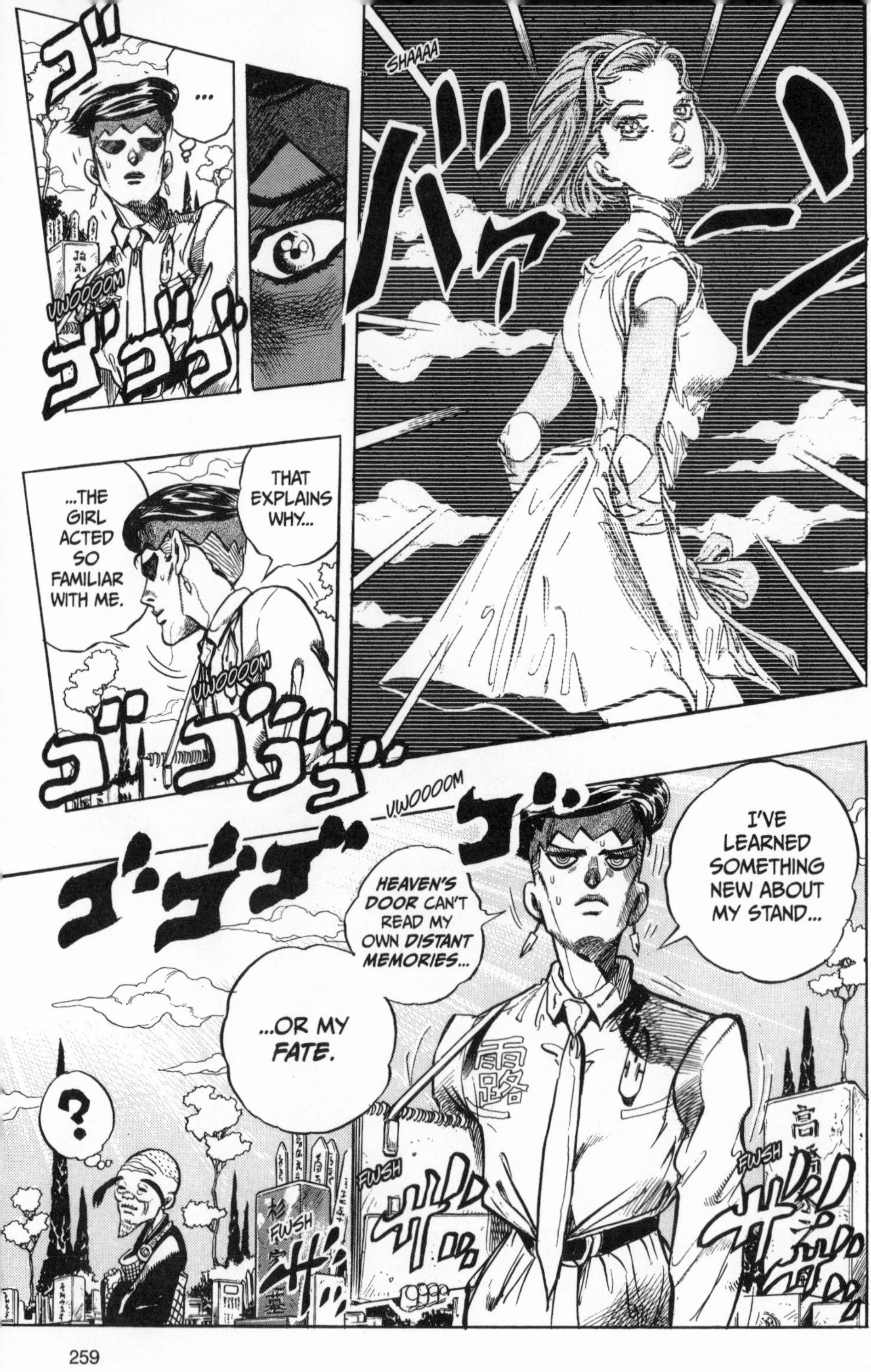
SHAAAA
...
VWOOOOM
THAT EXPLAINS WHY...
...THE GIRL ACTED SO FAMILIAR WITH ME.
VWOOOOM
VWOOOOM
I'VE LEARNED SOMETHING NEW ABOUT MY STAND...
HEAVEN'S DOOR CAN'T READ MY OWN DISTANT MEMORIES...
...OR MY FATE.
?
FWSH
FWSH
FWSH

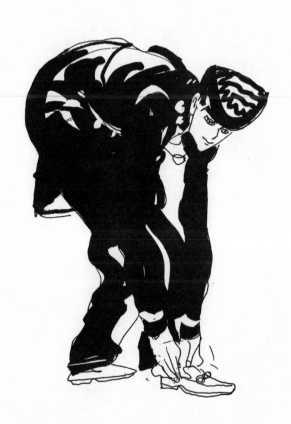

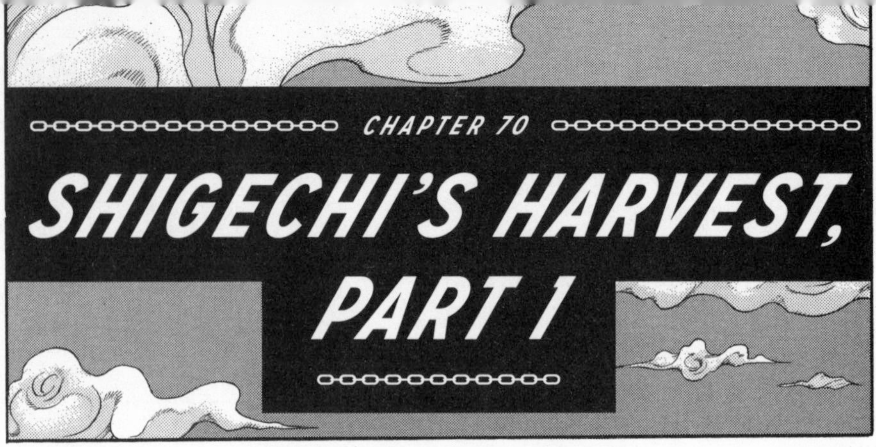
CHAPTER 70
SHIGECHI'S HARVEST, PART 1

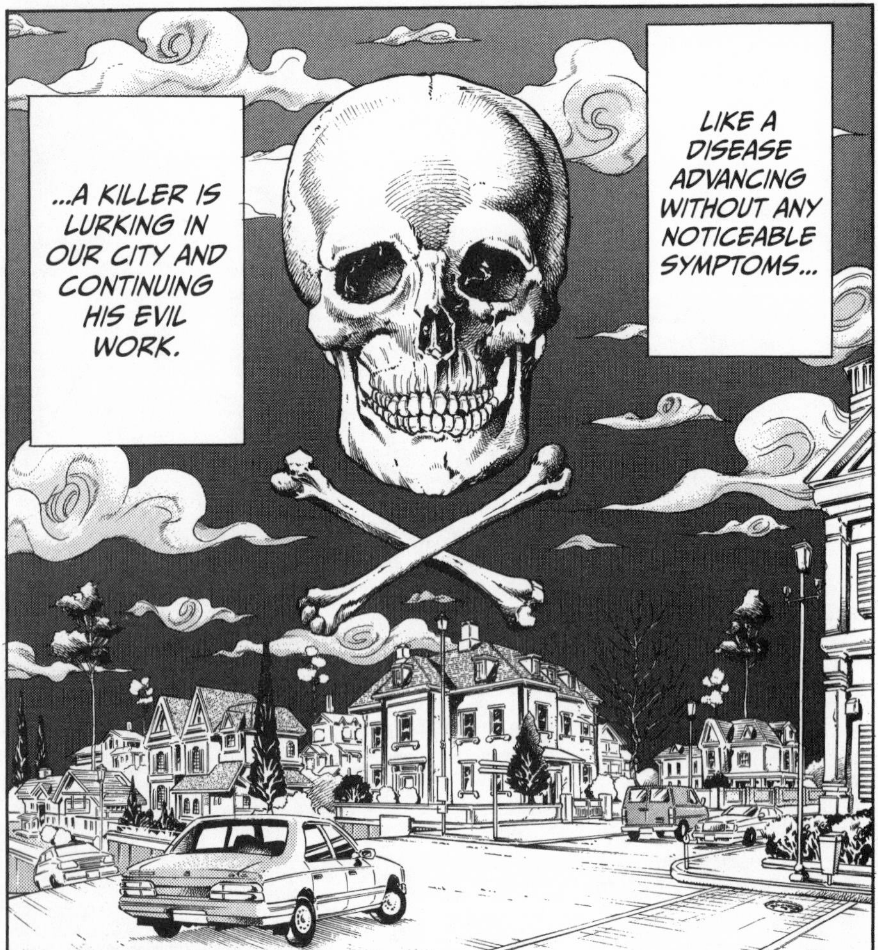
LIKE A DISEASE ADVANCING WITHOUT ANY NOTICEABLE SYMPTOMS...
...A KILLER IS LURKING IN OUR CITY AND CONTINUING HIS EVIL WORK.

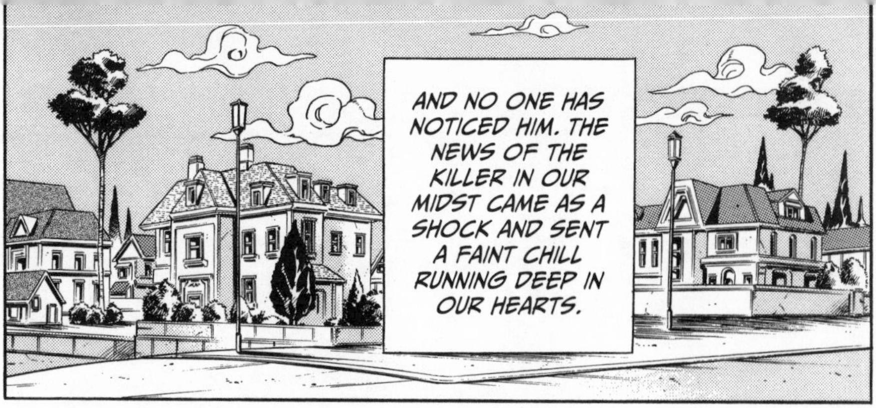
AND NO ONE HAS NOTICED HIM. THE NEWS OF THE KILLER IN OUR MIDST CAME AS A SHOCK AND SENT A FAINT CHILL RUNNING DEEP IN OUR HEARTS.

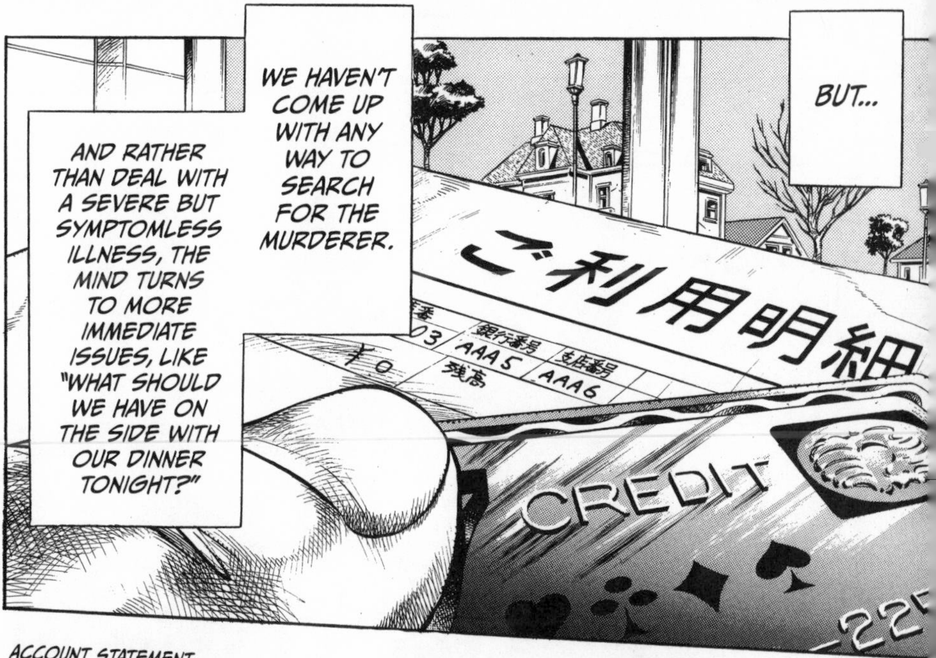
BUT...
WE HAVEN'T COME UP WITH ANY WAY TO SEARCH FOR THE MURDERER.
AND RATHER THAN DEAL WITH A SEVERE BUT SYMPTOMLESS ILLNESS, THE MIND TURNS TO MORE IMMEDIATE ISSUES, LIKE "WHAT SHOULD WE HAVE ON THE SIDE WITH OUR DINNER TONIGHT?"
ご利用明細
銀行番号
AAA5
支店番号
AAA6
¥0
残高
CREDIT

ACCOUNT STATEMENT

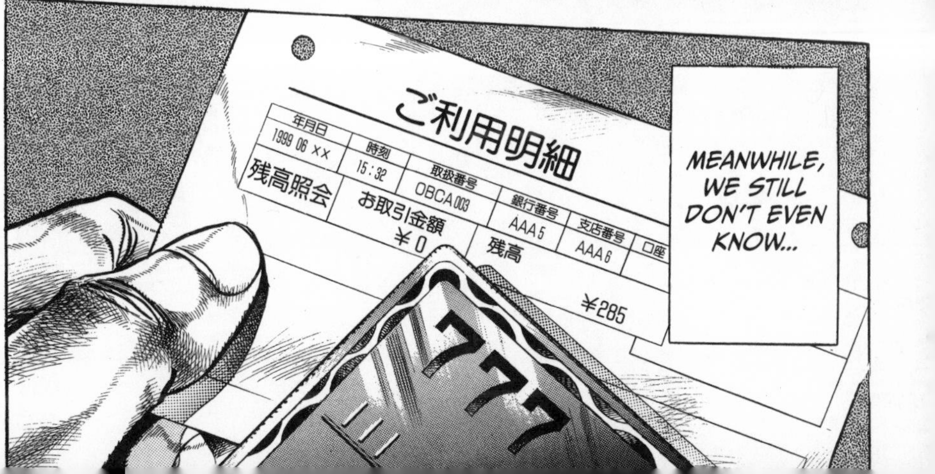
MEANWHILE, WE STILL DON'T EVEN KNOW...
ご利用明細
年月日
1999 06 ××
時刻
15 : 32
取扱番号
OBCA003
残高照会
お取引金額
¥0
銀行番号
AAA5
支店番号
AAA6
口座
残高
¥285

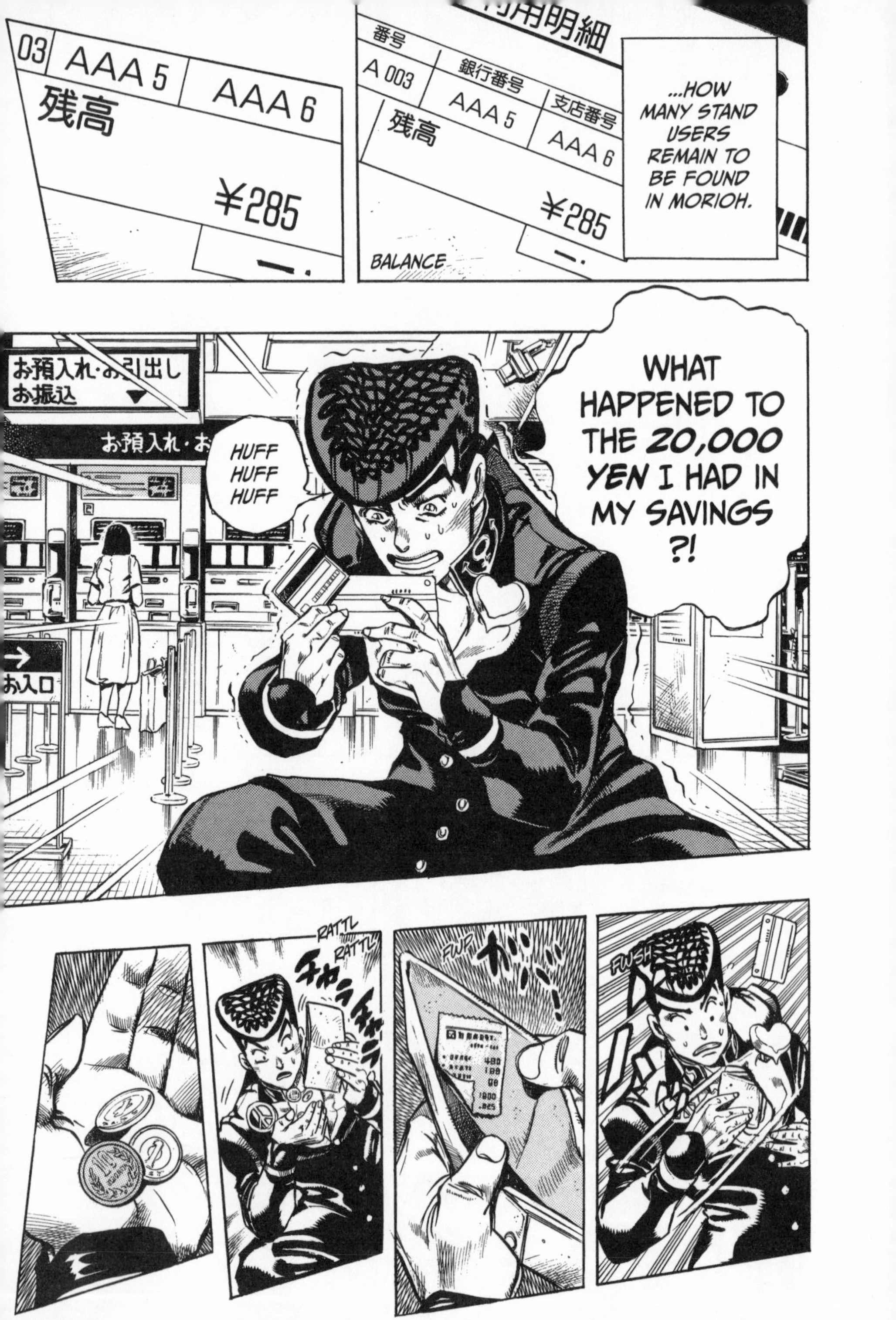

番号
A 003
銀行番号
AAA 5
支店番号
AAA 6
残高
¥285
BALANCE
...HOW MANY STAND USERS REMAIN TO BE FOUND IN MORIOH.
03
AAA 5
AAA 6
残高
¥285
お預入れ・お引出し
お振込
お預入れ・お
お入口
WHAT HAPPENED TO THE 20,000 YEN I HAD IN MY SAVINGS ?!
HUFF HUFF HUFF
FWSH
FWP
RATTL RATTL

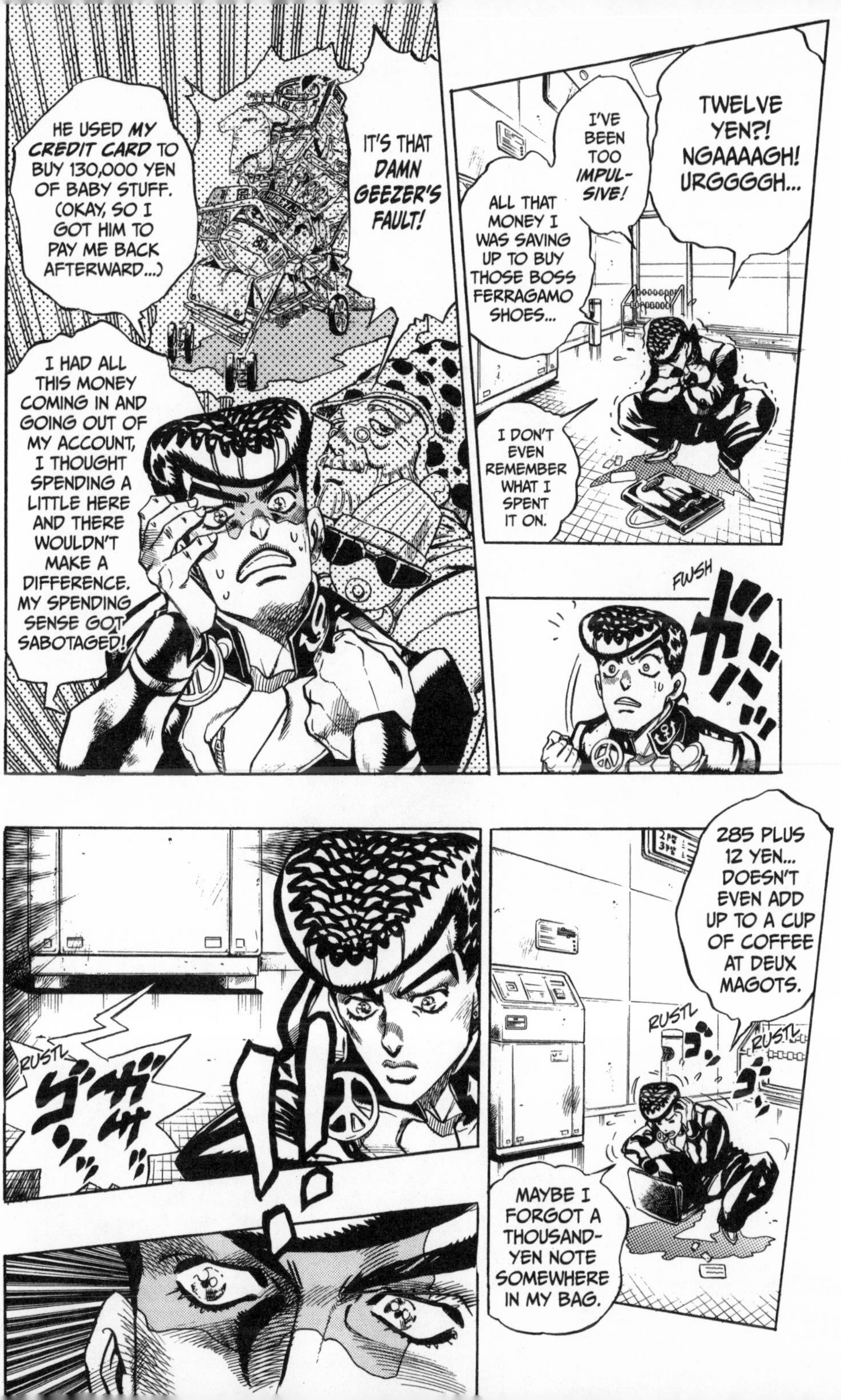
TWELVE YEN?! NGAAAAGH! URGGGGH...
I'VE BEEN TOO IMPUL-SIVE!
ALL THAT MONEY I WAS SAVING UP TO BUY THOSE BOSS FERRAGAMO SHOES...
I DON'T EVEN REMEMBER WHAT I SPENT IT ON.
FWSH
IT'S THAT DAMN GEEZER'S FAULT!
HE USED MY CREDIT CARD TO BUY 130,000 YEN OF BABY STUFF. (OKAY, SO I GOT HIM TO PAY ME BACK AFTERWARD...)
I HAD ALL THIS MONEY COMING IN AND GOING OUT OF MY ACCOUNT, I THOUGHT SPENDING A LITTLE HERE AND THERE WOULDN'T MAKE A DIFFERENCE. MY SPENDING SENSE GOT SABOTAGED!
285 PLUS 12 YEN... DOESN'T EVEN ADD UP TO A CUP OF COFFEE AT DEUX MAGOTS.
RUSTL
RUSTL
MAYBE I FORGOT A THOUSAND-YEN NOTE SOMEWHERE IN MY BAG.
RUSTL

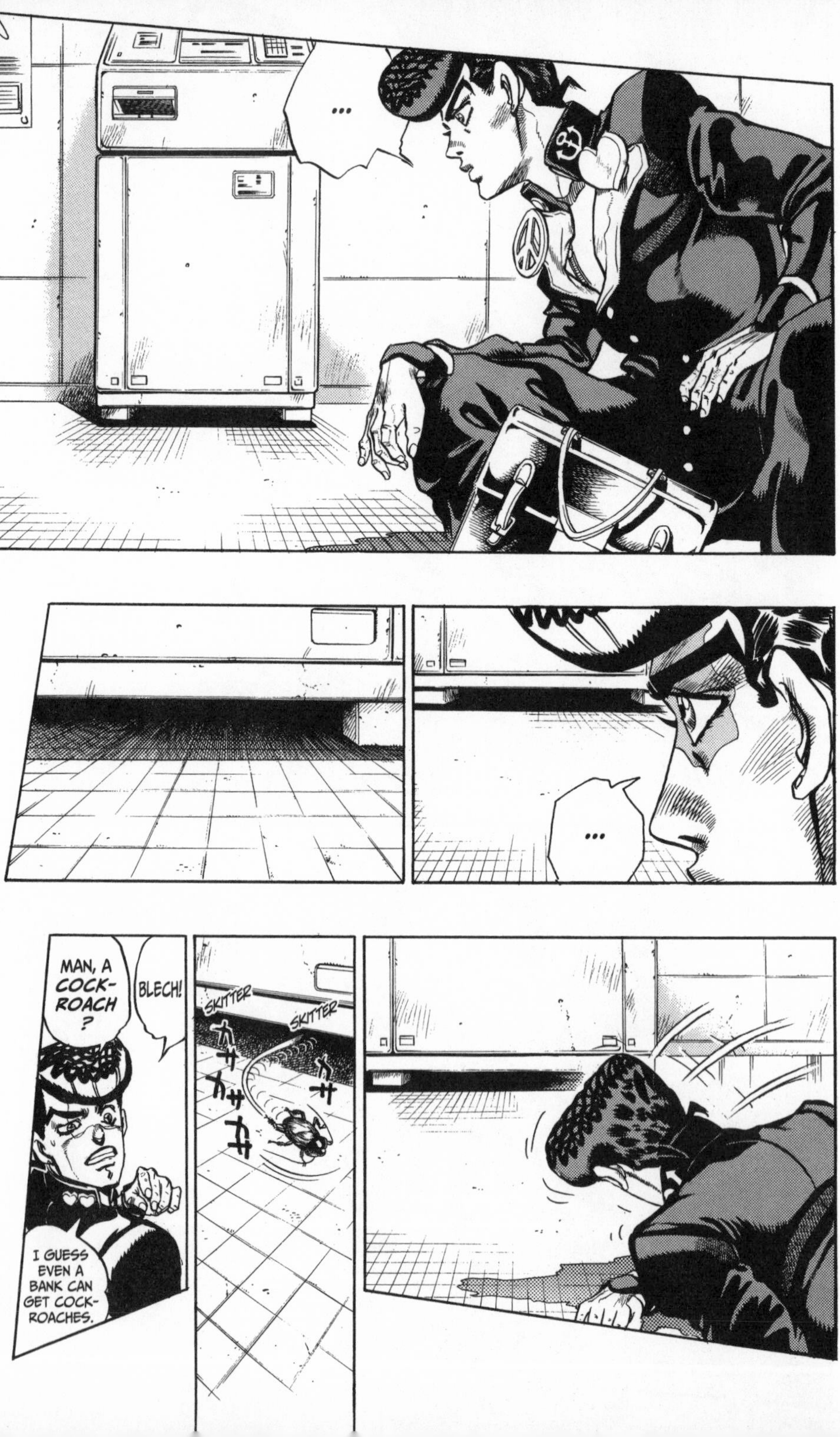
...
...
SKITTER
SKITTER
BLECH!
MAN, A COCK-
ROACH
?
I GUESS
EVEN A
BANK CAN
GET COCK-
ROACHES.

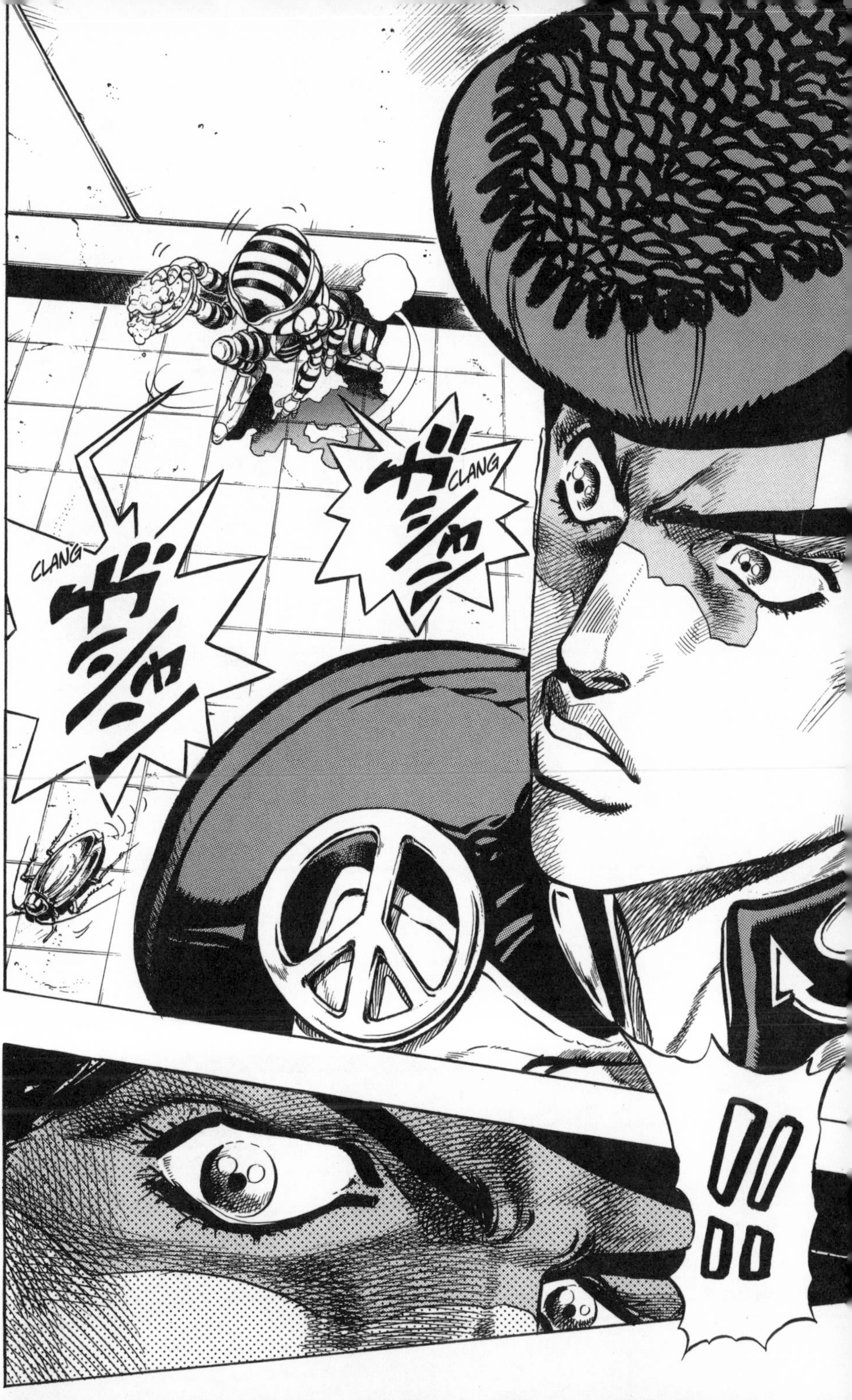

ガシャン
CLANG
ガシャン
CLANG
!!

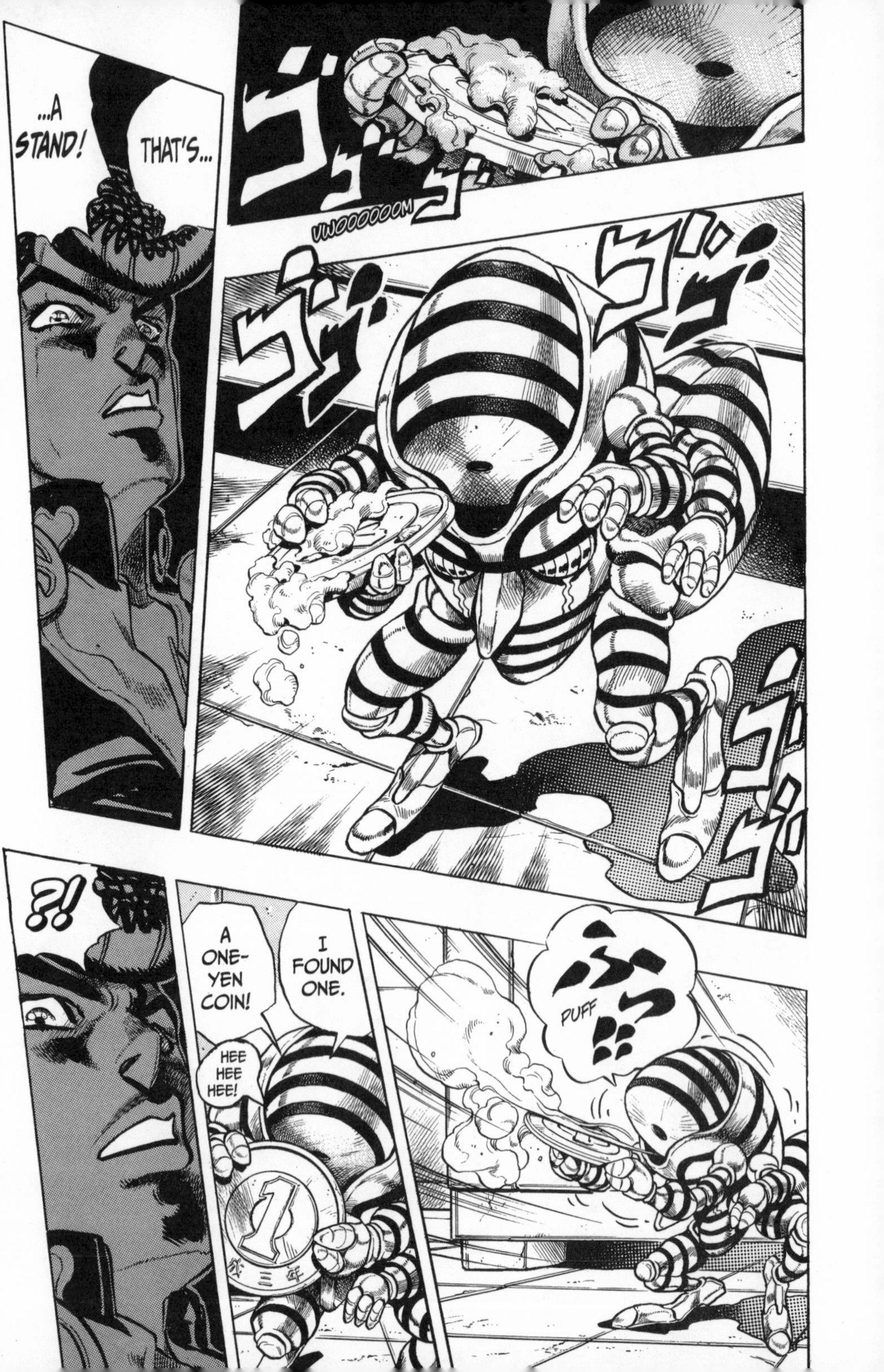
VWOOOOOOM
THAT'S...
...A STAND!
PUFF
I FOUND ONE.
A ONE-YEN COIN!
HEE HEE HEE!
?!

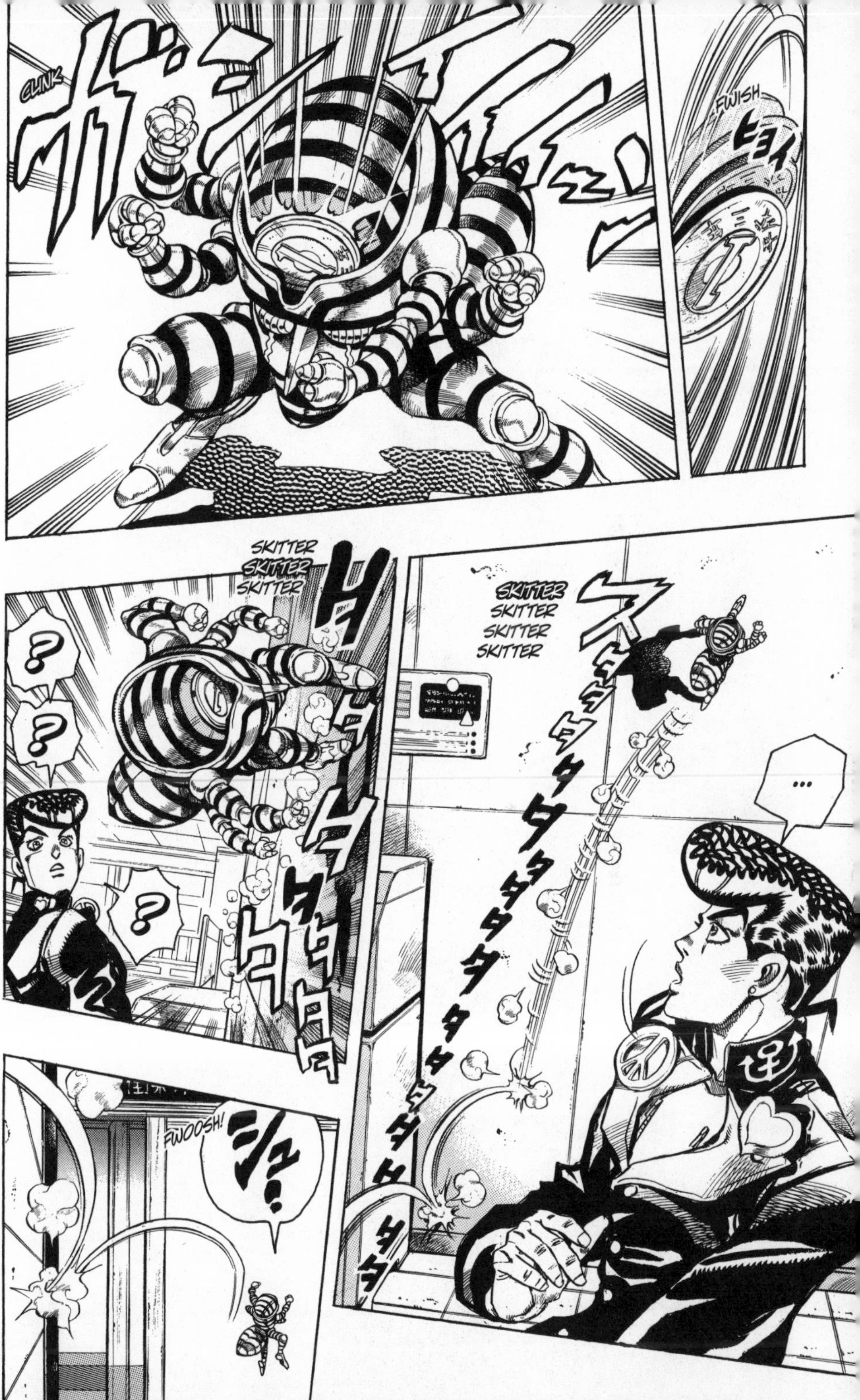
FWISH
ヒョイ
CLUNK
SKITTER
SKITTER
SKITTER
SKITTER
...
SKITTER
SKITTER
SKITTER
?
?
?
FWOOSH!
シュ

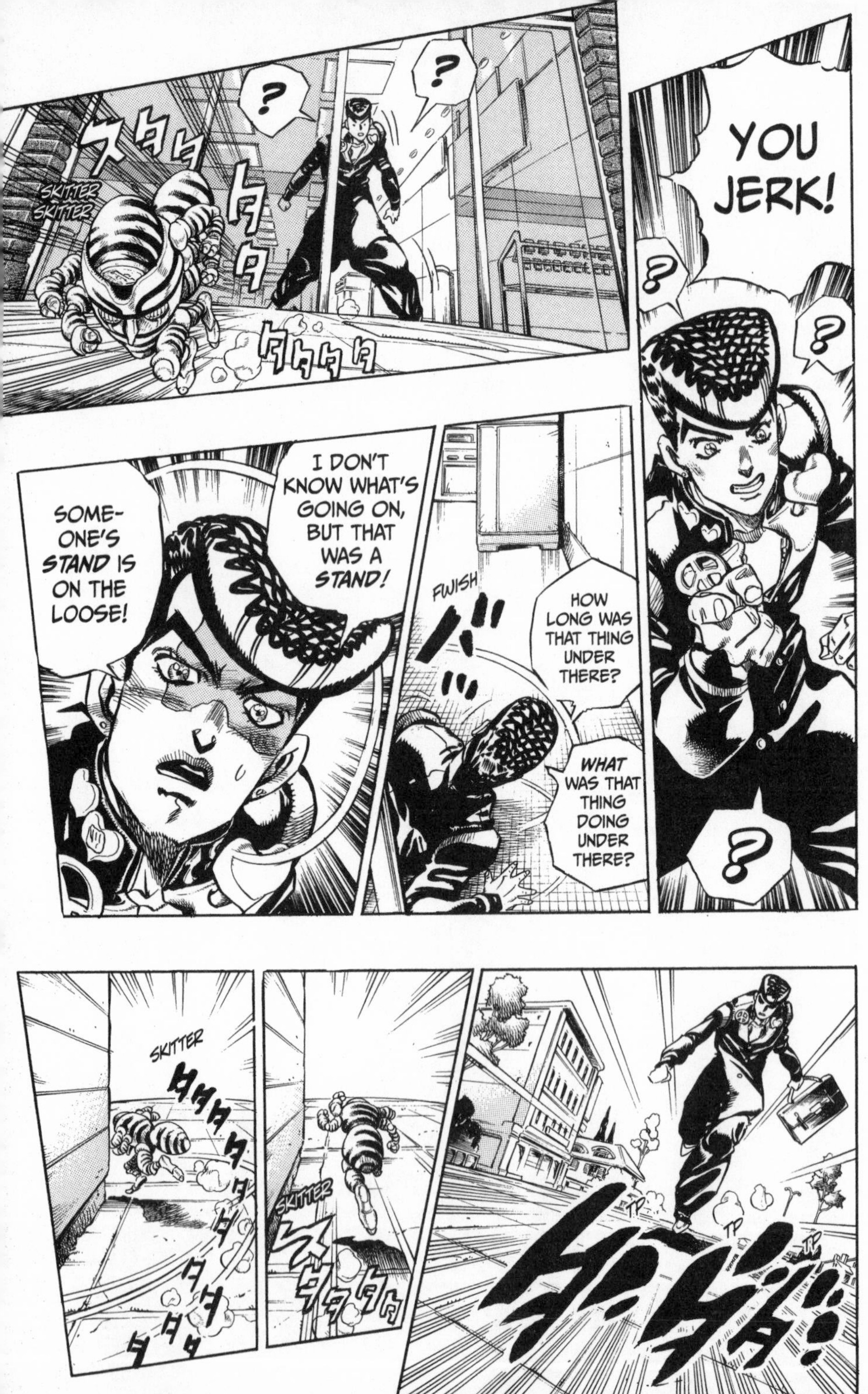

YOU JERK!
?
?
?
?
?
SKITTER SKITTER
HOW LONG WAS THAT THING UNDER THERE?
WHAT WAS THAT THING DOING UNDER THERE?
FWISH
I DON'T KNOW WHAT'S GOING ON, BUT THAT WAS A STAND!
SOME-ONE'S STAND IS ON THE LOOSE!
TP
TP
TP
SKITTER
SKITTER

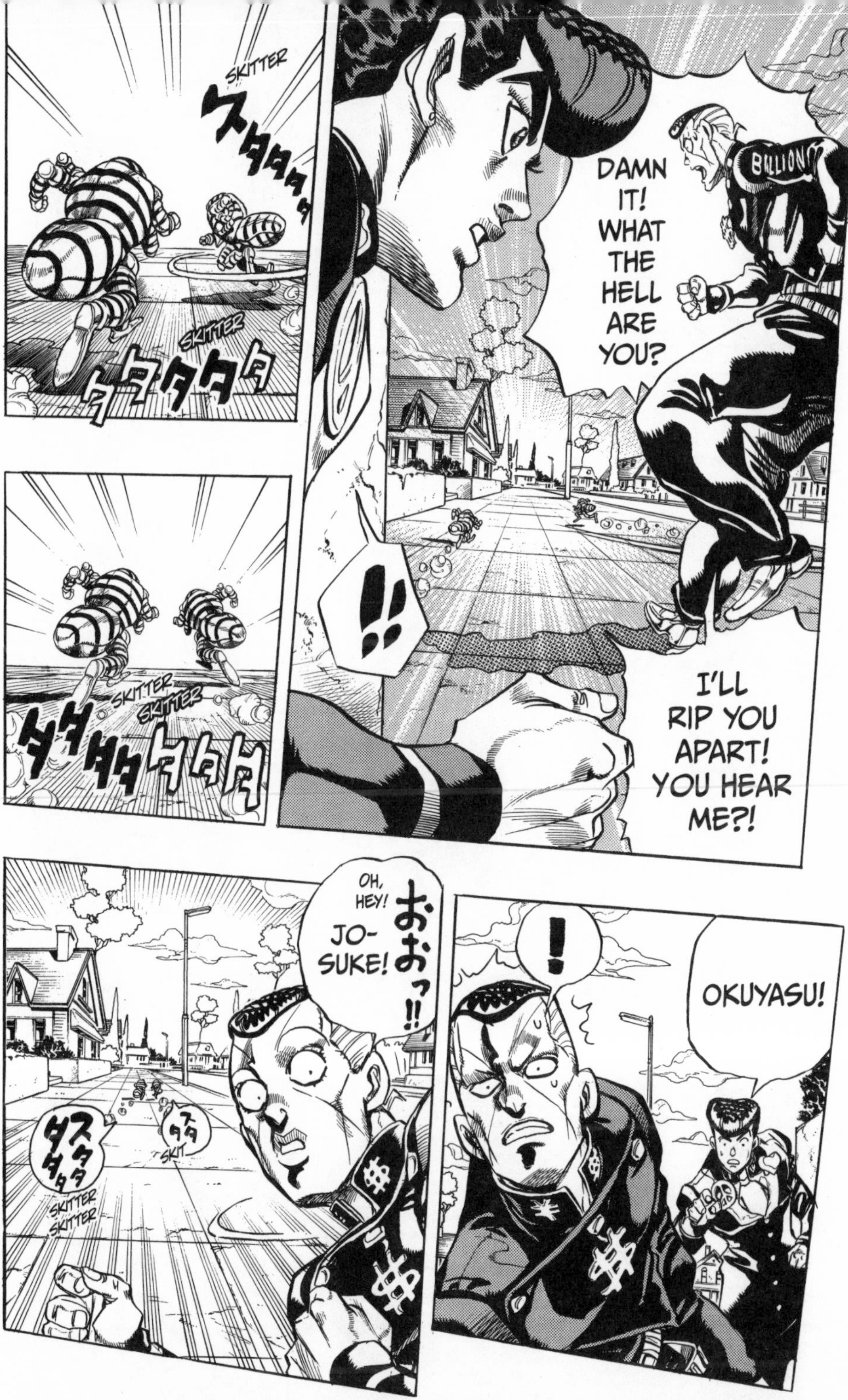
DAMN IT! WHAT THE HELL ARE YOU?
!!
I'LL RIP YOU APART! YOU HEAR ME?!
SKITTER
SKITTER
SKITTER
SKITTER
!
OKUYASU!
OH, HEY! JO-SUKE!
おおっ!!
SKIT
SKITTER
SKITTER

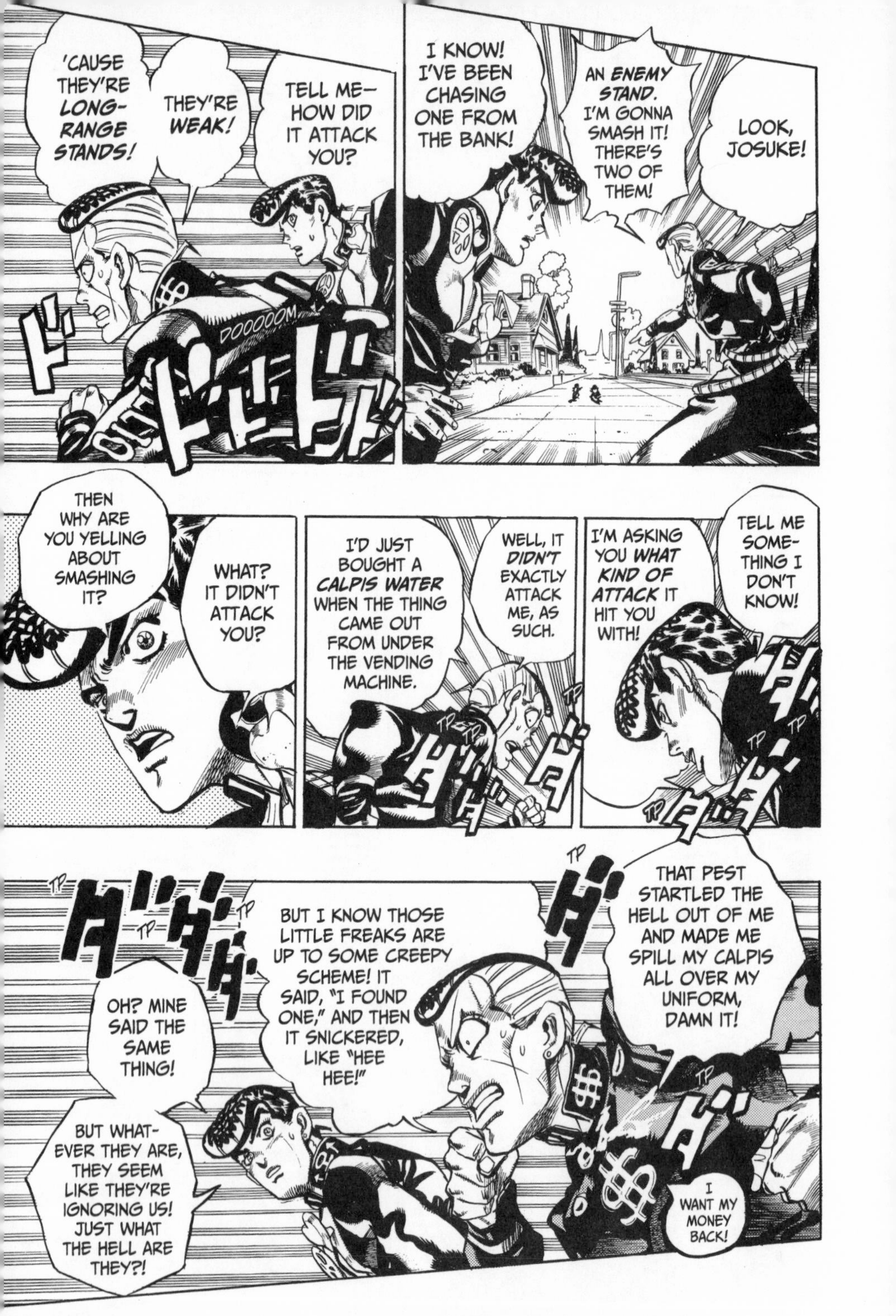
LOOK, JOSUKE!
AN *ENEMY STAND.* I'M GONNA SMASH IT! THERE'S TWO OF THEM!
I KNOW! I'VE BEEN CHASING ONE FROM THE BANK!
TELL ME—HOW DID IT ATTACK YOU?
THEY'RE *WEAK!*
'CAUSE THEY'RE *LONG-RANGE STANDS!*
DOOOOOM
TELL ME SOME-THING I DON'T KNOW!
I'M ASKING YOU *WHAT KIND OF ATTACK* IT HIT YOU WITH!
TP TP TP
WELL, IT *DIDN'T* EXACTLY ATTACK ME, AS SUCH.
I'D JUST BOUGHT A *CALPIS WATER* WHEN THE THING CAME OUT FROM UNDER THE VENDING MACHINE.
TP TP
WHAT? IT DIDN'T ATTACK YOU?
THEN WHY ARE YOU YELLING ABOUT SMASHING IT?
TP
THAT PEST STARTLED THE HELL OUT OF ME AND MADE ME SPILL MY CALPIS ALL OVER MY UNIFORM, DAMN IT!
TP
I WANT MY MONEY BACK!
BUT I KNOW THOSE LITTLE FREAKS ARE UP TO SOME CREEPY SCHEME! IT SAID, "I FOUND ONE," AND THEN IT SNICKERED, LIKE "HEE HEE!"
TP TP TP
OH? MINE SAID THE SAME THING!
BUT WHAT-EVER THEY ARE, THEY SEEM LIKE THEY'RE IGNORING US! JUST WHAT THE HELL ARE THEY?!

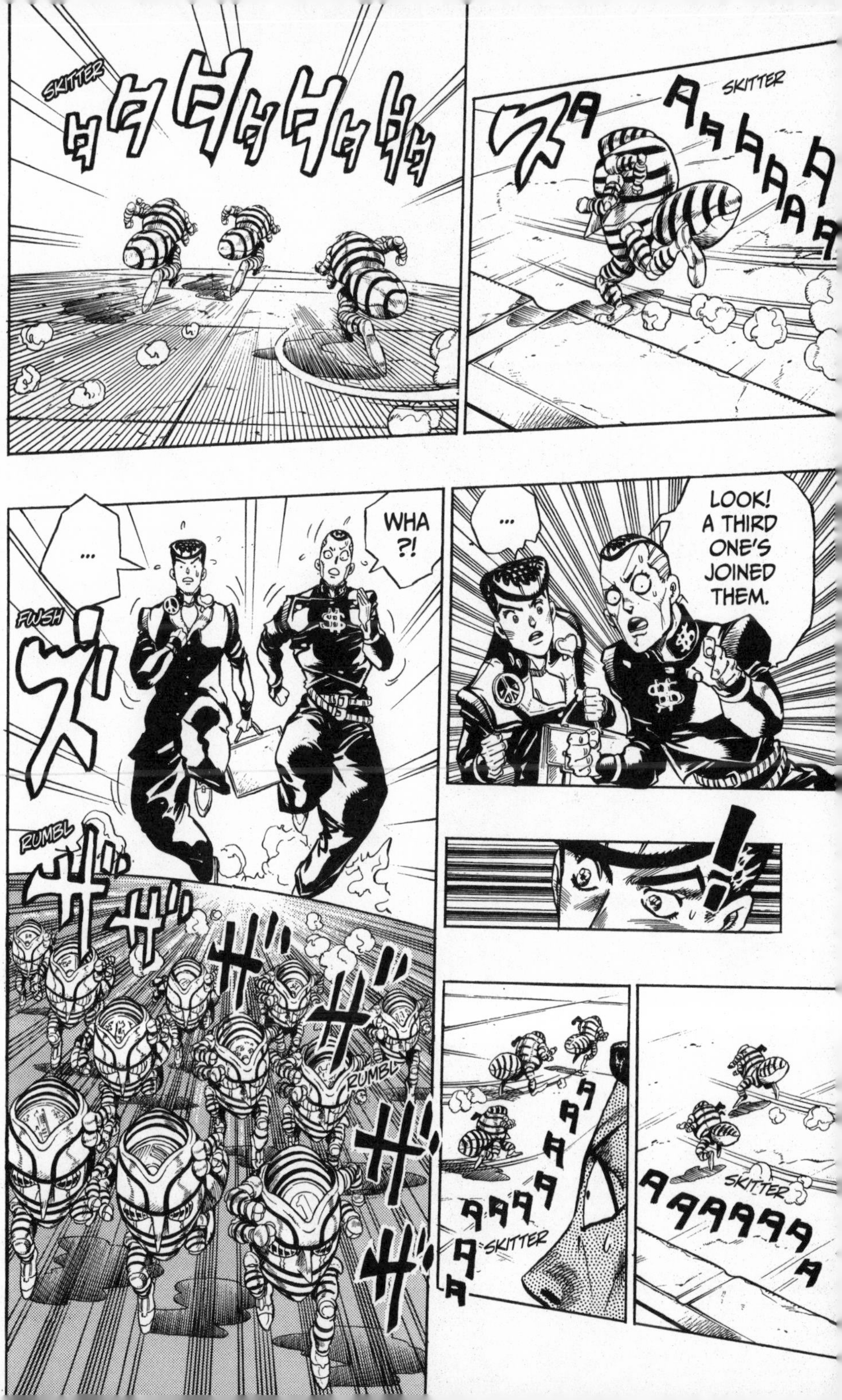
SKITTER
SKITTER
...
LOOK! A THIRD ONE'S JOINED THEM.
SKITTER
SKITTER
WHA ?!
...
FWSH
RUMBL
RUMBL

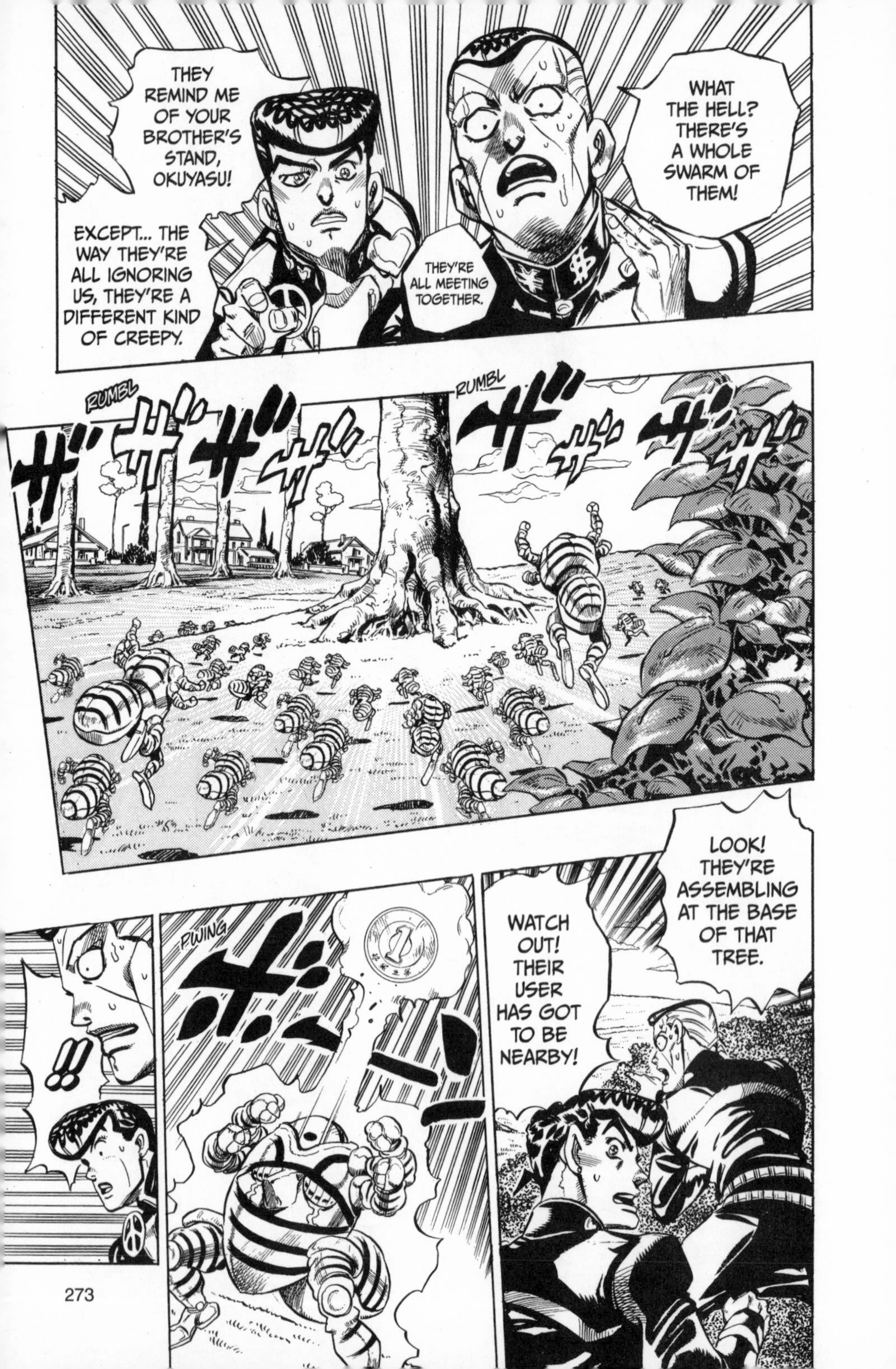
WHAT THE HELL? THERE'S A WHOLE SWARM OF THEM!
THEY'RE ALL MEETING TOGETHER.
THEY REMIND ME OF YOUR BROTHER'S STAND, OKUYASU!
EXCEPT... THE WAY THEY'RE ALL IGNORING US, THEY'RE A DIFFERENT KIND OF CREEPY.
RUMBL
RUMBL
LOOK! THEY'RE ASSEMBLING AT THE BASE OF THAT TREE.
WATCH OUT! THEIR USER HAS GOT TO BE NEARBY!
PWING
!!

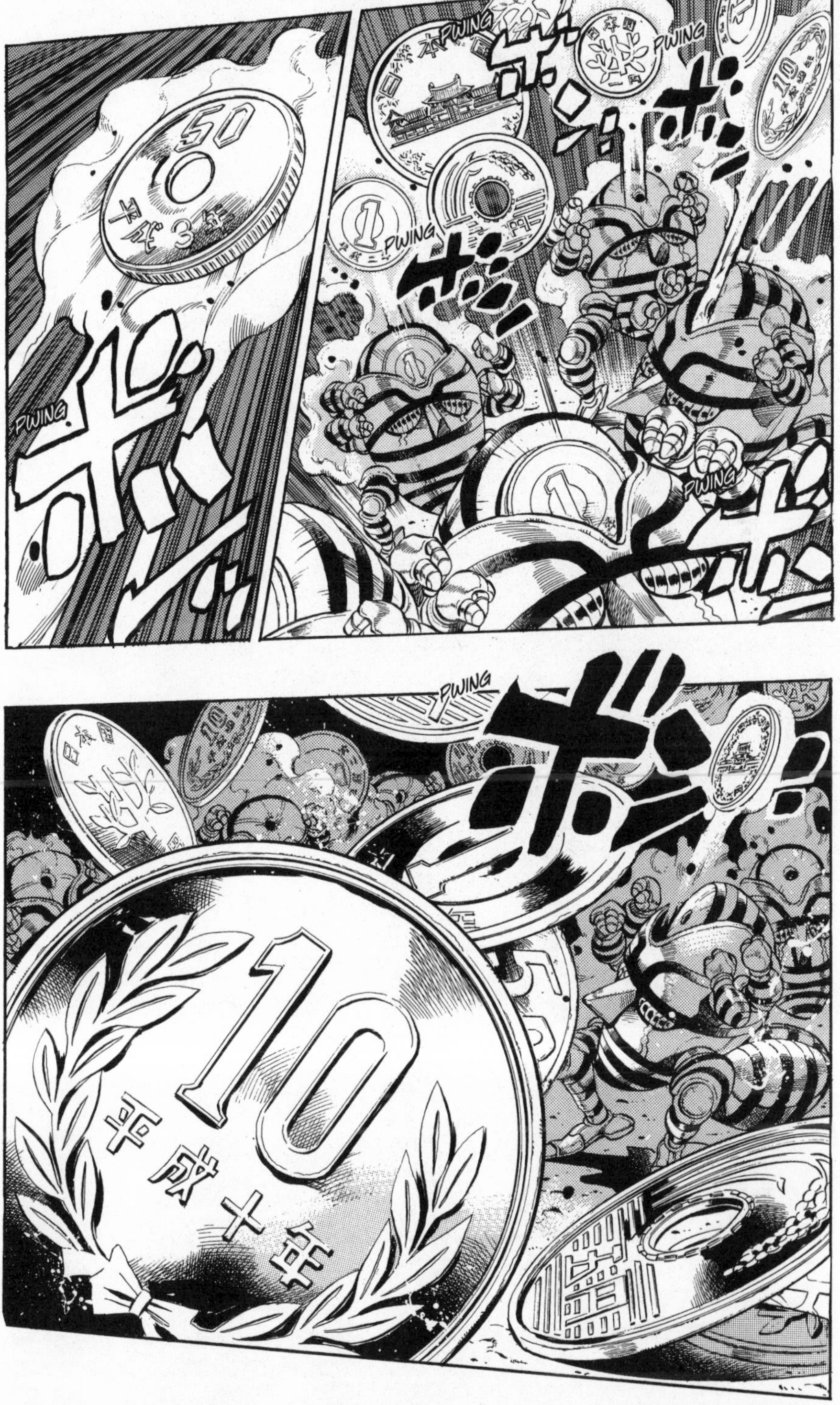
PWING
PWING
PWING
PWING
PWING
PWING
10
平成十年

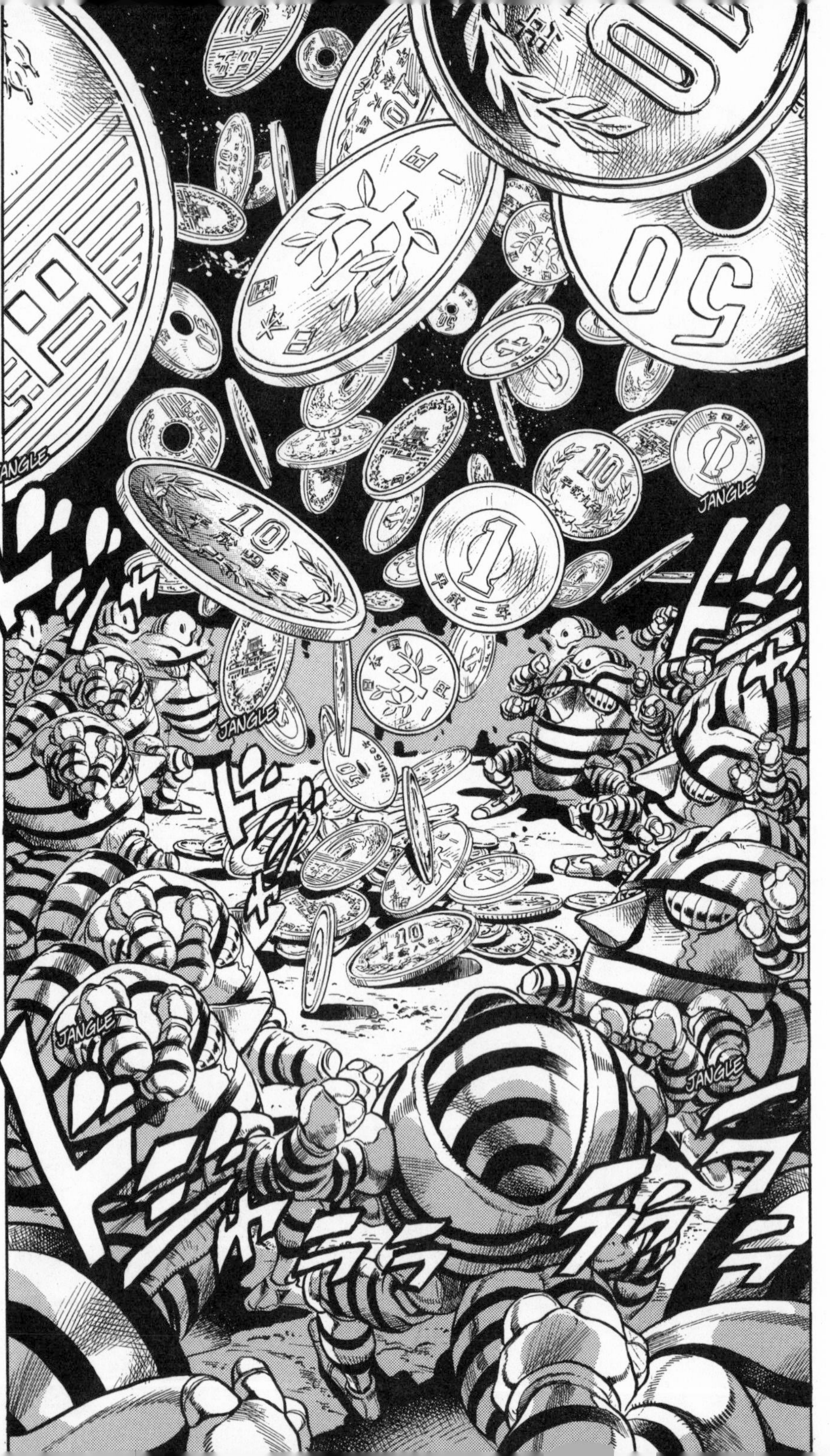
JANGLE
JANGLE
JANGLE
JANGLE
JANGLE

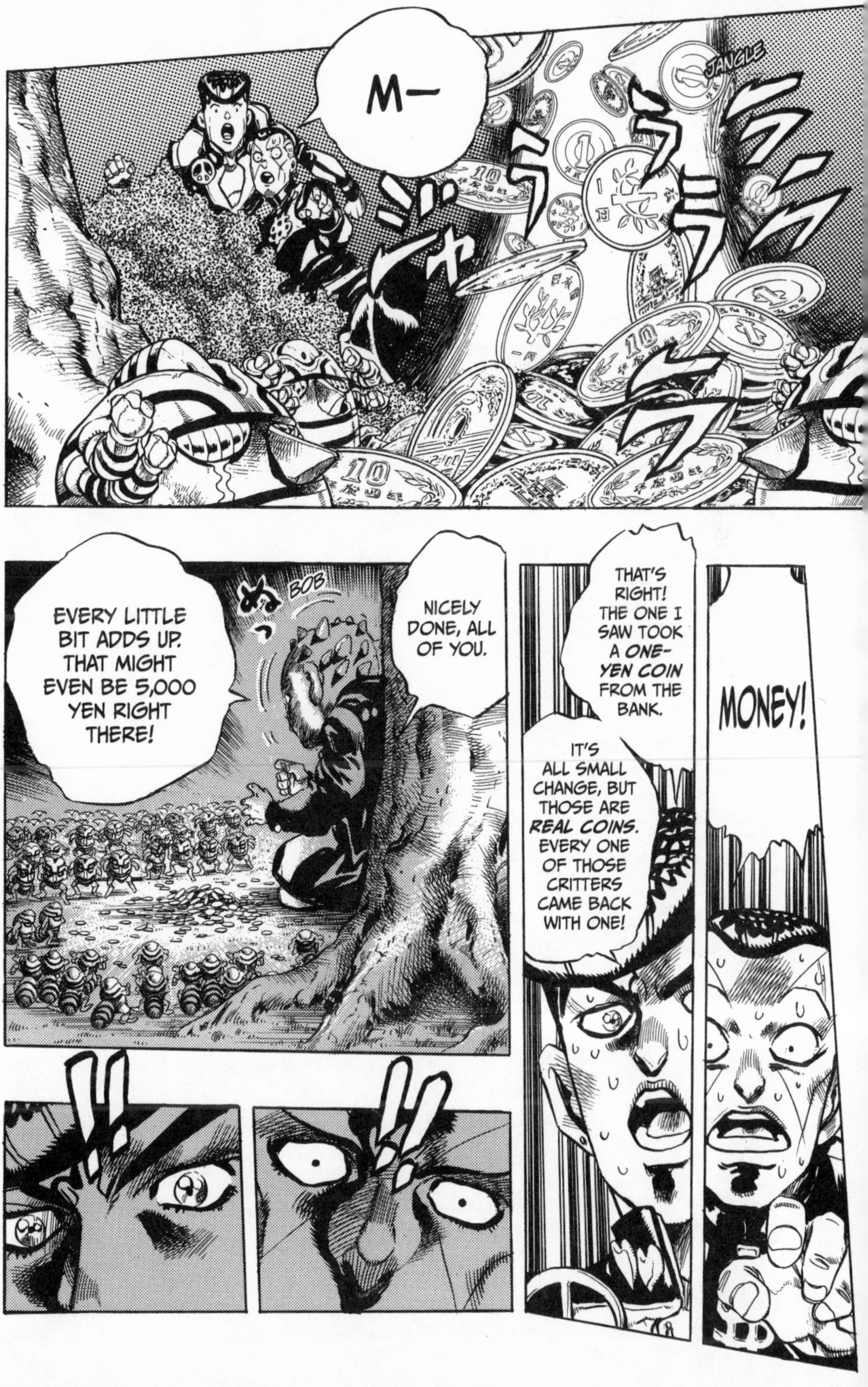
M—
JANGLE
MONEY!
THAT'S RIGHT! THE ONE I SAW TOOK A ONE-YEN COIN FROM THE BANK.
IT'S ALL SMALL CHANGE, BUT THOSE ARE REAL COINS. EVERY ONE OF THOSE CRITTERS CAME BACK WITH ONE!
NICELY DONE, ALL OF YOU.
BOB
EVERY LITTLE BIT ADDS UP. THAT MIGHT EVEN BE 5,000 YEN RIGHT THERE!

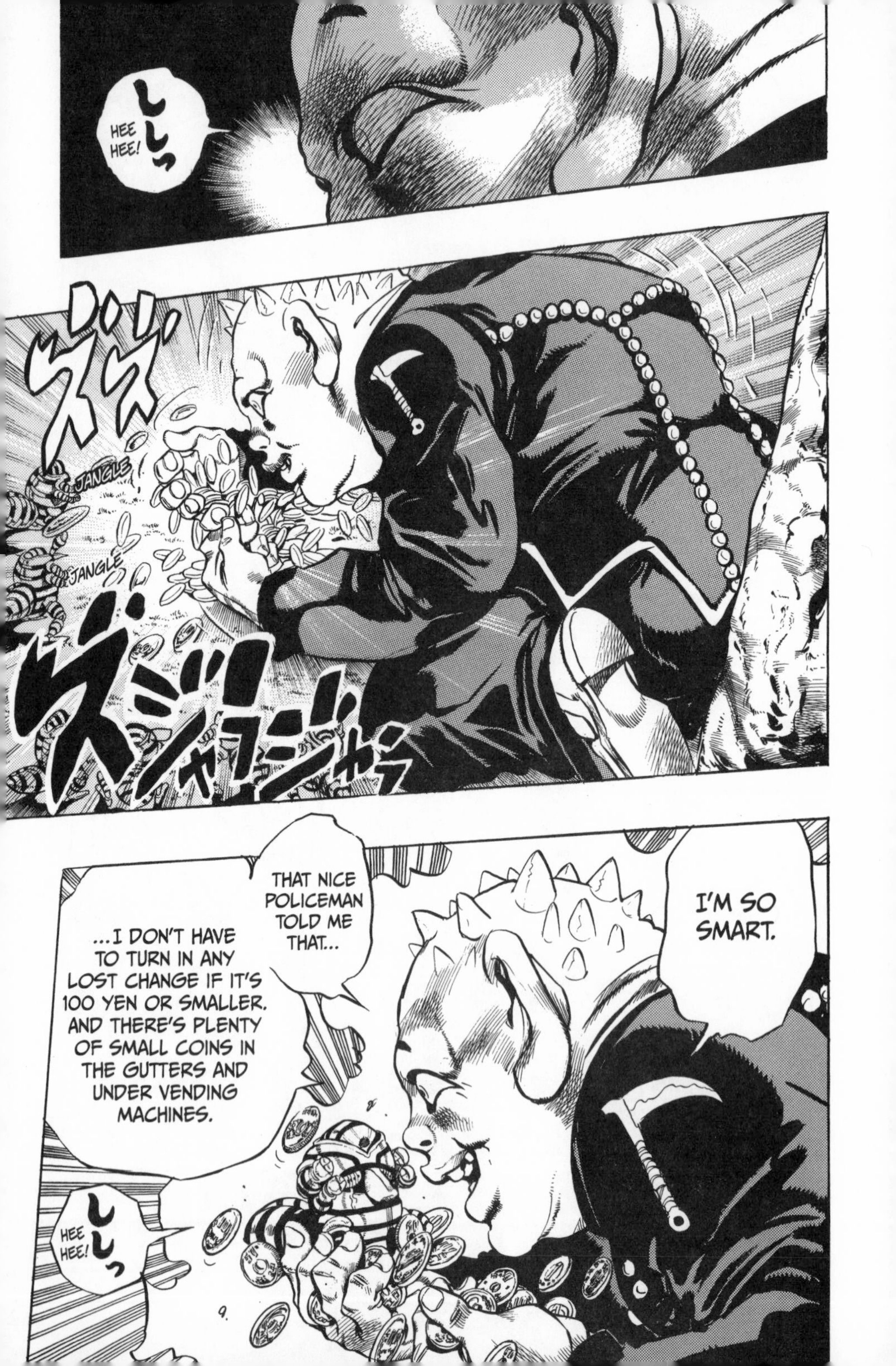
しし っ
HEE HEE!
JANGLE
JANGLE
I'M SO SMART.
THAT NICE POLICEMAN TOLD ME THAT...
...I DON'T HAVE TO TURN IN ANY LOST CHANGE IF IT'S 100 YEN OR SMALLER. AND THERE'S PLENTY OF SMALL COINS IN THE GUTTERS AND UNDER VENDING MACHINES.
しし っ
HEE HEE!

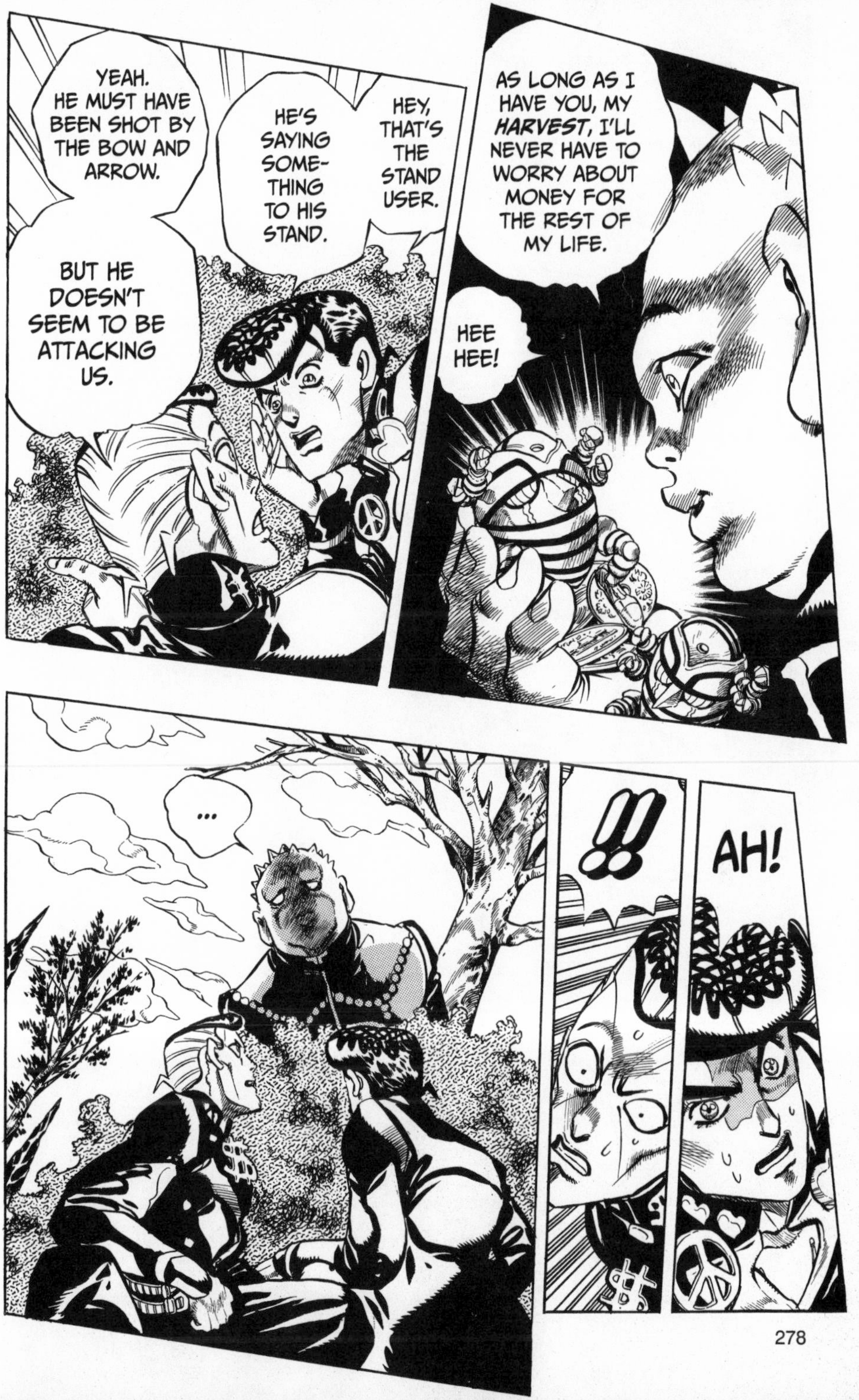
AS LONG AS I HAVE YOU, MY ***HARVEST***, I'LL NEVER HAVE TO WORRY ABOUT MONEY FOR THE REST OF MY LIFE.
HEE HEE!
HEY, THAT'S THE STAND USER.
HE'S SAYING SOME-THING TO HIS STAND.
YEAH. HE MUST HAVE BEEN SHOT BY THE BOW AND ARROW.
BUT HE DOESN'T SEEM TO BE ATTACKING US.
AH!
!!
...

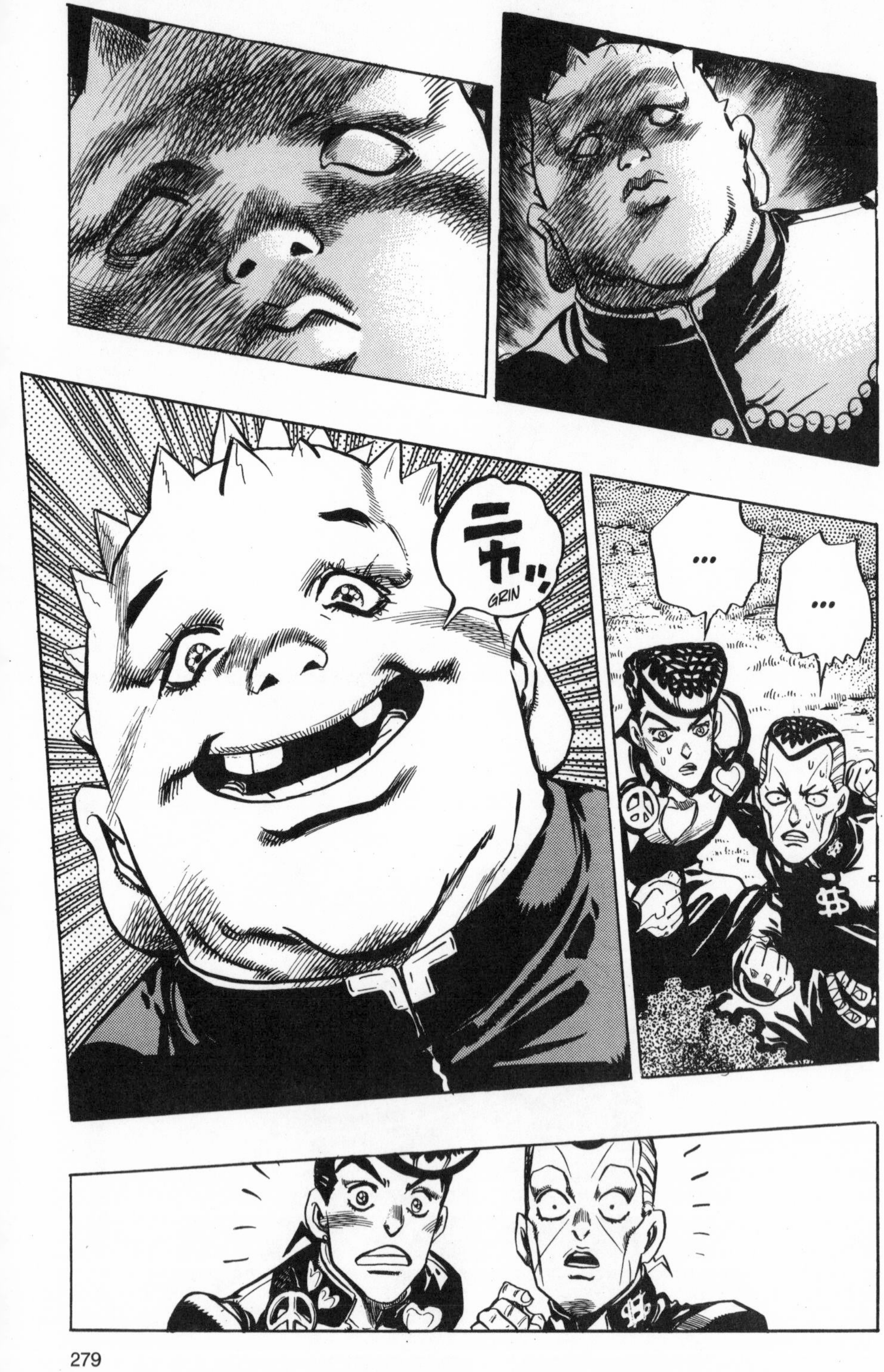
...
...
ニヤッ
GRIN

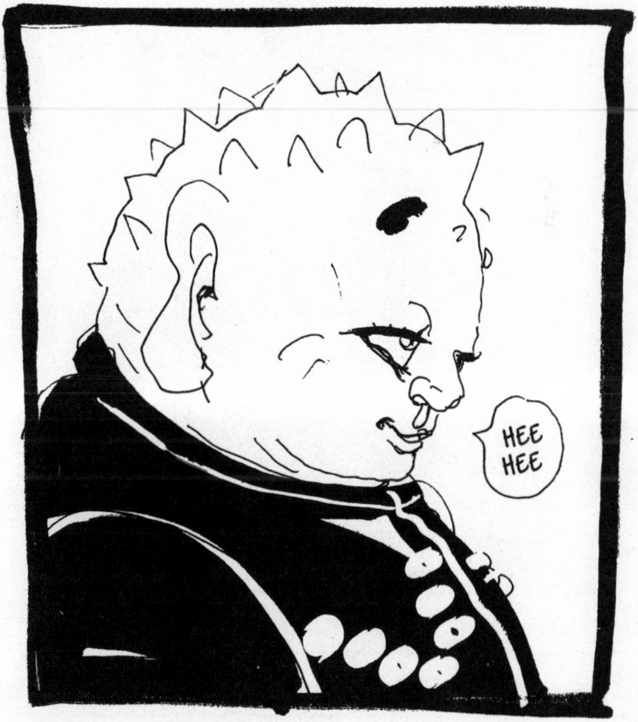
HEE HEE

CHAPTER 71

SHIGECHI'S HARVEST, PART 2

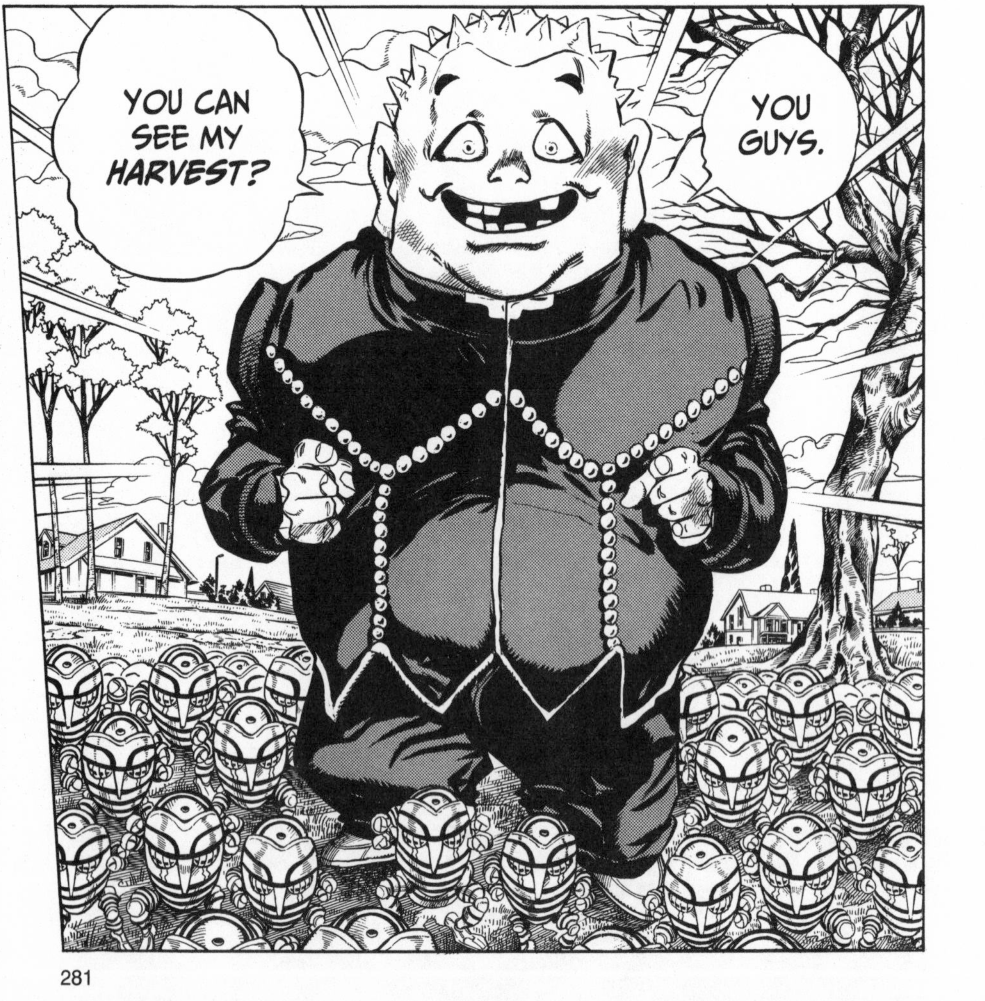
YOU GUYS.
YOU CAN SEE MY HARVEST?

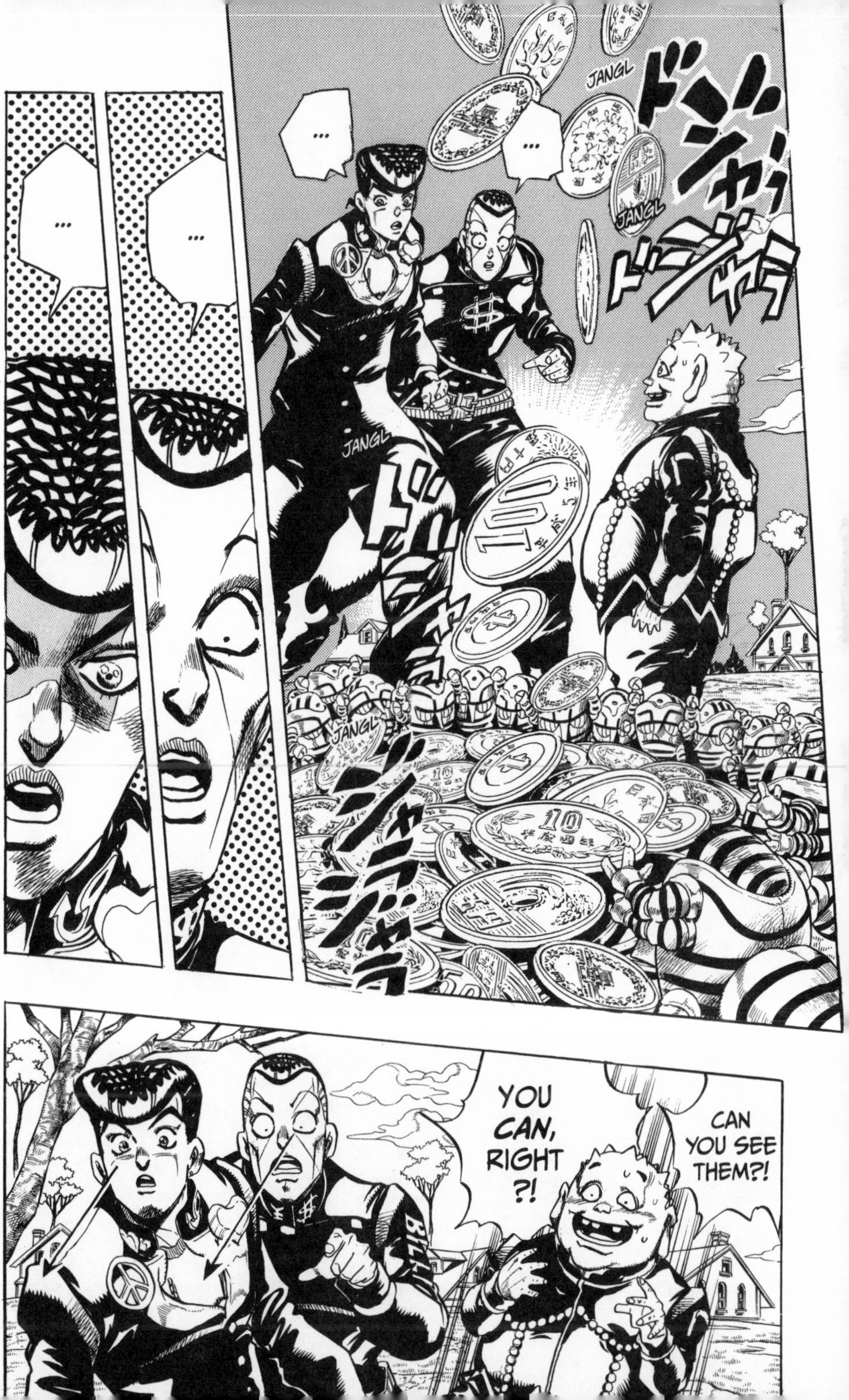
...
...
JANGL
ドンジャラ
JANGL
ドンジャラ
JANGL
JANGL
...
...
CAN YOU SEE THEM?!
YOU CAN, RIGHT ?!

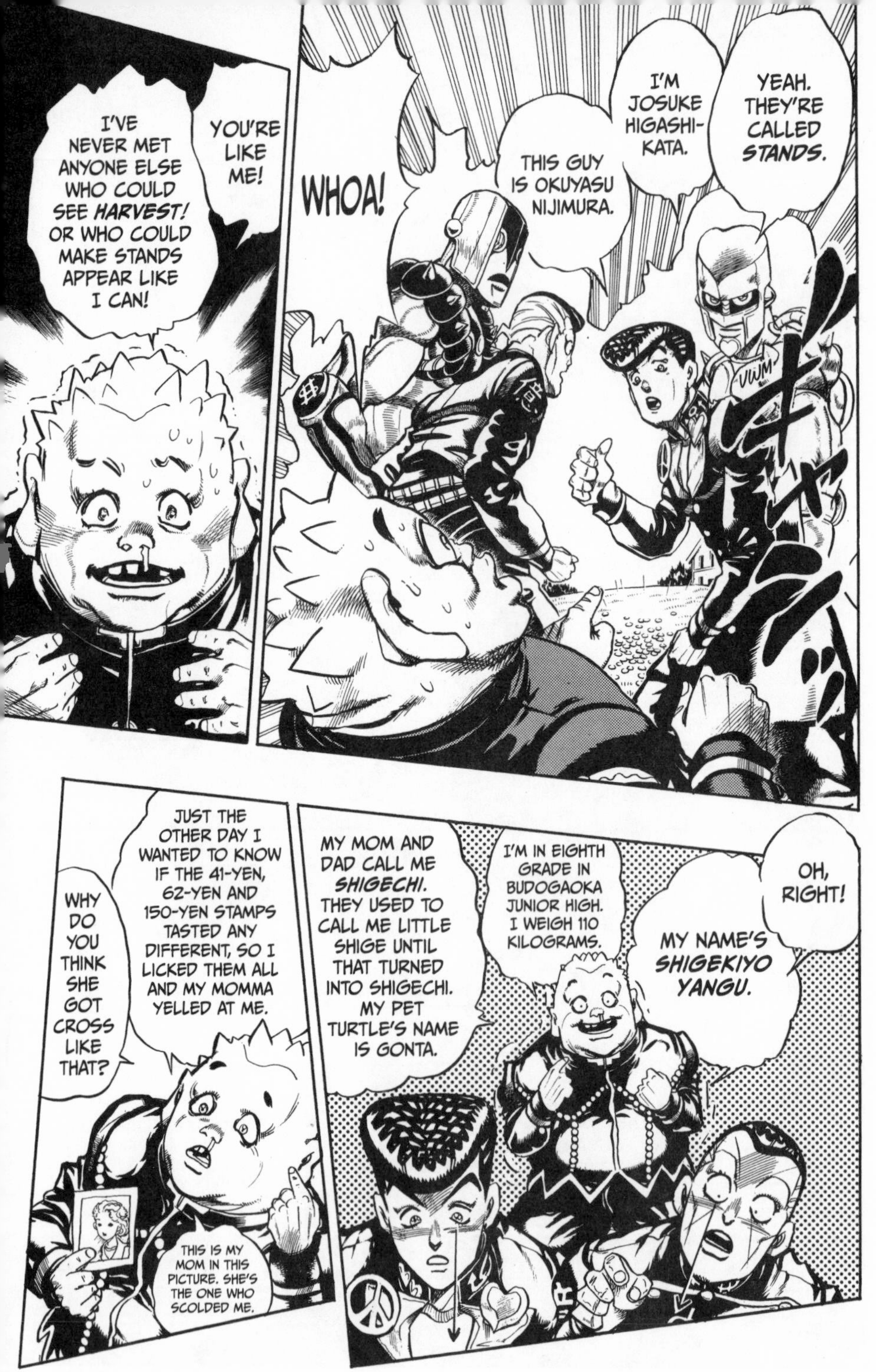
YEAH. THEY'RE CALLED STANDS.
I'M JOSUKE HIGASHI-KATA.
THIS GUY IS OKUYASU NIJIMURA.
WHOA!
VWM
YOU'RE LIKE ME!
I'VE NEVER MET ANYONE ELSE WHO COULD SEE HARVEST! OR WHO COULD MAKE STANDS APPEAR LIKE I CAN!
OH, RIGHT!
MY NAME'S SHIGEKIYO YANGU.
I'M IN EIGHTH GRADE IN BUDOGAOKA JUNIOR HIGH. I WEIGH 110 KILOGRAMS.
MY MOM AND DAD CALL ME SHIGECHI. THEY USED TO CALL ME LITTLE SHIGE UNTIL THAT TURNED INTO SHIGECHI. MY PET TURTLE'S NAME IS GONTA.
JUST THE OTHER DAY I WANTED TO KNOW IF THE 41-YEN, 62-YEN AND 150-YEN STAMPS TASTED ANY DIFFERENT, SO I LICKED THEM ALL AND MY MOMMA YELLED AT ME.
WHY DO YOU THINK SHE GOT CROSS LIKE THAT?
THIS IS MY MOM IN THIS PICTURE. SHE'S THE ONE WHO SCOLDED ME.

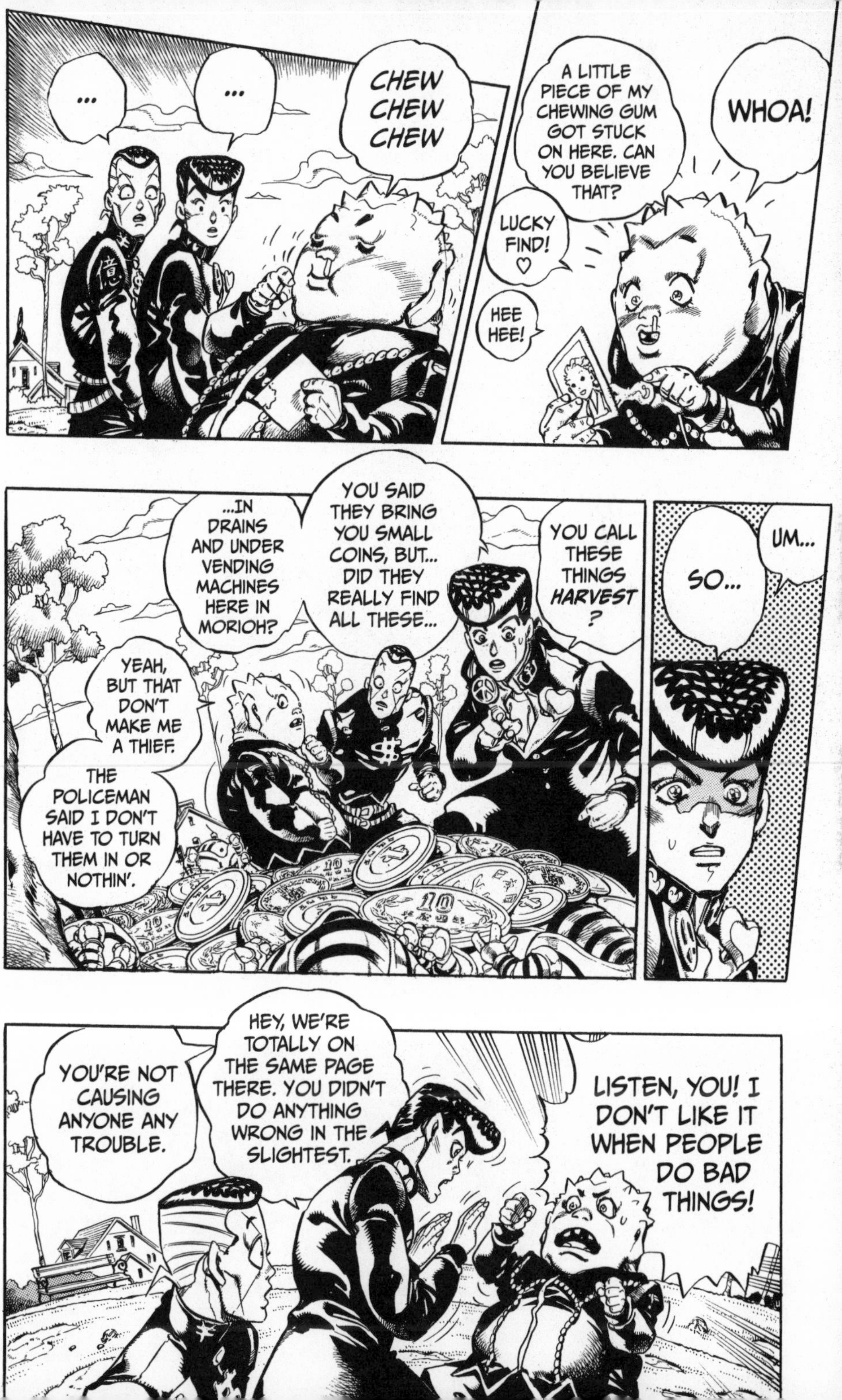
WHOA!
A LITTLE PIECE OF MY CHEWING GUM GOT STUCK ON HERE. CAN YOU BELIEVE THAT?
LUCKY FIND! ♡
HEE HEE!
CHEW CHEW CHEW
...
...
UM...
SO...
YOU CALL THESE THINGS *HARVEST*?
YOU SAID THEY BRING YOU SMALL COINS, BUT... DID THEY REALLY FIND ALL THESE...
...IN DRAINS AND UNDER VENDING MACHINES HERE IN MORIOH?
YEAH, BUT THAT DON'T MAKE ME A THIEF.
THE POLICEMAN SAID I DON'T HAVE TO TURN THEM IN OR NOTHIN'.
LISTEN, YOU! I DON'T LIKE IT WHEN PEOPLE DO BAD THINGS!
HEY, WE'RE TOTALLY ON THE SAME PAGE THERE. YOU DIDN'T DO ANYTHING WRONG IN THE SLIGHTEST.
YOU'RE NOT CAUSING ANYONE ANY TROUBLE.

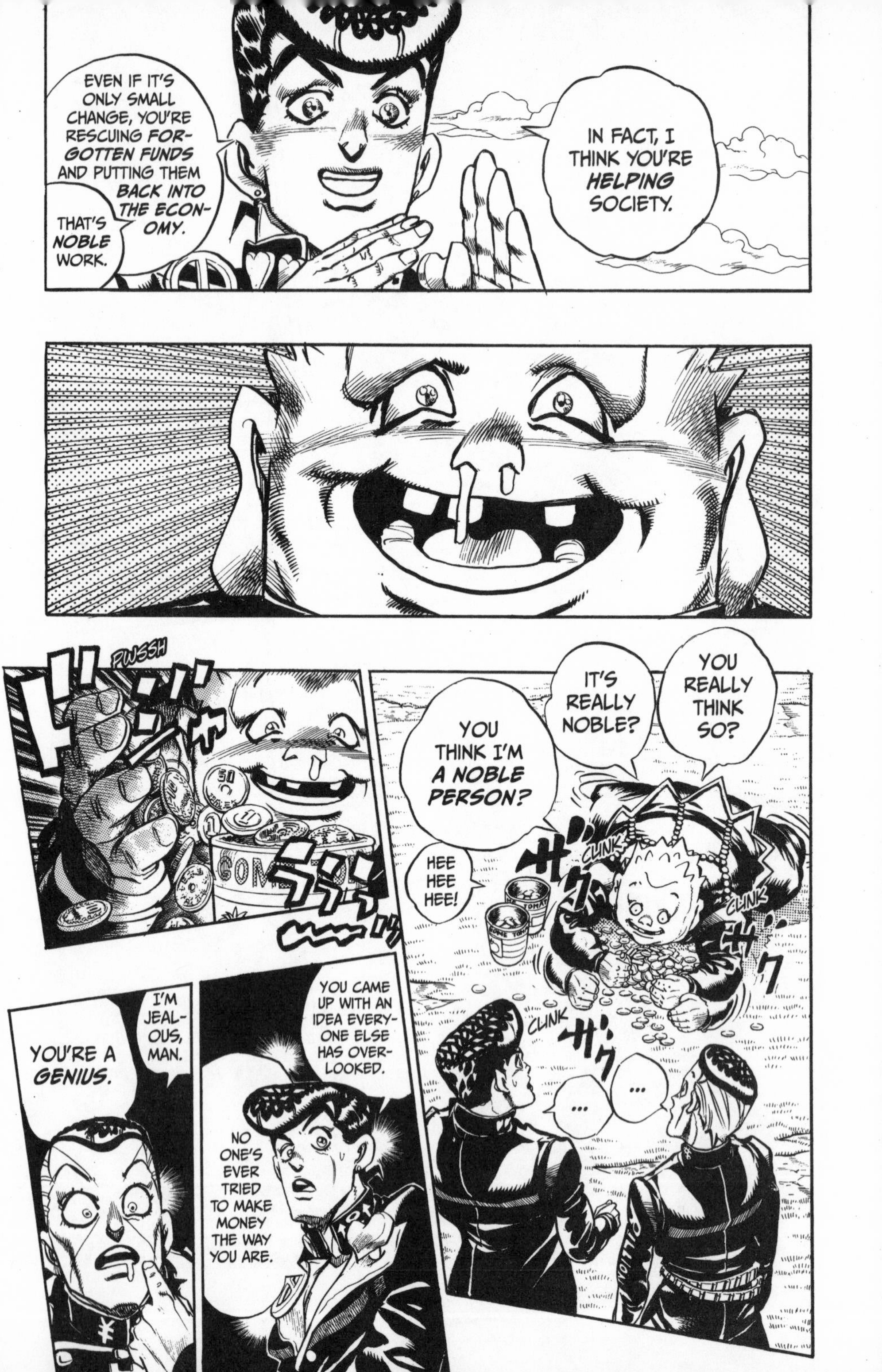
EVEN IF IT'S ONLY SMALL CHANGE, YOU'RE RESCUING FOR-GOTTEN FUNDS AND PUTTING THEM BACK INTO THE ECON-OMY.
THAT'S NOBLE WORK.
IN FACT, I THINK YOU'RE HELPING SOCIETY.
YOU REALLY THINK SO?
IT'S REALLY NOBLE?
YOU THINK I'M A NOBLE PERSON?
CLINK
HEE HEE HEE!
CLINK
CLINK
...
...
PWSSH
YOU CAME UP WITH AN IDEA EVERY-ONE ELSE HAS OVER-LOOKED.
NO ONE'S EVER TRIED TO MAKE MONEY THE WAY YOU ARE.
I'M JEAL-OUS, MAN.
YOU'RE A GENIUS.

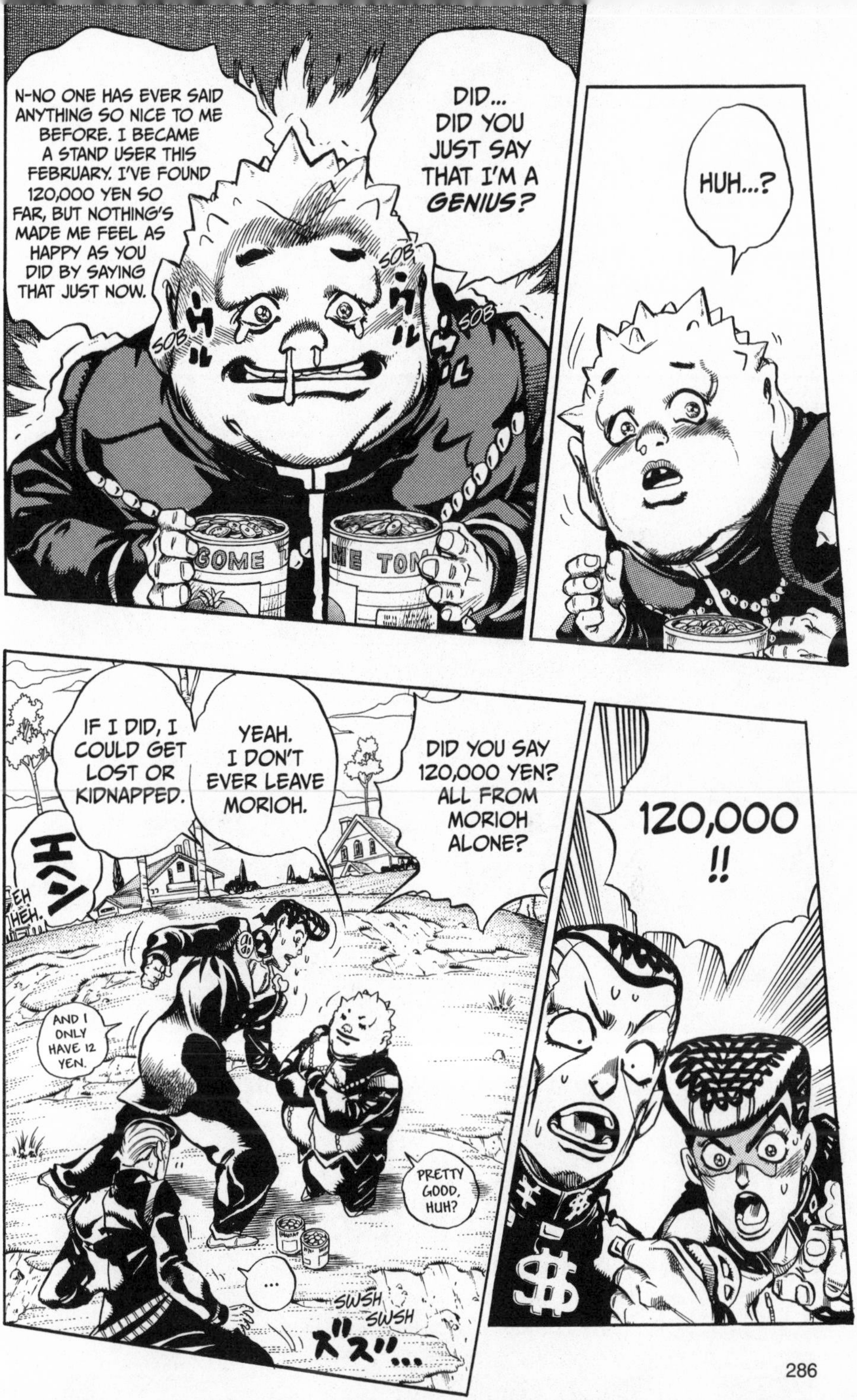
HUH...?
DID... DID YOU JUST SAY THAT I'M A GENIUS?
N-NO ONE HAS EVER SAID ANYTHING SO NICE TO ME BEFORE. I BECAME A STAND USER THIS FEBRUARY. I'VE FOUND 120,000 YEN SO FAR, BUT NOTHING'S MADE ME FEEL AS HAPPY AS YOU DID BY SAYING THAT JUST NOW.
SOB
SOB
SOB
120,000 !!
DID YOU SAY 120,000 YEN? ALL FROM MORIOH ALONE?
YEAH. I DON'T EVER LEAVE MORIOH.
IF I DID, I COULD GET LOST OR KIDNAPPED.
EH HEH.
AND I ONLY HAVE 12 YEN.
PRETTY GOOD, HUH?
...
SWSH SWSH

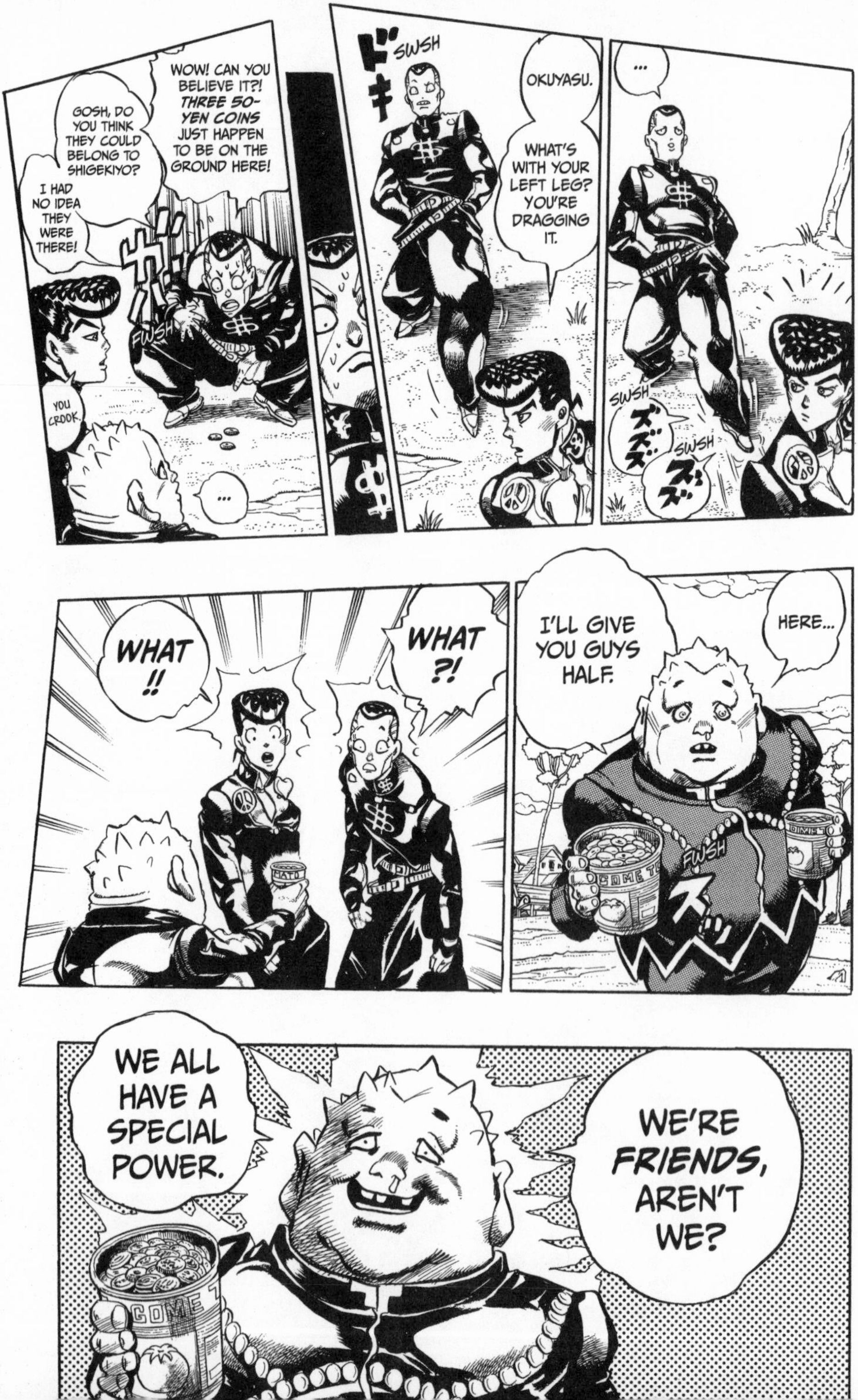
...
SWSH
SWSH
ドキ
SWSH
OKUYASU.
WHAT'S WITH YOUR LEFT LEG? YOU'RE DRAGGING IT.
WOW! CAN YOU BELIEVE IT?! *THREE 50-YEN COINS* JUST HAPPEN TO BE ON THE GROUND HERE!
GOSH, DO YOU THINK THEY COULD BELONG TO SHIGEKIYO?
I HAD NO IDEA THEY WERE THERE!
FWSH
YOU CROOK.
...
HERE...
I'LL GIVE YOU GUYS HALF.
FWSH
WHAT ?!
WHAT !!
WE'RE *FRIENDS,* AREN'T WE?
WE ALL HAVE A SPECIAL POWER.

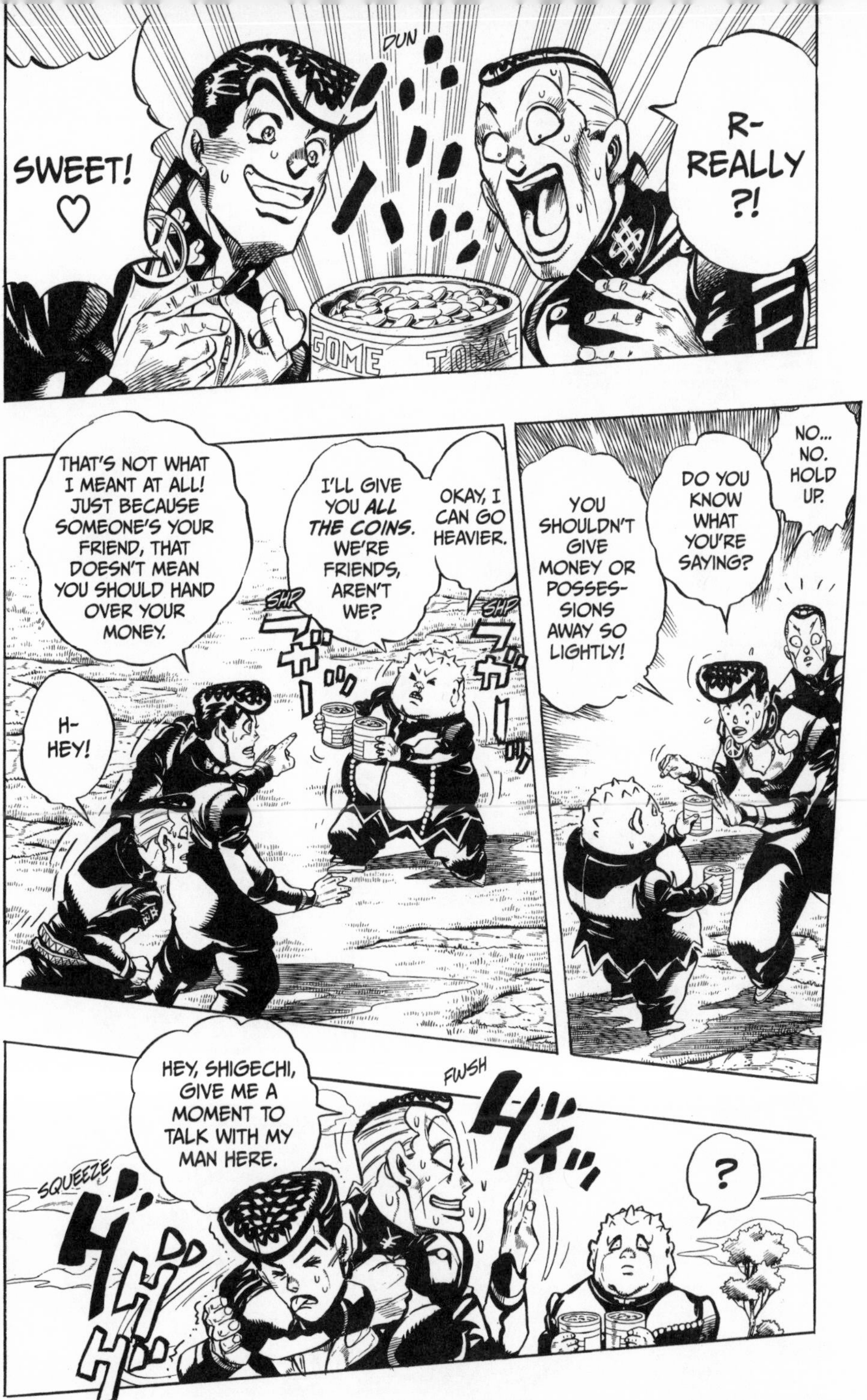
R-REALLY?!
DUN
SWEET! ♡
NO... NO. HOLD UP.
DO YOU KNOW WHAT YOU'RE SAYING?
YOU SHOULDN'T GIVE MONEY OR POSSESSIONS AWAY SO LIGHTLY!
OKAY, I CAN GO HEAVIER.
SHP
I'LL GIVE YOU *ALL THE COINS*. WE'RE FRIENDS, AREN'T WE?
SHP
THAT'S NOT WHAT I MEANT AT ALL! JUST BECAUSE SOMEONE'S YOUR FRIEND, THAT DOESN'T MEAN YOU SHOULD HAND OVER YOUR MONEY.
H-HEY!
?
FWSH
HEY, SHIGECHI, GIVE ME A MOMENT TO TALK WITH MY MAN HERE.
SQUEEZE

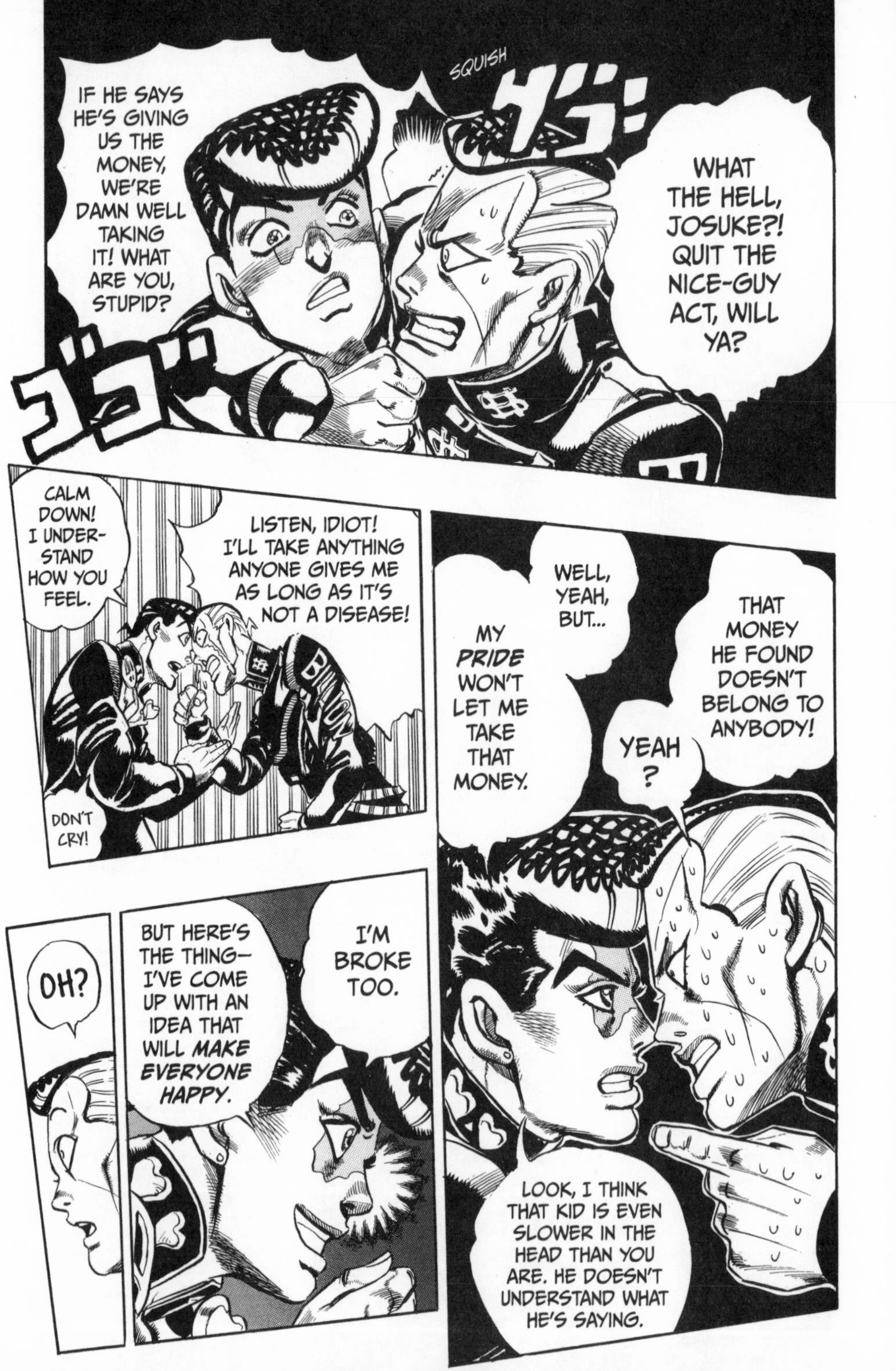
SQUISH
WHAT THE HELL, JOSUKE?! QUIT THE NICE-GUY ACT, WILL YA?
IF HE SAYS HE'S GIVING US THE MONEY, WE'RE DAMN WELL TAKING IT! WHAT ARE YOU, STUPID?
THAT MONEY HE FOUND DOESN'T BELONG TO ANYBODY!
WELL, YEAH, BUT...
MY *PRIDE* WON'T LET ME TAKE THAT MONEY.
YEAH?
LOOK, I THINK THAT KID IS EVEN SLOWER IN THE HEAD THAN YOU ARE. HE DOESN'T UNDERSTAND WHAT HE'S SAYING.
LISTEN, IDIOT! I'LL TAKE ANYTHING ANYONE GIVES ME AS LONG AS IT'S NOT A DISEASE!
CALM DOWN! I UNDER-STAND HOW YOU FEEL.
DON'T CRY!
I'M BROKE TOO.
BUT HERE'S THE THING— I'VE COME UP WITH AN IDEA THAT WILL ***MAKE EVERYONE HAPPY***.
OH?

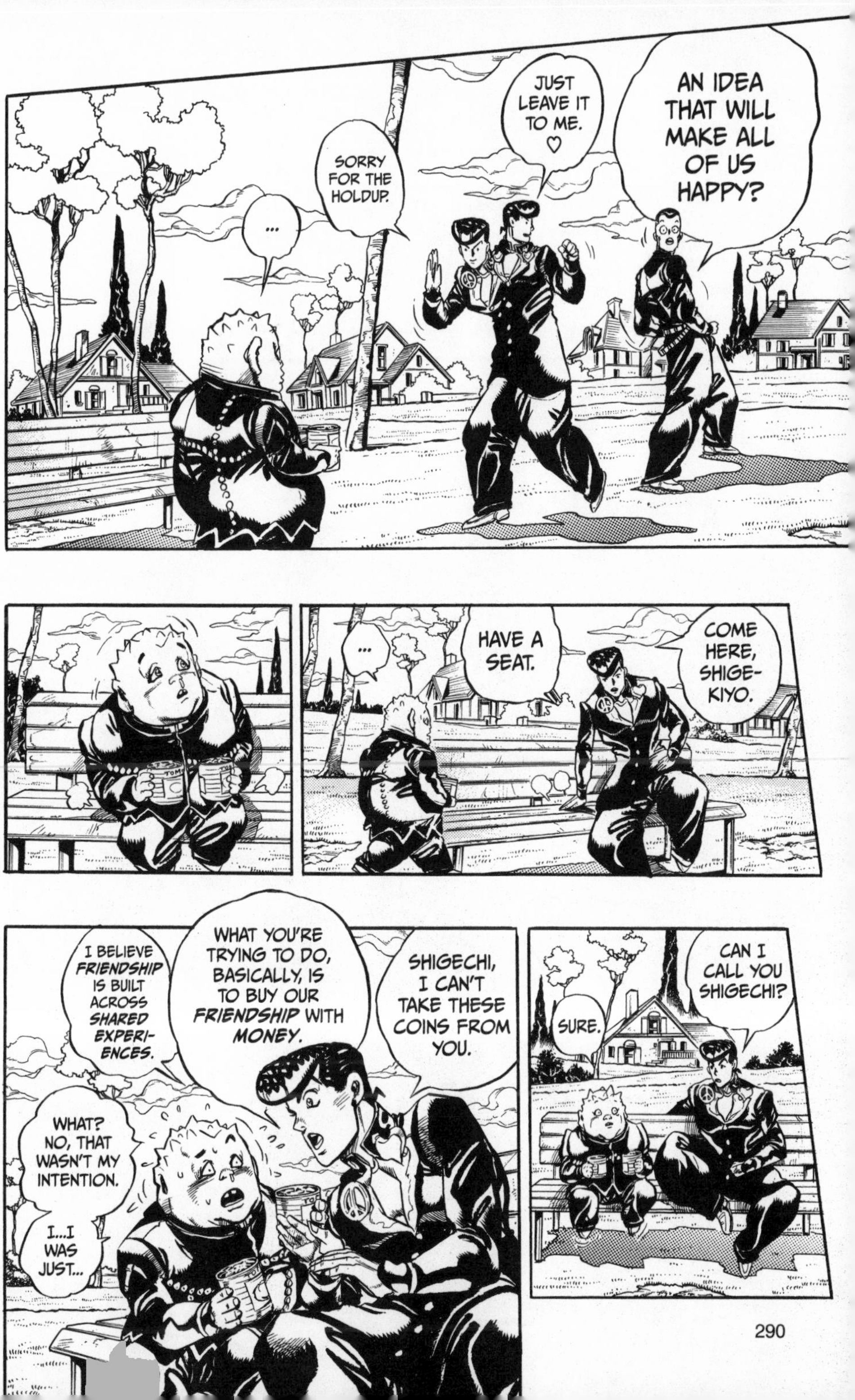

AN IDEA THAT WILL MAKE ALL OF US HAPPY?
JUST LEAVE IT TO ME. ♡
SORRY FOR THE HOLDUP.
...
COME HERE, SHIGE-KIYO.
HAVE A SEAT.
...
CAN I CALL YOU SHIGECHI?
SURE.
SHIGECHI, I CAN'T TAKE THESE COINS FROM YOU.
WHAT YOU'RE TRYING TO DO, BASICALLY, IS TO BUY OUR *FRIENDSHIP* WITH *MONEY*.
I BELIEVE *FRIENDSHIP* IS BUILT ACROSS *SHARED EXPERI-ENCES*.
WHAT? NO, THAT WASN'T MY INTENTION.
I...I WAS JUST...

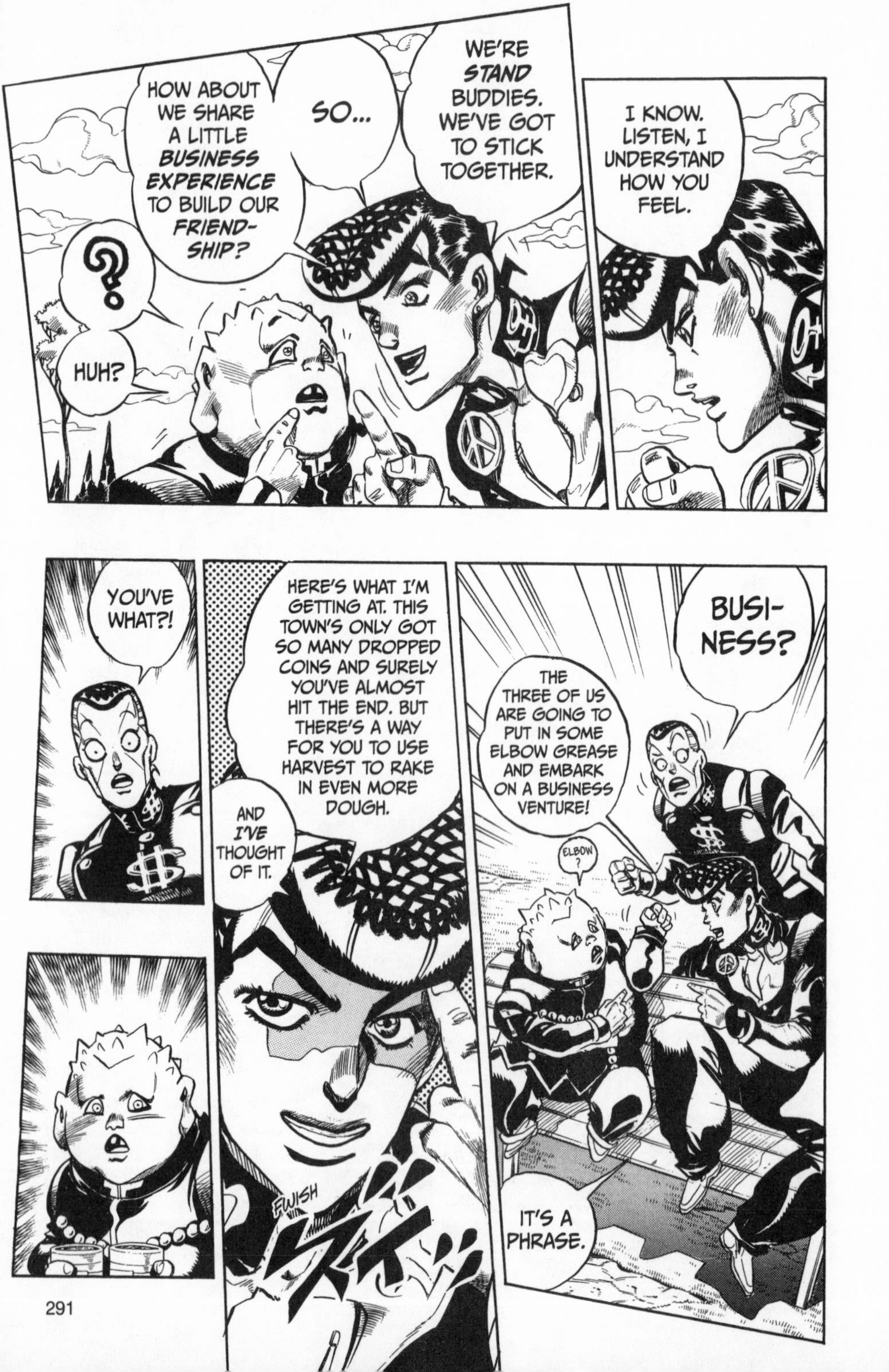
I KNOW. LISTEN, I UNDERSTAND HOW YOU FEEL.
WE'RE *STAND* BUDDIES. WE'VE GOT TO STICK TOGETHER.
SO...
HOW ABOUT WE SHARE A LITTLE *BUSINESS EXPERIENCE* TO BUILD OUR FRIEND-SHIP?
?
HUH?
BUSI-NESS?
THE THREE OF US ARE GOING TO PUT IN SOME ELBOW GREASE AND EMBARK ON A BUSINESS VENTURE!
ELBOW?
IT'S A PHRASE.
HERE'S WHAT I'M GETTING AT. THIS TOWN'S ONLY GOT SO MANY DROPPED COINS AND SURELY YOU'VE ALMOST HIT THE END. BUT THERE'S A WAY FOR YOU TO USE HARVEST TO RAKE IN EVEN MORE DOUGH.
AND *I'VE* THOUGHT OF IT.
FWISH
YOU'VE WHAT?!

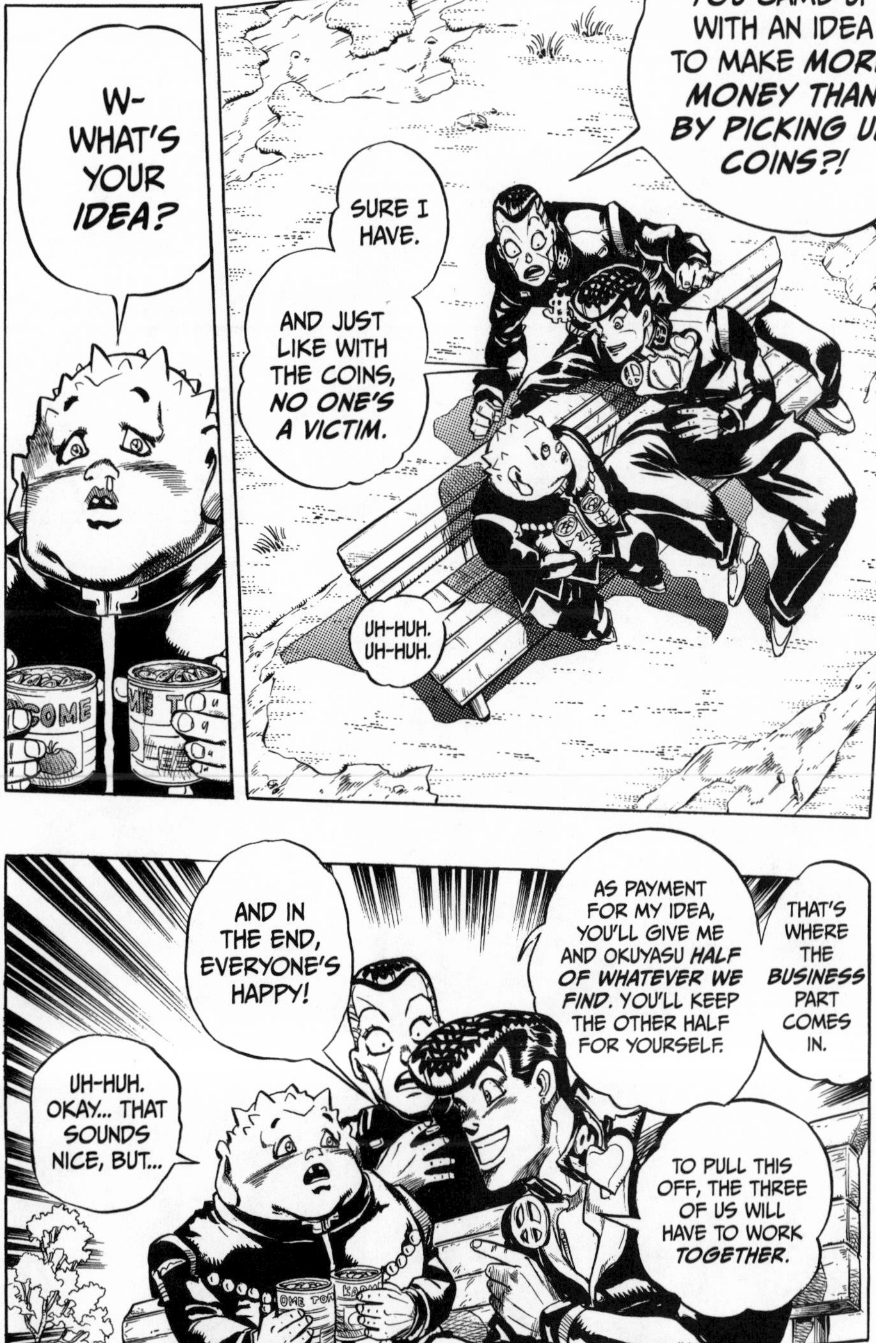
YOU CAME UP WITH AN IDEA TO MAKE MORE MONEY THAN BY PICKING UP COINS?!
SURE I HAVE.
AND JUST LIKE WITH THE COINS, NO ONE'S A VICTIM.
UH-HUH. UH-HUH.
W-WHAT'S YOUR IDEA?
THAT'S WHERE THE BUSINESS PART COMES IN.
AS PAYMENT FOR MY IDEA, YOU'LL GIVE ME AND OKUYASU HALF OF WHATEVER WE FIND. YOU'LL KEEP THE OTHER HALF FOR YOURSELF.
AND IN THE END, EVERYONE'S HAPPY!
TO PULL THIS OFF, THE THREE OF US WILL HAVE TO WORK TOGETHER.
UH-HUH. OKAY... THAT SOUNDS NICE, BUT...

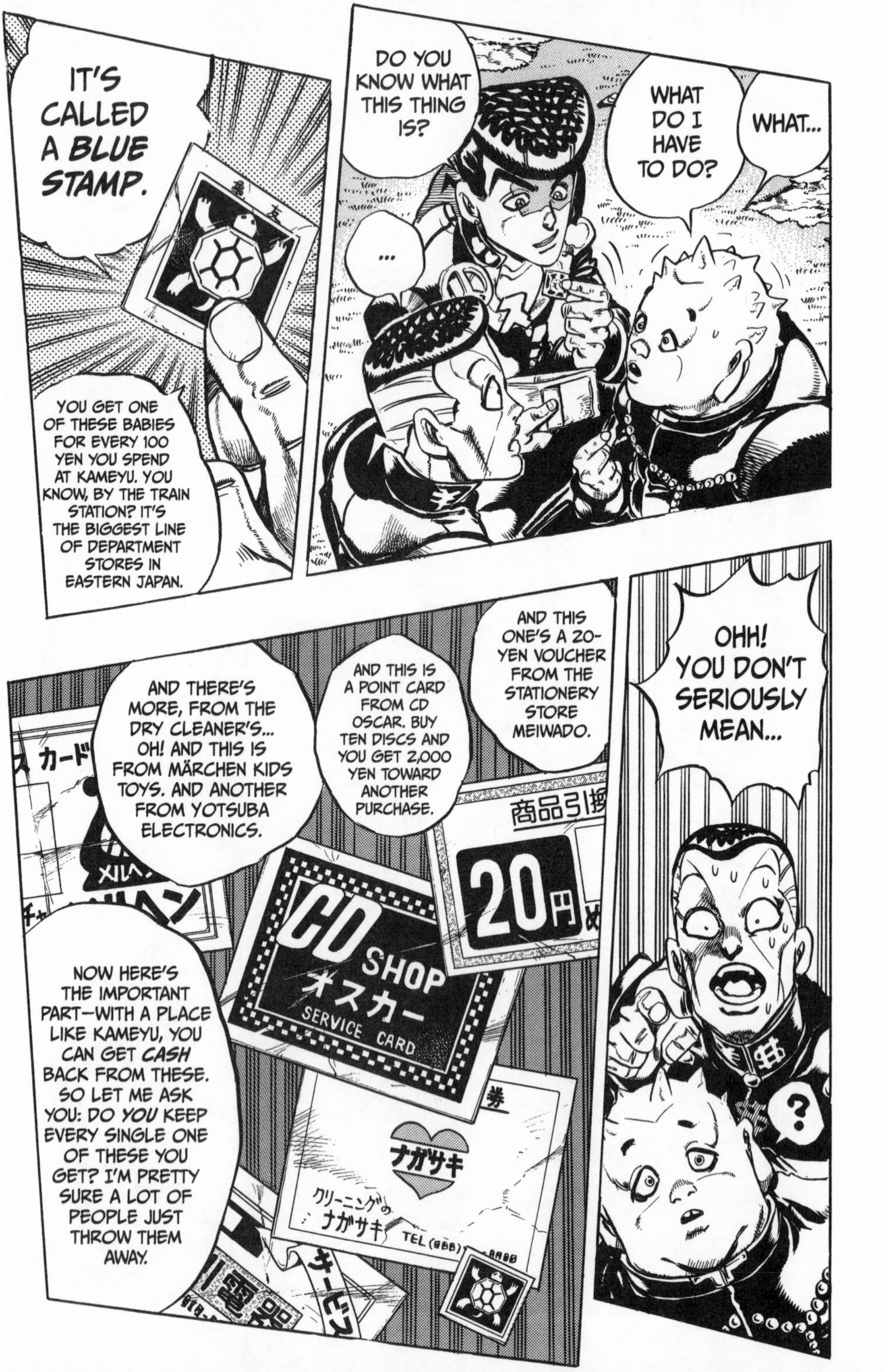
WHAT...
WHAT DO I HAVE TO DO?
DO YOU KNOW WHAT THIS THING IS?
...
IT'S CALLED A *BLUE STAMP.*
YOU GET ONE OF THESE BABIES FOR EVERY 100 YEN YOU SPEND AT KAMEYU. YOU KNOW, BY THE TRAIN STATION? IT'S THE BIGGEST LINE OF DEPARTMENT STORES IN EASTERN JAPAN.
OHH! YOU DON'T SERIOUSLY MEAN...
?
AND THIS ONE'S A 20-YEN VOUCHER FROM THE STATIONERY STORE MEIWADO.
AND THIS IS A POINT CARD FROM CD OSCAR. BUY TEN DISCS AND YOU GET 2,000 YEN TOWARD ANOTHER PURCHASE.
AND THERE'S MORE, FROM THE DRY CLEANER'S... OH! AND THIS IS FROM MÄRCHEN KIDS TOYS. AND ANOTHER FROM YOTSUBA ELECTRONICS.
商品引換
20円
CD SHOP オスカー
SERVICE CARD
NOW HERE'S THE IMPORTANT PART—WITH A PLACE LIKE KAMEYU, YOU CAN GET *CASH* BACK FROM THESE. SO LET ME ASK YOU: DO *YOU* KEEP EVERY SINGLE ONE OF THESE YOU GET? I'M PRETTY SURE A LOT OF PEOPLE JUST THROW THEM AWAY.
ナガサキ
クリーニングの
ナガサキ
TEL

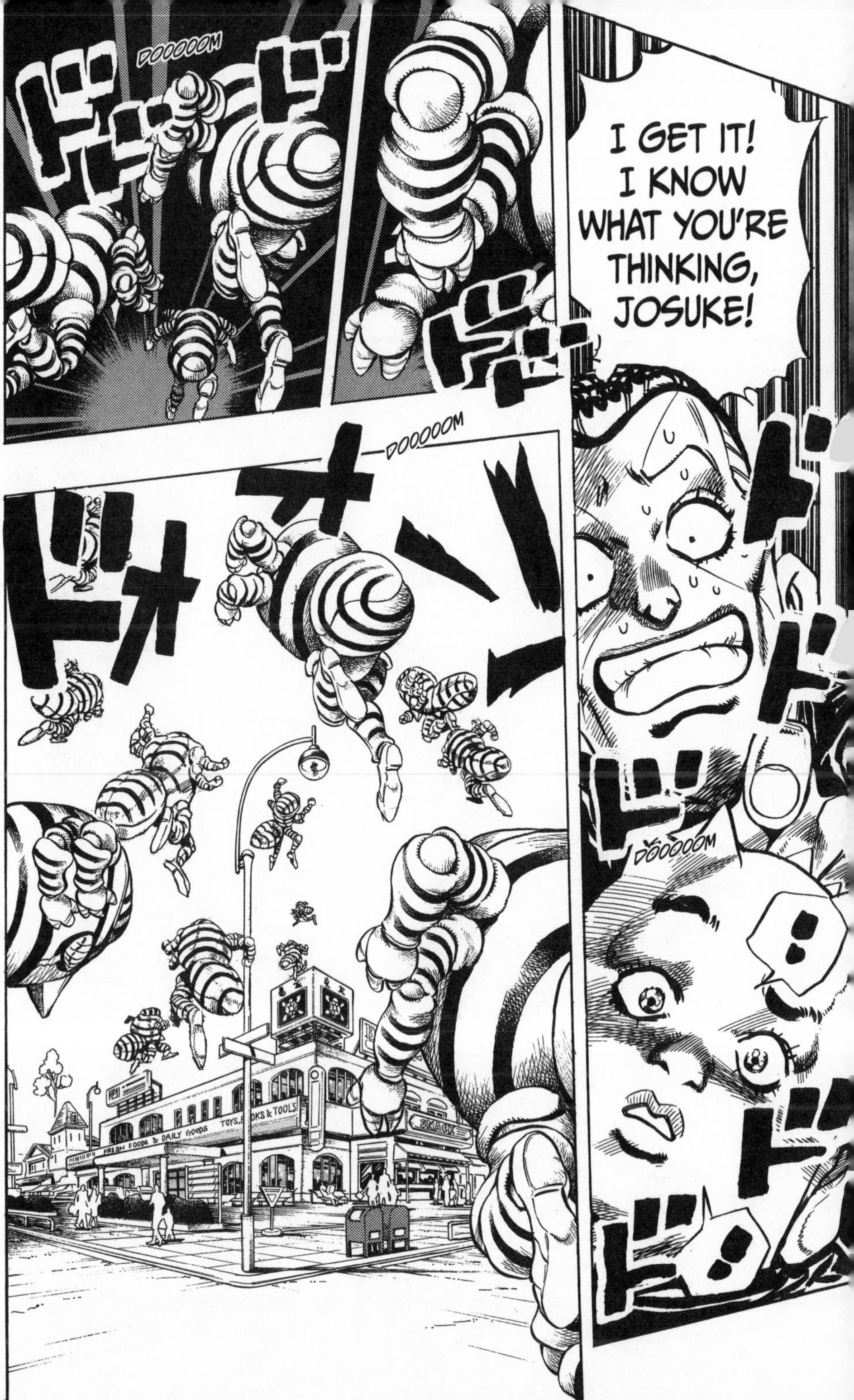
I GET IT! I KNOW WHAT YOU'RE THINKING, JOSUKE!
DOOOOOM
DOOOOOM
DOOOOOM
FRESH FOODS & DAILY GOODS
TOYS, BOOKS & TOOLS
SNACK

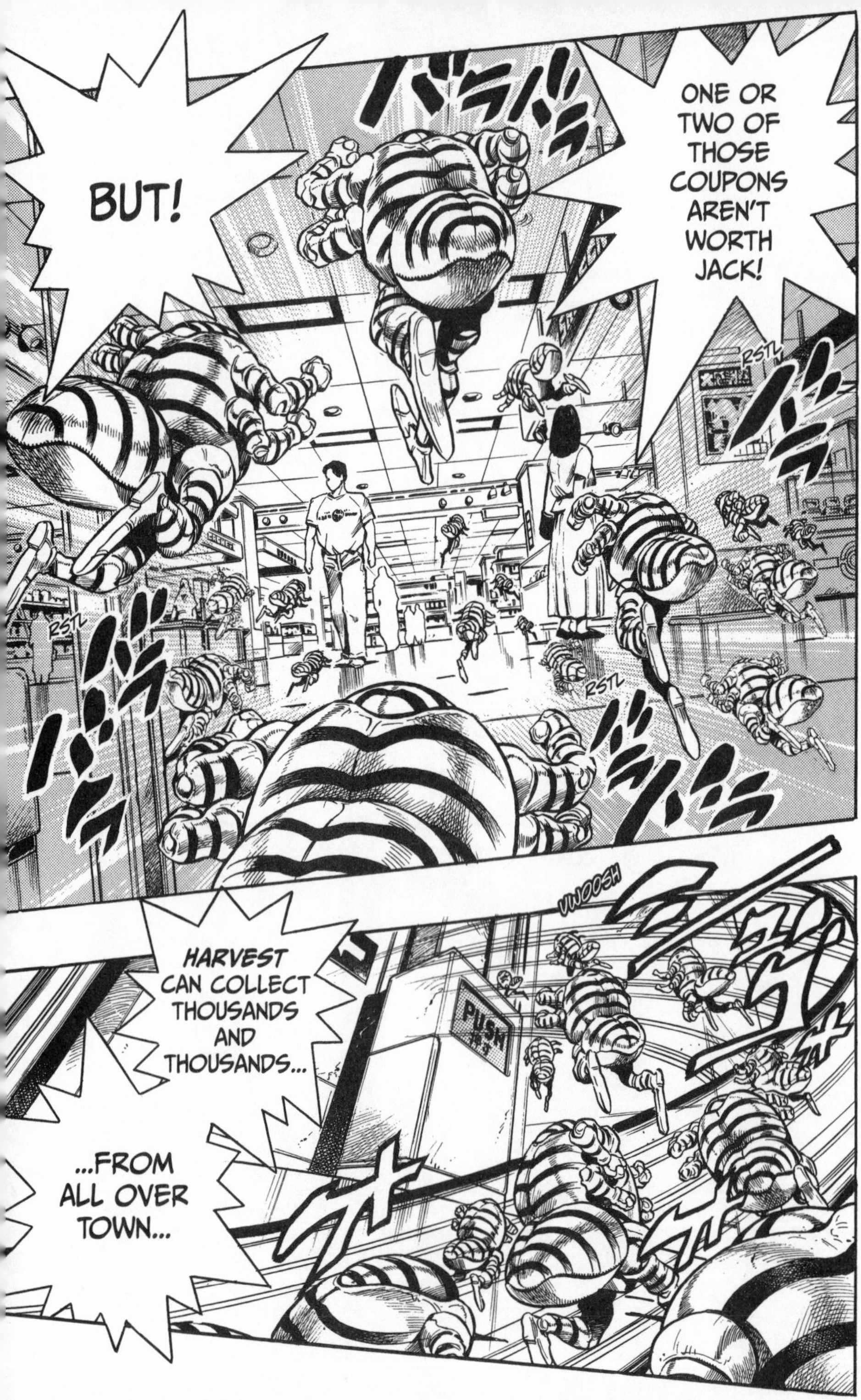
ONE OR TWO OF THOSE COUPONS AREN'T WORTH JACK!
BUT!
RSTL
RSTL
RSTL
VWOOSH
HARVEST CAN COLLECT THOUSANDS AND THOUSANDS...
...FROM ALL OVER TOWN...
PUSH

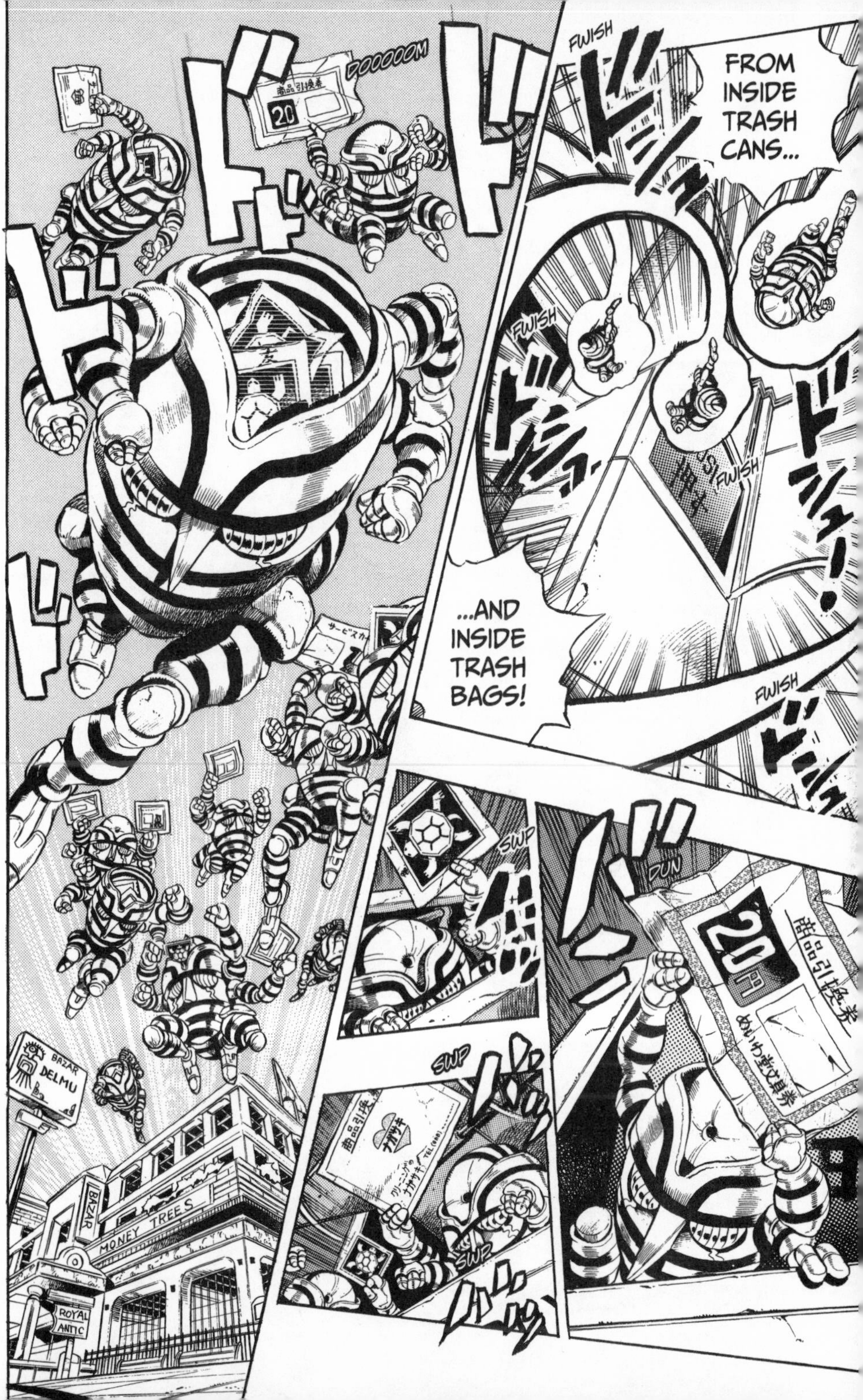

FWISH
FROM INSIDE TRASH CANS...
FWISH
FWISH
...AND INSIDE TRASH BAGS!
FWISH
DUN
20
商品引換券
SWP
SWP
商品引換
SWP
DOOOOOM
商品引換券
20
BAZAR
DELMU
BAZAR
MONEY TREES
ROYAL
ANTIC

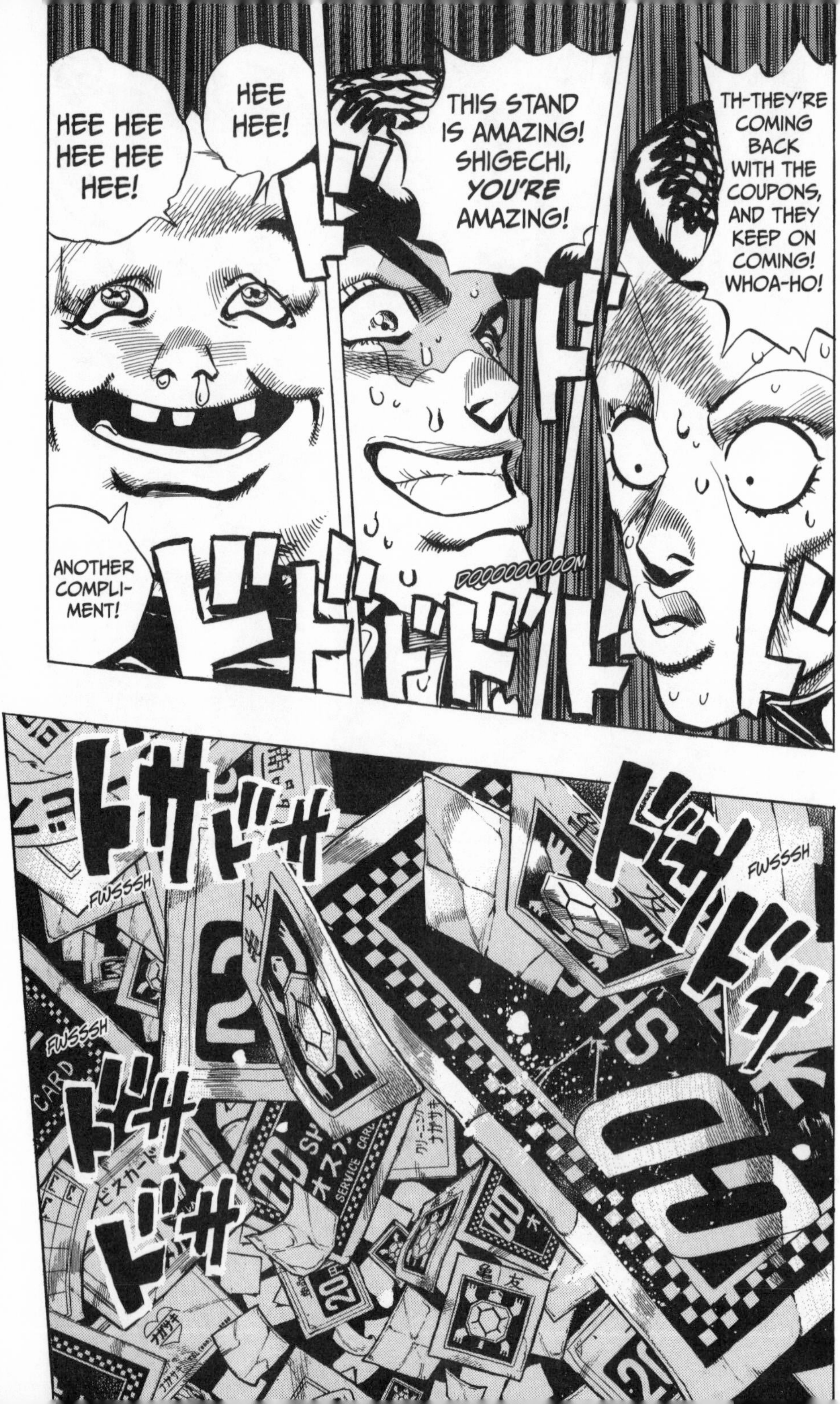
TH-THEY'RE COMING BACK WITH THE COUPONS, AND THEY KEEP ON COMING! WHOA-HO!
THIS STAND IS AMAZING! SHIGECHI, *YOU'RE* AMAZING!
DOOOOOOOOOM
HEE HEE!
HEE HEE HEE HEE HEE!
ANOTHER COMPLI-MENT!
FWSSSH
FWSSSH
FWSSSH

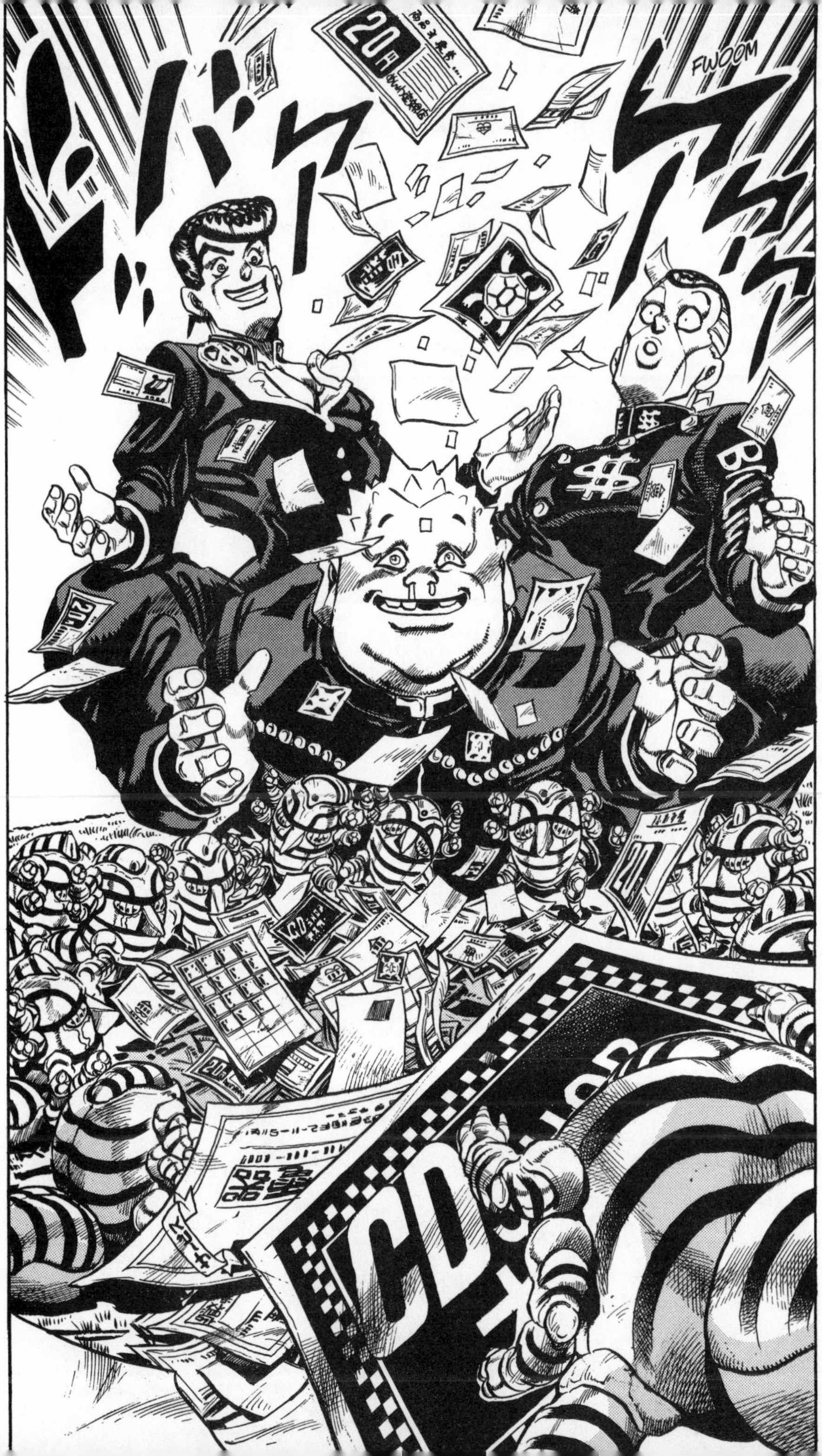
FWOOM
CD

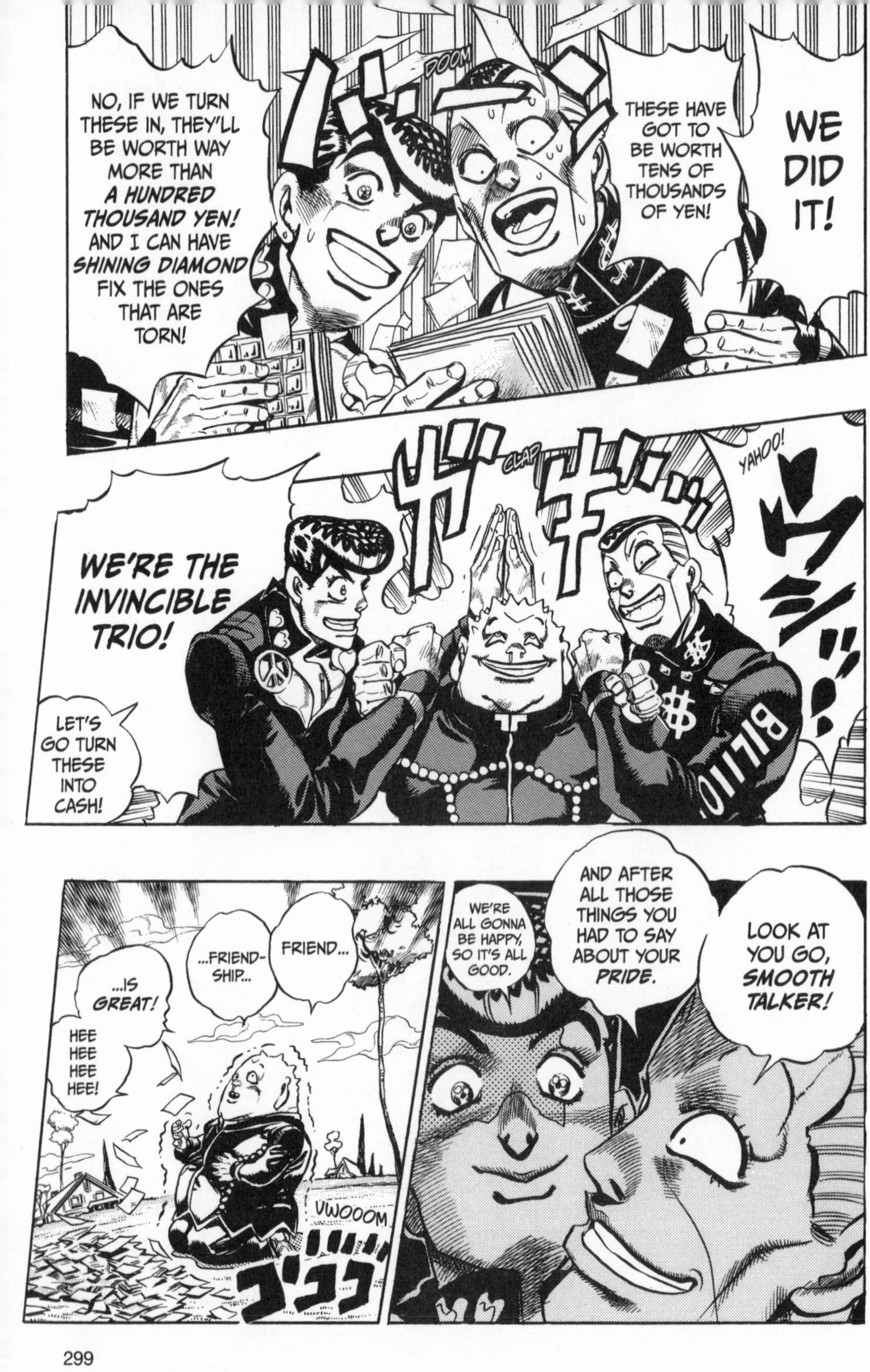
WE DID IT!
DOOM
THESE HAVE GOT TO BE WORTH TENS OF THOUSANDS OF YEN!
NO, IF WE TURN THESE IN, THEY'LL BE WORTH WAY MORE THAN *A HUNDRED THOUSAND YEN!* AND I CAN HAVE *SHINING DIAMOND* FIX THE ONES THAT ARE TORN!
YAHOO!
CLAP
WE'RE THE INVINCIBLE TRIO!
LET'S GO TURN THESE INTO CASH!
LOOK AT YOU GO, *SMOOTH TALKER!*
AND AFTER ALL THOSE THINGS YOU HAD TO SAY ABOUT YOUR *PRIDE.*
WE'RE ALL GONNA BE HAPPY, SO IT'S ALL GOOD.
FRIEND...
...FRIEND-SHIP...
...IS *GREAT!*
HEE HEE HEE HEE!
VWOOOM

10
平成八年

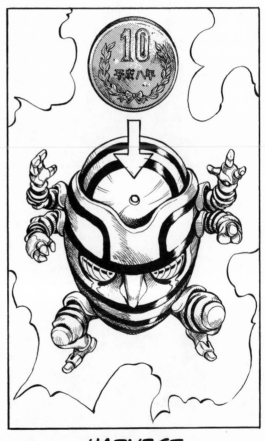

HARVEST

CHAPTER 72

SHIGECHI'S HARVEST, PART 3

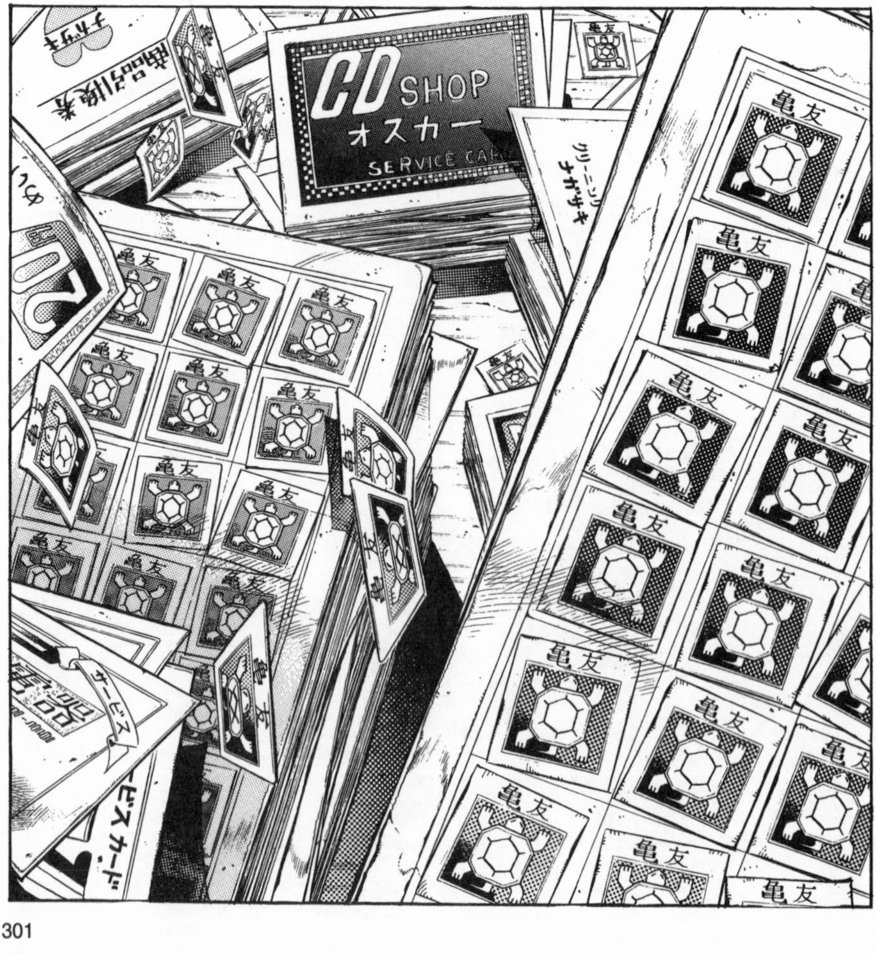
CD SHOP
オスカー
亀友

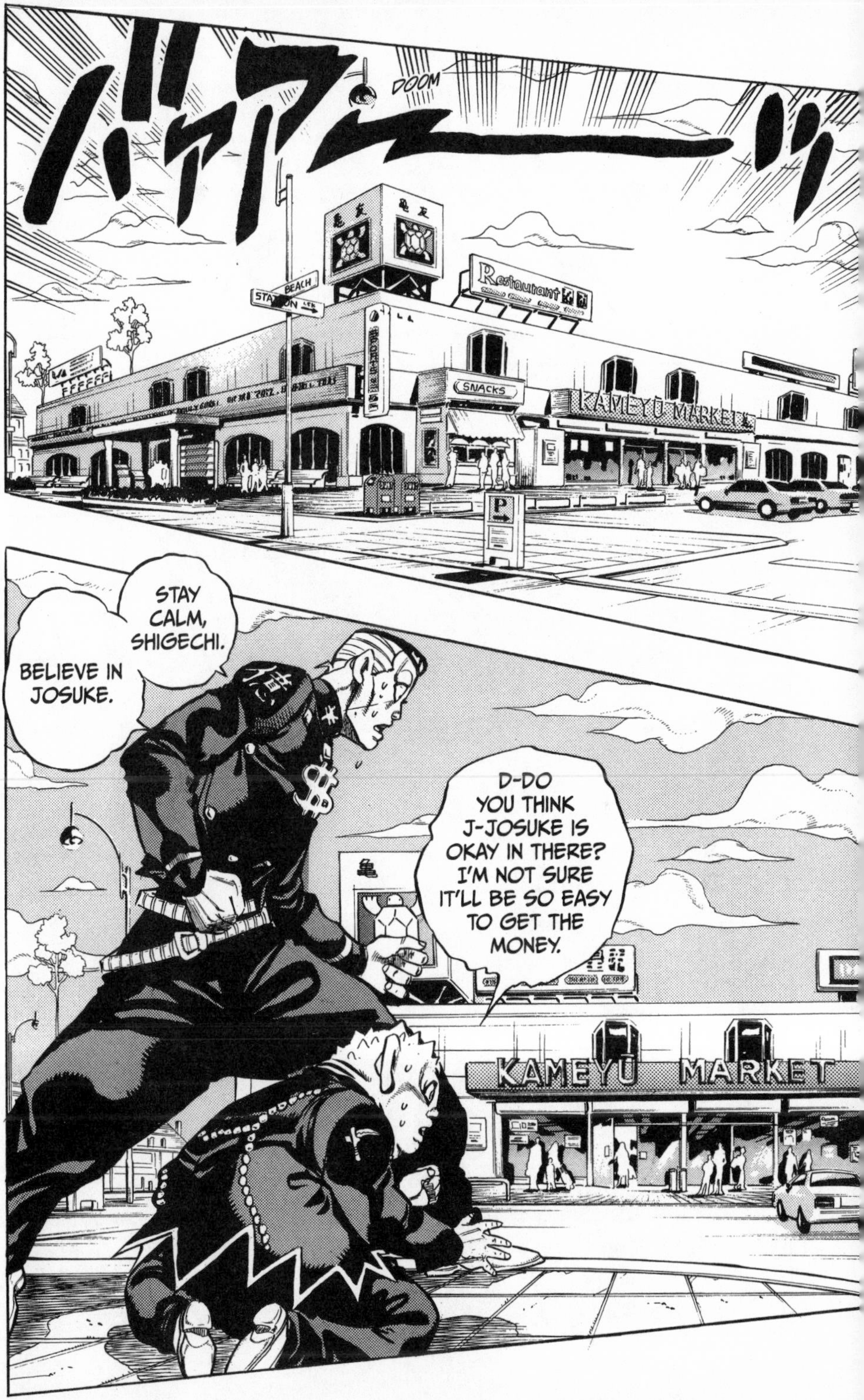
DOOM
BEACH
STATION
Restaurant
SNACKS
KAMEYU MARKET
P
D-DO YOU THINK J-JOSUKE IS OKAY IN THERE? I'M NOT SURE IT'LL BE SO EASY TO GET THE MONEY.
STAY CALM, SHIGECHI.
BELIEVE IN JOSUKE.
KAMEYU MARKET

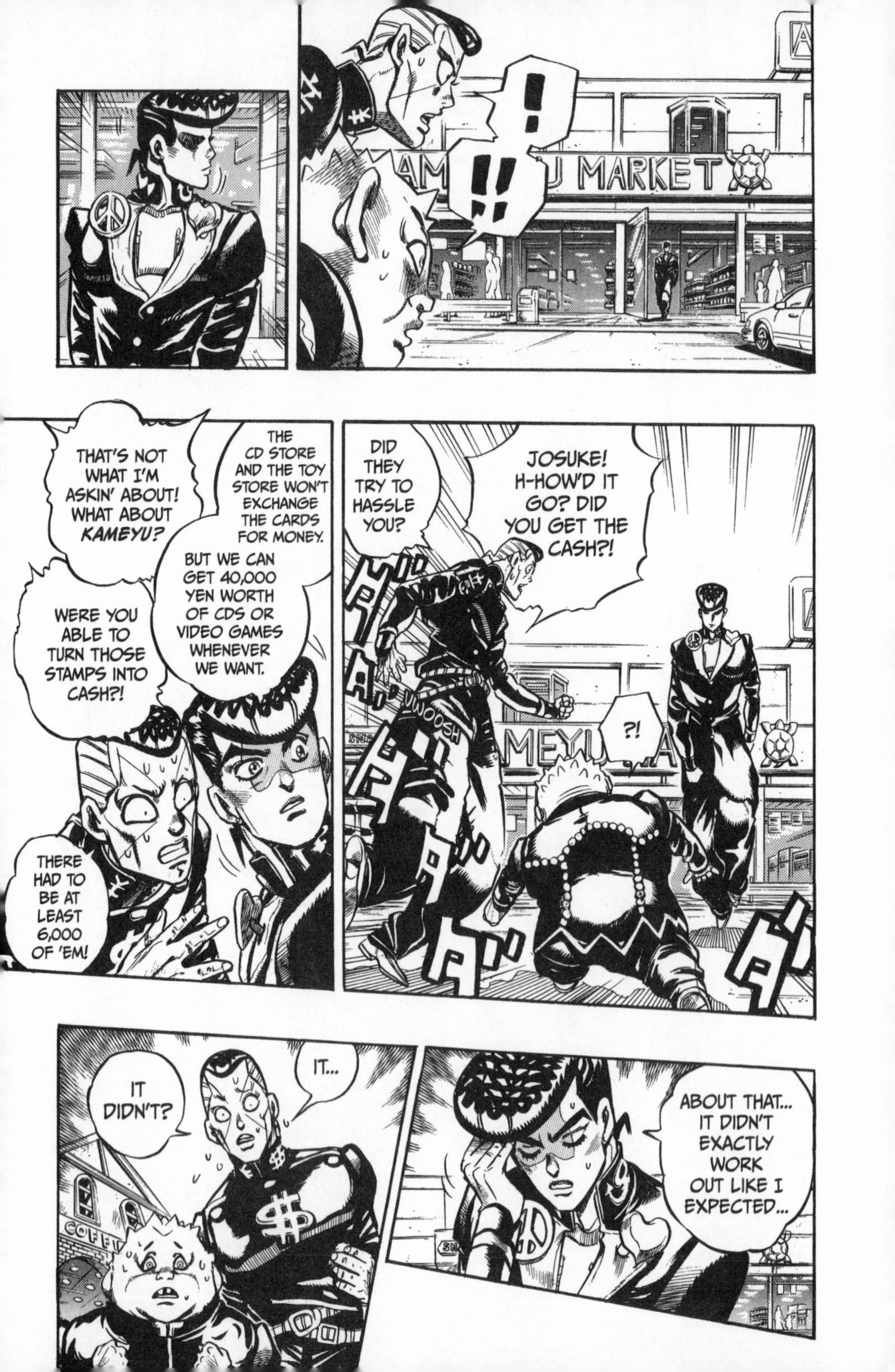
!
!!
JOSUKE! H-HOW'D IT GO? DID YOU GET THE CASH?!
DID THEY TRY TO HASSLE YOU?
VWOOSH
?!
THE CD STORE AND THE TOY STORE WON'T EXCHANGE THE CARDS FOR MONEY.
BUT WE CAN GET 40,000 YEN WORTH OF CDS OR VIDEO GAMES WHENEVER WE WANT.
THAT'S NOT WHAT I'M ASKIN' ABOUT! WHAT ABOUT *KAMEYU?*
WERE YOU ABLE TO TURN THOSE STAMPS INTO CASH?!
THERE HAD TO BE AT LEAST 6,000 OF 'EM!
ABOUT THAT... IT DIDN'T EXACTLY WORK OUT LIKE I EXPECTED...
IT...
IT DIDN'T?

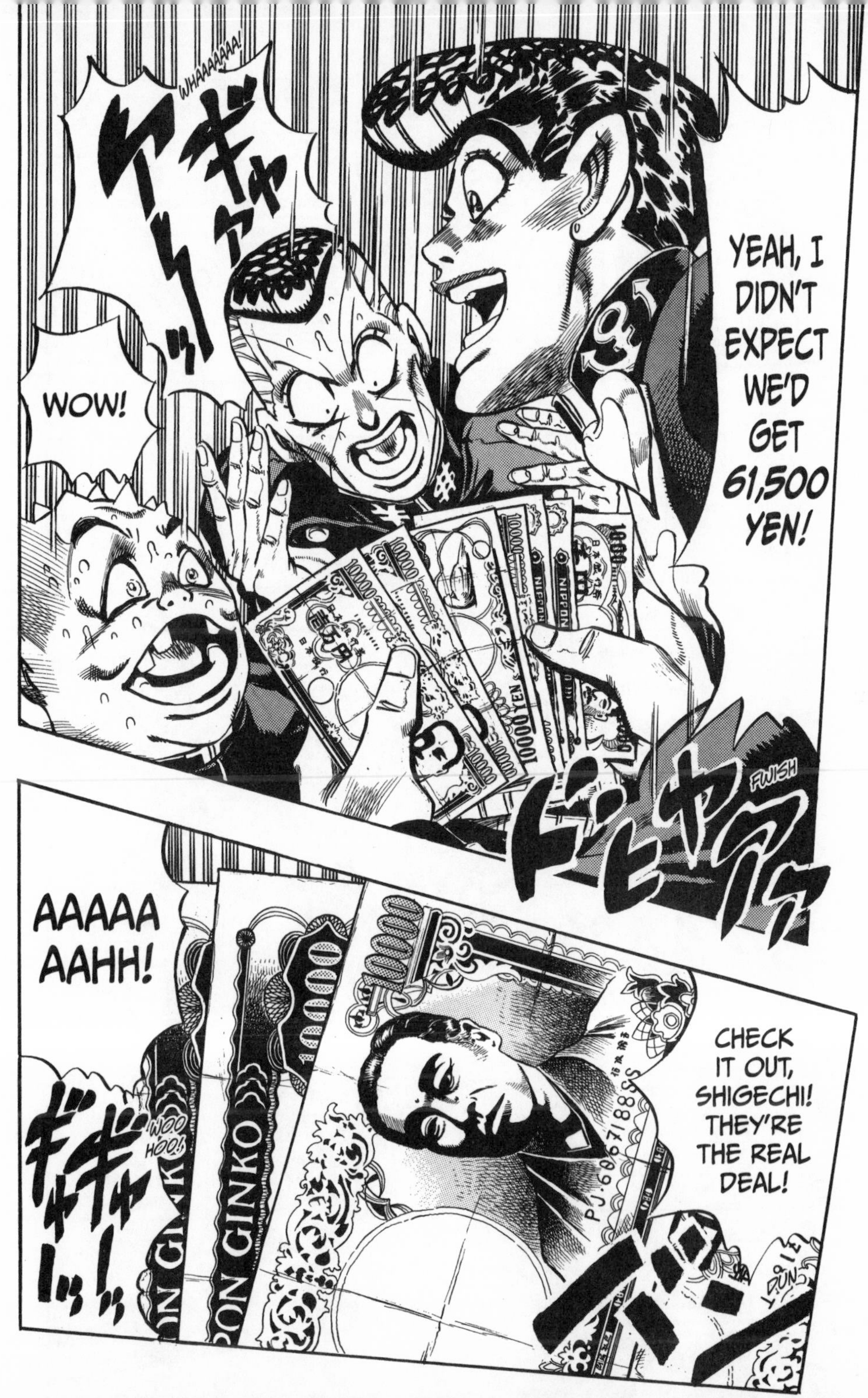
YEAH, I DIDN'T EXPECT WE'D GET 61,500 YEN!
WHAAAAAAA!
WOW!
FWISH
CHECK IT OUT, SHIGECHI! THEY'RE THE REAL DEAL!
DUN
AAAAAAAHH!
WOO HOO!

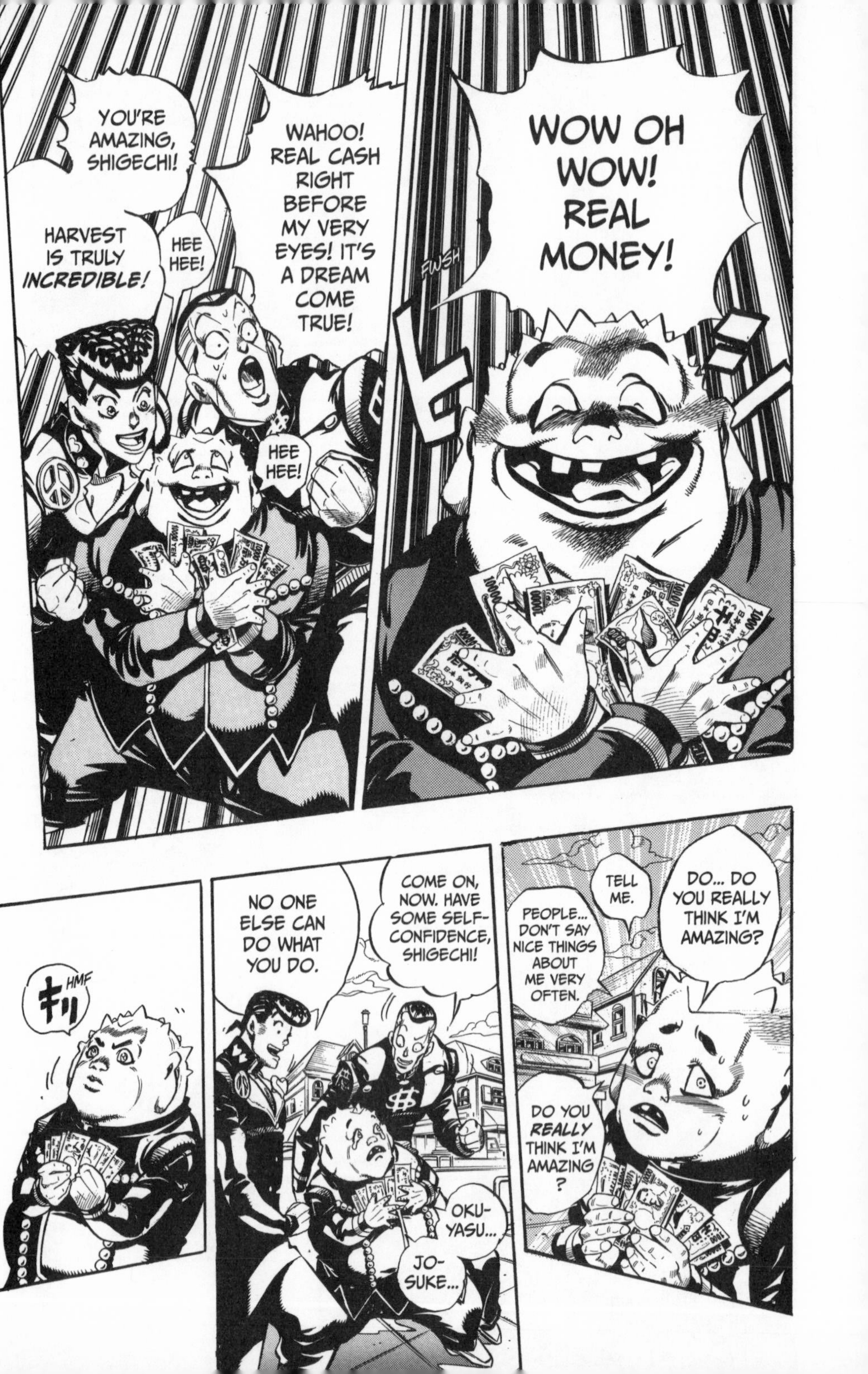
WOW OH WOW! REAL MONEY!
FWSH
WAHOO! REAL CASH RIGHT BEFORE MY VERY EYES! IT'S A DREAM COME TRUE!
YOU'RE AMAZING, SHIGECHI!
HEE HEE!
HARVEST IS TRULY INCREDIBLE!
HEE HEE!
DO... DO YOU REALLY THINK I'M AMAZING?
TELL ME.
PEOPLE... DON'T SAY NICE THINGS ABOUT ME VERY OFTEN.
DO YOU REALLY THINK I'M AMAZING?
COME ON, NOW. HAVE SOME SELF-CONFIDENCE, SHIGECHI!
NO ONE ELSE CAN DO WHAT YOU DO.
OKU-YASU...
JO-SUKE...
キリ
HMF

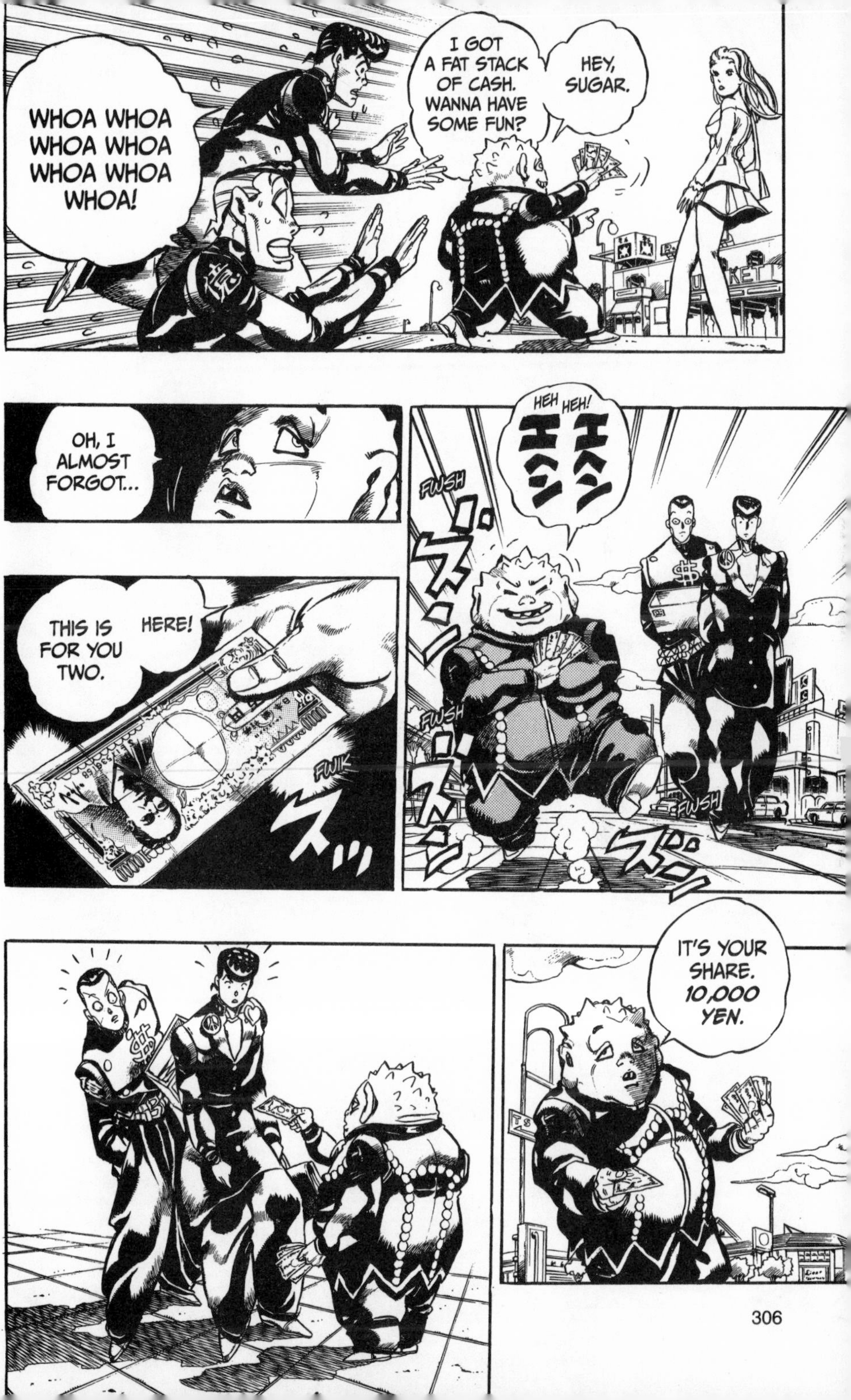
HEY, SUGAR.
I GOT A FAT STACK OF CASH. WANNA HAVE SOME FUN?
WHOA WHOA WHOA WHOA WHOA WHOA WHOA!
HEH HEH!
FWSH
FWSH
FWSH
OH, I ALMOST FORGOT...
HERE!
THIS IS FOR YOU TWO.
FWIK
IT'S YOUR SHARE. 10,000 YEN.

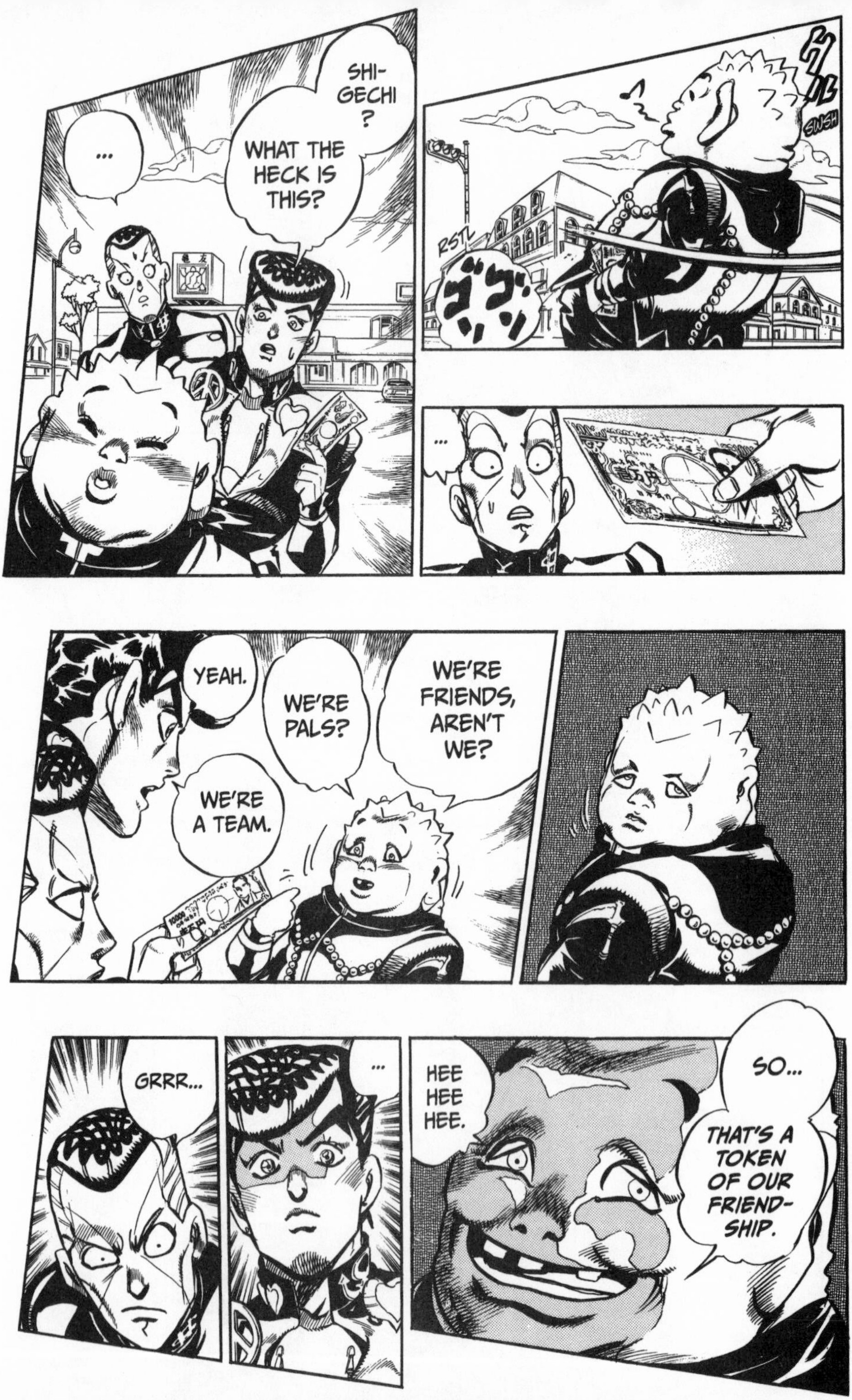
SWSH
RSTL
...
SHI-GECHI?
WHAT THE HECK IS THIS?
...
WE'RE FRIENDS, AREN'T WE?
WE'RE PALS?
YEAH.
WE'RE A TEAM.
SO...
THAT'S A TOKEN OF OUR FRIENDSHIP.
HEE HEE HEE.
...
GRRR...

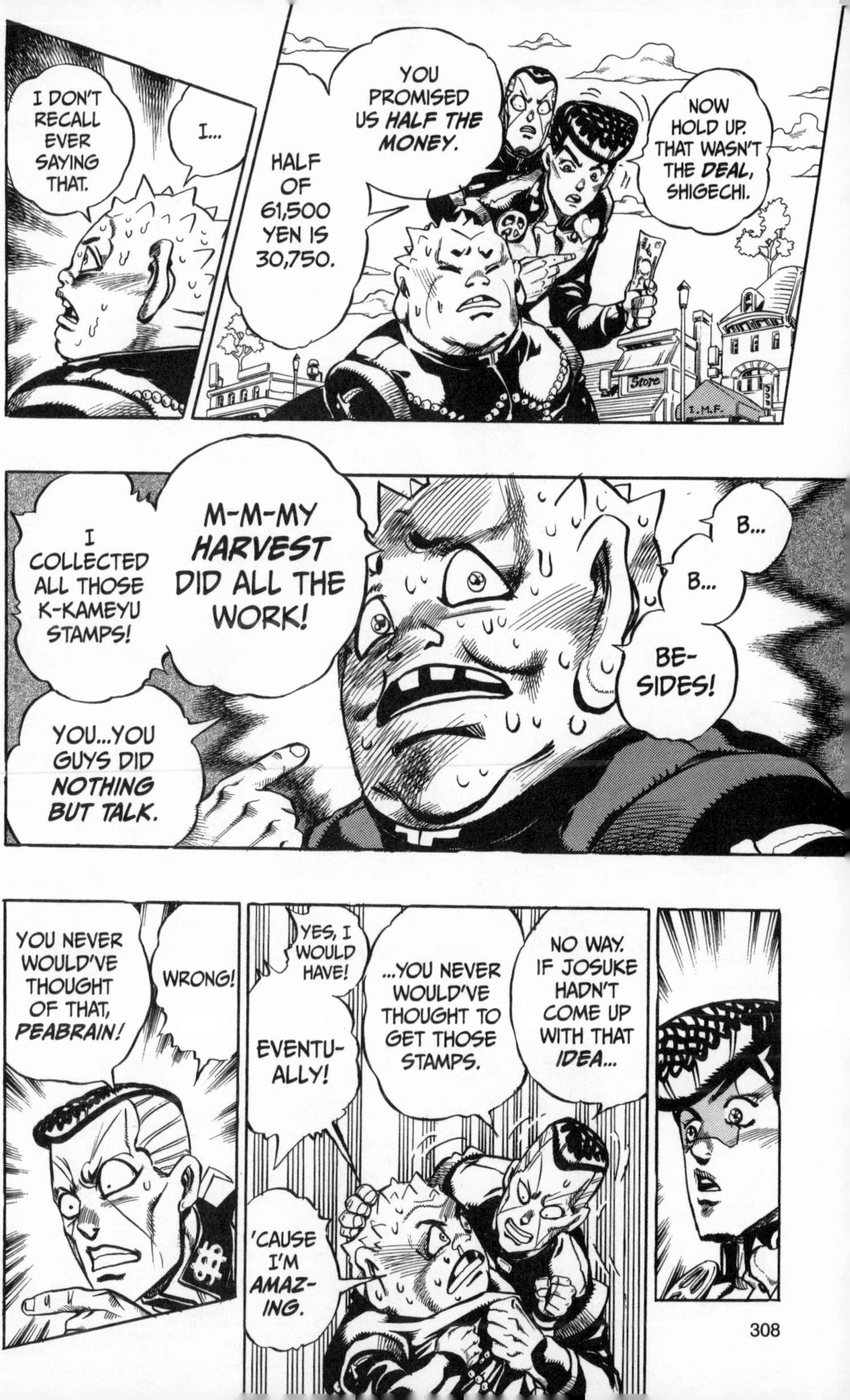
NOW HOLD UP. THAT WASN'T THE *DEAL*, SHIGECHI.
YOU PROMISED US *HALF THE MONEY*.
HALF OF 61,500 YEN IS 30,750.
Store
I.M.F.
I...
I DON'T RECALL EVER SAYING THAT.
B...
B...
BE-SIDES!
M-M-MY *HARVEST* DID ALL THE WORK!
I COLLECTED ALL THOSE K-KAMEYU STAMPS!
YOU...YOU GUYS DID *NOTHING BUT TALK*.
NO WAY. IF JOSUKE HADN'T COME UP WITH THAT *IDEA*...
...YOU NEVER WOULD'VE THOUGHT TO GET THOSE STAMPS.
YES, I WOULD HAVE!
EVENTU-ALLY!
'CAUSE I'M *AMAZ-ING*.
WRONG!
YOU NEVER WOULD'VE THOUGHT OF THAT, *PEABRAIN*!

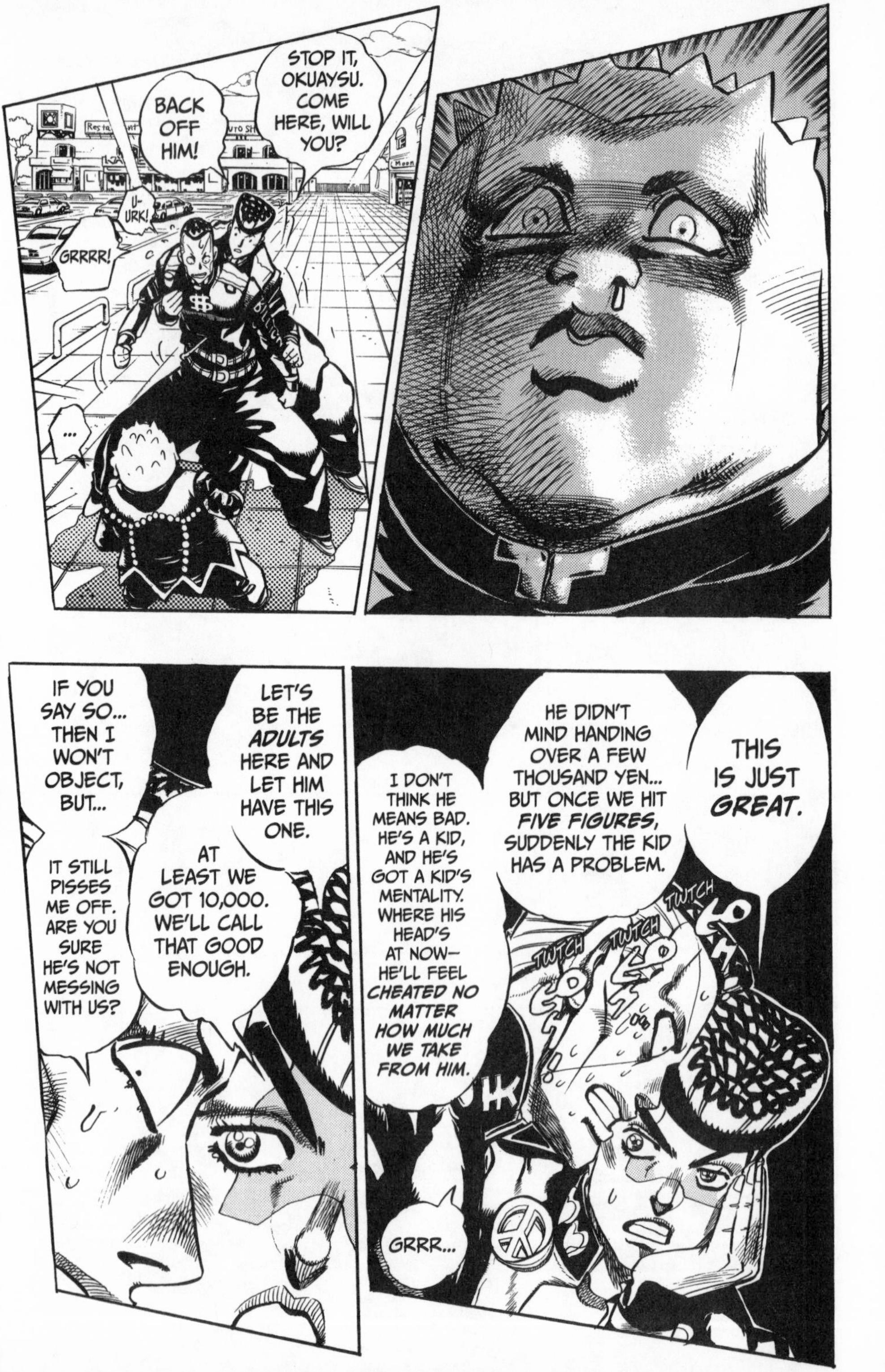
STOP IT, OKUAYSU. COME HERE, WILL YOU?
BACK OFF HIM!
U-URK!
GRRRR!
...
THIS IS JUST GREAT.
HE DIDN'T MIND HANDING OVER A FEW THOUSAND YEN... BUT ONCE WE HIT FIVE FIGURES, SUDDENLY THE KID HAS A PROBLEM.
I DON'T THINK HE MEANS BAD. HE'S A KID, AND HE'S GOT A KID'S MENTALITY. WHERE HIS HEAD'S AT NOW— HE'LL FEEL CHEATED NO MATTER HOW MUCH WE TAKE FROM HIM.
TWITCH
TWITCH
TWITCH
GRRR...
LET'S BE THE ADULTS HERE AND LET HIM HAVE THIS ONE.
IF YOU SAY SO... THEN I WON'T OBJECT, BUT...
AT LEAST WE GOT 10,000. WE'LL CALL THAT GOOD ENOUGH.
IT STILL PISSES ME OFF. ARE YOU SURE HE'S NOT MESSING WITH US?

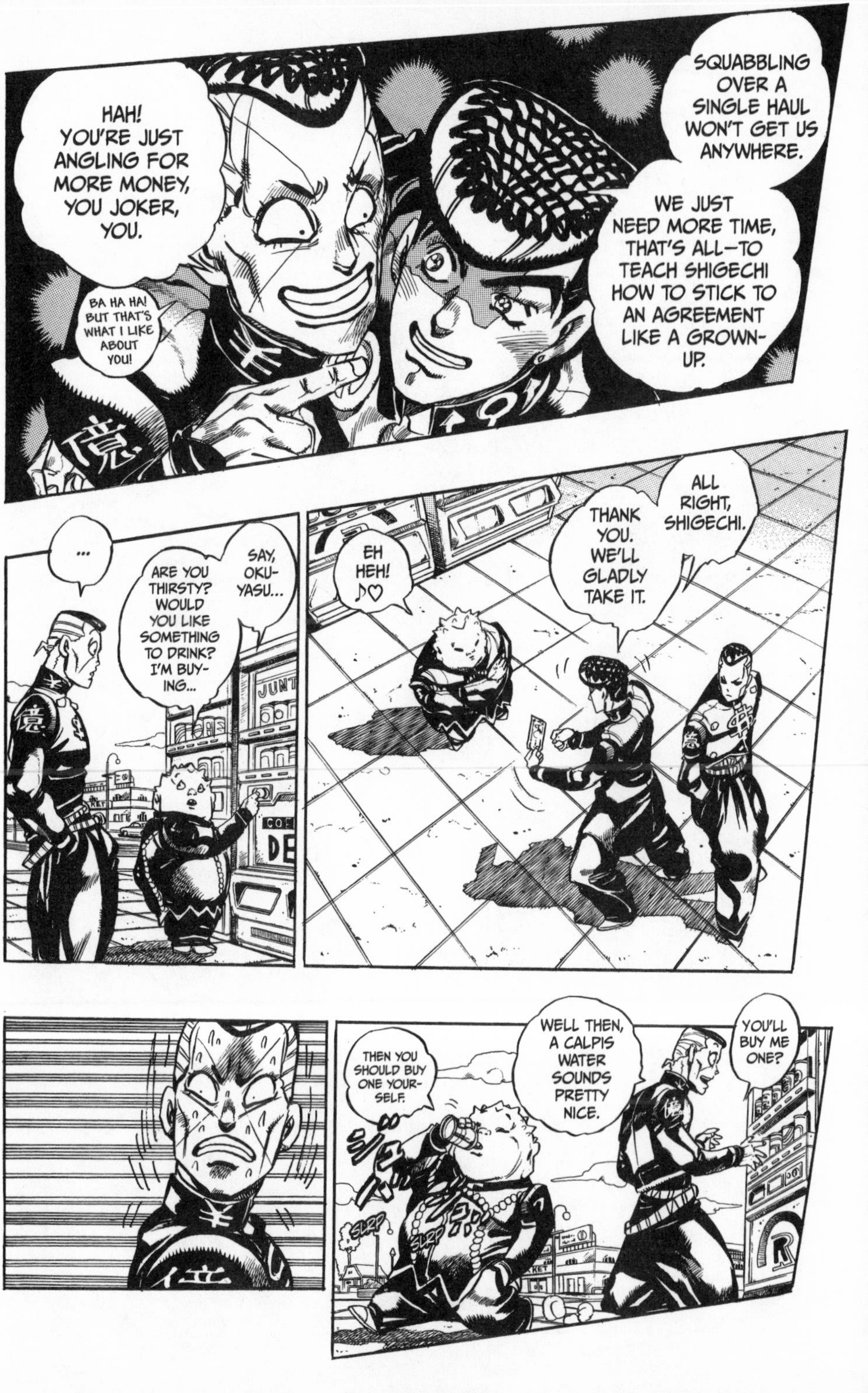
SQUABBLING OVER A SINGLE HAUL WON'T GET US ANYWHERE.
WE JUST NEED MORE TIME, THAT'S ALL—TO TEACH SHIGECHI HOW TO STICK TO AN AGREEMENT LIKE A GROWN-UP.
HAH! YOU'RE JUST ANGLING FOR MORE MONEY, YOU JOKER, YOU.
BA HA HA! BUT THAT'S WHAT I LIKE ABOUT YOU!
ALL RIGHT, SHIGECHI.
THANK YOU. WE'LL GLADLY TAKE IT.
EH HEH! ♪♡
SAY, OKU-YASU...
ARE YOU THIRSTY? WOULD YOU LIKE SOMETHING TO DRINK? I'M BUYING...
...
YOU'LL BUY ME ONE?
WELL THEN, A CALPIS WATER SOUNDS PRETTY NICE.
THEN YOU SHOULD BUY ONE YOURSELF.
SLRP
SLRP

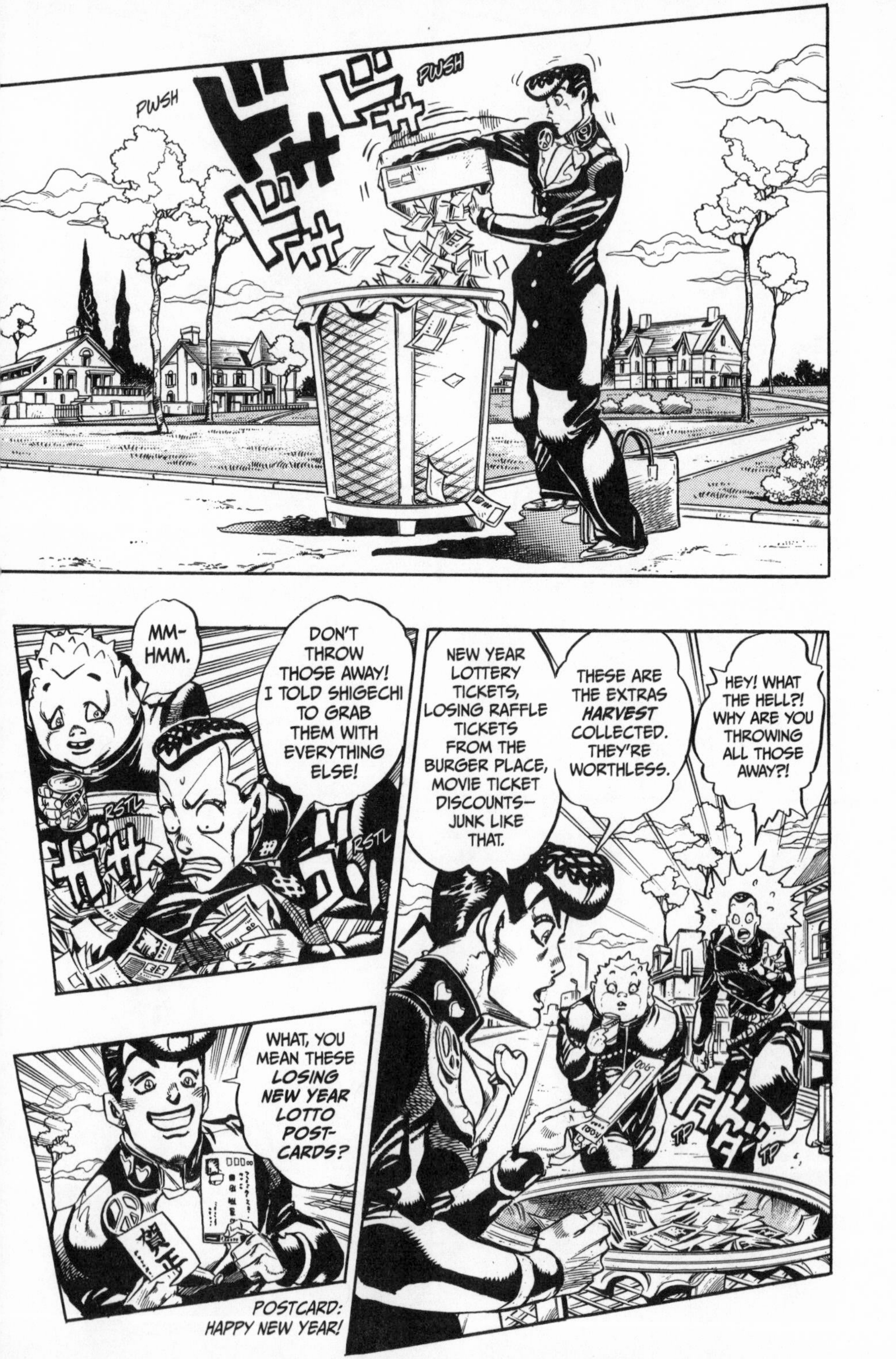
PWSH
PWSH
HEY! WHAT THE HELL?! WHY ARE YOU THROWING ALL THOSE AWAY?!
THESE ARE THE EXTRAS *HARVEST* COLLECTED. THEY'RE WORTHLESS.
NEW YEAR LOTTERY TICKETS, LOSING RAFFLE TICKETS FROM THE BURGER PLACE, MOVIE TICKET DISCOUNTS—JUNK LIKE THAT.
TP
TP
DON'T THROW THOSE AWAY! I TOLD SHIGECHI TO GRAB THEM WITH EVERYTHING ELSE!
MM-HMM.
RSTL
RSTL
WHAT, YOU MEAN THESE *LOSING NEW YEAR LOTTO* POST-CARDS?

POSTCARD: HAPPY NEW YEAR!

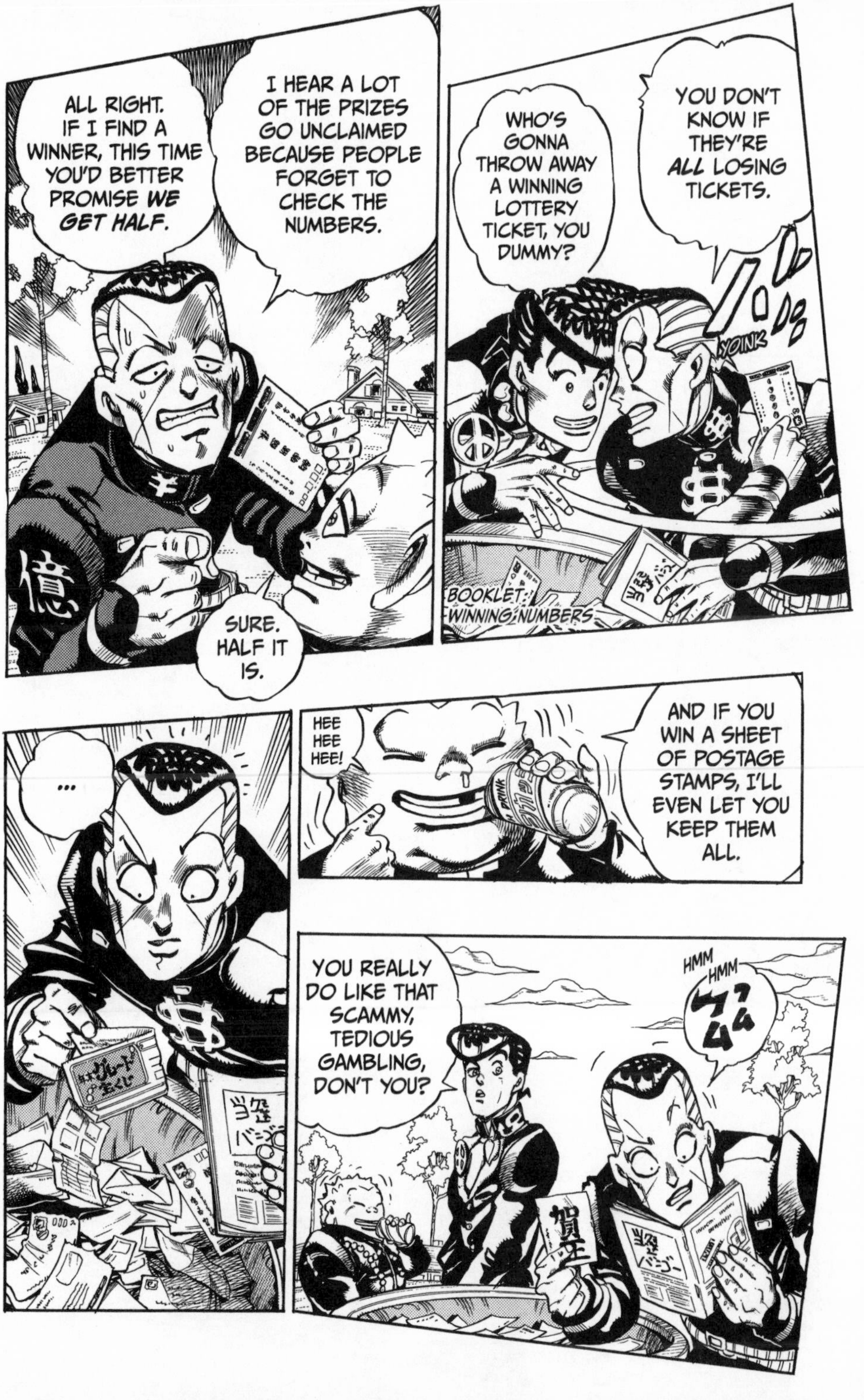
YOU DON'T KNOW IF THEY'RE ALL LOSING TICKETS.
WHO'S GONNA THROW AWAY A WINNING LOTTERY TICKET, YOU DUMMY?
YOINK
BOOKLET: WINNING NUMBERS
I HEAR A LOT OF THE PRIZES GO UNCLAIMED BECAUSE PEOPLE FORGET TO CHECK THE NUMBERS.
ALL RIGHT. IF I FIND A WINNER, THIS TIME YOU'D BETTER PROMISE WE GET HALF.
SURE. HALF IT IS.
AND IF YOU WIN A SHEET OF POSTAGE STAMPS, I'LL EVEN LET YOU KEEP THEM ALL.
HEE HEE HEE!
HMM HMM
YOU REALLY DO LIKE THAT SCAMMY, TEDIOUS GAMBLING, DON'T YOU?
...

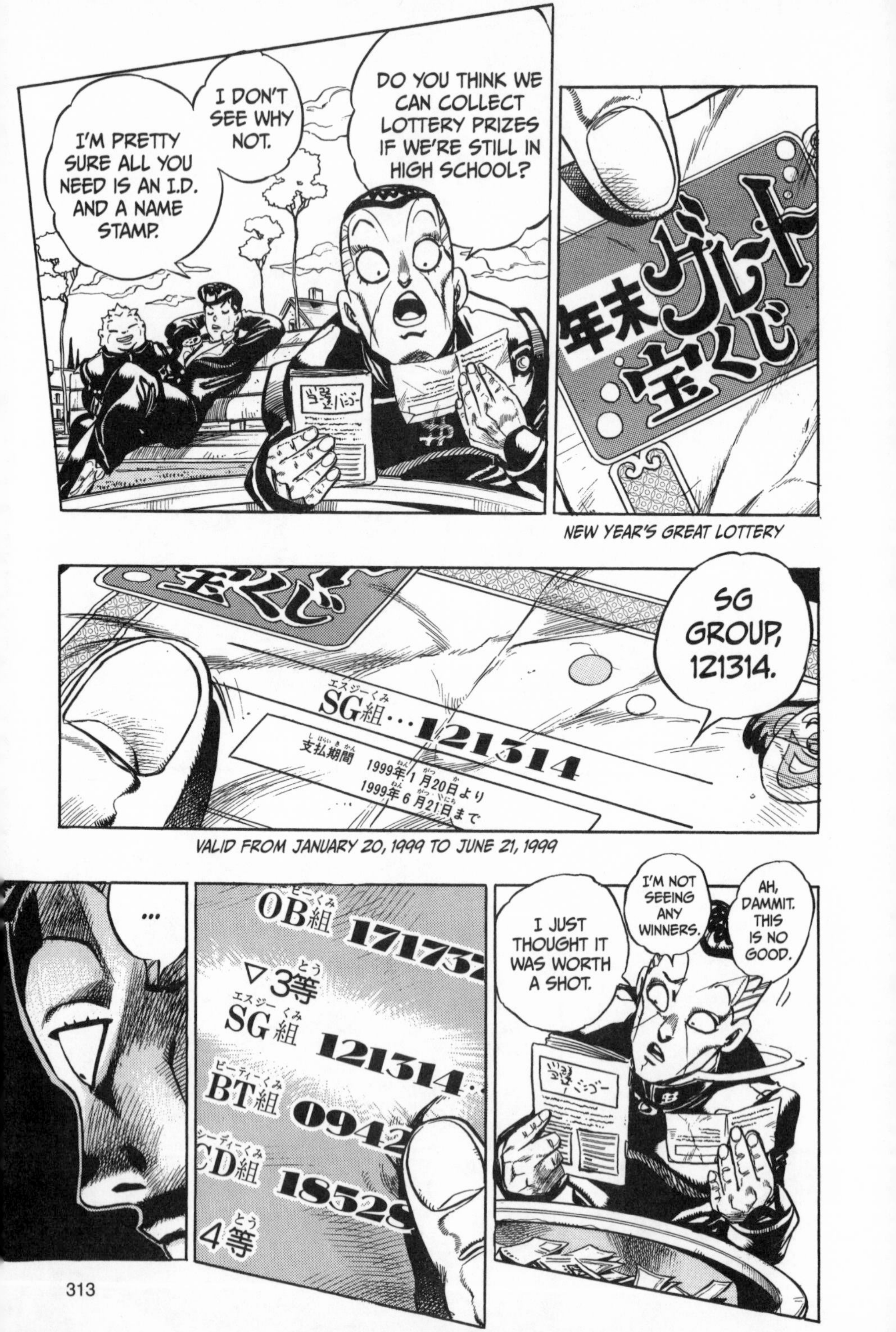

年末
宝くじ
NEW YEAR'S GREAT LOTTERY
DO YOU THINK WE CAN COLLECT LOTTERY PRIZES IF WE'RE STILL IN HIGH SCHOOL?
I DON'T SEE WHY NOT.
I'M PRETTY SURE ALL YOU NEED IS AN I.D. AND A NAME STAMP.
SG GROUP, 121314.
SG組…121314
支払期間 1999年1月20日より 1999年6月21日まで
VALID FROM JANUARY 20, 1999 TO JUNE 21, 1999
AH, DAMMIT. THIS IS NO GOOD.
I'M NOT SEEING ANY WINNERS.
I JUST THOUGHT IT WAS WORTH A SHOT.
OB組 17173
▽3等
SG組 121314
BT組 0942
CD組 1852
4等
...

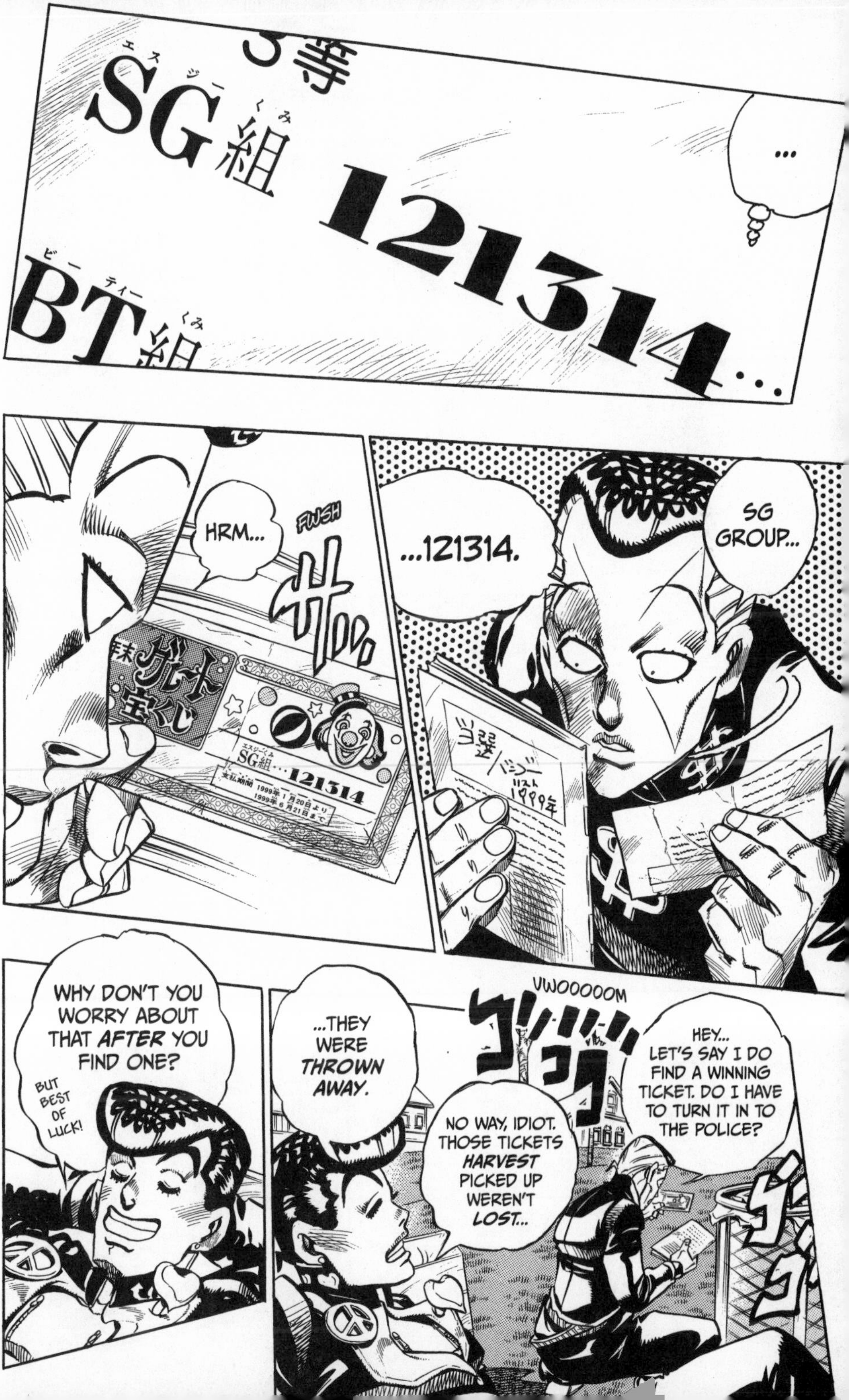
...
3等
SG組
121314...
BT組
SG GROUP...
...121314.
FWSH
HRM...
SG組…121314
支払期間 1999年 1月20日より 1999年 6月21日まで
HEY... LET'S SAY I DO FIND A WINNING TICKET. DO I HAVE TO TURN IT IN TO THE POLICE?
VWOOOOOM
NO WAY, IDIOT. THOSE TICKETS *HARVEST* PICKED UP WEREN'T *LOST*...
...THEY WERE *THROWN AWAY.*
WHY DON'T YOU WORRY ABOUT THAT *AFTER* YOU FIND ONE?
BUT BEST OF LUCK!

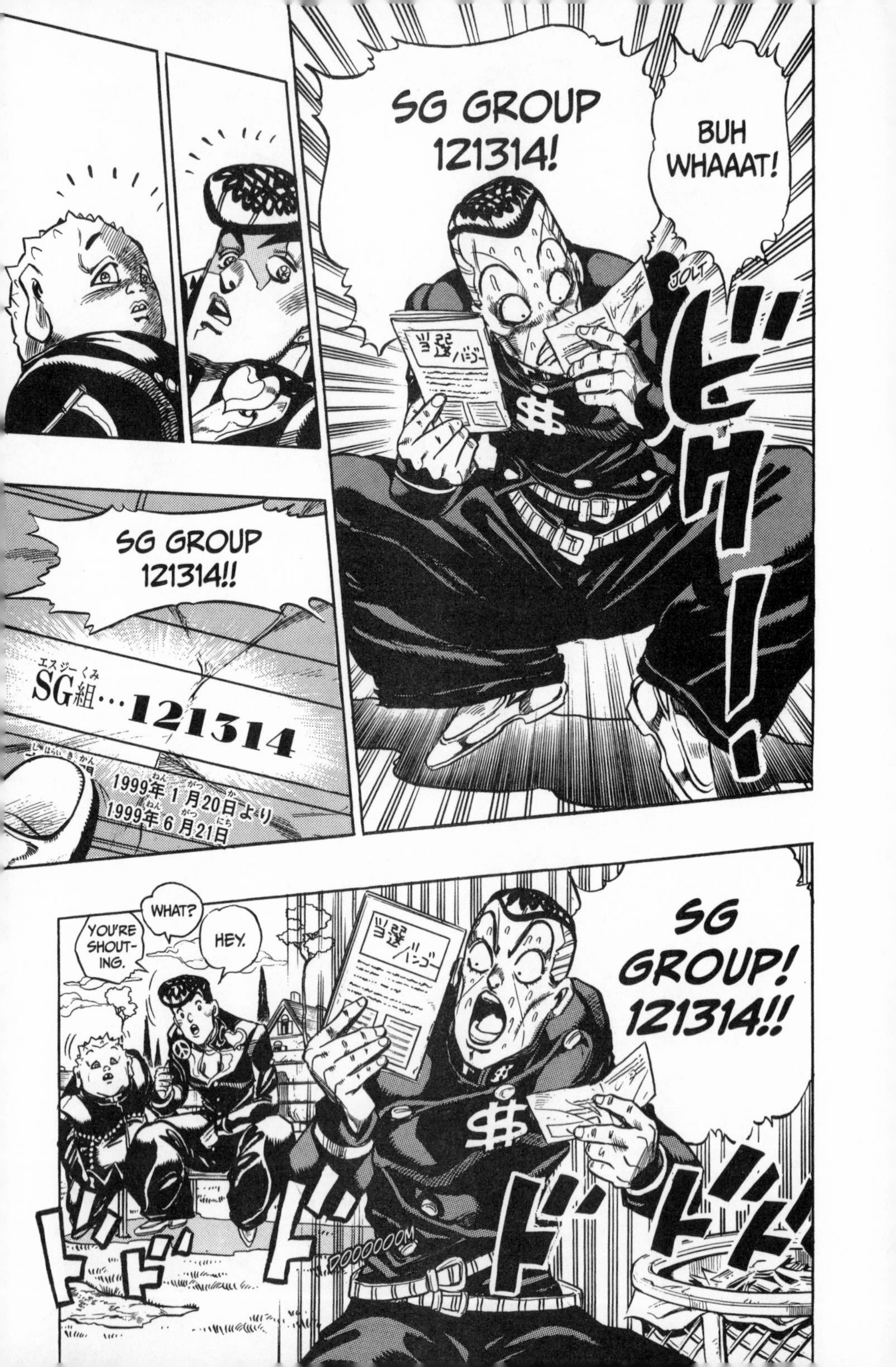
SG GROUP 121314!
BUH WHAAAT!
JOLT
ビクーッ!
SG GROUP 121314!!
SG組…121314
1999年1月20日より
1999年6月21日
SG GROUP! 121314!!
HEY.
WHAT?
YOU'RE SHOUT-ING.
ドドドドドド
DOOOOOOM

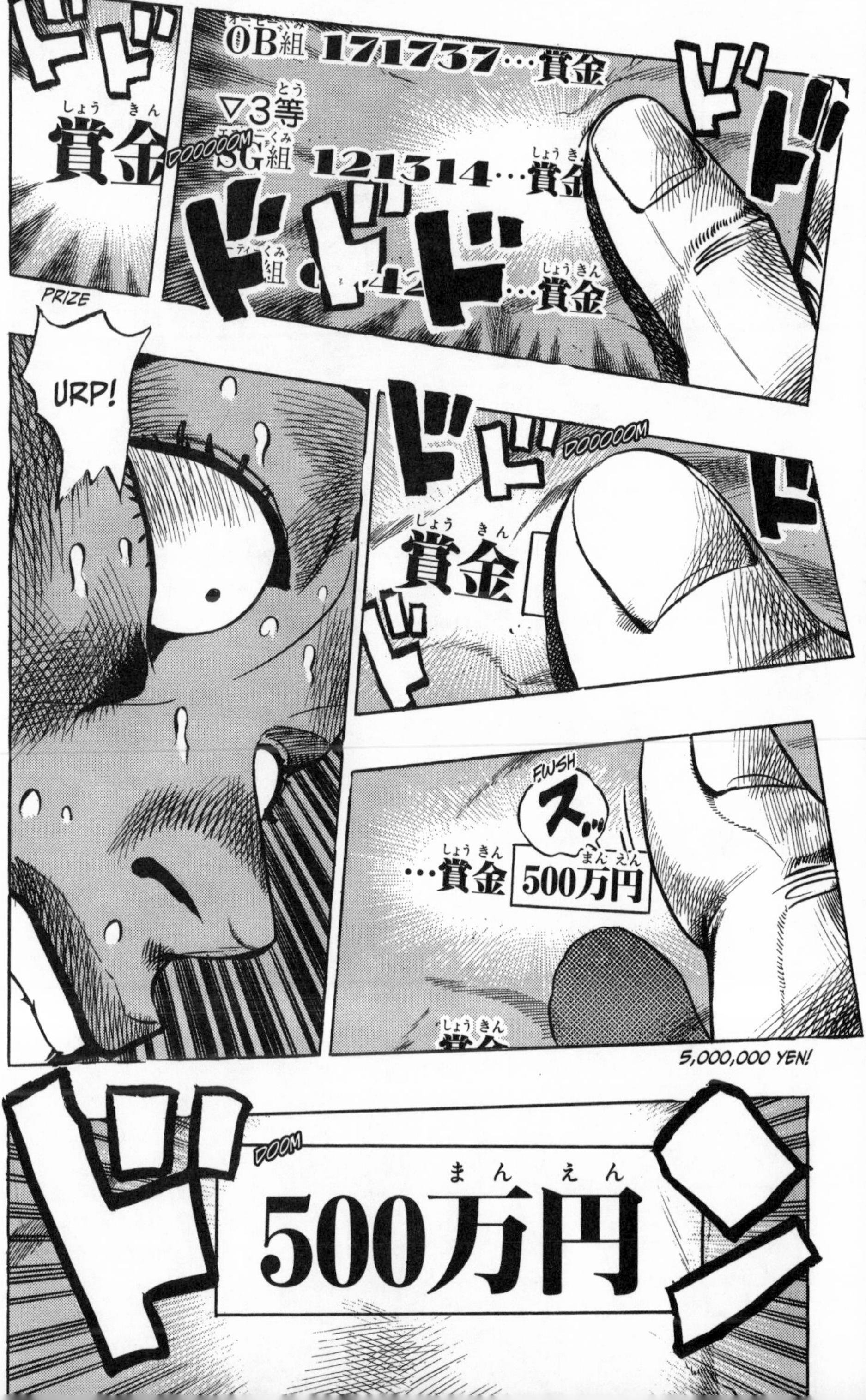
OB組 171737…賞金
▽3等
SG組 121314…賞金
…賞金
賞金
DOOOOOOM
PRIZE
DOOOOOM
賞金
FWSH
ス
…賞金 500万円
5,000,000 YEN!
URP!
DOOM
500万円

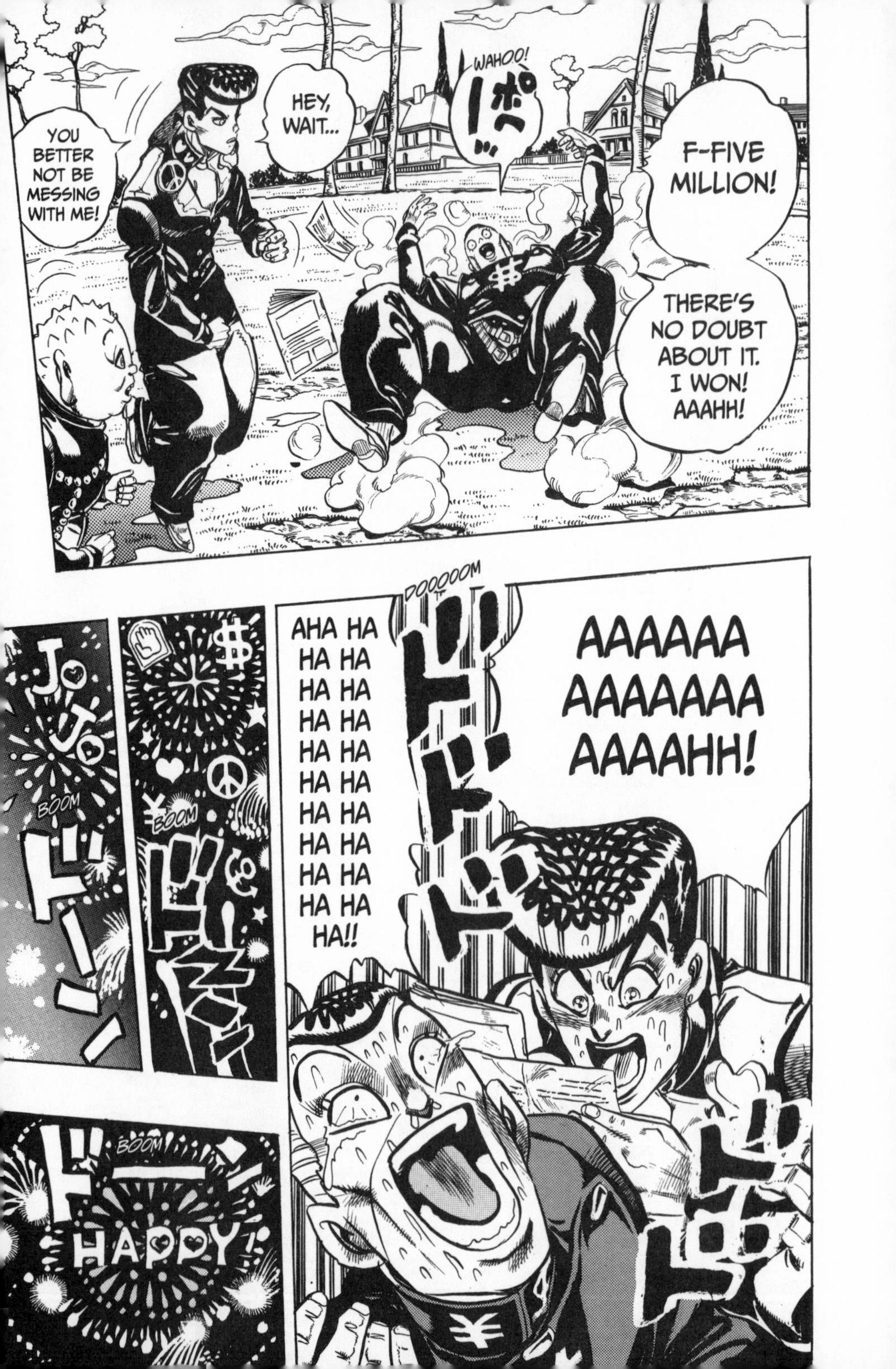
F-FIVE MILLION!
THERE'S NO DOUBT ABOUT IT. I WON! AAAHH!
WAHOO!
HEY, WAIT...
YOU BETTER NOT BE MESSING WITH ME!
AAAAAA AAAAAAA AAAAHH!
DOOOOOM
AHA HA HA HA HA HA HA HA HA HA HA HA HA HA HA HA HA HA HA HA HA!!
BOOM
JOJO
BOOM
BOOM
HAPPY!

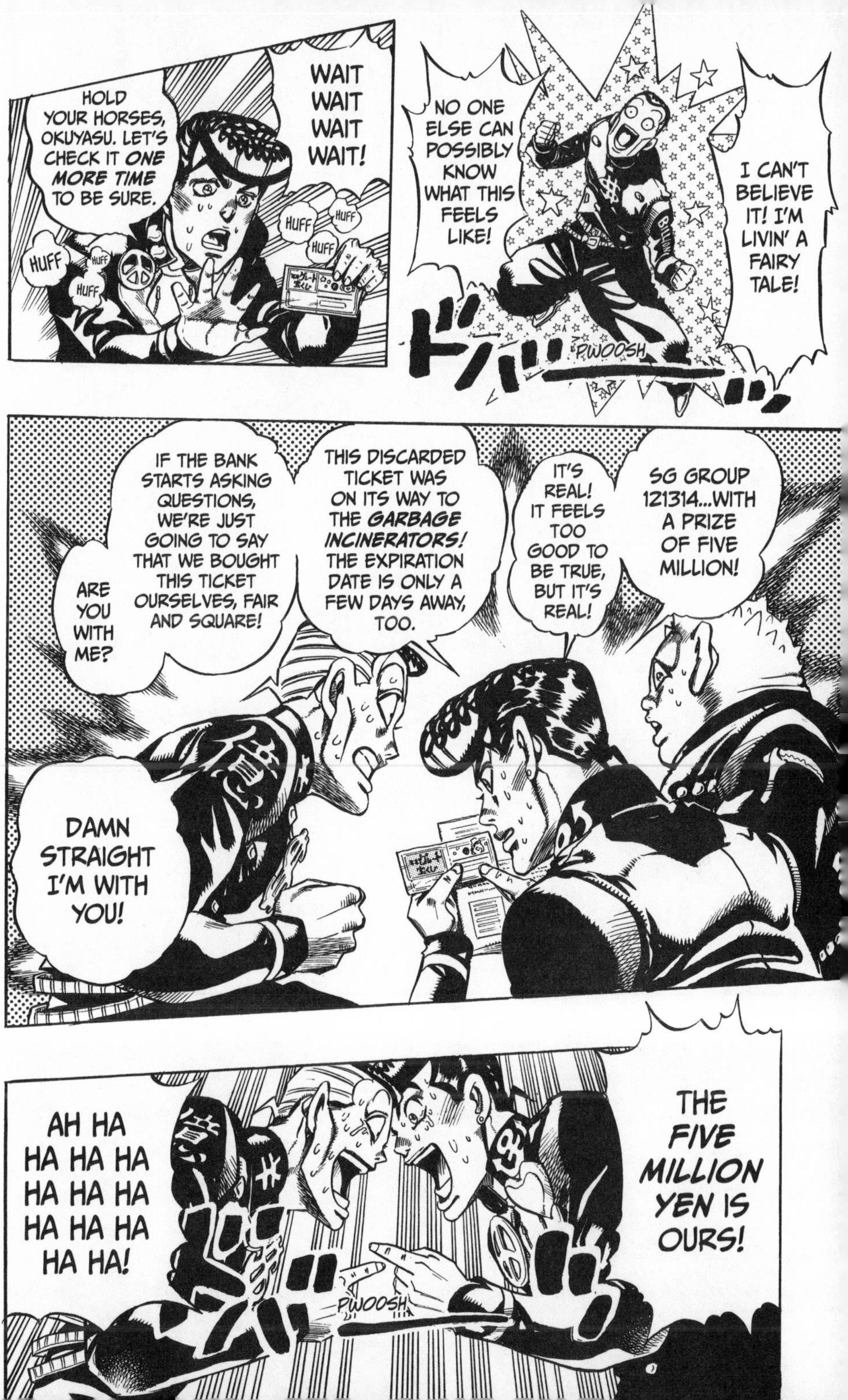
I CAN'T BELIEVE IT! I'M LIVIN' A FAIRY TALE!
NO ONE ELSE CAN POSSIBLY KNOW WHAT THIS FEELS LIKE!
PWOOSH
WAIT WAIT WAIT WAIT!
HOLD YOUR HORSES, OKUYASU. LET'S CHECK IT *ONE MORE TIME* TO BE SURE.
HUFF HUFF HUFF HUFF HUFF HUFF
SG GROUP 121314...WITH A PRIZE OF FIVE MILLION!
IT'S REAL! IT FEELS TOO GOOD TO BE TRUE, BUT IT'S REAL!
THIS DISCARDED TICKET WAS ON ITS WAY TO THE *GARBAGE INCINERATORS!* THE EXPIRATION DATE IS ONLY A FEW DAYS AWAY, TOO.
IF THE BANK STARTS ASKING QUESTIONS, WE'RE JUST GOING TO SAY THAT WE BOUGHT THIS TICKET OURSELVES, FAIR AND SQUARE!
ARE YOU WITH ME?
DAMN STRAIGHT I'M WITH YOU!
THE *FIVE MILLION YEN* IS OURS!
AH HA HA HA HA HA HA HA HA HA HA HA HA HA HA!
PWOOSH

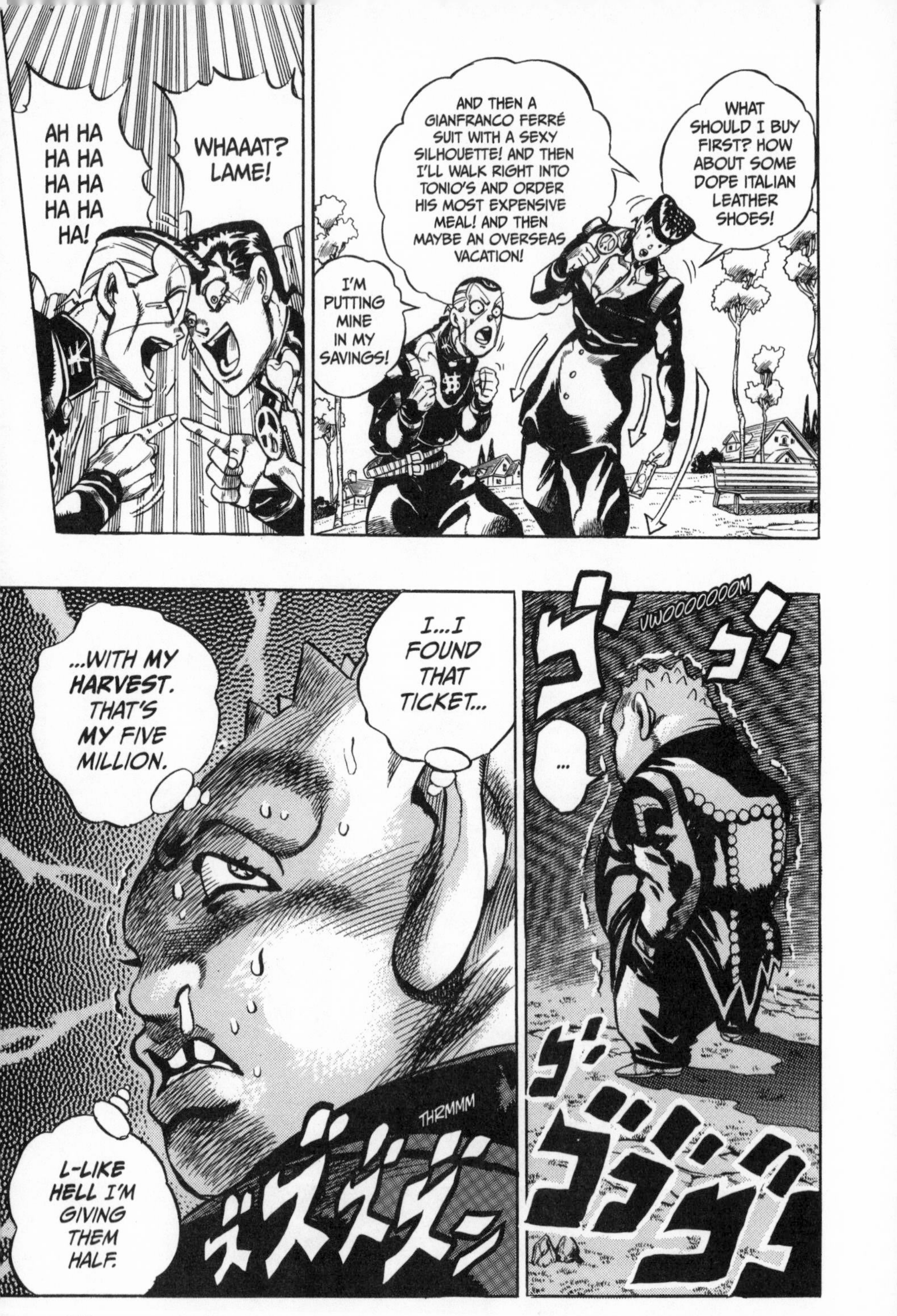
WHAT SHOULD I BUY FIRST? HOW ABOUT SOME DOPE ITALIAN LEATHER SHOES!
AND THEN A GIANFRANCO FERRÉ SUIT WITH A SEXY SILHOUETTE! AND THEN I'LL WALK RIGHT INTO TONIO'S AND ORDER HIS MOST EXPENSIVE MEAL! AND THEN MAYBE AN OVERSEAS VACATION!
I'M PUTTING MINE IN MY SAVINGS!
WHAAAT? LAME!
AH HA HA HA HA HA HA HA HA HA!
VWOOOOOOOM
...
I...I FOUND THAT TICKET...
...WITH MY HARVEST. THAT'S MY FIVE MILLION.
THRMMM
L-LIKE HELL I'M GIVING THEM HALF.

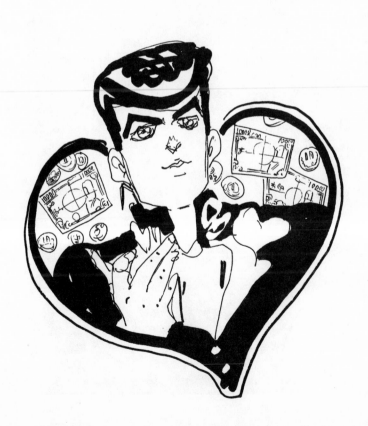

CHAPTER 73

SHIGECHI'S HARVEST, PART 4

BRAIN SALAD
BANK
BANK
BUDOGAOKA BANK

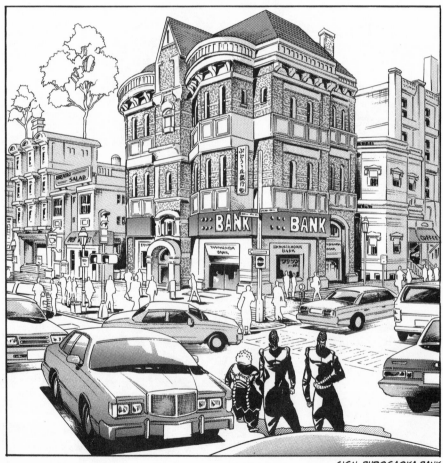

SIGN: BUDOGAOKA BANK

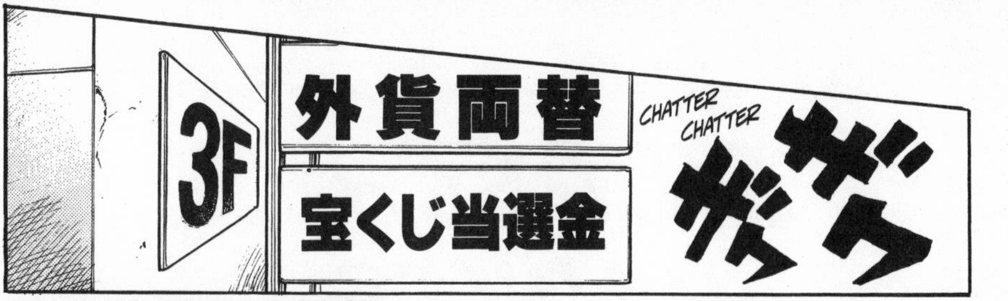
3F
外貨両替
宝くじ当選金
CHATTER CHATTER
ザワザワ

SIGN: FOREIGN CURRENCY EXCHANGE
LOTTERY PRIZE CLAIMS

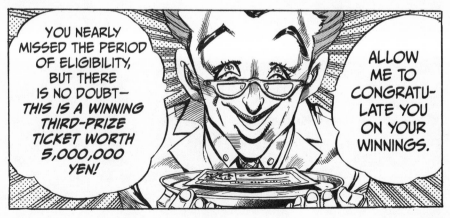

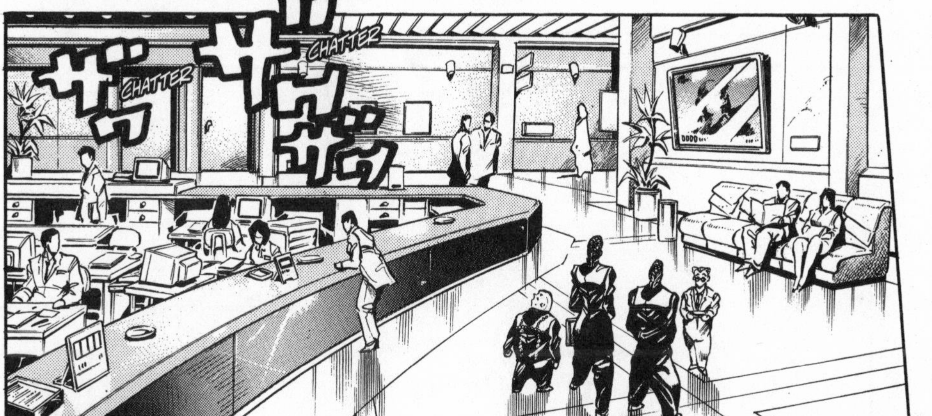
ザワ
CHATTER
ザワ
CHATTER
ザワ

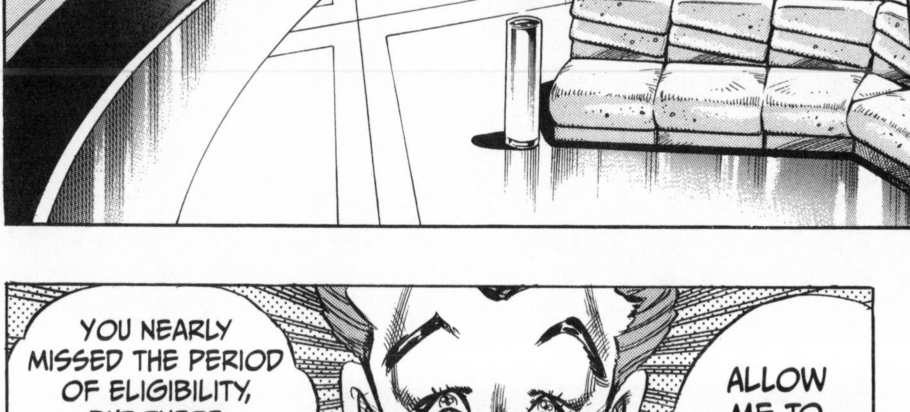
ALLOW ME TO CONGRATULATE YOU ON YOUR WINNINGS.
YOU NEARLY MISSED THE PERIOD OF ELIGIBILITY, BUT THERE IS NO DOUBT— THIS IS A WINNING THIRD-PRIZE TICKET WORTH 5,000,000 YEN!

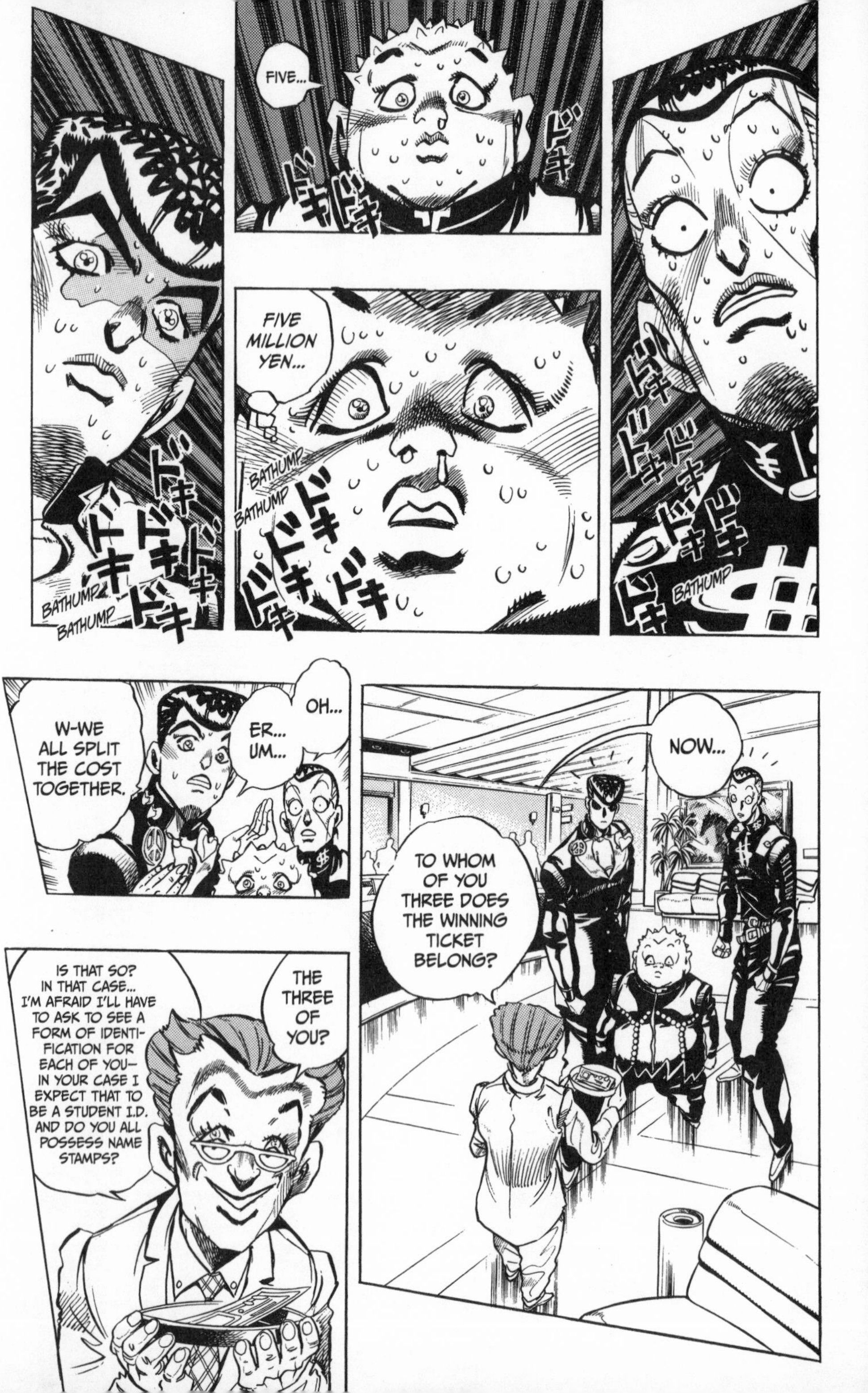
ドキドキ
BATHUMP
FIVE...
ドキドキ
FIVE MILLION YEN...
BATHUMP
BATHUMP
ドキドキ
BATHUMP
BATHUMP
NOW...
TO WHOM OF YOU THREE DOES THE WINNING TICKET BELONG?
OH...
ER... UM...
W-WE ALL SPLIT THE COST TOGETHER.
THE THREE OF YOU?
IS THAT SO? IN THAT CASE... I'M AFRAID I'LL HAVE TO ASK TO SEE A FORM OF IDENTIFICATION FOR EACH OF YOU— IN YOUR CASE I EXPECT THAT TO BE A STUDENT I.D. AND DO YOU ALL POSSESS NAME STAMPS?

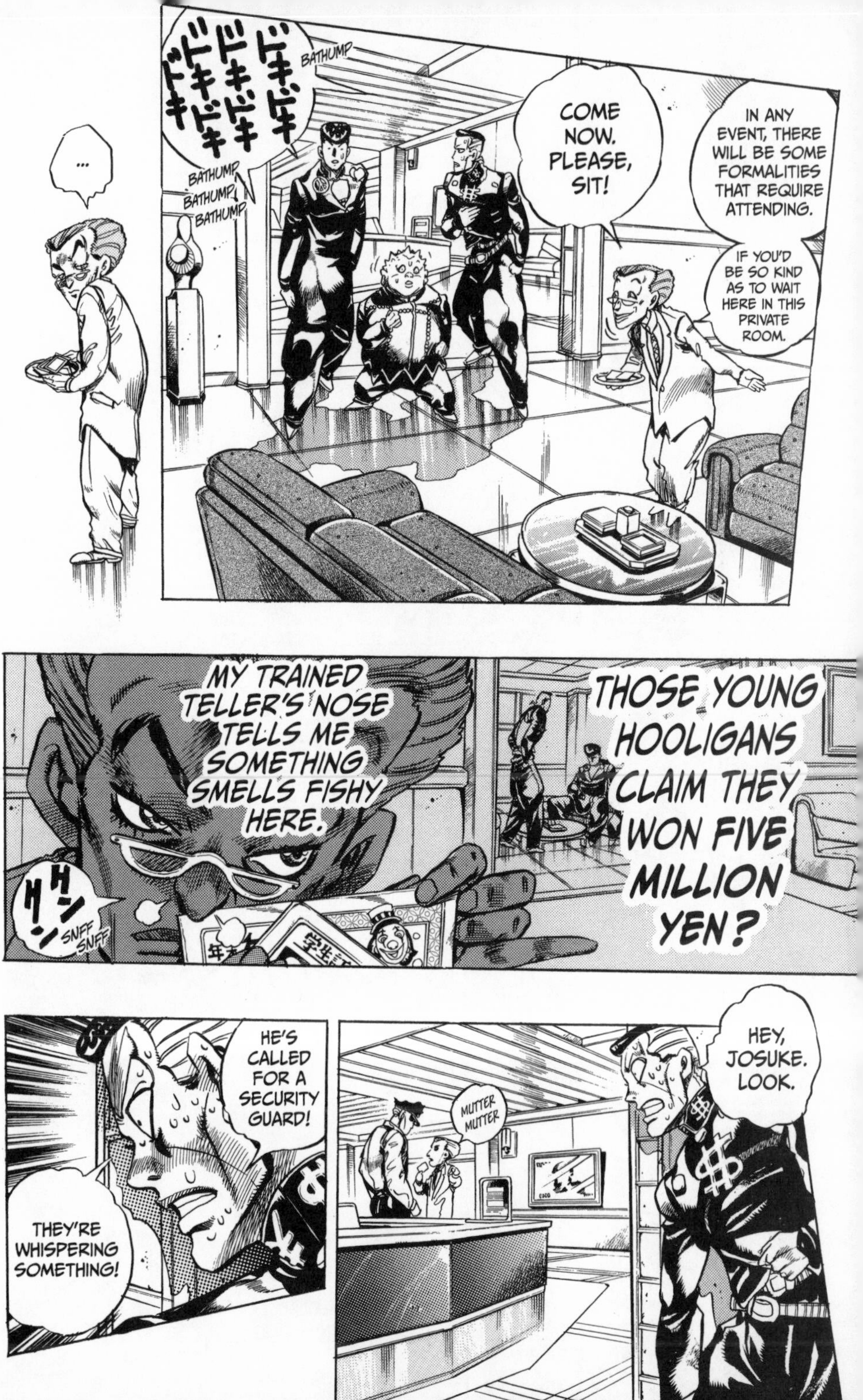

IN ANY EVENT, THERE WILL BE SOME FORMALITIES THAT REQUIRE ATTENDING.
IF YOU'D BE SO KIND AS TO WAIT HERE IN THIS PRIVATE ROOM.
COME NOW. PLEASE, SIT!
ドキドキドキドキドキドキドキドキ
BATHUMP
BATHUMP BATHUMP BATHUMP
...
THOSE YOUNG HOOLIGANS CLAIM THEY WON FIVE MILLION YEN?
MY TRAINED TELLER'S NOSE TELLS ME SOMETHING SMELLS FISHY HERE.
フンフン
SNFF SNFF
HEY, JOSUKE. LOOK.
MUTTER MUTTER
HE'S CALLED FOR A SECURITY GUARD!
THEY'RE WHISPERING SOMETHING!

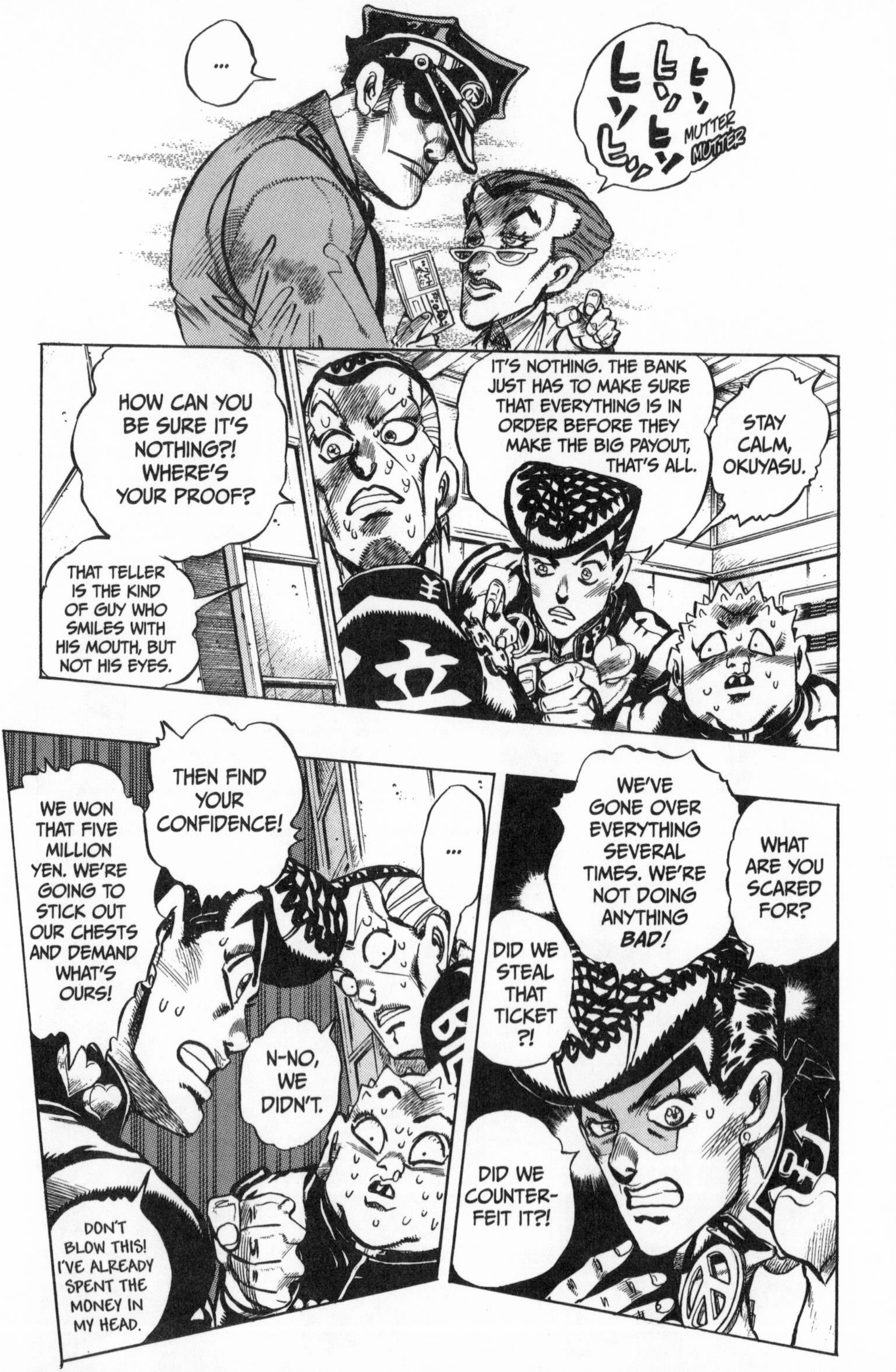
MUTTER MUTTER
...
STAY CALM, OKUYASU.
IT'S NOTHING. THE BANK JUST HAS TO MAKE SURE THAT EVERYTHING IS IN ORDER BEFORE THEY MAKE THE BIG PAYOUT, THAT'S ALL.
HOW CAN YOU BE SURE IT'S NOTHING?! WHERE'S YOUR PROOF?
THAT TELLER IS THE KIND OF GUY WHO SMILES WITH HIS MOUTH, BUT NOT HIS EYES.
WHAT ARE YOU SCARED FOR?
WE'VE GONE OVER EVERYTHING SEVERAL TIMES. WE'RE NOT DOING ANYTHING *BAD!*
DID WE STEAL THAT TICKET ?!
DID WE COUNTER-FEIT IT?!
...
THEN FIND YOUR CONFIDENCE!
WE WON THAT FIVE MILLION YEN. WE'RE GOING TO STICK OUT OUR CHESTS AND DEMAND WHAT'S OURS!
N-NO, WE DIDN'T.
DON'T BLOW THIS! I'VE ALREADY SPENT THE MONEY IN MY HEAD.

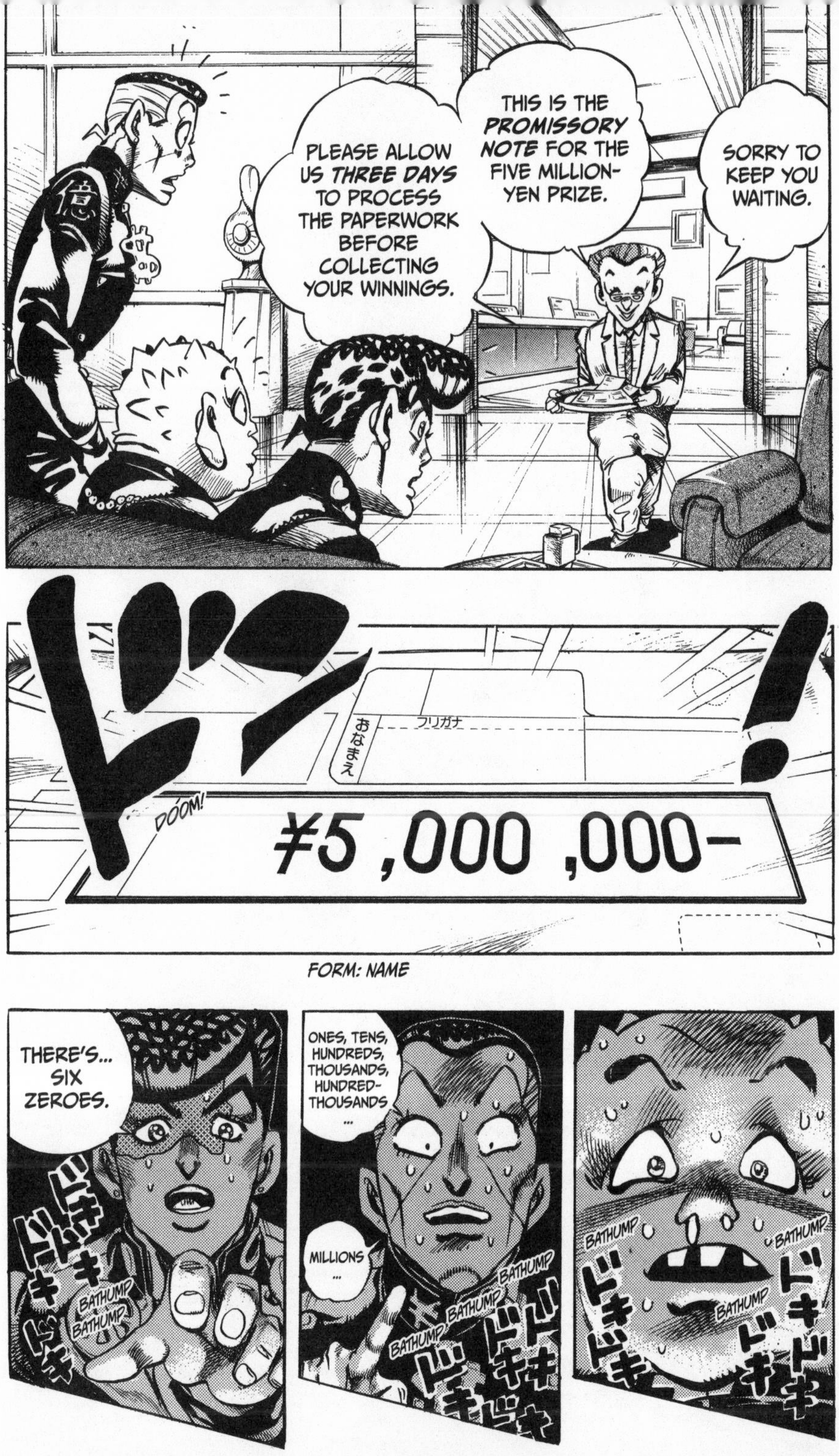
SORRY TO KEEP YOU WAITING.
THIS IS THE *PROMISSORY NOTE* FOR THE FIVE MILLION-YEN PRIZE.
PLEASE ALLOW US *THREE DAYS* TO PROCESS THE PAPERWORK BEFORE COLLECTING YOUR WINNINGS.
ドン!
DOOM!
フリガナ
おなまえ
¥5,000,000-
FORM: NAME
BATHUMP
BATHUMP
ONES, TENS, HUNDREDS, THOUSANDS, HUNDRED-THOUSANDS ...
MILLIONS ...
BATHUMP
BATHUMP
BATHUMP
THERE'S... SIX ZEROES.
BATHUMP
BATHUMP

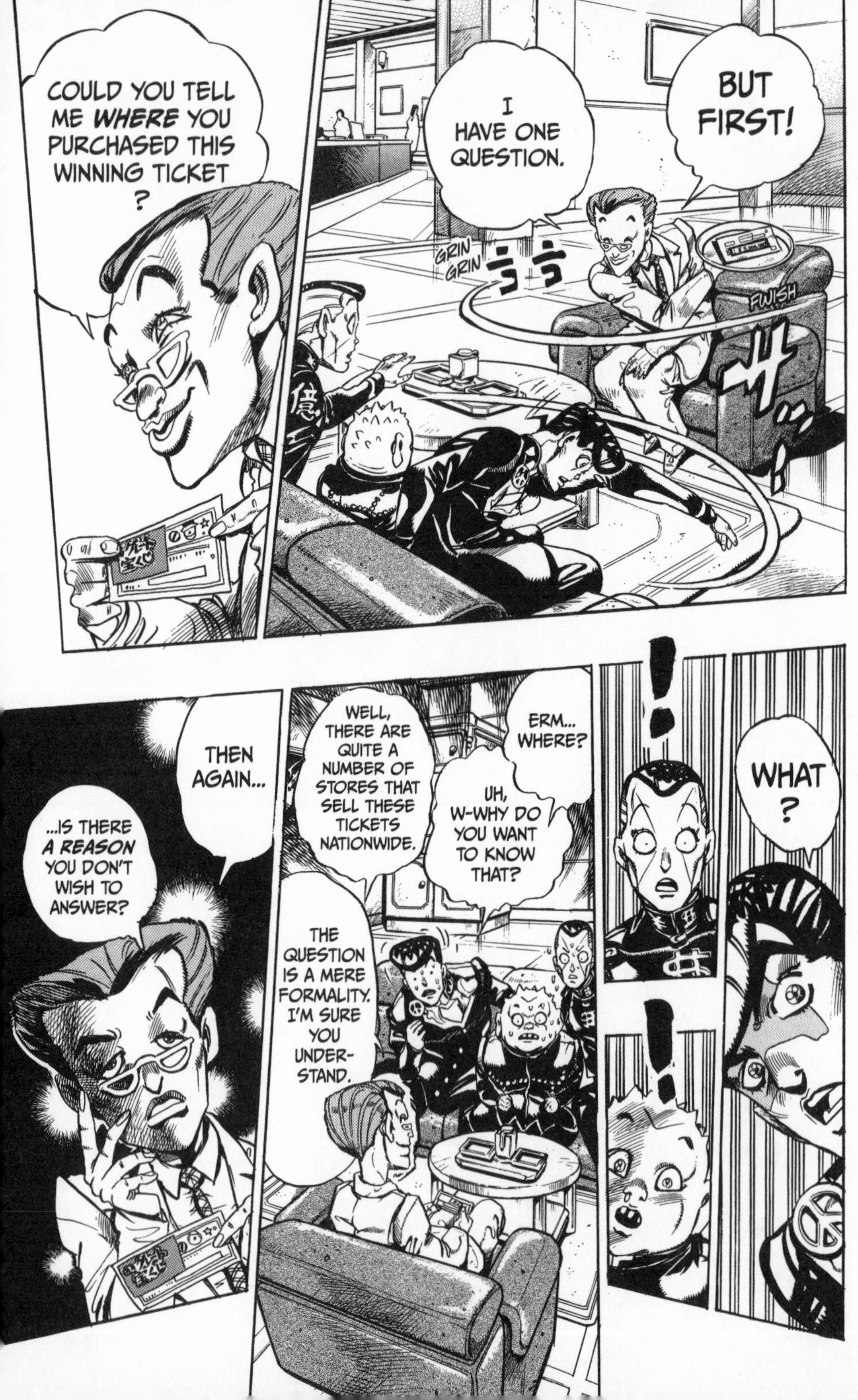
BUT FIRST!
I HAVE ONE QUESTION.
GRIN GRIN
FWISH
COULD YOU TELL ME WHERE YOU PURCHASED THIS WINNING TICKET ?
WHAT ?
ERM... WHERE?
UH, W-WHY DO YOU WANT TO KNOW THAT?
WELL, THERE ARE QUITE A NUMBER OF STORES THAT SELL THESE TICKETS NATIONWIDE.
THE QUESTION IS A MERE FORMALITY. I'M SURE YOU UNDER-STAND.
THEN AGAIN...
...IS THERE A REASON YOU DON'T WISH TO ANSWER?

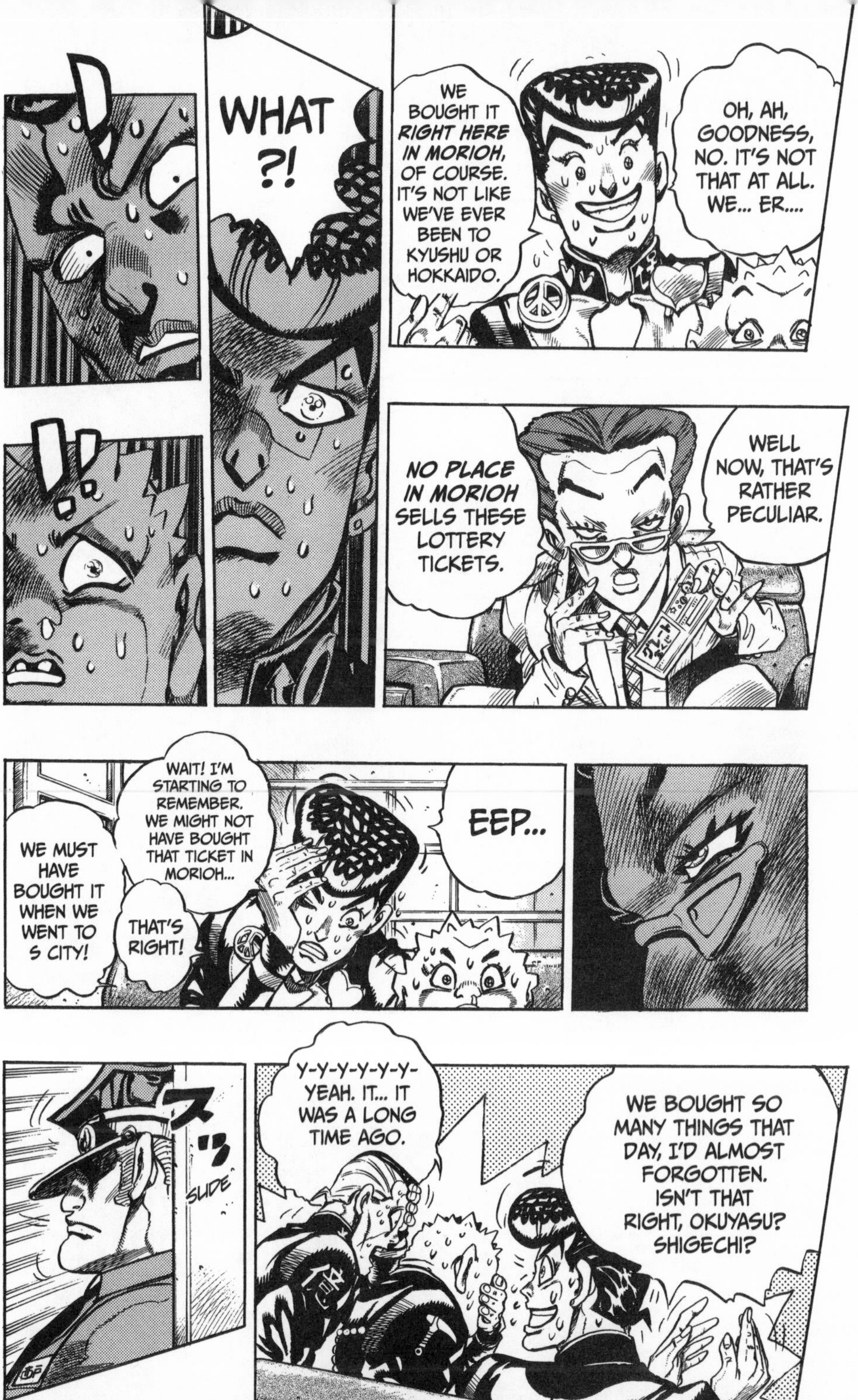
OH, AH, GOODNESS, NO. IT'S NOT THAT AT ALL. WE... ER....
WE BOUGHT IT *RIGHT HERE IN MORIOH*, OF COURSE. IT'S NOT LIKE WE'VE EVER BEEN TO KYUSHU OR HOKKAIDO.
WHAT ?!
WELL NOW, THAT'S RATHER PECULIAR.
NO PLACE IN MORIOH SELLS THESE LOTTERY TICKETS.
EEP...
WAIT! I'M STARTING TO REMEMBER. WE MIGHT NOT HAVE BOUGHT THAT TICKET IN MORIOH...
THAT'S RIGHT!
WE MUST HAVE BOUGHT IT WHEN WE WENT TO S CITY!
WE BOUGHT SO MANY THINGS THAT DAY, I'D ALMOST FORGOTTEN. ISN'T THAT RIGHT, OKUYASU? SHIGECHI?
Y-Y-Y-Y-Y-Y-YEAH. IT... IT WAS A LONG TIME AGO.
ス
SLIDE

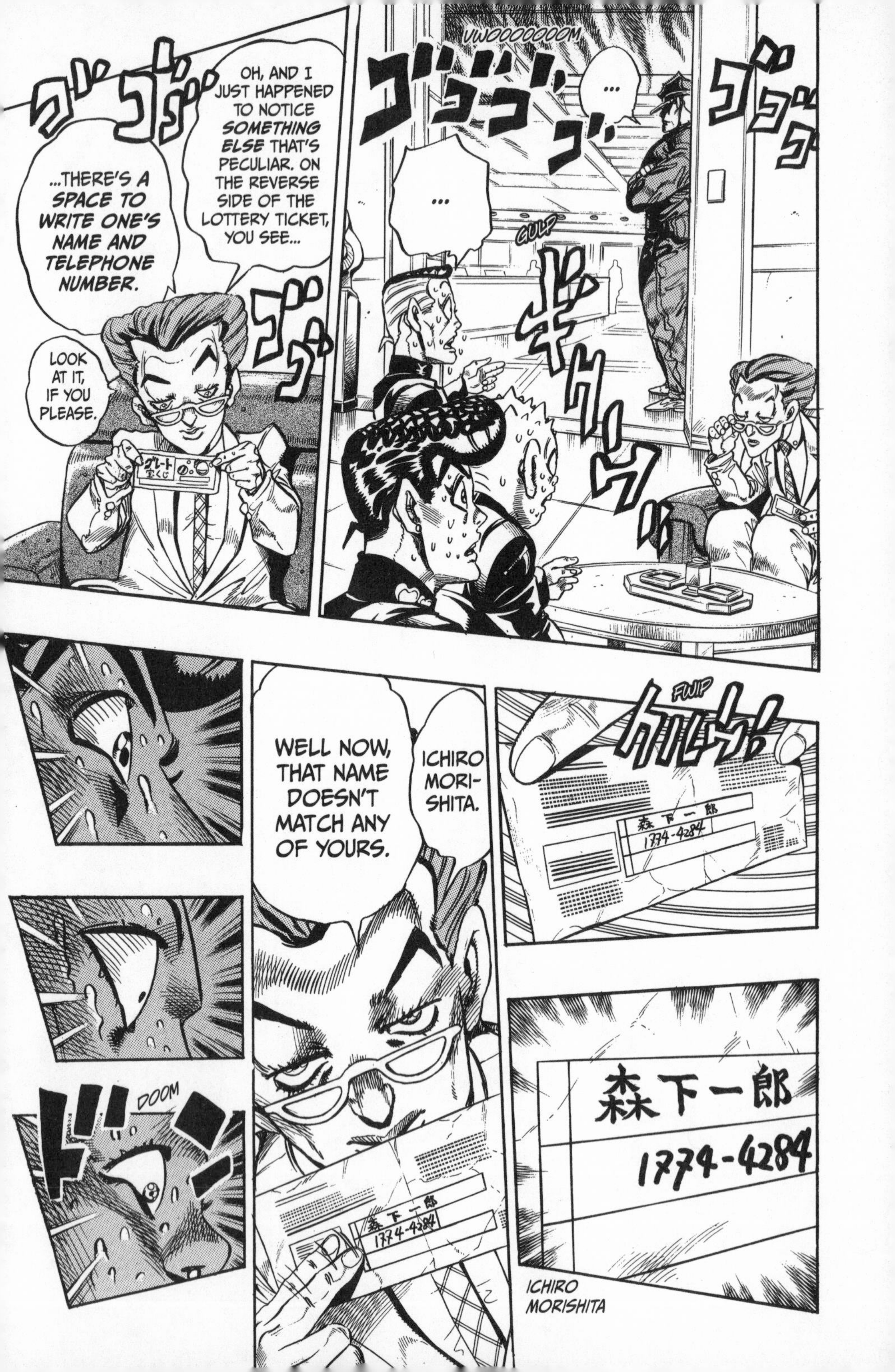
UWOOOOOOOM
...
...
GULP
OH, AND I JUST HAPPENED TO NOTICE SOMETHING ELSE THAT'S PECULIAR. ON THE REVERSE SIDE OF THE LOTTERY TICKET, YOU SEE...
...THERE'S A SPACE TO WRITE ONE'S NAME AND TELEPHONE NUMBER.
LOOK AT IT, IF YOU PLEASE.
FWIP
森下一郎
1774-4284
森下一郎
1774-4284
ICHIRO MORISHITA
ICHIRO MORISHITA.
WELL NOW, THAT NAME DOESN'T MATCH ANY OF YOURS.
DOOM

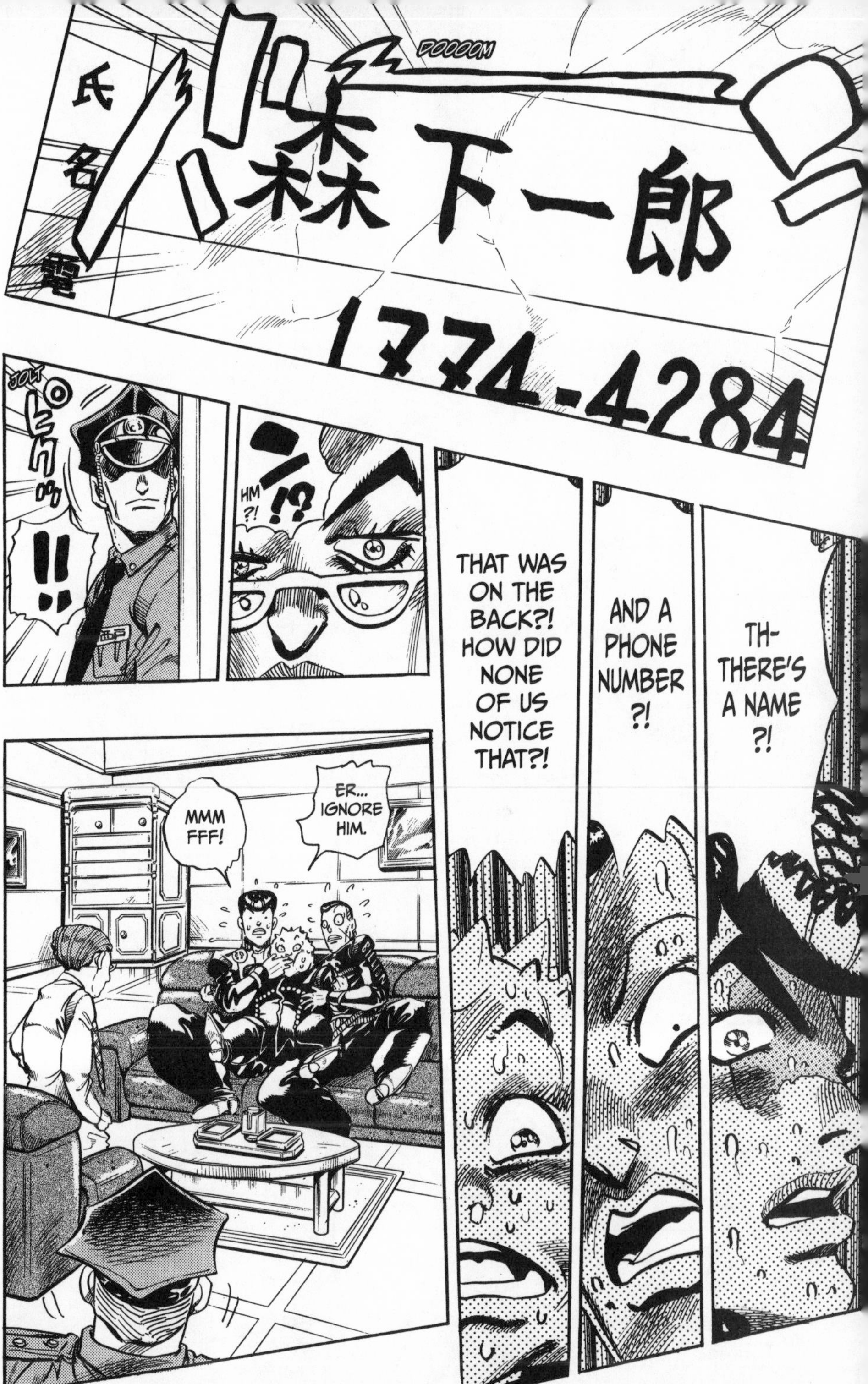
DOOOOM
氏名
森下一郎
電
1774-4284
TH- THERE'S A NAME?!
AND A PHONE NUMBER?!
THAT WAS ON THE BACK?! HOW DID NONE OF US NOTICE THAT?!
!?
HM ?!
JOLT
ピクッ
!!
ER... IGNORE HIM.
MMM FFF!

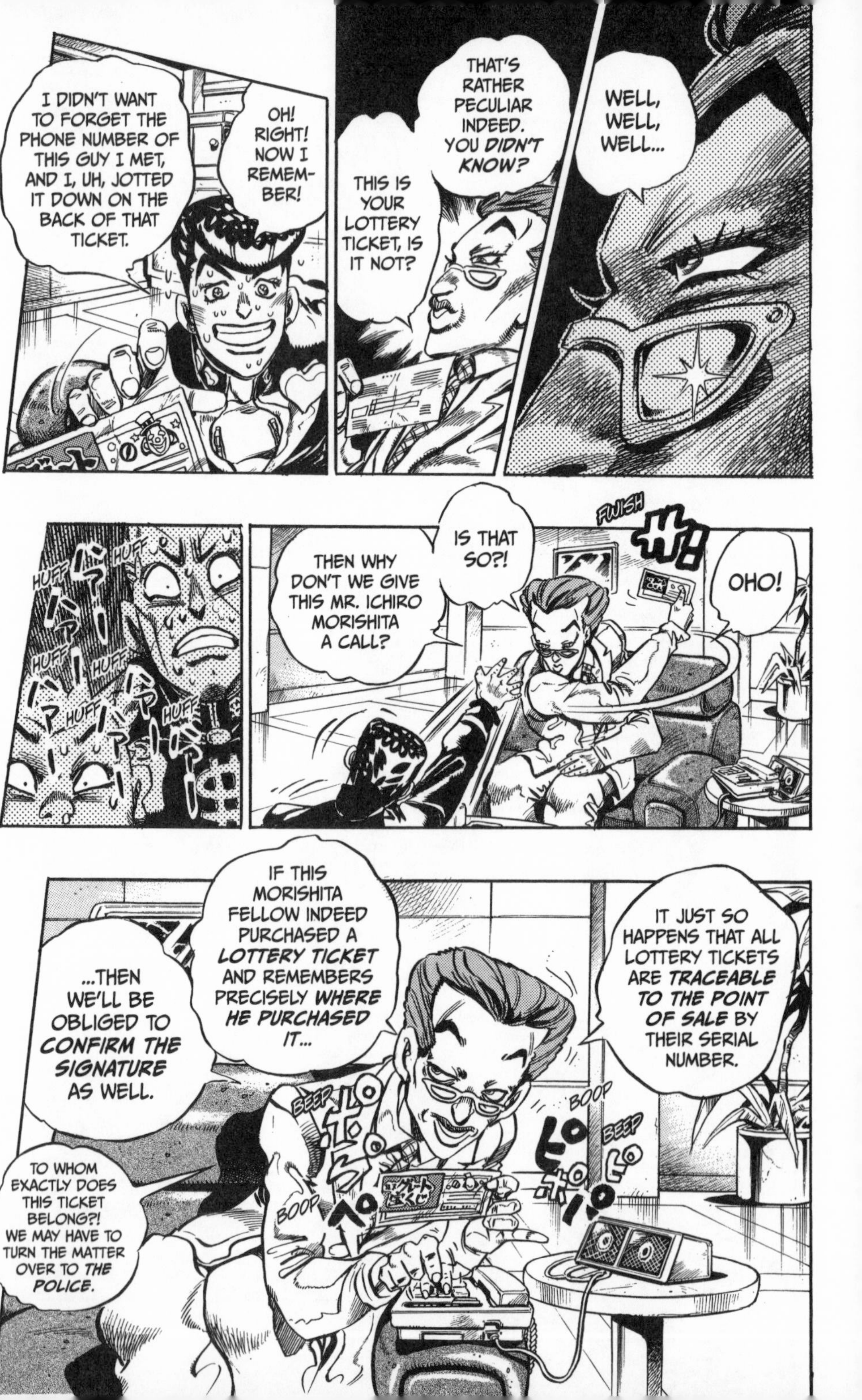
WELL, WELL, WELL...
THAT'S RATHER PECULIAR INDEED. YOU *DIDN'T KNOW?*
THIS IS YOUR LOTTERY TICKET, IS IT NOT?
OH! RIGHT! NOW I REMEMBER!
I DIDN'T WANT TO FORGET THE PHONE NUMBER OF THIS GUY I MET, AND I, UH, JOTTED IT DOWN ON THE BACK OF THAT TICKET.
FWISH
OHO!
IS THAT SO?!
THEN WHY DON'T WE GIVE THIS MR. ICHIRO MORISHITA A CALL?
HUFF
HUFF
HUFF
HUFF
HUFF
HUFF
IT JUST SO HAPPENS THAT ALL LOTTERY TICKETS ARE *TRACEABLE TO THE POINT OF SALE* BY THEIR SERIAL NUMBER.
IF THIS MORISHITA FELLOW INDEED PURCHASED A *LOTTERY TICKET* AND REMEMBERS PRECISELY *WHERE HE PURCHASED* IT...
...THEN WE'LL BE OBLIGED TO *CONFIRM THE SIGNATURE* AS WELL.
BOOP
BEEP
BEEP
BOOP
TO WHOM EXACTLY DOES THIS TICKET BELONG?! WE MAY HAVE TO TURN THE MATTER OVER TO *THE POLICE*.

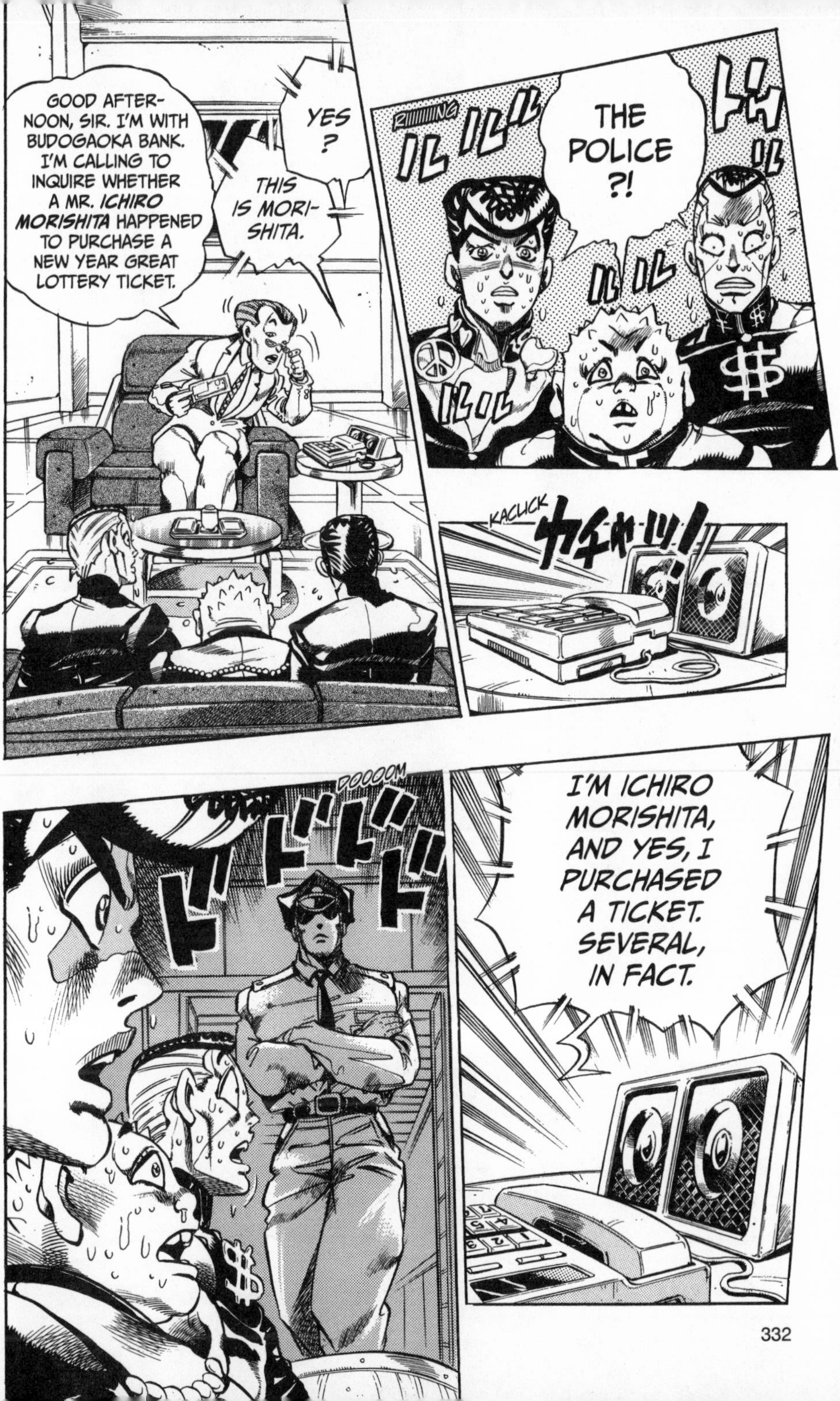
RIIIIING
THE POLICE ?!
KACLICK
YES ?
THIS IS MORI-SHITA.
GOOD AFTER-NOON, SIR. I'M WITH BUDOGAOKA BANK. I'M CALLING TO INQUIRE WHETHER A MR. ICHIRO MORISHITA HAPPENED TO PURCHASE A NEW YEAR GREAT LOTTERY TICKET.
I'M ICHIRO MORISHITA, AND YES, I PURCHASED A TICKET. SEVERAL, IN FACT.
DOOOOM

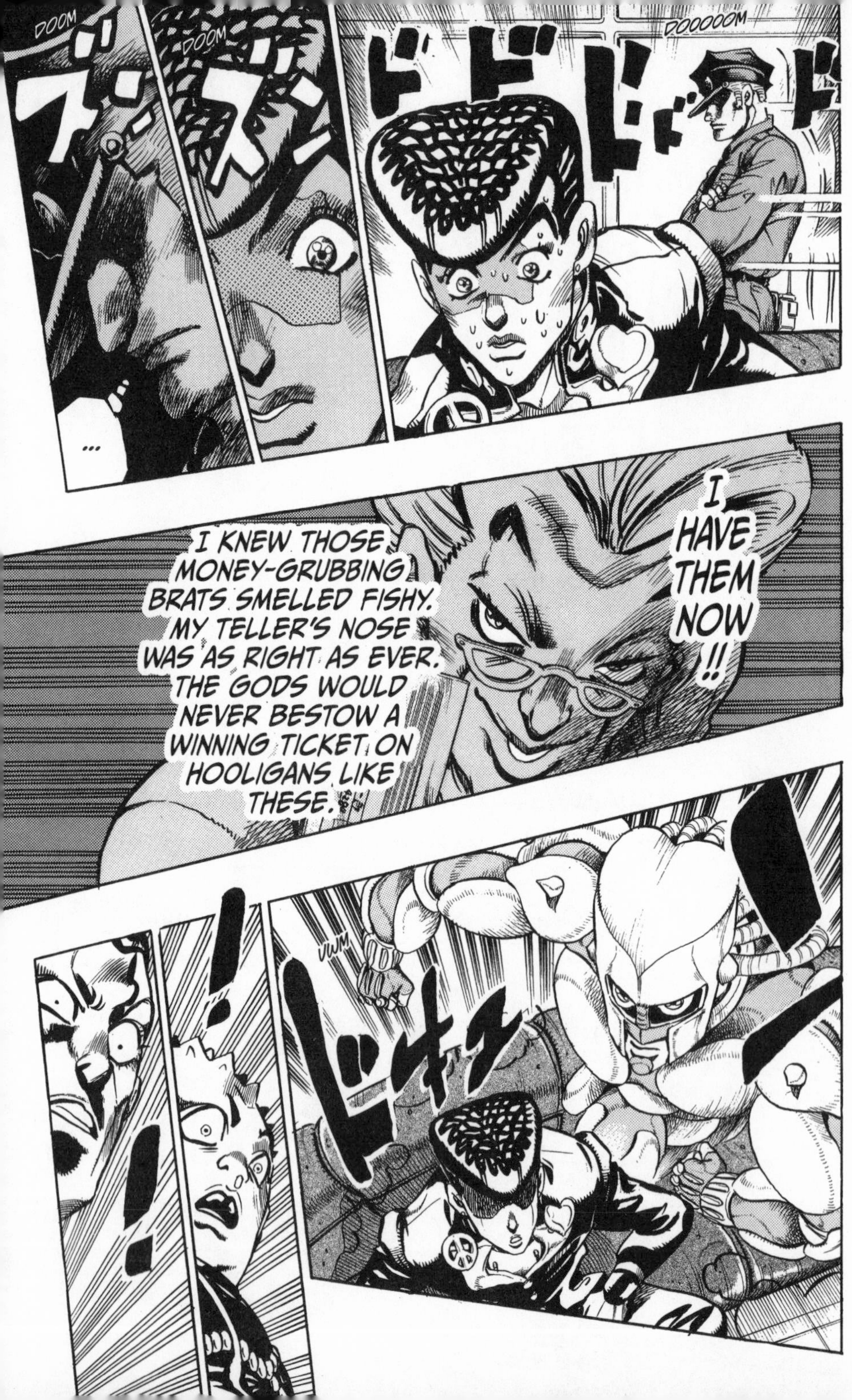

DOOOOOM
DOOM
DOOM
...
I HAVE THEM NOW!!
I KNEW THOSE MONEY-GRUBBING BRATS SMELLED FISHY. MY TELLER'S NOSE WAS AS RIGHT AS EVER. THE GODS WOULD NEVER BESTOW A WINNING TICKET ON HOOLIGANS LIKE THESE.
VWM

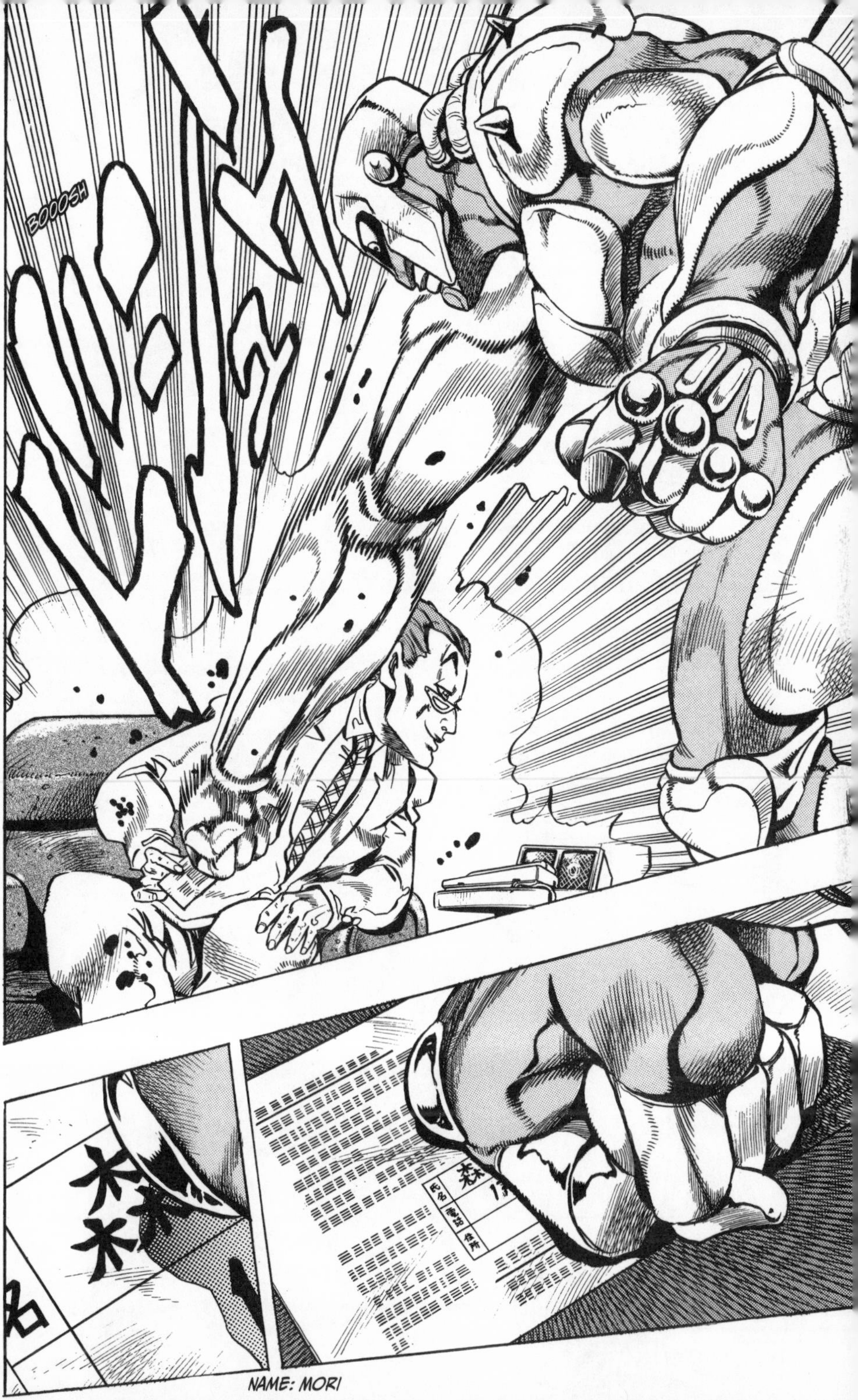
BOOOSH

NAME: MORI

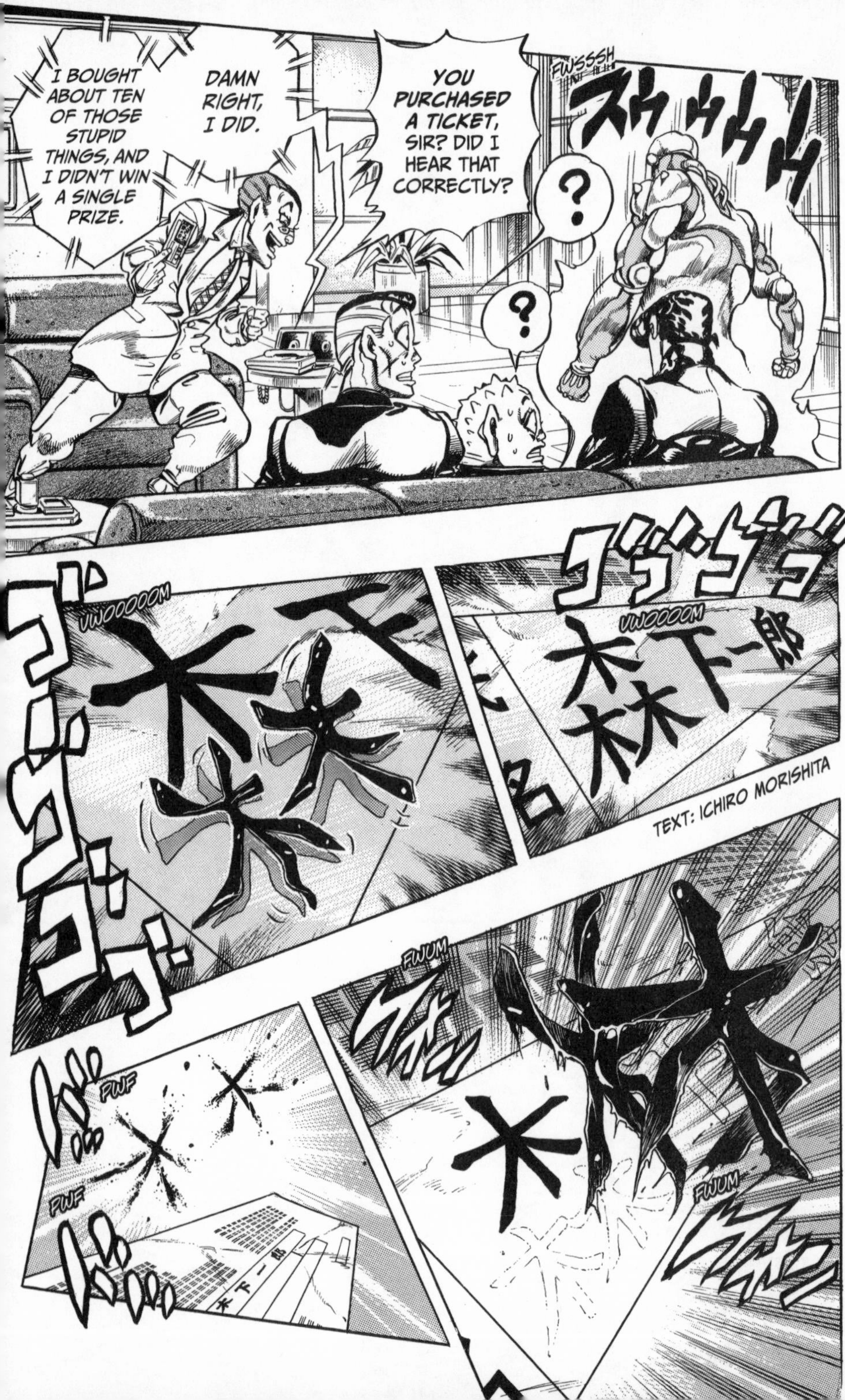
FWSSSH
?
?
YOU PURCHASED A TICKET, SIR? DID I HEAR THAT CORRECTLY?
DAMN RIGHT, I DID.
I BOUGHT ABOUT TEN OF THOSE STUPID THINGS, AND I DIDN'T WIN A SINGLE PRIZE.
VWOOOOM
TEXT: ICHIRO MORISHITA
VWOOOOOM
FWUM
FWUM
PWF
PWF

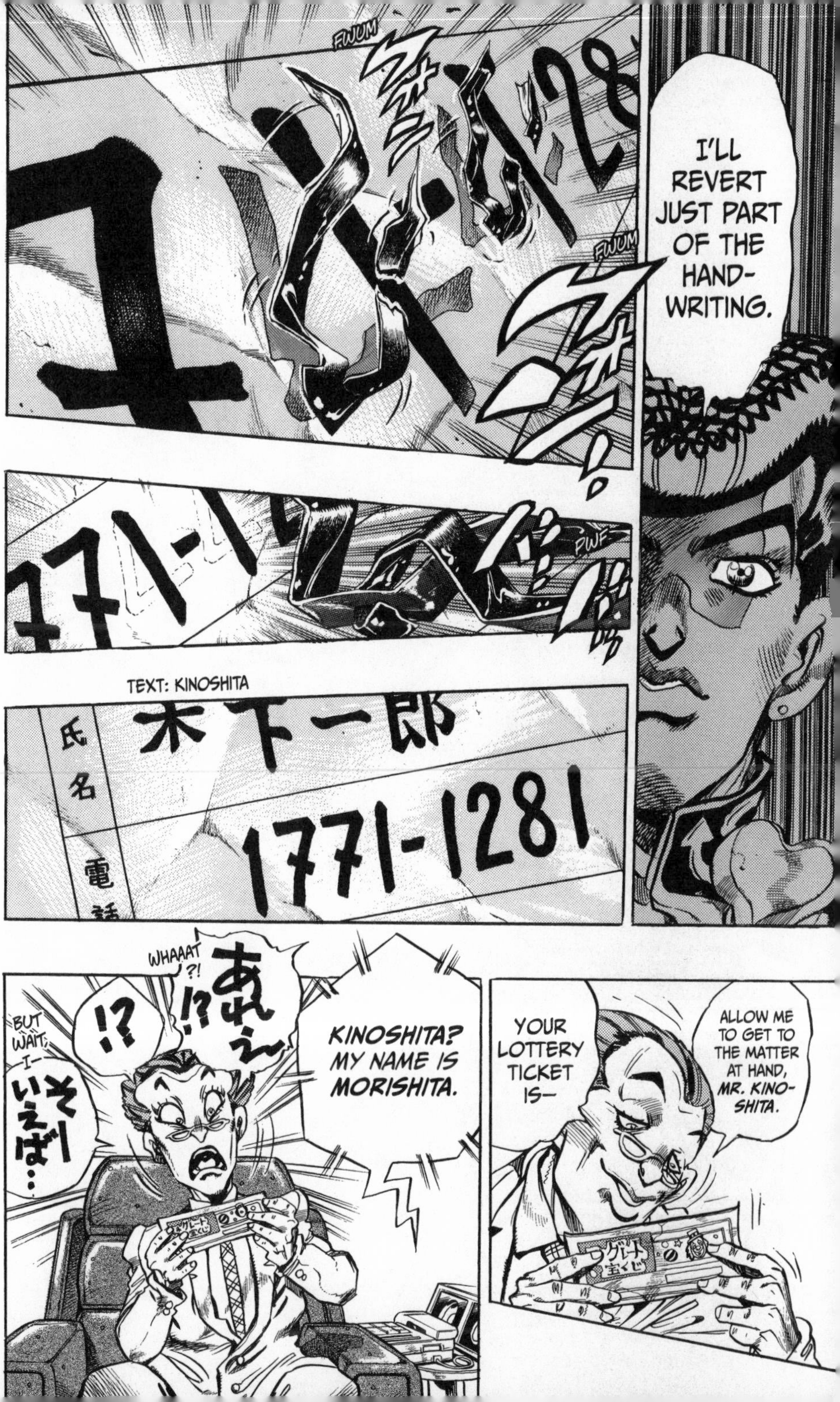
I'LL REVERT JUST PART OF THE HAND-WRITING.
FWUUM
FWUM
PWF
TEXT: KINOSHITA
木下一郎
氏名
電話
1771-1281
ALLOW ME TO GET TO THE MATTER AT HAND, MR. KINO-SHITA.
YOUR LOTTERY TICKET IS—
グレート宝くじ
KINOSHITA? MY NAME IS MORISHITA.
WHAAAT?!
あれえ〜
!?
!?
BUT WAIT, I—
そいえば…

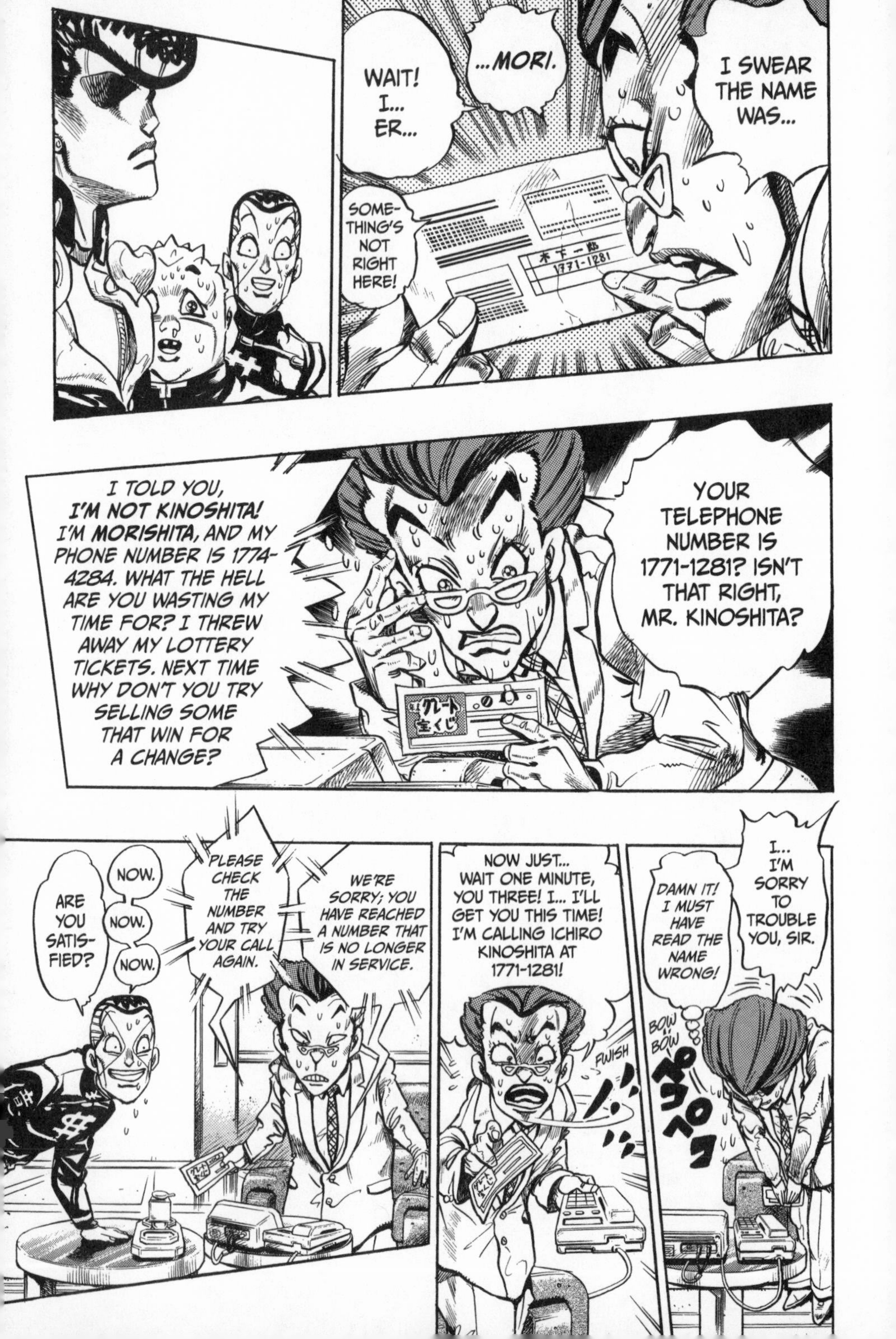
I SWEAR THE NAME WAS...
...MORI.
WAIT! I... ER...
SOMETHING'S NOT RIGHT HERE!
YOUR TELEPHONE NUMBER IS 1771-1281? ISN'T THAT RIGHT, MR. KINOSHITA?
I TOLD YOU, I'M NOT KINOSHITA! I'M MORISHITA, AND MY PHONE NUMBER IS 1774-4284. WHAT THE HELL ARE YOU WASTING MY TIME FOR? I THREW AWAY MY LOTTERY TICKETS. NEXT TIME WHY DON'T YOU TRY SELLING SOME THAT WIN FOR A CHANGE?
I... I'M SORRY TO TROUBLE YOU, SIR.
DAMN IT! I MUST HAVE READ THE NAME WRONG!
BOW BOW
NOW JUST... WAIT ONE MINUTE, YOU THREE! I... I'LL GET YOU THIS TIME! I'M CALLING ICHIRO KINOSHITA AT 1771-1281!
FWISH
WE'RE SORRY; YOU HAVE REACHED A NUMBER THAT IS NO LONGER IN SERVICE.
PLEASE CHECK THE NUMBER AND TRY YOUR CALL AGAIN.
NOW.
NOW.
NOW.
ARE YOU SATISFIED?

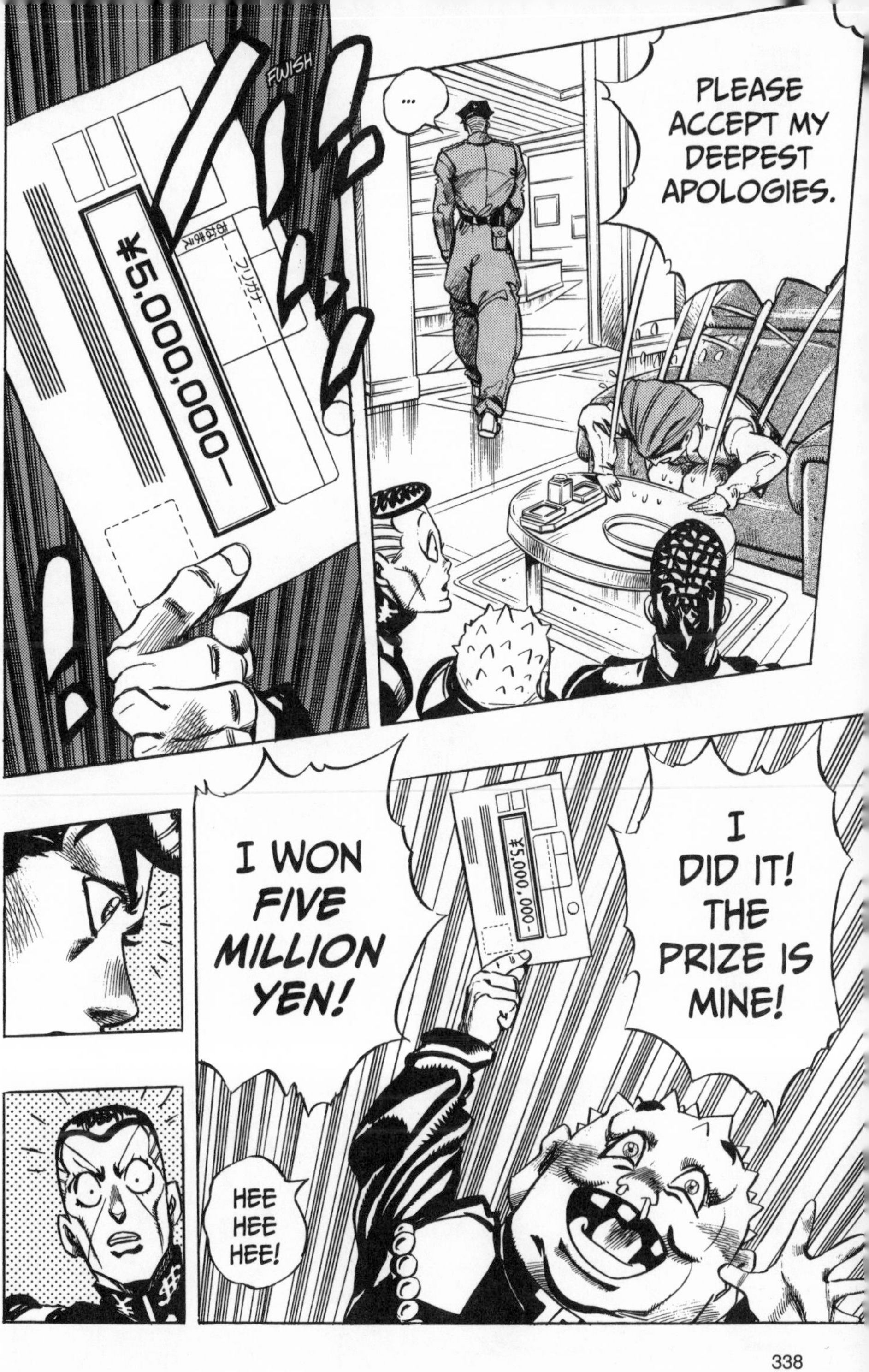
PLEASE ACCEPT MY DEEPEST APOLOGIES.
...
FWISH
¥5,000,000—
I DID IT! THE PRIZE IS MINE!
I WON FIVE MILLION YEN!
¥5,000,000-
HEE HEE HEE!

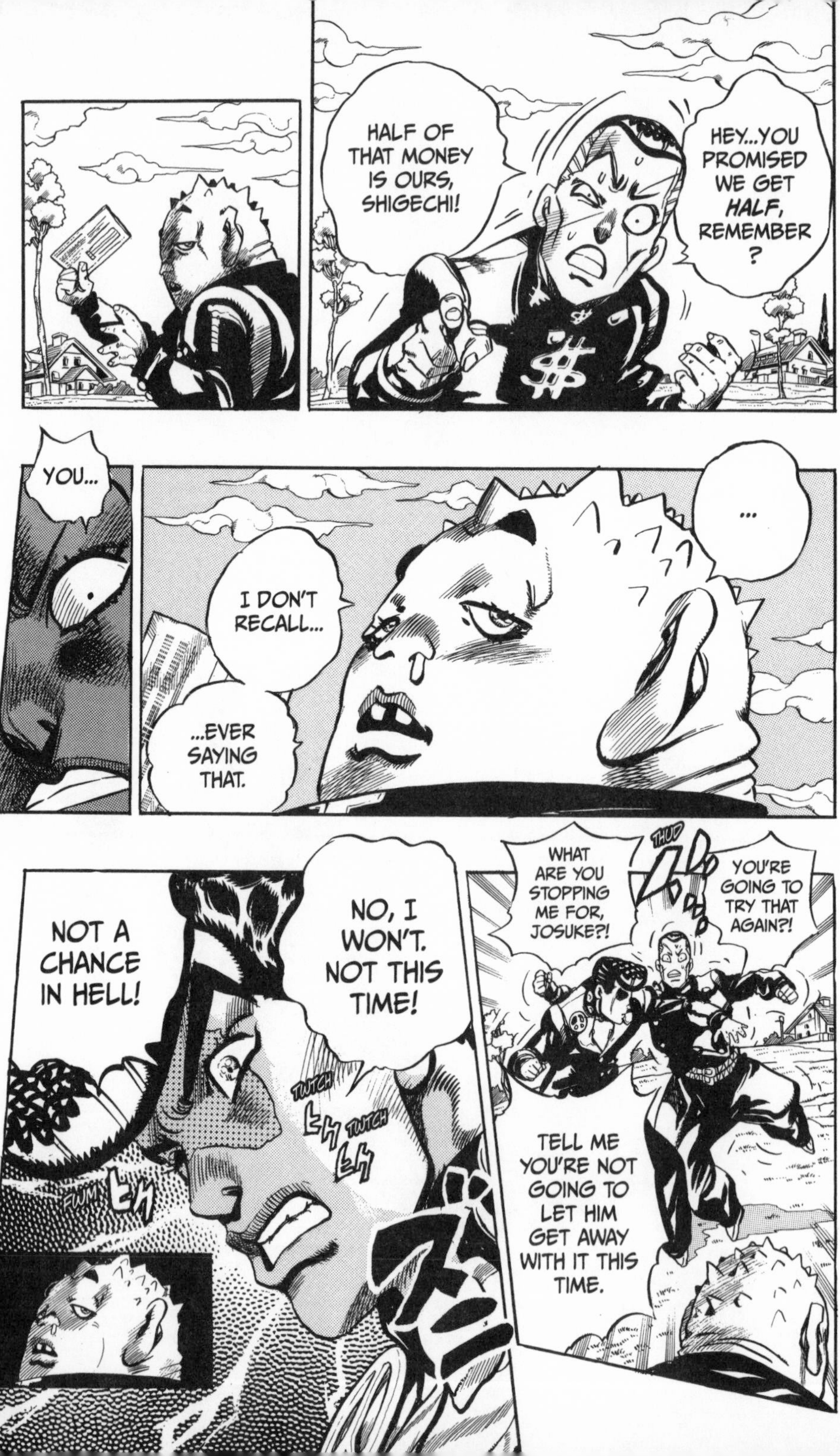
HALF OF THAT MONEY IS OURS, SHIGECHI!
HEY...YOU PROMISED WE GET HALF, REMEMBER?
...
I DON'T RECALL...
...EVER SAYING THAT.
YOU...
YOU'RE GOING TO TRY THAT AGAIN?!
THUD
WHAT ARE YOU STOPPING ME FOR, JOSUKE?!
TELL ME YOU'RE NOT GOING TO LET HIM GET AWAY WITH IT THIS TIME.
NO, I WON'T. NOT THIS TIME!
NOT A CHANCE IN HELL!
TWITCH
TWITCH
FWM

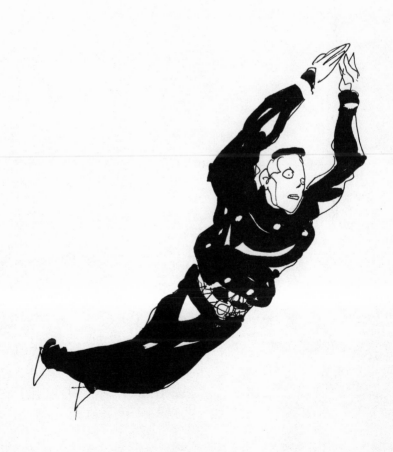

CHAPTER 74

SHIGECHI'S HARVEST, PART 5

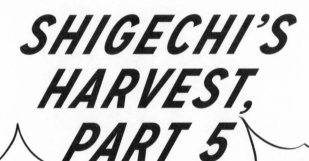

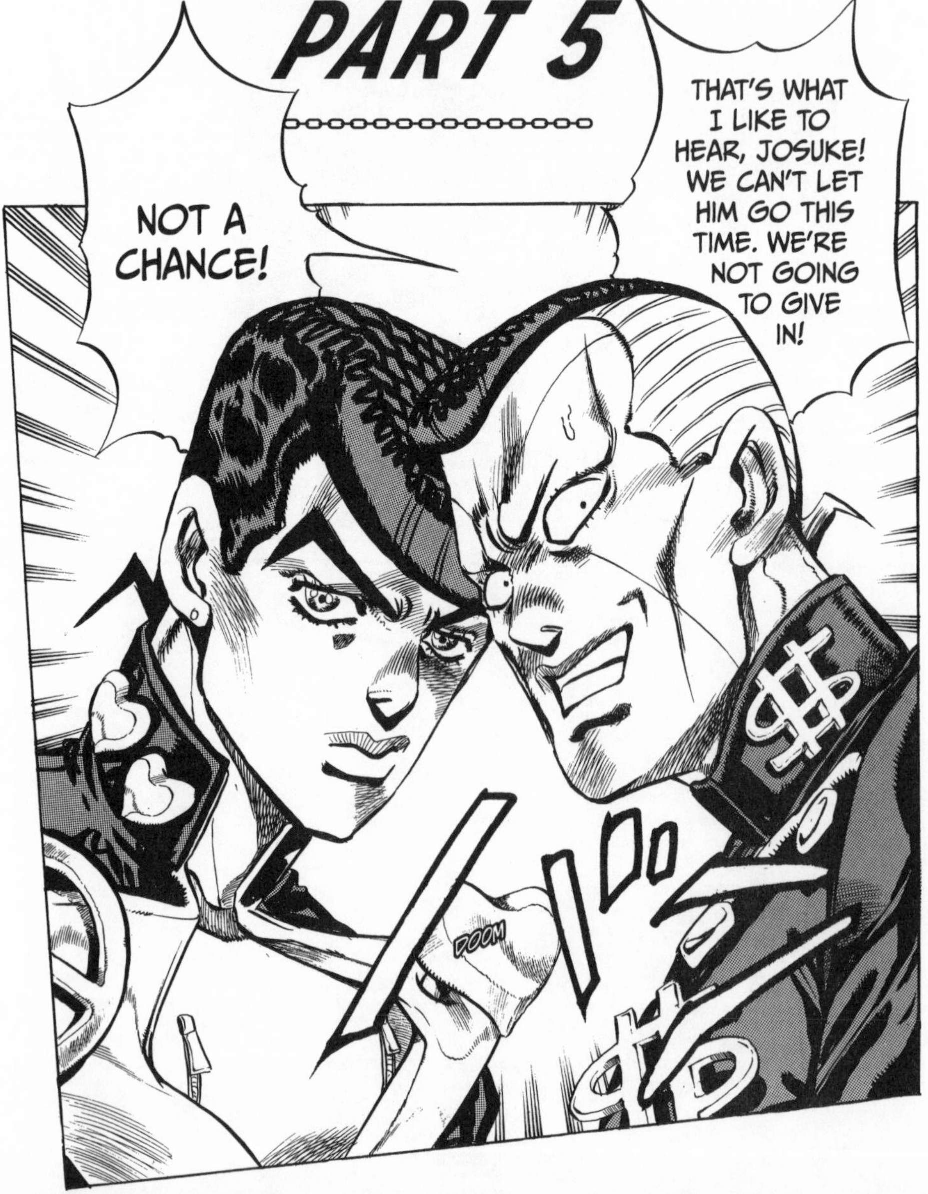
THAT'S WHAT I LIKE TO HEAR, JOSUKE! WE CAN'T LET HIM GO THIS TIME. WE'RE NOT GOING TO GIVE IN!
NOT A CHANCE!
DOOM

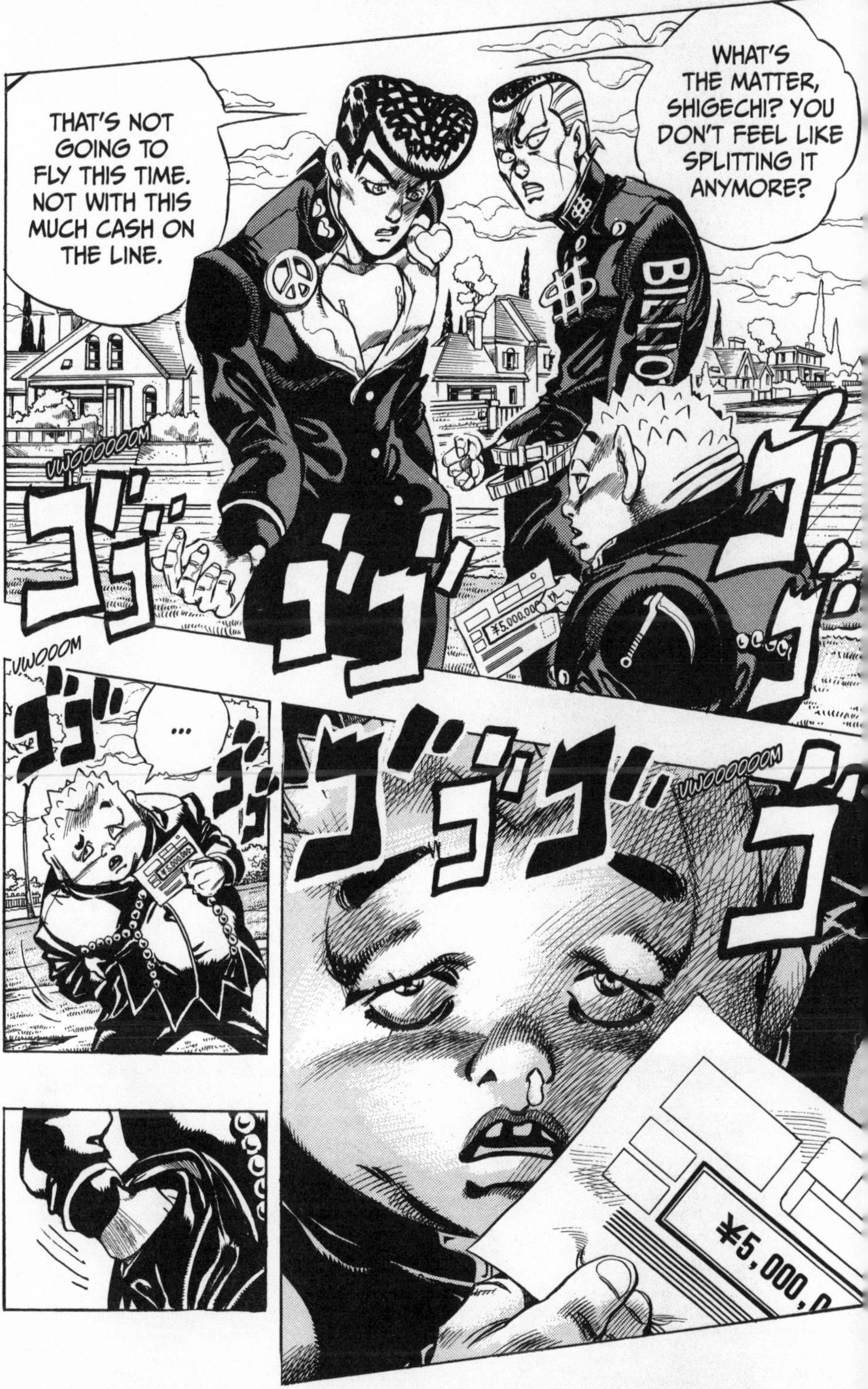
WHAT'S THE MATTER, SHIGECHI? YOU DON'T FEEL LIKE SPLITTING IT ANYMORE?
THAT'S NOT GOING TO FLY THIS TIME. NOT WITH THIS MUCH CASH ON THE LINE.
VWOOOOOOM
VWOOOOOOM
¥5,000,0
VWOOOM
...

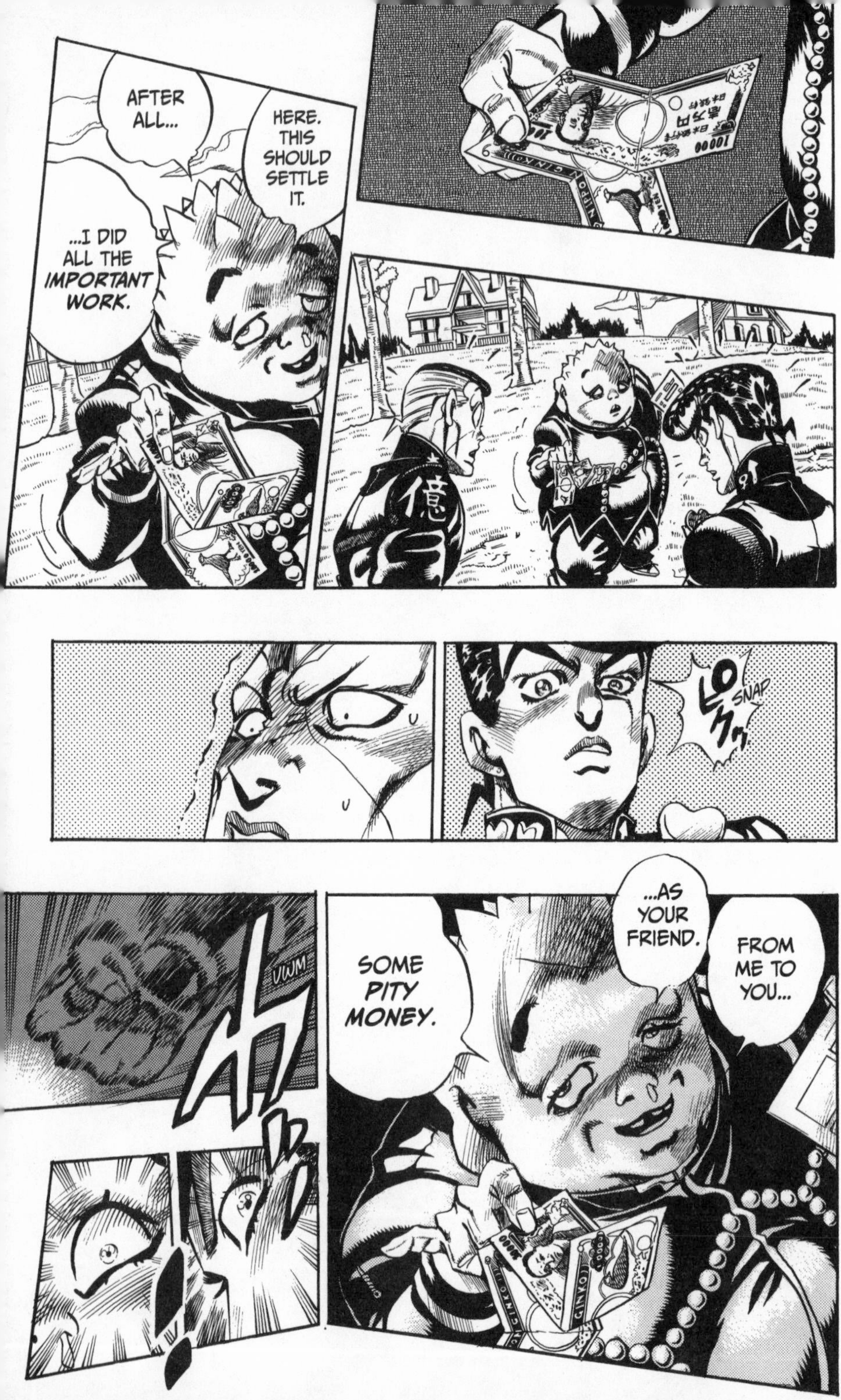
HERE. THIS SHOULD SETTLE IT.
AFTER ALL...
...I DID ALL THE IMPORTANT WORK.
SNAP
FROM ME TO YOU...
...AS YOUR FRIEND.
SOME PITY MONEY.
UWM

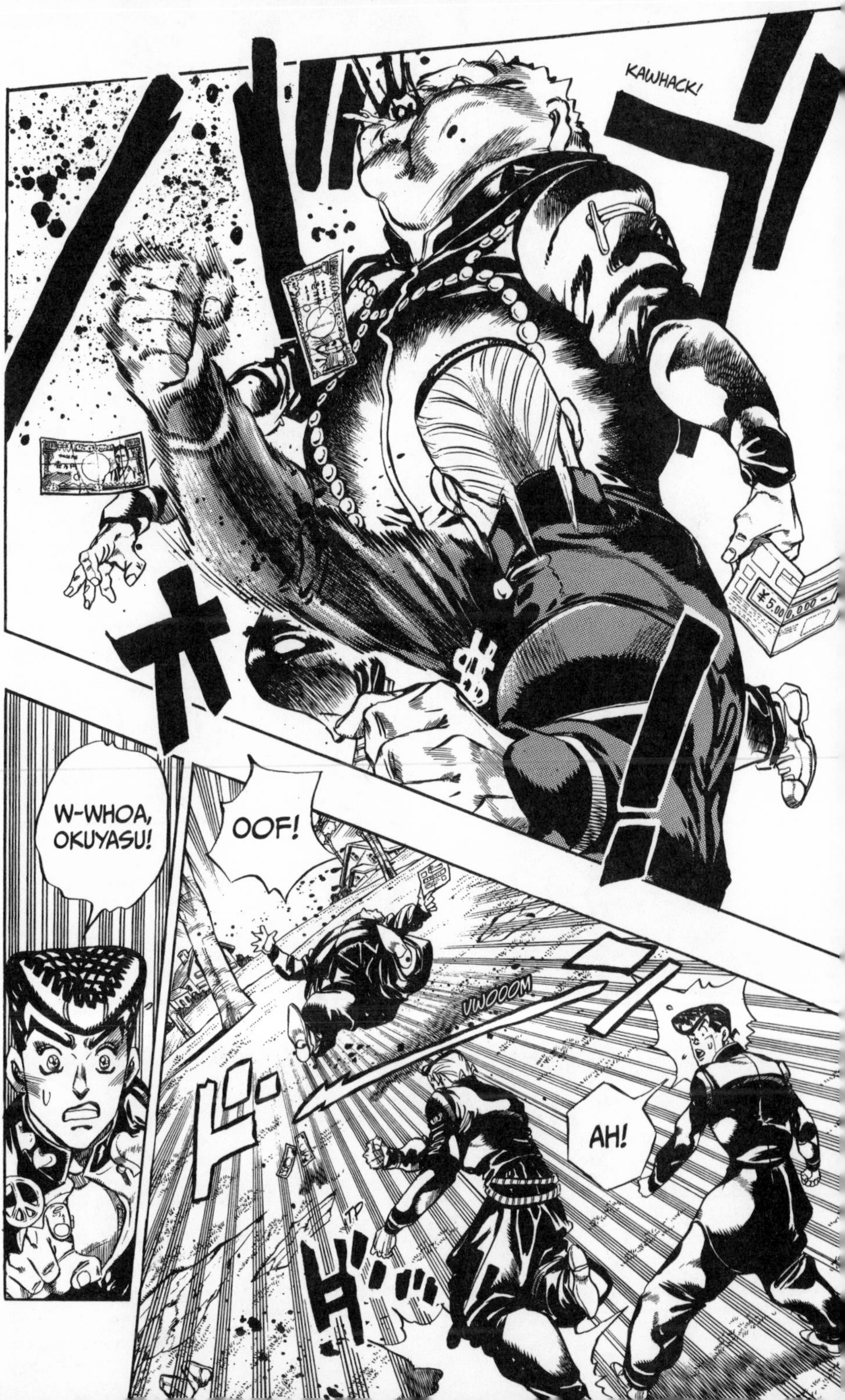
KAWHACK!
OOF!
VWOOOM
AH!
W-WHOA, OKUYASU!

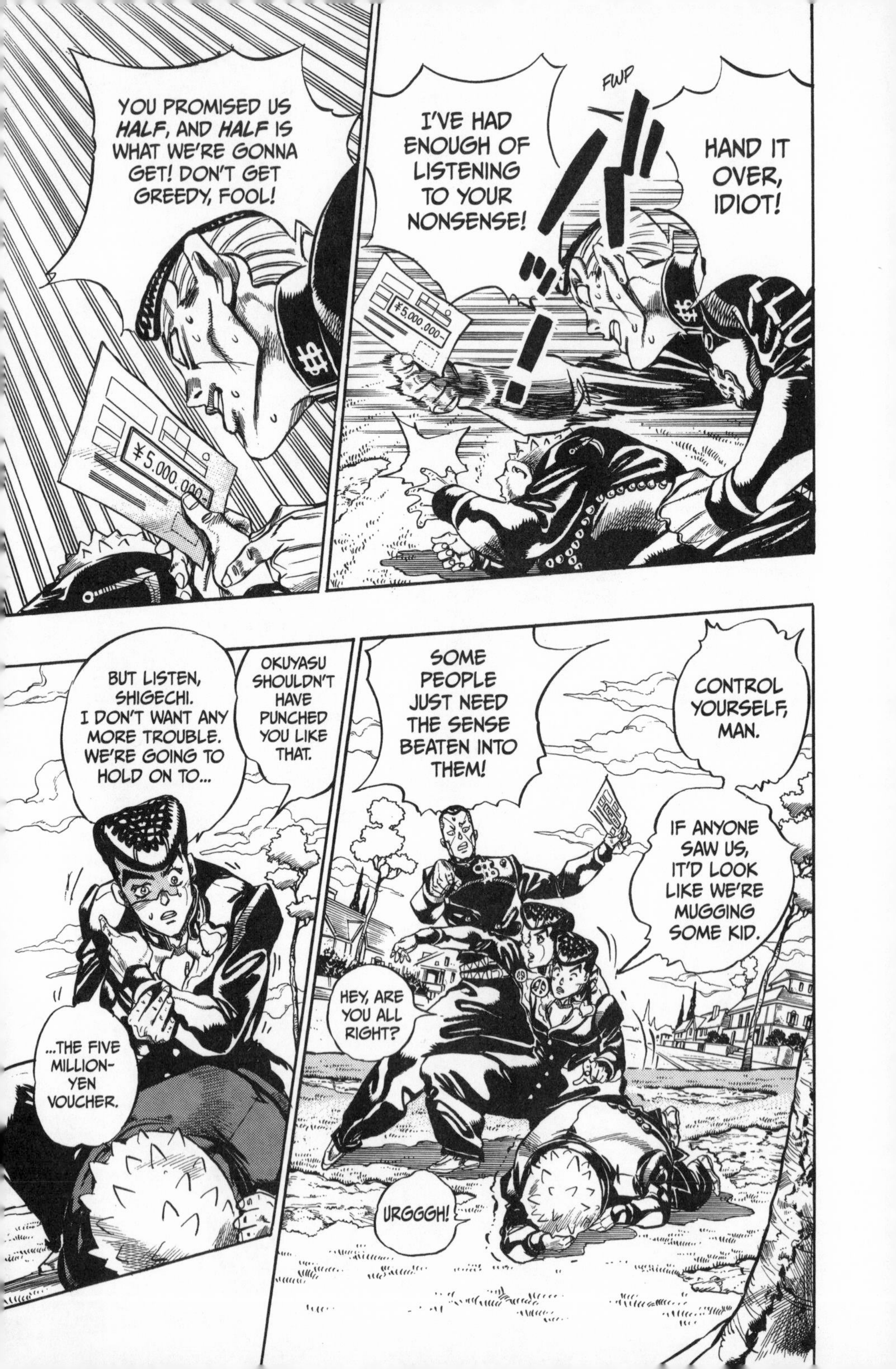
HAND IT OVER, IDIOT!
FWP
I'VE HAD ENOUGH OF LISTENING TO YOUR NONSENSE!
¥5,000,000-
YOU PROMISED US *HALF*, AND *HALF* IS WHAT WE'RE GONNA GET! DON'T GET GREEDY, FOOL!
¥5,000,000-
CONTROL YOURSELF, MAN.
SOME PEOPLE JUST NEED THE SENSE BEATEN INTO THEM!
IF ANYONE SAW US, IT'D LOOK LIKE WE'RE MUGGING SOME KID.
HEY, ARE YOU ALL RIGHT?
URGGGH!
OKUYASU SHOULDN'T HAVE PUNCHED YOU LIKE THAT.
BUT LISTEN, SHIGECHI. I DON'T WANT ANY MORE TROUBLE. WE'RE GOING TO HOLD ON TO...
...THE FIVE MILLION-YEN VOUCHER.

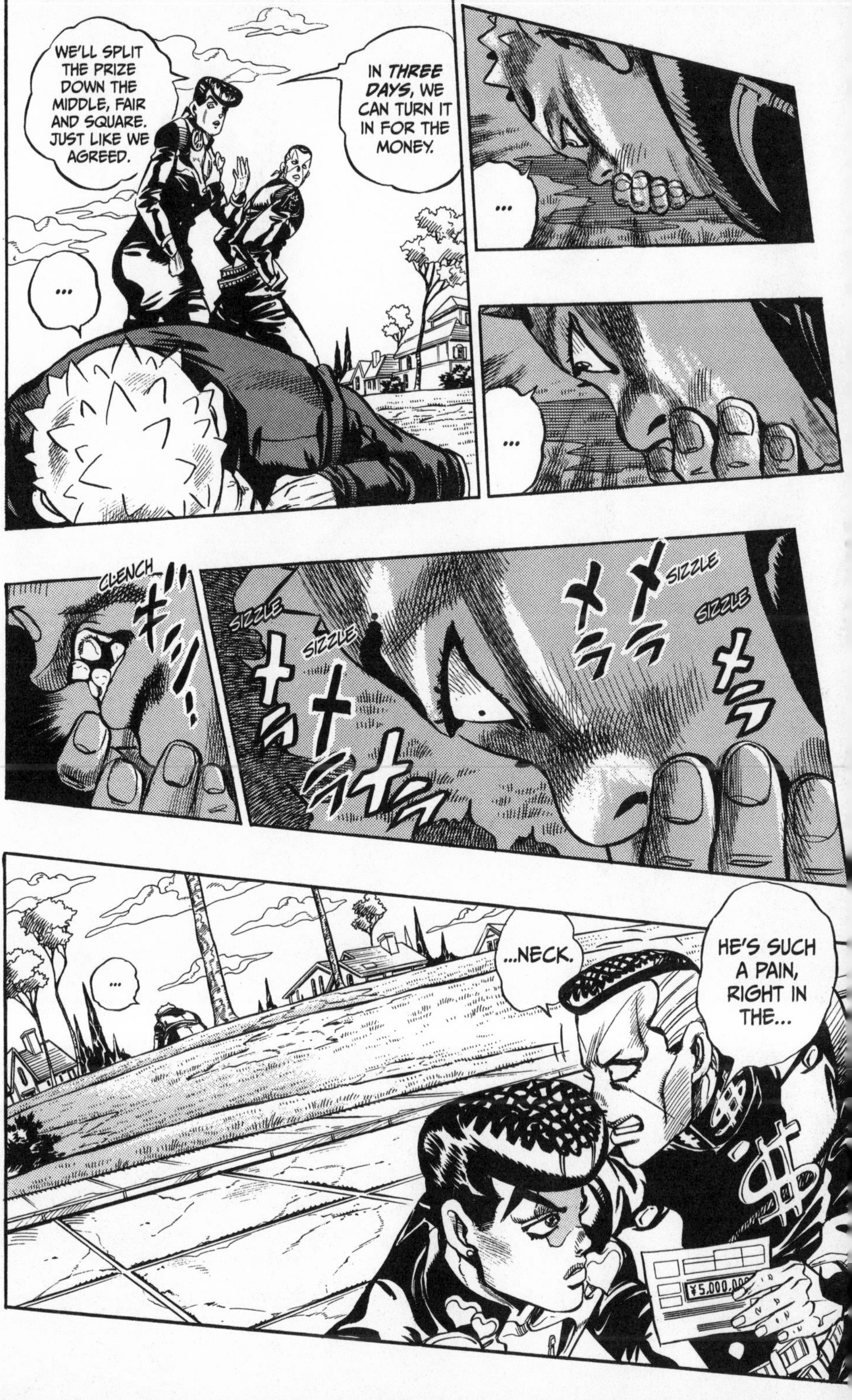
...
...
IN *THREE DAYS*, WE CAN TURN IT IN FOR THE MONEY.
WE'LL SPLIT THE PRIZE DOWN THE MIDDLE, FAIR AND SQUARE. JUST LIKE WE AGREED.
...
SIZZLE
SIZZLE
メラ
メラ
メラ
SIZZLE
SIZZLE
メラ
メラ
メラ
CLENCH
ギリ
HE'S SUCH A PAIN, RIGHT IN THE...
...NECK.
...

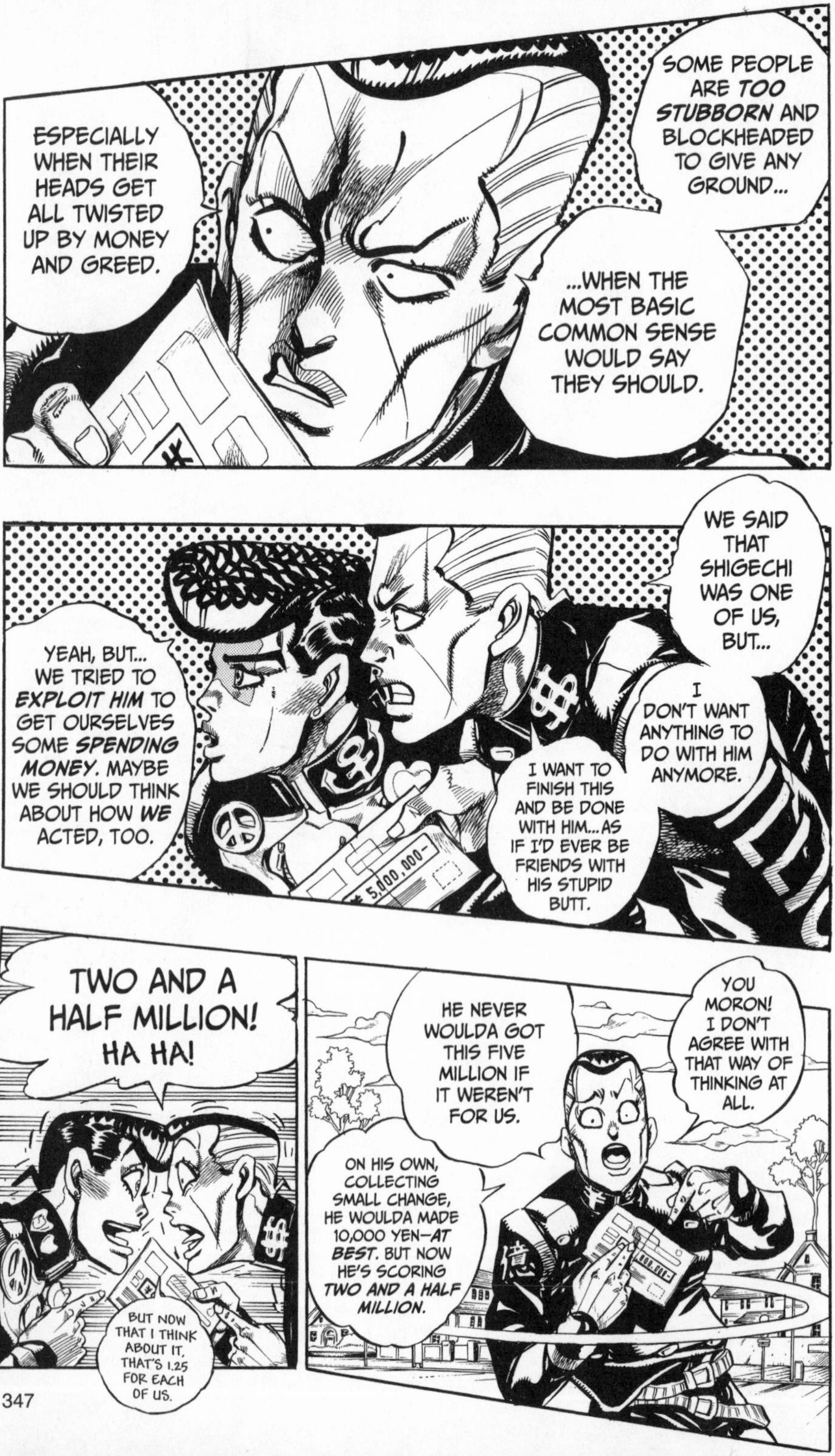
SOME PEOPLE ARE TOO STUBBORN AND BLOCKHEADED TO GIVE ANY GROUND...
...WHEN THE MOST BASIC COMMON SENSE WOULD SAY THEY SHOULD.
ESPECIALLY WHEN THEIR HEADS GET ALL TWISTED UP BY MONEY AND GREED.
WE SAID THAT SHIGECHI WAS ONE OF US, BUT...
I DON'T WANT ANYTHING TO DO WITH HIM ANYMORE.
I WANT TO FINISH THIS AND BE DONE WITH HIM...AS IF I'D EVER BE FRIENDS WITH HIS STUPID BUTT.
YEAH, BUT... WE TRIED TO EXPLOIT HIM TO GET OURSELVES SOME SPENDING MONEY. MAYBE WE SHOULD THINK ABOUT HOW WE ACTED, TOO.
YOU MORON! I DON'T AGREE WITH THAT WAY OF THINKING AT ALL.
HE NEVER WOULDA GOT THIS FIVE MILLION IF IT WEREN'T FOR US.
ON HIS OWN, COLLECTING SMALL CHANGE, HE WOULDA MADE 10,000 YEN—AT BEST. BUT NOW HE'S SCORING TWO AND A HALF MILLION.
TWO AND A HALF MILLION! HA HA!
BUT NOW THAT I THINK ABOUT IT, THAT'S 1.25 FOR EACH OF US.

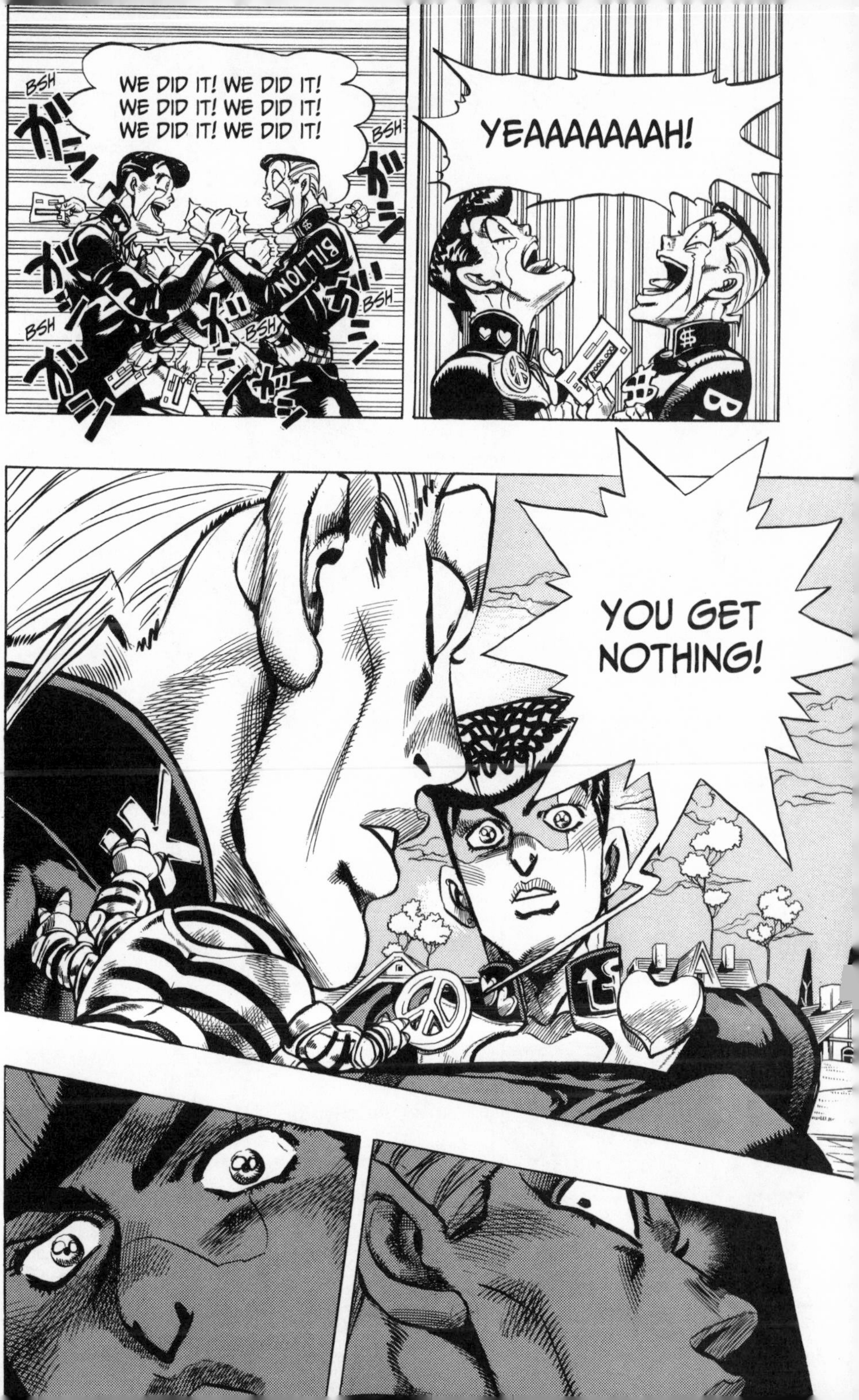
YEAAAAAAAH!
WE DID IT! WE DID IT! WE DID IT! WE DID IT! WE DID IT! WE DID IT!
BSH
BSH
BSH
BSH
BSH
YOU GET NOTHING!

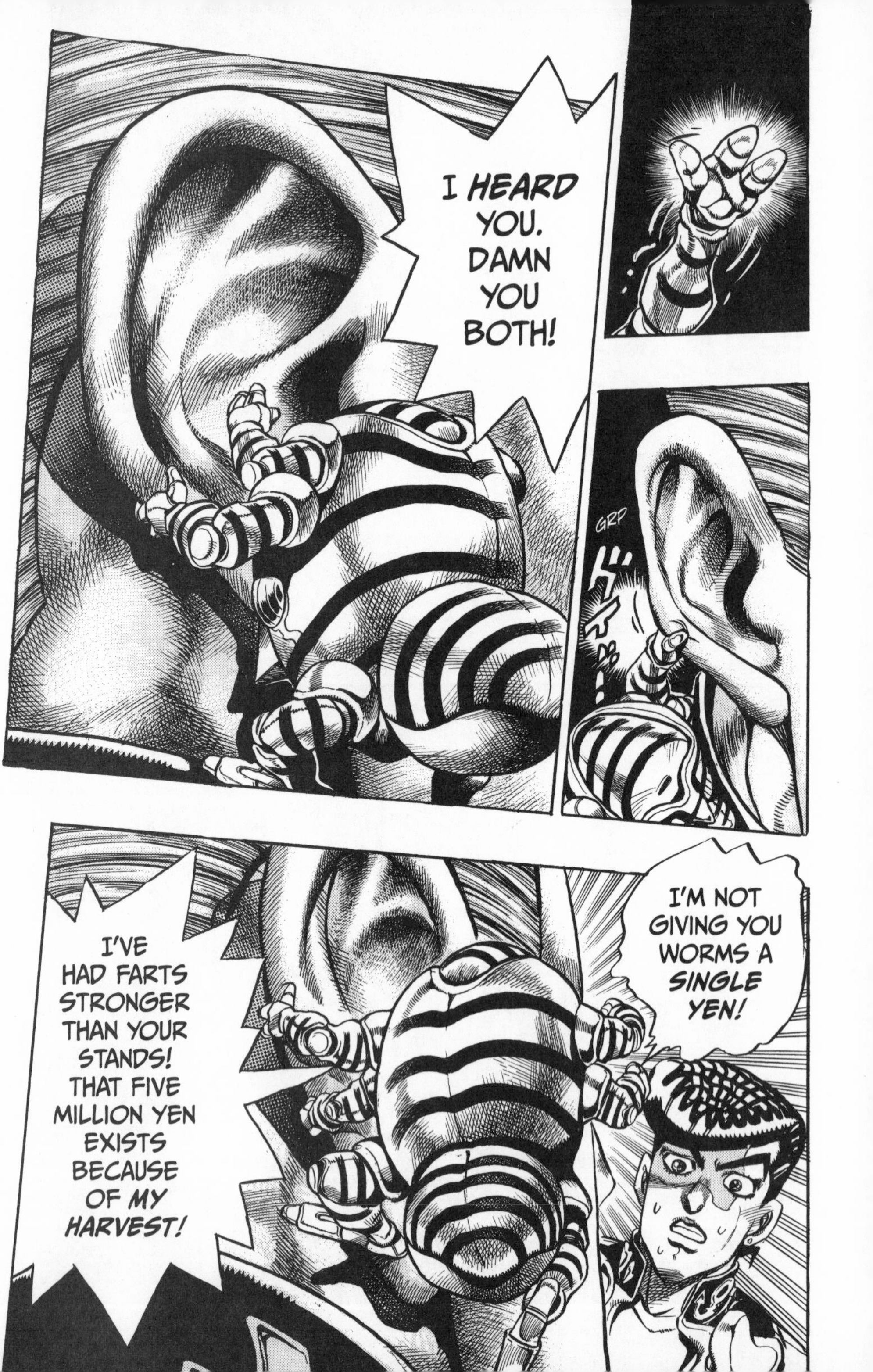
GRP
I HEARD YOU. DAMN YOU BOTH!
I'M NOT GIVING YOU WORMS A SINGLE YEN!
I'VE HAD FARTS STRONGER THAN YOUR STANDS! THAT FIVE MILLION YEN EXISTS BECAUSE OF MY HARVEST!

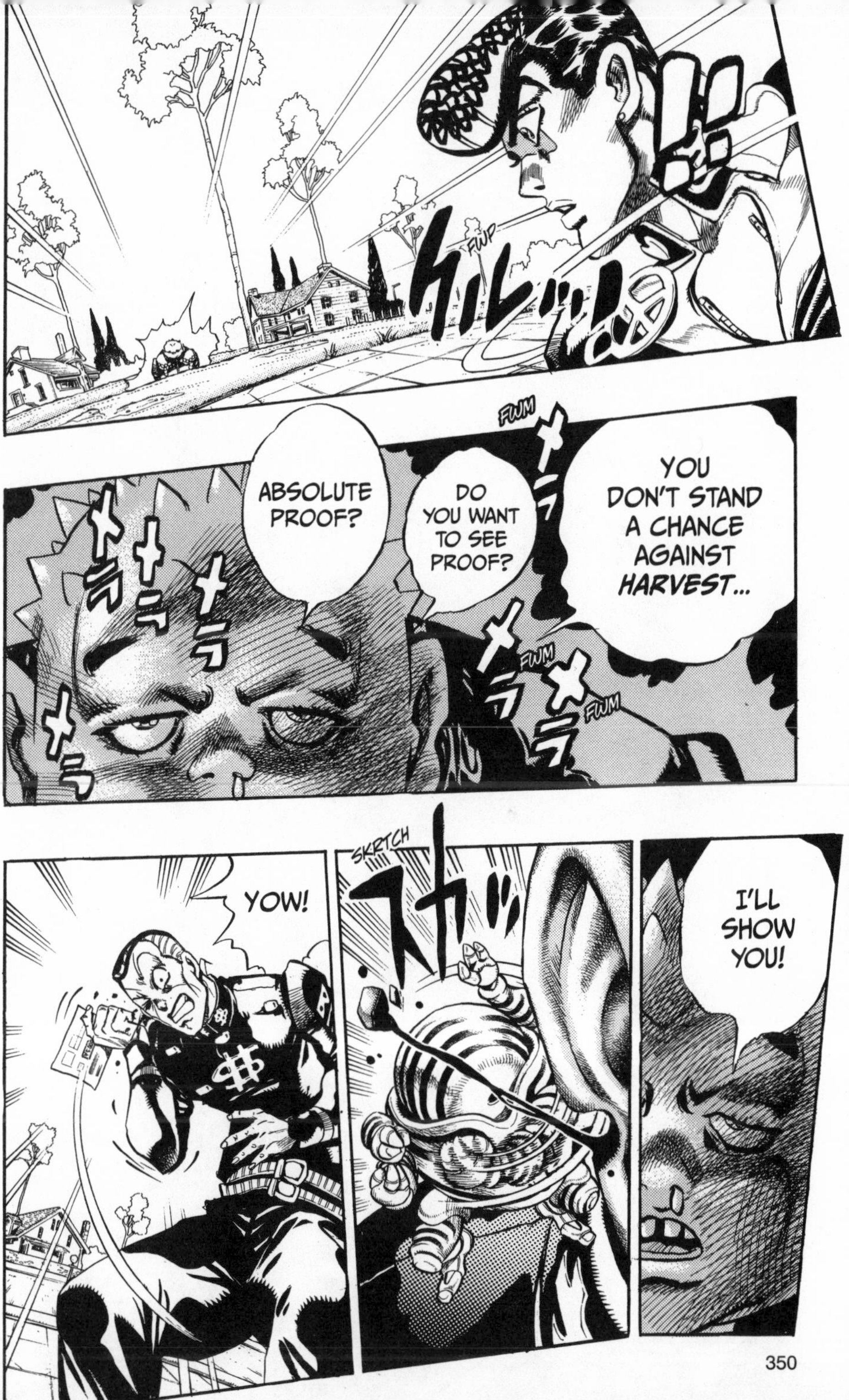
FWP
FWUM
YOU DON'T STAND A CHANCE AGAINST HARVEST...
FWUM
FWUM
DO YOU WANT TO SEE PROOF?
ABSOLUTE PROOF?
I'LL SHOW YOU!
SKRTCH
YOW!

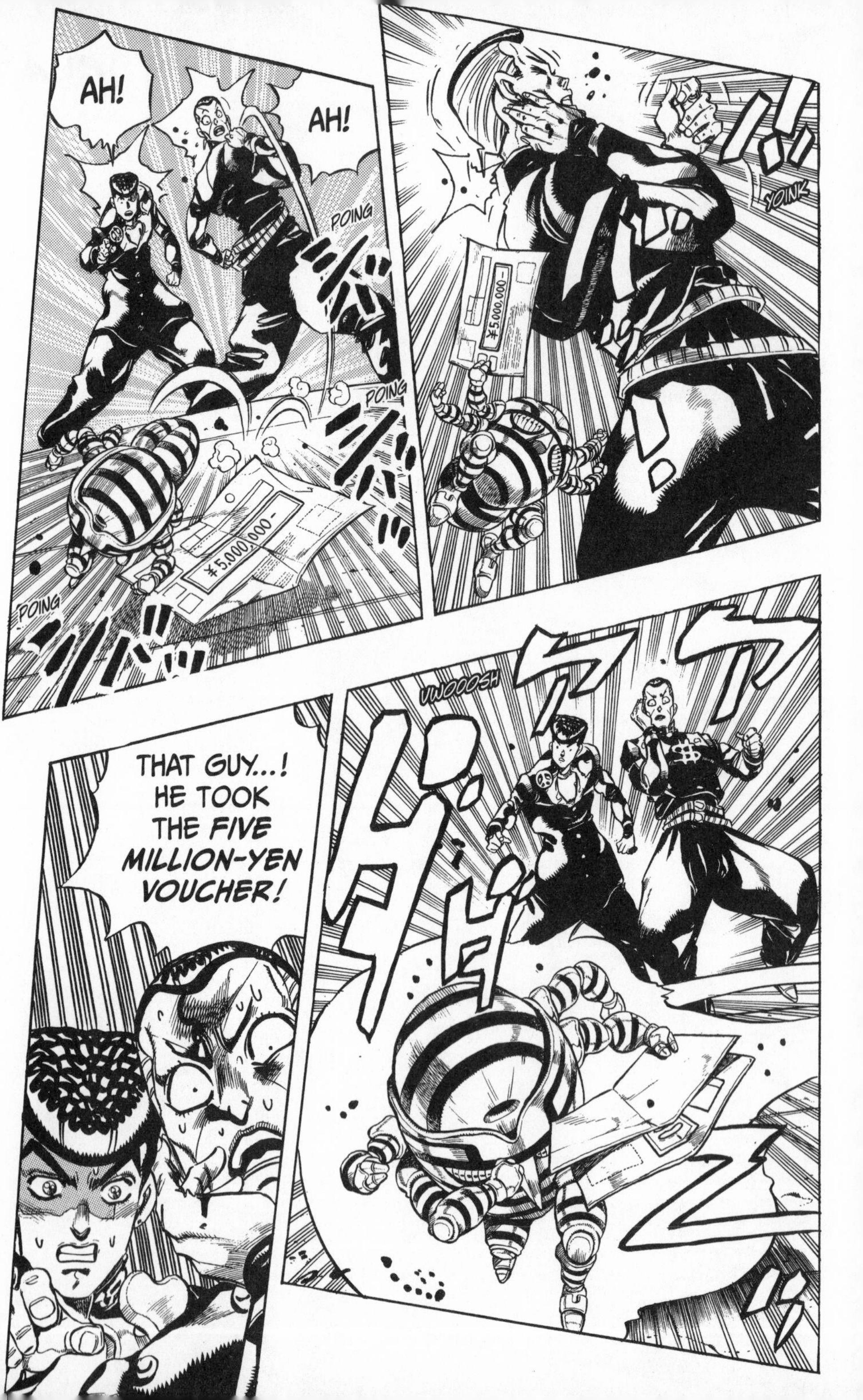

¥5,000,000-
YOINK
AH!
AH!
POING
POING
¥5,000,000-
POING
UWOOOSH
THAT GUY...! HE TOOK THE *FIVE MILLION-YEN VOUCHER!*

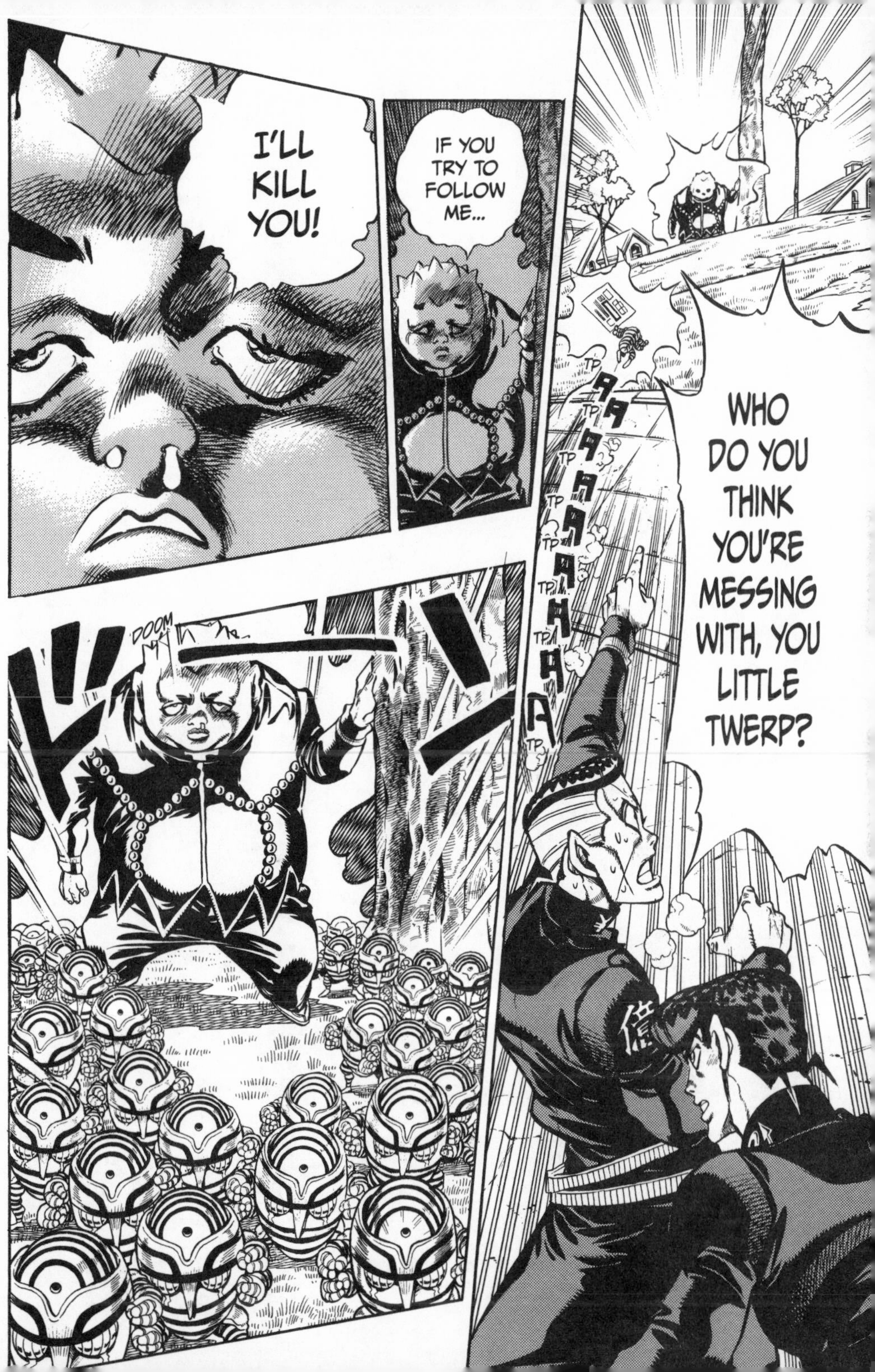
WHO DO YOU THINK YOU'RE MESSING WITH, YOU LITTLE TWERP?
TP TP TP TP TP TP TP TP
IF YOU TRY TO FOLLOW ME...
I'LL KILL YOU!
DOOM

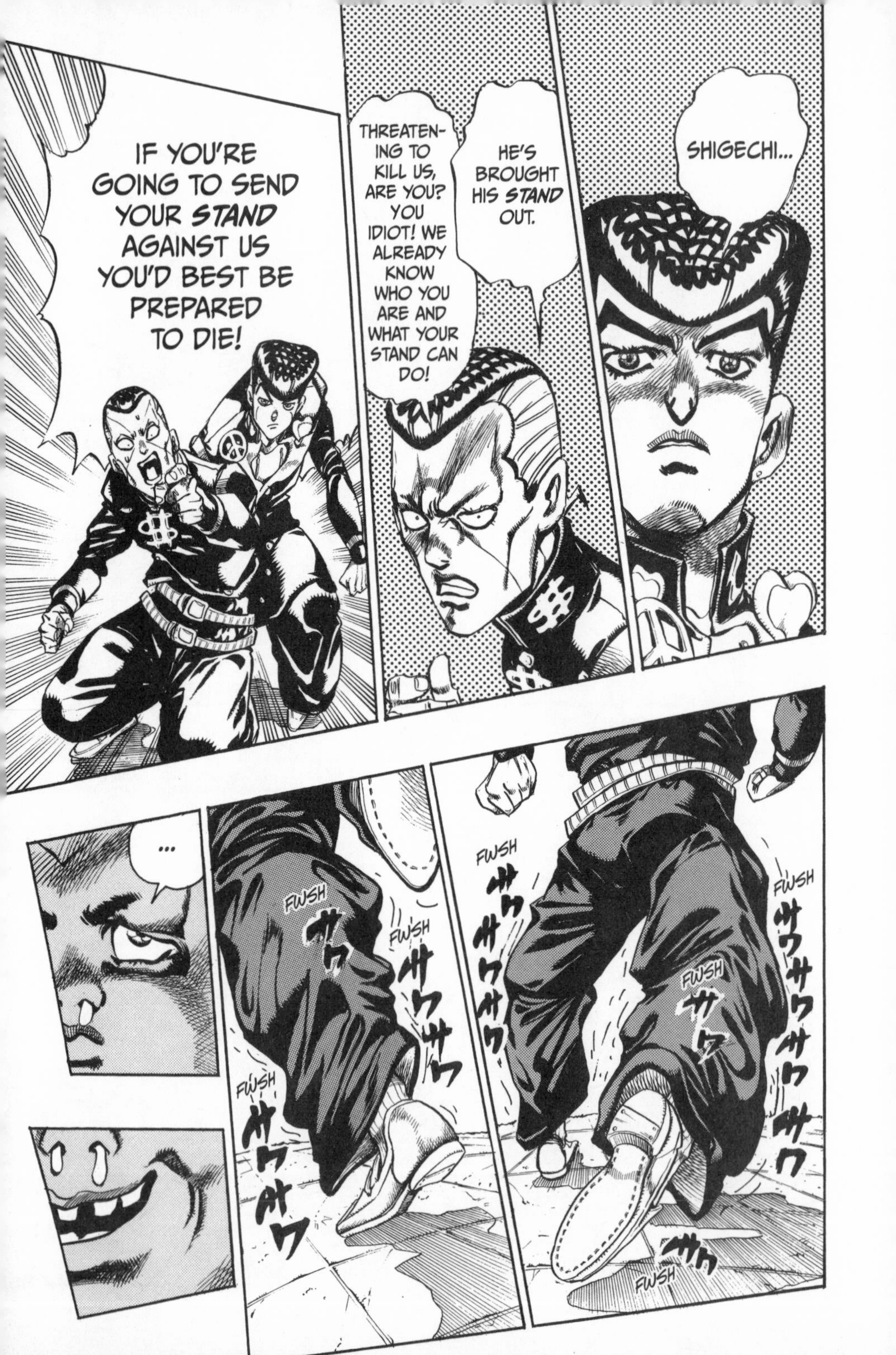
SHIGECHI...
HE'S BROUGHT HIS STAND OUT.
THREATENING TO KILL US, ARE YOU? YOU IDIOT! WE ALREADY KNOW WHO YOU ARE AND WHAT YOUR STAND CAN DO!
IF YOU'RE GOING TO SEND YOUR STAND AGAINST US YOU'D BEST BE PREPARED TO DIE!
FWSH
FWSH
FWSH
FWSH
FWSH
FWSH
FWSH
...

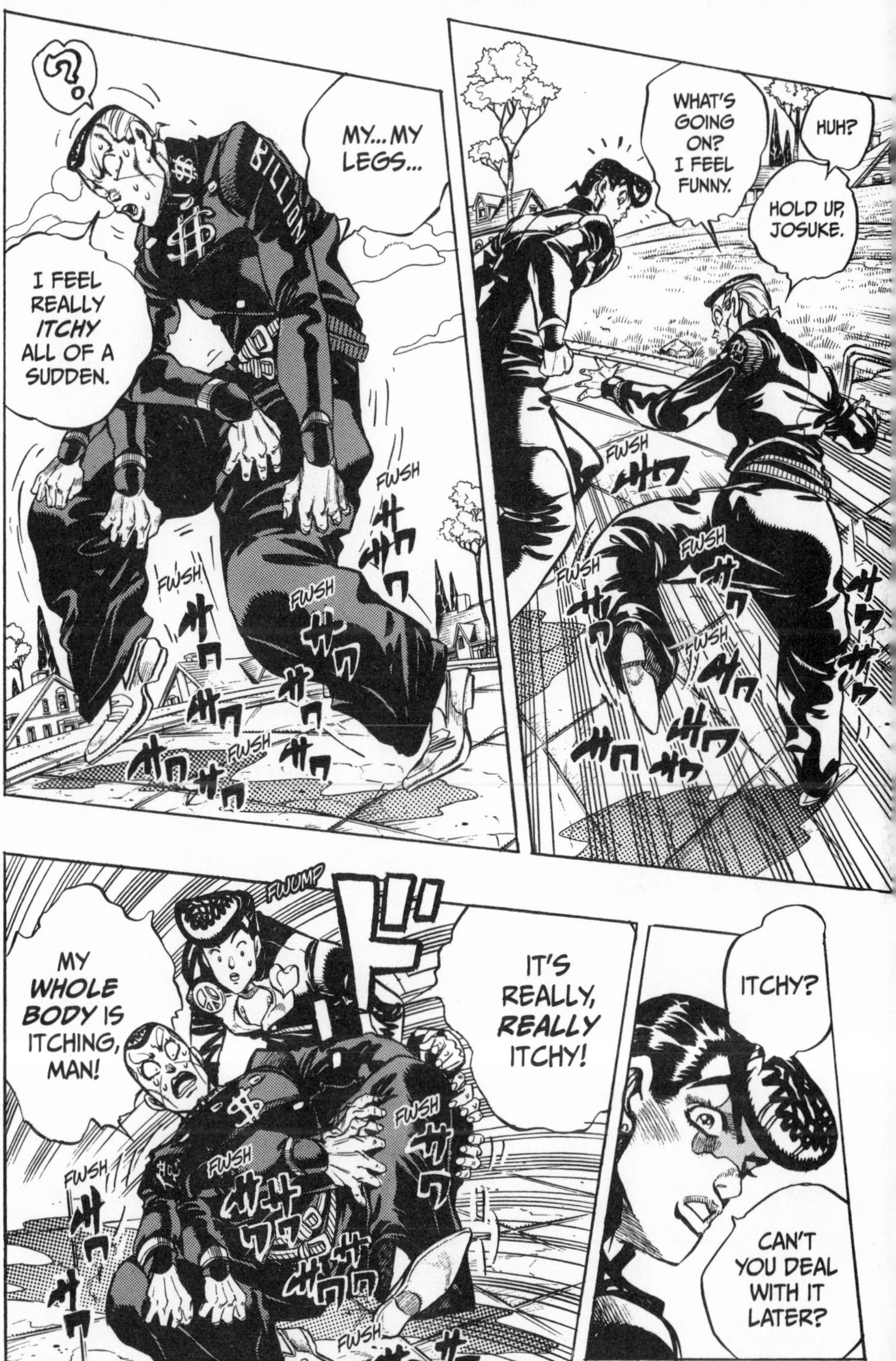
HUH?
HOLD UP, JOSUKE.
WHAT'S GOING ON? I FEEL FUNNY.
FWSH
FWSH
FWSH
FWSH
?
MY... MY LEGS...
I FEEL REALLY *ITCHY* ALL OF A SUDDEN.
FWSH
FWSH
FWSH
FWSH
ITCHY?
CAN'T YOU DEAL WITH IT LATER?
FWUMP
IT'S REALLY, *REALLY* ITCHY!
MY *WHOLE BODY* IS ITCHING, MAN!
FWSH
FWSH
FWSH
FWSH

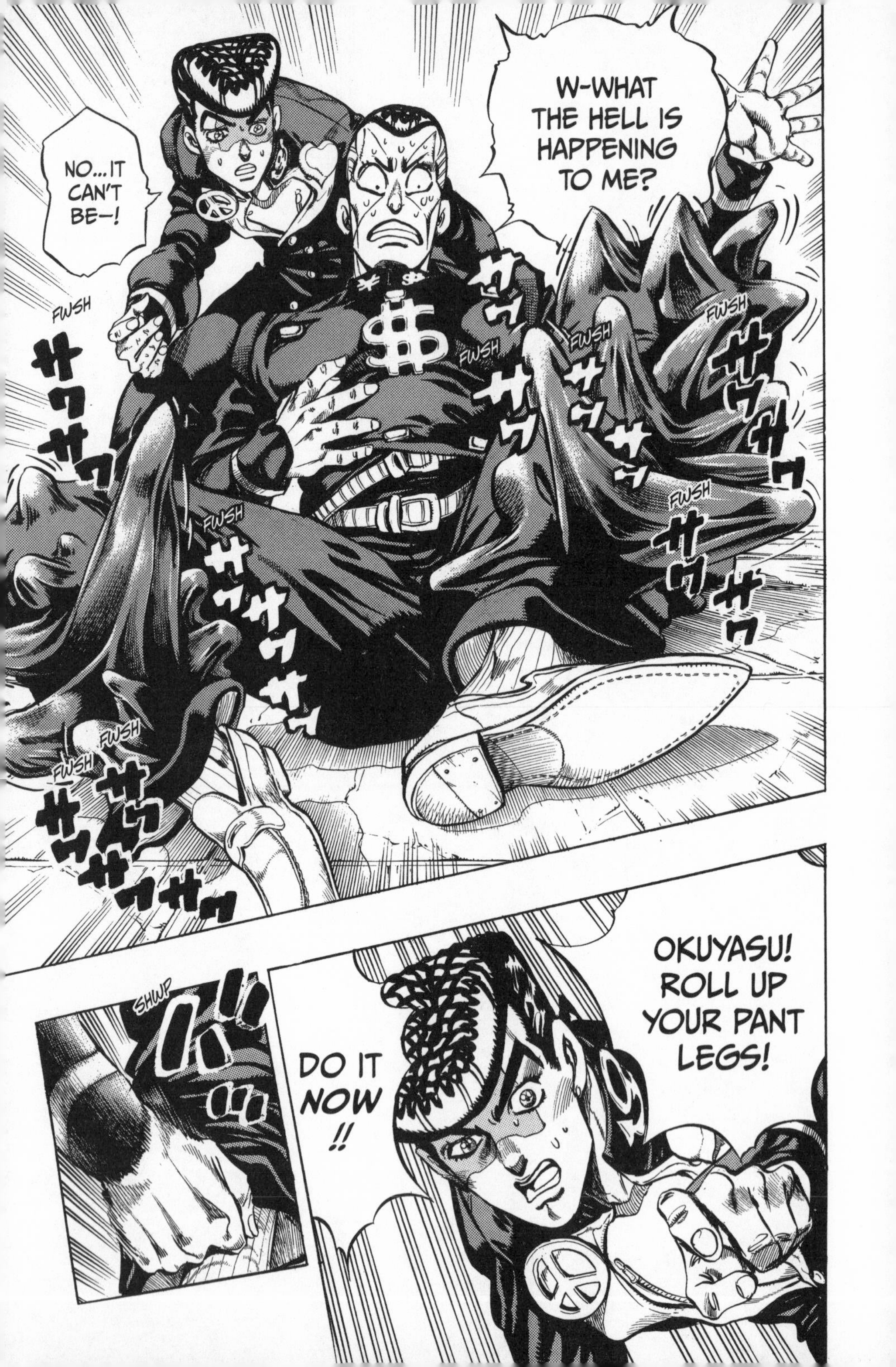
W-WHAT THE HELL IS HAPPENING TO ME?
NO...IT CAN'T BE–!
FWSH
FWSH
FWSH
FWSH
FWSH
FWSH
FWSH
FWSH
OKUYASU! ROLL UP YOUR PANT LEGS!
DO IT NOW!!
SHWP

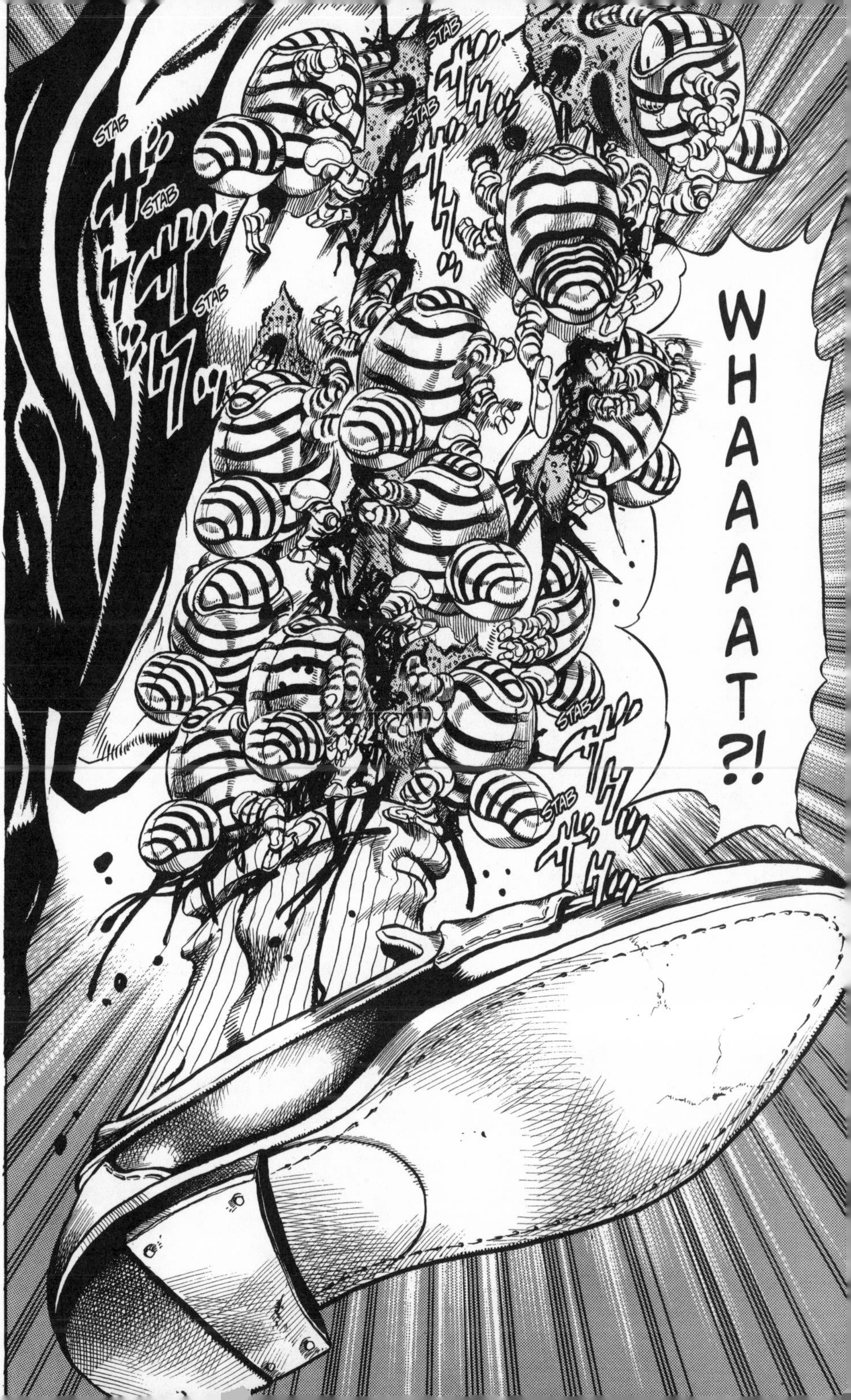
WHAAAAT?!
STAB
STAB
STAB
STAB
STAB
STAB
STAB

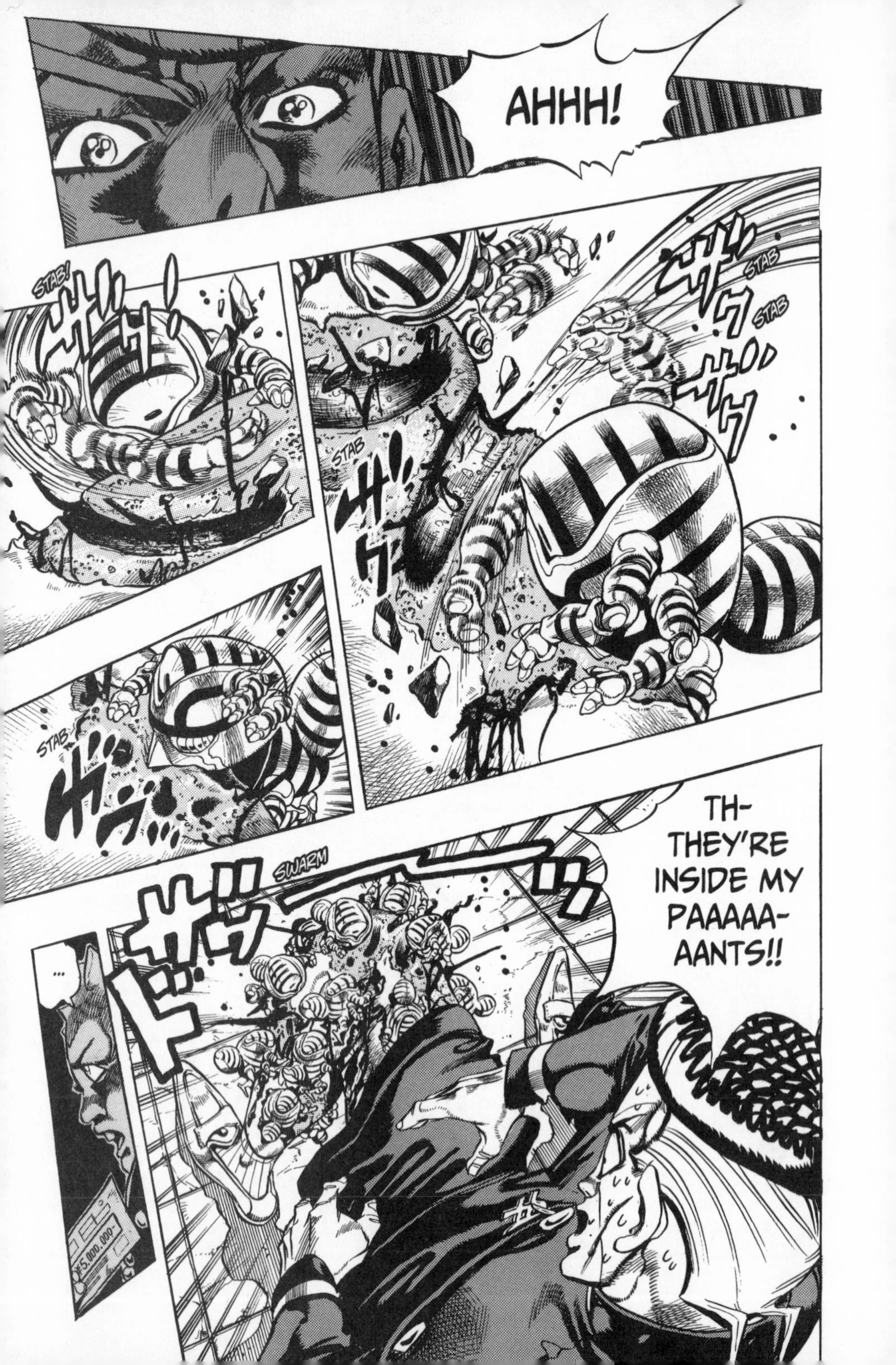
AHHH!
STAB
STAB
STAB
STAB!
STAB
TH-
THEY'RE
INSIDE MY
PAAAAA-
AANTS!!
SWARM
...

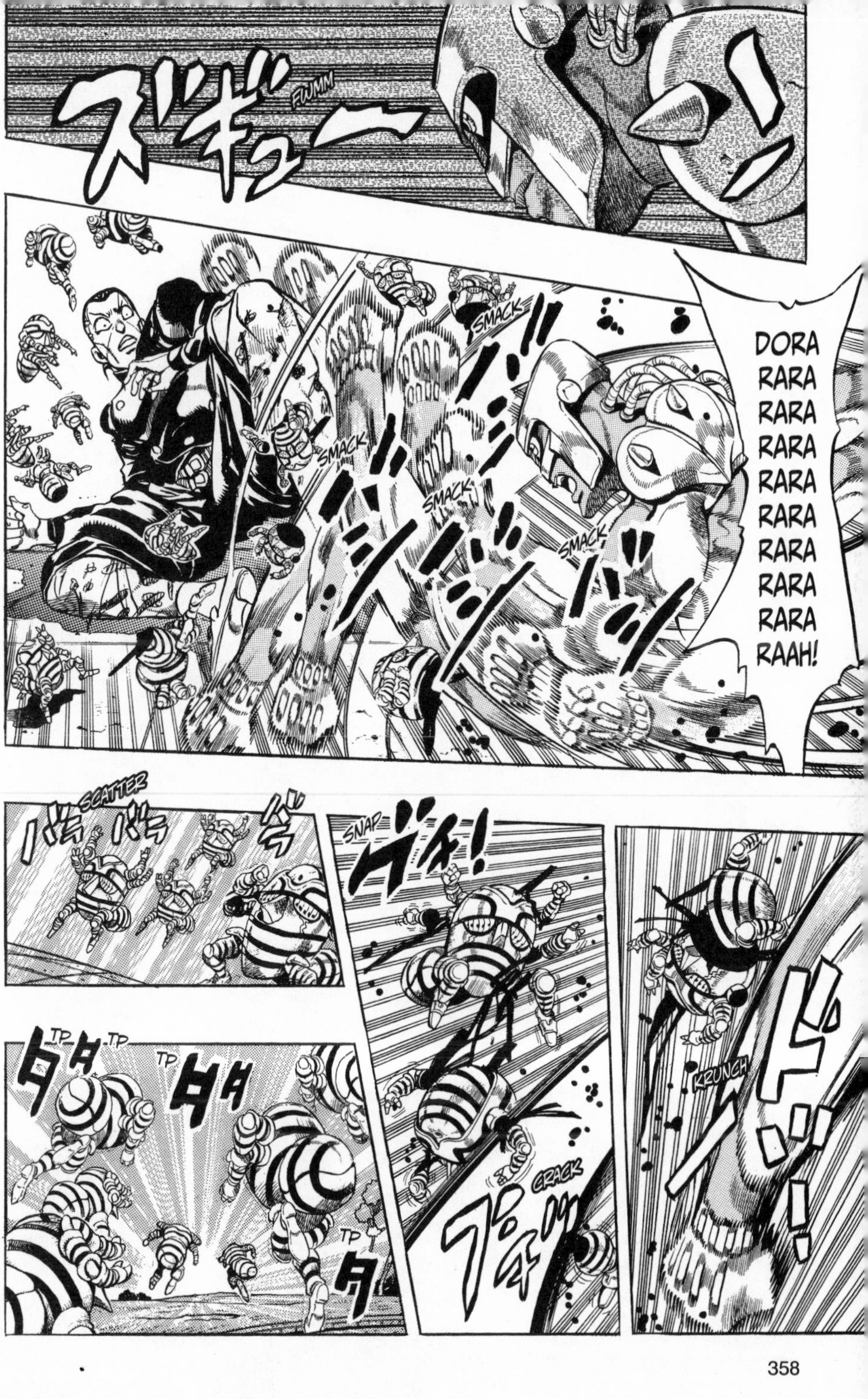
FWUMM
DORA RARA RARA RARA RARA RARA RARA RARA RARA RARA RAAH!
SMACK
SMACK
SMACK
SMACK
KRUNCH
SNAP
CRACK
SCATTER
TP
TP
TP
TP

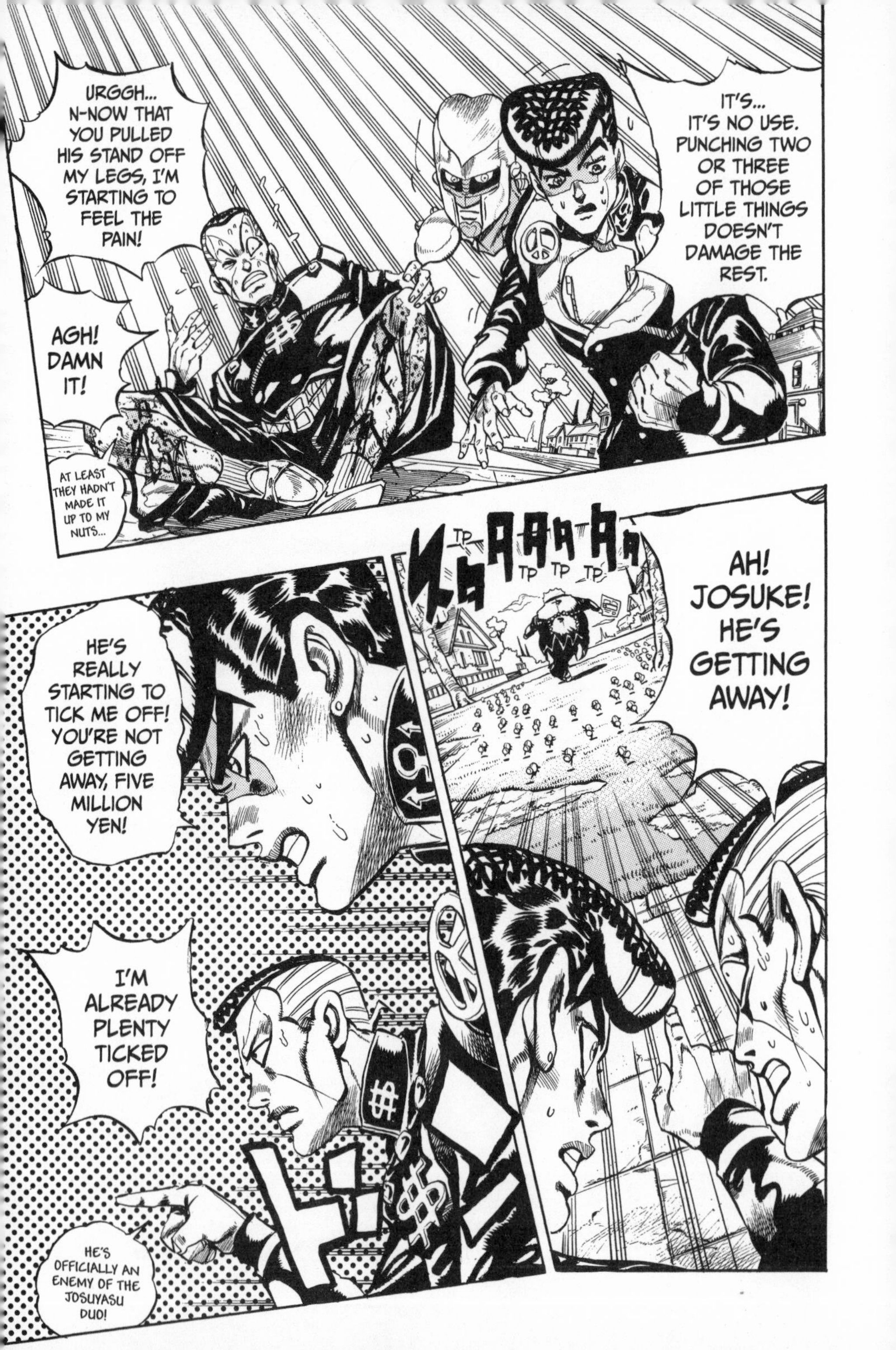
IT'S... IT'S NO USE. PUNCHING TWO OR THREE OF THOSE LITTLE THINGS DOESN'T DAMAGE THE REST.
URGGH... N-NOW THAT YOU PULLED HIS STAND OFF MY LEGS, I'M STARTING TO FEEL THE PAIN!
AGH! DAMN IT!
AT LEAST THEY HADN'T MADE IT UP TO MY NUTS...
TP TP TP TP
AH! JOSUKE! HE'S GETTING AWAY!
HE'S REALLY STARTING TO TICK ME OFF! YOU'RE NOT GETTING AWAY, FIVE MILLION YEN!
I'M ALREADY PLENTY TICKED OFF!
HE'S OFFICIALLY AN ENEMY OF THE JOSUYASU DUO!

C. D

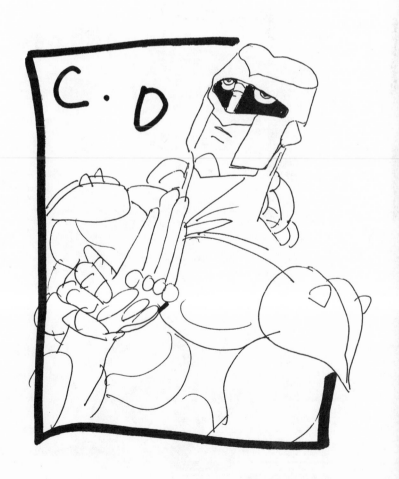

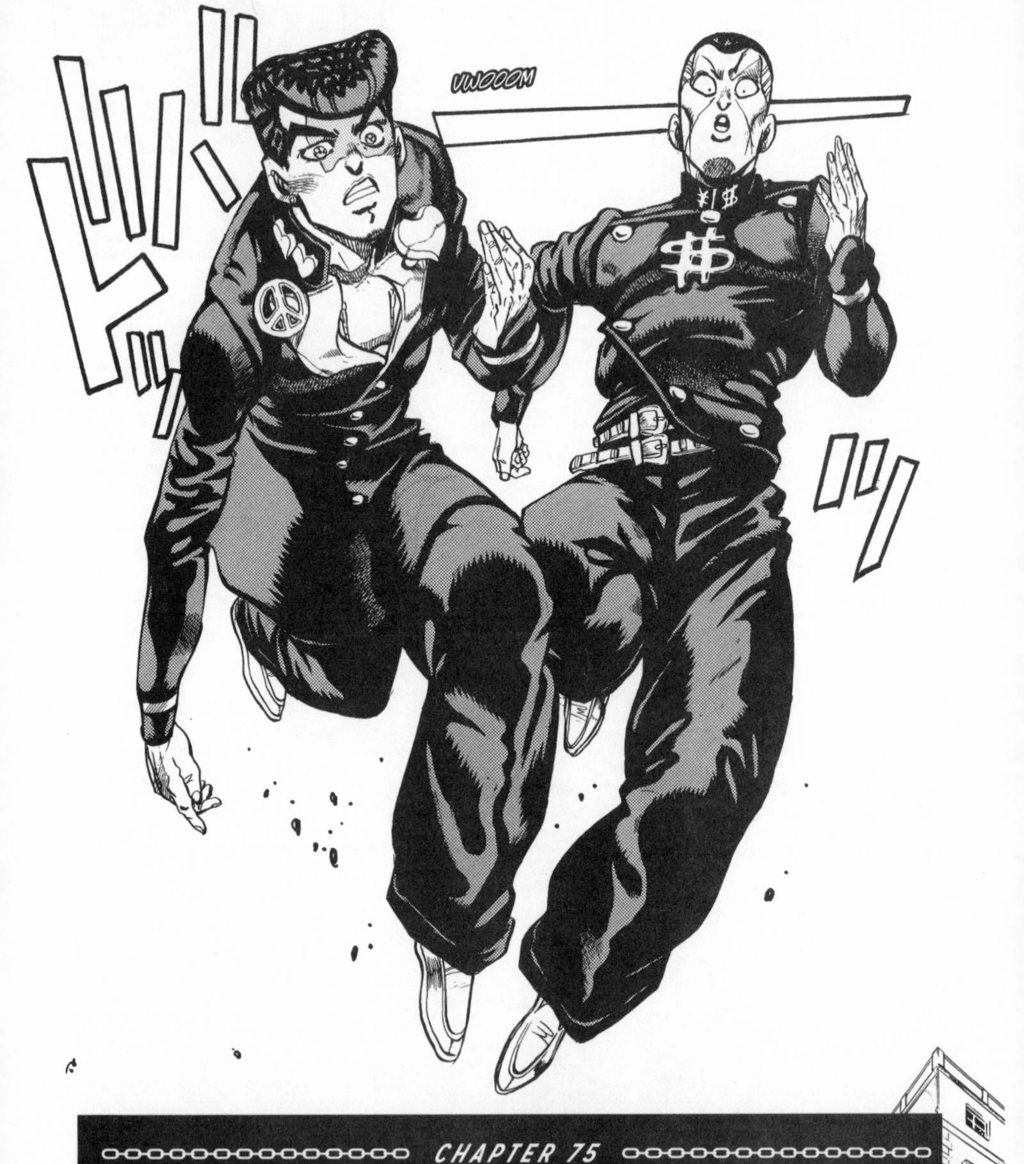
VWOOOM

CHAPTER 75

SHIGECHI'S HARVEST, PART 6

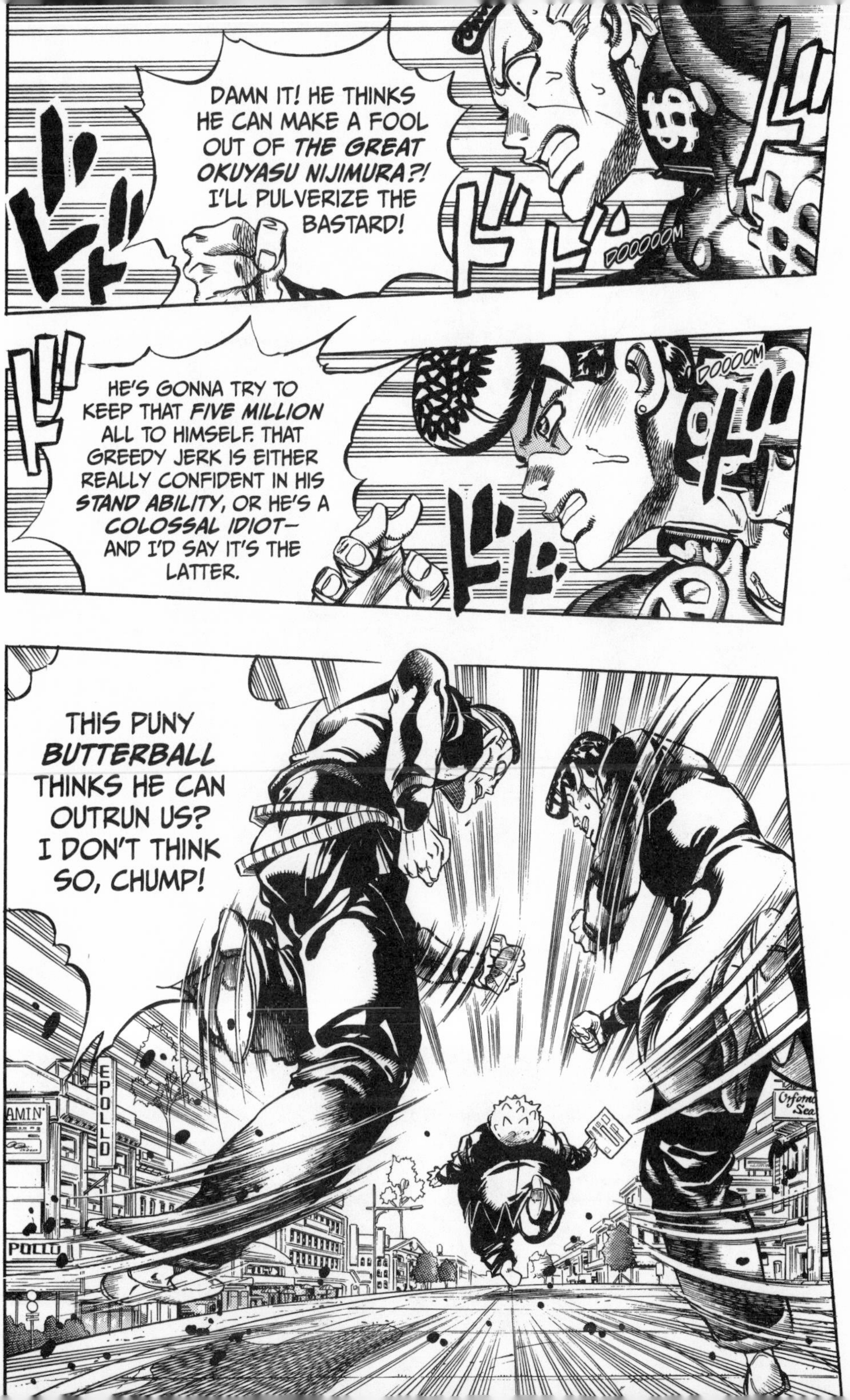
DAMN IT! HE THINKS HE CAN MAKE A FOOL OUT OF THE GREAT OKUYASU NIJIMURA?! I'LL PULVERIZE THE BASTARD!
DOOOOOM
DOOOOM
HE'S GONNA TRY TO KEEP THAT FIVE MILLION ALL TO HIMSELF. THAT GREEDY JERK IS EITHER REALLY CONFIDENT IN HIS STAND ABILITY, OR HE'S A COLOSSAL IDIOT— AND I'D SAY IT'S THE LATTER.
THIS PUNY BUTTERBALL THINKS HE CAN OUTRUN US? I DON'T THINK SO, CHUMP!
EPOLLO

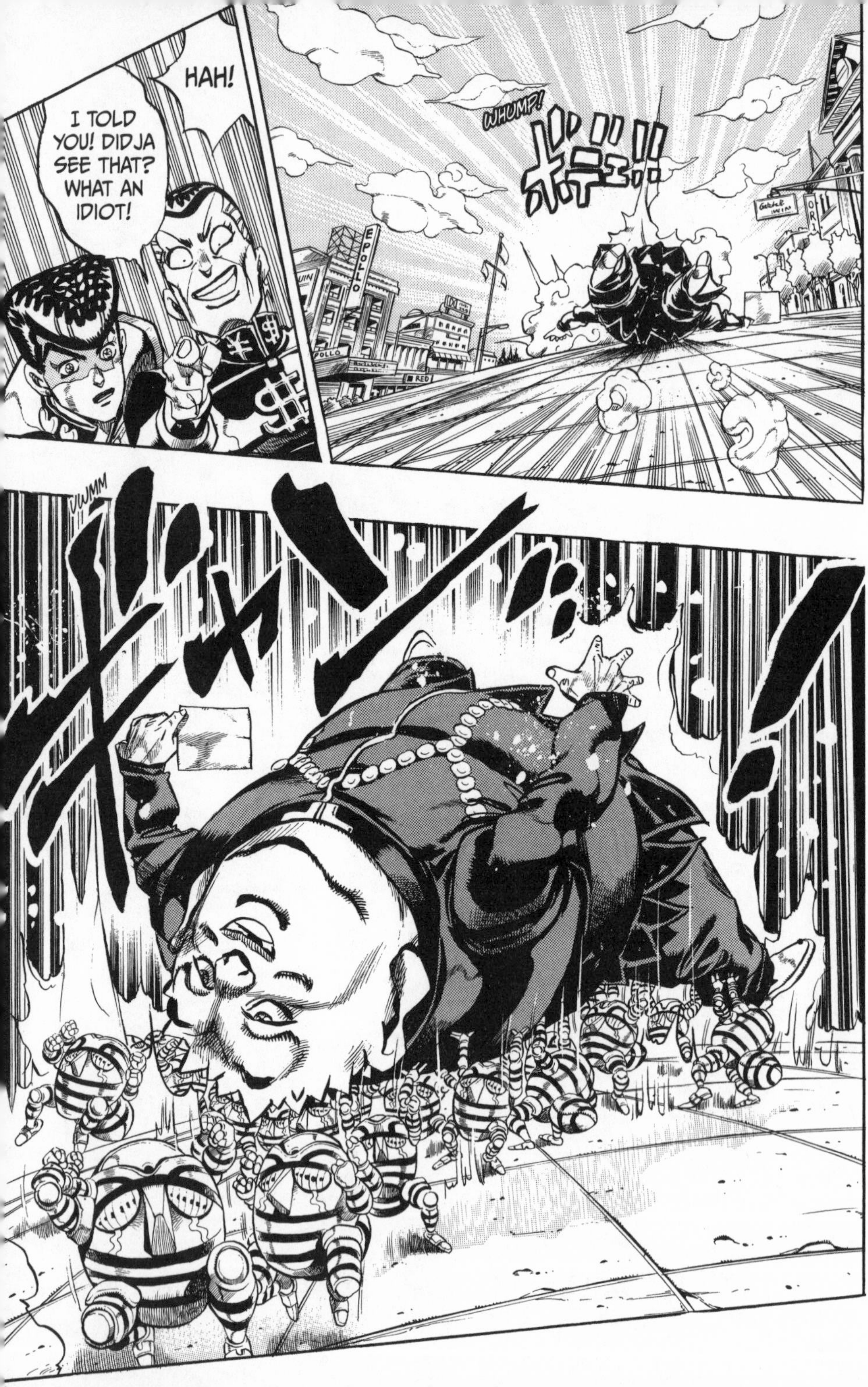
WHUMP!
ボデェ!!
HAH!
I TOLD YOU! DIDJA SEE THAT? WHAT AN IDIOT!
VWMM

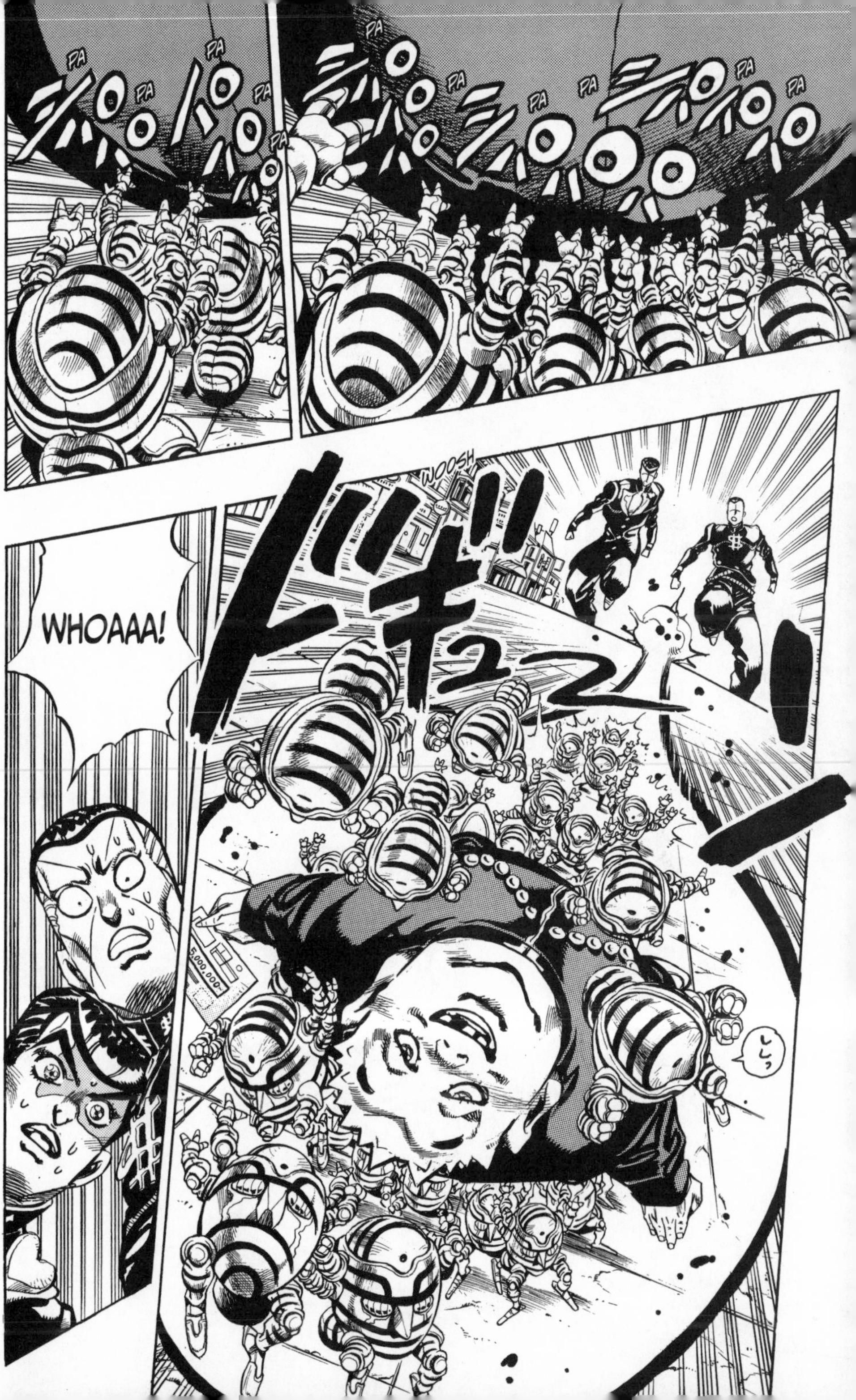
PA
PA
PA
PA
PA
PA
PA
PA
PA
PA
PA
WOOSH
WHOAAA!

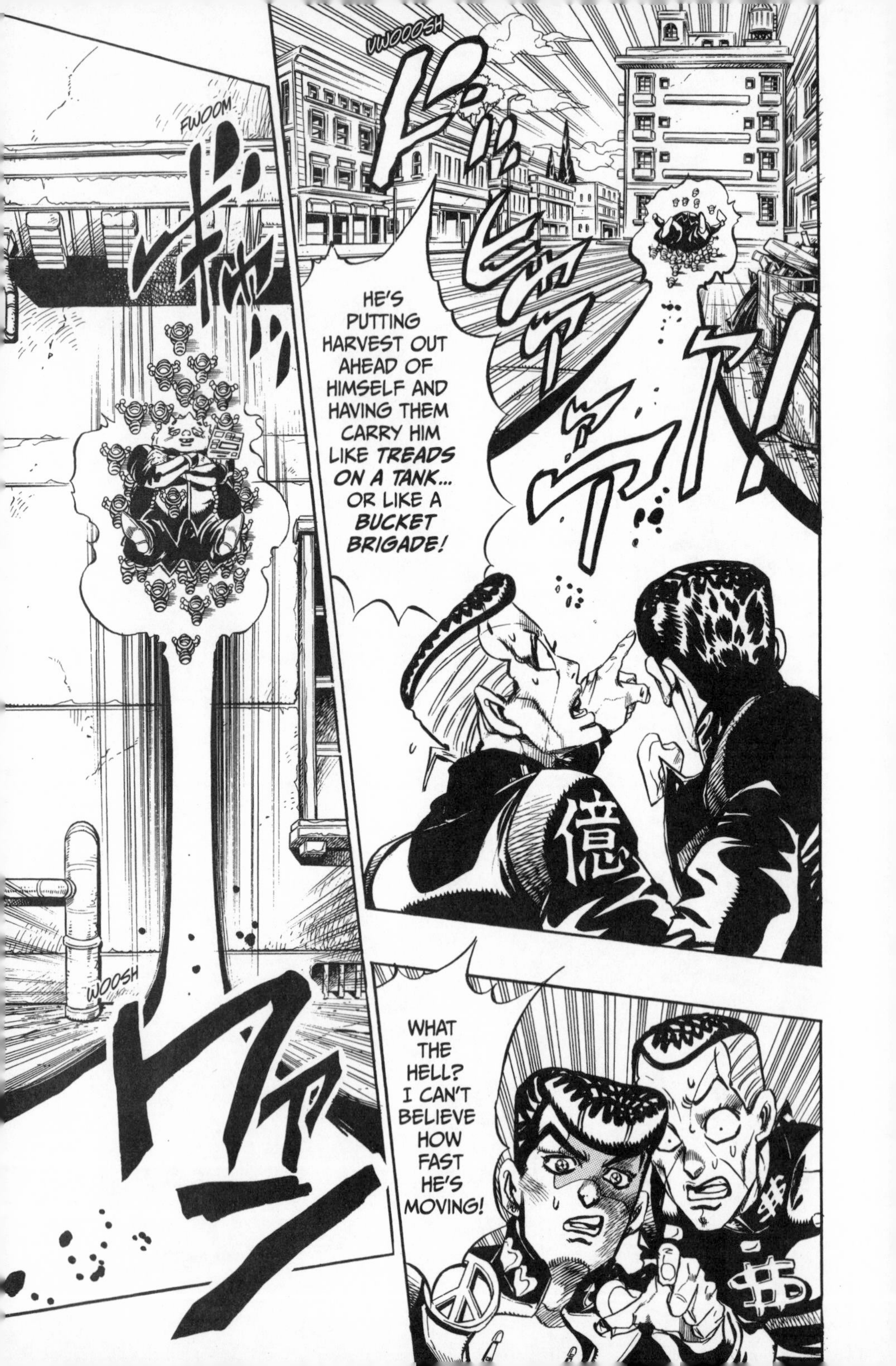
UWOOOSH
HE'S PUTTING HARVEST OUT AHEAD OF HIMSELF AND HAVING THEM CARRY HIM LIKE *TREADS ON A TANK*... OR LIKE A *BUCKET BRIGADE!*
WHAT THE HELL? I CAN'T BELIEVE HOW FAST HE'S MOVING!
FWOOM
WOOSH

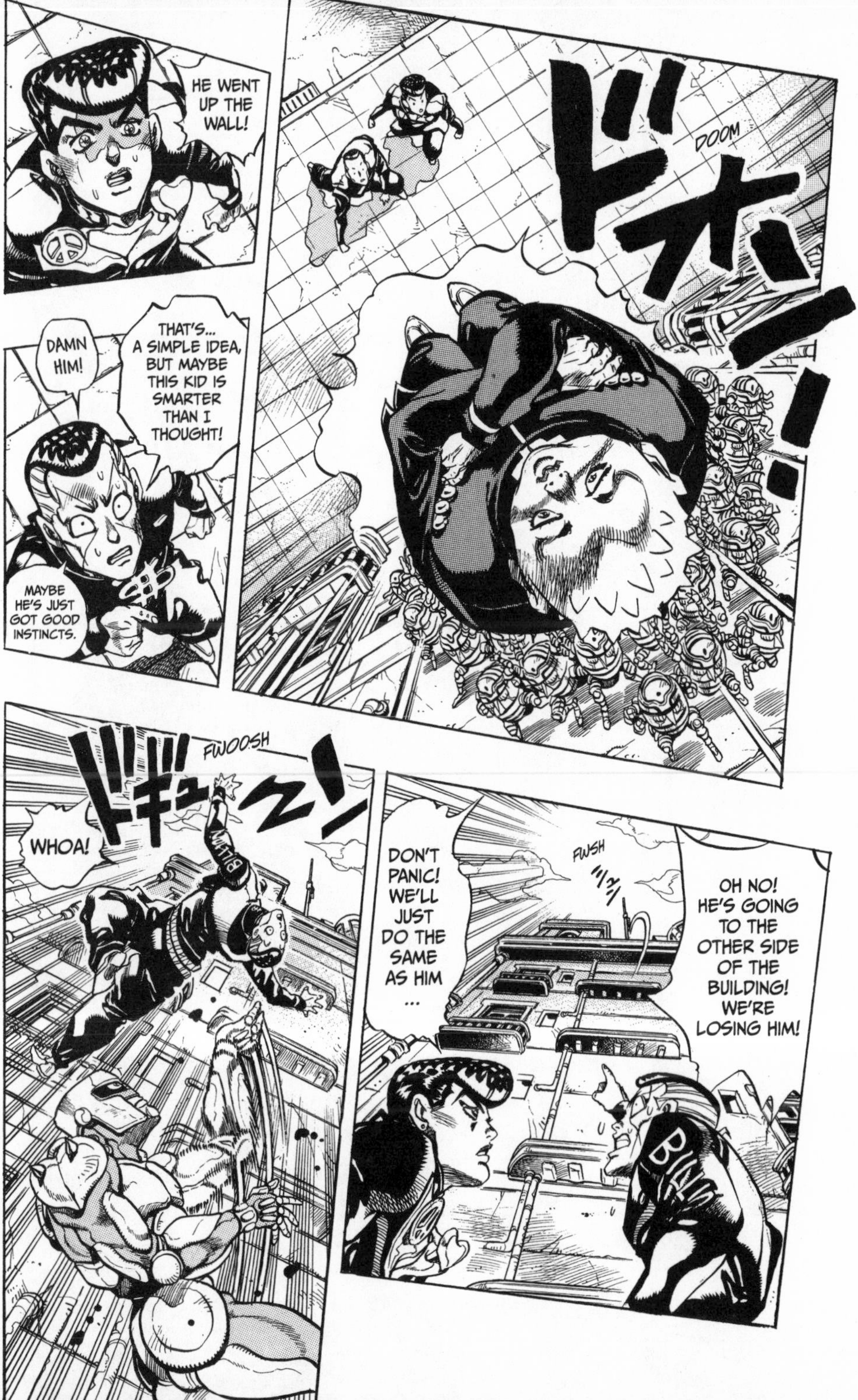
DOOM
HE WENT UP THE WALL!
THAT'S... A SIMPLE IDEA, BUT MAYBE THIS KID IS SMARTER THAN I THOUGHT!
DAMN HIM!
MAYBE HE'S JUST GOT GOOD INSTINCTS.
OH NO! HE'S GOING TO THE OTHER SIDE OF THE BUILDING! WE'RE LOSING HIM!
FWSH
DON'T PANIC! WE'LL JUST DO THE SAME AS HIM ...
FWOOSH
WHOA!

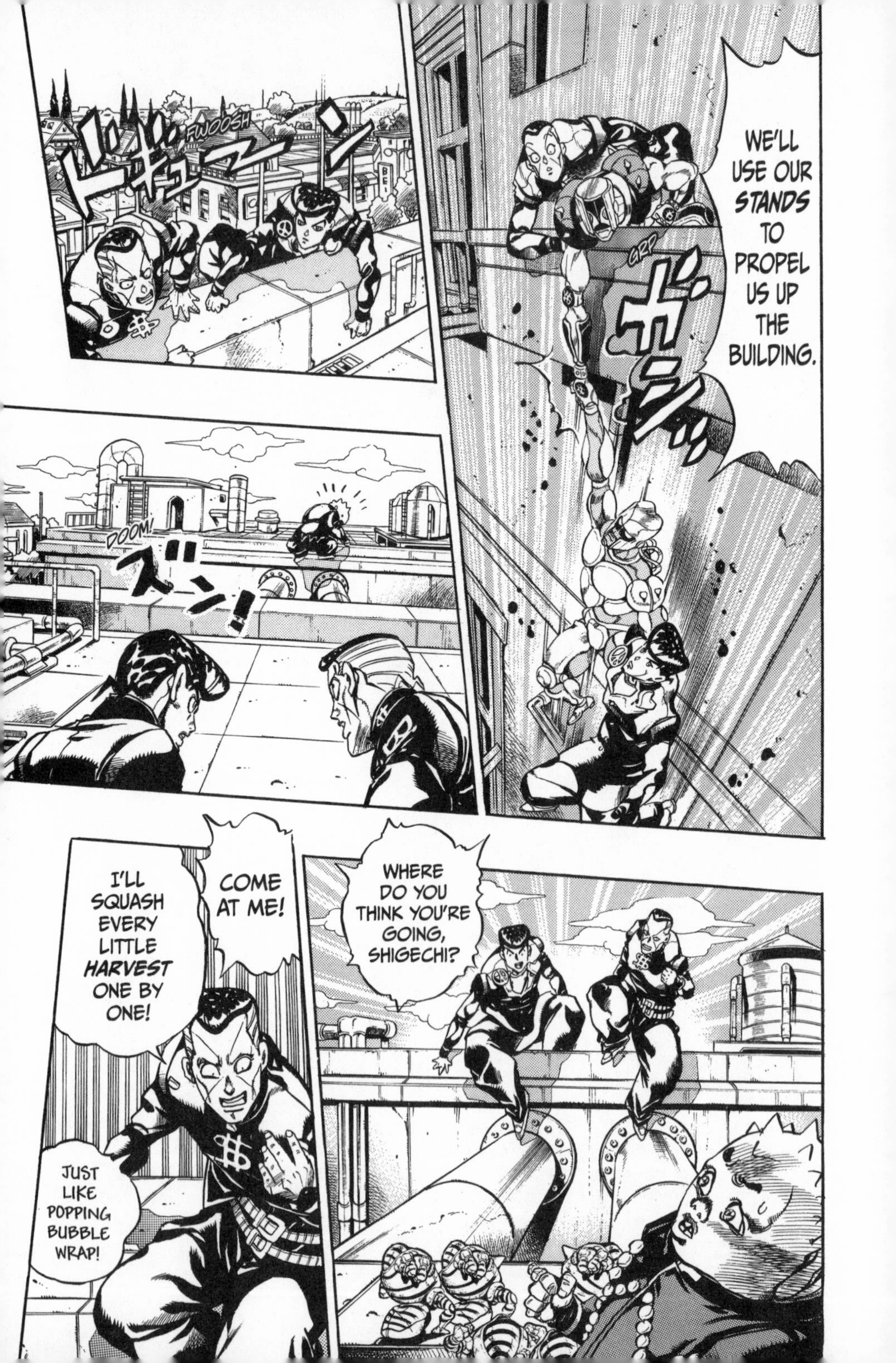
WE'LL USE OUR STANDS TO PROPEL US UP THE BUILDING.
GRP
FWOOSH
DOOM!
WHERE DO YOU THINK YOU'RE GOING, SHIGECHI?
COME AT ME!
I'LL SQUASH EVERY LITTLE HARVEST ONE BY ONE!
JUST LIKE POPPING BUBBLE WRAP!

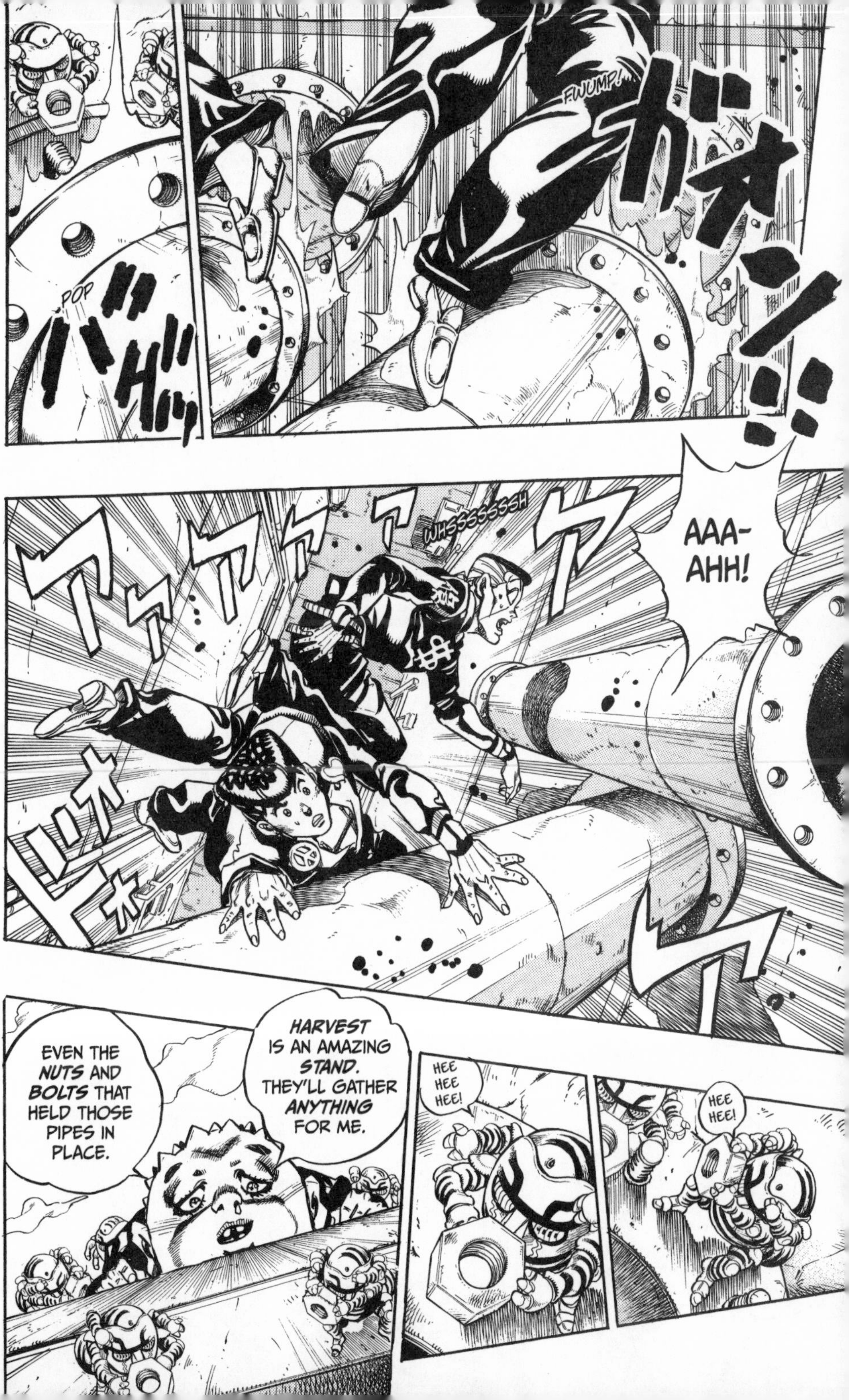
FWUMP!
POP
AAA-
AHH!
WHSSSSSSSH
HEE
HEE!
HEE
HEE
HEE!
HARVEST
IS AN AMAZING
STAND.
THEY'LL GATHER
ANYTHING
FOR ME.
EVEN THE
NUTS AND
BOLTS THAT
HELD THOSE
PIPES IN
PLACE.

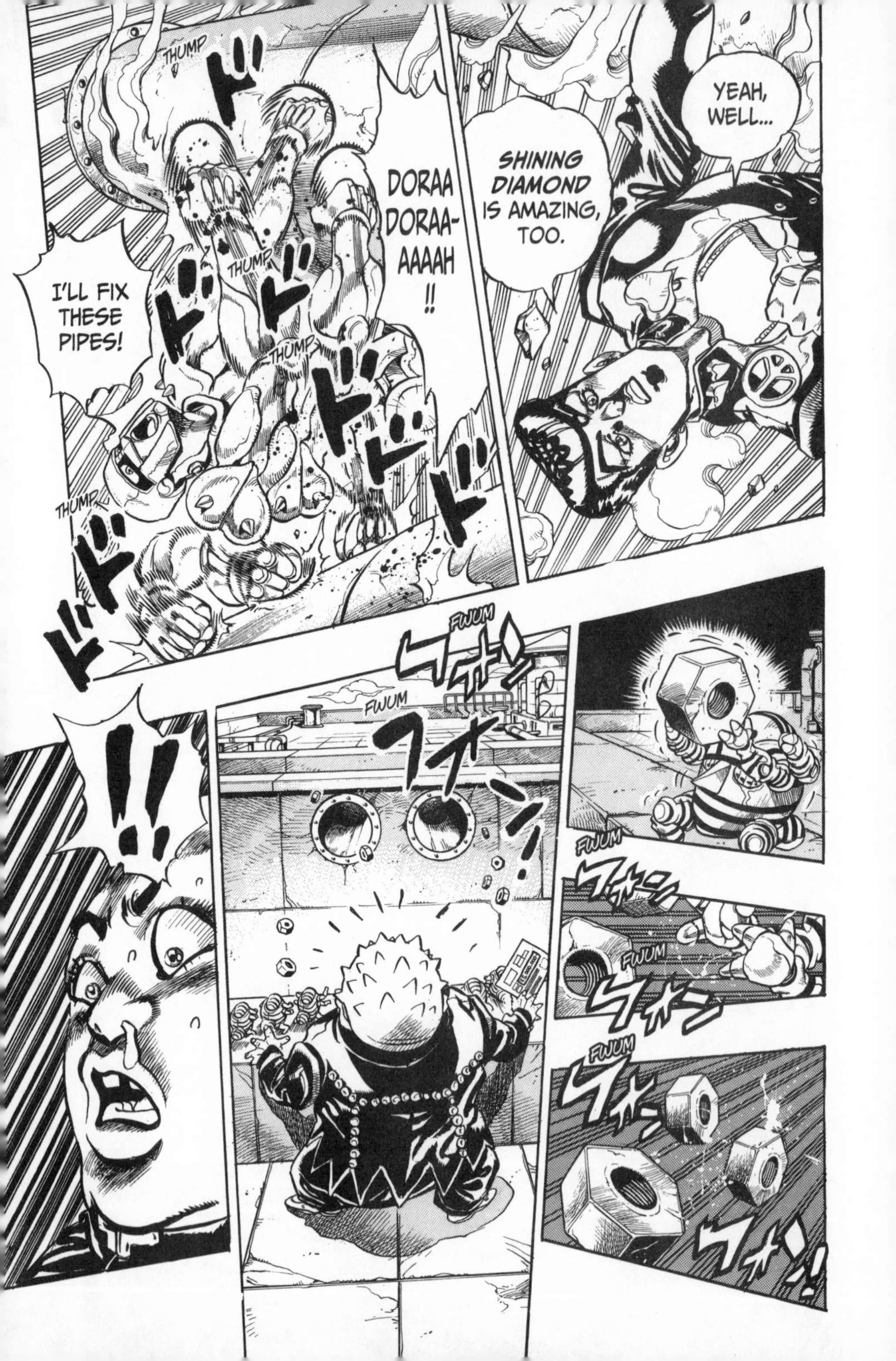
YEAH, WELL...
SHINING DIAMOND IS AMAZING, TOO.
THUMP
DORAA DORAA-AAAAH!!
THUMP
THUMP
I'LL FIX THESE PIPES!
THUMP
FWUM
FWUM
FWUM
FWUM
FWUM
!!

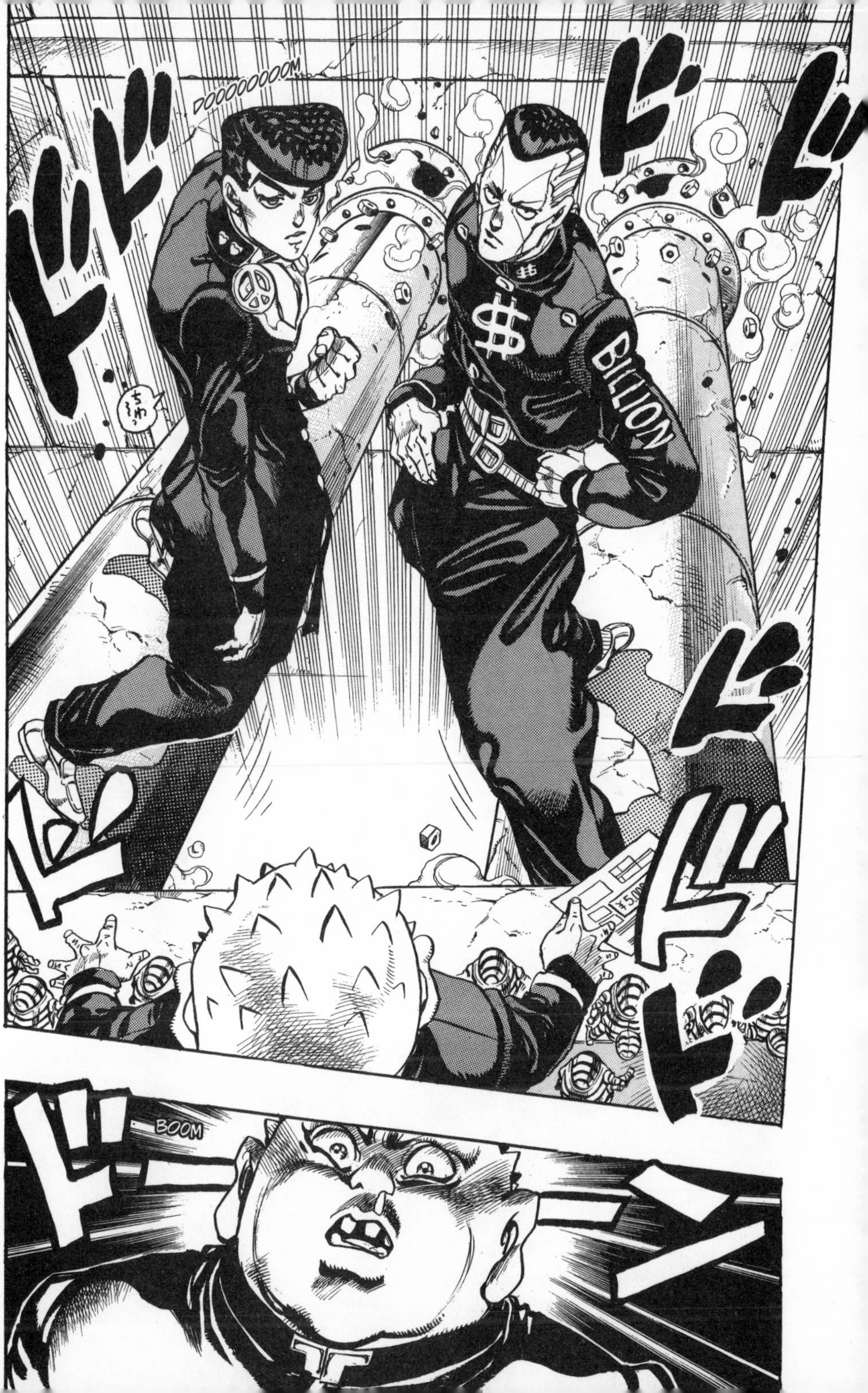
ドドドド
DOOOOOOOOOM
ちわ〜っ
BILLION
ドドドド
BOOM
ドン

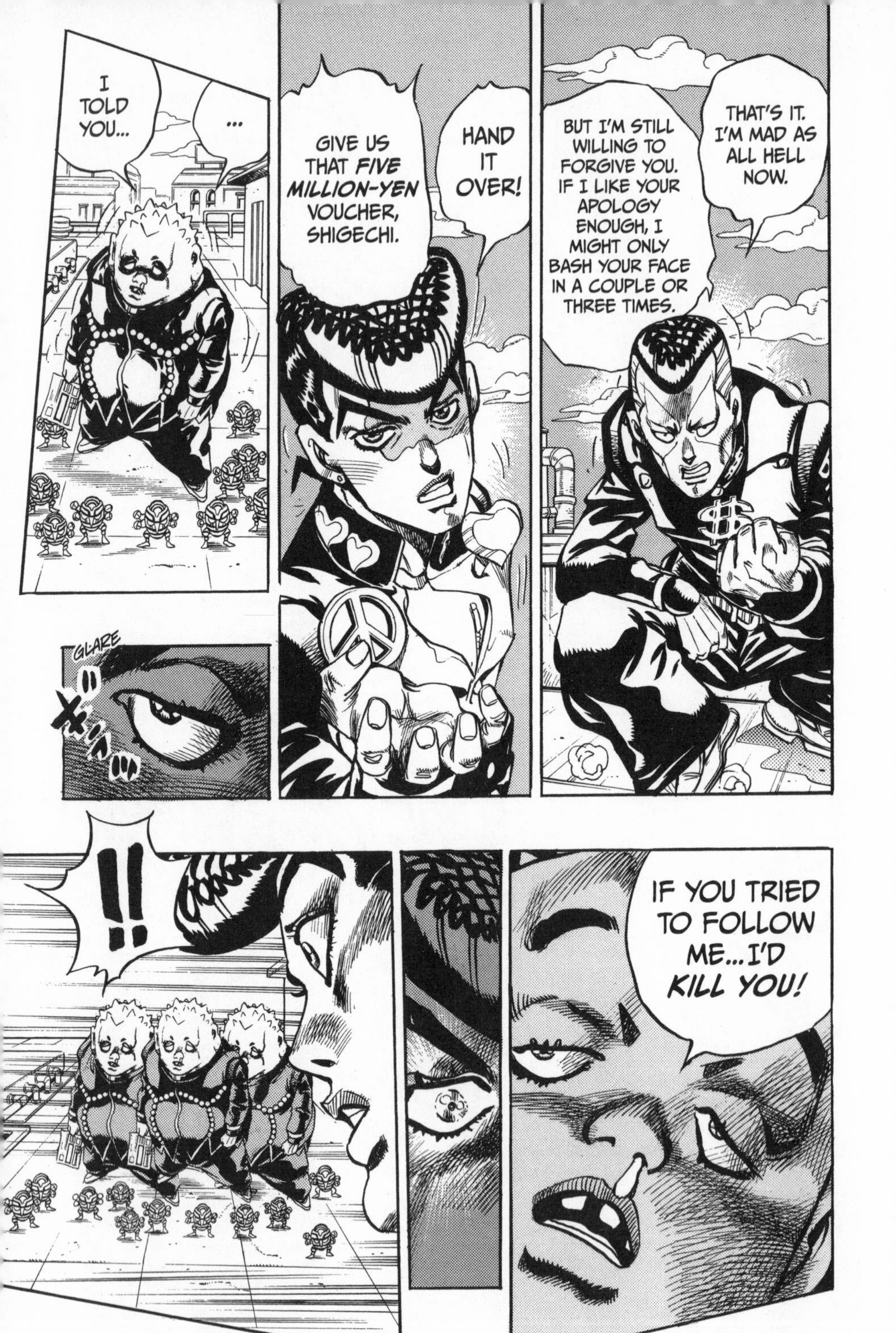

THAT'S IT. I'M MAD AS ALL HELL NOW.
BUT I'M STILL WILLING TO FORGIVE YOU. IF I LIKE YOUR APOLOGY ENOUGH, I MIGHT ONLY BASH YOUR FACE IN A COUPLE OR THREE TIMES.
HAND IT OVER!
GIVE US THAT *FIVE MILLION-YEN* VOUCHER, SHIGECHI.
...
I TOLD YOU...
GLARE
IF YOU TRIED TO FOLLOW ME...I'D *KILL YOU!*
!!

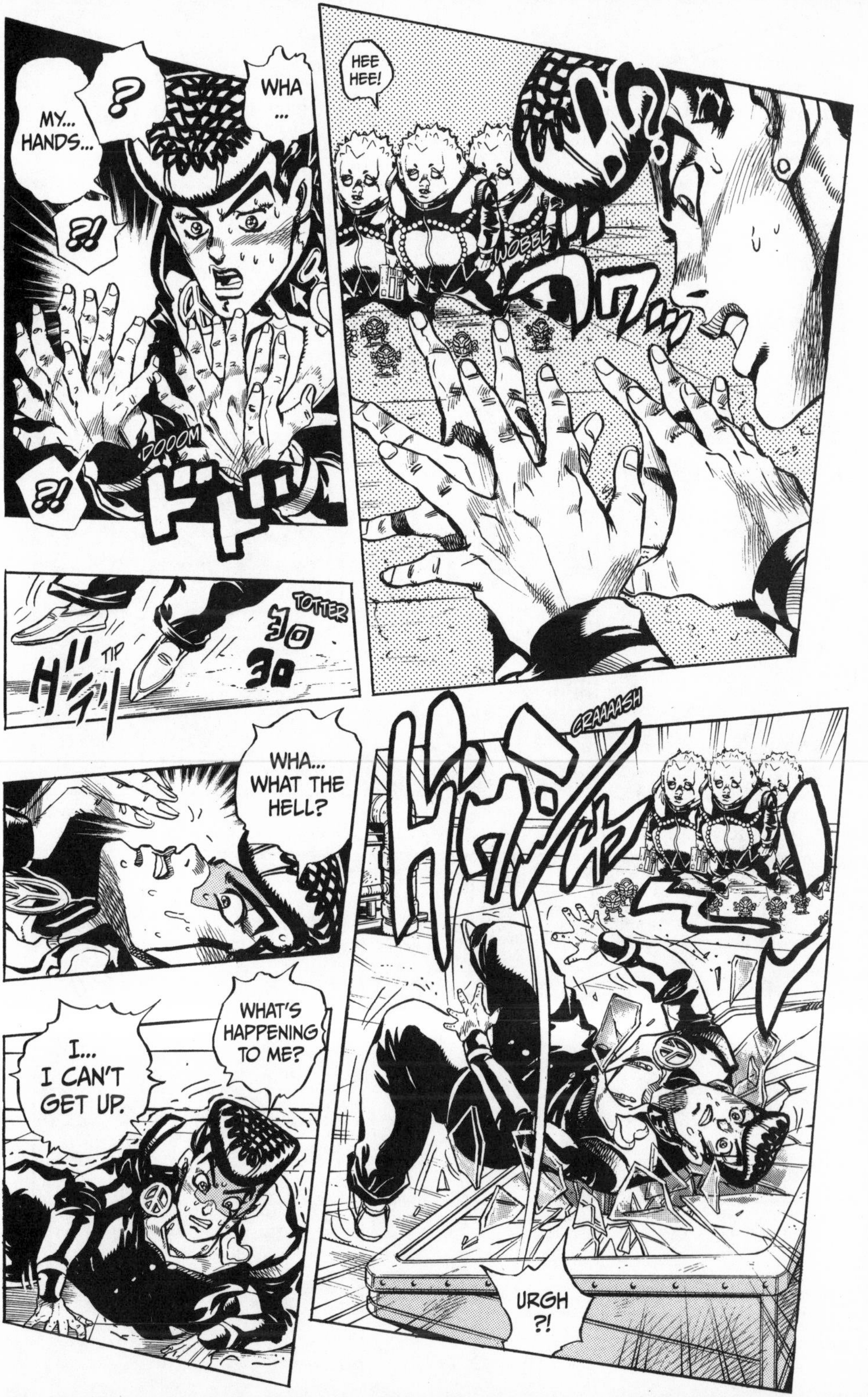
HEE HEE!
WOBBL
WHA ...
?
MY... HANDS...
?!
DOOOM
?!
TOTTER
TIP
CRAAAASH
URGH ?!
WHA... WHAT THE HELL?
WHAT'S HAPPENING TO ME?
I... I CAN'T GET UP.

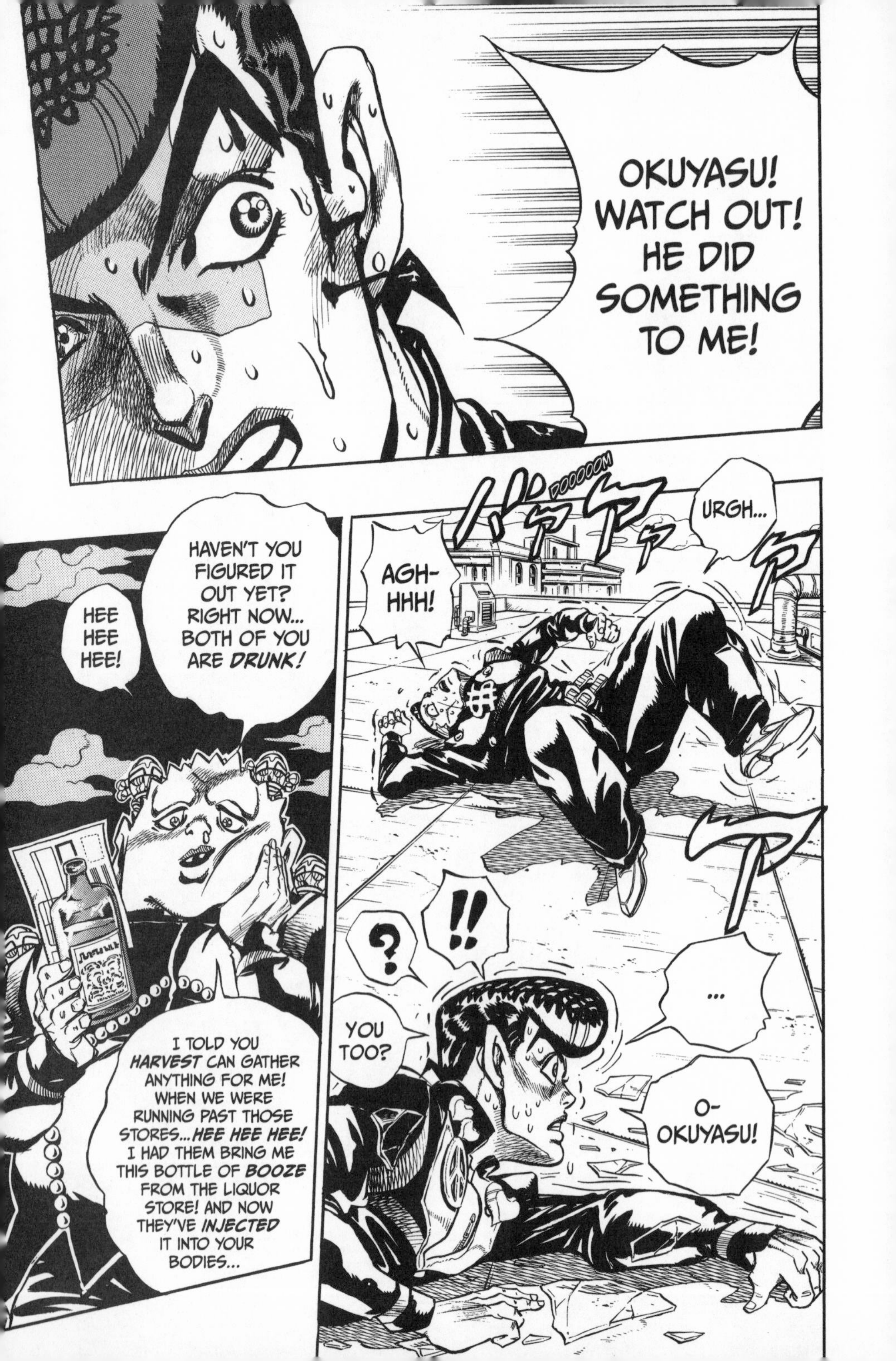
OKUYASU! WATCH OUT! HE DID SOMETHING TO ME!
URGH...
DOOOOOOM
AGH-HHH!
...
!!
?
O-OKUYASU!
YOU TOO?
HAVEN'T YOU FIGURED IT OUT YET? RIGHT NOW... BOTH OF YOU ARE *DRUNK!*
HEE HEE HEE!
I TOLD YOU *HARVEST* CAN GATHER ANYTHING FOR ME! WHEN WE WERE RUNNING PAST THOSE STORES... *HEE HEE HEE!* I HAD THEM BRING ME THIS BOTTLE OF *BOOZE* FROM THE LIQUOR STORE! AND NOW THEY'VE *INJECTED* IT INTO YOUR BODIES...

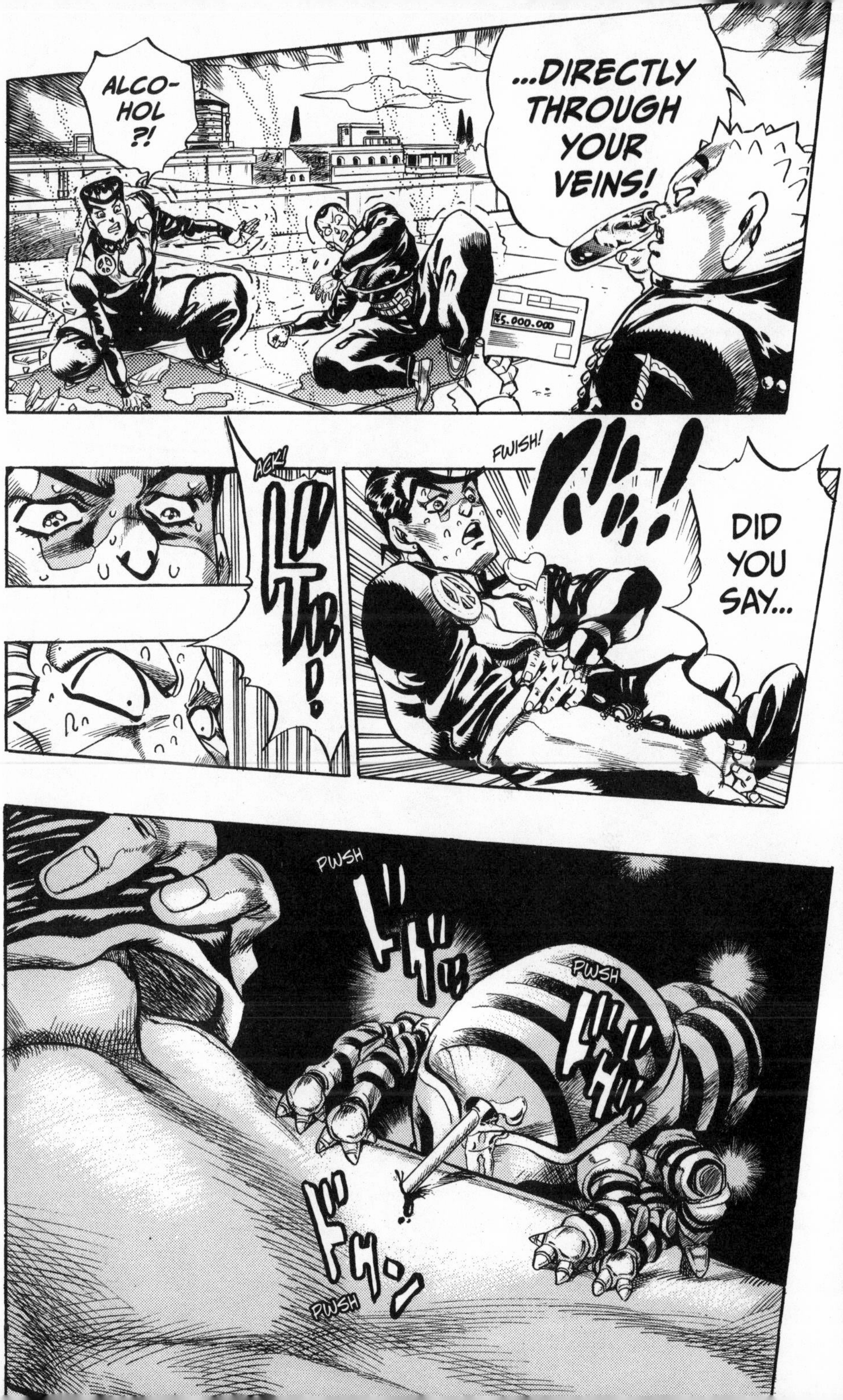
...DIRECTLY THROUGH YOUR VEINS!
¥5.000.000
ALCO-HOL?!
DID YOU SAY...
FWISH!
ACK!
PWSH
PWSH
PWSH

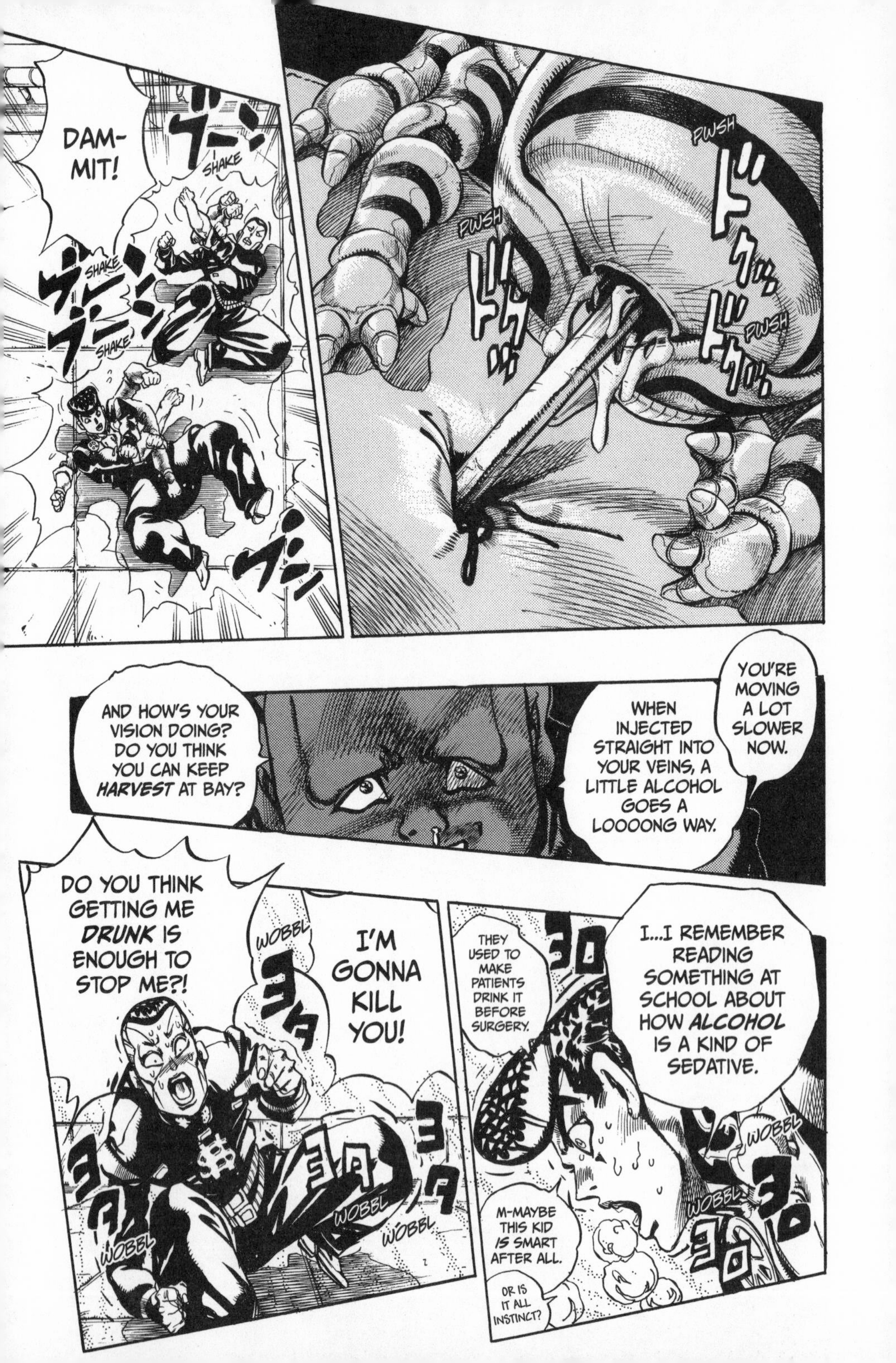
PWSH
PWSH
PWSH
DAM-MIT!
SHAKE
SHAKE
SHAKE
YOU'RE MOVING A LOT SLOWER NOW.
WHEN INJECTED STRAIGHT INTO YOUR VEINS, A LITTLE ALCOHOL GOES A LOOOONG WAY.
AND HOW'S YOUR VISION DOING? DO YOU THINK YOU CAN KEEP *HARVEST* AT BAY?
I...I REMEMBER READING SOMETHING AT SCHOOL ABOUT HOW *ALCOHOL* IS A KIND OF SEDATIVE.
THEY USED TO MAKE PATIENTS DRINK IT BEFORE SURGERY.
WOBBL
WOBBL
M-MAYBE THIS KID *IS* SMART AFTER ALL.
OR IS IT ALL INSTINCT?
DO YOU THINK GETTING ME *DRUNK* IS ENOUGH TO STOP ME?!
I'M GONNA KILL YOU!
WOBBL
WOBBL
WOBBL
WOBBL

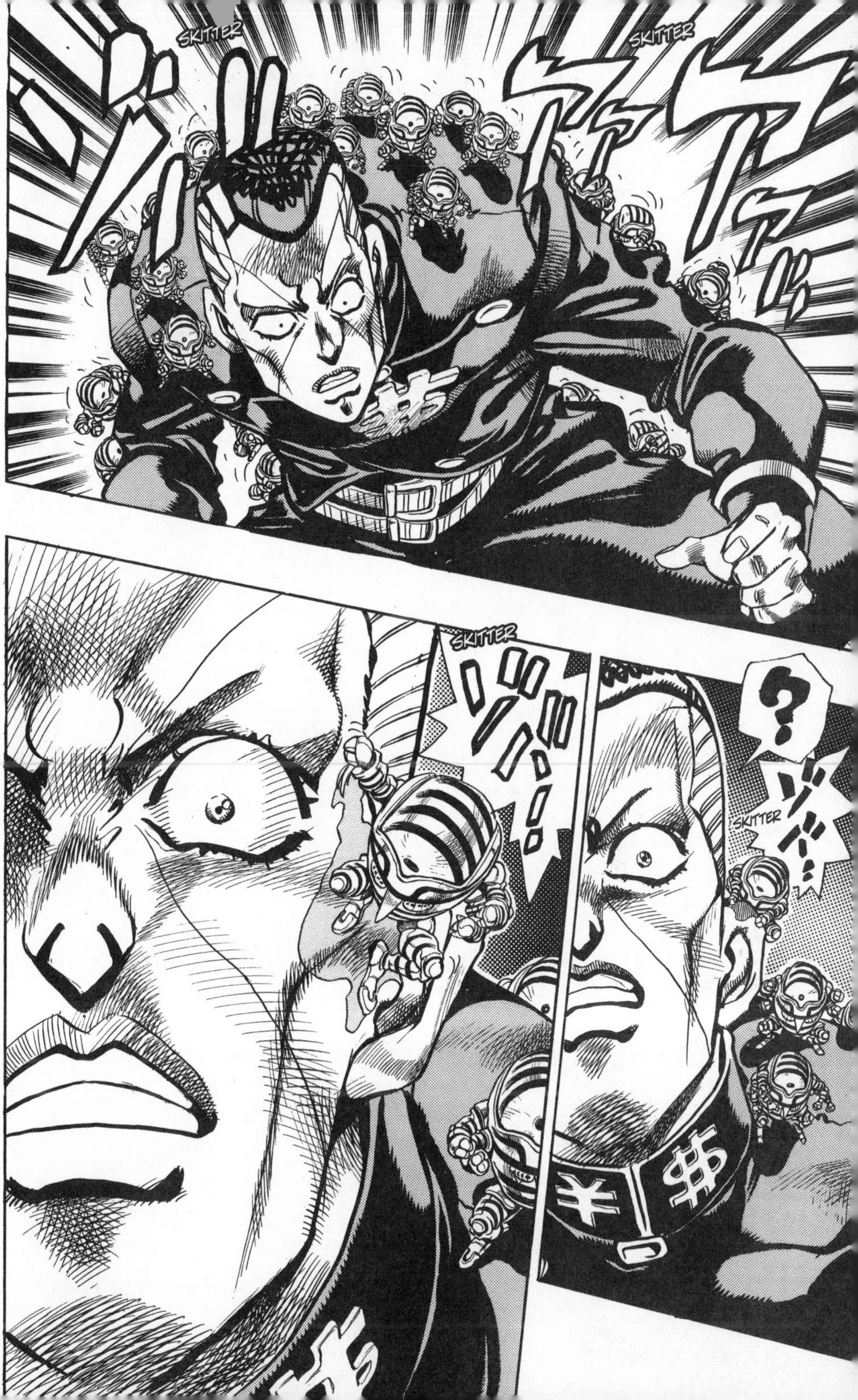
SKITTER
SKITTER
?
SKITTER
SKITTER

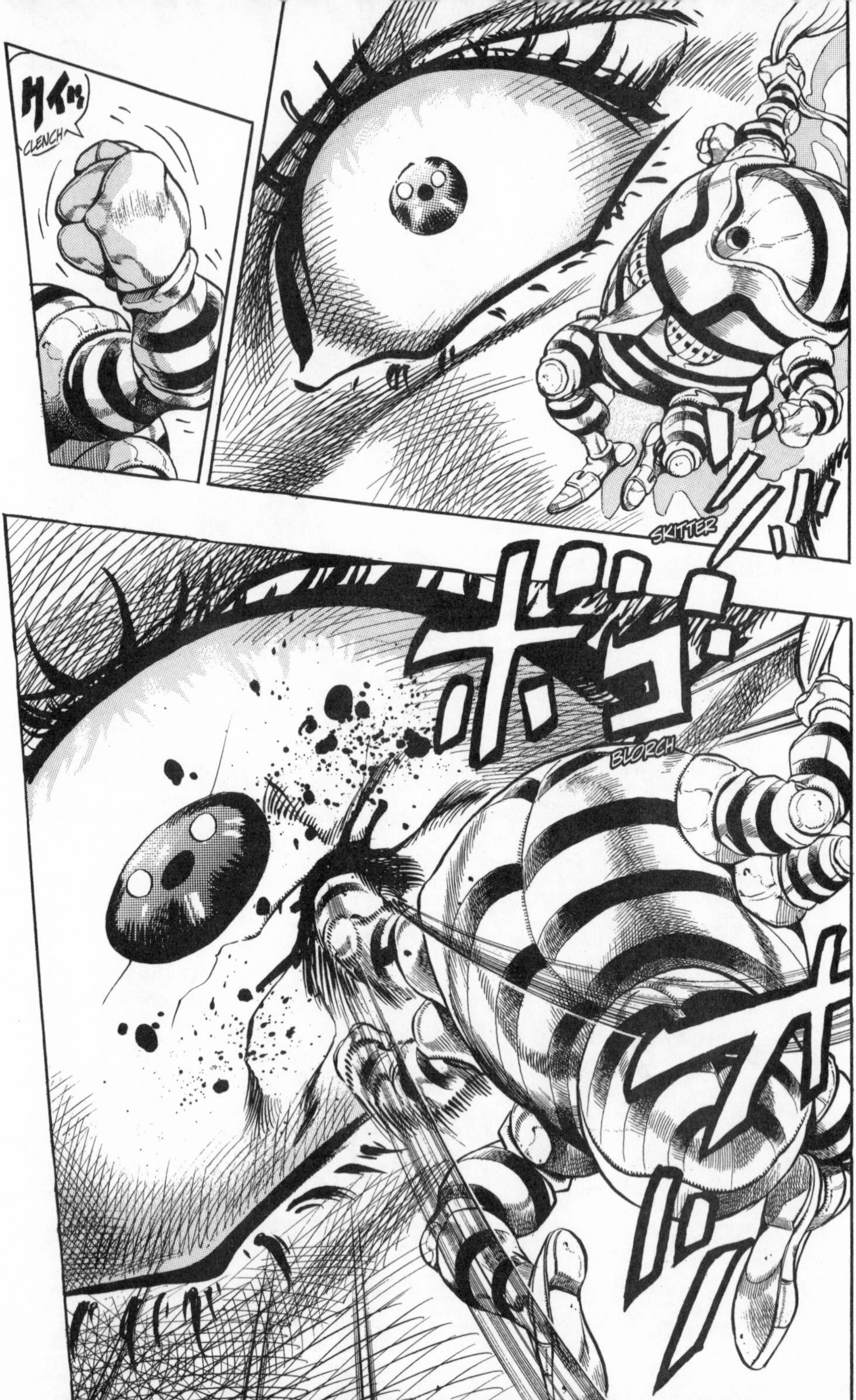
SKITTER
CLENCH
BLORCH

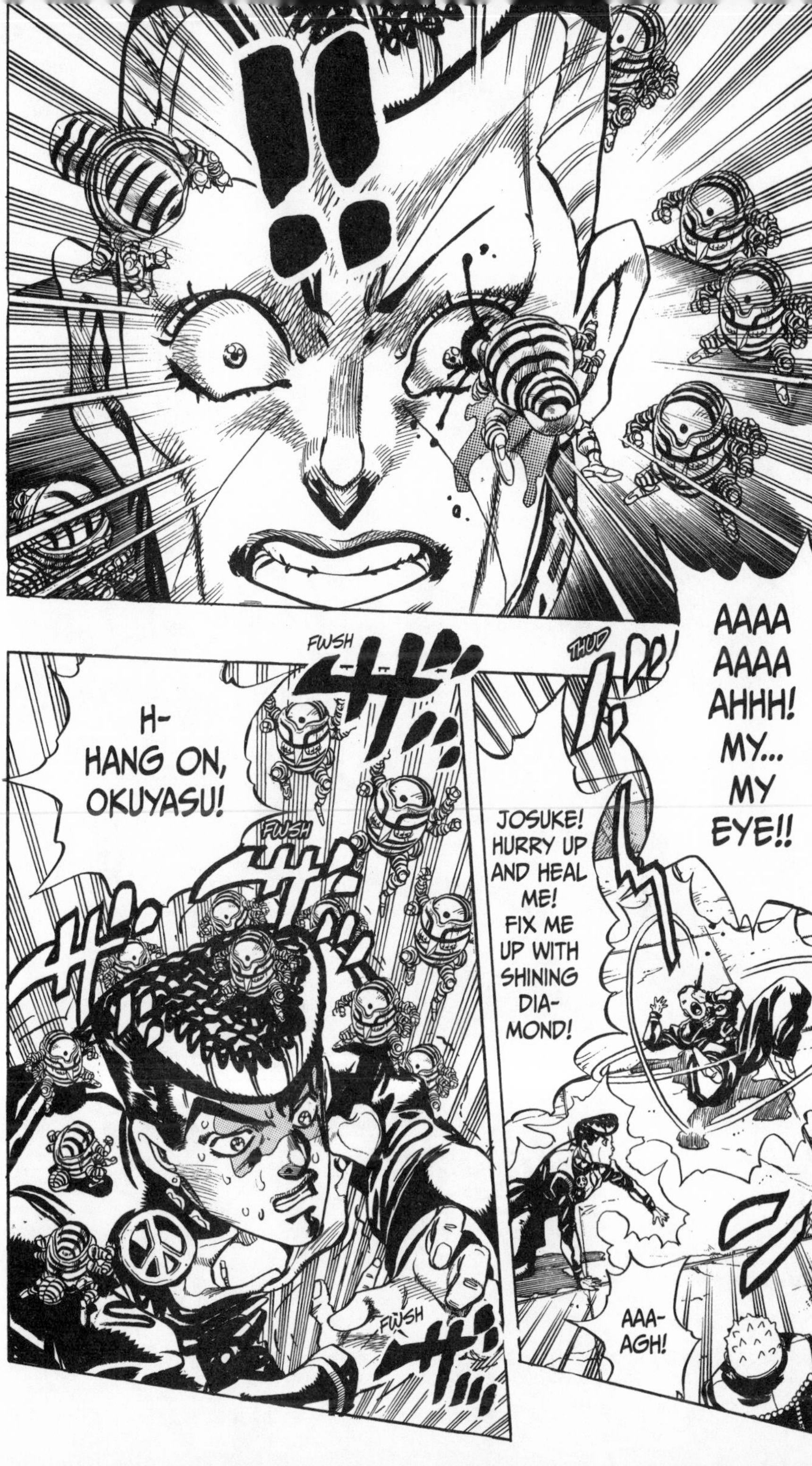
AAAA AAAA AHHH! MY... MY EYE!!
THUD
JOSUKE! HURRY UP AND HEAL ME! FIX ME UP WITH SHINING DIA-MOND!
AAA-AGH!
FWSH
H-HANG ON, OKUYASU!
FWSH
FWSH

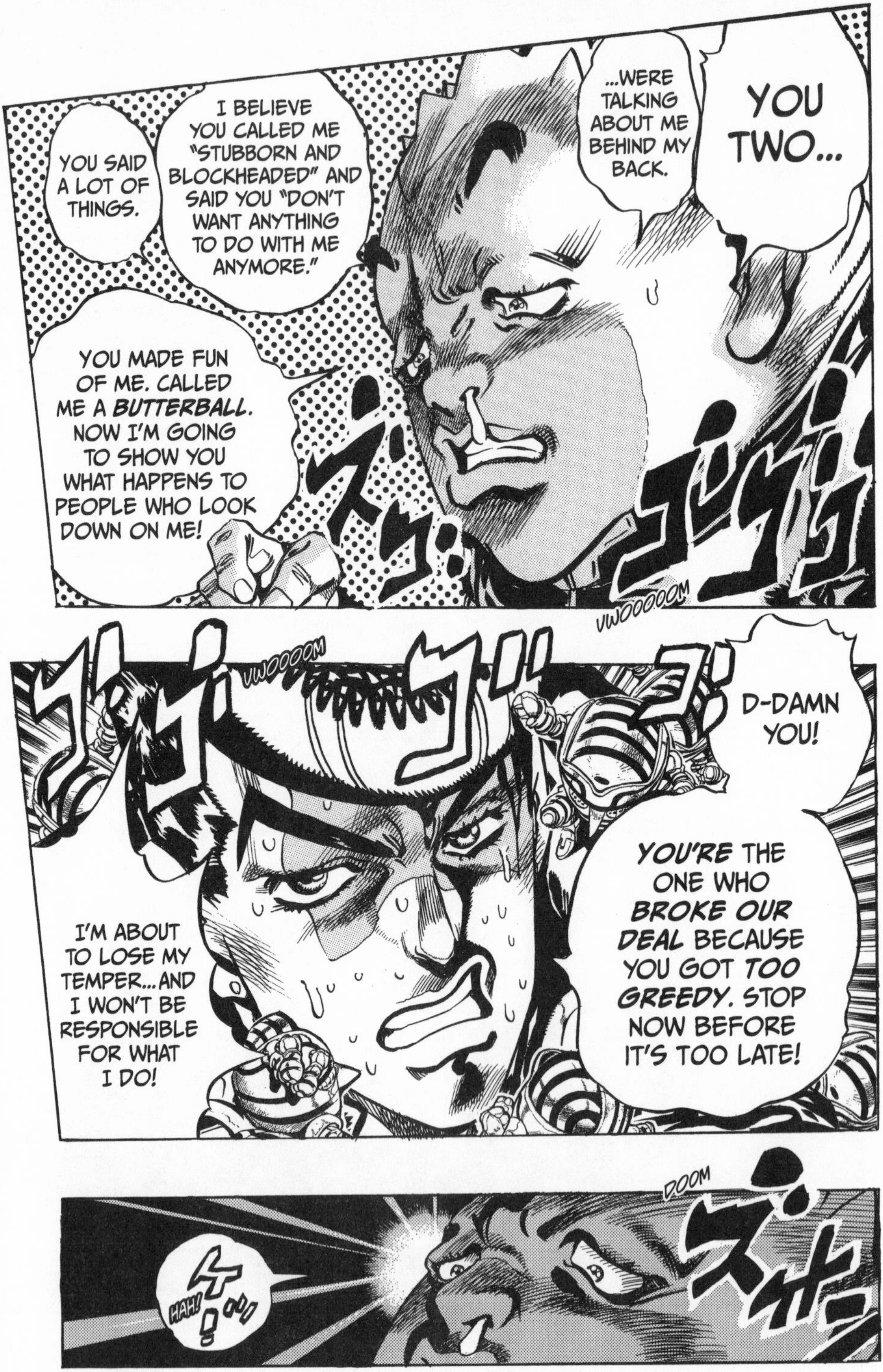
YOU TWO...
...WERE TALKING ABOUT ME BEHIND MY BACK.
I BELIEVE YOU CALLED ME "STUBBORN AND BLOCKHEADED" AND SAID YOU "DON'T WANT ANYTHING TO DO WITH ME ANYMORE."
YOU SAID A LOT OF THINGS.
YOU MADE FUN OF ME. CALLED ME A **BUTTERBALL**. NOW I'M GOING TO SHOW YOU WHAT HAPPENS TO PEOPLE WHO LOOK DOWN ON ME!
VWOOOOOM
D-DAMN YOU!
YOU'RE THE ONE WHO ***BROKE OUR DEAL*** BECAUSE YOU GOT ***TOO GREEDY***. STOP NOW BEFORE IT'S TOO LATE!
VWOOOOM
I'M ABOUT TO LOSE MY TEMPER...AND I WON'T BE RESPONSIBLE FOR WHAT I DO!
DOOM
HAH!

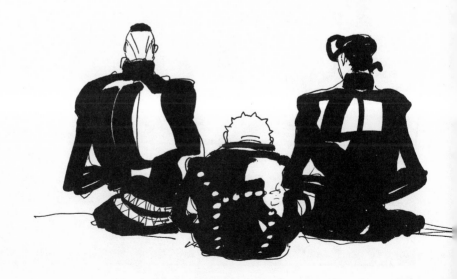

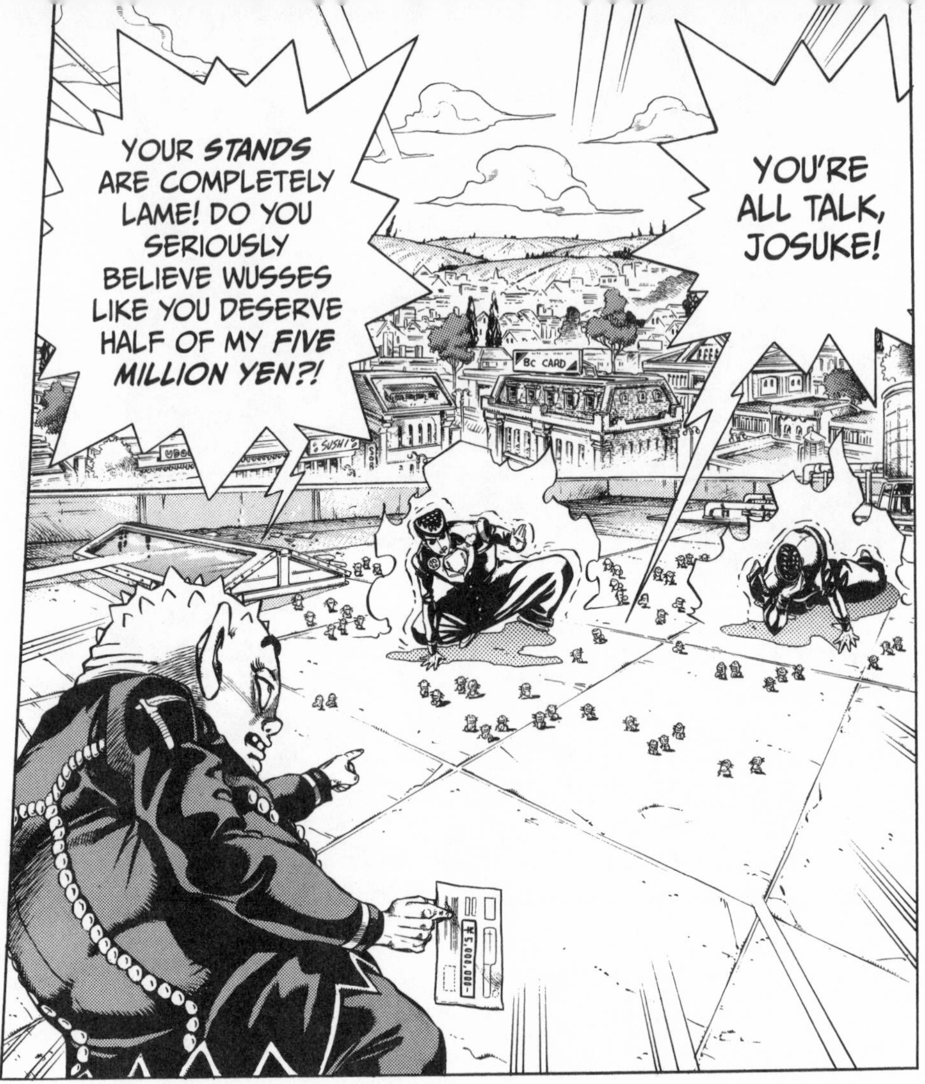

YOU'RE ALL TALK, JOSUKE!
YOUR STANDS ARE COMPLETELY LAME! DO YOU SERIOUSLY BELIEVE WUSSES LIKE YOU DESERVE HALF OF MY FIVE MILLION YEN?!
BC CARD
SUSHI
¥5,000,000-

CHAPTER 75

SHIGECHI'S HARVEST, PART 6

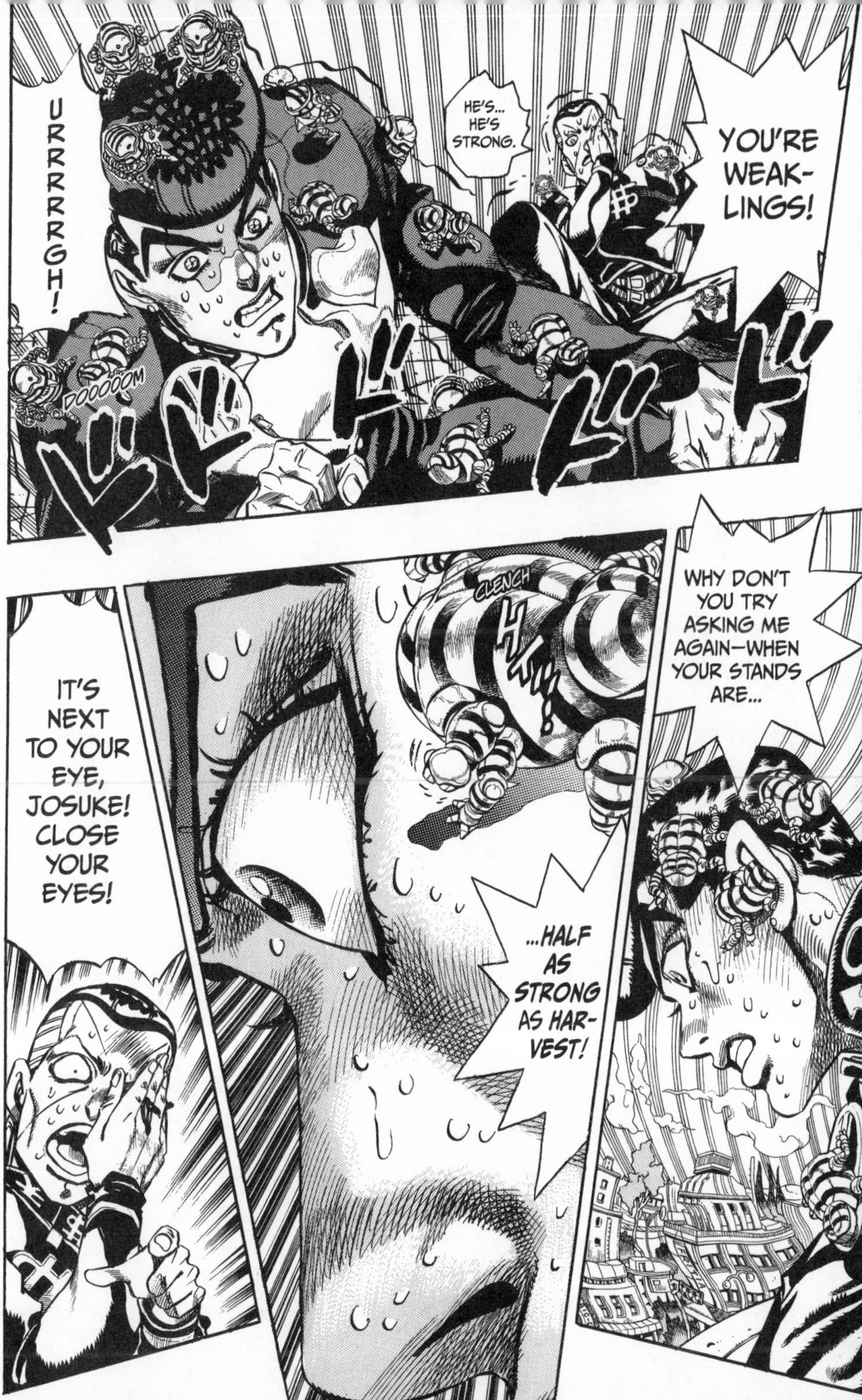
YOU'RE WEAK-LINGS!
HE'S... HE'S STRONG.
URRRRRGH!
DOOOOOM
WHY DON'T YOU TRY ASKING ME AGAIN—WHEN YOUR STANDS ARE...
CLENCH
...HALF AS STRONG AS HAR-VEST!
IT'S NEXT TO YOUR EYE, JOSUKE! CLOSE YOUR EYES!

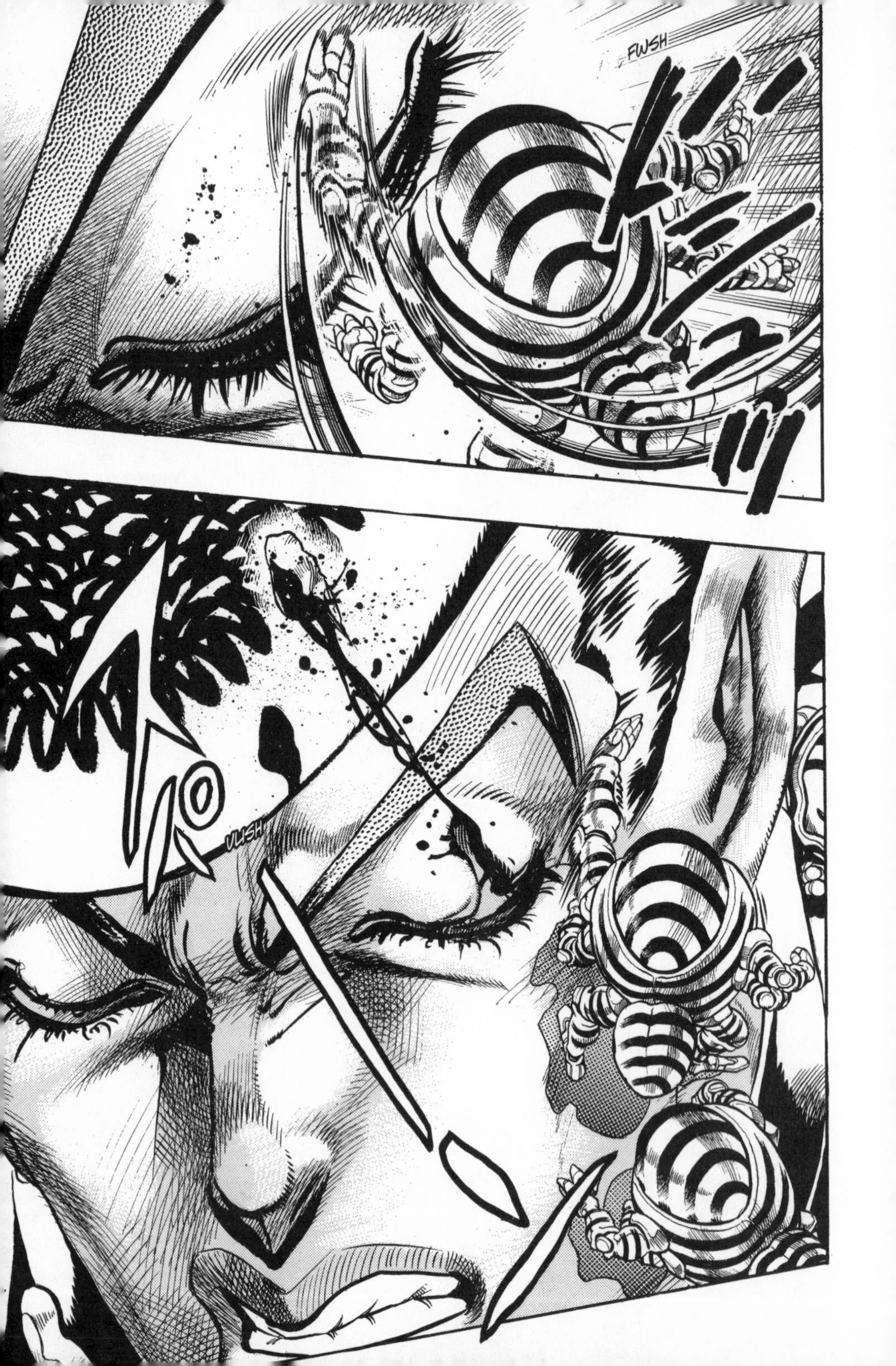
FWSH
VLISH

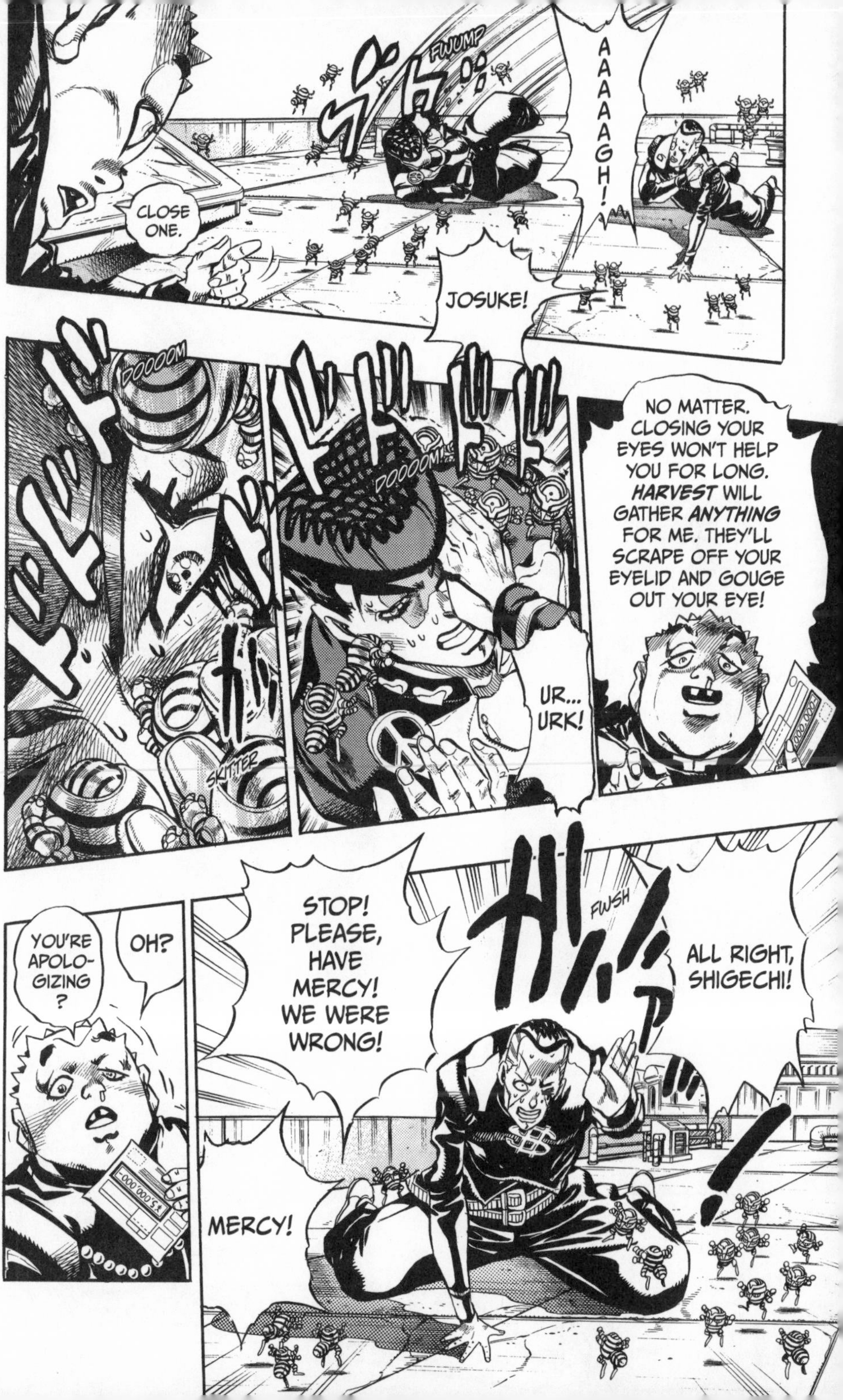
FWUMP
AAAAAGH!
CLOSE ONE.
JOSUKE!
NO MATTER. CLOSING YOUR EYES WON'T HELP YOU FOR LONG. *HARVEST* WILL GATHER *ANYTHING* FOR ME. THEY'LL SCRAPE OFF YOUR EYELID AND GOUGE OUT YOUR EYE!
DOOOOM
UR... URK!
DOOOOM
SKITTER
ALL RIGHT, SHIGECHI!
FWSH
STOP! PLEASE, HAVE MERCY! WE WERE WRONG!
MERCY!
OH?
YOU'RE APOLOGIZING?

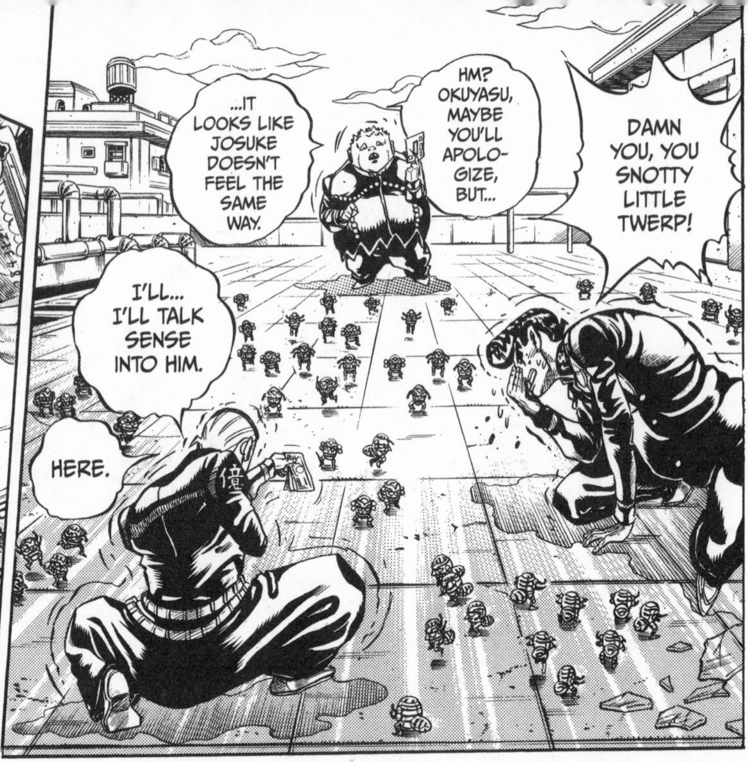
DAMN YOU, YOU SNOTTY LITTLE TWERP!
HM? OKUYASU, MAYBE YOU'LL APOLO-GIZE, BUT...
...IT LOOKS LIKE JOSUKE DOESN'T FEEL THE SAME WAY.
I'LL... I'LL TALK SENSE INTO HIM.
HERE.
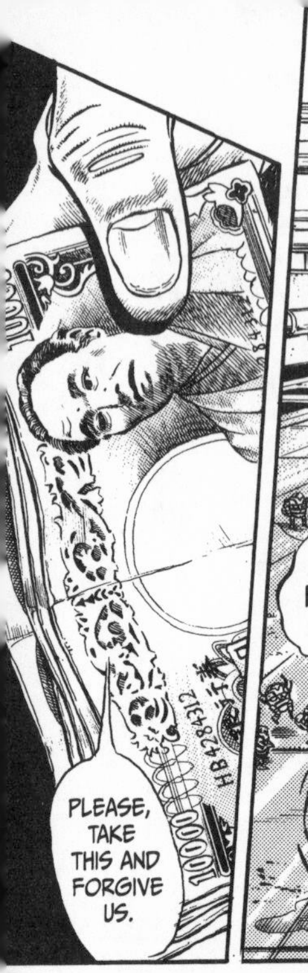
PLEASE, TAKE THIS AND FORGIVE US.
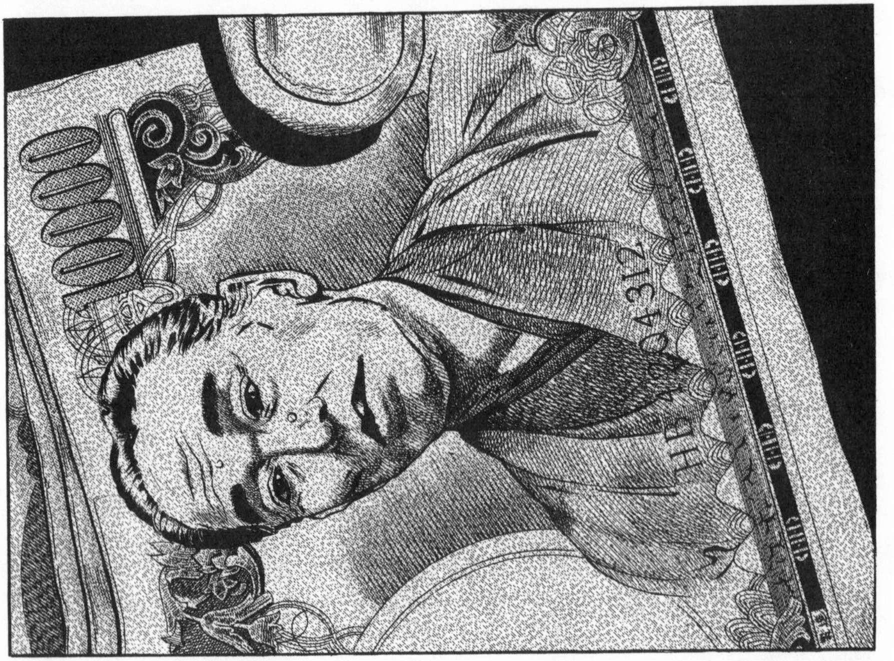

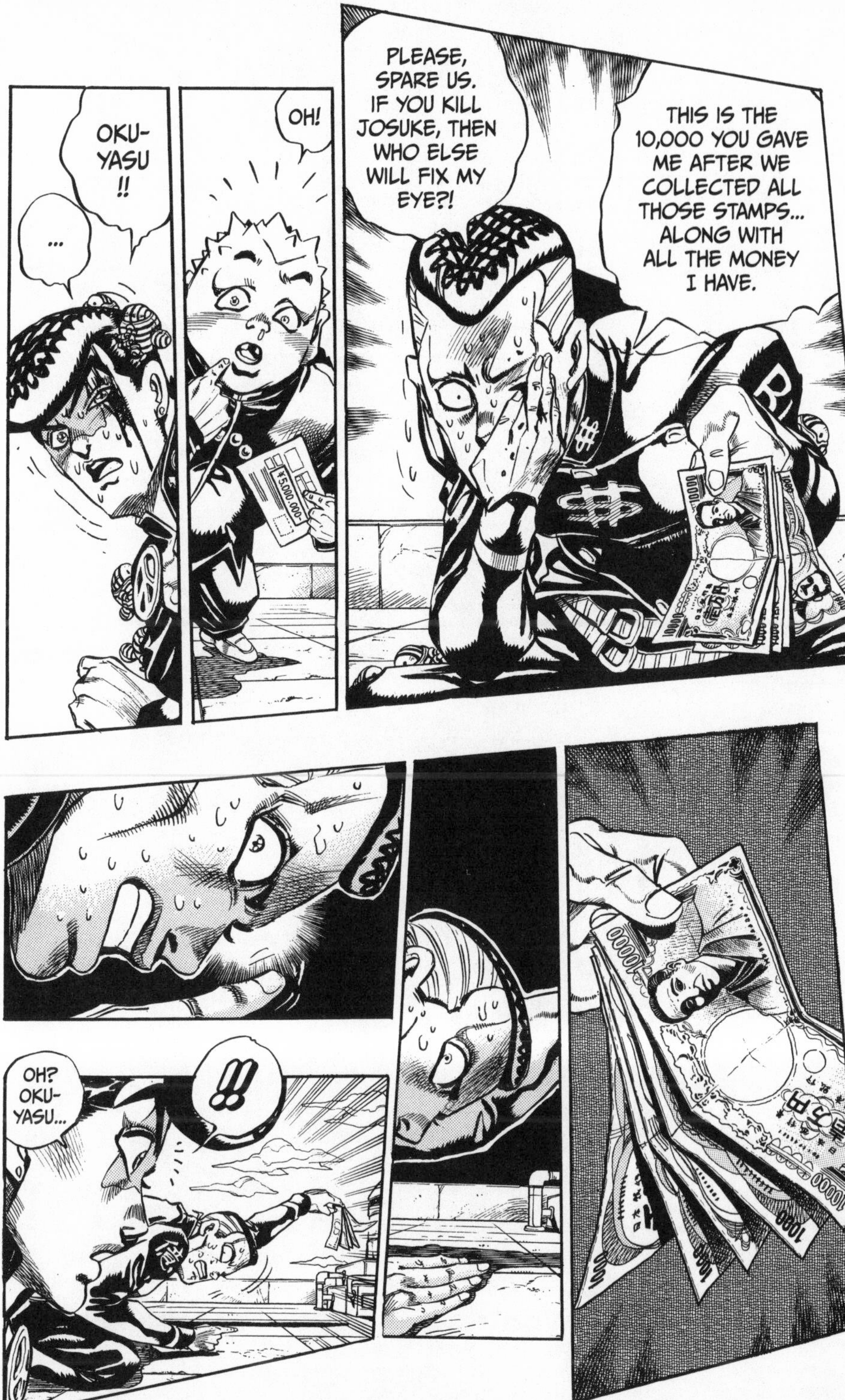
THIS IS THE 10,000 YOU GAVE ME AFTER WE COLLECTED ALL THOSE STAMPS... ALONG WITH ALL THE MONEY I HAVE.
PLEASE, SPARE US. IF YOU KILL JOSUKE, THEN WHO ELSE WILL FIX MY EYE?!
OH!
¥5,000,000
OKU-YASU !!
...
!!
OH? OKU-YASU...

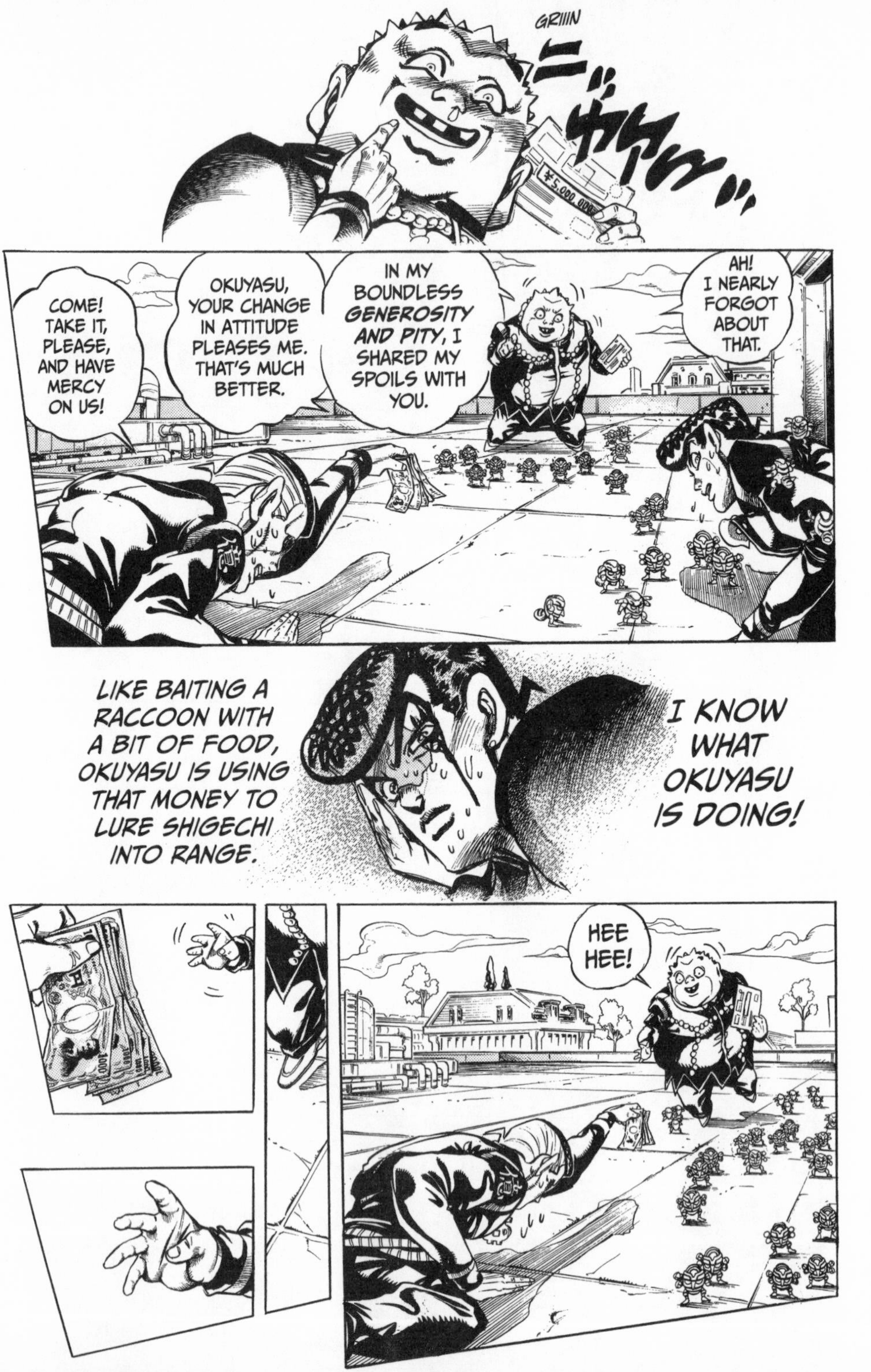
GRIIIN
AH! I NEARLY FORGOT ABOUT THAT.
IN MY BOUNDLESS *GENEROSITY AND PITY*, I SHARED MY SPOILS WITH YOU.
OKUYASU, YOUR CHANGE IN ATTITUDE PLEASES ME. THAT'S MUCH BETTER.
COME! TAKE IT, PLEASE, AND HAVE MERCY ON US!
I KNOW WHAT OKUYASU IS DOING!
LIKE BAITING A RACCOON WITH A BIT OF FOOD, OKUYASU IS USING THAT MONEY TO LURE SHIGECHI INTO RANGE.
HEE HEE!

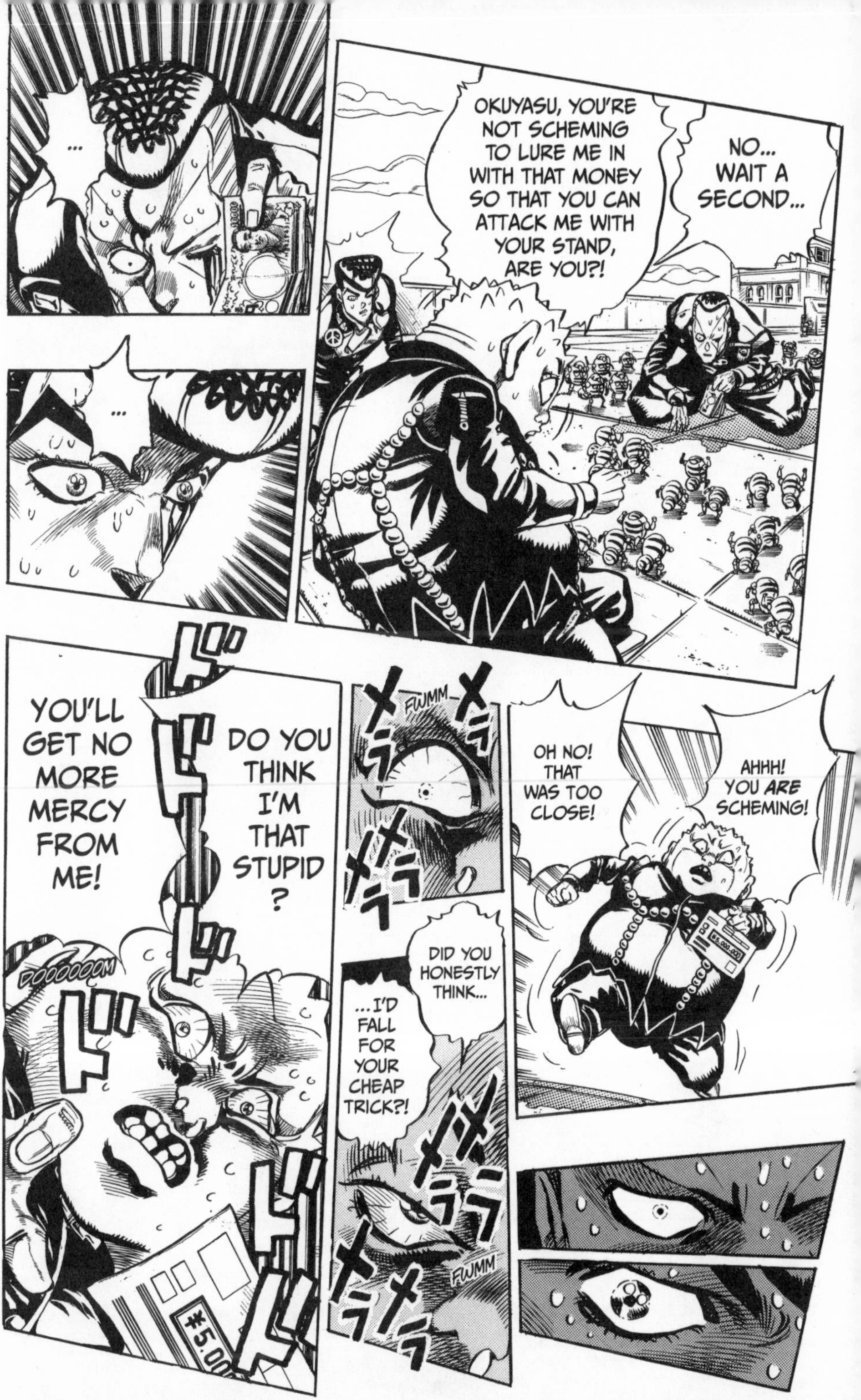
NO... WAIT A SECOND...
OKUYASU, YOU'RE NOT SCHEMING TO LURE ME IN WITH THAT MONEY SO THAT YOU CAN ATTACK ME WITH YOUR STAND, ARE YOU?!
...
...
AHHH! YOU *ARE* SCHEMING!
OH NO! THAT WAS TOO CLOSE!
FWUMM
DID YOU HONESTLY THINK...
...I'D FALL FOR YOUR CHEAP TRICK?!
FWUMM
DO YOU THINK I'M THAT STUPID?
YOU'LL GET NO MORE MERCY FROM ME!
DOOOOOOOM

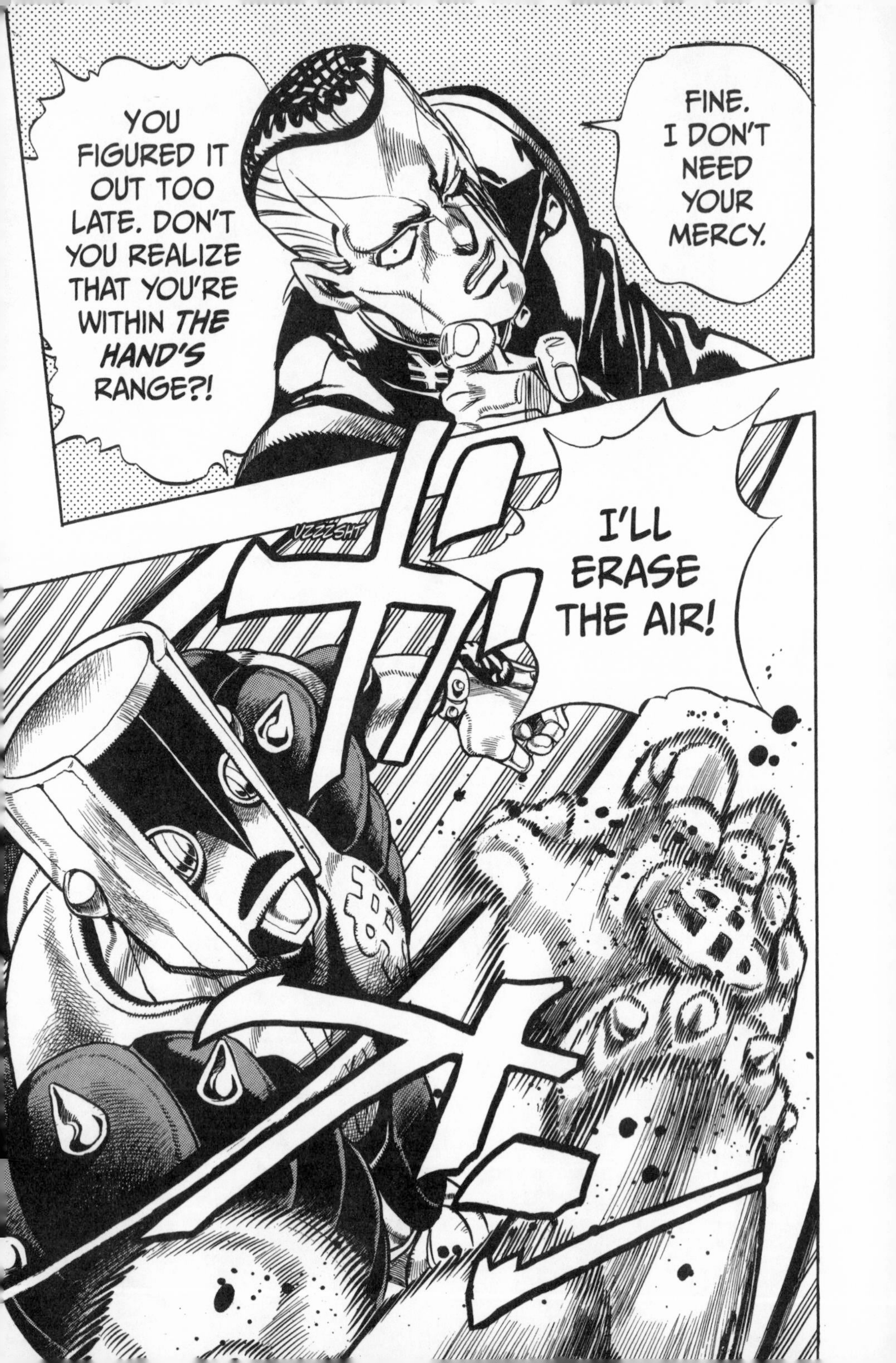
FINE. I DON'T NEED YOUR MERCY.
YOU FIGURED IT OUT TOO LATE. DON'T YOU REALIZE THAT YOU'RE WITHIN *THE HAND'S* RANGE?!
I'LL ERASE THE AIR!
VZZZSHT

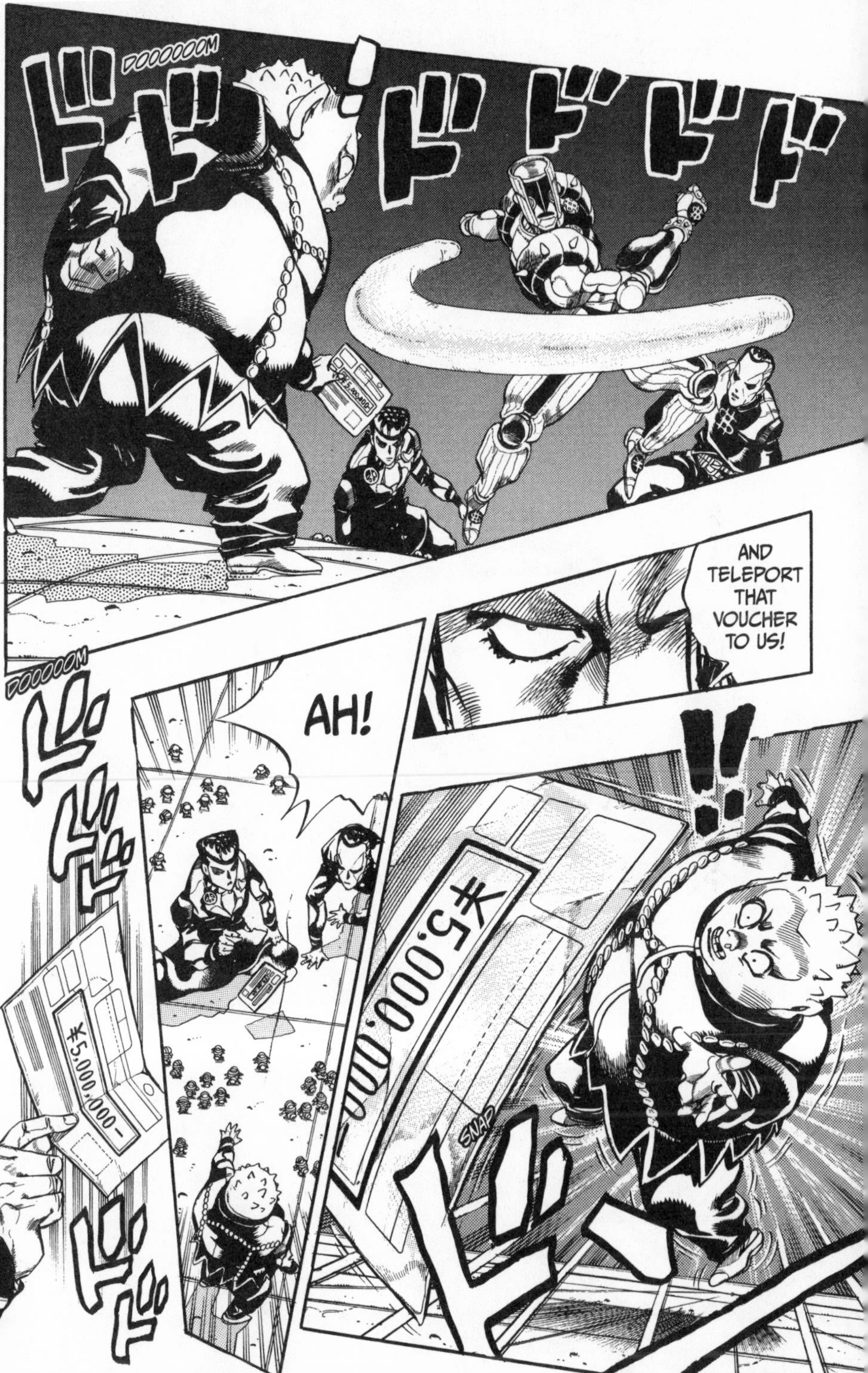
DOOOOOOM
ドドドドドドド
!
AND TELEPORT THAT VOUCHER TO US!
!!
¥5,000,000-
SNAP
AH!
DOOOOOM
ドドドドド
¥5,000,000-

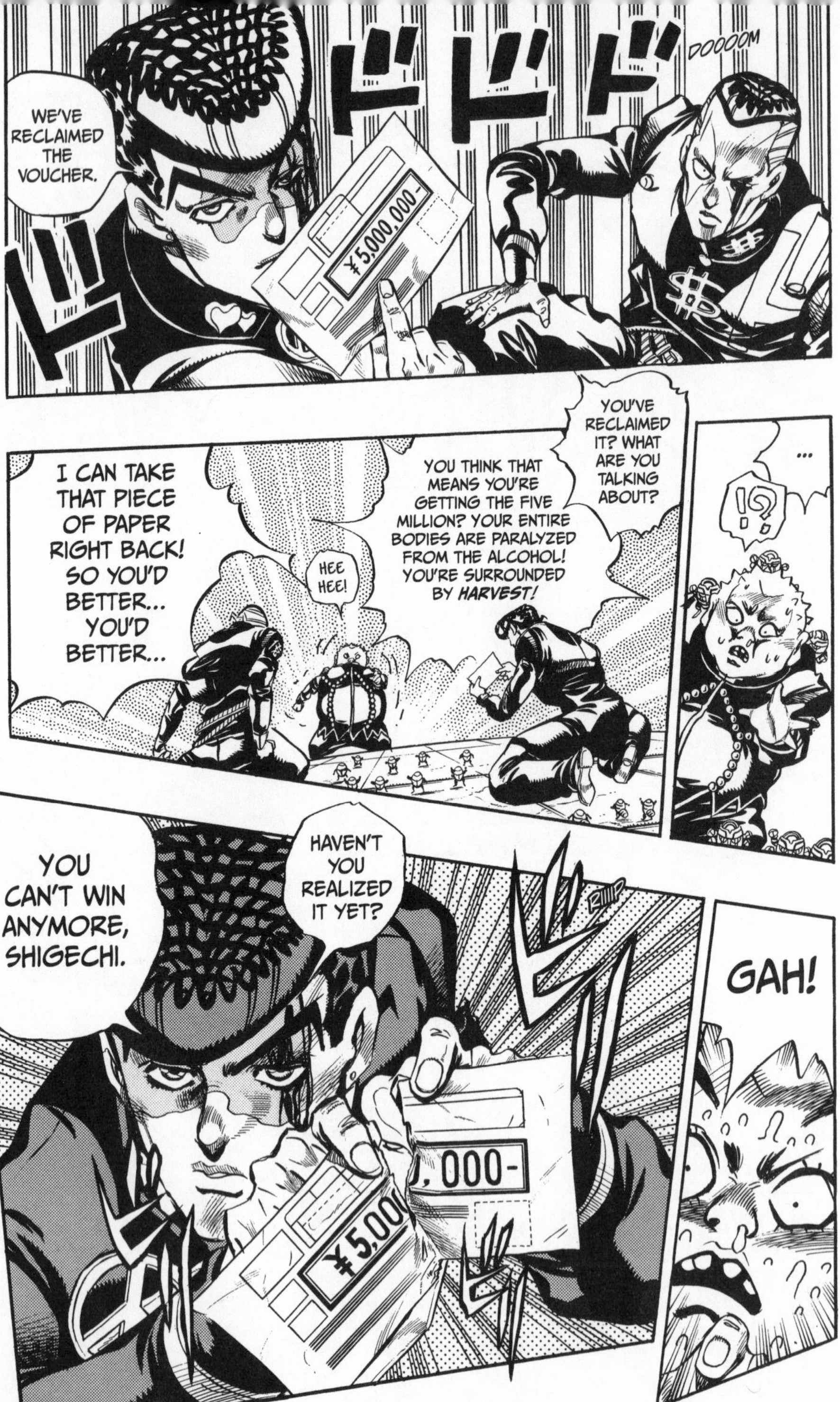

DOOOOM
ドドド
ドドド
WE'VE RECLAIMED THE VOUCHER.
¥5,000,000-
...
!?
YOU'VE RECLAIMED IT? WHAT ARE YOU TALKING ABOUT?
YOU THINK THAT MEANS YOU'RE GETTING THE FIVE MILLION? YOUR ENTIRE BODIES ARE PARALYZED FROM THE ALCOHOL! YOU'RE SURROUNDED BY *HARVEST!*
HEE HEE!
I CAN TAKE THAT PIECE OF PAPER RIGHT BACK! SO YOU'D BETTER... YOU'D BETTER...
GAH!
HAVEN'T YOU REALIZED IT YET?
YOU CAN'T WIN ANYMORE, SHIGECHI.

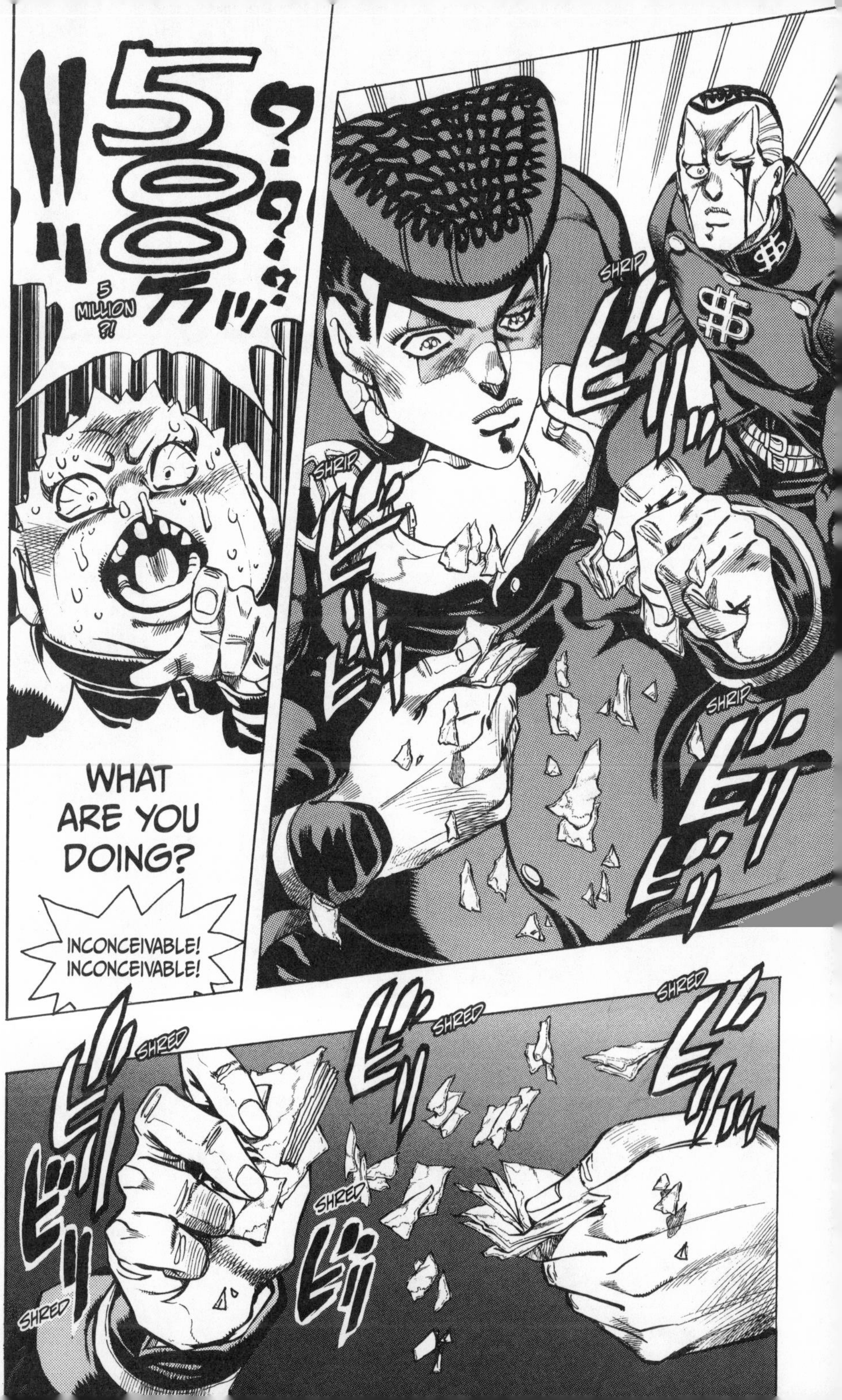
SHRIP
SHRIP
SHRIP
5 MILLION ?!
WHAT ARE YOU DOING?
INCONCEIVABLE! INCONCEIVABLE!
SHRED
SHRED
SHRED
SHRED
SHRED

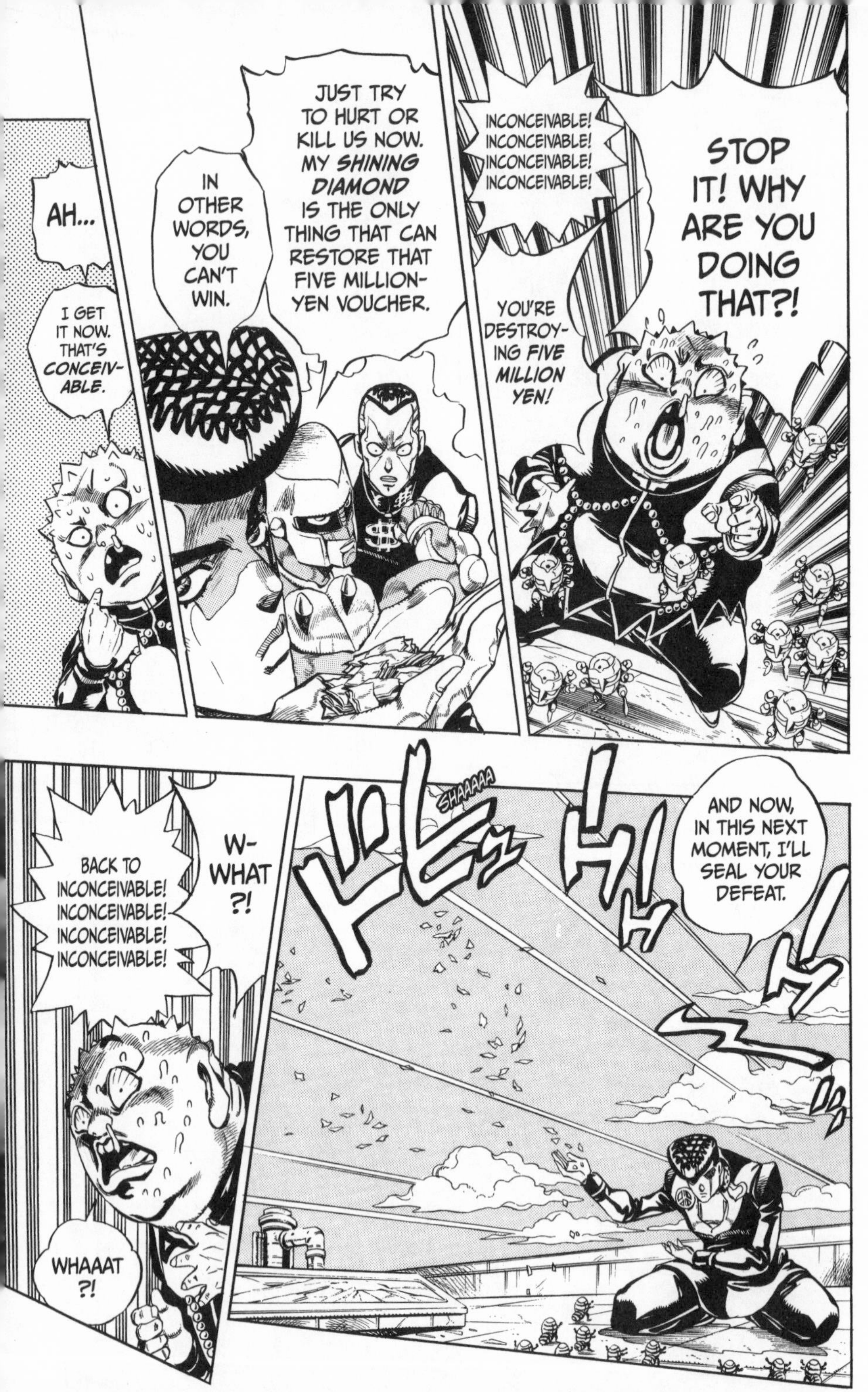
INCONCEIVABLE! INCONCEIVABLE! INCONCEIVABLE! INCONCEIVABLE!
STOP IT! WHY ARE YOU DOING THAT?!
YOU'RE DESTROYING FIVE MILLION YEN!
JUST TRY TO HURT OR KILL US NOW. MY SHINING DIAMOND IS THE ONLY THING THAT CAN RESTORE THAT FIVE MILLION-YEN VOUCHER.
IN OTHER WORDS, YOU CAN'T WIN.
AH...
I GET IT NOW. THAT'S CONCEIVABLE.
SHAAAAA
AND NOW, IN THIS NEXT MOMENT, I'LL SEAL YOUR DEFEAT.
W-WHAT?!
BACK TO INCONCEIVABLE! INCONCEIVABLE! INCONCEIVABLE! INCONCEIVABLE!
WHAAAT?!

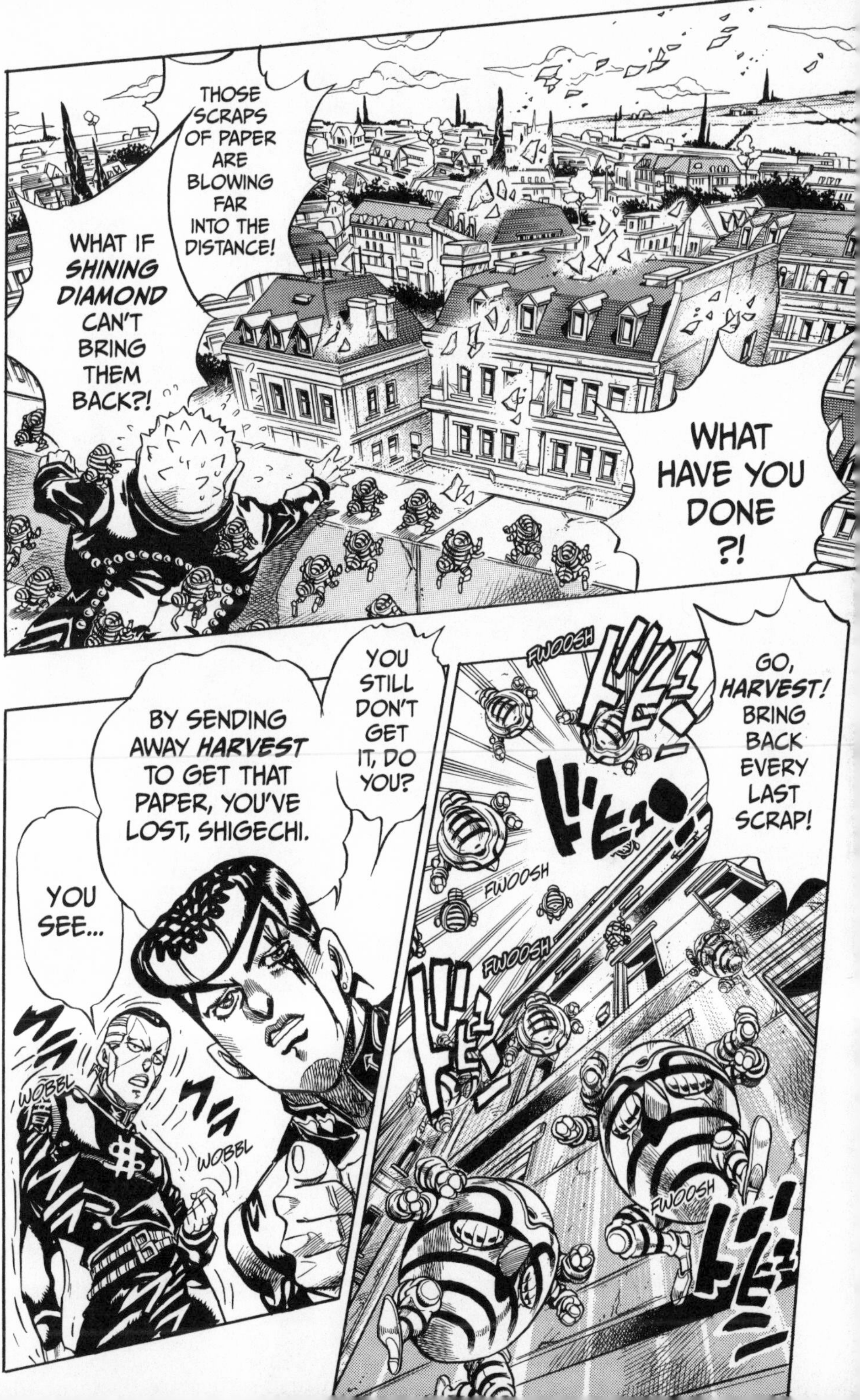
WHAT HAVE YOU DONE ?!
THOSE SCRAPS OF PAPER ARE BLOWING FAR INTO THE DISTANCE!
WHAT IF SHINING DIAMOND CAN'T BRING THEM BACK?!
GO, HARVEST! BRING BACK EVERY LAST SCRAP!
FWOOSH
FWOOSH
FWOOSH
FWOOSH
YOU STILL DON'T GET IT, DO YOU?
BY SENDING AWAY HARVEST TO GET THAT PAPER, YOU'VE LOST, SHIGECHI.
YOU SEE...
WOBBL
WOBBL

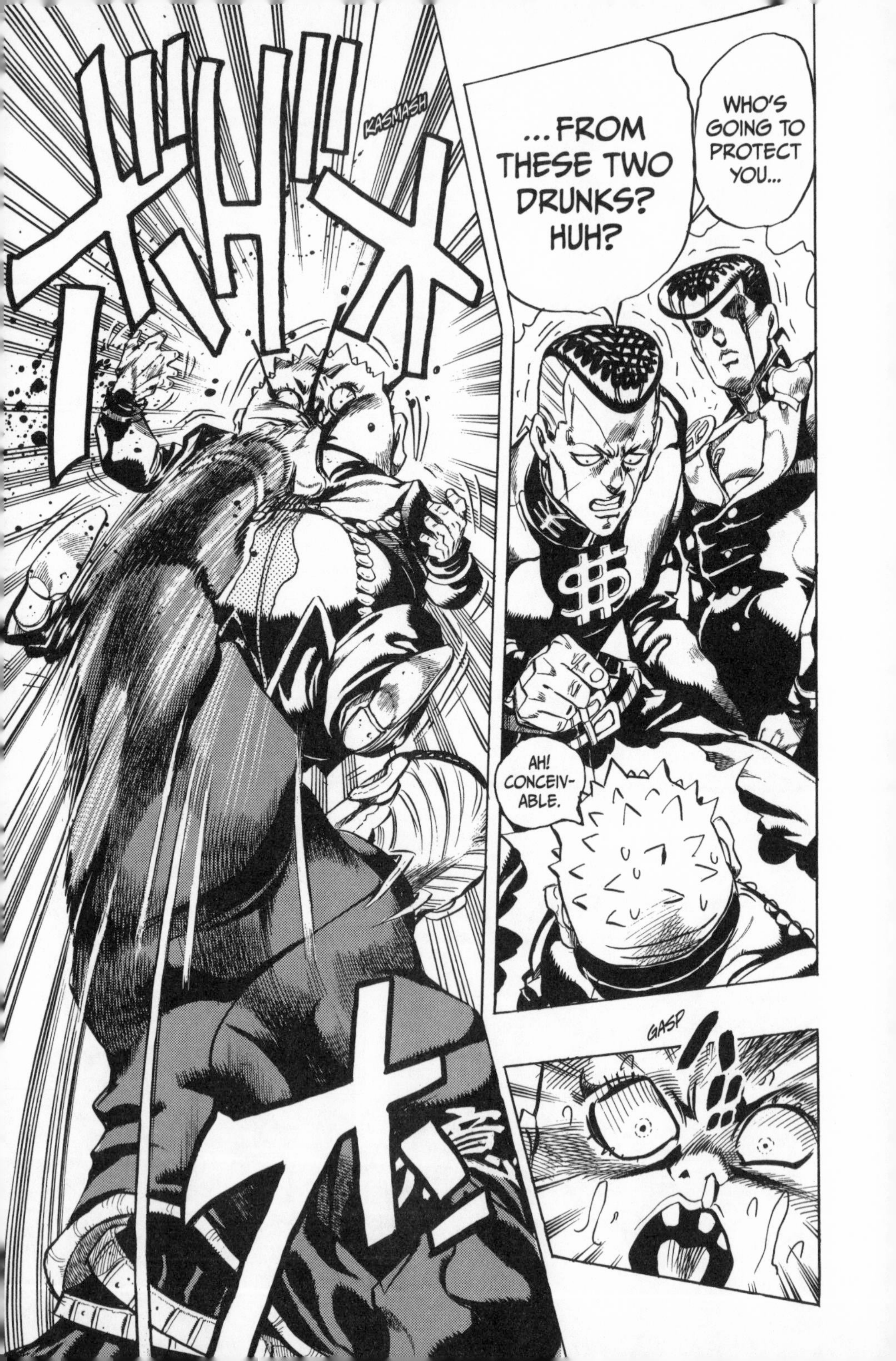
WHO'S GOING TO PROTECT YOU...
...FROM THESE TWO DRUNKS? HUH?
AH! CONCEIV-ABLE.
GASP
KASMASH

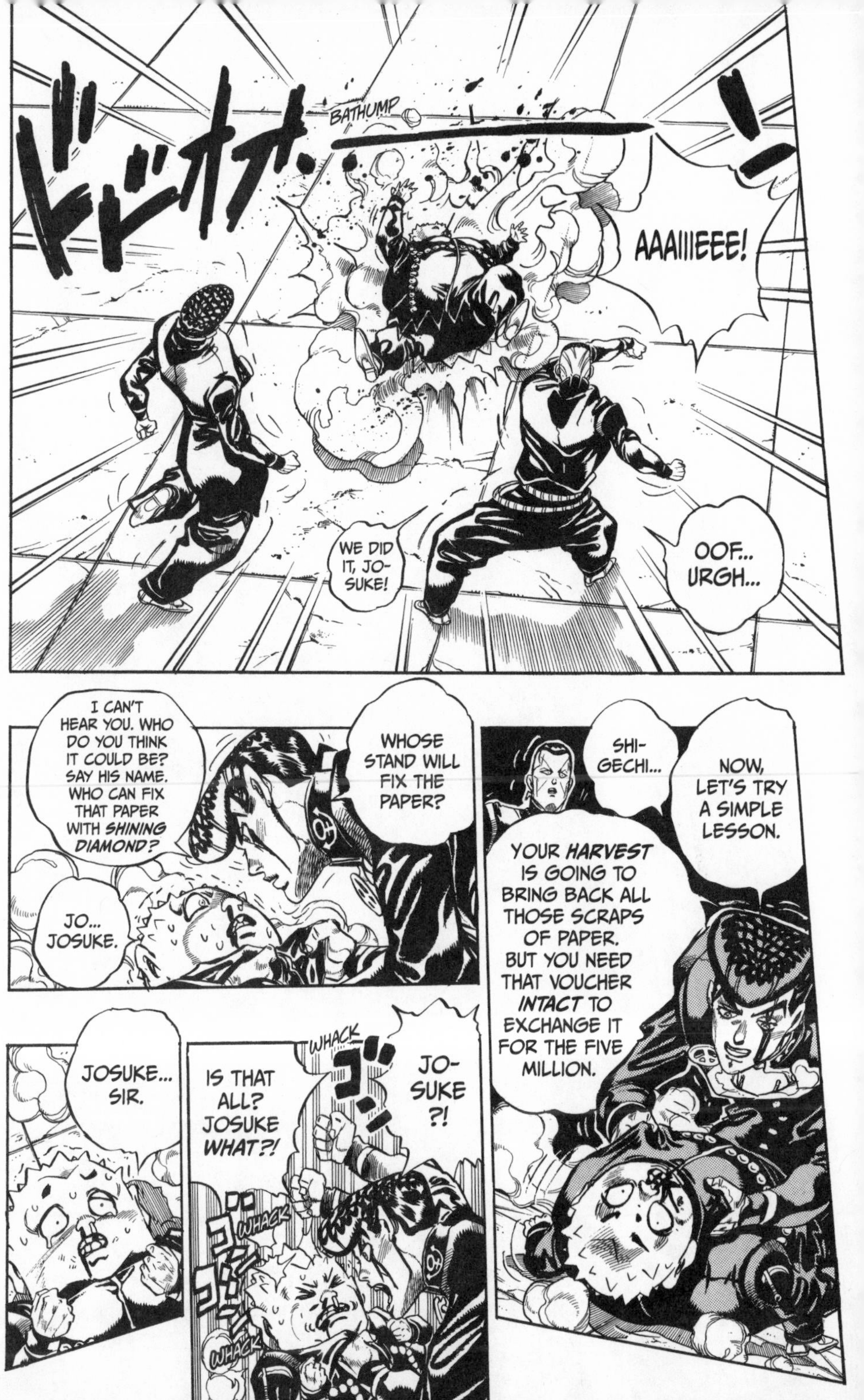
AAAIIIEEE!
BATHUMP
OOF... URGH...
WE DID IT, JO-SUKE!
NOW, LET'S TRY A SIMPLE LESSON.
SHI-GECHI...
YOUR *HARVEST* IS GOING TO BRING BACK ALL THOSE SCRAPS OF PAPER. BUT YOU NEED THAT VOUCHER *INTACT* TO EXCHANGE IT FOR THE FIVE MILLION.
WHOSE STAND WILL FIX THE PAPER?
I CAN'T HEAR YOU. WHO DO YOU THINK IT COULD BE? SAY HIS NAME. WHO CAN FIX THAT PAPER WITH *SHINING DIAMOND*?
JO... JOSUKE.
JO-SUKE?!
WHACK
IS THAT ALL? JOSUKE *WHAT?!*
WHACK
WHACK
JOSUKE... SIR.

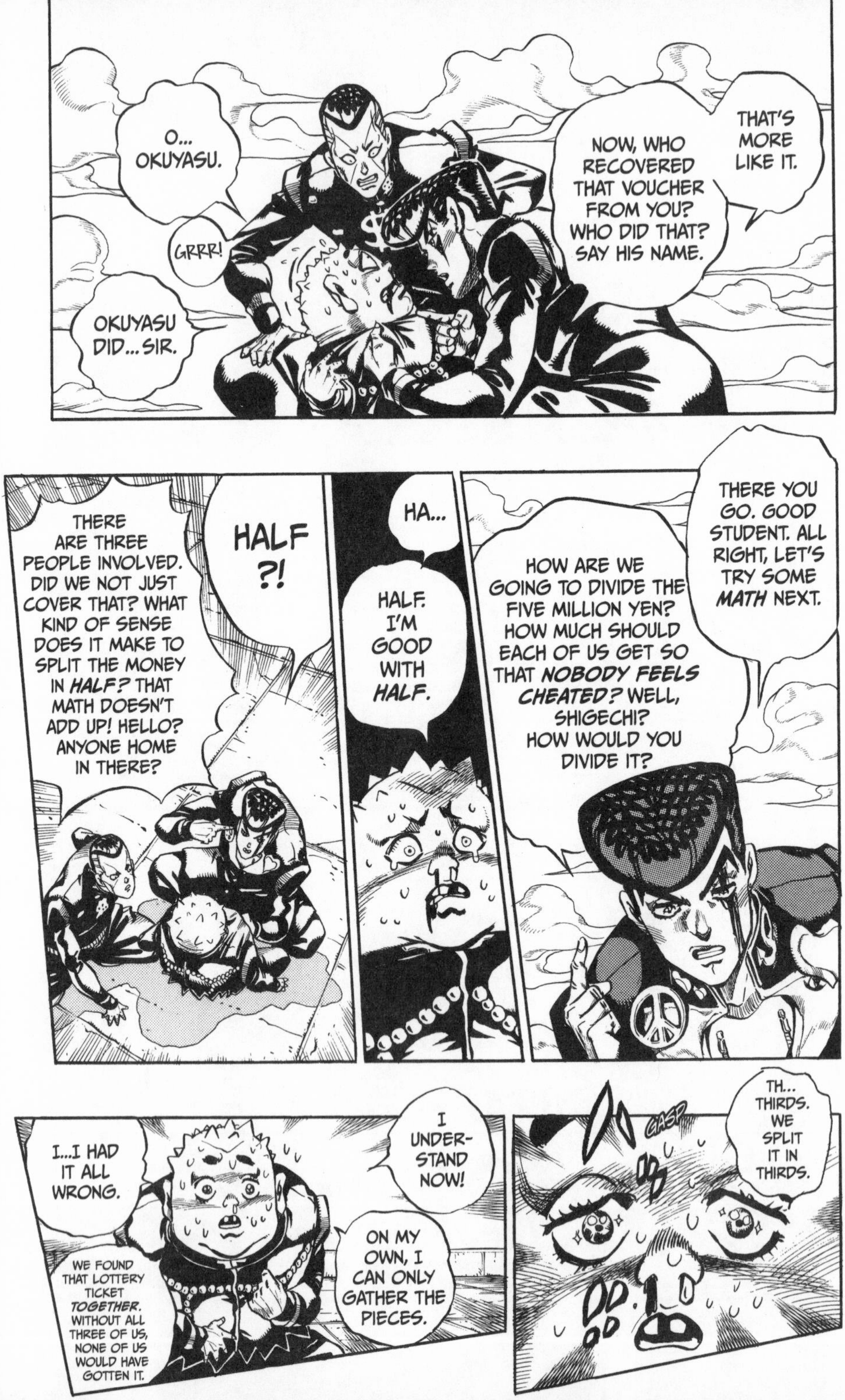
THAT'S MORE LIKE IT.
NOW, WHO RECOVERED THAT VOUCHER FROM YOU? WHO DID THAT? SAY HIS NAME.
O... OKUYASU.
GRRR!
OKUYASU DID... SIR.
THERE YOU GO. GOOD STUDENT. ALL RIGHT, LET'S TRY SOME *MATH* NEXT.
HOW ARE WE GOING TO DIVIDE THE FIVE MILLION YEN? HOW MUCH SHOULD EACH OF US GET SO THAT ***NOBODY FEELS CHEATED?*** WELL, SHIGECHI? HOW WOULD YOU DIVIDE IT?
HA...
HALF. I'M GOOD WITH ***HALF.***
HALF ?!
THERE ARE THREE PEOPLE INVOLVED. DID WE NOT JUST COVER THAT? WHAT KIND OF SENSE DOES IT MAKE TO SPLIT THE MONEY IN ***HALF?*** THAT MATH DOESN'T ADD UP! HELLO? ANYONE HOME IN THERE?
GASP
TH... THIRDS. WE SPLIT IT IN THIRDS.
I UNDER-STAND NOW!
I...I HAD IT ALL WRONG.
ON MY OWN, I CAN ONLY GATHER THE PIECES.
WE FOUND THAT LOTTERY TICKET ***TOGETHER.*** WITHOUT ALL THREE OF US, NONE OF US WOULD HAVE GOTTEN IT.

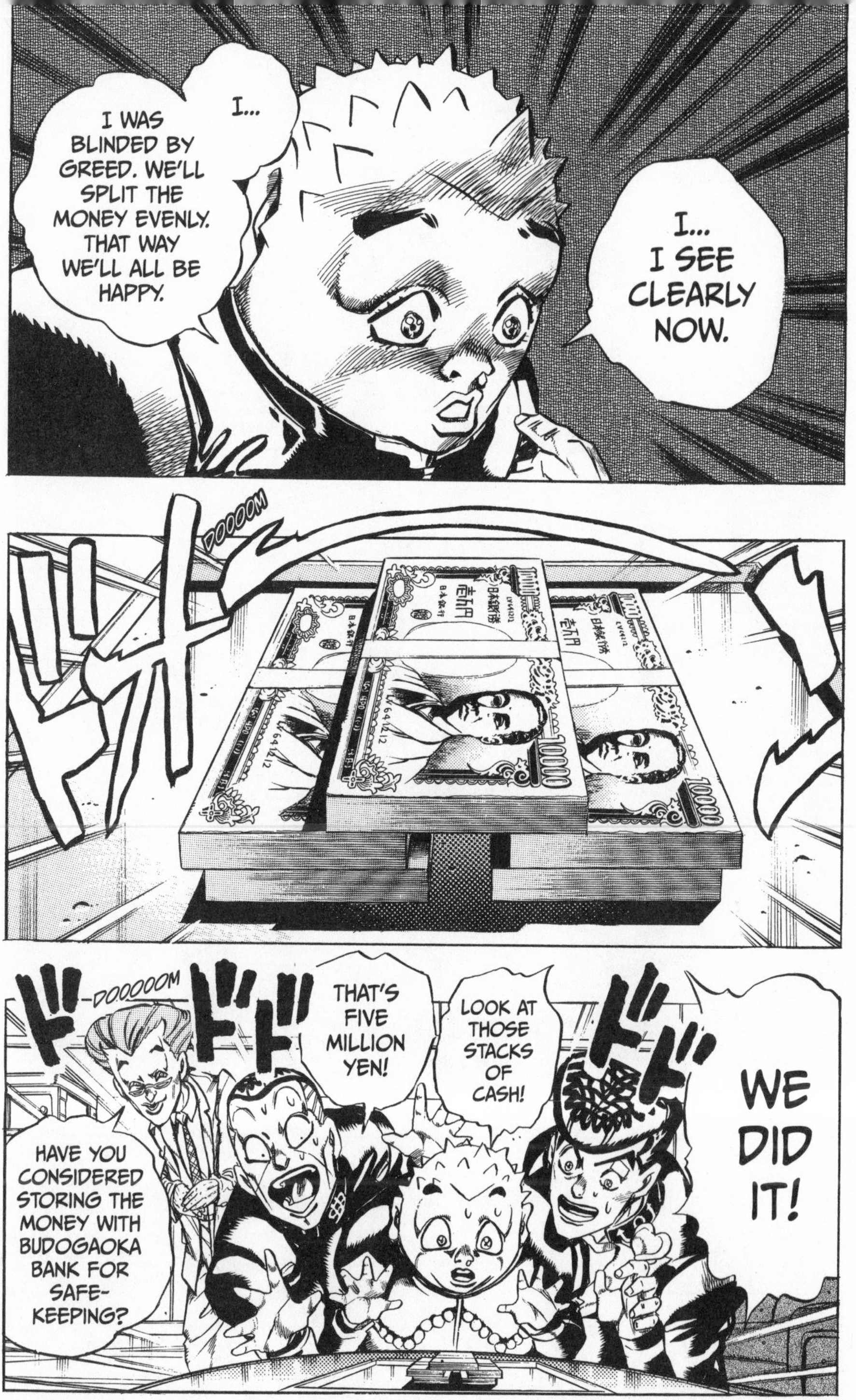
I... I SEE CLEARLY NOW.
I...
I WAS BLINDED BY GREED. WE'LL SPLIT THE MONEY EVENLY. THAT WAY WE'LL ALL BE HAPPY.
DOOOOM
WE DID IT!
LOOK AT THOSE STACKS OF CASH!
THAT'S FIVE MILLION YEN!
-DOOOOOOM
HAVE YOU CONSIDERED STORING THE MONEY WITH BUDOGAOKA BANK FOR SAFE-KEEPING?

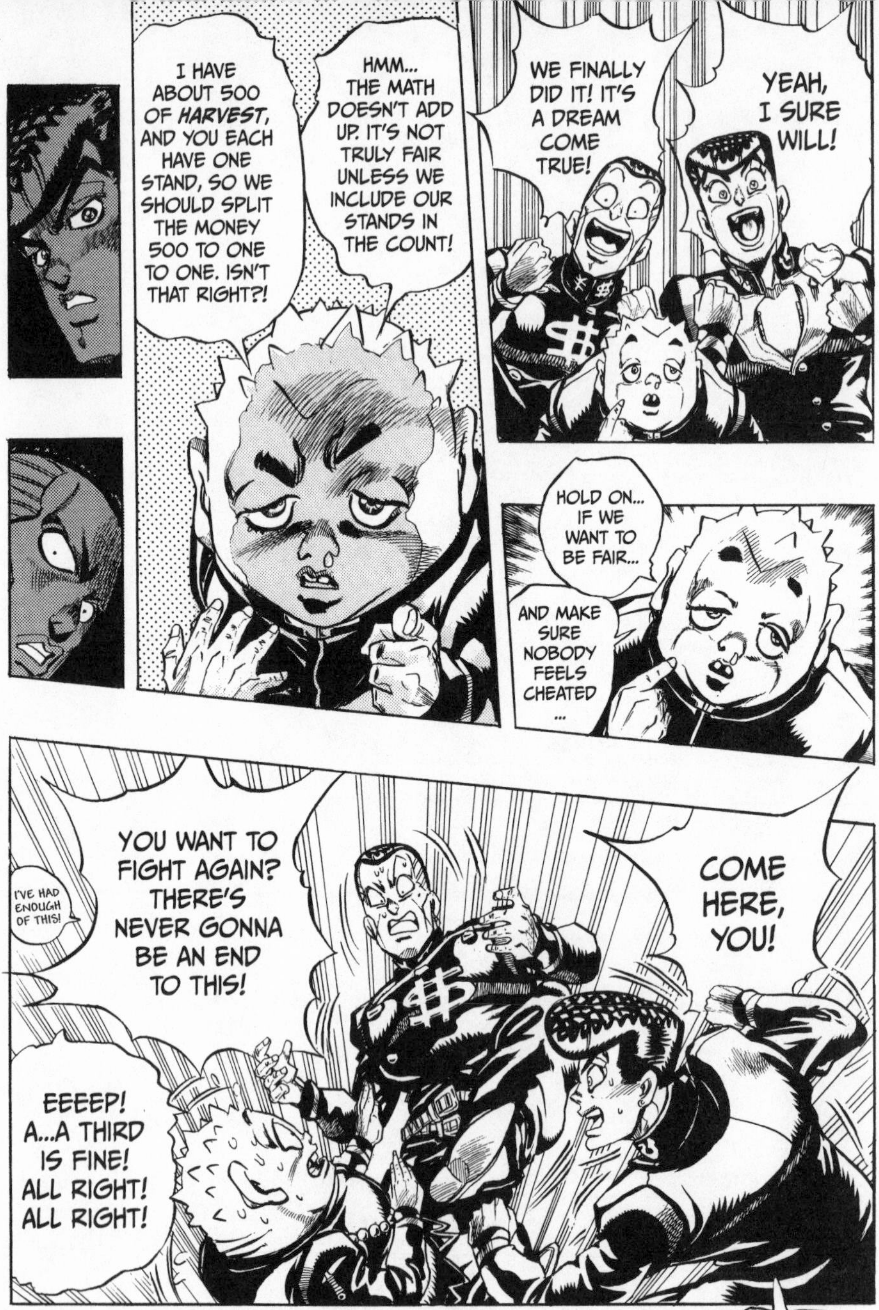
YEAH, I SURE WILL!
WE FINALLY DID IT! IT'S A DREAM COME TRUE!
HOLD ON... IF WE WANT TO BE FAIR...
AND MAKE SURE NOBODY FEELS CHEATED ...
HMM... THE MATH DOESN'T ADD UP. IT'S NOT TRULY FAIR UNLESS WE INCLUDE OUR STANDS IN THE COUNT!
I HAVE ABOUT 500 OF *HARVEST*, AND YOU EACH HAVE ONE STAND, SO WE SHOULD SPLIT THE MONEY 500 TO ONE TO ONE. ISN'T THAT RIGHT?!
COME HERE, YOU!
YOU WANT TO FIGHT AGAIN? THERE'S NEVER GONNA BE AN END TO THIS!
I'VE HAD ENOUGH OF THIS!
EEEEP! A...A THIRD IS FINE! ALL RIGHT! ALL RIGHT!
I GUESS IN THE END, I CAME OUT ALL RIGHT.
JOSUKE HIGASHIKATA'S CURRENT SAVINGS: 1,666,666 YEN
MAYBE THAT'S TOO MUCH MONEY FOR A HIGH SCHOOL FRESHMAN TO HAVE, BUT OH WELL! TO BE CONTINUED

PART 4, VOLUME 4 / END

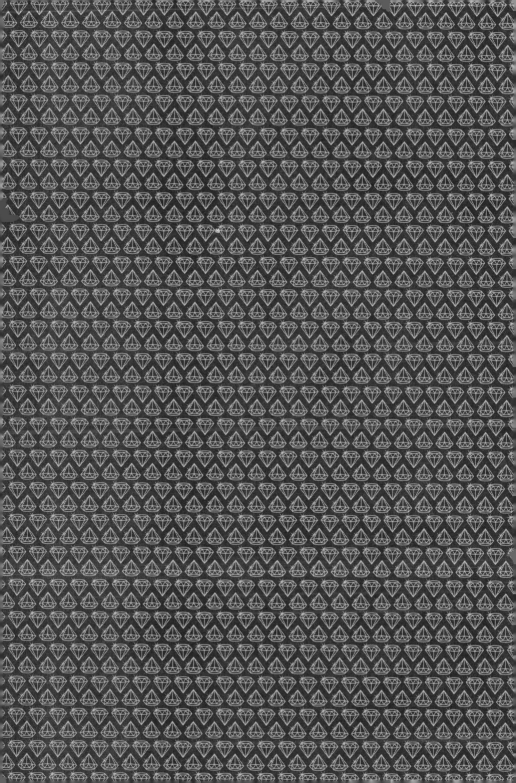

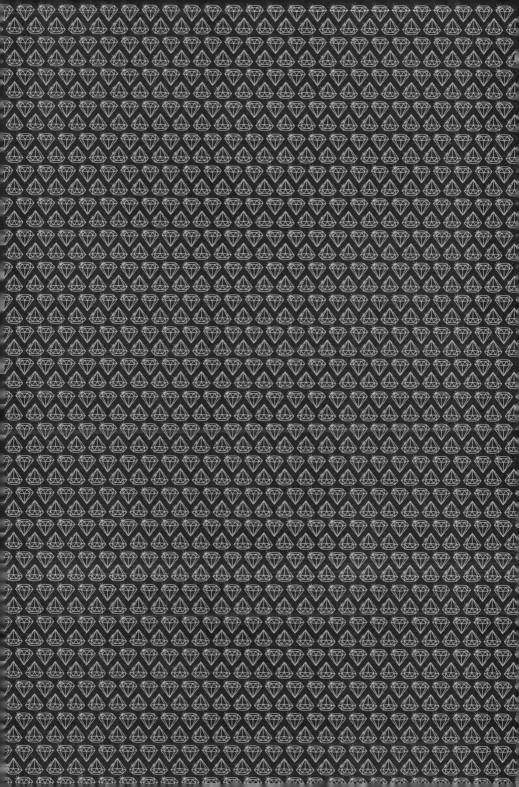

AUTHOR'S COMMENTS

The destruction of the environment is a topic that deeply weighs on my mind. A while ago I visited the town where I grew up and discovered that a mountain I remembered from my childhood had been completely erased—bulldozed away to clear room to develop a residential area. I'm sure the locals made a profit, and that's fine, but I think it's wrong to go so far as to change the topography.

Isn't that kind of thing a crime? I think it's a crime.

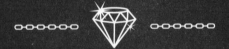

For a long time, I've felt bad for bicycles left sitting out to be drenched by the rain, but for the past few years, what I've really felt pity for are those blinking red lights on answering machines that let their owners know a message is waiting for them.

When I get back from a weeklong vacation and see that light, I wonder, "Were you really blinking this whole time?" I truly feel bad for those lights. I think they should at least be able to slack off while their owner isn't around to see. But then again, we all have our jobs to do, don't we?

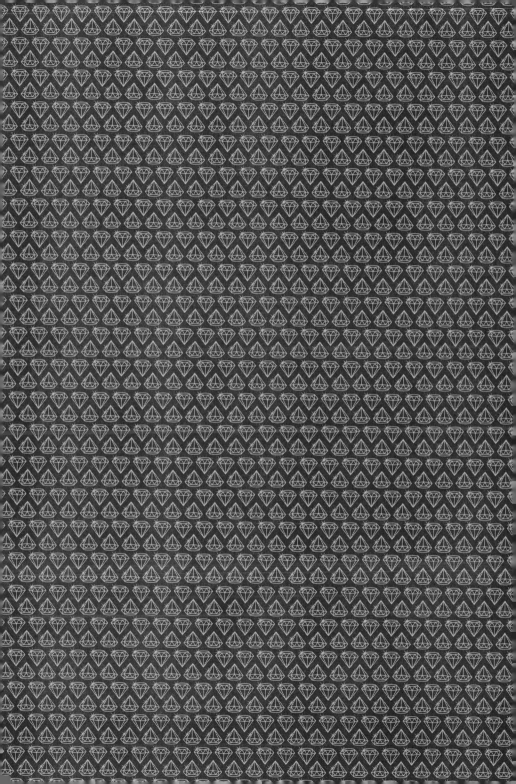

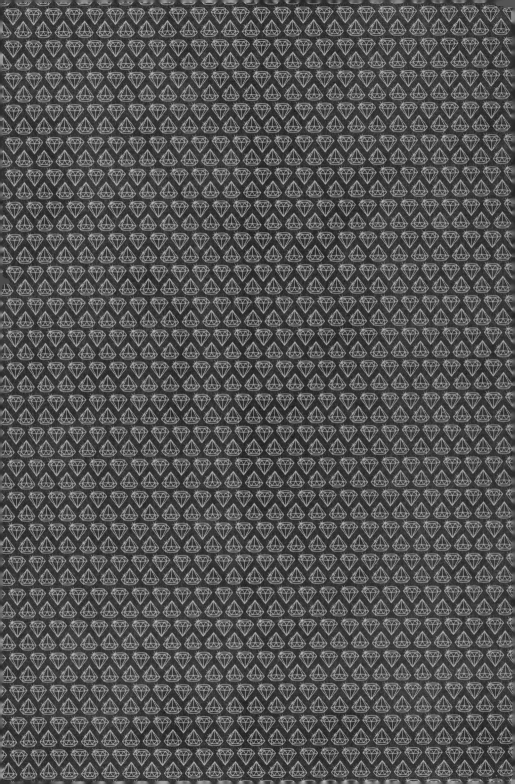

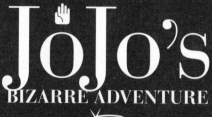

JoJo's
BIZARRE ADVENTURE

PART 4: DIAMOND IS UNBREAKABLE
VOLUME 4
BY HIROHIKO ARAKI

DELUXE HARDCOVER EDITION
Translation: Nathan A Collins
Touch-Up Art & Lettering: Mark McMurray
Design: Adam Grano
Editor: David Brothers

Printed in the U.S.A.

Published by VIZ Media, LLC
P.O. Box 77010
San Francisco, CA 94107

10 9 8 7 6 5 4 3 2 1
First printing, February 2020

viz.com   shonenjump.com

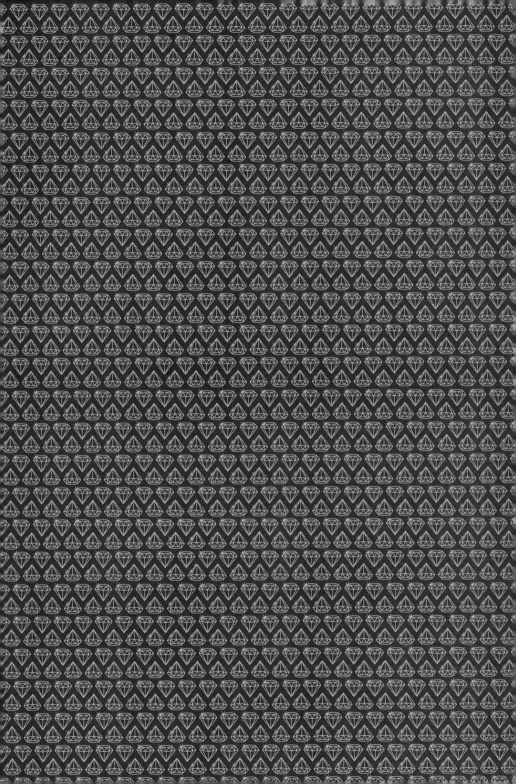

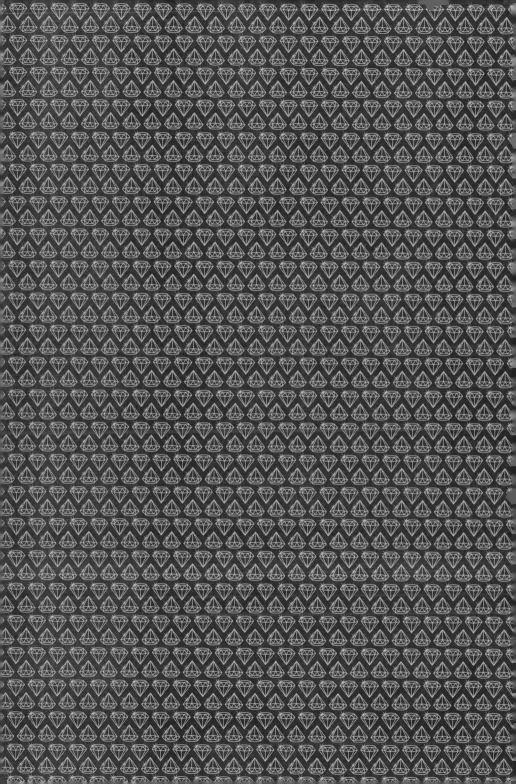

THIS IS THE LAST PAGE

JoJo's
BIZARRE ADVENTURE

has been printed in the original
Japanese format in order to preserve
the orientation of the original artwork.

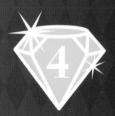

JoJo's

BIZARRE ADVENTURE

HIROHIKO ARAKI

PART 4 ★ DIAMOND IS UNBREAKABLE

JoJo's
BIZARRE ADVENTURE

PART 4 ★ DIAMOND IS UNBREAKABLE

CONTENTS

CHAPTER 57: Let's Go to the Manga Artist's House, Part 5 3

CHAPTER 58: Let's Go to the Manga Artist's House, Part 6 23

CHAPTER 59: Let's Go to the Manga Artist's House, Part 7 43

CHAPTER 60: Let's Go Hunting!, Part 1 63

CHAPTER 61: Let's Go Hunting!, Part 2 82

CHAPTER 62: Let's Go Hunting!, Part 3 101

CHAPTER 63: Let's Go Hunting!, Part 4 121

CHAPTER 64: Let's Go Hunting!, Part 5 141

CHAPTER 65: Rohan Kishibe's Adventure, Part 1 161

CHAPTER 66: Rohan Kishibe's Adventure, Part 2 181

CHAPTER 67: Rohan Kishibe's Adventure, Part 3 201

CHAPTER 68: Rohan Kishibe's Adventure, Part 4 221

CHAPTER 69: Rohan Kishibe's Adventure, Part 5 241

CHAPTER 70: Shigechi's Harvest, Part 1 261

CHAPTER 71: Shigechi's Harvest, Part 2 281

CHAPTER 72: Shigechi's Harvest, Part 3 301

CHAPTER 73: Shigechi's Harvest, Part 4 321

CHAPTER 74: Shigechi's Harvest, Part 5 341

CHAPTER 75: Shigechi's Harvest, Part 6 361

CHAPTER 76: Shigechi's Harvest, Part 7 381

Author's Comments 403

Credits 406

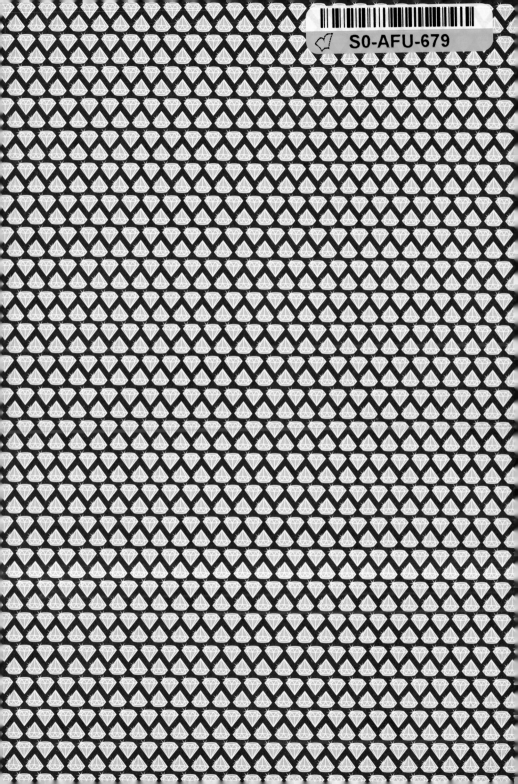